IMPORTANT

HERE IS YOUR REGISTRATION CODE TO ACCESS MCGRAW-HILL PREMIUM CONTENT AND MCGRAW-HILL ONLINE RESOURCES

For key premium online resources you need THIS CODE to gain access. Once the code is entered, you will be able to use the web resources for the length of your course.

Access is provided only if you have purchased a new book.

If the registration code is missing from this book, the registration screen on our website, and within your WebCT or Blackboard course will tell you how to obtain your new code. Your registration code can be used only once to establish access. It is not transferable

To gain access to these online resources

1. **USE** your web browser to go to: **www.mhhe.com/kw2e**
2. **CLICK** on "First Time User"
3. **ENTER** the Registration Code printed on the tear-off bookmark on the right
4. After you have entered your registration code, click on "Register"
5. **FOLLOW** the instructions to setup your personal UserID and Password
6. **WRITE** your UserID and Password down for future reference. Keep it in a safe place.

If your course is using WebCT or Blackboard, you'll be able to use this code to access the McGraw-Hill content within your instructor's online course.
To gain access to the McGraw-Hill content in your instructor's WebCT or Blackboard course simply log into the course with the user ID and Password provided by your instructor. Enter the registration code exactly as it appears to the right when prompted by the system. You will only need to use this code the first time you click on McGraw-Hill content.

These instructions are specifically for student access. Instructors are not required to register via the above instructions.

The McGraw-Hill Companies

McGraw-Hill Irwin

Thank you, and welcome to your McGraw-Hill/Irwin Online Resources.

Kinicki/Williams
Manaement: A Practical Introduction, 2/E
0-07-310051-X

3EF9-AQCP-VN3D-BE4K-FCBX

REGISTRATION CODE

REGISTRATION CODE

The McGraw-Hill Companies
McGraw-Hill Irwin

management

Kinicki/Williams website:
www.mhhe.com/kw2e

Cover

New York's Verrazano-Narrows Bridge, with runners during a New York City Marathon. When it opened in 1964, the Verrazano-Narrows Bridge was the world's longest suspension span. Today, its length is surpassed only by the Humber Bridge in England.

Located at the mouth of upper New York Bay, the bridge not only connects Brooklyn with Staten Island but is also a major link in the interstate highway system, providing the shortest route between the middle Atlantic states and Long Island.

Its monumental 693 foot high towers are 1-5/8 inches farther apart at their tops than at their bases because the 4,260-foot distance between them made it necessary to compensate for the earth's curvature. Each tower weighs 27,000 tons and is held together with three million rivets and one million bolts. Seasonal contractions and expansions of the steel cables cause the double-decked roadway to be 12 feet lower in the summer than in the winter.

Some great achievements of history were accomplished by individuals working quietly by themselves, such as scientific discoveries or works of art. But so much more has been achieved by people who were able to leverage their talents and abilities—and those of others—by being managers. None of the great architectural wonders of the world, such as this one, was built single-handedly by one person. Rather, all represent triumphs of management.

a practical introduction

Angelo Kinicki
Arizona State University

Brian K. Williams

Boston Burr Ridge, IL Dubuque, IA Madison, WI New York San Francisco St. Louis
Bangkok Bogotá Caracas Kuala Lumpur Lisbon London Madrid Mexico City
Milan Montreal New Delhi Santiago Seoul Singapore Sydney Taipei Toronto

MANAGEMENT: A PRACTICAL INTRODUCTION

Published by McGraw-Hill/Irwin, a business unit of The McGraw-Hill Companies, Inc., 1221 Avenue of the Americas, New York, NY, 10020.

This book is printed on acid-free paper.

3 4 5 6 7 8 9 0 CTP/CTP 0 9 8 7 6

ISBN-13: 978-0-07-292037-6
ISBN-10: 0-07-292037-8

Editorial director: *John E. Biernat*
Executive editor: *John Weimeister*
Developmental editor: *Sarah Reed*
Senior marketing manager: *Lisa Nicks*
Producer, Media technology: *Mark Molsky*
Senior project manager: *Christine A. Vaughan*
Senior production supervisor: *Rose Hepburn*
Production and Quark makeup: *Stacey C. Sawyer*
Lead designer: *Pam Verros*
Photo research coordinator: *Kathy Shive*
Photo researcher: *PoYee Oster*
Media project manager: *Betty Hadala*
Supplement producer: *Gina F. DiMartino*
Developer, Media technology: *Brian Nacik*
Cover photograph: *© David Zimmerman/Masterfile*
Typeface: *10.5/12 Times Roman*
Compositor: *GTS–Los Angeles, CA Campus*
Printer: *China Translation and Printing Services, Ltd.*

Library of Congress Cataloging-in-Publication Data

Kinicki, Angelo.
Management : a practical introduction / Angelo Kinicki, Brian K. Williams.-- 2nd ed
p. cm.
Includes bibliographical references and indexes.
ISBN 0-07-292037-8 (alk. paper)
1. Management. I. Williams, Brian K., 1938- II. Title.
HD31.K474 2006
658--dc22

2004065623

www.mhhe.com

brief toc

About the Authors

Angelo Kinicki is Professor and member of the Dean's Council of 100 Distinguished Scholars at Arizona State University. He joined the faculty in 1982, the year he received his doctorate in business administration from Kent State University. His specialty is organizational behavior.

Angelo is recognized for both his research and writing. He has published over 80 articles in a variety of leading academic and professional journals and has coauthored five textbooks (10, if multiple editions are counted). Angelo's success as a researcher also resulted in his being selected to serve on the editorial boards for the Academy of Management Journal, Journal of Vocational Behavior, and the Journal of Management. He also received the All-Time Best Reviewer Award from the Academy of Management Journal for the period 1996–1999.

Angelo's outstanding teaching performance resulted in his selection as the Graduate Teacher of the Year and the Undergraduate Teacher of the Year in the College of Business at Arizona State University. He was also acknowledged as the Instructor of the Year for Executive Education from the Center for Executive Development at ASU. One of Angelo's strengths is his ability to teach students at all levels within a university. He uses an interactive environment to enhance undergraduates' understanding about management and organizational behavior. He focuses MBAs on applying management concepts to solve complex problems, and PhD students learn the art and science of conducting scholarly research.

Angelo is also a busy consultant and speaker with companies around the world. His clients are many of the Fortune 500 companies as well as a variety of entrepreneurial firms. Much of his consulting work focuses on creating organizational change aimed at increasing organizational effectiveness and profitability. One of his most important and enjoyable pursuits is the practical application of his knowledge about management and organizational behavior.

Angelo and his wife, Joyce, have enjoyed living in the beautiful Arizona desert for 23 years but are natives of Cleveland, Ohio. They enjoy traveling, golfing, and hiking.

Brian Williams has been Managing Editor for college textbook publisher Harper & Row/Canfield Press in San Francisco; Editor-in-Chief for nonfiction trade-book publisher J. P. Tarcher in Los Angeles; Publications & Communications Manager for the University of California, Systemwide Administration, in Berkeley; and an independent writer and book producer based in the San Francisco and Lake Tahoe areas. He has a B.A. in English and M.A. in Communication from Stanford University. He has co-authored 20 books (47, counting revisions), which include such best-selling college texts as *Using Information Technology* with his wife, Stacey C. Sawyer, now being revised for its seventh edition with McGraw-Hill. He has also written a number of other information technology books, college success books, and health and social science texts. In his spare time, he and Stacey enjoy travel, music, cooking, hiking, and exploring the wilds of the American West.

Dedication

To Debby and Les Busfield, for their treasured friendship, for their commitment to their family, and for being model entrepreneurs.

–Love, A.K.

To Stacey, for her 19 years of steadfast, patient support and for her collaboration and shared adventures; to Sylvia, for her many years of being the apple of her father's eye; to Kirk, for being the son who continues to delight me.

–Much love, B.K.W.

What Reviewers Said about the First Edition of Management: A Practical Introduction

"I just finished reading the Kinicki & Williams text, and I LOVE IT! It is so readable and so practical! There's not too much information, but there is enough, and the examples they provide are just fabulous. I'm so excited to teach with it. There is so much to gain from this kind of text, and if [the students] start reading, I think they will enjoy it so much that they will continue to read."

–Cheri Maben-Crouch, Buena Vista University

"There is a good match between the objectives of the book and the course I teach. I like the overall approach to introducing the content and then reinforcing the key points not only at the end of the chapter but throughout the chapter.

–Larry Bohleber, University of Southern Indiana

"This text does a great job initially stating chapter objectives, reinforcing information, and continually helping students to make connections among the concepts."

–Mary Hogue, Kent State University

"You accomplished well the objective of introducing content followed by reinforcement of key ideas. You also provide practical advice and expanded topic coverage. It makes it easier for me to organize the course and to tailor different activities to individual students."

–David Leonard, Chabot College

"The presentation of the chapters is superior to the current text I'm using, and so is the writing style. I think your format would work better in trying to engage the students, and it would make the text more readable."

–Evgeniy Gentchev, Northwood University

"I am impressed that the text offers visual evidence of the authors' commitment to facilitating learning for a range of students rather than traditional students only."

–Tom Voigt Jr., Aurora University

"The text is well-written. Its style engages, and it is interesting. The approach actually goes beyond the management cycle to incorporate OB and OD concepts, which adds to its strength, in my judgment."

–Jeanne McNett, Assumption College

"[The book contains] very up-to-date examples that provide a real-world glimpse into the actual practices and issues facing modern organizations. I believe that this added dimension will further stimulate student interest in the material and its application outside the classroom."

–Barbara Petzall, Maryville University

"Separating the examples from the text is excellent! Current management textbooks have their chapters so full of examples that students often get overwhelmed and skip major chunks of reading. The quality of the information was up to par—current, to the point, familiar companies. Great approach!"

–Dmitriy Kalyagin, Chabot College

"The text has some very appealing features. I also like the way the information is presented in short, punchy soundbites."

–Annie Viets, University of Vermont

"I believe that an advantage of this text is in its layout/presentation. It does very well when presenting comparisons among topic areas."

–Douglas Micklich, Illinois State University

The Modern Way to Teach Management

The Second Edition of ***Management: A Practical Introduction***—a concepts book for the introductory course in management—uses instructor feedback to identify the most successful features of the first edition and to improve upon them. As with our first version, we hope this new edition will make a difference in the lives of our readers. By blending our two strengths—Angelo's scholarship, teaching, and management-consulting experience with Brian's writing and publishing background—we have tried to create a research-based yet highly readable, innovative, and practical text.

Our principal goal is simple to state but hard to execute: to make learning principles of management as easy and effective as possible. Accordingly, the book integrates writing, illustration, design, and magazine-like layout in **a program of learning that appeals to the visual sensibilities and respects the time crunch of today's students.** In an approach first tested in the first edition and fine-tuned based on instructor feedback, **basically we break down topics into easily grasped portions** coupled with **frequent use of various kinds of reinforcement.** Our hope, of course, is to produce a text that students will enjoy reading and provide them with practical benefits.

The text covers the principles that most management instructors have come to expect in an introductory text—planning, organizing, leadership, controlling—plus the issues that today's students need to be aware of and know in order to succeed: customer focus, globalism, diversity, ethics, information technology, entrepreneurship, work teams, the service economy, and small business.

Beyond these, our book **has four key features that make it unique:**

- **Student approach to learning**
- **Emphasis on practicality**
- **Imaginative writing for readability**
- **End-of-chapter resources**

A Student Approach to Learning

This purpose of this book is to make it as effective as possible for students to learn principles of management. Accordingly, the book integrates writing, illustration, design, and layout in a program of learning that appeals to the sensibilities of today's students. **Basically we structure topics into easily manageable portions** coupled with **frequent reinforcement.** Here's how it works:

Chapter Openings: Designed to Help Students Read with Purpose

Each chapter opening offers two features designed to help students focus their attention on what's important:

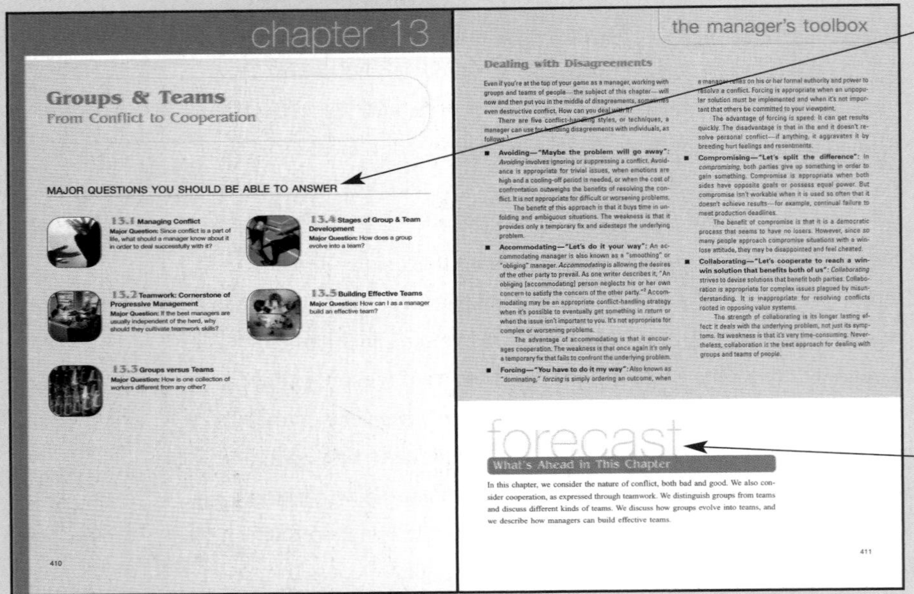

"Major Questions" Help Students Focus Their Attention
Each chapter begins with four to eight **Major Questions**—which correspond to the four to eight sections within the chapter. The Major Questions are worded so that they will be **provocative and motivational,** written to appeal to students' concern about "what's in it for me?" The intent is to help students read with purpose and to focus their attention on what they should be learning from each section.

"Forecast What's Ahead in This Chapter" provides a **brief overview of the chapter** to help give students a "preview" of the important topics to come.

Chapter Sections: Structured into Constituent Parts for Easier Learning

Within the body of the chapter, we have followed a strategy that essentially breaks down topic coverage into four to eight sections, with each section laid out in 2-, 4-, or 6-page blocs to offer **easily manageable units of study.**

"Major Question": Each section opens with a **Major Question,** which repeats one of the Major Questions from the chapter opening.

"The Big Picture" presents an **overview of the section** students are about to read.

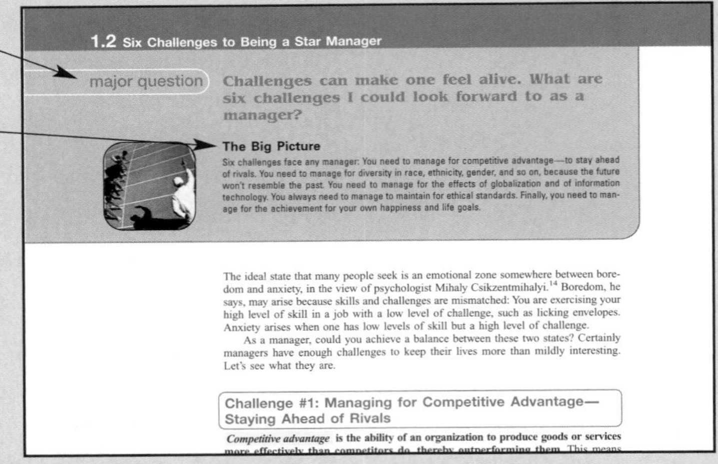

Within Each Section: **More Help for Student Readers**

The body of the text extends the concept of ease of learning using the following devices:

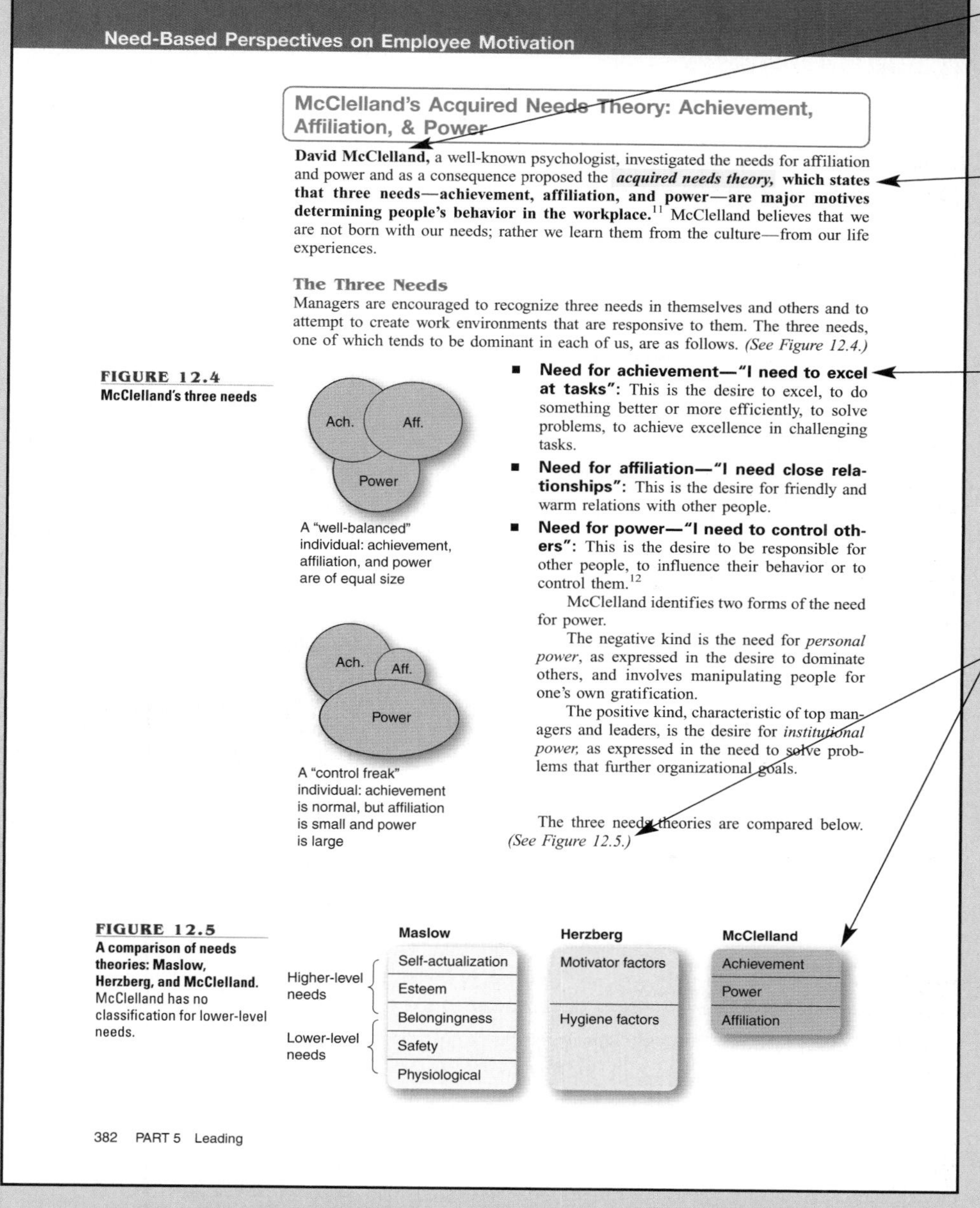

Need-Based Perspectives on Employee Motivation

McClelland's Acquired Needs Theory: Achievement, Affiliation, & Power

David McClelland, a well-known psychologist, investigated the needs for affiliation and power and as a consequence proposed the ***acquired needs theory,*** **which states that three needs—achievement, affiliation, and power—are major motives determining people's behavior in the workplace.**[11] McClelland believes that we are not born with our needs; rather we learn them from the culture—from our life experiences.

The Three Needs

Managers are encouraged to recognize three needs in themselves and others and to attempt to create work environments that are responsive to them. The three needs, one of which tends to be dominant in each of us, are as follows. *(See Figure 12.4.)*

FIGURE 12.4
McClelland's three needs

A "well-balanced" individual: achievement, affiliation, and power are of equal size

A "control freak" individual: achievement is normal, but affiliation is small and power is large

- **Need for achievement—"I need to excel at tasks":** This is the desire to excel, to do something better or more efficiently, to solve problems, to achieve excellence in challenging tasks.
- **Need for affiliation—"I need close relationships":** This is the desire for friendly and warm relations with other people.
- **Need for power—"I need to control others":** This is the desire to be responsible for other people, to influence their behavior or to control them.[12]

McClelland identifies two forms of the need for power.

The negative kind is the need for *personal power,* as expressed in the desire to dominate others, and involves manipulating people for one's own gratification.

The positive kind, characteristic of top managers and leaders, is the desire for *institutional power,* as expressed in the need to solve problems that further organizational goals.

The three needs theories are compared below. *(See Figure 12.5.)*

FIGURE 12.5
A comparison of needs theories: Maslow, Herzberg, and McClelland. McClelland has no classification for lower-level needs.

	Maslow	Herzberg	McClelland
Higher-level needs	Self-actualization	Motivator factors	Achievement
	Esteem		Power
Lower-level needs	Belongingness	Hygiene factors	Affiliation
	Safety		
	Physiological		

382 PART 5 Leading

- **Important People Names in Boldface:** The names of important management theorists and scholars appear in boldface.
- **Key Terms AND Definitions in Boldface:** Having both key terms and definitions boldfaced helps student understanding.
- **Frequent Use of Advance Organizers, Headings, & "Bite-Size" Text:** We make generous use of advance organizers, frequent headings, bulleted lists, and presentation of major ideas in bite-size form.
- **Illustrations Positioned Next to Discussion for Easy Reference:** We have tried to position figures close to the text reference so as to avoid "page flipping."

Helping Students Learn How to Learn: **Bonus Material**

Because focus groups and reviewers have told us that many students do not have the skills needed to succeed in college, we offer two other special features to help readers get a leg up:

- **"A One-Minute Guide to Success in This Class":** Appearing on page 1, immediately preceding Chapter 1, this one page of advice lays down four rules for student success in this class plus suggestions for how to use this book most effectively.
- **"Getting Control of Your Time: Dealing with the Information Deluge in College & in Your Career":** Appearing toward the end of Chapter 1, on pages 24–26, this section offers a crash course on acquiring time management skills, developing solid study habits, improving memory ability. Learning from lectures, and becoming an effective test taker.

Emphasis on Practicality

We would like this book to be a "keeper" for students, a resource for future courses and for their careers. Thus, we not only cover fundamental concepts of management but also offer a great deal of **practical advice.** This advice, of the sort found in general business magazines and the business sections of newspapers, is expressed not only in the text but also in the following:

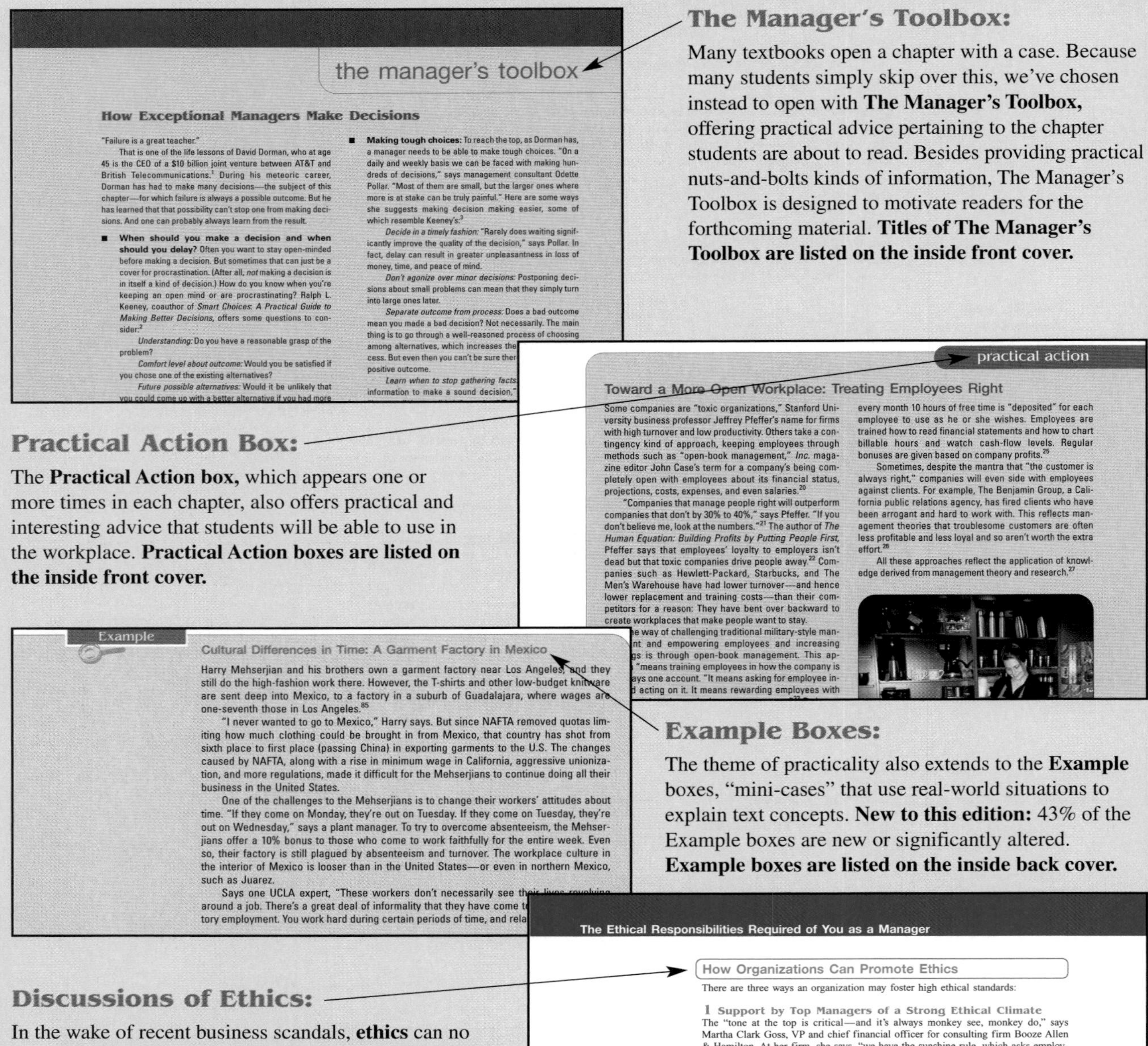

the manager's toolbox

How Exceptional Managers Make Decisions

"Failure is a great teacher."

That is one of the life lessons of David Dorman, who at age 45 is the CEO of a $10 billion joint venture between AT&T and British Telecommunications.[1] During his meteoric career, Dorman has had to make many decisions—the subject of this chapter—for which failure is always a possible outcome. But he has learned that that possibility can't stop one from making decisions. And one can probably always learn from the result.

- **When should you make a decision and when should you delay?** Often you want to stay open-minded before making a decision. But sometimes that can just be a cover for procrastination. (After all, *not* making a decision is in itself a kind of decision.) How do you know when you're keeping an open mind or are procrastinating? Ralph L. Keeney, coauthor of *Smart Choices: A Practical Guide to Making Better Decisions,* offers some questions to consider:[2]

  Understanding: Do you have a reasonable grasp of the problem?

  Comfort level about outcome: Would you be satisfied if you chose one of the existing alternatives?

  Future possible alternatives: Would it be unlikely that you could come up with a better alternative if you had more

- **Making tough choices:** To reach the top, as Dorman has, a manager needs to be able to make tough choices. "On a daily and weekly basis we can be faced with making hundreds of decisions," says management consultant Odette Pollar. "Most of them are small, but the larger ones where more is at stake can be truly painful." Here are some ways she suggests making decision making easier, some of which resemble Keeney's:[3]

  Decide in a timely fashion: "Rarely does waiting significantly improve the quality of the decision," says Pollar. In fact, delay can result in greater unpleasantness in loss of money, time, and peace of mind.

  Don't agonize over minor decisions: Postponing decisions about small problems can mean that they simply turn into large ones later.

  Separate outcome from process: Does a bad outcome mean you made a bad decision? Not necessarily. The main thing is to go through a well-reasoned process of choosing among alternatives, which increases the ... cess. But even then you can't be sure the... positive outcome.

  Learn when to stop gathering facts... information to make a sound decision,"...

The Manager's Toolbox:

Many textbooks open a chapter with a case. Because many students simply skip over this, we've chosen instead to open with **The Manager's Toolbox,** offering practical advice pertaining to the chapter students are about to read. Besides providing practical nuts-and-bolts kinds of information, The Manager's Toolbox is designed to motivate readers for the forthcoming material. **Titles of The Manager's Toolbox are listed on the inside front cover.**

practical action

Toward a More Open Workplace: Treating Employees Right

Some companies are "toxic organizations," Stanford University business professor Jeffrey Pfeffer's name for firms with high turnover and low productivity. Others take a contingency kind of approach, keeping employees through methods such as "open-book management," *Inc.* magazine editor John Case's term for a company's being completely open with employees about its financial status, projections, costs, expenses, and even salaries.[20]

"Companies that manage people right will outperform companies that don't by 30% to 40%," says Pfeffer. "If you don't believe me, look at the numbers."[21] The author of *The Human Equation: Building Profits by Putting People First,* Pfeffer says that employees' loyalty to employers isn't dead but that toxic companies drive people away.[22] Companies such as Hewlett-Packard, Starbucks, and The Men's Warehouse have had lower turnover—and hence lower replacement and training costs—than their competitors for a reason: They have bent over backward to create workplaces that make people want to stay.

...e way of challenging traditional military-style man... ...nt and empowering employees and increasing ...gs is through open-book management. This ap... "means training employees in how the company is ...ays one account. "It means asking for employee in... ...d acting on it. It means rewarding employees with every month 10 hours of free time is "deposited" for each employee to use as he or she wishes. Employees are trained how to read financial statements and how to chart billable hours and watch cash-flow levels. Regular bonuses are given based on company profits.[25]

Sometimes, despite the mantra that "the customer is always right," companies will even side with employees against clients. For example, The Benjamin Group, a California public relations agency, has fired clients who have been arrogant and hard to work with. This reflects management theories that troublesome customers are often less profitable and less loyal and so aren't worth the extra effort.[26]

All these approaches reflect the application of knowledge derived from management theory and research.[27]

Practical Action Box:

The **Practical Action box,** which appears one or more times in each chapter, also offers practical and interesting advice that students will be able to use in the workplace. **Practical Action boxes are listed on the inside front cover.**

Example

Cultural Differences in Time: A Garment Factory in Mexico

Harry Mehserjian and his brothers own a garment factory near Los Angeles, and they still do the high-fashion work there. However, the T-shirts and other low-budget knitware are sent deep into Mexico, to a factory in a suburb of Guadalajara, where wages are one-seventh those in Los Angeles.[85]

"I never wanted to go to Mexico," Harry says. But since NAFTA removed quotas limiting how much clothing could be brought in from Mexico, that country has shot from sixth place to first place (passing China) in exporting garments to the U.S. The changes caused by NAFTA, along with a rise in minimum wage in California, aggressive unionization, and more regulations, made it difficult for the Mehserjians to continue doing all their business in the United States.

One of the challenges to the Mehserjians is to change their workers' attitudes about time. "If they come on Monday, they're out on Tuesday. If they come on Tuesday, they're out on Wednesday," says a plant manager. To try to overcome absenteeism, the Mehserjians offer a 10% bonus to those who come to work faithfully for the entire week. Even so, their factory is still plagued by absenteeism and turnover. The workplace culture in the interior of Mexico is looser than in the United States—or even in northern Mexico, such as Juarez.

Says one UCLA expert, "These workers don't necessarily see th... around a job. There's a great deal of informality that they have come t... tory employment. You work hard during certain periods of time, and rela...

Example Boxes:

The theme of practicality also extends to the **Example** boxes, "mini-cases" that use real-world situations to explain text concepts. **New to this edition:** 43% of the Example boxes are new or significantly altered. **Example boxes are listed on the inside back cover.**

The Ethical Responsibilities Required of You as a Manager

How Organizations Can Promote Ethics

There are three ways an organization may foster high ethical standards:

1 Support by Top Managers of a Strong Ethical Climate

The "tone at the top is critical—and it's always monkey see, monkey do," says Martha Clark Goss, VP and chief financial officer for consulting firm Booze Allen & Hamilton. At her firm, she says, "we have the sunshine rule, which asks employees to consider how they would feel if they had to stand in front of partners [that is, top managers] and explain a particular business expense. It's a good rule, but only a guideline. People almost always follow the example of the senior partners."[33]

If top executives "wink at the problem" or "look the other way" in ethical matters, so will employees farther down the organization.

2 Ethics Codes & Training Programs

A *code of ethics* **consists of a formal written set of ethical standards guiding an organization's actions.** Most codes offer guidance on how to treat customers, suppliers, competitors, and other stakeholders. The purpose is to clearly state top management's expectations for all employees. As you might expect, most codes prohibit bribes, kickbacks, misappropriation of corporate assets, conflicts of interest, and "cooking the books"—making false accounting statements and other records. Other areas frequently covered in ethics codes are political contributions, workforce diversity, and confidentiality of corporate information.[34]

Discussions of Ethics:

In the wake of recent business scandals, **ethics** can no longer be considered impractical, if it ever could. We give ethics and social responsibility thorough coverage.

Web-based "Taking Something Practical Away from This Chapter" Essays

The Kinicki/Williams website (*www.mhhe.com/kw2e*) features expanded topic essays that provide students more insight into the text's lessons. *Examples:* "Encouraging Creativity." "Motivation through Goal Setting." "How to Reduce Stress." "Becoming an Effective Negotiator—Winning Tactics." "Online Job Hunting, Résumés, & Interviews."

Writing for Readability & Reinforcement

Research shows that textbooks written in a **people-oriented, imaginative style significantly improve students' ability to retain information.** Accordingly, we employ a number of journalistic devices to make the material as interesting as possible, as follows:

Biographical Sketches

Debby Krenek, when she was Editor in Chief of the *New York Daily News,* was the first woman in that management post in the newspaper's nearly eight decades of history. What brought about her rise, at age 43, to the top of the macho culture of daily journalism?

Here's one trait she demonstrated: While escorting a visitor through the cavernous newsroom in which she started 10 years before and later came to command, she stopped and pointed to a jumble of electrical cords behind a reporter's desk. "See this?" she said. "I'm the only person in the room who can tell you where all the electrical outlets are."

This knowledge might seem trivial, but in the newspaper business nothing must be allowed to prevent the presses from rolling on time. If a reporter's computer crashes shortly before deadline, for instance, it's vital that a new working terminal be found right away. Thus, Krenek made it a point to memorize the precise locations of all plugs and wires. "If everybody dropped dead," she said, "I could sit down and put the paper out."[4]

Colorful Facts

The ideal state that many people seek is an emotional zone somewhere between boredom and anxiety, in the view of psychologist Mihaly Csikzentmihalyi.[14] Boredom, he says, may arise because skills and challenges are mismatched: You are exercising your high level of skill in a job with a low level of challenge, such as licking envelopes. Anxiety arises when one has low levels of skill but a high level of challenge.

As a manager, could you achieve a balance between these two states? Certainly managers have enough challenges to keep their lives more than mildly interesting. Let's see what they are.

Apt Quotes

In the end, however, recall what Odette Pollar said: "If you truly like people and enjoy mentoring and helping others to grow and thrive, management is a great job."

Lively Tag Lines

Four Basic Strategy Types

Scholars **Raymond E. Miles** and **Charles C. Snow** suggest that organizations adapt one of four approaches when responding to uncertainty in their environment. They become *Defenders, Prospectors, Analyzers,* or *Reactors.*[13]

Defenders—"Let's Stick with What We Do Best, Avoid Other Involvements" Whenever you hear an organization's leader say that "We're sticking with the basics" or "We're getting back to our core business," that's the hallmark of a Defender organization. ***Defenders*** **are expert at producing and selling narrowly defined products or services.** Often they are old-line successful enterprises—such as Harley-Davidson motorcycles or Brooks Brothers clothiers—with a narrow focus. They do not tend to seek opportunities outside their present markets. They devote most of their attention to making refinements in their existing operations.

Prospectors—"Let's Create Our Own Opportunities, Not Wait for Them to Happen" A company described as "aggressive" is often a Prospector organization. ***Prospectors*** **focus on developing new products or services and in seeking out**

Photo Captions That Ask Questions to Spur Thinking

Wisdom from a star manager. Ann Fudge, renowned for her marketing expertise and people skills, was hired in 2003 to become chair and chief executive of Young & Rubicam Brands, as well as Y&R, its flagship ad agency. Not only is she one of the few African-American women to hold such a post, but she is also being called on to rescue an ailing advertising and communications giant ($4.7 billion in revenues in 2000) that two CEOs in three years had failed to do. Asked in a *Businessweek Online* interview whether people entering the workforce today are willing to make the sacrifices to rise to the top, she points out that one can't expect to move quickly through, since there are lots of roadblocks and challenges. "You've got to prove yourself," she says. "You're an Olympian. They're going to keep making it harder, and you're going to have to jump a higher hurdle. But when you do that, the sky is the limit. The question is whether you want to go through it." Do you think this is what you want to do?

End-of-Chapter Resources

The end-of-chapter **"Learning Portfolio"** continues our strategy of **repetition for learning reinforcement.** With this approach, the reader has several opportunities to focus on what's important and to grasp the most significant ideas in the chapter: in the Major Questions, the Forecast, the Major Questions again, the Big Picture, and the text itself. The Learning Portfolio offers further redundancy to help with memorizing ideas and concepts, as follows:

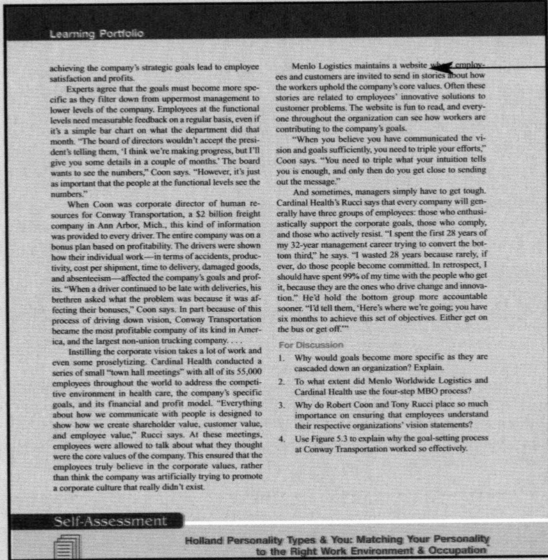

Learning Portfolio

achieving the company's strategic goals lead to employee satisfaction and profits.

Experts agree that the goals must become more specific as they filter down from uppermost management to lower levels of the company. Employees at the functional levels need measurable feedback on a regular basis, even if it's a simple bar chart on what the department did that month. "The board of directors wouldn't accept the president's telling them, 'I think we're making progress, but I'll give you some details in a couple of months.' The board wants to see the numbers," Coon says. "However, it's just as important that the people at the functional levels see the numbers."

When Coon was corporate director of human resources for Conway Transportation, a $2 billion freight company in Ann Arbor, Mich., this kind of information was provided to every driver. The entire company was on a bonus plan based on profitability. The drivers were shown how their individual work—in terms of accidents, productivity, cost per shipment, time to delivery, damaged goods, and absenteeism—affected the company's goals and profits. "When a driver continued to be late with deliveries, his brethren asked what the problem was because it was affecting their bonuses," Coon says. In part because of this process of driving down vision, Conway Transportation became the most profitable company of its kind in America, and the largest non-union trucking company. . . .

Instilling the corporate vision takes a lot of work and even some proselytizing. Cardinal Health conducted a series of small "town hall meetings" with all of its 55,000 employees throughout the world to address the competitive environment in health care, the company's specific goals, and its financial and profit model. "Everything about how we communicate with people is designed to show how we create shareholder value, customer value, and employee value," Rucci says. At these meetings, employees were allowed to talk about what they thought were the core values of the company. This ensured that the employees truly believe in the corporate values, rather than think the company was artificially trying to promote a corporate culture that really didn't exist.

Menlo Logistics maintains a website where employees and customers are invited to send in stories about how the workers uphold the company's core values. Often these stories are related to employees' innovative solutions to customer problems. The website is fun to read, and everyone throughout the organization can see how workers are contributing to the company's goals.

"When you believe you have communicated the vision and goals sufficiently, you need to triple your efforts," Coon says. "You need to triple what your intuition tells you is enough, and only then do you get close to sending out the message."

And sometimes, managers simply have to get tough. Cardinal Health's Rucci says that every company will generally have three groups of employees: those who enthusiastically support the corporate goals, those who comply, and those who actively resist. "I spent the first 28 years of my 32-year management career trying to convert the bottom third," he says. "I wasted 28 years because rarely, if ever, do those people become committed. In retrospect, I should have spent 99% of my time with the people who get it, because they are the ones who drive change and innovation." He'd hold the bottom group more accountable sooner. "I'd tell them, 'Here's where we're going; you have six months to achieve this set of objectives. Either get on the bus or get off.'"

For Discussion

1. Why would goals become more specific as they are cascaded down an organization? Explain.
2. To what extent did Menlo Worldwide Logistics and Cardinal Health use the four-step MBO process?
3. Why do Robert Coon and Tony Rucci place so much importance on ensuring that employees understand their respective organizations' vision statements?
4. Use Figure 5.3 to explain why the goal-setting process at Conway Transportation worked so effectively.

Self-Assessment

Holland Personality Types & You: Matching Your Personality to the Right Work Environment & Occupation

"Key Terms Used in This Chapter": The list of key terms is referenced by page number to their first appearance and definitions within the chapter.

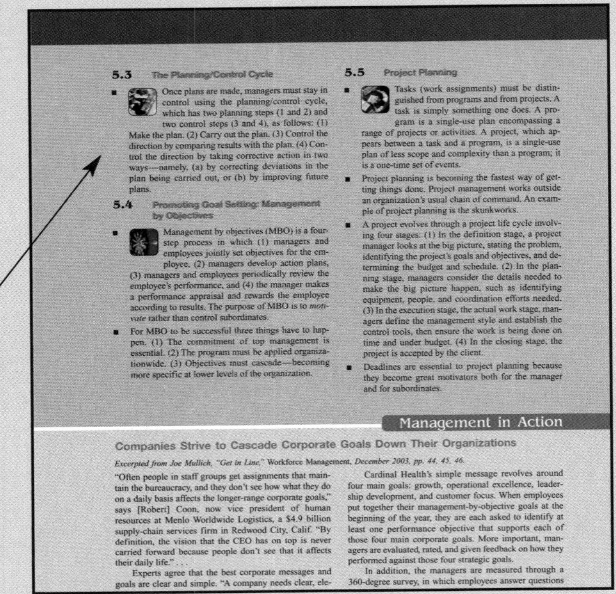

5.3 The Planning/Control Cycle

- Once plans are made, managers must stay in control using the planning/control cycle, which has two planning steps (1 and 2) and two control steps (3 and 4), as follows: (1) Make the plan. (2) Carry out the plan. (3) Control the direction by comparing results with the plan. (4) Control the direction by taking corrective action in two ways—namely, (a) by correcting deviations in the plan being carried out, or (b) by improving future plans.

5.4 Promoting Goal Setting: Management by Objectives

- Management by objectives (MBO) is a four-step process in which (1) managers and employees jointly set objectives for the employee, (2) managers develop action plans, (3) managers and employees periodically review the employee's performance, and (4) the manager makes a performance appraisal and rewards the employee according to results. The purpose of MBO is to *motivate* rather than control subordinates.
- For MBO to be successful three things have to happen. (1) The commitment of top management is essential. (2) The program must be applied organizationwide. (3) Objectives must cascade—becoming more specific at lower levels of the organization.

5.5 Project Planning

- Tasks (work assignments) must be distinguished from programs and from projects. A task is simply something one does. A program is a single-use plan encompassing a range of projects or activities. A project, which appears between a task and a program, is a single-use plan of less scope and complexity than a program; it is a one-time set of events.
- Project planning is becoming the fastest way of getting things done. Project management works outside an organization's usual chain of command. An example of project planning is the skunkworks.
- A project evolves through a project life cycle involving four stages: (1) In the definition stage, a project manager looks at the big picture, stating the problem, identifying the project's goals and objectives, and determining the budget and schedule. (2) In the planning stage, managers consider the details needed to make the big picture happen, such as identifying equipment, people, and coordination efforts needed. (3) In the execution stage, the actual work stage, managers define the management style and establish the control tools, then ensure the work is being done on time and under budget. (4) In the closing stage, the project is accepted by the client.
- Deadlines are essential to project planning because they become great motivators both for the manager and for subordinates.

Management in Action

Companies Strive to Cascade Corporate Goals Down Their Organizations

Excerpted from Joe Mullich, "Get in Line," Workforce Management, *December 2003, pp. 44, 45, 46.*

"Often people in staff groups get assignments that maintain the bureaucracy, and they don't see how what they do on a daily basis affects the longer-range corporate goals," says [Robert] Coon, now vice president of human resources at Menlo Worldwide Logistics, a $4.9 billion supply-chain services firm in Redwood City, Calif. "By definition, the vision that the CEO has on top is never carried forward because people don't see that it affects their daily life." . . .

Experts agree that the best corporate messages and goals are clear and simple. "A company needs clear, ele-

Cardinal Health's simple message revolves around four main goals: growth, operational excellence, leadership development, and customer focus. When employees put together their management-by-objective goals at the beginning of the year, they are each asked to identify at least one performance objective that supports each of those four main corporate goals. More important, managers are evaluated, rated, and given feedback on how they performed against those four strategic goals.

In addition, the managers are measured through a 360-degree survey, in which employees answer questions

"Summary": The Summary gives an **extensive reprise** of the chapter's subject matter—long enough to allow students a thorough before-the-test review but short enough that it does not replace the need to read the chapter itself.

"Management in Action": Presents a **recent case study** or situation along with **discussion questions. New to this edition:** 93% of these cases are new.

Management in Action cases

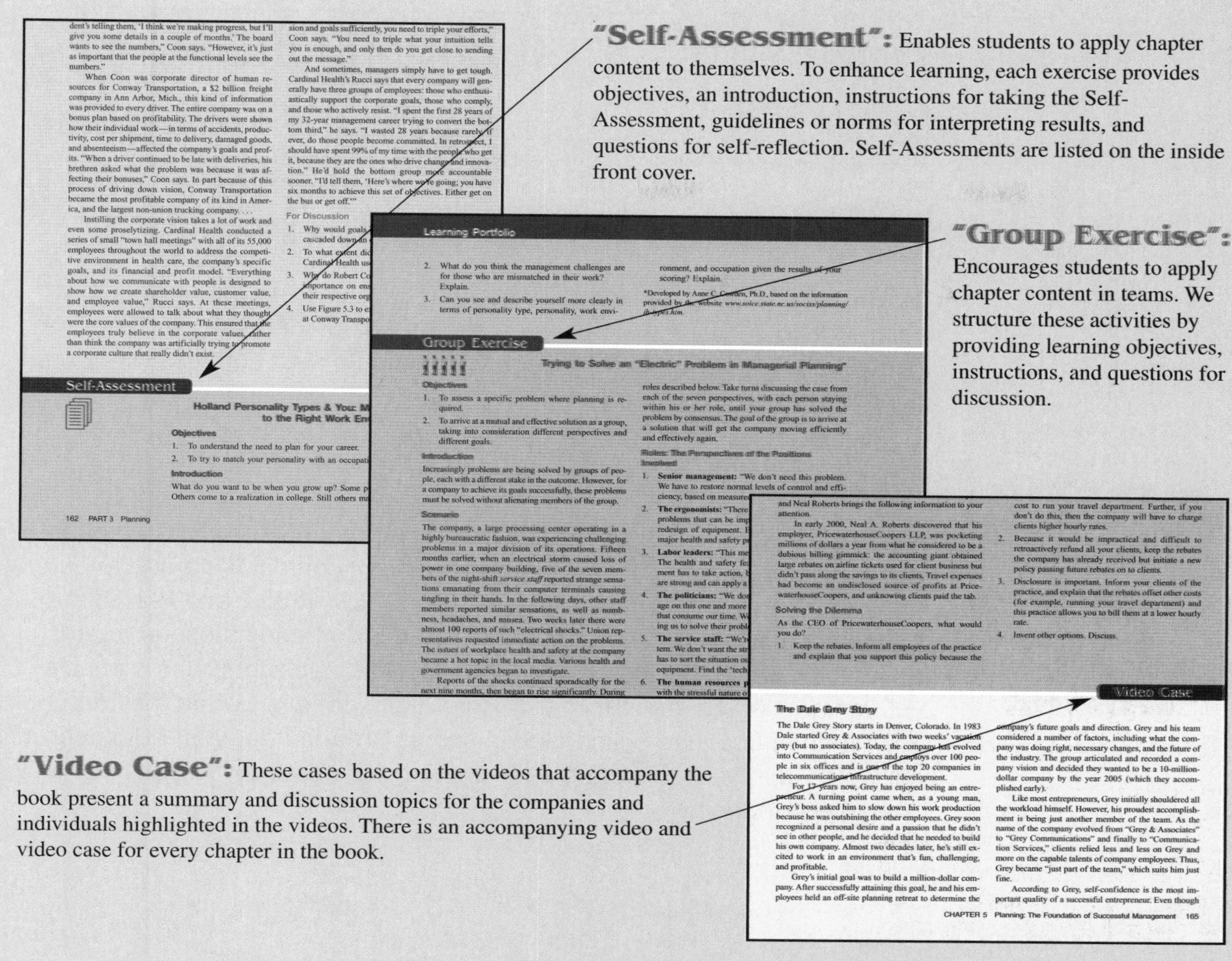

"Self-Assessment": Enables students to apply chapter content to themselves. To enhance learning, each exercise provides objectives, an introduction, instructions for taking the Self-Assessment, guidelines or norms for interpreting results, and questions for self-reflection. Self-Assessments are listed on the inside front cover.

"Group Exercise": Encourages students to apply chapter content in teams. We structure these activities by providing learning objectives, instructions, and questions for discussion.

"Video Case": These cases based on the videos that accompany the book present a summary and discussion topics for the companies and individuals highlighted in the videos. There is an accompanying video and video case for every chapter in the book.

"Ethical Dilemma": Presents **ethical situations,** often based on real events, that require students to think about how they would handle the dilemma. **New to this edition:** 50% of these cases are new.

Ethical Dilemma cases

For Instructors Creating Online Courses

McGraw-Hill offers management content for complete online courses, using online delivery systems such as WebCT, Blackboard, and PageOut, which enable instructors to exert complete control over course content and how it is presented to students.

WebCT & Blackboard

If your department or school is already using products such as WebCT and Blackboard, the McGraw-Hill management content is flexible enough to be used with any platform currently available. WebCT and Blackboard, for instance, allow you to set up online discussion and message boards to complement your office hours. Sophisticated tracking systems enable you to know which students need more attention (even when they don't ask for help) because online testing scores are recorded and automatically placed in your gradebook—and a special message will alert you to struggling students.

Create a custom course website with PageOut, free to instructors using a McGraw-Hill textbook.

To learn more, contact your McGraw-Hill publisher's representative or visit www.mhhe.com/solutions.

PageOut: McGraw-Hill's Course Management System

McGraw-Hill/Irwin's PageOut enables you to create a website for your management course that incorporates your course materials and syllabus and builds a custom website to your specifications. No thick how-to book, HTML coding, or graphic design knowledge is required. Simply fill in a series of boxes with simple English, click on one of our professional designs, and in no time your course is online. (For more information, go to *www.pageout.net.* Our PageOut product specialists are ready to take your course materials and build you your website.)

Key Supplements for Instructors

Instructor's Resource CD-ROM

This multimedia Instructor's Resource CD-ROM allows instructors to create dynamic classroom presentations by incorporating PowerPoint, videos, Test Bank, and every available print supplement.

Instructor's Manual

The Instructor's Manual, which new instructors praise as being easy to use, is unique in that it integrates both the text and the rest of the instructional package.

The Instructor's Manual contains the following for each chapter of the text:

Major Questions We repeat the Major Questions that begin each chapter.

Chapter Overview This gives an overall synopsis of the chapter.

Lecture Outline with Instructor Recommendations The detailed lecture outline contains marginal notes recommending where instructors may use examples, PowerPoint slides, figures, and Practical Action boxes in their presentation. It also references where exercises and assessments discussed in the Group & Video Resource Manual can be integrated into your course.

Key Terms Key terms are presented, along with their definitions.

Additional Critical Thinking Exercise An additional critical thinking exercise is included that requires students to analyze and apply chapter concepts as a way of getting more involved in the learning process.

Lecture Enhancers Short summaries of articles on the latest business and social issues are included to provide additional examples for classroom use.

Answers for Case Discussion Questions Suggested answers are provided for the Management in Action case study discussion questions.

Video Case Notes Teaching notes are presented on each end-of-chapter Video Case and offer suggested answers to the discussion questions presented in the text.

Test Bank

The Test Bank contains about 80–100 questions for each chapter: multiple choice, true/false, and essay. Each question also consists of a rationale and page number for the correct answer, as well as an indication of whether the question tests knowledge, understanding, or application.

PowerPoint

The PowerPoint presentation was created by Amanda Johnson and Angelo Kinicki. We offer two PowerPoint presentations for each chapter, depending on how you like to make use of this resource in your course. The first is a lecture outline consisting of principal concepts plus key terms and figures. The second includes additional and expanded figures as well as slides that illustrate and expand chapter concepts. This second presentation also contains Internet links to outside content. The PowerPoint is available on the Instructor's Resource CD and the Online Learning Center (explained below).

New to This Edition!

New Videos

Sixteen new videos on management issues accompany this edition and highlight companies such as SAS, Starbucks, BP, Amoco, JetBlue, and The Container Store. Most segments are 8–15 minutes long and are suitable for classroom, home, or lab viewing. Detailed notes regarding content, running time, suggestions for use, and answers are included in the Instructor's Manual. Video cases are also included at the end of each chapter that correspond to these videos.

New to This Edition!

The Group & Video Resource Manual: An Instructor's Guide to an Active Classroom

Authored by Amanda Johnson and Angelo Kinicki, the Group & Video Exercise Resource Manual was created to help instructors create a more lively and stimulating classroom environment. The manual contains interactive in-class group and individual exercises to accompany Build Your Management Skills assessments on the student CDOLC, additional group exercises for each chapter, and comprehensive notes and discussion questions to accompany the Manager's Hot Seat DVD, as well as notes for the Management Skill Booster and information on how to use the Team Learning Assistant.

This valuable guide includes information and material to help instructors successfully execute additional group exercises and the Manager's Hot Seat DVD into their classrooms. For each exercise, the manual includes learning objectives, unique PowerPoint slides to accompany the exercises, and comprehensive discussion questions to facilitate enhanced learning. The manual also includes lecturettes and associated PowerPoint slides to supplement and expand material presented in the text.

The Online Learning Center

www.mhhe.com/kw2e The Online Learning Center is a text-specific website available to both instructors and students. For instructors, it offers professional resources that apply to the course as a whole as well as specific materials pertaining to each chapter. It also features an instructor's bulletin board for sharing of ideas with students and downloadable (password-protected) supplements that accompany the text.

The Online Learning Center content can be accessed through the Kinicki/Williams website (*www.mhhe.com/kw2e*), through PageOut, or within a course management system such as WebCT or Blackboard.

New to This Edition!

The Manager's Hot Seat DVD

The Manager's Hot Seat is an interactive DVD that allows students to watch 15 real managers apply their years of experience in confronting issues. Students assume the role of the manager as they watch the video and answer multiple-choice questions that pop up during the segment, forcing them to make decisions on the spot. Students learn from the manager's mistakes and successes, and then do a report critiquing the manager's approach by defending their reasoning. The Hot Seat DVD is an optional package with this text.

New to This Edition!

Team Learning Assistant

TLA is a web-based system to facilitate team learning no matter what course you teach. It was developed at Boston University's Center for Team Learning with a grant from The General Electric Fund. If you are interested in incorporating a team-centered environment in your classroom or online course, this system facilitates effective team learning. Students in teams learn more when they are held accountable for their behavior and for meeting team learning goals. This system of web-based toolboxes for students, faculty, and program administrators facilitates a secure and reliable process of monitoring and maintaining team outcome data. Your McGraw-Hill sales representative can help you if you're interested in using this product with your Management course.

New to This Edition!

The Management Skill Booster

The Management Skill Booster is an Internet-based learning reinforcement system that delivers enjoyable interactive lessons to help students retain and practice what they learn in their Management course. The lessons are reinforced through quizzes, exercises, tips, and web links. Instructors can also use such resources as an online gradebook and student progress reports in this program.

Key Supplements for Students

The Online Learning Center

www.mhhe.com/kw2e Students may use the Online Learning Center (OLC) to exchange information and ideas with instructors via the instructor bulletin board. The OLC also offers self-grading quizzes to help students review material for each chapter, additional exercises, video clips, a Career Corner, and other professional resources. In addition, we present the online essays "Taking Something Practical Away from This Chapter." Also included on the OLC are Build Your Management Skills exercises, self-assessments, and Test Your Knowledge exercises on key management topics.

New to This Edition!

Student Study Guide

The new print Student Study Guide includes questions for review, key term review, and practice exercises. This is an excellent new tool to help students be successful in this course.

New to This Edition!

Downloading Material to Student PDAs—Study to Go

The new feature known as Study to Go enables students to download (at no charge) digital content from the Management website to their pocket PC or PDA. This gives them mobile access to flash cards, quizzes, and key terms from the book.

Acknowledgments

We could not have completed this product without the help of a great many others. The first edition was signed by Karen Mellon, to whom we are very grateful. Sincere thanks and gratitude go to our executive editor, John Weimeister, and his first-rate team at McGraw-Hill/Irwin. Key contributors included Sarah Reed, senior developmental editor; Lisa Nicks, senior marketing manager; Christine Vaughan, senior project manager; Pam Verros, senior designer; and Mark Molsky, media producer. We would also like to thank Stacey Sawyer for her work in producing and laying out this complicated book under a fast-paced schedule, Amanda Johnson for her wonderful work on the PowerPoint presentation and creating the Student Study Guide, Gayle Ross for her excellent work on the Instructor's Manual, Tony Chelte for authoring the Test Bank, Kim Wade for creating the Video Cases, Amit Shah for developing content for the Online Learning Center, and Paige Wolf for writing the teaching notes for the Manager's Hot Seat DVD segments.

Warmest thanks and appreciation go to the individuals who provided valuable input during the developmental stages of this edition, as follows:

John Anstey, University of Nebraska at Omaha
James Bell, Texas State University-San Marcos
Victor Berardi, Kent State University
Stephen Betts, William Paterson University
Larry Bohleber, University of Southern Indiana
Melanie Bookout, Greenville Technical College
Jon Bryan, Bridgewater State College
Glen Chapuis, St. Charles Community College
Ron Cooley, South Suburban College
Gary Corona, Florida Community College
Ajay Das, Baruch College
Lon Doty, San Jose State University
Ray Eldridge, Freed-Hardeman University
Judy Fitch, Augusta State University
David Foote, Middle Tennessee State University
Tony Frontera, Broome Community College
Michael Garcia, Liberty University
Evgeniy Gentchev, Northwood University
James Glasgow, Villanova University
Kris Gossett, Ivy Tech State College
Joyce Guillory, Austin Community College
Jack Heinsius, Modesto Junior College
Kim Hester, Arkansas State University
Mary Hogue, Kent State University
Rusty Juban, Southeastern Louisiana University
Dmitriy Kalyagin, Chabot College
Heesam Kang, Bacone College
David Leonard, Chabot College
Beverly Little, Western Carolina University
Tom Loughman, Columbus State University
Brenda McAleer, University of Maine at Augusta
David McArthur, University of Nevada Las Vegas
Joe McKenna, Howard Community College
Jeanne McNett, Assumption College
Spencer Mehl, Coastal Carolina Community College
Mary Meredith, University of Louisiana
Douglas Micklich, Illinois State University
Gregory Moore, Middle Tennessee State University
Barbara Petzall, Maryville University
Leah Ritchie, Salem State College
William Salyer, Morris College
Raymond Stoudt, DeSales University
Annie Viets, University of Vermont
Tom Voigt, Jr., Aurora University
Charles Warren, Salem State College
James Whelan, Manhattan College
Wendy Wysocki, Monroe County Community College

We would also like to thank the following colleagues who served as manuscript reviewers during the development of the first edition:

G. Stoney Alder, Western Illinois University
Phyllis C. Alderdice, Jefferson Community College
Maria Aria, Camden County College

James Bell, Texas State University-San Marcos
Danielle Beu, Louisiana Tech University
Larry Bohleber, University of Southern Indiana
Robert S. Boothe, University of Southern Mississippi
Roger Brown, Western Illinois University
Pamela Carstens, Coe College
Rod Christian, Mesa Community College
Mike Cicero, Highline Community College
Jack Cichy, Davenport University
Anthony Cioffi, Lorain County Community College
Deborah Clark, Santa Fe Community College
Sharon Clinebell, University of Northern Colorado
Kathleen DeNisco, Erie Community College
David Dore, San Francisco City College
Steven Dunphy, University of Akron
Subhash Durlabhji, Northwestern State University
Jack Dustman, Northern Arizona University
Joyce Guillory, Austin Community College
Charles T. Harrington, Pasadena City College
Santhi Harvey, Central State University
Heesam Kang, Bacone College
Jack Heinsius, Modesto Junior College
Edward Johnson, University of North Florida
Marcella Kelly, Santa Monica College
Rebecca Legleiter, Tulsa Community College
Mary Lou Lockerby, College of DuPage
Paul Londrigan, Charles So Mott Community College
Tom McFarland, Mount San Antonio College
Christine Miller, Tennessee Tech University
Rob Moorman, Creighton University
Robert Myers, University of Louisville
Francine Newth, Providence College
Jack Partlow, Northern Virginia Community College
Don A. Paxton, Pasadena City College
John Paxton, Wayne State College
Sheila Petcavage, Cuyahoga Community College
Barbara Rosenthall, Miami DadeCommunity College/Wolf son Campus I
Gary Ross, Barat College of DePaul University
Cindy Ruszkowski, Illinois State University
Diane R. Scott, Wichita State University
Marianne Sebok, Community College of Southern Nevada
Gerald F. Smith, University of Northern Iowa
Mark Smith, University of Southwest Louisiana
Jeff Stauffer, Ventura College
Virginia Anne Taylor, William Patterson University
Jerry Thomas, Arapahoe Community College
Robert Trumble, Virginia Commonwealth University
Anthony Uremovic, Joliet Junior College
Barry Van Hook, Arizona State University
Susan Verhulst, Des Moines Area Community College
Bruce C. Walker, University of Louisiana at Monroe
Allen Weimer, University of Tampa
John Whitelock, Community College of Baltimore/Catonsville Campus

The following professors also participated in an early focus group that helped drive the development of this text. We appreciate their suggestions and participation immensely:

Rusty Brooks, Houston Baptist University
Kerry Carson, University of Southwestern Louisiana
Sam Dumbar, Delgado Community College
Subhash Durlabhji, Northwestern State University
Robert Mullins, Delgado Community College
Carl Phillips, Southeastern Louisiana University
Allayne Pizzolatto, Nicholls State University
Ellen White, University of New Orleans

We would also like to thank the following students for participating in a very important focus group to gather feedback from the student reader's point of view:

Marcy Baasch,Triton College
Diana Broeckel, Triton College
Lurene Cornejo, Moraine Valley Community College
Dave Fell, Elgin Community College
Lydia Hendrix, Moraine Valley Community College
Kristine Kurpiewski, OaktonCommunityC,ollege
Michelle Monaco, Moraine Valley Community College
Shannon Ramey, Elgin Community College
Arpita Sikand, Oakton Community College

Finally, we would like to thank our wives, Joyce and Stacey, for being understanding, patient, and encouraging throughout the process of writing this edition. Your love and support helped us endure the trials of completing this text.

We hope you enjoy reading and applying the book. Best wishes for success in your career.

–Angelo Kinicki
–Brian K. Williams

contents

management

Kinicki/Williams website:
www.mhhe.com/kw2e

A One-Minute Guide to Success in This Class

Got one minute to read this section? It could mean the difference between getting an A instead of a B. Or a B instead of a C.

Four Rules for Success There are four rules that will help you be successful in this (or any other) course.

- **Rule 1:** Attend every class. No cutting allowed.
- **Rule 2:** Don't postpone studying, then cram the night before a test.
- **Rule 3:** Read or review lectures and readings more than once.
- **Rule 4:** Learn how to use this book.

How to Use This Book Most Effectively When reading this book, follow the steps below:

- Get an overview of the chapter by reading over the first page, which contains the section headings and Major Questions.
- Read "Forecast: What's Ahead in This Chapter."
- Look at the Major Question at the beginning of each section before you read it.
- Read the "The Big Picture," which summarizes the section.
- Read the section itself (which is usually only 2–6 pages), *trying silently to answer the Major Question.* This is important!
- After reading all sections, use the Key Terms and Summary at the end of the chapter to see how well you understand the major concepts. Reread any material you're unsure about.

If you follow these steps consistently, you'll probably absorb the material well enough that you won't have to cram before an exam; you'll need only to lightly review it before the test.

chapter 1

The Exceptional Manager

What You Do, How You Do It

MAJOR QUESTIONS YOU SHOULD BE ABLE TO ANSWER

1.1 Management: What It Is, What Its Benefits Are

Major Question: What are the rewards of being an exceptional manager—of being a star in my workplace?

1.2 Six Challenges to Being a Star Manager

Major Question: Challenges can make one feel alive. What are six challenges I could look forward to as a manager?

1.3 What Managers Do: The Four Principal Functions

Major Question: What would I actually *do*—that is, what would be my four principal functions as a manager?

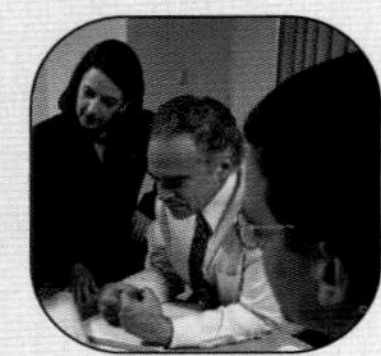

1.4 Pyramid Power: Levels & Areas of Management

Major Question: What are the levels and areas of management I need to know to move up, down, and sideways?

1.5 Roles Managers Must Play Successfully

Major Question: To be an exceptional manager, what roles must I play successfully?

1.6 The Skills Star Managers Need

Major Question: To be a terrific manager, what skills should I cultivate?

To Be a Star Manager, You Need a Personal Coach

Some day maybe you can afford to have a *personal career coach*—the kind long used by sports and entertainment figures and now adopted in the upper ranks of business.[1] These individuals "combine executive coaching and career consulting with marketing and negotiations," says one account. "They plot career strategy, help build networks of business contacts, . . . and shape their clients' images."[2]

Because planning a career is increasingly bewildering in today's work world, in the following pages we are going to try to act much like your personal career coach. In that spirit, it is our desire *to make this book as practical as possible for you.* For instance, the **Manager's Toolbox,** like this one, which appears at the beginning of every chapter, offers practical advice appropriate to the subject matter you are about to explore.

Five Rules for Staying Ahead in Your Career The purpose of this book is to help you become a successful manager—indeed, a *star manager*—an *exceptional manager,* as this chapter's title has it, whose performance is far superior to that of other managers. The first thing star managers learn is how to stay ahead in their careers.

The following strategies for staying ahead in the workplace of tomorrow are adapted from rules offered by professional career counselor Richard L. Knowdell, president of Career Research and Testing in San Jose, Calif.[3]

- **Take charge of your career, and avoid misconceptions:** Because you, not others, are in charge of your career, and it's an ongoing process, you should develop a career plan and base your choices on that plan. When considering a new job or industry, find out how that world *really* works, not what it's reputed to be. When considering a company you might want to work for, find out its corporate "style" or culture by talking to its employees.
- **Develop new capacities:** "Being good at several things will be more advantageous in the long run than being excellent at one narrow specialty," says Knowdell. "A complex world will not only demand *specialized knowledge* but also *general and flexible skills.*"
- **Anticipate and adapt to, even embrace, changes:** Learn to analyze, anticipate, and adapt to new circumstances in the world and in your own life. For instance, as technology changes the rules, *embrace* the new rules.
- **Keep learning:** "You can take a one- or two-day course in a new subject," says Knowdell, "just to get an idea of whether you want to use those specific skills and to see if you would be good at it. Then, if there is a match, you could seek out an extended course."
- **Develop your people and communications skills:** No matter how much communication technology takes over the workplace, there will always be a strong need for effectiveness in interpersonal relationships. In particular, learn to listen well.

forecast

What's Ahead in This Chapter

We describe the rewards, benefits, and privileges managers might expect. We also describe the six challenges to managers in today's world—not only staying ahead of rivals but also managing for diversity, globalization, information technology, ethical standards, and personal happiness and life goals. You'll be introduced to the four principal functions of management—planning, organizing, leading, and controlling—and levels and areas of management. We describe the three types of roles (interpersonal, informational, and decisional) and three skills (technical, conceptual, and human) required of a manager.

major question

What are the rewards of being an exceptional manager—of being a star in my workplace?

The Big Picture

Management is defined as the pursuit of organizational goals efficiently and effectively. Organizations, or people who work together to achieve a specific purpose, value managers because of the multiplier effect: Good managers have an influence on the organization far beyond the results that can be achieved by one person acting alone. Managers are well paid, with the CEOs and presidents of even small and midsize businesses earning good salaries and many benefits.

Debby Krenek, when she was Editor in Chief of the *New York Daily News,* was the first woman in that management post in the newspaper's nearly eight decades of history. What brought about her rise, at age 43, to the top of the macho culture of daily journalism?

Here's one trait she demonstrated: While escorting a visitor through the cavernous newsroom in which she started 10 years before and later came to command, she stopped and pointed to a jumble of electrical cords behind a reporter's desk. "See this?" she said. "I'm the only person in the room who can tell you where all the electrical outlets are."

This knowledge might seem trivial, but in the newspaper business nothing must be allowed to prevent the presses from rolling on time. If a reporter's computer crashes shortly before deadline, for instance, it's vital that a new working terminal be found right away. Thus, Krenek made it a point to memorize the precise locations of all plugs and wires. "If everybody dropped dead," she said, "I could sit down and put the paper out."[4]

If you had to put out this newspaper day after day, what would you consider a necessary component of managerial success? Attention to detail? Or only if that helps you achieve your important goals?

Attention to detail is not always a necessary attribute for success, but being prepared for surprises and change is. Continuing change—in the world and in the workplace—is a major theme of this book.

Another necessary attribute: people skills. Besides showing a mastery of the technical aspects of her profession, from reporting to presses to circulation, Krenek also had "emerged as a soft voice of reason and efficiency amid huge dysfunction," according to a magazine profile about her. "In an often anxious newsroom—rocked by a nasty . . . strike, two ownership changes, and a cavalcade of editors . . . —she's gently coaxed headline writers to move faster and nursed endangered projects, plus soothed tempers riled by her big-footed boss."[5]

The Art of Management Defined

Is being an exceptional manager—a star manager—a gift, like a musician having perfect pitch? Not exactly. But in good part it may be an art. Fortunately, it is one that is teachable.

Management, said one pioneer of management ideas, is "the art of getting things done through people."[6]

Getting things done. Through people. Thus, managers are task oriented, achievement oriented, and people oriented. And they operate within an ***organization*** **—a group of people who work together to achieve some specific purpose.**

More formally, ***management*** **is defined as (1) the pursuit of organizational goals efficiently and effectively by (2) integrating the work of people through (3) planning, organizing, leading, and controlling the organization's resources.**

Note the words *efficiently* and *effectively,* which basically mean "doing things right."

- ***Efficiency—the means:*** Efficiency is the means of attaining the organization's goals. **To be *efficient* means to use resources—people, money, raw materials, and the like—wisely and cost-effectively.**
- ***Effectiveness—the ends:*** Effectiveness is the organization's ends, the goals. **To be *effective* means to achieve results, to make the right decisions and to successfully carry them out so that they achieve the organization's goals.**

Good managers are concerned with trying to achieve both qualities. Often, however, organizations will erroneously strive for efficiency without being effective.

Example

Efficiency versus Effectiveness: Won't Someone Answer the Phone—*Please?*

We're all now accustomed to having our calls to companies answered not by people but by a recorded "telephone menu" of options. Certainly this arrangement is *efficient* for the companies, since they no longer need as many telephone receptionists. But it's not *effective* if it leaves us, the customers, fuming and not inclined to continue doing business.

This happened to Brian McConnell, but unlike a lot of us, he was able to do something about it. McConnell, of Roanoke, Va., found that he couldn't get past a bank's automated telephone system to talk to a real person. This was not the fault of the phone technology so much as of the bank's managers.

McConnell, president of a software firm, thereupon wrote a computer program that automatically phoned eight different numbers at the bank. People picking up the phone heard the recording, "This is an automated customer complaint. To hear a live complaint, press . . ."[7]

The cost for self-service via an automated phone system averages $1.85, whereas the cost of using a live customer-service representative is $4.50, according to the Gartner Group, an information technology analyst.[8] Nevertheless, automated technologies often don't allow completion of transactions, because of customer confusion and technological glitches, so this leads to "ping-ponging"—customers calling back trying to find a live representative or other means of contacting the company.

Thus, Scott Broetzmann, president of CustomerCare Measurement Consulting, a firm that does surveys on customer service, says that 90% of consumers say they want nothing to do with an automated telephone system. "They just don't like it," he says. The most telling finding is that 50% of those surveyed had become so aggravated that they were willing to pay an additional charge for customer service that avoids going through an automated phone system.[9]

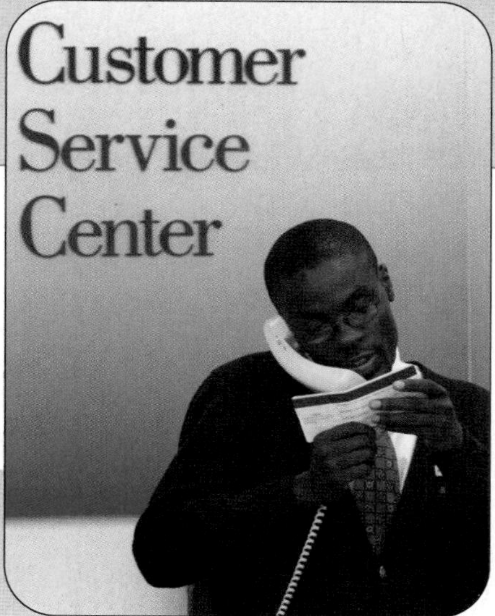

How often do you encounter organizations using their telephone systems more efficiently than effectively?

Why Organizations Value Managers: The Multiplier Effect

Good managers create value. Bad managers deplete it. The reason is that in being a manager you have a *multiplier effect:* Your influence on the organization is multiplied far beyond the results that can be achieved by just one person acting alone.

Of course, some great achievements of history, such as scientific discoveries or works of art, were accomplished by individuals working quietly by themselves. But so much more has been achieved by people who were able to leverage their talents and abilities by being managers. For instance, of the top 10 great architectural wonders of the world named by the American Institute of Architects, none was built single-handedly by one person. All were triumphs of management, although some reflected the vision of an individual. (The wonders are the Great Wall of China, the Great Pyramid, Machu Picchu, the Acropolis, the Coliseum, the Taj Mahal, the Eiffel Tower, the Brooklyn Bridge, the Empire State Building, and Frank Lloyd Wright's Falling Water house in Pennsylvania.)

Thus, while a solo operator such as a salesperson might accomplish many things and incidentally make a very good living, his or her boss could accomplish a great deal more—and could well earn two to seven times the income. And the manager will undoubtedly have a lot more influence.

Financial Rewards of Being a Star Manager

How well compensated are managers? According to the U.S. Bureau of Labor Statistics, the median weekly wage in 2003 for American workers of all sorts was $618—roughly $32,100 a year. Education pays: The average 2000 incomes for full-time workers with a bachelor's degree were $56,334 for men and $40,415 for women. (For high-school graduates, it was $34,303 for men and $24,970 for women.)

Sanford Weill. The former Citigroup CEO earned about $110,000 a day in 2003—equivalent to the yearly salary of a well-paid middle manager. He is shown here lecturing in Shanghai, China.

Business magazines frequently report on the astronomical earnings of top chief executive officers (CEOs), such as Sanford I. Weill, who headed Citigroup, the financial services company, for just nine months in 2003 and earned $30 million, or about $111,000 a day—*plus* $13.9 million worth of stock options.[10] However, this kind of compensation isn't common. In 2002, the average compensation of 365 top CEOs was $7.4 million.[11] More usual is the take-home pay for the head of a small business: the chief executive of a $3 million firm has an average base salary of $259,543 plus about $30,000 in cash incentives, and the chief executive of a $10 million company has a total compensation of $268,092.[12]

Managers farther down in the organization usually don't make this much, of course; nevertheless, they do fairly well compared to most workers. At the lower rungs, managers may make between $25,000 and $50,000 a year; in the middle levels, between $35,000 and $110,000.

There are also all kinds of fringe benefits and status rewards that go with being a manager, ranging from health insurance to stock options to large offices. And the higher you ascend in the management hierarchy, the more privileges may come your way: personal parking space, better furniture, lunch in the executive dining room, on up to—for those on the top rung of big companies—company car and driver, corporate jet, and even executive sabbaticals (months of paid time off to pursue alternative projects).

Psychological Rewards of Being a Manager

The rewards of being a manager go beyond money and status. Every successful goal accomplished provides you not only with personal satisfaction but also the satisfaction of all those employees you directed who helped you accomplish it.

Every promotion up the hierarchy of an organization stretches your abilities, challenges your talents and skills, and magnifies the range of your accomplishments. Every product or service you provide—the personal Hoover Dam or Empire State Building you build, as it were—becomes a monument to your accomplishments.

Points out Odette Pollar, who owns Time Management Systems, a productivity-improvement firm in Oakland, Calif.:[13]

> Managers are able to view the business in a broader context, to plan and grow personally. Managers can play more of a leadership role than ever before. This is an opportunity to counsel, motivate, advise, guide, empower, and influence large groups of people.
>
> These important skills can be used in business as well as in personal and volunteer activities. If you truly like people and enjoy mentoring and helping others to grow and thrive, management is a great job. ◆

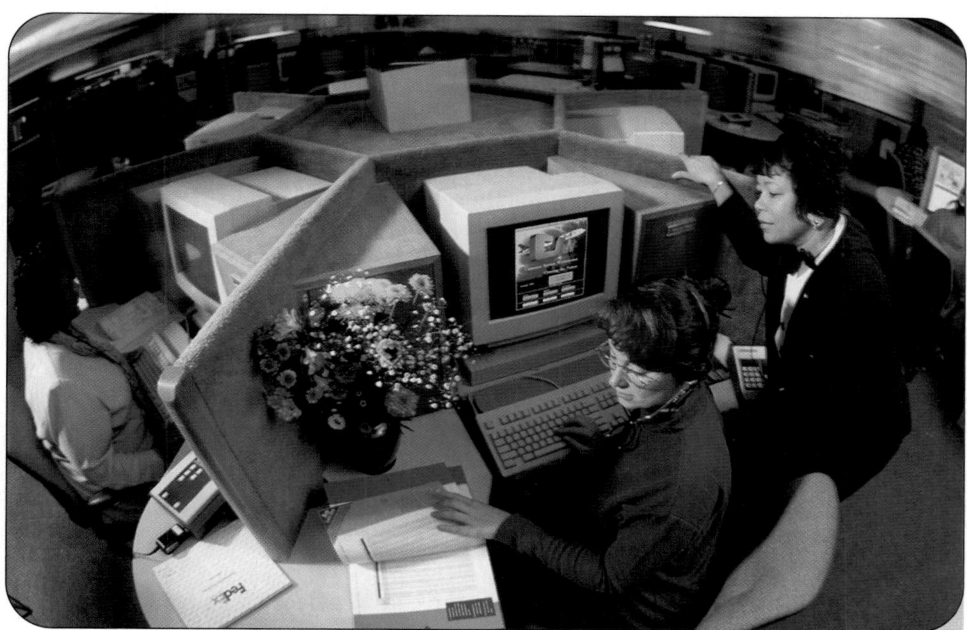

Rewards. One of the rewards of being a manager is providing counseling, advice, and empowerment to employees. Do these appeal to you?

major question

Challenges can make one feel alive. What are six challenges I could look forward to as a manager?

The Big Picture

Six challenges face any manager: You need to manage for competitive advantage—to stay ahead of rivals. You need to manage for diversity in race, ethnicity, gender, and so on, because the future won't resemble the past. You need to manage for the effects of globalization and of information technology. You always need to manage to maintain for ethical standards. Finally, you need to manage for the achievement for your own happiness and life goals.

The ideal state that many people seek is an emotional zone somewhere between boredom and anxiety, in the view of psychologist Mihaly Csikzentmihalyi.[14] Boredom, he says, may arise because skills and challenges are mismatched: You are exercising your high level of skill in a job with a low level of challenge, such as licking envelopes. Anxiety arises when one has low levels of skill but a high level of challenge.

As a manager, could you achieve a balance between these two states? Certainly managers have enough challenges to keep their lives more than mildly interesting. Let's see what they are.

Challenge #1: Managing for Competitive Advantage—Staying Ahead of Rivals

***Competitive advantage* is the ability of an organization to produce goods or services more effectively than competitors do, thereby outperforming them.** This means an organization must stay ahead in four areas: (1) being responsive to customers, (2) innovation, (3) quality, and (4) efficiency.

1 Being Responsive to Customers

The first law of business is: *take care of the customer.* Without customers—buyers, clients, consumers, shoppers, users, patrons, guests, investors, or whatever they're called—sooner or later there will be no organization. Nonprofit organizations are well advised to be responsive to their "customers," too, whether they're called citizens, members, students, patients, voters, rate-payers, or whatever, since they are the justification for the organizations' existence.

2 Innovation

Finding ways to deliver new or better goods or services is called *innovation.* No organization, for-profit or nonprofit, can allow itself to become complacent—especially when rivals are coming up with creative ideas. "Innovate or die" is an important adage for any manager.

We discuss innovation along with entrepreneurship in Chapter 3.

3 Quality

If your organization is the only one of its kind, customers may put up with products or services that are less than stellar (as they have with some airlines whose hub systems give them a near-monopoly on flights out of certain cities), but only because they have no choice. But if another organization comes along and offers a better-quality travel experience, TV program, cut of meat, computer software, or whatever, you may find your company falling behind. Making improvements in quality has become an important management idea in recent times, as we shall discuss.

Organizing: Discussed in Part 4 of This Book

Organizing **is defined as arranging tasks, people and other resources to accomplish the work.** College administrators must determine the tasks to be done, by whom, and what the reporting hierarchy is to be. Should the institution be organized into schools with departments, with department chairpersons reporting to deans who in return report to vice-presidents? Should the college hire more full-time instructors than part-time instructors? Should English professors teach just English literature or also composition, developmental English, and "first-year experience" courses?

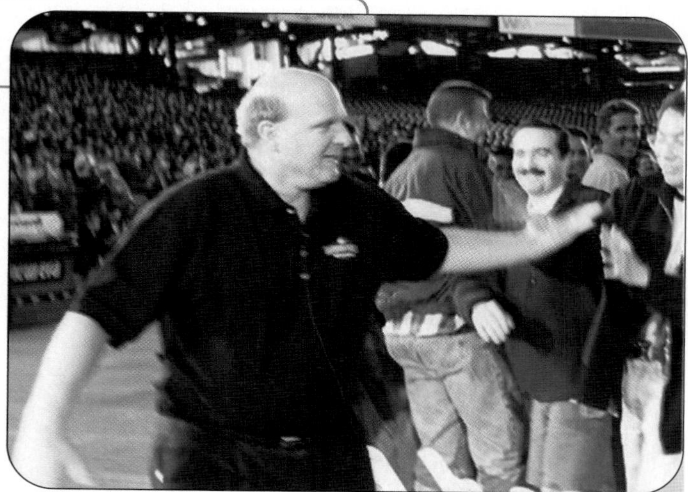

Leader. Steve Ballmer, CEO of Microsoft Corp., in 2001 was named the No. 1 CEO by *Worth* magazine.

Leading: Discussed in Part 5 of This Book

Leading **is defined as motivating, directing, and otherwise influencing people to work hard to achieve the organization's goals.** At your college, leadership begins, of course, with the president (who would be the chief executive officer, or CEO, in a for-profit organization). He or she is the one who must inspire faculty, staff, students, alumni, wealthy donors, and residents of the surrounding community to help realize the college's goals. As you might imagine, these groups often have different needs and wants, so an essential part of leadership is resolving conflicts.

Controlling: Discussed in Part 6 of This Book

Controlling **is defined as monitoring performance, comparing it with goals, and taking corrective action as needed.** Is the college discovering that fewer students are majoring in nursing than they did five years previously? Is the fault with a change in the job market? with the quality of instruction? with the kinds of courses offered? Are the Nursing Department's student recruitment efforts not going well? Should the department's budget be reduced? Under the management function of controlling, college administrators must deal with these kinds of matters. ◆

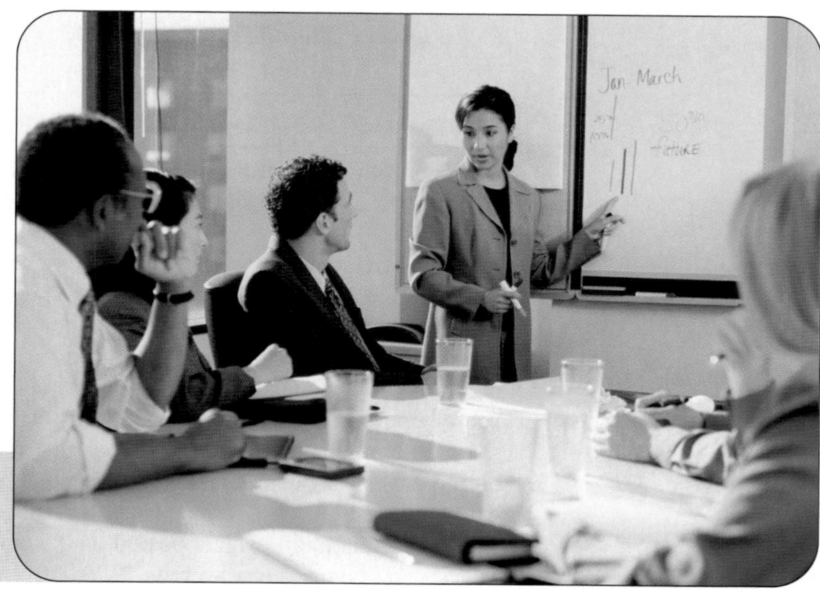

Which one of the four functions might this manager be performing?

major question **What are the levels and areas of management I need to know to move up, down, and sideways?**

The Big Picture

Within an organization, there are managers at three levels: *top, middle,* and *first-line.* Managers may also be *general managers,* or they may be *functional managers,* responsible for just one organizational activity, such as Research & Development, Marketing, Finance, Production, or Human Resources. Managers may work for for-profit, nonprofit, or mutual-benefit organizations.

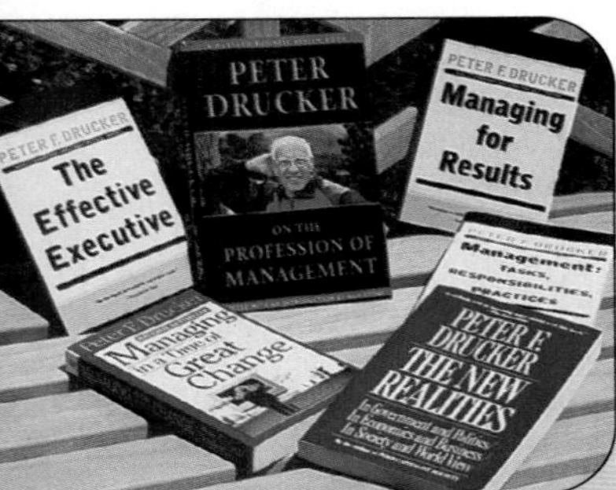

One of the most original management thinkers, Peter Drucker is also a prolific book writer.

The workplace of the future may resemble a symphony orchestra, says famed management theorist Peter Drucker.[26] Employees, especially so-called "knowledge workers"—those who have a great deal of technical skills—can be compared to concert musicians. Their managers can be seen as conductors.

In Drucker's analogy, musicians are used for some pieces of music—that is, work projects—and not others, and they are divided into different sections (teams) based on their instruments. The conductor's role is not to play each instrument better than the musicians but to lead them all through the most effective performance of a particular work.

This model is in sharp contrast to the traditional pyramidlike organizational model, where one leader sits at the top, with layers of managers beneath. We therefore need to take a look at the traditional arrangement first.

The Traditional Management Pyramid: Levels & Areas

A new Silicon Valley technology startup company staffed by young people in sandals and shorts may be so small and so loosely organized that only one or two members may be said to be a manager. General Motors or the U.S. Army, in contrast, has thousands of managers doing thousands of different things. Is there a picture we can draw that applies to all the different kinds of organizations that describes them in ways that make sense? Yes: by levels and by areas, as the following pyramid shows. *(See Figure 1.2 on the next page.)*

Three Levels of Management

Not everyone who works in an organization is a manager, of course, but those who are may be classified into three levels—top, middle, and first-line.

Top Managers

Their offices may be equipped with expensive leather chairs and have lofty views. Or, as with one Internet service provider (ISP), they may have plastic lawn chairs in the CEO's office and beat-up furniture in the lobby. Whatever their decor, an organization's top managers tend to have titles such as "chief executive officer (CEO)," "chief operating officer (COO)," "president," and "senior vice-president."

Some may be the stars in their fields, the men and women whose pictures appear on the covers of business magazines, people such as Carly Fiorina of Hewlett-Packard, who appeared on the cover of *Forbes* in mid-2003, and Steve Jobs of Apple Computer and Pixar Animation, who appeared on the cover of *Business Week* in early 2004.[27] Their salaries and bonuses can average $290,000 a year for CEOs and presidents of small and midsize companies to far over $1 million for top executives in large companies.

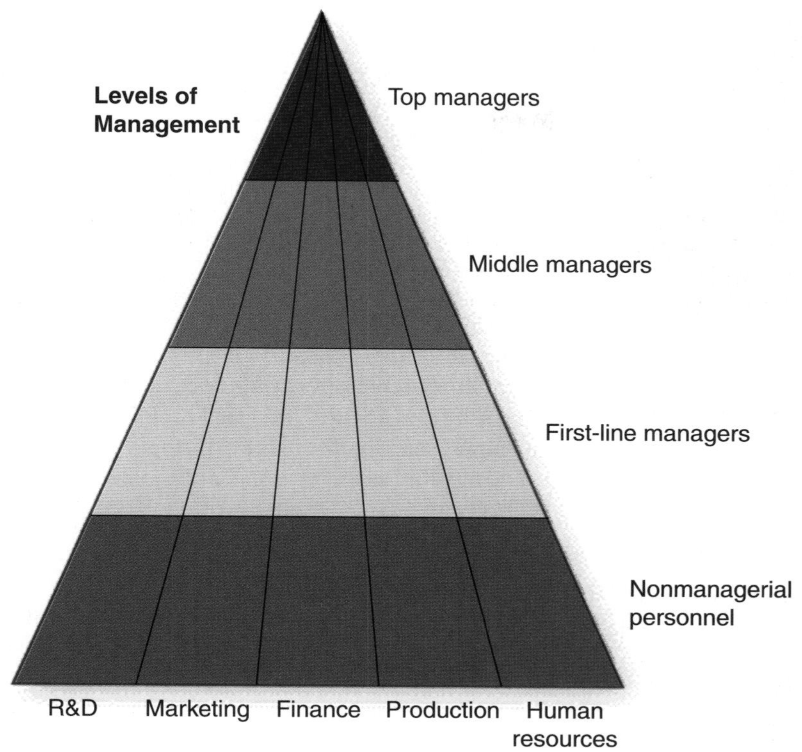

FIGURE 1.2

The levels and areas of management. Top managers make long-term decisions, middle managers implement those decisions, and first-line managers make short-term decisions.

Top managers **make long-term decisions about the overall direction of the organization and establish the objectives, policies, and strategies for it.** They need to pay a lot of attention to the environment outside the organization, being alert for long-run opportunities and problems and devising strategies for dealing with them. Thus, executives at this level must be future oriented, dealing with uncertain, highly competitive conditions.

These people stand at the summit of the management pyramid. But the nature of a pyramid, as business consultant Jack Falvey observes, is that the farther you climb, the less space remains at the top. Thus, most pyramid climbers never get to the apex.[28] However, that doesn't mean that you shouldn't try. Indeed, you might end up atop a much smaller pyramid of some other organization than the one you started out in—and happier with the result.

One kind of top manager. CEO Robert L. Nardelli, sitting to President George Bush's left, and two other Home Depot managers. Founded in 1978, Home Depot is the world's largest home improvement retailer and the second largest retailer in the United States, with $64.8 billion in sales in 2003. Nardelli was recruited from outside the company. Why do you think such a highly successful organization would go outside to recruit a top manager?

Middle Managers

Middle managers **implement the policies and plans of the top managers above them and supervise and coordinate the activities of the first-line managers below them.** In the nonprofit world, middle managers may have titles such as "clinic director," "dean of student services," and the like. In the for-profit world, the titles may be "division head," "plant manager," and "branch sales manager." Their salaries may range from $35,000 to $110,000 a year.

Sometimes the titles have become more creative, in accordance with the changing face of management. For instance, at Intuit, a California software company, Barb Karlin had the title of Director of Great People, which reflected the nature of her challenge—to recruit and retain programmers and other high-technology stars for her company. "I spent 19 years in marketing, bringing in new customers and keeping

Top managers of another sort. Entrepreneurs Larry Page (left) and Sergey Brin, former graduate students who founded the highly popular search engine Google six years earlier in a Menlo Park, Calif., garage, became instant billionaires before age 30 when they took their company public in 2004. Do you think a top manager is always adventurous?

them," she said. "Now I do it with employees instead of customers. The stakes are equally high: If you lose great people, you lose success. It's that simple."[29]

First-Line Managers

The job titles at the bottom of the managerial pyramid tend to be on the order of "department head," "foreman" or "forewoman," "team leader," or "supervisor"—clerical supervisor, production supervisor, research supervisor, and so on. Indeed, *supervisor* is the name often given to first-line managers as a whole. Their salaries may run from $25,000 to $50,000 a year.

Following the plans of middle and top managers, ***first-line managers*** **make short-term operating decisions, directing the daily tasks of nonmanagerial personnel,** who are, of course, all those people who work directly at their jobs but don't oversee the work of others.

No doubt the job of first-line manager will be the place where you would start your managerial career. This can be a valuable experience because it will be the training and testing ground for your management ideas.

Areas of Management: Functional Managers versus General Managers

We can represent the levels of management by slicing the organizational pyramid horizontally. We can also slice the pyramid vertically to represent the organization's departments or functional areas, as we did in Figure 1.2.

In a for-profit technology company, these might be *Research & Development, Marketing, Finance, Production,* and *Human Resources.* In a nonprofit college, these might be *Faculty, Student Support Staff, Finance, Maintenance,* and *Administration.* Whatever the names of the departments, the organization is run by two types of managers—functional and general. (These are line managers, with authority to direct employees. Staff managers mainly assist line managers, as we discuss later.)

Functional Managers

If your title is Vice President of Production, Director of Finance, or Administrator for Human Resources, you are a functional manager. **A *functional manager* is responsible for just one organizational activity.** Danamichele Brennan, now chief technology officer for McGettigan Partners, was previously with Rosenbluth Travel, where her title—indicative of the trend in some companies toward use of more flexible job titles—was Chief Travel Scientist. Her job was heading a research team that developed services to turn reservation agents into travel consultants. The goal: not just cheaper travel but better travel.[30] Leading this specialized sort of research-and-development activity makes her a functional manager.

General Managers

If you are working in a small organization of, say, 100 people and your title is Executive Vice President, you are probably a general manager over several departments, such as Production and Finance and Human Resources. **A *general manager* is responsible for several organizational activities.** At the top of the pyramid, general managers are those who seem to be the subject of news stories in magazines such as *Business Week, Fortune, Forbes, Inc.,* and *Fast Company.* Examples are big-company CEOs Kenneth I. Chenault of American Express, Craig Barrett of Intel, and Anne Mulcahy of Xerox Corp. It also includes small-company CEOs such as Gayle Martz, who heads Sherpa's Pet Trading Co., a $4 million New York company with 10 employees that sells travel carriers for dogs and cats. But not all general managers are in for-profit organizations.

Eleanor Josaitis, 69, is cofounder and head of Focus: Hope in Detroit, a nonprofit organization that feeds 43,000 people and runs a day-care center, a training program for machinists, and several for-profit companies with plant and equipment worth $10 million. In the role of a general manager, Josaitis oversees all aspects of the organization, including 850 employees, 51,000 volunteers, and a $46 million annual budget. "We made a conscious decision to run this organization with the sophistication of a business," said Josaitis. Thus, three principles govern Focus: Hope's approach to social change: *Think big. Demand results. Invite people to help.* All these principles reflect the strategic vision characteristic of a top-level general manager.[31]

A general manager is responsible for several organizational activities. Eleanor Josaitis of Focus: Hope oversees a nonprofit organization with a $46 million budget.

Managers for Three Types of Organizations: For-Profit, Nonprofit, Mutual-Benefit

There are three types of organizations classified according to the three purposes for which they are formed—*for-profit, nonprofit, and mutual-benefit.*[32]

1 For-Profit Organizations: For Making Money

For-profit, or business, organizations are formed to make money, or profits, by offering products or services. When most people think of "management," they think of business organizations, ranging from Allstate to Zenith, from Amway to Zagat.

2 Nonprofit Organizations: For Offering Services

Managers in nonprofit organizations are often known as "administrators." Nonprofit organizations may be either in the public sector, such as the University of California, or in the private sector, such as Stanford University. Either way, their purpose is to offer services to some clients, not to make a profit. Examples of such organizations are hospitals, colleges, and social-welfare agencies (the Salvation Army, the Red Cross).

One particular type of nonprofit organization is called the *commonweal organization.* Unlike nonprofit service organizations, which offer services to *some* clients, commonweal organizations offer services to *all* clients within their jurisdictions. Examples are the military services, the U.S. Postal Service, and your local fire and police departments.

3 Mutual-Benefit Organizations: For Aiding Members

Mutual-benefit organizations are voluntary collections of members—political parties, farm cooperatives, labor unions, trade associations, and clubs—whose purpose is to advance members' interests.

Do Managers Manage Differently for Different Types of Organizations?

If you become a manager, would you be doing the same types of things regardless of the type of organization? Generally you would be; that is, you would be performing the four management functions—planning, organizing, leading, and controlling—that we described in Section 1.3.

The single biggest difference, however, is that in a for-profit organization, the measure of its success is how much profit (or loss) it generates. In the other two types of organization, although income and expenditures are very important concerns, the measure of success is usually the effectiveness of the services delivered—how many students were graduated, if you're a college administrator, or how many crimes were prevented or solved, if you're a police chief. ◆

major question **To be an exceptional manager, what roles must I play successfully?**

The Big Picture

Managers tend to work long hours at an intense pace; their work is characterized by fragmentation, brevity, and variety; and they rely more on verbal than on written communication. According to management scholar Henry Mintzberg, managers play three roles—*interpersonal, informational,* and *decisional.* Interpersonal roles include figurehead, leader, and liaison activities. Informational roles are monitor, disseminator, and spokesperson. Decisional roles are entrepreneur, disturbance handler, resource allocator, and negotiator.

The Manager's Roles: Mintzberg's Useful Findings

Clearly, as *New York Daily News* Editor in Chief Debby Krenek's experience suggests, being a successful manager requires playing several different roles and exercising several different skills. What are they?

Maybe, you think, it might be interesting to shadow some managers to see what it is, in fact, they actually do. That's exactly what management scholar **Henry Mintzberg** did when, in the late 1960s, he followed five chief executives around for a week and recorded their working lives.[33] And what he found is valuable to know, since it applies not only to top managers but also to managers on all levels.

Multitasking. Multiple activities are characteristic of a manager—which is why so many managers carry a personal digital assistant to keep track of their schedules. Many students already use PDAs. Do you?

Consider this portrait of a manager's workweek: "There was no break in the pace of activity during office hours," reported Mintzberg about his subjects. "The mail (average of 36 pieces per day), telephone calls (average of five per day), and meetings (average of eight) accounted for almost every minute from the moment these executives entered their offices in the morning until they departed in the evening."[34]

Only five phone calls per day? And, of course, this was back in an era before e-mail, which nowadays can shower some executives with 100, even 300, messages a day. Obviously, the top manager's life is extraordinarily busy. Here are three of Mintzberg's findings, important for any prospective manager:

1 A Manager Relies More on Verbal Than on Written Communication

Writing letters, memos, and reports takes time. Most managers in Mintzberg's research tended to get and transmit information through telephone conversations and meetings. No doubt this is still true, although the technology of e-mail now makes it possible to communicate almost as rapidly in writing as with the spoken word.

2 A Manager Works Long Hours at an Intense Pace

"A true break seldom occurred," wrote Mintzberg about his subjects. "Coffee was taken during meetings, and lunchtime was almost always devoted to formal or informal meetings."

Long hours at work are standard, he found, with 50 hours being typical and up to 90 hours not unheard of. A 1999 survey by John P. Kotter of the Harvard Business School found that the general managers he studied worked just under 60 hours per week.[35]

A Mintzberg manager. Charles Schwab, founder of the financial services firm that bears his name. He relies more on verbal than on written communication, works long hours, and experiences an "interrupt-driven day." Interestingly, Schwab has achieved his success despite having had lifelong dyslexia, the common language-related learning disability characterized by difficulty sounding out letters and distinguishing words that sound familiar.

Are such hours really necessary? Three decades following the Mintzberg research, Linda Stroh, Director of Workplace Studies at Loyola University Chicago, did a study that found that people who work more also earn more. "Those managers who worked 61 hours or more per week had earned, on average, about two promotions over the past five years," she reported.[36] However, researchers at Purdue and McGill universities have found that more companies are allowing managers to reduce their working hours and spend more time with their families yet still advance their high-powered careers.[37]

3 A Manager's Work Is Characterized by Fragmentation, Brevity, & Variety

Only about a tenth of the managerial activities observed by Mintzberg took more than an hour; about half were completed in under 9 minutes. Phone calls averaged 6 minutes, informal meetings 10 minutes, and desk-work sessions 15 minutes. "When free time appeared," wrote Mintzberg, "ever-present subordinates quickly usurped it."

No wonder the executive's work time has been characterized as "the interrupt-driven day" and that many managers—such as the late Mary Kay Ash, head of the Mary Kay Cosmetics company—get up as early as 5 A.M. so that they will have a quiet period in which to work undisturbed.[38] No wonder that finding balance between work and family lives is an ongoing concern and that many managers—such as Dawn Lepore, executive V.P. of discount broker Charles Schwab & Co.—have become "much less tolerant of activities that aren't a good use of my time" and so have become better delegators.[39]

It is clear from Mintzberg's work that *time and task management* is a major challenge for every manager. The Practical Action box on the next page, "Managing Information Overload," offers some suggestions along this line, as does the box at the end of this chapter (page 24), "Getting Control of Your Time: Dealing with the Information Deluge in College & in Your Career."

practical action

Managing Information Overload: Keep Your Eye on the Big Picture

Chris Peters is a vice president of Microsoft, a company famous for its killer workdays, but he's known for keeping reasonable hours. How does he do it? Like other high achievers, he's able to get more work done in shorter time because he stays focused on things he *has* to do instead of unimportant things he might be doing.[40]

Stars like Peters keep their eye on the big picture. They "have this grasp of what the bottom line is, what 'the critical path' is, and they stay there rather than getting pulled off it all the time," says Carnegie Mellon professor Robert E. Kelley.[41] Stars keep their priorities straight by seeing projects through the eyes of the customers or the coworkers who depend on them. Says star manager Brian Graham, who sits out routine meetings and relies on coworkers to keep him informed, "The key for me is to know what not to do, and to always be looking for the path of quickest resolution."[42]

As a manager, how are you going to deal with information overload? College students already wrestle with this problem. Clearly, if you can come to grips with this beast now, you'll have developed some skills that can save your life in your career. Some strategies are given in the box ("Taking Something Practical Away from This Chapter") at the end of this chapter.

Three Types of Managerial Roles

Three Types of Managerial Roles: Interpersonal, Informational, & Decisional

From his observations and other research, Mintzberg concluded that managers play three broad types of roles or "organized sets of behavior": *interpersonal, informational,* and *decisional.*

1 Interpersonal Roles—Figurehead, Leader, & Liaison In their ***interpersonal roles,*** **managers interact with people inside and outside their work units. The three interpersonal roles include *figurehead, leader,* and *liaison* activities.** *(See Table 1.1, opposite.)*

2 Informational Roles—Monitor, Disseminator, & Spokesperson The most important part of a manager's job, Mintzberg believed, is information handling, because accurate information is vital for making intelligent decisions. In their three ***informational roles*** **—as *monitor, disseminator,* and *spokesperson*—managers receive and communicate information** with other people inside and outside the organization. *(See Table 1.1.)*

Frederick Smith (left), chairman and CEO of FedEx, is an example of a doer. When given a low grade on a graduate-school paper outlining his ideas for an overnight delivery service, he used his family's money to found that company.

3 Decisional Roles—Entrepreneur, Disturbance Handler, Resource Allocator, & Negotiator In their ***decisional roles,*** **managers use information to make decisions to solve problems or take advantage of opportunities. The four decision-making roles are *entrepreneur, disturbance handler, resource allocator,* and *negotiator.*** *(See Table 1.1.)*

Did anyone say a manager's job is easy? Certainly it's not for people who want to sit on the sidelines of life. Above all else, managers are *doers.* ◆

TABLE 1.1 **Three types of managerial roles: interpersonal, informational, and decisional**

Interpersonal Managerial Roles	**Figurehead role**	In your *figurehead role,* you show visitors around your company, attend employee birthday parties, and present ethical guidelines to your subordinates. In other words, you perform symbolic tasks that represent your organization.
	Leadership role	In your role of *leader,* you are responsible for the actions of your subordinates, since their successes and failures reflect on you. Your leadership is expressed in your decisions about training, motivating, and disciplining people.
	Liaison role	In your *liaison* role, you must act like a politician, working with other people outside your work unit and organization to develop alliances that will help you achieve your organization's goals.
Informational Managerial Roles	**Monitor role**	As a *monitor,* you should be constantly alert for useful information, whether gathered from newspaper stories about the competition or gathered from snippets of conversation with subordinates you meet in the hallway.
	Disseminator role	Workers complain they never know what's going on? That probably means their supervisor failed in the role of *disseminator.* Managers need to constantly disseminate important information to employees, as via e-mail and meetings.
	Spokesperson role	You are expected, of course, to be a diplomat, to put the best face on the activities of your work unit or organization to people outside it. This is the informational role of *spokesperson.*
Decisional Managerial Roles	**Entrepreneur role**	A good manager is expected to be an *entrepreneur,* to initiate and encourage change and innovation.
	Disturbance handler role	Unforeseen problems—from product defects to international currency crises—require you be a *disturbance handler,* fixing problems.
	Resource allocator role	Because you'll never have enough time, money, and so on, you'll need to be a *resource allocator,* setting priorities about use of resources.
	Negotiator role	To be a manager is to be a continual *negotiator,* working with others inside and outside the organization to accomplish your goals.

major question

To be a terrific manager, what skills should I cultivate?

The Big Picture

Good managers need to work on developing three principal skills. The first is *technical,* the ability to perform a specific job. The second is *conceptual,* the ability to think analytically. The third is *human,* the ability to interact well with people.

At the *New York Daily News,* Debby Krenek, introduced in the first section of this chapter, was preceded as Editor in Chief by a journalism legend, Pete Hamill, who exhorted his staff to make the tabloid newspaper a reflection of the exciting, ethnically diverse New York City that he saw on the streets. By contrast, Krenek was criticized by some subordinates for not having a grand vision for the paper. Does this mean that she lacks the right management stuff? Let's see what the "right stuff" might be.

In the mid-1970s, researcher **Robert Katz** found that through education and experience managers acquire three principal skills—*technical, conceptual,* and *human.*[43]

1 Technical Skills—The Ability to Perform a Specific Job

Krenek clearly had acquired the job-specific knowledge needed to function in the world of newspapers (as opposed to another industry—tax law, engineering, or restaurant work, say). Indeed, she has a college degree in journalism from Texas A&M and worked as a copy editor and reporter for two Texas newspapers before moving to New York.

***Technical skills* consist of the job-specific knowledge needed to perform well in a specialized field.** Having the requisite technical skills seems to be most important at the lower levels of management—that is, among first-line managers.

2 Conceptual Skills—The Ability to Think Analytically

Krenek also had the "big picture" knowledge of all the steps that had to happen for the *Daily News* to be daily news—for the paper to be off the presses and on the trucks at the same time every day. Indeed, she suggested that she could almost get the *News* out by herself, if she had to.

***Conceptual skills* consist of the ability to think analytically, to visualize an organization as a whole and understand how the parts work together.** Conceptual skills are particularly important for top managers, who must deal with problems that are ambiguous but that could have far-reaching consequences.

3 Human Skills—The Ability to Interact Well with People

This may well be the most difficult set of skills to master. ***Human skills* consist of the ability to work well in cooperation with other people to get things done.** These skills—the ability to motivate, to inspire trust, to communicate with others—are necessary for managers of all levels. But because of the range of people, tasks, and problems in an organization, developing your human-interacting skills may turn out to be an ongoing, lifelong effort. Krenek has an easy-going manner, and she had tried to improve the paper's morale with such simple gestures as compliments and champagne toasts. Although she was criticized for lacking the magnetism and flair of her predecessor, Pete Hamill himself observed that she was able to resist "the pervasive sourness" of the company culture of the *News.* One veteran reporter praised her for having a skill that other managers "don't have: an ability to get along with people. And, unlike the others, she actually listens."[44]

But how successful was she with her boss, real-estate magnate and publisher Mortimer Zuckerman? At first, perhaps because early on she adopted a "no surprises" policy of talking with him regularly throughout the day, Zuckerman praised her as both a "wonderful person" and an adept manager. In fact, he lauded her as being capable enough to run a Fortune 500 company—indeed, even the Pentagon.

But ultimately Zuckerman seems to have lost confidence in her. This shows that in real life even the most talented and skillful of managers can find themselves on the wrong side of their boss if they let their guard down. Despite all Zuckerman's praise, a few years later Krenek found herself fired. And she learned about it not from her boss but from a *Daily News* editor who read the news in a gossip column of a rival publication and called her about it at 1 A.M. When she telephoned Zuckerman to ask about the rumor, the publisher replied, "I can neither confirm nor deny it."[45]

What happened? The dismissal was apparently related to the fact that the *Daily News*'s fierce rival, the *New York Post,* had gained circulation as a result of a per-copy newsstand price cut. This was not a matter over which Krenek had much control. What could she have done better?

In nearly all respects, Krenek had what it takes to be a star manager. But all it takes is failure in one area to lose this status. ◆

Wisdom from a star manager. Ann Fudge, renowned for her marketing expertise and people skills, was hired in 2003 to become chair and chief executive of Young & Rubicam Brands, as well as Y&R, its flagship ad agency. Not only is she one of the few African-American women to hold such a post, but she is also being called on to rescue an ailing advertising and communications giant ($4.7 billion in revenues in 2000) that two CEOs in three years had failed to do. Asked in a *Businessweek Online* interview whether people entering the workforce today are willing to make the sacrifices to rise to the top, she points out that one can't expect to move quickly through, since there are lots of roadblocks and challenges. "You've got to prove yourself," she says. "You're an Olympian. They're going to keep making it harder, and you're going to have to jump a higher hurdle. But when you do that, the sky is the limit. The question is whether you want to go through it." Do you think this is what you want to do?

Taking Something Practical Away from This Chapter

Getting Control of Your Time: Dealing with the Information Deluge in College & in Your Career

One great problem most college students face—and that all managers face—is how to manage their time. This first box describes skills that will benefit you in college and later in your career.

"I've managed to ratchet my schedule down so I can have an outside life," says Doug Shoemaker, a San Francisco architect who tries to be home by 6:00 every night. "I'm a highly organized guy, I really focus on tasks, and I get them done."[46]

Professionals and managers all have to deal with this central problem: how not to surrender their lives to their jobs. The place to start, however, is in college. If you can learn to manage time while you're still a student, you'll find it will pay off not only in higher grades and more free time but also in more efficient information-handling skills that will serve you well as a manager later on.

Developing Study Habits: Finding Your "Prime Study Time"

Each of us has a different energy cycle. The trick is to use it effectively. That way your hours of best performance will coincide with your heaviest academic demands. For example, if your energy level is high during the evenings, you should plan to do your studying then.

Make a Study Schedule First make a master schedule that shows all your regular obligations—especially classes and work—for the entire school term. Then insert the times during which you plan to study. Next write in major academic events, such as term paper due dates and when exams will take place. At the beginning of every week, schedule your study sessions. Write in the specific tasks you plan to accomplish during each session.

Find Some Good Places to Study Studying means first of all avoiding distractions. Avoid studying in places that are associated with other activities, particularly comfortable ones, such as lying in bed or sitting at a kitchen table.

Avoid Time Wasters, but Reward Your Studying While clearly you need to learn to avoid distractions so that you can study, you must also give yourself frequent rewards so that you will indeed be *motivated* to study. You should study with the notion that, after you finish, you will give yourself a reward. The reward need not be elaborate. It could be a walk, a snack, or some similar treat.

Improving Your Memory Ability

Memorizing is, of course, one of the principal requirements of staying in college. And it's a great help for success in life afterward.

Beyond getting rid of distractions, there are certain techniques you can adopt to enhance your memory.

Space Your Studying, Rather Than Cramming Cramming—making a frantic, last-minute attempt to memorize massive amounts of material—is probably the least effective means of absorbing information. Indeed, it may actually tire you out and make you even more anxious before the test. Research shows that it is best to space out your studying of a subject on successive days. This is preferable to trying to do it all during the same number of hours on one day.[47] It is repetition that helps move information into your long-term memory bank.

Review Information Repeatedly—Even "Overlearn" It By repeatedly reviewing information—"rehearsing"—you can improve both your retention and your understanding of it.[48] Overlearning can improve your recall substantially. Overlearning is continuing to repeatedly review material even after you appear to have absorbed it.

Use Memorizing Tricks There are several ways to organize information so that you can retain it better. The table opposite shows how to establish associations between items you want to remember. *(See Figure 1.3.)*

How to Improve Your Reading Ability: The SQ3R Method

SQ3R Stands for *survey, question, read, recite, and review*[49] The strategy here is to break a reading assignment into small segments and master each before moving on. The five steps of the SQ3R method are as follows:

***Survey* the Chapter before You Read It** Get an overview of the chapter or other reading assignment before you begin reading it. If you have a sense what the material is about before you begin reading it, you can predict where it is going. Many textbooks offer some "preview"-type material—a list of objectives or an outline of topic headings at the beginning of the chapter. Other books offer a summary at the end of the chapter. This book offers "The Big Picture" at the beginning of each section. It also offers a Summary at the end of each chapter. The strategy for reading this book is presented on page 1.

***Question* the Segment in the Chapter before You Read It** This step is easy to do, and the point, again, is to get involved in the material. After surveying the entire chapter, go to the first segment—section, subsection, or even paragraph, depending on the level of difficulty and density of information. Look at the topic heading of that segment. In your mind, restate the heading as a question.

After you have formulated the question, go to steps 3 and 4 (read and recite). Then proceed to the next segment and restate the heading here as a question. For instance, consider the section heading in this chapter that reads "What Managers Do: The Four Principal Functions." You

- **Mental and physical imagery:** Use your visual and other senses to construct a personal image of what you want to remember. Indeed, it helps to make the image humorous, action-filled, sexual, bizarre, or outrageous in order to establish a personal connection. Example: To remember the name of the 21st president of the United States, Chester Arthur, you might visualize an author writing the number "21" on a wooden chest. This mental image helps you associate chest (Chester), author (Arthur), and 21 (21st president).
- **Acronyms and acrostics:** An acronym is a word created from the first letters of items in a list. For instance, Roy G. Biv helps you remember the colors of the rainbow in order: red, orange, yellow, green, blue, indigo, violet. An acrostic is a phrase or sentence created from the first letters of items in a list. For example, *Every Good Boy Does Fine* helps you remember that the order of musical notes on the stave is E-G-B-D-F.
- **Location:** Location memory occurs when you associate a concept with a place or imaginary place. For example, you could learn the parts of a computer system by imagining a walk across campus. Each building you pass could be associated with a part of the computer system.
- **Word games:** Jingles and rhymes are devices frequently used by advertisers to get people to remember their products. You may recall the spelling rule "*I* before *E* except after *C* or when sounded like *A* as in *neighbor* or *weigh*." You can also use narrative methods, such as making up a story.

FIGURE 1.3 Some memorizing tricks

could ask yourself, "What *are* the four functions of a manager?" For the heading in Chapter 2 "Two Overarching Perspectives about Management & Four Practical Reasons for Studying Them," ask "What *are* the types of management perspectives, and what are reasons for studying them?"

***Read* the Segment about Which You Asked the Question** Now read the segment you asked the question about. Read with purpose, to answer the question you formulated. Underline or color-mark sentences you think are important, if they help you answer the question. Read this portion of the text more than once, if necessary, until you can answer the question. In addition, determine whether the segment covers any other significant questions, and formulate answers to these, too. After you have read the segment, proceed to step 4. (Perhaps you can see where this is all leading. If you read in terms of questions and answers, you will be better prepared when you see exam questions about the material later.)

***Recite* the Main Points of the Segment** Recite means "say aloud." Thus, you should speak out loud (or softly) the answer to the principal question about the segment and any other main points. Make notes on the principal ideas, so you can look them over later. Now that you have actively studied the first segment, move on to the second segment and do steps 2–4 for it. Continue doing this through the rest of the segments until you have finished the chapter.

***Review* the Entire Chapter by Repeating Questions** After you have read the chapter, go back through it and review the main points. Then, without looking at the book, test your memory by repeating the questions.

Clearly the SQ3R method takes longer than simply reading with a rapidly moving color marker or underlining pencil. However, the technique is far more effective because it requires your *involvement and understanding*. This is the key to all effective learning.

Learning from Lectures

Does attending lectures really make a difference? Research shows that students with grades of B or above were more apt to have better class attendance than students with grades of C− or below.[50]

Regardless of the strengths of the lecturer, here are some tips for getting more out of lectures.

Take Effective Notes by Listening Actively Research shows that good test performance is related to good note taking.[51] And good note taking requires that you *listen actively*—that is, participate in the lecture process. Here are some ways to take good lecture notes:

- **Read ahead and anticipate the lecturer:** Try to anticipate what the instructor is going to say, based on your previous reading. Having background knowledge makes learning more efficient.
- **Listen for signal words:** Instructors use key phrases such as "The most important point is . . . ," "There are four reasons for . . . ," "The chief reason . . . ," "Of special importance . . . ," "Consequently . . . ." When you hear such signal phrases, mark your notes with an asterisk (*), or write *Imp* (for "Important").
- **Take notes in your own words:** Instead of just being a stenographer, try to restate the lecturer's thoughts in your own words. This makes you pay attention to the lecture and organize it in a way that is meaningful to you. In addition, don't try to write everything down. Just get the key points.
- **Ask questions:** By asking questions during the lecture, you participate in it and increase your understanding. Although many students are shy about asking questions, most professors welcome them.

Becoming an Effective Test Taker

Besides having knowledge of the subject matter, you can acquire certain skills that will help during the test-taking process. Some suggestions:[52]

Review Your Notes Regularly Most students, according to one study, do take good notes, but they don't use them effectively. That is, they wait to review their notes until just before final exams, when the notes have lost much of their meaning.[53] Make it a point to review your notes regularly, such as the afternoon after the lecture or once or twice a week. We cannot emphasize enough how important this kind of reviewing is.

Reviewing: Study Information That Is Emphasized & Enumerated Because you won't always know whether an exam will be an objective test or an essay test, you need to prepare for both. Here are some general tips.

- **Review material that is emphasized:** In the lectures, this consists of any topics your instructor pointed out as being significant or important. It also includes anything he or she spent a good deal of time discussing or specifically advised you to study. In the textbook, pay attention to key terms (often emphasized in *italic* or **boldface** type), their definitions, and their examples. In addition, of course, material that has a good many pages given over to it should be considered important.
- **Review material that is enumerated:** Pay attention to any numbered lists, both in your lectures and in your notes. Enumerations often provide the basis for essay and multiple-choice questions.
- **Review other tests:** Look over past quizzes, as well as the discussion questions or review questions provided at the end of chapters in many textbooks.

Prepare by Doing Final Reviews & Budgeting Your Test Time Learn how to make your energy and time work for you. Whether you have studied methodically or must cram for an exam, here are some tips:

- **Review your notes:** Spend the night before the test reviewing your notes. Then go to bed without interfering with the material you have absorbed (as by watching television). Get up early the next morning, and review your notes again.
- **Find a good test-taking spot:** Make sure you arrive at the exam with any pencils or other materials you need. Get to the classroom early, or at least on time, and find a quiet spot. If you don't have a watch, sit where you can see a clock. Again review your notes. Avoid talking with others, so as not to interfere with the information you have learned or to increase your anxiety.
- **Read the test directions:** Many students don't do this and end up losing points because they didn't understand precisely what was required of them. Also, listen to any verbal directions or hints your instructor gives you before the test.
- **Budget your time:** Here is an important test strategy: Before you start, read through the entire test and figure out how much time you can spend on each section. There is a reason for budgeting your time: you would hate to find you have only a few minutes left and a long essay still to be written. Write the number of minutes allowed for each section on the test booklet or scratch sheet and stick to the schedule. The way you budget your time should correspond to how confident you feel about answering the questions.

Objective Tests: Answer Easy Questions & Eliminate Options Some suggestions for taking objective tests, such as multiple-choice, true/false, or fill-in, are as follows:

- **Answer the easy questions first:** Don't waste time stewing over difficult questions. Do the easy ones first, and come back to the hard ones later. (Put a check mark opposite those you're not sure about.) Your unconscious mind may have solved them in the meantime, or later items may provide you with the extra information you need.
- **Answer all questions:** Unless the instructor says you will be penalized for wrong answers, try to answer all questions. If you have time, review all the questions and make sure you have written the responses correctly.
- **Eliminate the options:** Cross out answers you know are incorrect. Be sure to read all the possible answers, especially when the first answer is correct. (After all, other answers could also be correct, so that "All of the above" may be the right choice.) Be alert that subsequent questions may provide information pertinent to earlier questions. Pay attention to options that are long and detailed, since answers that are more detailed and specific are likely to be correct. If two answers have the opposite meaning, one of the two is probably correct.

Essay Tests: First Anticipate Answers & Prepare an Outline Because time is limited, your instructor is likely to ask only a few essay questions during the exam. The key to success is to try to anticipate beforehand what the questions might be and memorize an outline for an answer. Here are the specific suggestions:

- **Anticipate 10 probable essay questions:** Use the principles we discussed above of reviewing lecture and textbook material that is *emphasized* and *enumerated.* You will then be in a position to identify 10 essay questions your instructor may ask. Write out these questions.
- **Prepare and memorize informal essay answers:** For each question, list the main points that need to be discussed. Put supporting information in parentheses. Circle the key words in each main point and below the question put the first letter of the key word. Make up catch phrases, using acronyms, acrostics, or word games, so that you can memorize these key words. Test yourself until you can recall the key words the letters stand for and the main points the key words represent.

Key Terms Used in This Chapter

collaborative computing, 11
competitive advantage, 8
conceptual skills, 22
controlling, 13
databases, 10
decisional roles, 20
e-business, 10
e-commerce, 10
e-mail, 10
effective, 5
efficient, 5
first-line manager, 16
four management functions, 12
functional manager, 16
general manager, 16
human skills, 22
informational roles, 20
innovation, 8
Internet, 10
interpersonal roles, 20
knowledge management, 11
leading, 13
management, 4
management process, 12
middle manager, 15
organization, 4
organizing, 13
planning, 12
project management software, 10
technical skills, 22
telecommuting, 11
top manager, 15
videoconferencing, 11

Summary

1.1 Management: What It Is, What Its Benefits Are

-  Management is defined as the pursuit of organizational goals, efficiently and effectively. Efficiently means to use resources wisely and cost-effectively. Effectively means to achieve results, to make the right decisions and successfully carry them out to achieve the organization's goals.

1.2 Six Challenges to Being a Star Manager

- 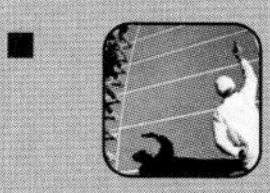 Challenge #1, managing for competitive advantage, means an organization must stay ahead in four areas: being responsive to customers; innovating new products or services; offering better quality; being more efficient.
- Challenge #2 is managing for diversity among different genders, ages, races, and ethnicities.
- Challenge #3 is managing for globalization, the expanding universe.
- Challenge #4 is managing for computers and telecommunications—information technology.
- Challenge #5 is managing for right and wrong, or ethical standards.
- Challenge #6 is managing for your own happiness and life goals.

1.3 What Managers Do: The Four Principal Functions

-  The four management functions are represented by the abbreviation POLC: *planning, organizing, leading, controlling.*
- The first function is defined as setting goals and deciding how to achieve them.
- The second function is defined as arranging tasks, people, and other resources to accomplish the work.
- The third function is defined as motivating, directing, and otherwise influencing people to work hard to achieve the organization's goals.
- The fourth function is defined as monitoring performance, comparing it with goals, and taking corrective action as needed.

1.4 Pyramid Power: Levels & Areas of Management

-  Within an organization, there are managers at three levels: top, middle, and first-line.
- Top managers make long-term decisions about the overall direction of the organization and establish the objectives, policies, and strategies for it.
- Middle managers implement the policies and plans of their superiors and supervise and coordinate the activities of the managers below them.
- First-line managers make short-term operating decisions, directing the daily tasks of nonmanagement personnel.
- There are three types of organizations classified according to the three different purposes for which they are formed. (1) For-profit organizations are formed to make money by offering products or services. (2) Nonprofit organizations offer services to some, but not to make a profit. (3) Mutual-benefit

organizations are voluntary collections of members created to advance members' interests.

1.5 Roles Managers Must Play Successfully

-  The Mintzberg study shows that, first, a manager relies more on verbal than on written communication; second, managers work long hours at an intense pace; and, third, a manager's work is characterized by fragmentation, brevity, and variety.
- From this, Mintzberg concluded that managers play three broad types of roles: interpersonal, informational, and decisional.
- In the first role, the manager acts as figurehead, leader, and liaison.
- In the second role, the manager acts as monitor, disseminator, and spokesperson.
- In the third role, the manager acts as entrepreneur, disturbance handler, resource allocator, and negotiator.

1.6 The Skills Star Managers Need

-  The three skills that star managers cultivate are technical, conceptual, and human.
- The first set of skills consists of job-specific knowledge needed to perform well in a specialized field.
- The second set of skills consists of the ability to think analytically, to visualize an organization as a whole, and to understand how the parts work together.
- The third set of skills consists of the ability to work well in cooperation with other people to get things done.

Management in Action

Successful Managers Learn the Balance Between Seeking Input & Making Decisions on Their Own

Excerpted from Carol Hymowitz, "In the Lead: The Confident Boss Doesn't Micromanage or Delegate Too Much," The Wall Street Journal, *March 11, 2003, p. B1.*

David D'Alessandro, chief executive of John Hancock Financial Services, Boston, once worked for a manager who constantly second-guessed his employees' work and forbade them from talking to anyone above him without telling him about the conversation.

"He spent half his day fielding reports from employees about whom they had spoken to," says Mr. D'Alessandro. "And he perpetuated the myth that only he could do things right."

Mr. D'Alessandro also has observed managers who, by contrast, delegate responsibilities to so many different subordinates that no one is in charge.

In either case, employees end up feeling stifled, passive, unfocused, and unwilling to take risks. "Whether you are micromanaging or diluting your authority, it's a sign of insecurity," he says.

The challenge for managers is to know when to be hands-on and when to let go and rely on subordinates. They also must understand that with each advance of the ranks, they must change the way they weigh the need to both delegate and to make decisions about things big and small.

Mr. D'Alessandro's instincts are to be a hands-on manager. But he has no strict rule about not getting involved in day-to-day tasks; sometimes he needs to jump in to keep things on track, or simply to get some peace of mind. But he has learned how to strike that important balance between helping out and trusting.

While president of John Hancock's insurance divisions, a job he took in 1991, Mr. D'Alessandro had to make sure his direct reports met weekly and monthly operations goals. He was overseeing about 8,000 employees and had nine direct reports, including heads of sales, finance, product development, and marketing for the insurance business.

"I had to believe they could do it on their own and give them the authority to do that, at least until they proved they had bad judgment," he says.

Whenever he was worried about meeting sales targets, he'd be tempted to jump in and do a subordinate's job. "Sometimes I'd want to go to the offices in the field and find things out for myself," he says. "But if I did that, people would say I was crazy—and they'd be right."

Instead he asked questions, such as why a Seattle report once showed sales down 16%. "But I wouldn't ask 40 questions like that," he says. "My point was to let people know they better be on their toes and know everything about their business."

When Mr. D'Alessandro moved to the helm of John Hancock in 2000, however, he realized he needed a management style that was even more consensual, considering the experience and expertise of those he managed.

"Each of the people who reports to me is so smart and more knowledgeable in their individual areas than I am," he says, "it would be insulting for me to ask them the Seattle kind of question. My job now is to patiently listen, hear their various views on whether we should do this deal or that strategy, and then reach a judgment."

Only when he sees problems threatening a particular project's chances of success will he go around his direct reports. "I'll make a discreet call to someone I know who is lower down," he says.

Others have earned their leadership stripes by learning how to rely on others while asserting their authority.

Debra Cafaro walked into a crisis when she was named chairman and chief executive of Ventas, a real-estate investment trust in Louisville, Ky, in 1999. She had to depend on her small team of managers but also show her ability to make tough decisions. The company, which owns nursing homes and hospitals, was originally named Vencor but had split into two companies in the wake of Medicare cutbacks in the 1990s. Ventas owned the properties and facilities that Vencor operated. Within weeks of Ms. Cafaro's arrival, the Justice Department launched an investigation at both companies over Medicare billing fraud, and Vencor filed for bankruptcy protection. Vencor's creditors then threatened lawsuits against Ventas. . . . At Ventas, she reached a settlement with the Justice Department, refinanced company debt, and helped Vencor restructure.

A lawyer by training, Cafaro sought advice from several outside attorneys, but she also worked closely with her company's general counsel and a few other executives. "We'd assemble; I'd play devil's advocate and ask a lot of questions," says Ms. Cafaro, who prefers that subordinates voice strong views. "Of ten, the group would divide over two possible directions—and debate each other," she says. "In the end, I had to make a judgment, and I never shrank from that."

For Discussion

1. Using Figure 1.1, p. 12, as a guide, describe which functions of management were displayed by David D'Alessandro and Debra Cafaro.
2. Based on Mr. D'Alessandro's and Ms. Cafaro's experiences, what type of managerial behavior is expected from top managers?
3. Which of the three types of managerial roles did Mr. D'Alessandro and Ms. Cafaro display?
4. Assume you are a manager faced with making a decision. What factors would you consider in determining whether or not to ask your employees for input as opposed to making the decision on your own?
5. The leaders depicted in this case displayed which of the three critical skills identified by Robert Katz—technical, conceptual, human? Explain.

Can You Pass the CEO Test?

Objectives

1. To assess whether or not you have "it" at this time to be a CEO.
2. To assess whether or not you want to be a CEO.
3. To see what seems to be expected of a CEO.

Introduction

The Chief Executive Officer of a company is the person in charge, the top star. This person has tremendous power and, consequently, experiences incredible pressures. Not everyone is cut out to be a CEO or aspires to be one. Many people would not want the stress and expectations for greatness that come with the job.

Instructions

Take the following quiz at *www.mbajungle.com/monthlysurvey/ceotest.cfm* to "test" whether you have "it" or not. Leading a successful company requires a combination of talents and skills that few people seem to have—some people have it, some don't. Here's your chance to find out where you stand.

Accompanying the quiz is an article by John Scaizi for the MBA Jungle Online magazine. Read it; then take the test and see if you are a potential rising star. Once you have completed the test and have submitted your responses, ask yourself the following questions and be prepared to discuss them.

Questions for Discussion

1. Do you want to be a CEO? Explain.
2. Do you want to climb the corporate ladder to become a star?
3. At what level in the organization do you think you would be comfortable?
4. What are the ethics behind #7, #8, #11, # 15, and #16?
5. How would you describe what it takes to be a CEO?

Group Exercise

How Well Do Managers Manage Their Time?*

Objectives

To see how time is allocated in a top management position.

To start to think about how you might spend your time in a top management position.

To see what you think about this kind of job and what functions are performed.

Introduction

Managers must allocate their time appropriately. If as a manager you continuously misallocate your time in terms of work coordination, your company will not reach its goals or, at the very least, you will not achieve your own goals and may become a liability to the organization. So, you must understand how to allocate your time wisely.

Instructions

The following is from Charles Handy's *Understanding Organizations:*

A senior manager's diary: One senior division manager sat down to review what he regarded as the major responsibilities of his job. He listed six key areas for himself:

1. Relations with head office: communicating with the top managers.
2. Long-term and strategic planning: the plans that position the company over time.
3. Operational responsibilities for particular ongoing activities: the day-to-day activities of the company.
4. Co-coordinating function: working with other parts of the company to complete a task or tasks.
5. Standard setting, performance, morale priorities: setting up quality standards and other types of standards, operationalizing performance appraisals, and developing a climate where employees want to work.
6. External relations: working with customers, watching what competitors are doing, dealing with pressure groups, working with suppliers.

As a group, estimate in percentages how you think this senior manager allocated his time to these six key areas. (The senior manager's percentages are included at the end of this exercise.)

1.	%	4.	%
2.	%	5.	%
3.	%	6.	%

What areas would you add to his list? Why?

Questions for Discussion

1. How do your percentages compare to the senior division manager's time allocation?
2. Why do you think that 1, 3, and 4 take so much of his time?
3. In this changing world do you think that more time should be spent on 2, 5, and 6?
4. How do managers "know" how to allocate their time? In his position, would you allocate your time differently? Why or why not?

Answers

After outlining the six key areas of responsibility in his job, the division manager then analyzed his diary for the previous three months and came up with the following approximate percentages of time spent on each of the key areas:

1.	20 %	4.	25%
2.	10 %	5.	5 %
3.	35 %	6.	5 %

*Adapted and modified by Anne Cowden, Ph.D., from Charles Handy's *Understanding Organizations* (New York: Penguin, 1993), p. 338.

Ethical Dilemma

To Delay or Not to Delay?

You have been hired by a vice president of a national company to create an employee attitude survey, to administer it to all employees, and to interpret the results. You have known this vice president for over 10 years and have worked for her on several occasions. She trusts and likes you, and you trust and like her. You have completed your work and now are ready to present the findings and your interpretations to the vice president's management team. The vice president has told you that she wants your honest interpretation of the results, because she is planning to make changes based on the results. Based on this discussion, your report clearly identifies several strengths and weaknesses that need to be addressed. For example, employees feel that they are working too hard and that management does not care about providing good customer service. At the meeting you will be presenting the results and your interpretations to a group of 15 managers. You also have known most of these managers for at least 5 years.

You show up for the presentation armed with slides, handouts, and specific recommendations. Your slides are loaded on the computer, and most of the participants have arrived. They are drinking coffee and telling you how excited they are about hearing your presentation. You also are excited to share your insights. Ten minutes before the presentation is set to begin, the vice president takes you out of the meeting room and says she wants to talk with you about your presentation. The two of you go to another office, and she closes the door. She then tells you that her boss's boss decided to come to the presentation unannounced. She feels that he is coming to the presentation solely looking for negative information in your report. He does not like the vice president and wants to replace her with one of his friends. If you present your results as planned, it will provide this individual with the information he needs to create serious problems for the vice president. Knowing this, the vice president asks you to find some way to delay your presentation. You have 10 minutes to decide what to do.

Solving the Dilemma

What would you do?

1. Deliver the presentation as planned.
2. Give the presentation but skip over the negative results.
3. Go back to the meeting room and announce that your spouse has had an accident at home and you must leave immediately. You tell the group that you just received this message and that you will contact the vice president to schedule a new meeting.
4. Invent other options. Discuss.

Video Case

The McFarlane Companies

While in high school, Todd McFarlane dreamed of playing major league baseball. When his dream didn't come true, he decided he had to go to college and earn a living. But McFarlane didn't want to just go to "work" every day; he wanted to do something he enjoyed. As a teenager, he liked to draw comic book superheroes. While in high school and college, he taught himself to draw. After sending out hundreds of samples and receiving hundreds of rejections, he was offered a job at Marvel Comics. At first working for meager pay on obscure comics, meeting deadlines with high-quality work earned him a reputation as an excellent worker. He was given the opportunity to work on well-known comics like *Batman, The Hulk,* and *Spider Man.* He brought *Spider Man* from relative obscurity to the number one comic book with record sales. Over time, McFarlane became the highest paid artist in the industry. However, he quickly became frustrated with the restrictions he faced at Marvel. He wanted to try new ideas but was discouraged by the lack of excitement at the company. He decided it was time to quit and start his own comic book business, and so he persuaded several of his best coworkers to come with him.

Industry insiders expected his company to last a year at most. But McFarlane never considered failure, and he did anything but fail. His first comic, *Spawn,* sold 1.7 million copies—and the rest is history. Today, he's creating comics, producing movies, directing music videos, and running one of the most successful toy companies in the world. His path to success was similar to that of other entrepreneurs who learned about their business working for a large company.

Entrepreneurs like McFarlane, however, face many challenges in the business environment. He takes advantage of the latest in technology to creatively make toys, movies, and video games. The Internet provides a way to reach his key customers. McFarlane loves to see rivals turn out shoddy goods because they can't compete with his high-quality toys and other products that are well worth the extra few cents.

What about his major league dream? Part of McFarlane's dream started coming true when he bought Mark McGuire's record-breaking 70th home run ball, with a price tag of $3 million. When the record was broken the next year by Barry Bonds, McFarlane had to reevaluate. He combined McGuire's ball with other McGuire and Sammy Sosa balls he had purchased to form the McFarlane collection. He sent the collection on a tour of every major league stadium. In addition to providing great public relations for the firm, this move helped develop a relationship with people in professional sports and management that led to licensing rights to produce major league toys. The $3 million ball will likely lead to $20 million in profit.

Did his boyhood dreams come true? Well, he doesn't have a baseball career, but every toy contract with a major league team includes what you might call a signing bonus—the right for McFarlane to hit batting practice in every ballpark that shows his collection. While that's not the same as being a player, McFarlane's not complaining.

Discussion Questions

1. Review the six major challenges facing today's managers. Which of these has Todd McFarlane faced? Provide evidence from the video to support your answer.
2. Managers are classified into three basic levels. What are they? In which level would you place Todd McFarlane?
3. Managers need to develop three principle skill sets—technical, conceptual, and human skills. Define each of these skill sets and provide examples of McFarlane's proficiency (or lack thereof) in each of these areas.

chapter 2

Management Theory

Essential Background for the Successful Manager

MAJOR QUESTIONS YOU SHOULD BE ABLE TO ANSWER

2.1 Evolving Viewpoints: How We Got to Today's Management Outlook

Major Question: What's the payoff in studying different management perspectives, both yesterday's and today's?

2.2 Classical Viewpoint: Scientific & Administrative Management

Major Question: If the name of the game is to manage work more efficiently, what can the classical viewpoint teach me?

2.3 Behavioral Viewpoint: Behaviorism, Human Relations, & Behavioral Science

Major Question: To understand how people are motivated to achieve, what can I learn from the behavioral viewpoint?

2.4 Quantitative Viewpoints: Management Science & Operations Research

Major Question: If the manager's job is to solve problems, how might the two quantitative approaches help?

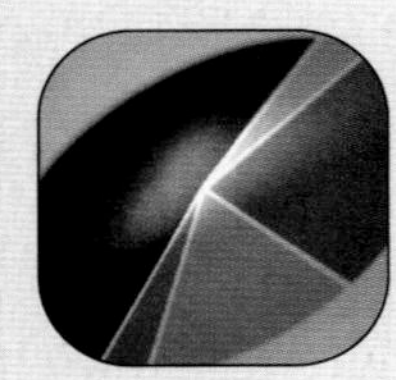

2.5 Systems Viewpoint

Major Question: How can the exceptional manager be helped by the systems viewpoint?

2.6 Contingency Viewpoint

Major Question: In the end, is there one best way to manage in all situations?

2.7 Quality-Management Viewpoint

Major Question: Can the quality-management viewpoint offer guidelines for true managerial success?

2.8 The Learning Organization

Major Question: Organizations must learn or perish. How do I build a learning organization?

the manager's toolbox

Mindfulness over Mindlessness: Being a Learner in a Learning Organization

Learn or die. Isn't that the challenge for us as individuals? It's the same with organizations. Thus has arisen the concept of the "learning organization," in which employees continually expand their ability to achieve results by obtaining the right knowledge and changing their behavior.

Throughout your career, you will have to constantly be a learner, evaluating all kinds of beliefs and theories—including those described in this chapter. However, one barrier to learning that all of us need to be aware of is *mindlessness.* Instead we need to adopt the frame of mind that Harvard psychology professor Ellen Langer has called *mindfulness,* a form of active engagement.

We've all experienced mindlessness. We misplace our keys. We write checks in January with the previous year's date. Mindlessness is characterized by the three following attributes:

- **Entrapment in old categories:** An avid tennis player, Langer says that at a tennis camp she, like all other students, was taught *exactly* how to hold her racquet and toss the ball when making a serve. But later, when watching a top tennis championship, she observed that none of the top players served the way she was taught and that all served slightly differently.[1]

  The significance: There is no one right way of doing things. In a conditional, or mindful, way of teaching, an instructor doesn't say "This is THE answer" but rather "This is ONE answer." Thus, all information—even in the hard sciences and mathematics, where it may seem as though there is just one correct answer—should be regarded with open-mindedness, since there may be exceptions. That is, you should act as though the information is true only for certain uses or under certain circumstances.

- **Automatic behavior:** Langer tells of the time she used a new credit card in a department store. Noticing that Langer hadn't signed the card yet, the cashier returned it to her to sign the back. After passing the credit card through the imprinting machine, the clerk handed her the credit card receipt to sign, which Langer did. Then, says Langer, the cashier "held the form next to the newly signed card to see if the signatures matched."[2]

  In automatic behavior, we take in and use limited signals from the world around us without letting other signals penetrate as well. By contrast, mindfulness is being open to new information—including that not specifically assigned to you. Mindfulness requires you engage more fully in whatever it is you're doing.

- **Acting from a single perspective:** Most people, says Langer, typically assume that other people's motives and intentions are the same as theirs. For example, she says, "If I am out running and see someone walking briskly, I assume she is trying to exercise and would run if only she could," when actually she may be intending to get her exercise only from walking.

For most situations, many interpretations are possible. "Every idea, person, or object is potentially simultaneously many things depending on the perspective from which it is viewed," says Langer.[3] Trying out different perspectives gives you *more choices in how to respond;* a single perspective that produces an automatic reaction reduces your options.

Developing mindfulness means consciously adapting: Being open to novelty. Being alert to distinctions. Being sensitive to different contexts. Being aware of multiple perspectives. Being oriented in the present.

forecast

What's Ahead in This Chapter

This chapter gives you a short overview of the three principal *historical* perspectives or viewpoints on management—*classical, behavioral,* and *quantitative.* It then describes the three principal *contemporary* viewpoints—*systems, contingency,* and *quality-management.* Finally, we consider the concept of *learning organizations.*

major question

What's the payoff in studying different management perspectives, both yesterday's and today's?

The Big Picture

Management began as an art but is evolving into a science. Two principal perspectives are the *historical* and the *contemporary*. Studying management theory provides a guide to action, a source of new ideas, clues to the meaning of your managers' decisions, and clues to the meaning of outside events.

It's a story seen over and over again in the movies: The amateur comes onto the scene and confounds the experts by achieving the goal everyone has been working for—catching the killer, winning the client, finding the Aztec gold, or whatever. And he or she usually does so not because of experience but because of a combination of wits, intuition, alertness, and luck.

Does this happen in real life? Of course—at least sometimes. Indeed, innovations sometimes come from people who aren't experts. The first workable personal computer, for instance, was invented by two college dropouts, Steve Jobs and Stephen Wozniak, not by the engineers at IBM or Hewlett-Packard. Unlike in the movies, however, most of the time to be a good manager it usually helps to have knowledge—to be an expert.

Is Management an Art or a Science?

There's no question that the practice of management can be an art. Debby Krenek, formerly of the *New York Daily News,* has a background in journalism, not business. Bill Gates, the founder of Microsoft Corp. and today the richest man in the world, had no training in management—in fact, he was a college dropout (from Harvard) with a background in computer science. Great managers, like great painters or actors, are those who have the right mix of intuition, judgment, and experience.

But management is also a science. That is, rather than being performed in a seat-of-the-pants, trial-and-error, make-it-up-as-you-go-along kind of way—which can lead to some truly horrendous mistakes—management can be approached deliberately, rationally, systematically. That's what the scientific method is, after all—a logical process, embodying four steps:

1. You observe events and gather facts.
2. You pose a possible solution or explanation based on those facts.
3. You make a prediction of future events.
4. You test the prediction under systematic conditions.

Throughout the book, we describe various scientific tools that managers use to solve problems.

Two Overarching Perspectives about Management & Four Practical Reasons for Studying Them

In this chapter, we describe two overarching perspectives about management:

- **Historical: The *historical perspective* includes three viewpoints—*classical, behavioral,* and *quantitative.***

- **Contemporary:** **The** ***contemporary perspective*** **also includes three viewpoints—*systems, contingency,* and *quality-management.***

This is supposed to be a practical book. But what could be more practical than studying different approaches to management to see which seem to work best? After all, as philosopher George Santayana said, "Those who cannot remember the past are condemned to repeat it."

Indeed, there are four good reasons for studying theoretical perspectives:

1. **Guide to action:** Knowing management perspectives helps you develop a set of principles, a blueprint, that will guide your actions.
2. **Source of new ideas:** Being aware of various perspectives can also provide new ideas when you encounter new situations.
3. **Clues to meaning of your managers' decisions:** It can help you understand the focus of your organization, where the top managers are "coming from."
4. **Clues to meaning of outside events:** Finally, it may allow you to understand events outside the organization that could affect it or you. ◆

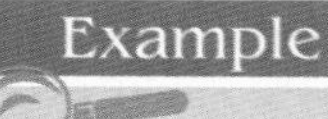

How Understanding Theory Can Help You: Is the Pyramid Hierarchy Useful or Useless?

Is there a reason for having the kind of management hierarchy that we described in Chapter 1? The idea that the company is shaped like a pyramid, with the CEO at the top and everybody else in layers below, is a legacy with strong roots in the military bureaucracy. German sociologist Max Weber thought bureaucracy was actually a rational approach to organizations, and in his day it probably was an improvement over the organizational arrangements then in place, as we'll discuss. The traditional pyramid hierarchy and bureaucracy have had a past history of great success in large corporations such as the Coca-Cola Company.

Knowing what you know about the pyramid hierarchy, can you think of any problems posed by the traditional organization chart? Could a hierarchy of boxes with lines showing who works in what department and who reports to whom actually become a corporate straitjacket?

That's what Lars Kolind, CEO of Danish digital hearing-aid producer Oticon, thought. He took Oticon's organization chart and simply threw it away. "He unilaterally abolished the old pyramid," says one account. In the new "spaghetti organization," as it came to be called, there was "no formal organization, no departments, no functions, no paper, no permanent desks."[4] All employees worked at mobile workstations, all desks were on wheels, and everybody worked on projects, that were always subject to reorganization. Why such deliberate disorganization? Because if you want to have a company that is fast, agile, and innovative, as CEO Kolind does, you might want to have a flexible organizational structure that allows for fast reaction time.

Oticon has only 150 employees, however. Here's the challenge: Could the same be done with a large company such as Coca-Cola, with its hundreds of thousands of employees?

We return to a discussion of types of organization in Chapter 8.

major question

If the name of the game is to manage work more efficiently, what can the classical viewpoint teach me?

The Big Picture

The *three historical management viewpoints* we will describe include (1) the classical, described in this section; (2) the behavioral; and (3) the quantitative. The classical viewpoint, which emphasized ways to manage work more efficiently, had two approaches: (a) scientific management and (b) administrative management. *Scientific management,* pioneered by Frederick W. Taylor and Frank and Lillian Gilbreth, emphasized the scientific study of work methods to improve the productivity of individual workers. *Administrative management,* pioneered by Henry Fayol and Max Weber, was concerned with managing the total organization.

Bet you've never heard of a "therblig," although it may describe some physical motions you perform from time to time—perhaps when you have to wash dishes. A made-up word you won't find in most dictionaries, *therblig* was coined by Frank Gilbreth and is, in fact, "Gilbreth" spelled backward, with the "t" and the "h" reversed. It refers to one of 17 basic motions. By identifying the therbligs in a job, as in the tasks of a bricklayer (which he had once been), Frank and his wife, Lillian, were able to eliminate motions while simultaneously reducing fatigue.

The Gilbreths were a husband-and-wife team of industrial engineers who were pioneers in one of the classical approaches to management, part of the historical perspective. As we mentioned, there are *three historical management viewpoints* or approaches. *(See Figure 2.1, opposite page.)* They are

- Classical
- Behavioral
- Quantitative

In this section, we describe the classical perspective of management, which originated during the early 1900s. **The *classical viewpoint,* which emphasized finding ways to manage work more efficiently, had two branches—*scientific* and *administrative***—each of which is identified with particular pioneering theorists. In general, classical management assumes that *people are rational.* Let's compare the two approaches.

Adam Smith. Another voice in the classical viewpoint, the Scottish economist authored *An Inquiry into the Nature and Causes of the Wealth of Nations* (often called simply *The Wealth of Nations*) in 1776. Considered to be the founder of modern economics, he was one of the first to imagine a system for creating wealth and improving the lives of everyone. Whereas other thinkers believed that fixed resources had to be divided among competing individuals and groups, Smith believed that resources could be expanded so that everyone could become richer. Such wealth, he suggested, was created through the efforts of entrepreneurs working to improve their lives, which led to the provision of goods and services and jobs for others. For this to occur, he believed, it was necessary for people to have the freedom to own land or property and the freedom to keep the profits they acquired from working the land or running a business. In other words, people had to know they would be rewarded, which could give them incentive to work hard to create the wealth, which would provide plenty of food and products that would benefit everyone.

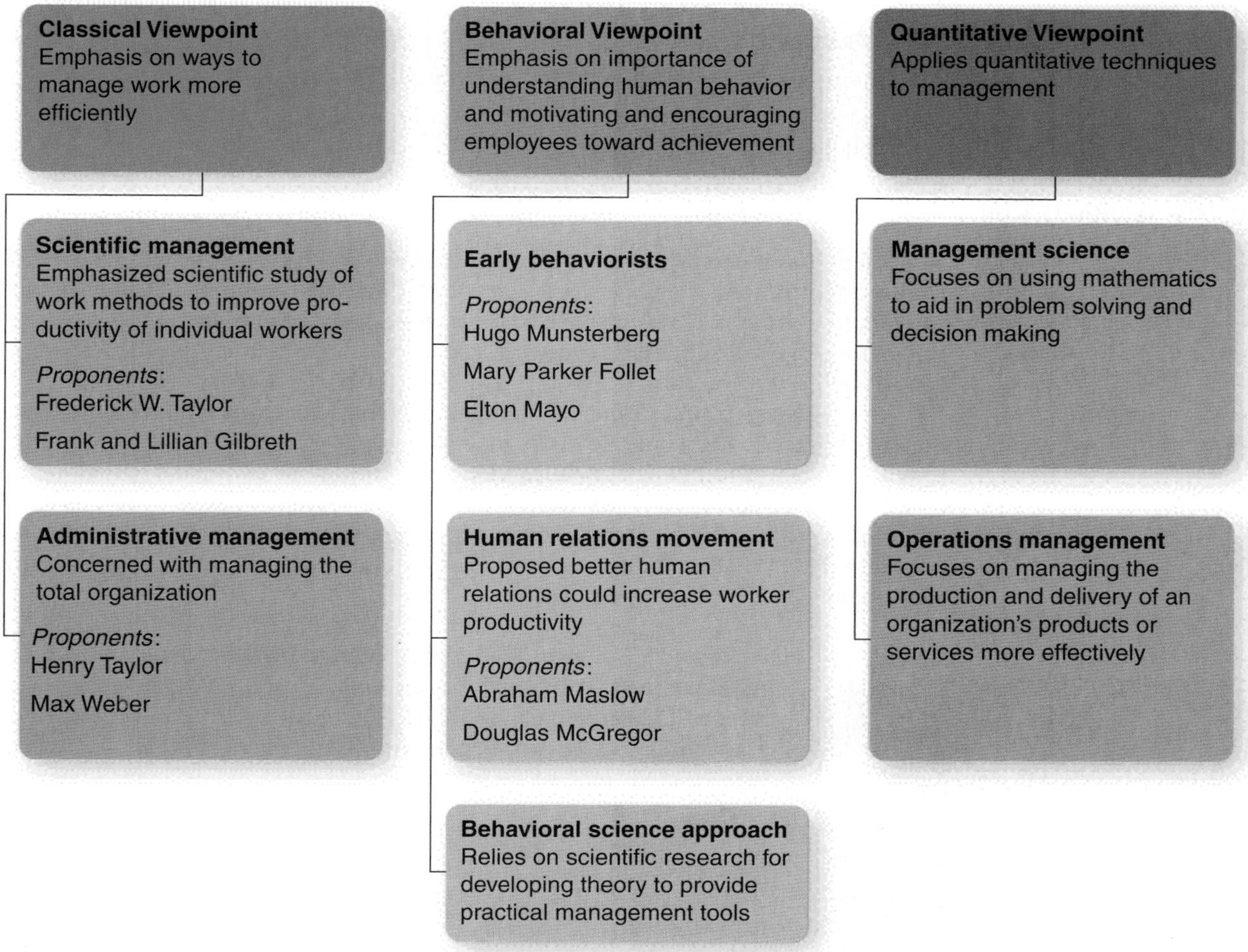

Classical Viewpoint
Emphasis on ways to manage work more efficiently

- **Scientific management**
  Emphasized scientific study of work methods to improve productivity of individual workers
  Proponents:
  Frederick W. Taylor
  Frank and Lillian Gilbreth
- **Administrative management**
  Concerned with managing the total organization
  Proponents:
  Henry Taylor
  Max Weber

Behavioral Viewpoint
Emphasis on importance of understanding human behavior and motivating and encouraging employees toward achievement

- **Early behaviorists**
  Proponents:
  Hugo Munsterberg
  Mary Parker Follet
  Elton Mayo
- **Human relations movement**
  Proposed better human relations could increase worker productivity
  Proponents:
  Abraham Maslow
  Douglas McGregor
- **Behavioral science approach**
  Relies on scientific research for developing theory to provide practical management tools

Quantitative Viewpoint
Applies quantitative techniques to management

- **Management science**
  Focuses on using mathematics to aid in problem solving and decision making
- **Operations management**
  Focuses on managing the production and delivery of an organization's products or services more effectively

FIGURE 2.1 **The historical perspective.** Three viewpoints are shown.

Scientific Management: Pioneered by Taylor & the Gilbreths

The problem for which scientific management emerged as a solution was this: In the expansive days of the early 20th century, labor was in such short supply that managers were hard pressed to raise the productivity of workers. ***Scientific management*** **emphasized the scientific study of work methods to improve the productivity of individual workers.** Two of its chief proponents were **Frederick W. Taylor** and the team of **Frank and Lillian Gilbreth.**

Frederick Taylor & the Four Principles of Scientific Management

No doubt there are some days when you haven't studied, or worked, as efficiently as you could. This could be called "underachieving," or "loafing," or what Taylor called it—*soldiering,* deliberately working at less than full capacity. Known as "the father of scientific management," Taylor was an American engineer who believed that managers could eliminate soldiering by applying four principles of science:

Frederick W. Taylor from Philadelphia, called the father of scientific management. He published *The Principles of Scientific Management* in 1911.

1. Evaluate a task by scientifically studying each part of the task (not use old rule-of-thumb methods).
2. Carefully select workers with the right abilities for the task.
3. Give workers the training and incentives to do the task with the proper work methods.
4. Use scientific principles to plan the work methods and ease the way for workers to do their jobs.

Taylor based his system on *motion studies,* in which he broke down each worker's job at a steel company, say, into basic physical motions and then trained workers to use the methods of their best-performing coworkers. In addition, he suggested employers institute a *differential rate system,* in which more efficient workers earned higher wages.

Although "Taylorism" met considerable resistance from employees fearing that working harder would lead to lost jobs except for the highly productive few, Taylor believed that by raising production both labor and management could increase profits to the point where they no longer would have to quarrel over them. If used correctly, the principles of scientific management can enhance productivity, and such innovations as motion studies and differential pay are still used today.

Frank & Lillian Gilbreth & Industrial Engineering

Lillian and Frank Gilbreth, industrial engineers who pioneered time and motion studies.

As mentioned, Frank and Lillian Gilbreth were a husband-and-wife team of industrial engineers who lectured at Purdue University in the early 1900s. Their experiences in raising twelve children—to whom they applied some of their ideas about improving efficiency (such as printing the Morse Code on the back of the bathroom door so that family members could learn it while doing other things)—later were popularized in a book, two movies, and a TV sitcom, *Cheaper by the Dozen*. The Gilbreths expanded on Taylor's motion studies—for instance, by using movie cameras to film workers at work in order to isolate the parts of a job.

Lillian Gilbreth, who received a Ph.D. in psychology, was the first woman to be a major contributor to management science.

Administrative Management: Pioneered by Fayol & Weber

Scientific management is concerned with the jobs of individuals. ***Administrative management* is concerned with managing the total organization.** Among the pioneering theorists were **Henry Fayol** and **Max Weber.**

Henry Fayol & the Functions of Management

Fayol was not the first to investigate management behavior, but he was the first to systematize it. A French engineer and industrialist, he became known to American business when his most important work, *General and Industrial Management,* was translated into English in 1930.

Fayol was the first to identify the major functions of management (p. 12)—planning, organizing, leading, and controlling, as well as coordinating—the first four of which you'll recognize as the functions providing the framework for this and most other management books.

Max Weber & the Rationality of Bureaucracy

In our time, the word "bureaucracy" has come to have negative associations: impersonality, inflexibility, red tape, a molasseslike response to problems. But to German sociologist Max Weber, a *bureaucracy* was a rational, efficient, ideal organization based on principles of logic. After all, in Weber's Germany in the late 19th century, many people were in positions of authority (particularly in the government) not because of their abilities but because of their social status. The result, Weber wrote, was that they didn't perform effectively.

A better-performing organization, he felt, should have five positive bureaucratic features:

1. A well-defined hierarchy of authority
2. Formal rules and procedures
3. A clear division of labor
4. Impersonality
5. Careers based on merit

Weber's work was not translated into English until 1947, but, as we mentioned in the box on page 35, it came to have an important influence on the structure of large corporations, such as General Motors.

The Problem with the Classical Viewpoint: Too Mechanistic

The essence of the classical viewpoint was that work activity was amenable to a rational approach, that through the application of scientific methods, time and motion studies, and job specialization it was possible to boost productivity. Indeed, these concepts are still in use today, the results visible to you every time you visit McDonald's or Pizza Hut.

The flaw in the classical viewpoint, however, is that it is mechanistic: it tends to view humans as cogs within a machine, not taking into account the importance of human needs. Behavioral theory addressed this problem, as we explain next. ◆

Scientific management. Carmakers have broken down automobile manufacturing into its constituent tasks. This reflects the contributions of the school of scientific management. Is there anything wrong with this approach? How could it be improved?

major question

To understand how people are motivated to achieve, what can I learn from the behavioral viewpoint?

The Big Picture

The second of the three historical management perspectives was the *behavioral* viewpoint, which emphasized the importance of understanding human behavior and of motivating employees toward achievement. The behavioral viewpoint developed over three phases: (1) *Early behaviorism* was pioneered by Hugo Munsterberg, Mary Parker Follett, and Elton Mayo. (2) The *human relations movement* was pioneered by Abraham Maslow (who proposed a hierarchy of needs) and Douglas McGregor (who proposed a Theory X and Theory Y view to explain managers' attitudes toward workers). (3) The *behavioral science approach* relied on scientific research for developing theories about behavior useful to managers.

The ***behavioral viewpoint*** **emphasized the importance of understanding human behavior and of motivating employees toward achievement.** The behavioral viewpoint developed over three phases: (1) early behaviorism, (2) the human relations movement, and (3) behavioral science.

The Early Behaviorists: Pioneered by Munsterberg, Follett, & Mayo

The three people who pioneered behavioral theory were **Hugo Munsterberg, Mary Parker Follett,** and **Elton Mayo.**

Hugo Munsterberg & the First Application of Psychology to Industry

Called "the father of industrial psychology," German-born Hugo Munsterberg had a Ph.D. in psychology and a medical degree and joined the faculty at Harvard University in 1892. Munsterberg suggested that psychologists could contribute to industry in three ways. They could:

1. Study jobs and determine which people are best suited to specific jobs
2. Identify the psychological conditions under which employees do their best work
3. Devise management strategies to influence employees to follow management's interests

His ideas led to the field of *industrial psychology,* the study of human behavior in workplaces, which is still taught in colleges today.

Mary Parker Follett thought managers and employees should work together cooperatively.

Mary Parker Follett & Power Sharing Among Employees & Managers

A Massachusetts social worker and social philosopher, Mary Parker Follett was lauded on her death in 1933 as "one of the most important women America has yet produced in the fields of civics and sociology." Instead of following the usual hierarchical arrangement of managers as order givers and employees as order takers, Follett thought organizations should become more democratic, with managers and employees working cooperatively.

Among her most important ideas were the following:

1. Organizations should be operated as "communities," with managers and subordinates working together in harmony.

2. Conflicts should be resolved by having managers and workers talk over differences and find solutions that would satisfy both parties—a process she called *integration*.
3. The work process should be under the control of workers with the relevant knowledge, rather than of managers, who should act as facilitators.

With these and other ideas, Follett anticipated some of today's concepts of "self-managed teams," "worker empowerment," and "interdepartmental teams"—that is, members of different departments working together on joint projects.

Elton Mayo & the Supposed "Hawthorne Effect"

Do you think workers would be more productive if they thought they were receiving special attention? This was the conclusion drawn by a Harvard research group in the late 1920s.

Conducted by Elton Mayo and his associates at Western Electric's Hawthorne (Chicago) plant, what came to be called the *Hawthorne studies* began with an investigation into whether workplace lighting level affected worker productivity. (This was the type of study that Taylor or the Gilbreths might have done.) In later experiments, other variables were altered, such as wage levels, rest periods, and length of workday. Worker performance varied but tended to increase over time, leading Mayo and his colleagues to hypothesize what came to be known as the *Hawthorne effect*—namely, that employees worked harder if they received added attention, if they thought that managers cared about their welfare and that supervisors paid special attention to them.

Ultimately, the Hawthorne studies were faulted for being poorly designed and not having enough empirical data to support the conclusions. Nevertheless, they succeeded in drawing attention to the importance of "social man" (social beings) and how managers using good human relations could improve worker productivity. This in turn led to the so-called *human relations movement* in the 1950s and 1960s.

Western Electric's Hawthorne plant, where Elton Mayo and his team conducted their studies in the 1920s. Do you think you'd perform better in a robotlike job if you thought your supervisor cared about you and paid more attention to you?

The Human Relations Movement: Pioneered by Maslow & McGregor

Douglas McGregor suggested managers need to be aware of their own attitudes toward their employees.

The two theorists who contributed most to the ***human relations movement*** **—which proposed that better human relations could increase worker productivity**—were Abraham Maslow and Douglas McGregor.

Abraham Maslow & the Hierarchy of Needs

What motivates you to perform: Food? Security? Love? Recognition? Self-fulfillment? Probably all of these, Abraham Maslow would say, although some needs must be satisfied before others. The chairman of the psychology department at Brandeis University and one of the earliest researchers to study motivation, in 1943 Maslow proposed his famous *hierarchy of human needs:* physiological, safety, social, esteem, and self-actualization[5] (as we discuss in detail in Chapter 12).

Douglas McGregor & Theory X versus Theory Y

Having been for a time a college president (at Antioch College in Ohio), Douglas McGregor came to realize that it was not enough for managers to try to be liked; they also needed to be aware of their attitudes toward employees.[6] Basically, McGregor suggested in a 1960 book, these attitudes could be either "X" or "Y."

Theory X represents a pessimistic, negative view of workers. In this view, workers are considered to be irresponsible, to be resistant to change, to lack ambition, to hate work, and to want to be led than to lead.

Theory Y represents the outlook of human relations proponents—an optimistic, positive view of workers. In this view, workers are considered to be capable of accepting responsibility, self-direction, and self-control and of being imaginative and creative.

The principal contribution offered by the Theory X/Theory Y perspective is that it can help managers avoid falling into the trap of the *self-fulfilling prophecy*. This is the idea that if a manager expects a subordinate to act in a certain way, the worker may, in fact, very well act that way, thereby confirming the manager's expectations: The prophecy that the manager made is fulfilled.

Theory Y? Debra Stark (third from left) built her Concord, Mass.–based Debra's Natural Gourmet store into a $2.5 million business by assigning each of her 26 employees, whom she calls "coworkers," a management role, such as monitoring product turnover. Each quarter, Stark distributes 20% of her after-tax profits among everyone, divided according to not only hours worked and salary level but also "how I see they're interacting with customers, each other, and me."

The Systems Viewpoint
Regards the organization as systems of interrelated parts that operate together to achieve a common purpose

The Contingency Viewpoint
Emphasizes that a manager's approach should vary according to—i.e., be contingent on—the individual and environmental situation

The Quality-Management Viewpoint
Three approaches

Quality control
Strategy for minimizing errors by managing each state of production

Proponent:
Walter Shewart

Quality assurance
Focuses on the performance of workers, urging employees to strive for "zero defects"

Total quality management
Comprehensive approach dedicated to continuous quality improvement, training, and customer satisfaction

Proponents:
W. Edwards Deming
Joseph M. Juran

FIGURE 2.2 **The contemporary perspective.** Three viewpoints

3. ***Transformation processes*** **are the organization's capabilities in management and technology that are applied to converting inputs into outputs.** The main activity of the organization is to transform inputs into outputs.
4. ***Feedback*** **is information about the reaction of the environment to the outputs that affects the inputs.** Are the customers buying or not buying the product? That information is feedback.

Checkout system. Customers use a self-service scanning system, which allows them to check themselves out at this Home Depot. Self-scanning checkout is an automated process that enables shoppers to scan, bag, and pay for their purchases without human assistance. The store's computer records the input, which is used for accounting, restocking store inventory, and weeding out products that don't sell well.

The four parts of a system are illustrated below. *(See Figure 2.3.)*

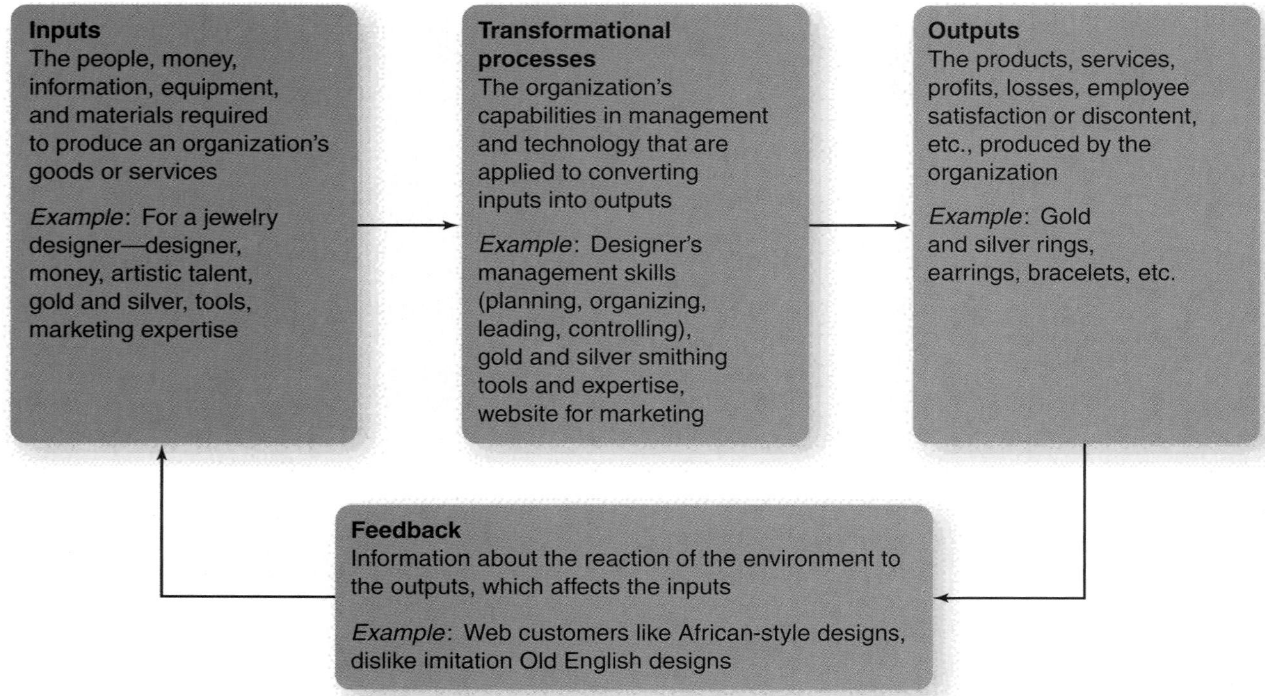

Inputs
The people, money, information, equipment, and materials required to produce an organization's goods or services
Example: For a jewelry designer—designer, money, artistic talent, gold and silver, tools, marketing expertise
Transformational processes
The organization's capabilities in management and technology that are applied to converting inputs into outputs
Example: Designer's management skills (planning, organizing, leading, controlling), gold and silver smithing tools and expertise, website for marketing
Outputs
The products, services, profits, losses, employee satisfaction or discontent, etc., produced by the organization
Example: Gold and silver rings, earrings, bracelets, etc.
Feedback
Information about the reaction of the environment to the outputs, which affects the inputs
Example: Web customers like African-style designs, dislike imitation Old English designs

FIGURE 2.3 The four parts of a system

Open & Closed Systems

Nearly all organizations are, at least to some degree, open systems rather than closed systems. An ***open system*** **continually interacts with its environment. A *closed system* has little interaction with its environment;** that is, it receives very little feedback from the outside. The classical management viewpoint often considered an organization a closed system. So does the management science perspective, which simplifies organizations for purposes of analysis. However, any organization that ignores feedback from the environment opens itself up to possibly spectacular failures.

The history of management is full of accounts of organizations whose services or products failed because they weren't open enough systems and didn't have sufficient feedback. One of the most famous gaffes was the introduction of the 1959 Edsel by the Ford Motor Co. despite mixed reactions about the car's eccentric styling by customers given a preview look at the vehicle. ◆

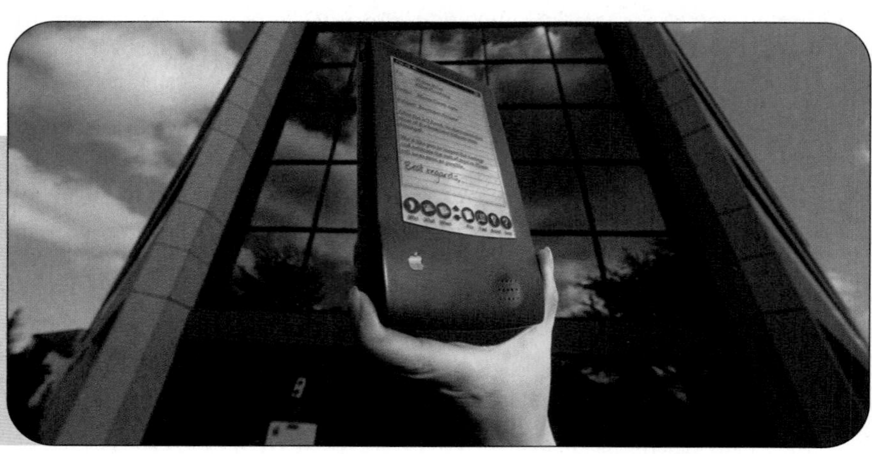

Closed system. The Apple Newton Messagepad, a personal digital assistant released in 1993 and killed in 1998, probably failed because of being developed as a closed system, with inadequate feedback from consumers before launch. It was panned for being too expensive, too large, and having faulty handwriting recognition. (It still survives because of the efforts of Newton enthusiasts, not Apple.)

Example

Open & Closed Systems: Marketing to Generation Y

Are generations really different? However fuzzy the notion of what a "generation" is, we have been accustomed to hearing them labeled: the Baby Boomers (born between 1945 and 1962), then Generation X (born 1963 to 1978), and now Generation Y (born 1979 to 1994). Generation Y—also tagged the Echo Boomers and the Millennium Generation—consists of 60 million people. While this is not as huge as the 72 million Baby Boomers, it is a great deal larger than the 17 million in Gen X, and no marketer can afford to ignore a demographic bulge of this size. But how to discover what's cool and what's not to this generation?

Having grown up with the Internet, Gen Yers are accustomed to high-speed information, research shows, which has made fashions faster changing, with young consumers inclined to switch brand loyalties in a millisecond. So far, however, Tommy Hilfiger has stayed ahead of the style curve. "When Hilfiger's distinctive logo-laden shirts and jackets started showing up on urban rappers in the early '90s," says a *Business Week* account, "the company started sending researchers into music clubs to see how this influential group wore the styles. It bolstered its traditional mass-media ads with unusual promotions. . . . Knowing its customers' passion for computer games, it sponsored a Nintendo competition and installed Nintendo terminals in its stores." By having constant feedback—an open system—with young consumers, Hilfiger has been rewarded: Its jeans are the No. 1 brand in this age group.[14] Indeed, designers like Hilfiger, Nike, and DKNY have even refused to crack down on the pirating of their logos for T-shirts and baseball hats in the inner cities in order to maintain the "got to be cool" presence of their brands.[15]

By contrast, Levi's, a veritable icon of Baby Boomer youth, was jolted awake in 1997 when its market share slid, and the company's researchers found the brand was losing popularity among teens. "We all got older, and as a consequence, we lost touch with teenagers," said David Spangler, director of market research. Levi's thereupon opened up its relatively closed system by instituting ongoing teen panels to keep tabs on emerging trends. Generation Y "is a generation that must be reckoned with," says Spangler. "They are going to take over the country."

Although Levi's has struggled to regain its luster, the end of 2003 capped the seventh consecutive year of declining sales. Earlier that year, it closed its last remaining North American manufacturing plants, joining most American apparel makers in shipping clothing-making jobs overseas.[16]

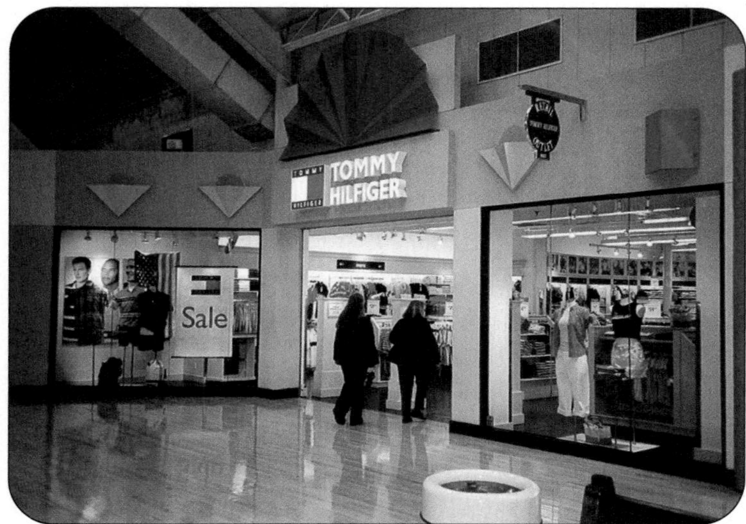

Open system. How do you stay successful? So far Tommy Hilfiger clothes have stayed popular because the firm constantly interacts with prospective customers.

major question

In the end, is there one best way to manage in all situations?

The Big Picture

The second viewpoint in the contemporary perspective, the contingency viewpoint, emphasizes that a manager's approach should vary according to the individual and environmental situation.

The classical viewpoints advanced by Taylor and Fayol assumed that their approaches had universal applications—that they were "the one best way" to manage organizations. The contingency viewpoint began to develop when managers discovered that under some circumstances better results could be achieved by breaking the one-best-way rule.

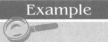

Example

The Contingency Viewpoint: When Does Using Data-Mining Software to Build Business Make Sense?

Most managers believe that technology increases productivity, a notion that Taylor and the Gilbreths might subscribe to. But does it always? Consider the use of data-mining software to increase business.

Gary Loveman, a former Harvard Business School professor, is now CEO of gambling giant Harrah's Entertainment, which owns or manages 25 casinos. Over the past six years, he has helped to build Harrah's into what will soon probably be the world's largest gaming company. He has done this not by courting high rollers, as other gambling casinos do, but by, as one article describes it, "looking for frequent shoppers—the teachers, doctors, and accountants who walk through the doors to play the odds, again and again and again."[17]

The means of building business from this customer base, Loveman explained in a famous paper (and later book), "Diamonds in the Data Mine," was through the use of data-mining software, a computer-assisted process of sifting through and analyzing vast amounts of data in order to extract meaning and discover new knowledge.[18] Loveman identified its best customers through its Total Rewards incentive program and taught them to respond to the casino's marketing efforts in a way that added to their individual value.

But does data mining always boost productivity? New software from startups such as Visible Path Corp. and Spoke Software Inc. is designed to enable companies to make faster sales by identifying and mining electronic networks of personal contacts. They allow people to get introductions to people they don't know, based on mathematical formulas that analyze tidbits of data in electronic calendars, phone logs, sales records, company databases, and the like. Thus, for example, software could compare millions of electronic address books to find whether a former college classmate of yours who became an accountant who once did business with Starbucks could help you meet chairman Howard Schultz to help pitch a business deal.

Such software might seem a beneficial business-networking tool. However, the potential downside, one writer points out, is that a world "in which salespeople are using higher-powered electronic networking tools would inevitably be a world in which more pushy people engage in more intrusive behavior."[19] Such aggressive relationship mining might well backfire by angering and humiliating the very people you are trying to reach. (From an ethical standpoint, these tools also raise prickly privacy issues.)

So, should you or should you not adopt data-mining tools for your business? The answer, according to the contingency viewpoint: it depends.

The *contingency viewpoint* emphasizes that a manager's approach should vary according to—that is, be contingent on—the individual and the environmental situation.

A manager subscribing to the Gilbreth approach might try to get workers to build a better mousetrap, say, by simplifying the steps. A manager of the Theory X/Theory Y persuasion might try to use motivational techniques to boost worker productivity. But the manager following the contingency viewpoint would simply ask, "What method is the best to use under these particular circumstances?" ◆

practical action

Toward a More Open Workplace: Treating Employees Right

Some companies are "toxic organizations," Stanford University business professor Jeffrey Pfeffer's name for firms with high turnover and low productivity. Others take a contingency kind of approach, keeping employees through methods such as "open-book management," *Inc.* magazine editor John Case's term for a company's being completely open with employees about its financial status, projections, costs, expenses, and even salaries.[20]

"Companies that manage people right will outperform companies that don't by 30% to 40%," says Pfeffer. "If you don't believe me, look at the numbers."[21] The author of *The Human Equation: Building Profits by Putting People First,* Pfeffer says that employees' loyalty to employers isn't dead but that toxic companies drive people away.[22] Companies such as Hewlett-Packard, Starbucks, and The Men's Warehouse have had lower turnover—and hence lower replacement and training costs—than their competitors for a reason: They have bent over backward to create workplaces that make people want to stay.

One way of challenging traditional military-style management and empowering employees and increasing earnings is through open-book management. This approach "means training employees in how the company is run," says one account. "It means asking for employee input and acting on it. It means rewarding employees with bonuses when the goals they create are met."[23] By learning the key numbers, employees are able to use their heads instead of just doing their jobs and going home. "Whether or not you have equity ownership, open-book management helps employees to feel, think, and act like owners," says Gary T. Brown, director of human resources for Springfield ReManufacturing Corp., a rebuilder of truck engines in Springfield, Mo.[24] "True open-book management means asking employees what the goals should be."

CompuWorks, a Pittsfield, Mass., computer systems-integration company, cultivates employee loyalty by piling on personal and team recognition, as in giving the Wizard of the Week award to the employee who goes beyond the call of duty. It also operates the Time Bank, into which every month 10 hours of free time is "deposited" for each employee to use as he or she wishes. Employees are trained how to read financial statements and how to chart billable hours and watch cash-flow levels. Regular bonuses are given based on company profits.[25]

Sometimes, despite the mantra that "the customer is always right," companies will even side with employees against clients. For example, The Benjamin Group, a California public relations agency, has fired clients who have been arrogant and hard to work with. This reflects management theories that troublesome customers are often less profitable and less loyal and so aren't worth the extra effort.[26]

All these approaches reflect the application of knowledge derived from management theory and research.[27]

Starbucks. Offering better pay, health insurance, and even stock options, Starbucks' approach to employees results in a turnover rate of only 60%—compared with 140% average for hourly workers in the fast-food business.

major question

Can the quality-management viewpoint offer guidelines for true managerial success?

The Big Picture

The quality-management viewpoint, the third category under contemporary perspectives, consists of *quality control, quality assurance,* and especially the movement of *total quality management (TQM),* dedicated to continuous quality improvement, training, and customer satisfaction.

Malcolm Baldrige National Quality Award. U.S. Commerce Secretary Donald Evans (left) and President George W. Bush (right) pose with Baldrige Award winners Alfred G. Stubblefield (second left) and John Heer, top executives for Baptist Hospital Inc., which was recognized for exceptional quality and performance excellence.

During the 1960s and 1970s, word got around among buyers of American cars that one shouldn't buy a "Monday car" or a "Friday car"—cars built on the days when absenteeism and hangovers were highest among dissatisfied auto workers. The reason, supposedly, was that, despite the efforts of quantitative management, the cars produced on those days were the most shoddily made of what were coming to look like generally shoddy products.

The energy crisis of 1973 showed different possibilities, as Americans began to buy more fuel-efficient cars made in Japan. Consumers found they could not only drive farther on a gallon of gas but that the cars were better made and needed repair less often. Eventually American car manufacturers began to adopt Japanese methods, leading to such slogans as "At Ford, Quality Is Job One." Today the average American car lasts eight or nine years compared to five or six 20 years ago.[28]

Although not a "theory" as such, the ***quality-management viewpoint,*** **which includes quality control, quality assurance, and total quality management,** deserves to be considered because of the impact of this kind of thinking on contemporary management perspectives.

Quality Control & Quality Assurance

Quality **refers to the total ability of a product or service to meet customer needs.** Quality is seen as one of the most important ways of adding value to products and services, thereby distinguishing them from those of competitors. Two traditional strategies for ensuring quality are quality control and quality assurance.

Quality Control

Quality control **is defined as the strategy for minimizing errors by managing each stage of production.** Quality control techniques were developed in the 1930s at Bell Telephone Labs by **Walter Shewart,** who used statistical sampling to locate errors by testing just some (rather than all) of the items in a particular production run.

Quality Assurance

Developed in the 1960s, ***quality assurance*** **focused on the performance of workers, urging employees to strive for "zero defects."** Quality assurance has been less successful because often employees have no control over the design of the work process.

Total Quality Management: Creating an Organization Dedicated to Continuous Improvement

In the years after World War II, the imprint "Made in Japan" on a product almost guaranteed that it was cheap and flimsy. That began to change with the arrival in Japan of two Americans, **W. Edwards Deming** and **Joseph M. Juran.**

W. Edwards Deming (right), shown with Kenzo Sasaoka, president of Yokogawa Hewlett-Packard, in Japan, 1982.

W. Edwards Deming

Desperate to rebuild its war-devastated economy, Japan eagerly received mathematician W. Edwards Deming's lectures on "good management." Deming believed that quality stemmed from "constancy of purpose"—steady focus on an organization's mission—along with statistical measurement and reduction of variations in production processes. However, he also emphasized the human side, saying that managers should stress teamwork, try to be helpful rather than simply give orders, and make employees feel comfortable about asking questions.

In addition, Deming proposed his so-called "85–15 rule"—namely, when things go wrong, there is an 85% chance that the system is at fault, only a 15% chance that the individual worker is at fault. (The "system" would include not only machinery and equipment but also management and rules.) Most of the time, Deming thought, managers erroneously blamed individuals when the failure was really in the system.

Joseph M. Juran

Another pioneer with Deming in Japan's quality revolution was Joseph M. Juran, who defined quality as "fitness for use." By this he meant that a product or service should satisfy a customer's real needs. Thus, the best way to focus a company's efforts, Juran suggested, was to concentrate on the real needs of customers.

TQM: What It Is

From the work of Deming and Juran has come the strategic commitment to quality known as total quality management. ***Total quality management (TQM)*** **is a comprehensive approach—led by top management and supported throughout the organization—dedicated to continuous quality improvement, training, and customer satisfaction.**

The four components of TQM are as follows:

1. **Make Continuous Improvement a Priority** TQM companies are never satisfied. They make small, incremental improvements an everyday priority in all areas of the organization. By improving everything a little bit of the time all the time, the company can achieve long-term quality, efficiency, and customer satisfaction.
2. **Get Every Employee Involved** To build teamwork and trust, TQM companies see that every employee is involved in the continuous improvement process. This requires that workers must be trained and empowered to find and solve problems. The goal is to build teamwork, trust, and mutual respect.
3. **Listen to & Learn from Customers & Employees** TQM companies pay attention to their customers, the people who use their products or services. In addition, employees within the companies listen and learn from other employees, those outside their own work areas.
4. **Use Accurate Standards to Identify & Eliminate Problems** TQM organizations are always alert to how competitors do things better, then try to improve on them—a process known as benchmarking. Using these standards, they apply statistical measurements to their own processes to identify problems. ◆

major question

Organizations must learn or perish. How do I build a learning organization?

The Big Picture

Learning organizations actively create, acquire, and transfer knowledge within themselves and are able to modify their behavior to reflect new knowledge. There are three ways you as a manager can help build a learning organization.

Ultimately, the lesson we need to take from the theories, perspectives, and viewpoints we have described is this: We need to keep on learning. Organizations are the same way: Like people, they must continually learn new things or face obsolescence. A key challenge for managers, therefore, is to establish a culture that will enhance their employees' ability to learn—to build so-called learning organizations.

Learning organizations, says Massachusetts Institute of Technology professor **Peter Senge,** who coined the term, are places "where people continually expand their capacity to create the results they truly desire, where new and expansive patterns of thinking are nurtured, where collective aspiration is set free, and where people are continually learning how to learn together."[29]

The Learning Organization: Handling Knowledge & Modifying Behavior

More formally, a ***learning organization*** **is an organization that actively creates, acquires, and transfers knowledge within itself and is able to modify its behavior to reflect new knowledge.**[30] Note the three parts:

1. **Creating & Acquiring Knowledge** In learning organizations, managers try to actively infuse their organizations with new ideas and information, which are the prerequisites for learning. They acquire such knowledge by constantly scanning their external environments, by not being afraid to hire new talent and expertise when needed, and by devoting significant resources to training and developing their employees.
2. **Transferring Knowledge** Managers actively work at transferring knowledge throughout the organization, reducing barriers to sharing information and ideas among employees. Electronic Data Systems (EDS), for instance, practically invented the information-technology services industry, but by 1996 it was slipping behind competitors—missing the onset of the Internet wave, for example. When a new CEO, Dick Brown, took the reins in 1999, he changed the culture from "fix the problem yourself" to sharing information internally.[31]
3. **Modifying Behavior** Learning organizations are nothing if not results oriented. Thus, managers encourage employees to use the new knowledge obtained to change their behavior to help further the organization's goals.[32]

How to Build a Learning Organization: Three Roles Managers Play

To create a learning organization, managers must perform three key functions or roles: (1) *build a commitment to learning,* (2) *work to generate ideas with impact,* and (3) *work to generalize ideas with impact.*[33]

1. **You Can Build a Commitment to Learning** To instill in your employees an intellectual and emotional commitment to the idea of learning, you as a manager need to lead the way by investing in it, publicly promoting it, creating rewards and symbols of it, and similar activities. In publicly promoting it, for example, you can disseminate videos and readings to employees, be a presenter or participant at training seminars, or share with other managers management practices you've learned.
2. **You Can Work to Generate Ideas with Impact** As a manager, you need to try to generate ideas with impact—that is, ideas that add value for customers, employees, and shareholders—by increasing employee competence through training, experimenting with new ideas, and engaging in other leadership activities.

   Soon after Dick Brown became new CEO of EDS, he saw that the company had to be reinvented as a cool brand to make people feel good about working there. His marketing director decided to launch a new campaign at the biggest media event of all: the Super Bowl. EDS ran an ad showing rugged cowboys riding herd on 10,000 cats. The message: "We ride herd on complexity."
3. **You Can Work to Generalize Ideas with Impact** Besides generating ideas with impact, you can also generalize them—that is, reduce the barriers to learning among employees and within your organization. You can create a climate that reduces conflict, increases communication, promotes teamwork, rewards risk taking, reduces the fear of failure, and increases cooperation. In other words, you can create a psychologically safe and comforting environment that increases the sharing of successes, failures, and best practices.

We consider the learning organization again in Chapter 8. 

Example

A Learning Organization: Apple & Steve Jobs's Experimental Mindset

Experimental mindset—support for trying new things—is an important factor in facilitating learning. An example of a company employing this learning factor is Apple Computer.

Apple—and its headstrong chairman, Steve Jobs—have made plenty of mistakes. In 2000, after bringing the trend-setting iMac personal computer to market, Jobs commissioned a good-looking, cube-shaped, fanless Mac with a high price tag—so high, in fact, that consumers were turned off in droves, and the product was withdrawn in a matter of months. Macs were also developed without CD burners, just at a time that students were starting to burn CDs of their favorite songs.

Realizing their mistake, Jobs ordered Apple's developers to create the iTunes music program to help customers manage their growing PC music collections. "That led to the concept of the iPod," says a *Business Week* account. "If people were going to maintain the bulk of their music on their PCs, they'd want a portable device to take it with them."[34]

Looking for the necessary components, Apple found PortalPlayer had the technology for the insides and Toshiba had a small disk drive that could hold thousands of songs. Despite the high price of $399 when the iPod debuted in October 2001, the product was extremely profitable. Sales surged even more after a Windows-compatible iPod by Hewlett-Packard came out in mid-2002—a revolution in Apple's way of thinking, since it used to resist licensing its technology to cloners and as a result had lost market share to Microsoft.

Then Jobs took on the even bigger task of persuading the major record labels to make their music available for inexpensive legal downloads on one website—what became the Apple Music Store. When iTunes was unveiled in April 2003, it was clear Apple had a hit: a million songs were sold the first week.

Can Jobs and Apple learn from the past to grow their market, as in moving into movie downloads? "A dozen years ago," says *Business Week,* Jobs "was the washed-up former CEO of Apple, the *enfant terrible* of tech with little hope of doing anything of consequence again. Now he's hailed for changing the world of music—and has the opportunity to do much more."

Key Terms Used in This Chapter

administrative management, 38
behavioral science, 43
behavioral viewpoint, 40
classical viewpoint, 36
closed system, 48
contemporary perspective, 35
contingency viewpoint, 51
feedback, 47
historical perspective, 34
human relations movement, 42
inputs, 46
learning organization, 54
management science, 44
open system, 48
operations management, 45
outputs, 46
quality, 52
quality assurance, 52
quality control, 52
quality-management viewpoint, 52
quantitative management, 44
scientific management, 37
subsystems, 46
system, 46
systems viewpoint, 46
total quality management (TQM), 53
transformation process, 47

Summary

2.1 Evolving Viewpoints: How We Got to Today's Management Outlook

- Management is an art, but it is also a science. In this chapter we describe two overarching theoretical perspectives on management: (1) The historical perspective includes three viewpoints—classical, behavioral, and quantitative. (2) The contemporary perspective also includes three viewpoints—systems, contingency, and quality-management.
- There are four good reasons for studying theoretical perspectives. They provide (1) a guide to action, (2) a source of new ideas, (3) clues to the meaning of your managers' decisions, and (4) clues to the meaning of outside ideas.

2.2 Classical Viewpoint: Scientific & Administrative Management

- The first of the historical perspectives includes the classical viewpoints, which emphasized finding ways to manage work more efficiently. It had two branches, scientific and administrative.
- Scientific management emphasized the scientific study of work methods to improve productivity of individual workers. It was pioneered by Frederick W. Taylor, who offered four principles of science that could be applied to management, and by Frank and Lillian Gilbreth, who refined motion studies that broke job tasks into physical motions.
- Administrative management was concerned with managing the total organization. Among its pioneers were Henry Fayol, who identified the major functions of management (planning, organizing, leading, and controlling), and Max Weber, who identified five positive bureaucratic features in a well-performing organization.
- The problem with the classical viewpoint is that it is too mechanistic, viewing humans as cogs in a machine.

2.3 Behavioral Viewpoint: Behaviorism, Human Relations, & Behavioral Science

- The second of the historical perspectives, the behavioral viewpoint emphasized the importance of understanding human behavior and of motivating employees toward achievement. It developed over three phases.
- The first phase, early behaviorism, had three pioneers. Hugo Munsterberg suggested that psychologists could contribute to industry by studying jobs, identifying the psychological conditions for employees to do their best work, and devising strategies to influence employees to follow management's interests.
- Mary Parker Follett thought organizations should be democratic, with employees and managers working together.
- Elton Mayo hypothesized a so-called Hawthorne effect, suggesting that employees worked harder if they received added attention from managers.
- The second phase was the human relations movement, which suggested that better human relations could increase worker productivity. It was pioneered by Abraham Maslow, who proposed a hierarchy of human needs (physiological, safety, social, esteem, and self-actualization). Another pioneer was Douglas McGregor, who proposed a Theory X (managers have

pessimistic, negative view of workers) versus Theory Y (managers have optimistic, positive view of workers) and suggested that managers could avoid the self-fulfilling prophecy of expecting workers to behave a certain way and then being unsurprised when they acted that way.

- The third phase was the behavioral science approach, which relies on scientific research for developing theories about human behavior that can be used to provide practical tools for managers.

2.4 Quantitative Viewpoints: Management Science & Operations Research

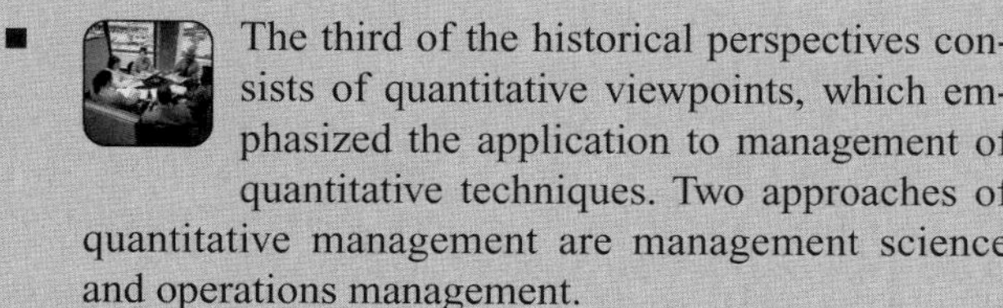

- The third of the historical perspectives consists of quantitative viewpoints, which emphasized the application to management of quantitative techniques. Two approaches of quantitative management are management science and operations management.
- Management science focuses on using mathematics to aid in problem solving and decision making.
- Operations management focuses on managing the production and delivery of an organization's products or services more effectively.

2.5 Systems Viewpoint

- We turn from study of the historical management perspectives to the contemporary management perspectives, which includes three viewpoints: (1) systems, (2) contingency, and (3) quality-management.
- The systems viewpoint regards the organization as a system of interrelated parts or collection of subsystems that operate together to achieve a common purpose. A system has four parts: inputs, outputs, transformation processes, and feedback. A system can be open, continually interacting with its environment, or closed, having little such interaction.

2.6 Contingency Viewpoint

- The second viewpoint in the contemporary perspective is the contingency viewpoint, which emphasizes that a manager's approach should vary according to the individual and the environmental situation.

2.7 Quality-Management Viewpoint

- The third category in the contemporary perspective is the quality-management viewpoint, which includes (1) quality control, (2) quality assurance, and (3) total quality management.
- Quality refers to the total ability of a product or service to meet customer needs. Two traditional strategies for ensuring quality are quality control and quality assurance. Quality control is defined as the strategy for minimizing errors by managing each stage of production. Quality assurance focuses on the performance of workers, urging employees to strive for "zero defects."
- Total quality management (TQM) is a comprehensive approach—led by top management and supported throughout the organization—dedicated to continuous quality improvement, training, and customer satisfaction. The four components of TQM are (1) make continuous improvement a priority, (2) get every employee involved, (3) listen to and learn from customers and employees, and (4) use accurate standards to identify and eliminate problems.

2.8 The Learning Organization

- A learning organization is an organization that actively creates, acquires, and transfers knowledge within itself and is able to modify its behavior to reflect new knowledge.
- Three roles that managers must perform to build a learning organization are (1) build a commitment to learning, (2) work to generate ideas with impact, and (3) work to generalize ideas with impact.

Management in Action

Toyota Relies on a Variety of Management Theories to Cut Costs & Increase Profits

Excerpted from Brian Bremner and Chester Dawson, "Can Anything Stop Toyota?" Business Week, *November 17, 2003, pp. 116, 117, 120, 122.*

BusinessWeek

Yoi kangae, yoi shina! That's Toyota-speak for "Good thinking means good products." The slogan is emblazoned on a giant banner hanging across the company's Takaoka assembly plant, an hour outside the city of Nagoya. Plenty of good thinking has gone into the high-tech ballet that's performed here 17 hours a day. Six separate car models—from the Corolla compact to the new youth-oriented Scion xB—glide along on a single production line in any of a half-dozen colors. Overhead, car doors flow by on a conveyor belt that descends to floor level and drops off the right door in the correct color for each vehicle. This efficiency means Takaoka workers can build a car in just 20 hours.

The combination of speed and flexibility is world class. More important, a similar dance is happening at 30 Toyota plants worldwide, with some able to make as many as eight different models on the same line. That is leading to a monster increase in productivity and market responsiveness—all part of the company's obsession with what President Fujio Cho calls "the criticality of speed." . . .

Of course, the carmaker has always moved steadily forward: its executives created the doctrine of *kaizen,* or continuous improvement. "They find a hole, and they plug it," says auto-industry consultant Maryann Keller. "They methodically study problems, and they solve them." But in the past few years, Toyota has accelerated these gains, raising the bar for the entire industry. Consider: . . .

- Toyota has launched a joint program with its suppliers to radically cut the number of steps needed to make cars and car parts. In the past year alone, the company chopped $2.6 billion out of its $113 billion in manufacturing costs without any plant closures or layoffs. Toyota expects to cut an additional $2 billion out of its cost base this year.
- Toyota is putting the finishing touches on a plan to create an integrated, flexible, global manufacturing system. In this new network, plants from Indonesia to Argentina will be designed both to customize cars for local markets and to shift production to quickly satisfy any surges in demand from markets worldwide. By tapping, say, its South African plant to meet a need in Europe, Toyota can save itself the $1 billion normally needed to build a new factory. . . .

Toyota has always valued frugality. It still turns down the heat at company-owned employee dormitories during working hours and labels its photocopy machines with the cost per copy to discourage overuse. But cost-cutting was often a piecemeal affair. With CCC21 [Construction of Cost Competitiveness for the 21st Century], Cho set a bold target of slashing prices on all key components for new models by 30%, which meant working with suppliers and Toyota's own staff to ferret out excess. "Previously, we tried to find waste here and there," says Cho. "But now there is a new dimension of proposals coming in."

In implementing CCC21, no detail is too small. For instance, Toyota designers took a close look at the grip handles mounted above the doors inside most cars. By working with suppliers, they managed to cut the number of parts in these handles to five from 34, which helped cut procurement costs by 40%. As a plus, the change slashed the time needed for installation by 75%—to three seconds. "The pressure is on to cut costs at every stage," says Takashi Araki, a project manager at parts maker Aisin Seiki Co.

Just as Cho believes he can get far more out of suppliers, he thinks Toyota can make its workers vastly more productive. This is classic *kaizen,* but these days it has gone into overdrive. In the middle of the Kentucky plant, for instance, a *Kaizen* Team of particularly productive employees works in a barrackslike structure. The group's sole job is coming up with ways to save time and money. Georgetown employees, for instance, recommended removing the radiator support base—the lower jaw of the car—until the last stage of assembly. That way, workers can step into the engine compartment to install parts instead of having to lean over the front end and risk straining their backs. "We used to have to duck into the car to install something," explains Darryl Ashley, 41, a soft-spoken Kentucky native who joined Toyota nine years ago. . . .

It was once company doctrine that Lexus could be made only in Japan. No longer. Production of the RX 330 SUV started in Cambridge [Ontario, Canada] on Sept. 26 [2003]. If the Canadian hands can deliver the same quality as their Japanese counterparts, Toyota will be able to chop shipping costs by shifting Lexus production to the market where the bulk of those cars are sold.

The Japanese bosses put the Canadians through their paces. The 700 workers on the RX 330 line trained for 12 weeks, including stints in Japan for 200 of them. There, the Canadians managed to beat Japanese teams in quality assessment on a mock Lexus line. Cambridge has taken Toyota's focus on *poka-yoke,* or foolproofing measures, to another level. The plant has introduced "Circle L" stations where workers must double- and triple-check parts that customers have complained about—anything from glove boxes to suspension systems. "We know that if we can get this right, we may get to build other Lexus models," says Jason Birt, a 28-year-old Lexus line worker.

The Cambridge workers are aided by a radical piece of manufacturing technology being rolled out to Toyota plants worldwide. The system, called the Global Body Line, holds vehicle frames in place while they're being welded, using just one master brace instead of the dozens of separate braces required in a standard factory. No big deal? Perhaps, but the system is half as expensive to install. Analysts say it lets Toyota save 75% of the cost of refitting a production line to build a different car, and it's key to Toyota's ability to make multiple models on a single line. Better yet, the brace increases the rigidity of the car early in production, which boosts the accuracy of welds and makes for a more stable vehicle. "The end results are improved quality, shortened welding lines, reduced capital investment, and less time to launch new vehicles," says Atsushi Niimi, president of Toyota Motor Manufacturing North America.

Cho and his managers are not just reengineering how Toyota makes its cars—they want to revolutionize how it creates products. With the rise of e-mail and teleconferencing, teams of designers, engineers, product planners, workers, and suppliers rarely all convened in the same place. Under Cho, they're again required to work face to face, in a process Toyota calls *obeya*—literally, "big room." This cuts the time it takes to get a car from the drawing board to the showroom. It took only 19 months to develop the 2003 Solara. That's better than 22 months for the latest Sienna minivan, and 26 months for the latest Camry—well below the industry average of about three years.

For Discussion

1. Is Toyota making changes more reflective of managerial art or managerial science? Explain your rationale.
2. What advice would Frederick Taylor probably offer managers at Toyota?
3. To what extent is Toyota's approach to cost reduction and productivity enhancement consistent with Mary Parker Follett's teachings? Explain.
4. How is Toyota using management science and operations management techniques to reduce costs and increase productivity? Explain.
5. Are the changes being made at Toyota consistent with recommendations derived from a quality-management viewpoint?

Self-Assessment

What Is Your Level of Self-Esteem?

Objectives

1. To get to know yourself a bit better.
2. To help you assess your self-esteem.

Introduction:

Self-esteem, confidence, self-worth, and self-belief are all important aspects of being a manager in any organizational structure. However, the need for strong self-esteem is especially vital today because organizations demand that a manager manage people not as appendages of machines (as in Scientific Management) but as individuals who possess skills, knowledge, and self-will. Managers used to operate from a very strong position of centralized power and authority. However, in our modern organizational settings power is shared, and knowledge is to some extent "where you find it." To manage effectively in this situation, managers need strong self-esteem.

Instructions:

To assess your self-esteem, answer the following questions. For each item, indicate the extent to which you agree or disagree by using the following scale. Remember, there are no right or wrong answers.

1 = strongly disagree
2 = disagree
3 = neither agree nor disagree
4 = agree
5 = strongly agree

Questions

1. I generally feel as competent as my peers.	1 2 3 4 5
2. I usually feel I can achieve whatever I want.	1 2 3 4 5
3. Whatever happens to me is mostly in my control.	1 2 3 4 5
4. I rarely worry about how things will work out.	1 2 3 4 5
5. I am confident that I can deal with most situations.	1 2 3 4 5
6. I rarely doubt my ability to solve problems.	1 2 3 4 5
7. I rarely feel guilty for asking others to do things.	1 2 3 4 5
8. I am rarely upset by criticism.	1 2 3 4 5
9. Even when I fail, I still do not doubt my basic ability.	1 2 3 4 5
10. I am very optimistic about my future.	1 2 3 4 5

11. I feel that I have quite a lot to offer an employer. 1 2 3 4 5
12. I rarely dwell for very long on personal setbacks. 1 2 3 4 5
13. I am always comfortable in disagreeing with my boss. 1 2 3 4 5
14. I rarely feel that I would like to be somebody else. 1 2 3 4 5

TOTAL SCORE______

Arbitrary Norms

High Self-esteem = 56–70

Moderate Self-esteem = 29–55

Low Self-esteem = 14–28

Questions for Discussion

1. Do you agree with the assessment? Why or why not?
2. How might you go about improving your self-esteem?
3. Can you survive today without having relatively good confidence in yourself?

Group Exercise

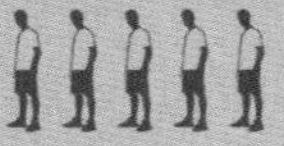

Who Are the Most Admired Companies & Why?*

Objectives

1. To assess your group's awareness of the most admired companies in the United States (as of 2004).
2. To discover the different perceptions of these companies and their management practices.
3. To understand how companies achieve the reputation they have earned.

Introduction

For decades *Fortune* magazine has asked top managers who they think are the most-admired and best-managed companies in the United States. Over the years we have moved from a time when Frederick Taylor and Henry Ford tied productivity to profit to the current understanding of the effect of the other "bottom lines" that must be considered to assess how well a company is managed (for example, companies' effect on the environment). Only six companies have held the number-1 spot on this *Fortune* list since 1983. They are IBM (5 times), Merck (15 times), Rubbermaid (11 times), Coca-Cola (13 times), General Electric (9 times), and Wal-Mart (2 times). However, only three of these were in the top 10 in 2004.

Instructions

Eight key attributes of reputation are used to rank the companies (there are 500 in all):

innovation
financial soundness
employee talent
use of corporate assets
long-term investment value
social responsibility
quality of management
quality of products/services

Following is a list, in random order, of the top 10 most-admired companies for 2004. Each member of your group is to guess these companies' rankings based on the attributes listed above. (Number 1 is the highest ranking and number 10 is the lowest ranking.) Group members should then compare their rankings and come to a consensus. (If time permits, locate additional information about each company on the Internet before you complete your group rankings.)

Here are the companies, in random order:

1. IBM
2. Dell
3. Berkshire Hathaway
4. Southwest Airlines
5. FedEx
6. Microsoft
7. Wal-Mart
8. Starbucks
9. General Electric
10. Johnson & Johnson

Questions for Discussion

1. Why did you as an individual rank the companies as you did? Explain.
2. How different was the group ranking from your own ranking? Why?
3. Why did the group order its ranking in the way it did?
4. What concepts from the chapter could you use to explain why these companies are so well managed and admired?

Answers

1. Wal-Mart
2. Berkshire Hathaway
3. Southwest Airlines
4. General Electric
5. Dell
6. Microsoft
7. Johnson & Johnson
8. Starbucks
9. FedEx
10. IBM

*This exercise was adapted from *www.leadersdirect.com/howareyou/html.*

Ethical Dilemma

Should Medical Devices Be Used as an Aid in Marketing Products?

Excerpted from Joan O'C. Hamilton, "Journey to the Center of the Mind: 'Functional' MRI Is Yielding a Clearer Picture of What Thoughts Look Like," Business Week, *April 19, 2004, pp. 78–80.*

[Magnetic resonance imaging (MRI)] technology has been used since the 1980s to detect injury or disease in patients suffering from symptoms such as seizures, paralysis, or severe headaches. But in just the past few years, manufacturers have developed stronger MRI magnets and more sophisticated software that can sort through a flood of subtle signals the scans collect.

. . . Imaging technology has leaped far beyond its roots of looking for lumps and shadows. Psychiatrists are now studying the mental activities of patients suffering from depression and other emotional ills. Basic researchers are rolling thousands of healthy subjects . . . into MRI machines in order to explore the very essence of the mind, asking them to think, decide, feel, and learn inside the scanners. Pharma companies hope the new "functional" MRI (fMRI) technology will enhance drug development. Law enforcement experts hope it could become a more accurate lie detector. Even our most private tastes and impulses are under scrutiny as so-called neuromarketing takes off.

. . . Unlike other brain-scanning technologies such as positron emission tomography (PET), which exposes patients to radiation, fMRI simply tracks the response in the brain tissue to magnetic fields. It's noninvasive and believed to be harmless. That means even very young children can be scanned—and scanned repeatedly as they grow older.

. . . One intriguing, yet controversial use of fMRI is probing consumer preferences—a technique sometimes called *neuromarketing*. At California Institute of Technology, researcher Stephen R. Quartz is using fMRI to explore how the brain perceives a cool product vs. an uncool one. Among portable MP3 players, "the [Apple] iPod is by far the market leader. What about that gives us a different signal in the brain?" he asks. Quartz also has formed a company that will offer services to Hollywood studios, imaging the brains of test audiences as they view movie trailers to see which generate the most brain buzz.

Solving the Dilemma

You are part of a committee on medical ethics organized to vote on whether fMRI should be used in capacities other than medicine—i.e., law enforcement and consumer marketing. How would you vote?

1. Absolutely not. It is wrong to use medical technology in any other capacity than healing.
2. Absolutely not. I don't think anyone should be able to peek into my own private thoughts and preferences.
3. Yes, but only if the brain scan data is made public. It could be of scientific interest and could be used to combat social issues such as racism and terrorism. It would also be extremely useful for law enforcement, because it would help determine what really went on in the mind of a criminal.
4. Invent other options. Discuss.

Video Case

Now Who's Boss?

Jonathan Tisch, chairman and CEO of Loews Hotels, was in for an eye-opening experience. As a child he worked at various jobs in the hotel industry, but as CEO he was woefully unprepared to take on the tasks of desk clerk, bellhop, cook, housekeeper, and more. Tisch performed the jobs of various staff members at his Loews Miami Beach Hotel, all filmed and turned into a television program for The Learning Channel. Tisch was impressed with the dedication, diligence, and hard work shown by the hotel staff. He was also surprised at the extent to which technology was integrated into hotel functions. Using the computer to check guests into the hotel was an arduous experience, with the line of customers growing impatient as he struggled to learn the system. What has not changed, however, is the fundamental nature of the hospitality business. When guests arrive, they're tired, cranky, and irritable. They want a clean room quickly, relaxation by the pool, and smooth service from friendly, helpful staff.

The hotel staff who trained and supervised Tisch in his new jobs were brutally honest, but they kept a touch of humor. More than once Tisch was given a failing grade and told he wouldn't be able to handle the job in real life. Tisch performed each job for about half a day and left with a newfound respect for the employees who keep the hotel running smoothly. As a housekeeper, Tisch just didn't know his standards, and his supervisor, Sara Roiz, didn't hesitate to tell him so. Tisch was especially impressed with the physical challenges faced by the housekeepers, who enter a room never knowing what to expect and often receive no tips for their service.

When Tisch returned to his job as CEO, he informed senior executives that they would share similar experiences. Top managers assumed the roles of subordinates in each of their departments and gained a new appreciation for what it takes to keep an organization running.

Discussion Questions

1. Summarize the contributions of Frederick Taylor and Mary Parker Follett to contemporary management. Which of these two individuals would be most willing, as was CEO Jonathan Tisch, to perform the job of his or her subordinate?
2. Based on what you've seen in the video, does CEO Jonathan Tisch have a Theory Y or a Theory X view of human nature?
3. Is Lowes Miami Beach Hotel a learning organization? Use evidence from the video to support your answer.

then-prevailing wages. The reason: He recognized that his promise to build a car affordable to the masses would be hypocritical if he didn't pay his own workers enough to buy it themselves.[6]

Internal & External Stakeholders

Should a company be principally responsible to just its stockholders? Perhaps we need a broader term to indicate all those with a stake in an organization. That term, appropriately, is ***stakeholders*** **—the people whose interests are affected by an organization's activities.**

Managers operate in two organizational environments, both made up of various stakeholders. *(See Figure 3.1.)* As we describe in the rest of this section, the two environments are these:

- Internal stakeholders
- External stakeholders

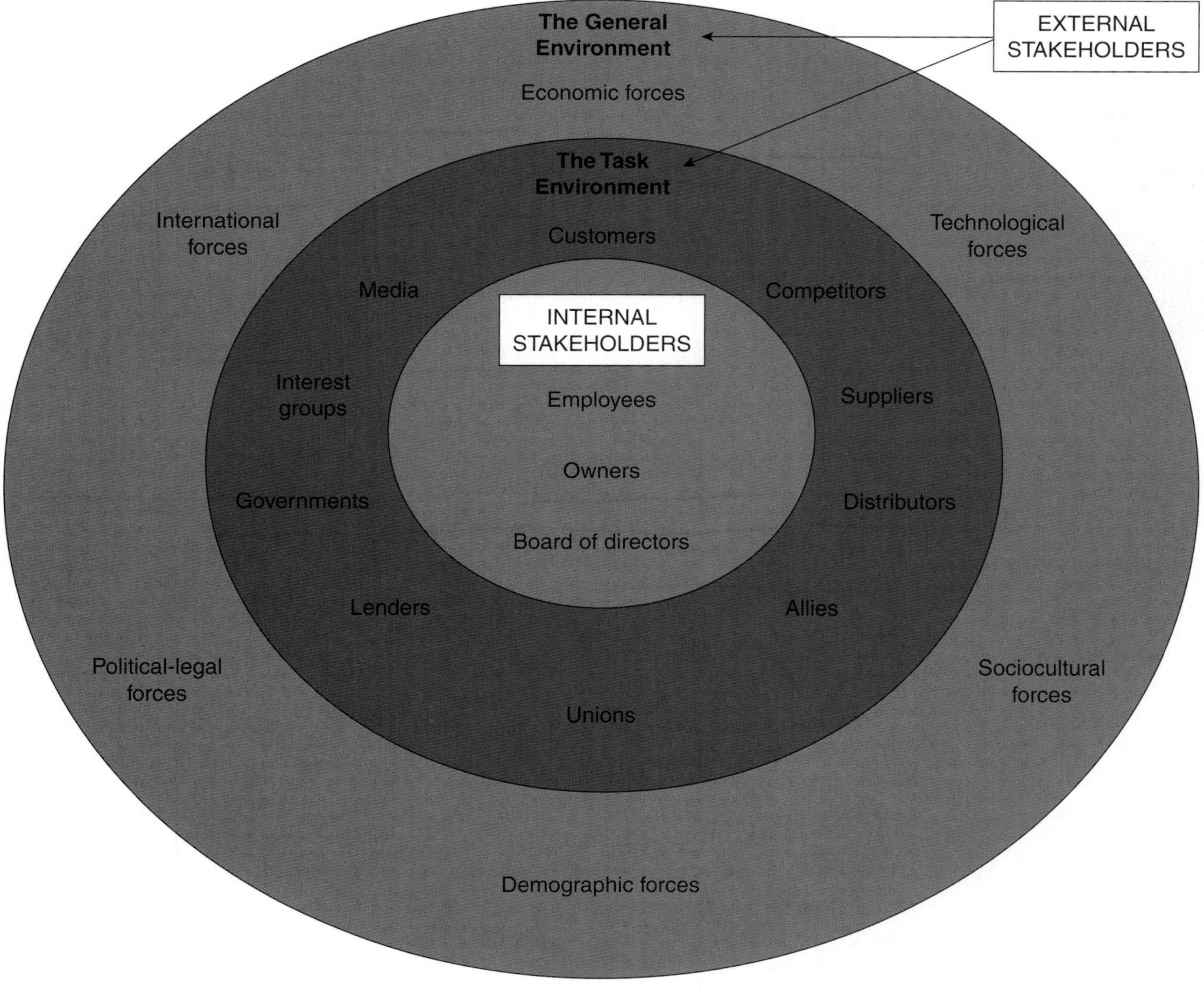

FIGURE 3.1

The organization's environment. The two main groups are internal and external stakeholders

Internal Stakeholders

Whether small or large, the organization to which you belong has people in it that have an important stake in how it performs. These ***internal stakeholders* consist of employees, owners, and the board of directors, if any.** Let us consider each in turn.

Employees

As a manager, could you run your part of the organization if you and your employees were constantly in conflict? Labor history, of course, is full of accounts of just that. But such conflict may lower the performance of the organization, thereby hurting everyone's stake. In many of today's forward-looking organizations, employees are considered "the talent"—the most important resource.

For instance, at Trilogy Software, a small, fast-growing software firm in Austin, Texas, workers aren't really considered "employees." "They're all shareholders," says former U.S. Labor Secretary Robert Reich in an article about cutting-edge kinds of companies. "They're all managers. They're all partners. That's how [Joe] Liemandt, Trilogy's CEO, has chosen to run his company—and that's what makes it successful."[7]

Owners

The ***owners* of an organization consist of all those who can claim it as their legal property,** such as Wal-Mart's stockholders. In the for-profit world, if you're running a one-person graphic design firm, the owner is just you—you're what is known as a sole proprietorship. If you're in an Internet startup with your brother-in-law, you're both owners—you're a partnership. If you're a member of a family running a car dealership, you're all owners—you're investors in a privately owned company. If you work for an airline that is partly owned by its employees, as United Airlines is (55% employee owned), you are one of the joint owners—you're part of an Employee Stock Ownership Plan (ESOP). And if you've bought a few shares of stock in a company whose shares are listed for sale on the New York Stock Exchange, such as General Motors, you're one of thousands of owners—you're a stockholder. In all these examples, of course, the goal of the owners is to make a profit.

Board of Directors

Who hires the chief executive of a for-profit or nonprofit organization? In a corporation, it is the *board of directors,* whose members are elected by the stockholders to see that the company is being run according to their interests. In nonprofit organizations, such as universities or hospitals, the board may be called the *board of trustees* or *board of regents.* Board members are very important in setting the organization's overall strategic goals and in approving the major decisions and salaries of top management.

Not all firms have a board of directors. A lawyer, for instance, may operate as a sole proprietor, making all her own decisions. A large corporation might have eight or so members of its board of directors. Some of these directors (inside directors) may be top executives of the firm. The rest (outside directors) are elected from outside the firm. ◆

Employees or owners? United Airlines is 55% employee-owned, through a device known as the Employee Stock Ownership Plan, in which employees become owners by buying a company's stock. Although the idea was conceived nearly 50 years ago, there are only about 11,500 ESOPs today out of the hundreds of thousands of publicly and privately owned businesses. Why do you suppose more companies aren't owned by their employees?

practical action

"It's a Career, Not a Job": The Different Career Paths

As a manager, it's not enough that you be aware of all the changing trends and responsibilities in the workplace. You also need to have a sense of where you're going.

No doubt what you're looking for is something about which you can say "It's not just a job, it's a career," as the slogan goes. Your *career path* is the sequence of jobs and occupations you follow during your career.

Michael J. Driver has suggested there are different possible career paths, among them the *linear career, the steady-state career,* and the *spiral career.*[8]

The Linear Career: Climbing the Stairs The *linear career* resembles the traditional view of climbing the stairs in an organization's hierarchy. That is, you move up the organization in a series of jobs—generally in just one functional area, such as finance—each of which entails more responsibility and requires more skills.

The legendary Roberto C. Goizueta of Coca-Cola Co., who started out as a chemist with a Havana-based Coke subsidiary, spent his entire career with the company, rising through the technical side before he became chairman and CEO. Some top executives may change companies during their ascent, as Lee Iaccoca did from Ford to Chrysler, but their careers are still always upwardly mobile—that is, linear.

Of course, it's possible that a linear career will *plateau.* That is, you'll rise to a certain level and then remain there; there will be no further promotions. Career plateaus actually happen a lot and need not signify disgrace, since they happen even to very successful managers. After all, the higher you get in the hierarchy, the fewer the managerial positions above you and the more intense the competition for them.

Another possibility, of course, is the *declining career,* in which a person reaches a certain level and then after a time begins descending back to the lower levels. This could come about, for instance, because technology changes the industry you're in and you're not willing or able to learn the necessary new skills. It can also happen because people have addiction problems, for example, causing them to take their eye off the career ball. Or they are victims of age, gender, or racial discrimination.

The Steady-State Career: Staying Put The *steady-state career* is almost the opposite of a linear career: you discover early in life that you're comfortable with a certain occupation and you stay with it. Or you accept a promotion for a while, decide you don't like the responsibility, and take a step down.

This kind of career is actually fairly commonplace: sales representatives, computer programmers, graphic artists, accountants, insurance agents, or physicians, for example, may decide they are perfectly happy being "hands-on" professionals rather than managers.

The Spiral Career: Holding Different Jobs That Build on One Another The *spiral career* is, like the linear career, upwardly mobile. However, on this career path, you would have a number of jobs that are fundamentally different yet still build on one another, giving you more general experience and the skills to advance in rank and status. Nowadays this route may actually give you a better chance of reaching the top than the linear career because it provides such a broad base of experience.

For example, an engineer might start out in a company's research and development department, then become a product manager in the marketing department, then move into sales, all the while gradually moving up the organization chart.

Of course, it's possible that you might (like some salespeople, actors, chefs, or construction workers) favor a variant called the *transitory career.* That is, you're the kind of person that doesn't want the responsibility that comes with promotion. You're a free spirit that likes the variety of experience that comes with continually shifting sideways from job to job or place to place (or you're afraid of making the commitment to doing any one thing).

major question

Who are stakeholders important to me outside the organization?

The Big Picture

The external environment of stakeholders consists of the task environment and the general environment. The task environment consists of customers, competitors, suppliers, distributors, strategic allies, employee associations, local communities, financial institutions, government regulators, special-interest groups, and the mass media. The general environment consists of economic, technological, sociocultural, demographic, political-legal, and international forces.

In the first section we described the environment inside the organization. Here let's consider the environment outside it, which consists of ***external stakeholders*** **— people or groups in the organization's external environment that are affected by it.** This environment consists of:

- The task environment
- The general environment

The Task Environment

The ***task environment*** **consists of 11 groups that present you with daily tasks to handle: customers, competitors, suppliers, distributors, strategic allies, employee organizations, local communities, financial institutions, government regulators, special-interest groups, and mass media.**

1 Customers

The first law of business, we've said, is *take care of the customer.* ***Customers*** **are those who pay to use an organization's goods or services.** Customers may be the focus not only of for-profit organizations but also nonprofit ones. A 1998 survey found that, with crime rates falling, police forces scored the biggest four-year gain in customer (citizen) satisfaction of all industries and services.[9]

Example

Taking Care of Customers: L.L. Bean's No Questions Asked

Only a handful of companies stand by their products for a lifetime—Parker Pens, Williams-Sonoma cookware, Zippo cigarette lighters, for example. For more than 90 years, L.L. Bean, the Freeport, Maine, mail-order seller of clothing and outdoor gear, has had an unconditional guarantee that it will give a replacement, refund, or charge credit and even pay shipping on a Bean product if a customer is dissatisfied with it—no matter when it was bought. No proof of purchase is required. No product defect need be cited. Even 30-year-old worn-out hiking boots can be exchanged.

Why don't more companies have such lifetime warranties or total-satisfaction guarantees? "Companies are worried about customers cheating them," says one writer. "That's nonsense. People cheat bad companies, because they think the companies have cheated them. Nobody cheats top companies."[10]

2 Competitors

Is there any line of work you could enter in which there would *not* be ***competitors*** **—people or organizations that compete for customers or resources,** such as talented employees or raw materials? Every organization has to be actively aware of its competitors. Florist shops and delicatessens must be aware that customers can buy the same products at Safeway or Kroegers.

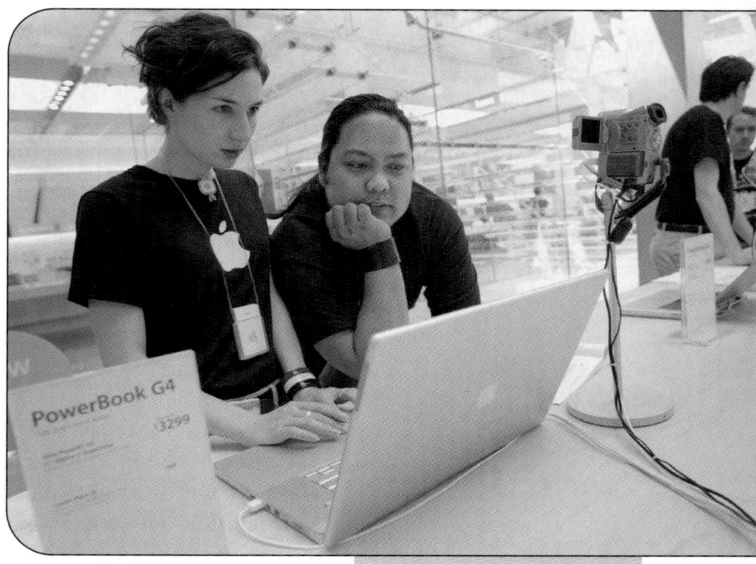

Apple manufactures and sells its personal computers not only over the Internet but also through its own stores. Does doing so give the company a competitive advantage over Internet sellers of PCs, such as Dell and IBM?

3 Suppliers

A *supplier* is a person or an organization that provides supplies—that is, raw materials, services, equipment, labor, or energy—to other organizations. Suppliers in turn have their own suppliers: the publisher of this book buys the paper on which it is printed from a paper merchant, who in turn is supplied by several paper mills, who in turn are supplied wood for wood pulp by logging companies with forests in the United States or Canada.

4 Distributors

A *distributor* is a person or an organization that helps another organization sell its goods and services to customers. Publishers of magazines, for instance, don't sell directly to newsstands; rather, they go through a distributor, or wholesaler. Tickets to Outkast, The Dave Matthews Band, or other artist's performance might be sold to you directly by the concert hall, but they are also sold through such distributors as TicketMaster, Tower Records, and Blockbuster Video.

Distributors can be quite important because in some industries (such as movie theaters and magazines) there is not a lot of competition, and the distributor has a lot of power over the ultimate price of the product. However, the rise in popularity of the Internet has allowed manufacturers of personal computers, for example, to cut out the "middleman"—the distributor—and to sell to customers directly.

5 Strategic Allies

Companies, and even nonprofit organizations, frequently link up with other organizations (even competing ones) in order to realize strategic advantages. The term ***strategic allies*** **describes the relationship of two organizations who join forces to achieve advantages neither can perform as well alone.**

In 1999, several major drug companies, normally fierce competitors, discussed joining to pursue basic research out of fear that small biotech firms might monopolize crucial gene information and then charge the big companies huge fees for access to it.[11]

6 Employee Organizations: Unions & Associations

As a rule of thumb, labor unions (such as the United Auto Workers or the Teamsters Union) tend to represent hourly workers; professional associations (such as the National Education Association or the Newspaper Guild) tend to represent salaried workers. Nevertheless, during a labor dispute, the salary-earning reporters in the Newspaper Guild might well picket in sympathy with the wage-earning circulation-truck drivers in the Teamsters Union.

In recent years, the percentage of the labor force represented by unions has steadily declined (from 35% in the 1950s to 12.9% in 2004).[12] Moreover, union agendas have changed. Strikes and violence are pretty much out. Benefits, stock ownership, and campaigns for "living-wage" ordinances are in.[13]

7 Local Communities

Local communities are obviously important stakeholders, as becomes evident not only when a big organization arrives but also when it leaves, sending government officials scrambling to find new industry to replace it. Schools and municipal governments rely on the organization for their tax base. Families and merchants depend on its employee payroll for their livelihoods. In addition, everyone from the United Way to the Little League may rely on it for some financial support.[14]

When Fruit of the Loom, the 153-year-old underwear maker, decided in 2003 to shift its factory from Cameron County in South Texas to Honduras, it was only the latest apparel maker to send jobs offshore. Other companies that had departed in the preceding four years were Levi's and Wrangler jeans, Carter baby clothes, Converse sneakers, Dickies uniforms, Vanity Fair lingerie, North Face parkas, and Haggar slacks. The latest loss was a blow not only to the 800 Fruit of the Loom textile workers. For Cameron County (population 335,000), an area suffering from 33% unemployment rates, it was a disaster. For former mill worker Lupita Sanchez and her husband, this meant their annual income dropped from $35,000 a year, plus benefits, to $13,000—well below the poverty line of $21,959 for a family of five.[15]

Although exporting jobs offshore may have certain benefits (the "consumer surplus" economists speak of that results from lower prices far outweighing the cost of lost jobs or wages), there are serious costs to workers even when they find new jobs. As economist Jeff Madrick points out, "There are long periods of unemployment, retraining costs, and costs of search for a job. And the new jobs usually pay less than the old ones. In the meantime, skills are lost as well."[16]

Broadcaster and columnist Lou Dobbs, who is generally probusiness, believes that corporations, which are benefiting financially from the new global marketplace and cheaper labor in foreign countries, aren't giving enough back to local communities. "Corporate giving in 2002 declined over the previous year when adjusted for inflation," he writes.[17]

8 Financial Institutions

Want to launch a small start-up company? As Visa, MasterCard, and Discover continue to flood mailboxes with credit-card offers, some entrepreneurs have found it convenient to use multiple cards to fund new enterprises. Joe Liemandt of Trilogy Software charged up 22 cards to finance his startup.

Established companies also often need loans to tide them over when revenues are down or to finance expansion, but they rely for assistance on lenders such as commercial banks, investment banks, and insurance companies.

9 Government Regulators

The preceding groups are external stakeholders in your organization since they are clearly affected by its activities. But why would ***government regulators*** **—regulatory agencies that establish ground rules under which organizations may operate**—be considered stakeholders?

We are talking here about an alphabet soup of agencies, boards, and commissions that have the legal authority to prescribe or proscribe the conditions under which you may conduct business. To these may be added local and state regulators on the one hand and foreign governments and international agencies (such as the World Trade Organization, which oversees international trade and standardization efforts) on the other.

Such government regulators can be said to be stakeholders because not only do they affect the activities of your organization, they are in turn affected by it. The Federal Aviation Agency (FAA), for example, specifies how far planes must stay apart to prevent

From investor to CEO. Peter Thiel was a money man, running a special type of high-risk investment company called a *hedge fund,* when Max Levchin, then working in online security, approached him in 1998 about investing in a company that would specialize in safeguards for transferring money through wireless devices. Thiel thought it would be fun to run a company and became CEO. Their company, PayPal, evolved from a person-to-person site (as for enabling people to pay each other back online for dinner) to a person-to-business site that enables almost anything to be bought and sold over the Internet. PayPal was acquired by online auction giant eBay for $1.5 billion in 2002.

midair collisions. But when the airlines want to add more flights on certain routes, the FAA may have to add more flight controllers and radar equipment, since those are the agency's responsibility.

10 Special-Interest Groups

"The Gap, a San Francisco-based national clothing chain, was slammed with high-profile demonstrations on Saturday by activists protesting its labor policies in the Mariana Islands . . . ," read the newspaper account.[18] Any organization can become the target of a special-interest group, as The Gap was by an outfit called Global Exchange, which denounced the chain's use of below-minimum-wage labor (so-called sweatshop labor) in its factory on Saipan, which is U.S. territory.

***Special-interest groups* are groups whose members try to influence specific issues,** some of which may affect your organization. Examples are Mothers Against Drunk Driving, the National Organization for Women, and the National Rifle Association. Special-interest groups may try to exert political influence, as in contributing funds to lawmakers' election campaigns or in launching letter-writing efforts to officials. Or they may organize picketing and *boycotts*—holding back their patronage—of certain companies, as some African-American groups did in recent years to protest reports of racism at Texaco and at Denny's restaurants.

11 Mass Media

On March 24, 1989, when the tanker *Exxon Valdez* ran aground in Prince William Sound, it dumped 11 million gallons of North Slope crude oil into the water, blackening 1,500 miles of magnificent Gulf of Alaska coastline. This was not only one of the nation's worst environmental disasters; for the Exxon Corporation it was the start of a gigantic public-relations nightmare that never seemed to end. Even 15 years later, the news media were running prominent stories on the effects of the incident, once again bringing it to public attention.[19]

Exxon's troubles were not the fault of the press. But no manager can afford to ignore the power of the mass media—print, radio, TV, and the Internet—to rapidly and widely disseminate news both bad and good. Thus, most companies, universities, hospitals, and even government agencies have a public-relations person or department to communicate effectively with the press. In addition, top-level executives often receive special instruction on how to best deal with the media.

The March for Women's Lives. In April 2004, an estimated 1,150,000 people, according to organizers, from across the U.S. and nearly 60 countries gathered in Washington, D.C., to show support for reproductive rights and freedom for all women. A contingent of abortion opponents assembled along the route to protest. Many managers have to deal with "external stakeholders" of special-interest groups such as these.

The General Environment

Beyond the task environment is the ***general environment,*** **or *macroenvironment,* which includes six forces: economic, technological, sociocultural, demographic, political-legal, and international.**

You may be able to control some forces in the task environment, but you can't control those in the general environment. Nevertheless, they can profoundly affect your organization's task environment without your knowing it, springing nasty surprises on you. Clearly, then, as a manager you need to keep your eye on the far horizon because these forces of the general environment can affect long-term plans and decisions.

1 Economic Forces

Economic forces **consist of the general economic conditions and trends—unemployment, inflation, interest rates, economic growth—that may affect an organization's performance.** These are forces in your nation and region and even the world over which you and your organization probably have no control.

Are banks' interest rates going up in the United States? Then it will cost you more to borrow money to open new stores or build new plants. Is your region's unemployment rate rising? Then maybe you'll have more job applicants to hire from, yet you'll also have fewer customers with money to spend. Are natural resources getting scarce in an important area of supply? Then your company will need to pay more for them or switch to alternative sources.

One indicator that managers often pay attention to is productivity growth. Rising productivity leads to rising profits, lower inflation, and higher stock prices. In recent times, companies have been using information technology to cut costs, resulting in productivity growing at an annual rate of 3–3.5%, rather than the expected 2–2.5%.[20]

2 Technological Forces

Technological forces **are new developments in methods for transforming resources into goods or services.** For example, think what the U.S. would have been like if the elevator, air-conditioning, the combustion engine, and the airplane had not been invented. No doubt changes in computer and communications technology—especially the influence of the Internet—will continue to be powerful technological forces during your managerial career. But other technological currents may affect you as well.

For example, biotechnology may well turn health and medicine upside down in the coming decades. Researchers can already clone animals, and some reports say they are close to doing the same with humans.

Socio-carbo forces. Should this man be smiling? For a while in 2004, the low-carb Dr. Atkins diet became such a craze that bakery products suffered and beef prices rose. Any industry can be affected by changes in sociocultural forces.

3 Sociocultural Forces

"I have one client who has tattoos of all kinds of stuff on her body," says Doug, owner of Doug's Tattoos in Oakland, Calif. "There's no theme to it. She has favorite cartoon names, her children's and grandchildren's names—just anything she likes at the time."[21]

Some day, of course, our descendants will view these customs as old-fogyish and quaint. That's how it is with sociocultural changes. ***Sociocultural forces*** **are influences and trends originating in a country's, a society's, or a culture's human relationships and values that may affect an organization.**

Entire industries have been rocked when the culture underwent a lifestyle change that affected their product or service. The interest in health and fitness, for instance, led to a decline in sales of cigarettes, whiskey, red meat, and eggs. And it led to a boost in sales of athletic shoes, spandex clothing, and Nautilus and other exercise machines. The Robert Atkins low-carbohydrate, high-protein diet has been around for years, but only recently—in part because scientific studies supported its efficacy—has it swept the country. The result has been spiraling prices for beef and eggs and panic among purveyors of high-carb products such as bread and pasta.[22]

4 Demographic Forces

Demographics derives from the ancient Greek word for "people"—*demos*—and deals with statistics relating to human populations. Age, gender, race, sexual orientation, occupation, income, family size, and the like are known as demographic characteristics when they are used to express measurements of certain groups. ***Demographic forces*** **are influences on an organization arising from changes in the characteristics of a population, such as age, gender, or ethnic origin.** In the United States, for instance, more women and minorities continue to join the workforce, making it more diverse.

A dozen years ago, for instance, the part of South-Central Los Angeles that experienced urban riots (following the acquittal of four white cops in the beating of black motorist Rodney King) was dominated by African-Americans. Today nearly two thirds of South-Central is Hispanic, with many recent immigrants from Mexico and Central America. The area also is the first rung on the ladder of success for immigrants from Russia, Korea, China, Thailand, Israel, Iran, Italy, and Jamaica.[23]

5 Political-Legal Forces

Political-legal forces **are changes in the way politics shape laws and laws shape the opportunities for and threats to an organization.** In the United States, whatever political view tends to be dominant at the moment may be reflected in how the government handles antitrust issues, in which one company tends to monopolize a particular industry. Should Microsoft, for instance, be allowed to dominate the market for personal-computer operating systems?

As for legal forces, some countries have more fully developed legal systems than others. And some countries have more lawyers per capita. (The United States has an estimated 25% of the world's lawyers, according to University of Wisconsin law professor Marc Galanter—not the 70% figure repeated for years by some conservative political figures.[24]) American companies may be more willing to use the legal system to advance their interests, as in suing competitors to gain competitive advantage. But they must also watch that others don't do the same to them.

Microsoft founder Bill Gates. Microsoft has been repeatedly accused of anticompetitive practices, both in the United States and, more recently, in the European Union. Why is competition so important to a free-market system?

6 International Forces

International forces **are changes in the economic, political, legal, and technological global system that may affect an organization.**

This category represents a huge grab bag of influences. How does the economic integration of the European Union create threats and opportunities for American companies? U.S. companies that do significant business in Europe are subject to regulation by the European Union (EU). In 2004, for instance, the EU ruled that Microsoft Corp. had abusively wielded its Windows software monopoly and ordered it to produce a version of Windows without Microsoft's own digital media player included. Microsoft supporters complained that the ruling stepped on U.S. turf and interfered with a successful American industry.[25] We consider global concerns in Chapter 4.

How well Americans can handle international forces depends a lot on their training. The American Council on Education says there is a "dangerous" shortage of experts in non-European cultures and languages. The council urges that schools teach a wider variety of languages and that instruction begin as early as kindergarten, since waiting until students are in college to begin instruction in more obscure languages hinders their ability to become fluent speakers.[26] ◆

major question **What does the successful manager need to know about ethics and values?**

The Big Picture

Managers need to be aware of what constitutes ethics, values, the four approaches to ethical dilemmas, and how organizations can promote ethics.

"It's a tough issue, choosing between being a law-abiding person and losing your job," says lawyer Gloria Allred, who represented a woman fired for complaining about running her boss's office football pool.[27] Imagine having to choose between *economic performance* and *social performance,* which in business is what most ethical conflicts are about.[28] This is known as an ***ethical dilemma,*** **a situation in which you have to decide whether to pursue a course of action that may benefit you or your organization but that is unethical or even illegal.**

Defining Ethics & Values

Most of us assume we know what "ethics" and "values" mean, but do we? Let's consider them.

Ethics

Ethics **are the standards of right and wrong that influence behavior.** These standards may vary among countries and among cultures. ***Ethical behavior*** **is behavior that is accepted as "right" as opposed to "wrong" according to those standards.**

What are the differences among a tip, a gratuity, a gift, a donation, a commission, a consulting fee, a kickback, a bribe? Regardless of the amount of money involved, each one may be intended to reward the recipient for providing you with better service, either anticipated or performed. However, while giving a member of the International Olympic Committee (IOC) several thousand dollars to help steer the 2002 Olympic Winter Games to Salt Lake City may be considered unethical behavior in the United States, it may be considered perfectly ethical under the standards of the IOC member's own country.

Olympics on the carpet. Robert Garff, who chaired the Salt Lake Organizing Committee, which brought the 2002 Olympic Winter Games to Utah, holds his head as he releases a report investigating the ethics of his committee's actions. The committee was alleged to have bribed Olympic officials (with Donny Osmond photos, music CDs, and cash). Do you think ethical behavior is the most important part of doing business?

Values

Ethical dilemmas often take place because of an organization's ***value systems,*** **the pattern of values within an organization.** ***Values*** **are the relatively permanent and deeply held underlying beliefs and attitudes that help determine a person's behavior,** such as the belief that "Fairness means hiring according to ability, not family background." Values and value systems are the underpinnings for ethics and ethical behavior.

Organizations may have two important value systems that can conflict: (1) the value system stressing financial performance versus (2) the value system stressing cohesion and solidarity in employee relationships.[29]

Four Approaches to Deciding Ethical Dilemmas

How do alternative values guide people's decisions about ethical behavior? Here are four approaches, which may be taken as guidelines:

1 The Utilitarian Approach: For the Greatest Good

Ethical behavior in the ***utilitarian approach*** **is guided by what will result in the greatest good for the greatest number of people.** Managers often take the utilitarian approach, using financial performance—such as efficiency and profit—as the best definition of what constitutes "the greatest good for the greatest number."[30]

Thus, a utilitarian "cost-benefit" analysis might show that in the short run the firing of thousands of employees may improve a company's bottom line and provide immediate benefits for the stockholders. The drawback of this approach, however, is that it may result in damage to workforce morale and the loss of employees with experience and skills—actions not so readily measurable in dollars.

2 The Individual Approach: For Your Greatest Self-Interest Long Term, Which Will Help Others

Ethical behavior in the ***individual approach*** **is guided by what will result in the individual's best *long-term* interests, which ultimately are in everyone's self-interest.** The assumption here is that you will act ethically in the short run to avoid others harming you in the long run.

The flaw here, however, is that one person's short-term self-gain may *not,* in fact, be good for everyone in the long term. After all, the manager of an agribusiness that puts chemical fertilizers on the crops every year will always benefit, but the fishing industries downstream could ultimately suffer if chemical runoff reduces the number of fish. Indeed, this is one reason why Puget Sound Chinook, or king salmon, are now threatened with extinction in the Pacific Northwest.[31]

3 The Moral-Rights Approach: Respecting Fundamental Rights Shared by Everyone

Ethical behavior in the ***moral-rights approach*** **is guided by respect for the fundamental rights of human beings,** such as those expressed in the U.S. Constitution's Bill of Rights. We would all tend to agree that denying people the right to life, liberty, privacy, health and safety, and due process is unethical. Thus, most of us would have no difficulty condemning the situation of immigrants illegally brought into the United States and then effectively enslaved—as when made to work seven days a week as maids.

The difficulty, however, is when rights are in conflict, such as employer and employee rights. Should employees on the job have a guarantee of privacy? Actually, it is legal for employers to listen to business phone calls and monitor all non-spoken personal communications.[32]

4 The Justice Approach: Respecting Impartial Standards of Fairness

Ethical behavior in the ***justice approach*** **is guided by respect for impartial standards of fairness and equity.** One consideration here is whether an organization's policies—such as those governing promotions or sexual harassment cases—are administered impartially and fairly regardless of gender, age, sexual orientation, and the like.

Fairness can often be a hot issue. For instance, many employees are loudly resentful when a corporation's CEO is paid a salary and bonuses worth hundreds of times more than what they receive—even when the company performs poorly—and when fired is then given a "golden parachute," or extravagant package of separation pay and benefits.

How Organizations Can Promote Ethics

There are three ways an organization may foster high ethical standards:

1 Support by Top Managers of a Strong Ethical Climate

The "tone at the top is critical—and it's always monkey see, monkey do," says Martha Clark Goss, VP and chief financial officer for consulting firm Booze Allen & Hamilton. At her firm, she says, "we have the sunshine rule, which asks employees to consider how they would feel if they had to stand in front of partners [that is, top managers] and explain a particular business expense. It's a good rule, but only a guideline. People almost always follow the example of the senior partners."[33]

If top executives "wink at the problem" or "look the other way" in ethical matters, so will employees farther down the organization.

2 Ethics Codes & Training Programs

A ***code of ethics*** **consists of a formal written set of ethical standards guiding an organization's actions.** Most codes offer guidance on how to treat customers, suppliers, competitors, and other stakeholders. The purpose is to clearly state top management's expectations for all employees. As you might expect, most codes prohibit bribes, kickbacks, misappropriation of corporate assets, conflicts of interest, and "cooking the books"—making false accounting statements and other records. Other areas frequently covered in ethics codes are political contributions, workforce diversity, and confidentiality of corporate information.[34]

Nike Code of Conduct

NIKE INC. WAS FOUNDED ON A I-IANDSI-TAKE.

Implicit in that act was the determination that we would build our business with all of our partners based on trust, teamwork, honesty and mutual respect. We expect all of our business partners to operate on the same principles

At the core of the NIKE corporate ethic is the belief that we are a company comprised of many different kinds of people, appreciating individual diversity, and dedicated to equal opportunity for each individual.

NIKE designs, manufactures and markets products for sports and fitness consumers. At every step in that process, we are driven to do not only what is required by law, but what is expected of s leader. We expect our business partners to do the same. NIKE partners with contractors who share our commitment to best practices and continuous improvement in:

1. Management practices that respect the rights of all employees, including the right to free association and collective bargaining
2. Minimizing our impact on the environment
3. Providing a safe and healthy work place
4. Promoting the health and well-being of all employees

Contractors must recognize the dignity of each employee, and the right to a work place free of harassment, abuse or corporal punishment. Decisions on hiring, salary, benefits, advancement, termination or retirement must be based solely on the employee's ability to do the job. There shall be no discrimination based on race, creed, gender, marital or maternity status, religious or political beliefs, age or sexual orientation.

Wherever NIKE operates around the globe we are guided by this Code of Conduct and we bind our contractors to these principles. Contractors must post this Code in all major workspaces, translated into the language of the employee, and must train employees on their rights and obligations as defined by this Code and applicable local laws.

While these principles establish the spirit of our partnerships, we also bind our partners to specific standards of conduct. The core standards are set forth below.

Forced Labor
The contractor does not use forced labor in any form – prison, indentured, bonded or otherwise.

Child Labor
The contractor does not employ any person below the age of 18 to produce footwear. The contractor does not employ any person below the age of 16 to produce apparel, accessories or equipment. If at the time Nike production begins, the contractor employs people of the legal working age who are at least 15, that employment may continue, but the contractor will not hire any person going forward who is younger than the Nike or legal age limit, whichever is higher. To further ensure these age standards are complied with, the contractor does not use any form of homework for Nike production.

Compensation
The contractor provides each employee at least the minimum wage, or the prevailing industry wage, whichever is higher, provides each employee a clear, written accounting for every pay period, and does not deduct from employee pay for disciplinary infractions.

Benefits
The contractor provides each employee all legally mandated benefits.

Hours of Work/Overtime
The contractor complies with legally mandated work hours; uses overtime only when each employee is fully compensated according to local law; informs each employee at the time of hiring if mandatory overtime is a condition of employment; and on a regularly scheduled basis provides one day off in seven, and requires no more than 60 hours of work per week on a regularly scheduled basis, or complies with local limits if they are lower.

Environment, Safety and Health (ES&H)
The contractor has written environmental, safety and health policies and standards, and implements a system to minimize negative impacts on the environment, reduce work-related injury and illness, and promote the general health of employees.

Documentation and Inspection
The contractor maintains on file all documentation needed to demonstrate compliance with this Code of Conduct and required laws; agrees to make these documents available for Nike or its designated monitor; and agrees to submit to inspections with or without prior notice.

Nike's Code. Despite its code of conduct, the athletic-shoe company had to deal with negative websites questioning its treatment of workers in less-developed countries. The company responded with a website of its own showing pictures of its overseas manufacturing facilities and describing the benefits offered employees. Still, a code of ethics is not always a guarantee of ethical behavior. A collector's item is the 64-page "Enron Code of Ethics," which includes sections on conflicts of interest. The Houston-based energy company was greatly criticized for its irregular financial dealings, which brought tremendous losses to shareholders and employees. If you were considering being hired by a new company, how could you tell whether it really tended to act ethically?

In addition, about 45% of the 1,000 largest U.S. corporations now provide ethics training.[35] The approaches vary, but one way is to use a case approach to present employees with ethical dilemmas. By clarifying expectations, this kind of training may reduce unethical behavior.[36]

Whistleblower. Tobacco industry whistleblower Jeffrey Wigand (right) testifies in March 2000 before a Rhode Island Senate committee while the state's Lt. Gov. Jeffrey J. Fogarty looks on. Wigand was a chemist for Brown & Williamson who had learned about the tobacco company's discovery of the relationship between nicotine and addiction, which it had consistently denied. Whistleblowing is not for everyone; close to half of all whistleblowers are fired. Given this fact, what would it take for you to become a whistleblower?

3 Rewarding Ethical Behavior: Protecting Whistleblowers

It's not enough to simply punish bad behavior; managers must also reward good ethical behavior, as in encouraging (or at least not discouraging) whistleblowers.

A *whistleblower* is an employee who reports organizational misconduct to the public, such as health and safety matters, waste, corruption, or overcharging of customers. For instance, the law that created the Occupational Safety and Health Administration allows workers to report unsafe conditions, such as "exposure to toxic chemicals; the use of dangerous machines, which can crush fingers; the use of contaminated needles, which expose workers to the AIDS virus; and the strain of repetitive hand motion, whether at a computer keyboard or in a meatpacking plant."[37]

The law prohibits employers from firing employees who report workplace hazards, although one study found that about two-thirds of those who complained lost their jobs anyway.[38] Clearly, top managers have to stress that the organization's ethics policy is more than just window dressing.

Ethics Teaching in College In the wake of all the white-collar scandals, such as those at Enron, WorldCom, and Tyco, that shook the corporate world in the early 2000s, many business departments and schools in colleges and universities have required more education in ethics. The Haas School of Business at the University of California at Berkeley, for example, offers a program that includes seven new ethics courses, and the program requires first-year students to visit executives in jail.

"Schools bear some responsibility for the behavior of executives," says Fred J. Evans, dean of the College of Business and Economics at California State University at Northridge. "If you're making systematic errors in the [business] world, you have to go back to the schools and ask, 'What are you teaching?'"[39]

At issue, however, is the most effective kind of instruction in the subject. "You have five profit-oriented classes during the semester where you're learning about free markets and shareholder maximization," says one student, "and then there's one mandatory ethics course. It's an abrupt transition . . . And you wonder if it can really prepare you for the real world."[40]

At the University of Pittsburgh's Joseph M. Katz Graduate School of Business, the faculty decided that having a separate ethics class was a lot like telling students they could be bad during the week if they just went to church on Sunday. As a result, every class at the school is now steeped in ethics.

This is also the approach we try to take in this book—teaching ethics throughout, not just in one place, and offering real-world Ethical Dilemmas at the end of each chapter. Although in the business world you might be advised to "Get a good lawyer and accountant so you can justify what you're doing," as many executives have learned to their sorrow, even this expertise may be of no help if what you're doing is in violation of basic values. ◆

major question **Is being socially responsible really necessary?**

The Big Picture

Managers need to be aware of the viewpoints supporting and opposing social responsibility, four managerial approaches to social responsibility, and whether being and doing good pays off financially for the organization.

If ethical responsibility is about being a good individual citizen, social responsibility is about being a good organizational citizen. More formally ***social responsibility*** **is a manager's duty to take actions that will benefit the interests of society as well as of the organization.** An example of social responsibility is ***philanthropy,*** **donating money to worthwhile recipients,** such as charities and schools. Companies may also make donations of their products, services, expertise, or employees' time.

Example

Social Responsibility: As You Sow Works to Create Corporate Consciousness

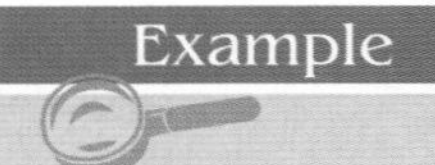

Some companies already believe that doing well and doing good are worthwhile business goals. For example, Bagel Works, a six-store bagel chain headquartered in Keene, N.H., invests part of its profits in such projects as affordable housing, conservation, farming, downtown revitalization, and education. It fully recycles and tries to pay employees close to a livable wage.[41]

What's in it for Bagel Works and its cofounders, Richard French, now 40, and Jennifer Pearl, 37? "Some could argue that we may be able to make more money," says French. "But if we weren't doing some of these things, we might have a lesser quality of employee or more turnover." Moreover, he says, it has increased customer loyalty.[42]

French and Pearl seem to have developed socially responsible business practices from the beginning. Other firms may need a nudge. Dell Inc., for instance, became the first major personal computer maker to commit to specific goals for recycling old computers. The Gap developed ways to rate the working conditions in the factories of its overseas contractors. Home Depot stopped selling old-growth and tropical lumber. Coca-Cola and Pepsi agreed to use some recycled plastic in their bottles.

All came to such socially responsible positions through the efforts of San Francisco-based As You Sow Foundation, which despite its name is not a foundation but more like a consulting firm. Its goal: to show corporations, through shareholder resolutions or discussions with management, that better treatment of workers and of the environment can provide business benefits. It brings its influence to bear not by being do-gooders, says Conrad McKerron, director of As You Sow's corporate social responsibility program, but by talking about long-term value. "In the age of globalization," he says, "the most valuable thing these companies have is their brand name. We stress over and over that getting these controversies [about treatment of workers and the environment] behind them will help maintain long-term value."[43]

At the least, socially conscious businesses aren't any less profitable as a group. Often, in fact, they have a competitive edge: in one survey of 2,000 people, 76% said they'd switch from their current brand to one associated with a good cause if price and quality were equal.[44]

Social responsibility rests at the top of a pyramid of a corporation's obligations, right up there with economic, legal, and ethical responsibilities. That is, while some people might consider that a company's first duty is to make a profit, most would hold that it is equally important that it obey the law, be ethical, and be a good corporate citizen.[45]

Is Social Responsibility Worthwhile? Opposing & Supporting Viewpoints

In the old days of cutthroat capitalism, social responsibility was hardly thought of. A company's most important goal was to make money pretty much any way it could, and the consequences be damned. Today for-profit enterprises generally make a point of "putting something back" into society as well as taking something out.

Not everyone, however, agrees with these new priorities. Let's consider the two viewpoints.

Against Social Responsibility

"Few trends could so thoroughly undermine the very foundations of our free society," argues free-market economist Milton Friedman, "as the acceptance by corporate officials of social responsibility other than to make as much money for their stockholders as possible."[46]

Friedman represents the view that, as he says, "The social responsibility of business is to make profits." That is, unless a company focuses on maximizing profits, it will become distracted and fail to provide goods and services, benefit the stockholders, create jobs, and expand economic growth—the real social justification for the firm's existence.

This view would presumably support the efforts of companies to set up headquarters in name only in offshore Caribbean tax havens (while keeping their actual headquarters in the U.S.) in order to minimize their tax burden.

For Social Responsibility

"A large corporation these days not only may engage in social responsibility," says famed economist Paul Samuelson, "it had damned well better to try to do so."[47] That is, a company must be concerned for society's welfare as well as for corporate profits.

Beyond the fact of ethical obligation, the rationale for this view is that since businesses create problems (environmental pollution, for example), they should help solve them. Moreover, they often have the resources to solve problems in ways that the nonprofit sector does not. Finally, being socially responsible gives businesses a favorable public image that can help head off government regulation.

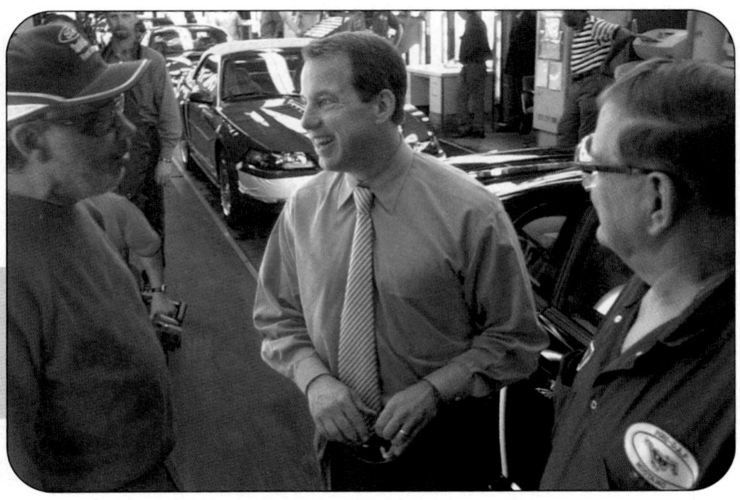

Social conscience. Ford Motor Co. CEO William Clay Ford (center) talks with assembly line workers. In 2003, he donated his bonus to help pay college tuition for Ford employees.

Four Managerial Approaches to Social Responsibility

The two extremes in managers' approaches to social responsibility range from "Do nothing" to "Do a lot."[48] Or, stated another way, from "obstructionist" to "proactive," as follows.[49]

Four Approaches to Social Responsibility

Obstructionist: "Just make money, forget any social responsibility."

Defensive: "Just do what the law requires, no more."

Accommodative: "Do the minimum that's ethically required."

Proactive: "Be a leader in social responsibility."

1 The Obstructionist Manager

Managers in an obstructionist organization not only resist being socially responsible, they also behave unethically—maybe even illegally—whenever they think they can get away with it, or deny wrong-doing if found out. In the ***obstructionist approach,*** **managers put economic gain first and resist social responsibility as being outside the organization's self-interest.**

Illegal drug dealers certainly represent the obstructionist approach. But so do some entirely legal companies. In 1999, according to a grand jury indictment, Waste Management, the largest trash hauler in the United States, hired Joseph Lauricella, who tried to undermine another company by swiping confidential data, sabotaging potential deals, and spreading rumors that tied the other company to illegal dumping and drug trafficking.[50]

2 The Defensive Manager

In the ***defensive approach,*** **managers make the minimum commitment to social responsibility—obeying the law but doing nothing more.** The defensive approach probably represents Milton Friedman's position: Companies are in business to make money, and they shouldn't distract themselves by doing anything else.

3 The Accommodative Manager

In the ***accommodative approach,*** **managers do more than the law requires, if asked, and demonstrate moderate social responsibility.** For months in 1998, Intel battled privacy groups that claimed its new Pentium III chip's hardwired identification number would give websites the power to monitor a user's every move online, until the company finally yielded and released the chip with the ID number turned off.[51]

4 The Proactive Manager

In the ***proactive approach,*** **managers actively lead the way in being socially responsible for all stakeholders, using the organization's resources to identify and respond to social problems.** For example, Merck & Co., the pharmaceutical concern, spent millions developing a drug (Mectizan) to fight river blindness, then distributed it free in the West African countries in which the disease is mainly found.[52]

Sorry Sears. Sometimes even major companies are obstructionist. In the most serious ethical breach in its history, Sears, Roebuck and Co. was discovered in 1999 to have secretly violated federal law for a decade. It even, suggested U.S. Justice Department lawyers, may have put its illegal practice in its procedures manual. Sears allegedly used unenforceable agreements to collect debts that legally no longer existed with some bankrupt credit-card holders. "The company's 111 years old," said the relatively new CEO at the time, Arthur Martinez, "and I'm the guy in the chair when we plead guilty to a criminal offense. Wonderful."

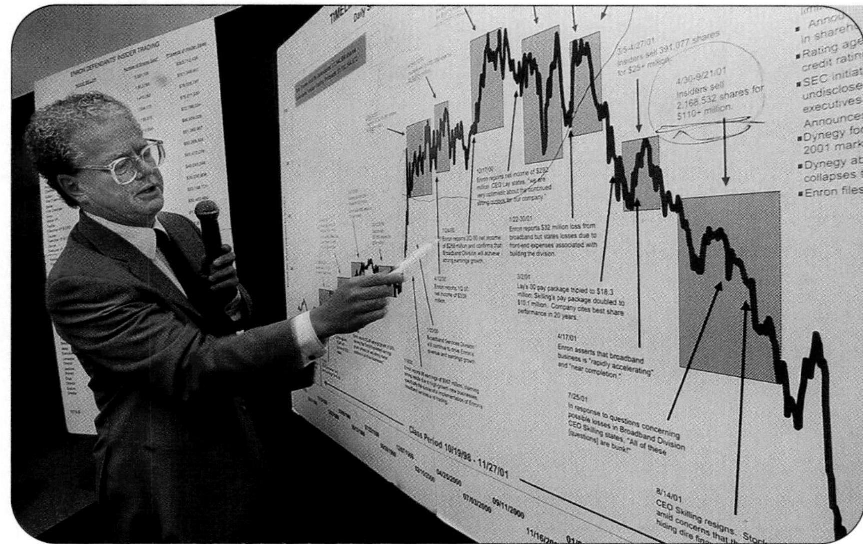

Enron demise detailed. Attorney William Lerach at a news conference shows the rising and falling share price for the Texas energy company. Lerach was representing Amalgamated Bank, which was suing Enron executives and directors and the company's auditor, Arthur Andersen. The suit alleged that Enron executives inflated earnings to drive up share prices, resulting in $1.1 billion in proceeds for them. What would you expect Enron's share price to be today as you read this—higher or lower than in 2002?

Bottom Line: Does Being Good Pay Off Financially?

From a hard-headed manager's point of view, does ethical behavior and high social responsibility pay off financially? Here's what the research shows.

Effect on Stock Price

Not all illegalities by a company will hurt its stock price, but the announcement of certain kinds of illegalities will—specifically tax evasion, bribery, or violations of government contracts.[53] In general, however, the damage to the stock price lasts for only a few days, as investors turn their attention to the company's future prospects.

Effect on Sales Growth

The announcement of a company's conviction for illegal activity may have only a short-term effect on the stock price. However, it has been shown to diminish a company's sales growth for a much longer period of time—indeed, for several years.[54]

Effect on Customers

According to one survey, 88% of the respondents said they were more apt to buy from companies that are socially responsible than from companies that are not.[55]

Effect on Job Applicants

Another study found that as a company's reputation is enhanced by acts of social responsibility, making it seem to be a more attractive employer, it attracts more applicants.

Ethical behavior and social responsibility are more than just admirable ways of operating. They give an organization a clear competitive advantage. ◆

major question

What trends in workplace diversity should managers be aware of?

The Big Picture

One of today's most important management challenges is working with stakeholders of all sorts who vary widely in diversity—in age, gender, race, religion, ethnicity, sexual orientation, capabilities, and socioeconomic background. Managers should also be aware of the differences between internal and external dimensions of diversity and barriers to diversity.

"Coors Cares," says one of the beer company's slogans.

Didn't it always? Actually, in the 1980s the Coors family's funding of right-wing causes—they helped start the conservative Heritage Foundation—gave the brewer such a bad reputation with minorities and unions that it devastated it financially. Today Coors still gives steady support to the political right. Ironically, however, the company goes far beyond government requirements in embracing sensitivity, diversity, and other politically left policies.

Inside Coors, workers get training in sexual harassment and attend diversity workshops. "Employees can choose among eight 'resource councils'—groups representing gays, women, and Native Americans, among others," says a *Time* article. It also claims to offer "the first corporate mammography program in the country." In addition, it sets aside a specific share of purchases for minority-owned firms. Outside it provides sponsorship of such programs as the Mi Casa resource center for women, a black-heritage festival, and a marathon gay dance party. It is one of the three out of four Fortune 500 companies to have diversity programs to help attract and keep minorities.[57]

Coors and other companies have discovered they can benefit from a singular fact: minority markets buy more goods and services than any country that trades with the United States.[58] In this section, we describe one of the most important management challenges—dealing with diversity.

How to Think about Diversity: Which Differences Are Important?

***Diversity* represents all the ways people are unlike and alike—the differences and similarities in age, gender, race, religion, ethnicity, sexual orientation, capabilities, and socioeconomic background.** Note here that diversity is not synonymous with differences. Rather, it encompasses both differences and similarities. This means that as a manager you need to manage both simultaneously.

To help distinguish the important ways in which people differ, diversity experts Lee Gardenswartz and Anita Rowe have identified a "diversity wheel" consisting of four layers of diversity: (1) personality, (2) internal dimensions, (3) external dimensions, and (4) organizational dimensions. *(See Figure 3.2.)*

Let's consider these four layers:

Personality

At the center of the diversity wheel is personality. It is at the center because ***personality* is defined as the stable physical and mental characteristics responsible for a person's identity.** We cover the dimension of personality in Chapter 11.

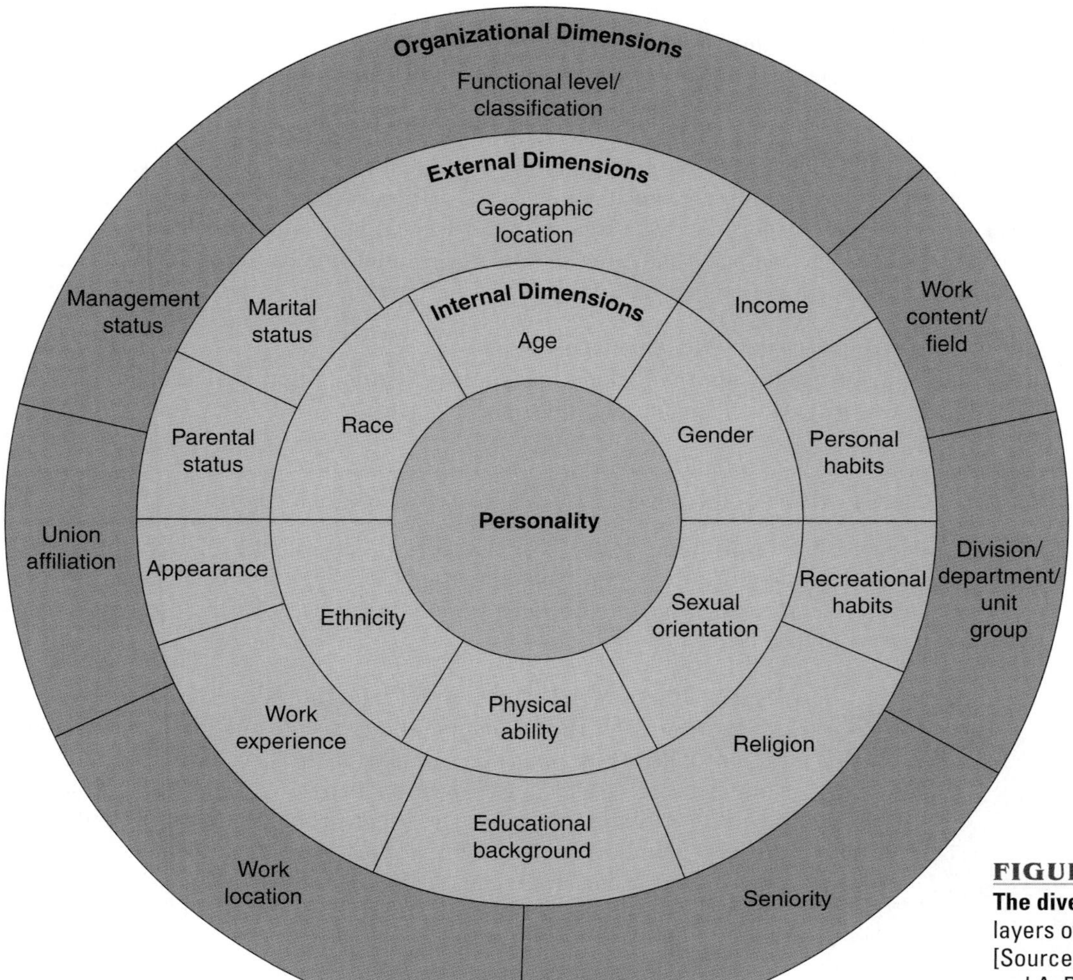

FIGURE 3.2

The diversity wheel. Four layers of diversity [Source: L. Gardenswartz and A. Rowe, *Diverse Teams at Work: Capitalizing on the Power of Diversity* (New York: McGraw-Hill, 1994), p. 33 © 1994. Reproduced with permission of The McGraw-Hill Companies. Internal dimensions and external dimensions are adapted from M. Loden and J. B. Rosener, *Workforce America! Managing Employee Diversity as a Vital Resource,* (Homewood, IL: Business One Irwin, 1991).]

Internal Dimensions

Internal dimensions of diversity **are those human differences that exert a powerful, sustained effect throughout every stage of our lives:** gender, age, ethnicity, race, sexual orientation, physical abilities.[59] These are referred to as the *primary* dimensions of diversity because they are not within our control for the most part. Yet they strongly influence our attitudes and expectations and assumptions about other people, which in turn influence our own behavior.

What characterizes internal dimensions of diversity is that they are visible and salient in people. And precisely because these characteristics are so visible, they may be associated with certain stereotypes—for example, that black people work in menial jobs. For instance, an African-American female middle manager reports that, while on vacation and sitting by the pool at a resort, she was approached by a 50ish white male who "demanded that I get him extra towels. I said, 'Excuse me?' He then said, 'Oh, you don't work here,' with no shred of embarrassment or apology in his voice."[60]

External Dimensions

External dimensions of diversity **include an element of choice; they consist of the personal characteristics that people acquire, discard, or modify throughout their lives:** educational background, marital status, parental status, religion, income, geographic location, work experience, recreational habits, appearance, personal habits.

They are referred to as the *secondary* dimensions of diversity because we have a greater ability to influence or control them than we do internal dimensions.

These external dimensions also exert a significant influence on our perceptions, behavior, and attitudes. If you are not a believer in the Muslim religion, for example, you may not perceive the importance of some of its practices—as with some managers at Atlanta-based Argenbright Security Inc., who sent seven Muslim female employees home for wearing Islamic head scarves at their security jobs at Dulles International Airport. Because wearing head scarves in no way affected their job performance, the company had to reimburse the women for back pay and other relief in a settlement negotiated with the Equal Employment Opportunity Commission.[61]

Organizational Dimensions

Organizational dimensions include management status, union affiliation, work location, seniority, work content, and division or department.

Trends in Workforce Diversity

How is the U.S. workforce apt to become more diverse in the 21st century? Let's examine five categories on the internal dimension—*age, gender, race/ethnicity, sexual orientation, and physical/mental abilities*—and one category on the external dimension, *educational level.*

Age: More Older People in the Workforce

The most significant demographic event, suggests management philosopher Peter Drucker, "is that in the developed countries the number and proportion of younger people is rapidly shrinking. . . . Those shrinking numbers of younger people will have to both drive their economies and help support much larger numbers of older people."[62] In Europe and Japan, births are not keeping pace with deaths. Italy, for example, could drop from 60 million to 20 million by the end of the 21st century.

The United States is the only developed economy to have enough young people, suggests Drucker, and that is only because immigrants to the United States still have large families. Even so, the median age of the American worker is expected to reach 40.6 years by 2005, quite a change from 34.3 in 1980.[63]

Diversity enriches. A diverse population in a company can provide ideas, experience, and points of view that strengthen the business culture.

Gender: More Women Working

Nearly half the new entrants into the workforce in the years 1990–2005 were expected to be women.[64] In addition, the percentage of women in executive, managerial, and administrative jobs has been increasing. For instance, in 2000, Gen X women—those ages 25–34—made up 51% of total employment in such jobs, up from 38% in 1983.[65]

Traditionally, however, women have been concentrated in relatively low-paying occupations; the average working woman's family would earn $4,205 more per year if women were paid as much as men with comparable job qualifications, according to one study.[66] In general, women earn 76 cents for every $1 a man is paid. Women executives do even less well: 69 cents for every dollar made by a male executive.[67] The obstacles to women's progress are known as the so-called ***glass ceiling*** **—the metaphor for an invisible barrier preventing women and minorities from being promoted to top executive jobs.** For instance, women made up only 15.7% of corporate officers of Fortune 500 companies in 2002, versus 84.3% men who hold posts as chairman, vice chairman, CEO, president, or senior or executive vice president.[68]

What factors are holding women back? Three that are mentioned are negative stereotypes, lack of mentors, and limited experience in line or general management.[69]

Interestingly, however, several studies have suggested that female managers outshine their male counterparts on almost every measure, from motivating others to fostering communication to producing high-quality work to goal-setting to mentoring employees.[70] Indeed, one study, by Catalyst, an advocacy group for women in business, found that companies with more women executives have better financial performance.[71] We discuss this further in a later chapter.

The color of Coca-Cola. Kimberly Orton (left) speaks during a November 2000 news conference in Atlanta, where Coke is headquartered. The company agreed to pay $192.5 million to settle a class-action racial discrimination suit that alleged that it had discriminated against blacks in pay, promotions, and performance evaluations. Looking on are Linda Ingram (second from left), Elvenyia Barton-Gibson, and George Eddings Jr. Do you think a lawsuit is the best wake-up call for an organization practicing discrimination?

Race & Ethnicity: More People of Color in the Workforce

In the years 1990–2005, people of color are expected to have contributed 34.7% of new entrants to the workforce (Hispanics 15.7%, African-Americans 13%, Asians and other races 6%).[72] Unfortunately, three trends show that American businesses need to do a lot better by this population.

First, people of color, too, have hit the glass ceiling. For example, African-Americans held only 6.4% and Hispanics only 4.5% of all executive, managerial, and administrative jobs in 2000.[73]

Second, they have not been paid equally with whites. In 1993, for example, college-educated black men employed as executives, administrators, and professionals had a median income that was 86% of that for their white peers.[74]

Third, their chances for success have been hurt by perceived discrimination, as shown, for example, by a study of 200 black managers and 139 Hispanic employees.[75] African-Americans also have been found to receive lower performance ratings than whites have.[76]

In the wake of the September 11, 2001, terrorist attacks on New York's World Trade Center and the Pentagon, Arab Americans also alleged discrimination. "We have people being targeted at work who have lived in this country for 25 years with no record of any violation," said one regional director of the American-Arab Anti-Discrimination Committee. Among the complaints: getting fired after they had been questioned—but cleared—by the FBI, employers disregarding religious and racial slurs at work, bans on turbans and head scarves, and prohibitions of daily prayer and foot-washing rituals.[77]

Sexual Orientation: Gays & Lesbians Become More Visible

Gays and lesbians make up, by some estimates, 6% of the U.S. population. Between a quarter and two-thirds report being discriminated against at work (with negative attitudes directed toward them held more by men than by women[78]). One 2003 study found that 41% of gay employees said they had been harassed, pressured to quit, or denied a promotion because of their sexual orientation.[79] Homosexual workers report higher levels of stress compared with heterosexual workers, and one source of this may be the fact that in 36 states homosexuality is still a legitimate legal basis for firing an employee. Finally, gay and bisexual male workers were found to earn 11%–27% less than equally qualified heterosexual counterparts.[80]

How important is the issue of sexual preference? Once again, if managers are concerned about hiring and keeping workplace talent, they shouldn't ignore the motivation and productivity of 6% of the workforce. Many employers are recognizing this: 95% of the top 500 U.S. companies now offer policies prohibiting discrimination based on sexual preference, and 70% offer domestic partner benefits for same-sex couples.[81]

Disability. Everyone recognizes the wheelchair as signifying that a person is partly disabled, but other disabilities are not so easily identified—and may not invite understanding. Do you think that mental disabilites, for example, should be accommodated in employment? If you were subject to mood swings, would you think that would prevent you from doing your job effectively?

People with Differing Physical & Mental Abilities

One out of six Americans has a physical or mental disability, according to the U.S. Department of Labor. Since 1992 we have had the ***Americans with Disabilities Act,* which prohibits discrimination against the disabled** and requires organizations to reasonably accommodate an individual's disabilities. Despite what we've all heard about organizations having to spend hundreds of thousands of dollars building wheelchair ramps and the like, the costs actually aren't that great: half the disability accommodations cost less than $50 and 69% cost less than $500.[82]

Even so, disabled people have difficulty finding work. Although two-thirds of people with disabilities want to work, roughly two-thirds are unemployed. (Among blind adults, for example, about 70% are out of work.[83]) Those who are working tend to be in part-time, low-status jobs with little chance for advancement. Moreover, they earn up to 35% less than their more fully abled counterparts.[84] Here, too, is a talent pool that managers will no doubt find themselves tapping into in the coming years.

Educational Levels: Mismatches Between Education & Workforce Needs.

Two important mismatches between education and workplace are these:

- **College graduates may be in jobs for which they are overqualified:** About 27% of people working have a college degree. But some are ***underemployed* — working at jobs that require less education than they have**—such as tending bar, managing video stores, or other jobs that someone with less education could do.

  It is estimated that a quarter of the workforce (not all of them college graduates) is underemployed, a condition associated with higher absenteeism, arrest rates, and unmarried parenthood and with lower motivation, job involvement, and psychological well-being.[85]

- **High-school dropouts and others may not have the literacy skills needed for many jobs:** Among 16- to 24-year-olds in the United States, 10.9% were high school dropouts in 2000.[86] In addition, an estimated 73 million adult Americans are illiterate, meaning unable to use "printed and written information to function in society, to achieve one's goals, and to develop one's knowledge and potential."[87] In addition, more than two-thirds of the American workforce reads below ninth-grade level—a problem because about 70% of on-the-job reading materials are written at or above that level.[88]

Barriers to Diversity

Some barriers are erected by diverse people themselves. In the main, however, most barriers are put in their paths by organizations.[89] When we speak of "the organization's barriers," we are, of course, referring to the *people* in the organization—especially those who may have been there for a while—who are resistant to making it more diverse.

Resistance to change in general is an attitude that all managers come up against from time to time, and resistance to diversity is simply one variation. It may be expressed in the following six ways.

1 Stereotypes & Prejudices

***Ethnocentrism* is the belief that one's native country, culture, language, abilities, or behavior is superior to those of another culture.** (An example is embodied in the title of the Wesley Snipes/Woody Harrelson movie about urban basketball hustlers: *White Men Can't Jump.*) When differences are viewed as being weaknesses—which is what many stereotypes and prejudices ultimately come down to—this may be expressed as a concern that diversity hiring will lead to a sacrifice in competence and quality.

2 Fear of Reverse Discrimination

Some employees are afraid that attempts to achieve greater diversity in their organization will result in reverse discrimination—that more black or Asian employees will be promoted to fire captain or police lieutenant, for example, over the heads of supposedly more qualified whites.

3 Resistance to Diversity Program Priorities

Some companies such as 3M offer special classes teaching tolerance for diversity, seminars in how to get along.[90] Some employees may see diversity programs as distracting them from the organization's "real work." In addition, they may be resentful of diversity-promoting policies that are reinforced through special criteria in the organization's performance appraisals and reward systems.

4 Unsupportive Social Atmosphere

Diverse employees may be excluded from office camaraderie and social events.

5 Lack of Support for Family Demands

In most families (63%, according to the Bureau of Labor Statistics), both parents work; in 29.5% only the father works, and in 4.5% only the mother works. But more and more women are moving back and forth between being at-home mothers and in the workforce, as economic circumstances dictate.[91] Yet in a great many households, it is still women who primarily take care of children, as well as other domestic chores. When organizations aren't supportive in offering flexibility in hours and job responsibilities, these women may find it difficult to work evenings and weekends or to take overnight business trips.

6 Lack of Support for Career-Building Steps

Organizations may not provide diverse employees with the types of work assignments that will help qualify them for positions in senior management. In addition, organizations may fail to provide the kind of informal training or mentoring that will help them learn the political savvy to do networking and other activities required to get ahead. ◆

OUR GLOBAL DIVERSITY VISION

Johnson & Johnson's Credo sets forth our responsibilities to our employees. It recognizes their dignity and merit, their individuality, and the requirement for equal opportunity in employment, development and advancement for those qualified. From these principles, modified over the years, Johnson & Johnson has fostered and encouraged the development of a diverse workforce - a workforce for the future. ▼ While we can point with pride to a commitment to diversity deeply rooted in our value system, we recognize that our employees, customers and communities, then, were far different from those of today. However, our commitment to these core stakeholders as they have evolved and as Johnson & Johnson has evolved is as strong as ever. ▼ Today's customers and employees come from all over the world and represent different ages, cultures, genders, races and physical capabilities. Through their life experiences, they provide a diversity of thought and perspective that must be reflected in our corporate culture.

Our global diversity vision is to become
THE EMPLOYER OF CHOICE
IN A DYNAMIC GLOBAL ENVIRONMENT.

To achieve this vision, we must build a workforce that is increasingly skilled, diverse, motivated and committed to dynamic leadership. This workforce should reflect our diverse customer base and be knowledgeable of the markets we serve. ▼ Being the Employer of Choice in a Dynamic Global Environment means embracing the differences and similarities of all our employees and prospective employees. It also means the execution of innovative diversity and marketing initiatives to ensure our ability to recruit, develop, retain and promote exceptional talent from an array of backgrounds and geographies, while continuing our pursuit of excellence. ▼ Our goal is to ensure our ability to meet the demands of a changing world with a vision worthy of our values and our commitment to be the leader in health care across the globe. When we achieve our vision, diversity becomes one of our most important competitive advantages.

Johnson & Johnson

Global diversity vision. Johnson & Johnson publishes this expression of the health products company's desire "to become the employer of choice" in its employment policies.

major question Do I have what it takes to be an entrepreneur?

The Big Picture

Entrepreneurship, a necessary attribute of business, means taking risks to create a new enterprise. It is expressed through two kinds of innovators, the entrepreneur and the intrapreneur.

The entrepreneur. Niklas Zennström, one-half of the team that created popular file-sharing program Kazaa, hopes his latest invention, Skype, will turn telecommunications on its ear.

Niklas Zennström, 38, born in Sweden, and Janus Friis, 27, of Denmark, already have a track record. Their popular file-sharing program Kazaa, which allows users to get things for free, whether music or videos, has been downloaded more times than any other software in history, with more than 315 million copies residing in personal computers all over the world.[92] It has also made Zennström and Friis among the chief enemies of the music business, to the point where they sold off Kazaa to avoid further legal hassles.

Kazaa (named for a Thai restaurant, Sawaddee Ka, the pair frequented in Amsterdam) is based on the concept of distributed, or peer-to-peer (P2P), computing, which allows people to access one another's personal computers for storage or computing capacity. Kazaa proved superior to Napster, the original free-music exchange concept, because Napster was based on centralized server computers that kept track of what files sat on which users' computers. This meant that as users increased, Napster had to add more servers. Kazaa, by contrast, allowed computer users to negotiate among each other, avoiding the use of centralized servers.

Now Zennström, the money and business-development partner, and Friis, in charge of product brainstorming, are taking the P2P concept and applying it to making free Internet PC-to-PC telephone calls. Their company, called Skype, routes calls over an Internet connection, avoiding the traditional voice phone network. What makes Skype different from other Internet phone services is that it doesn't rely on a centralized infrastructure to maintain the directory of users and route calls. Rather, the P2P phone network consists of the users themselves, with each Skype subscriber helping to route calls between users.

Similar to an instant-messenging program, Skype provides you with a directory to search for other people who have registered with the service. If you click on a user, his or her computer will start ringing; if you both have voice headsets or microphones, you can have a crystal-clear connection. The principal drawback is that both parties have to be hooked up to the Internet. In the future, as wireless Internet services (such as Wi-Fi) spread, making calls available to cellphones and laptops, this could become less of a problem.[93]

How will Skype make money if calls are free? Zennström and Friis hope to charge for some services in the future, such as conference calls (now the first 5 hours are free), voice mailboxes, connections to the regular telephone networks, and placing ads on the screen interface.

Entrepreneurship Defined: Taking Risks in Pursuit of Opportunity

Zennström and Friis didn't think up all the components of Kazaa and Skype—they hired others to solve the the technical details. But they are the entrepreneurs, the men with the idea, the risk takers.

So is Chip Conley, who has made a success in the offbeat but expanding business of "boutique" hotels, each of which, unlike Hiltons and Hyatts, has its own one-of-a-kind charm. Conley likes magazines because they provide inspired themes for the hotels he buys and renovates. For instance, he says the Nob Hill Lambourne in San Francisco, which is oriented toward health-conscious travelers, resembles the magazine *Men's Health;* the hotel offers algae shakes, vitamins instead of chocolates on the pillows, and an on-call psychologist. The Hotel Rex, modeled on *The New Yorker,* features a book-lined cocktail lounge, old leather furniture, and poetry readings.[94]

The most successful entrepreneurs become wealthy and make the covers of business magazines: Fred Smith of Federal Express. Debbie Fields of Mrs. Field's Cookies. Anita Roddick of The Body Shop. Michael Dell of Dell Computers. Failed entrepreneurs may benefit from the experience to live to fight another day—as did Henry Ford, twice bankrupt before achieving success with Ford Motor Co.

What Entrepreneurship Is

***Entrepreneurship* is the process of taking risks to try to create a new enterprise.** There are two types of entrepreneurship:

- **The entrepreneur: An *entrepreneur* is someone who sees a new opportunity for a product or service and launches a business to try to realize it.** Most entrepreneurs run small businesses with fewer than 100 employees.
- **The intrapreneur: An *intrapreneur* is someone who works inside an existing organization who sees an opportunity for a product or service and mobilizes the organization's resources to try to realize it.** This person might be a researcher or a scientist but could also be a manager who sees an opportunity to create a new venture that could be profitable.

Example of an Intrapreneur: Art Fry & 3M's Post-it Notes

Example

One of the most famous instances of intrapreneurship occurred at 3M Corp., a company famous for pumping out new products, when 3M employee Art Fry conceived of Post-it Notes, those bright-colored "sticky notes" that people use to post messages on walls and mark books. The company had invented an experimental adhesive for which it could find no use. Meanwhile, when attending church, Fry found that the bits of paper he used to mark hymns in his hymnbook kept slipping out. It dawned on him that 3M's experimental glue could provide adhesive-backed paper that would stick for a long time but could be easily removed without damaging the book.

Coming up with the product was only the first step. Market surveys were negative. Office-supply distributors thought the notion useless. Fry thereupon started giving samples to executives and secretaries at 3M, who began using the sticky paper and soon were hooked. Later Fry used the same approach with other executives and secretaries throughout the United States. After 12 years, the orders began to flow, and Post-its became a winning product for 3M.[95]

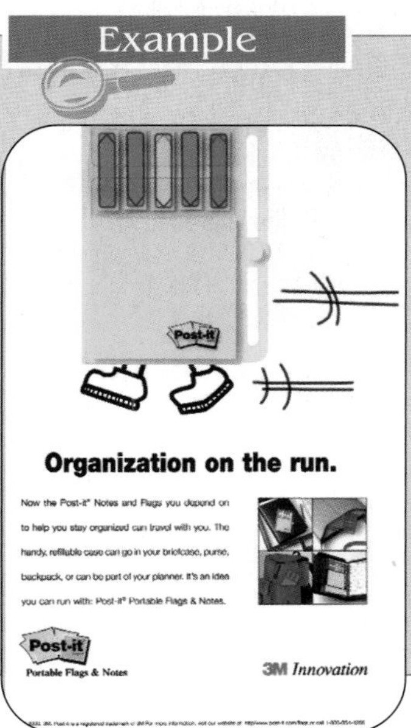

Organization on the run.
Post-it
Portable Flags & Notes
3M Innovation

Up and away. Gary Ream, president and partner of Woodward Camp, transformed this aging gymnastics camp in central Pennsylvania into an extreme-sports summer retreat. First he offered BMX lessons, then coached in-line skaters and skateboarders, then began hosting competitions, which attracted the attention of sports TV channel ESPN and generated further publicity.

How Do Entrepreneurs & Managers Differ?

While the entrepreneur is not necessarily an inventor, he or she "always searches for change, responds to it, and exploits it as an opportunity," Peter Drucker points out.[96] How does this differ from being a manager?

Being an entrepreneur is what it takes to *start* a business; being a manager is what it takes to *grow or maintain* a business. As an entrepreneur/intrapreneur, you initiate new goods or services; as a manager you coordinate the resources to produce the goods or services.

The examples of success we mentioned above—Chip Conley, Fred Smith, Debbie Fields, Anita Roddick, Michael Dell—are actually *both* entrepreneurs and effective managers. Some people, however, find they like the start-up part but hate the management part. For example, Stephen Wozniak, entrepreneurial co-founder with Steve Jobs of Apple Computer, abandoned the computer industry completely and went back to college. Jobs, by contrast, went on to launch another business, Pixar, which among other things became the animation factory that made the movies *Toy Story* and *Finding Nemo*.

Entrepreneurial companies have been called "gazelles" for the two attributes that make them successful: *speed and agility*. "Gazelles have mastered the art of the quick," says Alan Webber, founding editor of *Fast Company* magazine. "They have internal approaches and fast decision-making approaches that let them move with maximum agility in a fast-changing business environment."[97]

Is this the kind of smart, innovative world you'd like to be a part of? Most people prefer the security of a job and a paycheck. Indeed, even young people—those ages 25–34—who might be expected to be attracted to the entrepreneurial life are about 40% less likely to be self-employed than their parents, according to the Bureau of Labor Statistics.[98]

Entrepreneurs do seem to have psychological characteristics that are different from managers, as follows:[99]

- **Characteristic of both—high need for achievement:** Both entrepreneurs and managers have a high need for achievement. However, entrepreneurs certainly seem to be motivated to pursue moderately difficult goals through their own efforts in order to realize their ideas and, they hope, financial rewards. Managers, by contrast, are more motivated by promotions and organizational rewards of power and perks.
- **Also characteristic of both—belief in personal control of destiny:** If you believe "I am the captain of my fate, the master of my soul," you have what is known as ***internal locus of control,*** **the belief that you control your own destiny,** that external forces will have little influence. (External locus of control means the reverse—you believe you don't control your destiny, that external forces do.) Both entrepreneurs and managers like to think they have personal control over their lives.

- **Characteristic of both, but especially of entrepreneurs—high energy level and action orientation:** Rising to the top in an organization probably requires that a manager put in long hours. For entrepreneurs, however, creating a new enterprise may require an extraordinary investment of time and energy. In addition, while some managers may feel a sense of urgency, entrepreneurs are especially apt to be impatient and to want to get things done as quickly as possible, making them particularly action oriented.
- **Characteristic of both, but especially of entrepreneurs—high tolerance for ambiguity:** Every manager needs to be able to make decisions based on ambiguous—that is, unclear or incomplete—information. However, entrepreneurs must have more tolerance for ambiguity because they are trying to do things they haven't done before.
- **More characteristic of entrepreneurs than managers—self-confidence and tolerance for risk:** Managers must believe in themselves and be willing to make decisions; however, this statement applies even more to entrepreneurs. Precisely because they are willing to take risks in the pursuit of new opportunities—indeed, even risk personal financial failure—entrepreneurs need the confidence to act decisively.

Of course, not all entrepreneurs have this kind of faith in themselves. So-called *necessity* entrepreneurs are people such as laid-off corporate workers, discharged military people, immigrants, and divorced homemakers who suddenly must earn a living and are simply trying to replace lost income and are hoping a job comes along. These make up about 11% of entrepreneurs. However, so-called *opportunity* entrepreneurs—the other 89%—are those who start their own business out of a burning desire rather than because they lost a job. Unlike necessity types, they tend to be more ambitious and to start firms that can lead to high-growth businesses.

Which do you think you would be more happier doing—being an entrepreneur or being a manager?[100] ◆

Meg Whitman, eBay CEO. Pierre Omidyar was the entrepreneurial founder of the online auction company, but Whitman is the professional manager who, in one fan's words, "has taken a brilliant idea, and with execution, monitoring, and constant improvement, made it infinitely better."

Key Terms Used in This Chapter

accommodative approach, 82
Americans with Disabilities Act, 88
code of ethics, 78
competitors, 71
customers, 70
defensive approach, 82
demographic forces, 75
distributor, 71
diversity, 84
economic forces, 74
ethnocentrism, 88
entrepreneur, 91
entrepreneurship, 91
ethical behavior, 76
ethical dilemma, 76
ethics, 76
external dimensions of diversity, 85
external stakeholders, 70
general environment, 74
glass ceiling, 86
government regulators, 72
individual approach, 77
internal dimensions of diversity, 85
internal locus of control, 92
internal stakeholders, 68
international forces, 75
intrapreneur, 91
justice approach, 77
macroenvironment, 74
moral-rights approach, 77
obstructionist approach, 82
owners, 68
personality, 84
philanthropy, 80
political-legal forces, 75
proactive approach, 82
sociocultural forces, 74
social responsibility, 80
special-interest groups, 73
stakeholders, 67
strategic allies, 71
supplier, 71
task environment, 70
technological forces, 74
underemployed, 88
utilitarian approach, 77
value system, 76
values, 76
whistleblower, 79

Summary

3.1 The Community of Stakeholders Inside the Organization

- Managers operate in two organizational environments—internal and external—both made up of shareholders, the people whose interests are affected by the organization's activities. The first, or internal, environment, also includes employees, owners, and the board of directors.

3.2 The Community of Stakeholders Outside the Organization

- The external environment of stakeholders consists of the task environment and the general environment.
- The task environment consists of 11 groups that present the manager with daily tasks to deal with. (1) Customers are those who pay to use an organization's goods and services. (2) Competitors are people or organizations that compete for customers or resources. (3) Suppliers are people or organizations that provide supplies—raw materials, services, equipment, labor, or energy—to other organizations. (4) Distributors are people or organizations that help another organization sell its goods and services to customers. (5) Strategic allies describe the relationship of two organizations who join forces to achieve advantages neither can perform as well alone. (6) Employee organizations consist of labor unions and employee associations. (7) Local communities consist of residents, companies, governments, and nonprofit entities that depend on the organization's taxes, payroll, and charitable contributions. (8) Financial institutions are commercial banks, investment banks, and insurance companies that deal with the organization. (9) Government regulators are regulatory agencies that establish the ground rules under which the organization operates. (10) Special-interest groups are groups whose members try to influence specific issues that may affect the organization. (11) The mass media are print, radio, TV, and Internet sources that affect the organization's public relations.
- The general environment includes six forces. (1) Economic forces consist of general economic conditions and trends—unemployment, inflation, interest rates, economic growth—that may affect an organization's performance. (2) Technological forces are new developments in methods for transforming resources into

Ethical Dilemma

Should Job Applicants Reveal Their Chronic Illnesses to Potential Employers?

Based on Joann S. Lublin, "Should Job Hunters Reveal Chronic Illness? The Pros and Cons," The Wall Street Journal, *January 13, 2004, p. B1.*

You've just graduated from college and are excited to begin job hunting. You have many exciting prospects, but there is one thing holding you back—you were recently diagnosed with scleroderma. This chronic connective tissue disease is progressive and typically kills patients within 10 years. Your doctor is positive about your prognosis; however, you have already experienced some of the effects, such as swelling and stiffening in your fingers. Federal disability laws bar employers from asking about an applicant's health. However, the U.S. Supreme Court ruled that a company can refuse to hire an applicant whose medical condition might adversely affect the performance of a specific job function.

Solving the Dilemma

Knowing a company might be reluctant to hire you based on your condition, what would you do?

1. Don't immediately mention your disease during the interview. Instead, play up your abilities, experience, and enthusiasm for the job. If you get hired, you can explain your illness and make up for missed work owing to medical appointments and flare-ups by working on weekends.
2. Bring up your disease right away. You don't have to provide vivid details about your symptoms, but it is important for your employer to know you have a chronic disease and how it will affect you.
3. Don't mention your disease at all. If you get the job and have a flare-up and need to take sick days, it is your business.
4. Invent other options. Discuss.

Video Case

Joe-to-Go

Jerry Andrews was a typical soccer dad—hauling kids to games, bringing snacks, and cheering on the sidelines. One day he volunteered to bring coffee to an early morning game. Only later he realized how difficult it would be to carry a dozen cups of coffee, especially with the leg braces he wore as a result of childhood polio. Later he and his friends discussed the problem and Andrews's idea of a disposable thermos bag. One thing led to another, resulting in a major entrepreneurial idea. They decided to call the bag "Joe-to-Go."

Entrepreneurship is filled with pitfalls and roadblocks. Successful entrepreneurs must be passionate, action-oriented, and energetic. They must have self-direction and be able to tolerate uncertainty but must also be practical and willing to seek advice when needed.

Andrews knew intuitively who his customers would be. But he still needed help to turn his idea into a viable product. Outside design and production experts helped Andrews create just the right product. He also sought advice from accountants, lawyers, market researchers, insurance agents, and small-business advisors. Retailers who could reach customers and tell them about the benefits of a thermos bag were vital. Fortunately, his only investor was an experienced salesperson eager to find customers for the new product. Everywhere they promoted the product, people loved it—but nobody was buying. Finally, Dunkin' Donuts saw the potential of selling more coffee, and perhaps more donuts, by using Joe-to-Go. Other companies soon followed.

Andrews decided to license his product and is paid a fixed amount for every box sold. Companies are free to label the box anything they like. Some keep the "Joe-to-Go" name, others use their own name. A major victory came when Starbucks began to carry the product. When he would go to a Starbucks that didn't carry his product, Andrews would bring one out and show it off. Orders then followed.

It took a great deal of patience, persistence, and hard work to make Joe-to-Go a success. Those who own their businesses face a trade-off between increased freedom and decreased security. Fortunately, there are always new opportunities and new challenges.

Discussion Questions

1. Identify some of the internal stakeholders in Jerry Andrews's Joe-to-Go enterprise.
2. Identify groups in the external task environment that affected the success of Joe-to-Go.
3. Is Jerry Andrews an entrepreneur or an intrapreneur?
4. Describe some of the personality characteristics that led to Andrews's success.
5. What is the primary reason independently owned and operated small businesses fail?

chapter 4

Global Management

Managing Across Borders

MAJOR QUESTIONS YOU SHOULD BE ABLE TO ANSWER

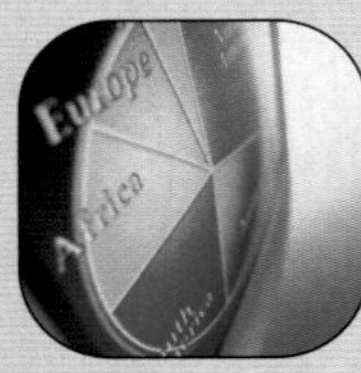

4.1 Globalization: The Collapse of Time & Distance

Major Question: What three important developments of globalization will probably affect me?

4.2 You & International Management

Major Question: Why learn about international management, and what characterizes the successful international manager?

4.3 Why & How Companies Expand Internationally

Major Question: Why do companies expand internationally, and how do they do it?

4.4 Economic & Political-Legal Differences

Major Question: How may foreign countries differ in their economic, political, and legal characteristics?

4.5 The World of Free Trade: Regional Economic Cooperation

Major Question: What are barriers to free trade, and what major organizations and trading blocs promote trade?

4.6 The Importance of Understanding Cultural Differences

Major Question: What are the principal areas of cultural differences?

the manager's toolbox

Being a Star Road Warrior

Since business travelers who fly 100,000-plus miles a year are no longer a rare breed, should you prepare for the possibility of joining them?

As we discuss in this chapter, globalization has collapsed time and distance. Managers must be prepared to work for organizations that operate not only countrywide but worldwide. To stay connected with colleagues, employees, clients, and suppliers, you may have to travel a lot.

Business travel can have its rewards. Many people enjoy going to different cities, meeting new people, encountering new cultures. In one survey, people who took business trips of five nights or more said that being on the road provided certain escapes: from their everyday workplace (35% of those polled); from putting out work "fires" (20%); from frequent meetings (12%); from coworker distractions (11%).[1]

Two lessons that business travelers have learned are the following.

- **Frequent travel may be needed because personal encounters are essential for teamwork:** "Flying is a waste of time, but it's a necessary evil," says management consultant Jeff Bowden, who flies about 500,000 miles a year. "I've done well financially, so I've been very lucky. I laugh at people who think they can be successful without flying."[2]

  Scott Collins lives in Michigan, where his $100,000 salary goes far. But he works at Netscape Communications in Mountain View, Calif., in the heart of Silicon Valley, and travels the 2,000 miles between home and workplace a couple of times a month. The reason: Phones, e-mail, and videoconferencing aren't entirely feasible. Teamwork requires personal encounters.

  "Paradoxically, location matters more than ever in high-tech," says futurist Paul Saffo. "To be a player in Silicon Valley, you have to be in people's faces."[3]

  The same is true in most other industries.

- **Frequent travel requires frequent adjustments:** How do you cope if you travel all the time? Management consultant Bowden keeps sets of clothes in Tampa, Los Angeles, and Vancouver, British Columbia. He is away so much that he has a problem getting rid of his household trash. If he puts his garbage cans out Tuesday morning, he may not be home to wheel them in. So he has learned to dispose of the trash in a trash can en route to the airport.

  Vicki Schubert-Martin, who works in the software industry, travels about 250,000 miles a year, which keeps her away from her Denver home about five days a week. To keep up her health, she maintains a high-fiber diet while on the road. She keeps a close relationship with her husband by phoning him daily and spending weekends hiking, biking, and seeing movies with him. "It's a matter of keeping a healthy attitude about it," she says.[4]

forecast

What's Ahead in This Chapter

This chapter covers the importance of globalization—the rise of the global village, of one big market, of both worldwide megafirms and minifirms. We also describe the characteristics of the successful international manager, why and how companies expand internationally, and some of the economic and political-legal differences between countries. We describe the barriers to free trade and the major organizations promoting trade. Finally, we describe some of the cultural differences you may encounter if you become an international manager.

major question **What three important developments of globalization will probably affect me?**

The Big Picture

Globalization, the trend of the world economy toward becoming a more interdependent system, is reflected in three developments: the rise of the "global village" and e-commerce, the trend of the world's becoming one big market, and the rise of both megafirms and Internet-enabled minifirms worldwide.

Barry Salzman, president of DoubleClick International, a worldwide Internet advertising firm headquartered in New York, spends about 75% of his time traveling. "He takes a laptop and four battery packs so that he can wade through the 200 e-mail messages he averages daily," says one description. "He carries two mobile phones because he is on call, day or night, to handle problems anywhere in the world."[5]

Here is a manager who heads an Internet company—which can reach all corners of the globe in milliseconds. Yet he spends most of his time traveling because it's the only way he can see to manage his 13 offices worldwide.

Can you visualize yourself operating like this? Like Salzman, you are living in a world being rapidly changed by ***globalization*** **—the trend of the world economy toward becoming a more interdependent system.** Time and distance, which have been under assault for 150 years, have now virtually collapsed, as reflected in three important developments we shall discuss:[6]

1. The rise of the "global village" and electronic commerce.
2. The world's becoming one market instead of many national ones.
3. The rise of both megafirms and Internet-enabled minifirms worldwide.

The Rise of the "Global Village" & Electronic Commerce

The hallmark of great civilizations has been their great systems of communications. In the beginning, communications was based on transportation: the Roman Empire had its network of roads, as did other ancient civilizations, such as the Incas. Later the great European powers had their farflung navies. In the 19th century, the United States and Canada unified North America by building transcontinental railroads. Later the airplane reduced travel time between continents.

Interacting internationally. China is a global trading colossus, with imports and exports totaling $851 billion in 2003. Japan is its top trading partner; the United States is its second.

From Transportation to Communication

Transportation began to yield to the electronic exchange of information. Beginning in 1844, the telegraph ended the short existence of the Pony Express and, beginning in 1876, found itself in competition with the telephone. The amplifying vacuum tube, invented in 1906, led to commercial radio. Television came into being in England in 1925. During the 1950s and 1960s, as television exploded throughout the world, communications philosopher Marshall McLuhan posed the notion of a "global village," where we all share our hopes, dreams, and fears in a "worldpool" of information. **The *global village* refers to the "shrinking" of time and space as air travel and the electronic media have made it easier for the people of the globe to communicate with one another.**

Then the world became even faster and smaller. Fifteen years ago, cellphones, pagers, fax, and voice-mail links barely existed. When AT&T launched the first cellular communications system in 1983, it predicted fewer than a million users by 2000. By the end of 1993, however, there were more than 16 million cellular phone subscribers in the United States.[7] And as of the end of 2003, there were nearly 142 million.[8]

The Net, the Web, & the World

And then came the Internet, the worldwide computer-linked "network of networks," where today 729 million people log on every week throughout the world (only 35.8% of them English speaking).[9] The Net might have remained the province of academicians had it not been for the contributions of Tim Berners-Lee, who came up with the coding system, linkages, and addressing scheme that debuted in 1991 as the World Wide Web. "He took a powerful communications system [the Internet] that only the elite could use," says one writer, "and turned it into a mass medium."[10]

The arrival of the Web quickly led to ***e-commerce,* or electronic commerce, the buying and selling of products and services through computer networks.** Total U.S. e-commerce sales to consumers topped $918 billion by the end of 2003, or about 1.5% of consumer retail spending.[11] Indeed, online shopping is growing even faster than the increase in computer use.[12]

Example

Worldwide E-Commerce: Amazon.com

In 1994, Jeffrey Bezos left a successful career on Wall Street with a plan to exploit the potential for electronic retailing on the World Wide Web by launching an online bookstore called Amazon.com.

Bezos realized that no bookstore with four walls could possibly stock the more than 2.5 million books that are now active and in print. Moreover, he saw that an online bookstore wouldn't have to make the same investment in retail clerks, store real estate, or warehouse space (in the beginning, Amazon.com ordered books from the publisher *after* Amazon took an order), so it could pass savings along to customers in the form of discounts. In addition, he appreciated that there would be opportunities to obtain demographic information about customers in order to offer personalized services, such as books of interest to them. Finally, Bezos saw that there could be a good deal of online interaction: customers could post reviews of books they read and could reach authors by e-mail to provide feedback.

Amazon.com sold its first book in July 1995 and by the end of 1998 had served 6.2 million customers in more than 100 countries. Later the firm began expanding into nonbook areas, such as online retailing of music CDs, toys, electronics, drugs, cosmetics, and pet supplies. It reported its first full-year profit in 2003.[13]

One Big World Market: The Global Economy

"We are seeing the results of things started in 1988 and 1989," said Rosabeth Moss Kantor of the Harvard Business School a decade later.[14] It was in the late 1980s when the Berlin Wall came down, signaling the beginning of the end of communism in Eastern Europe. It was also when countries of the Pacific Rim began to open their economies to foreign investors. Finally, the trend toward governments deregulating their economies began sweeping the globe. These three events set up conditions by which goods, people, and money could move more freely throughout the world—a

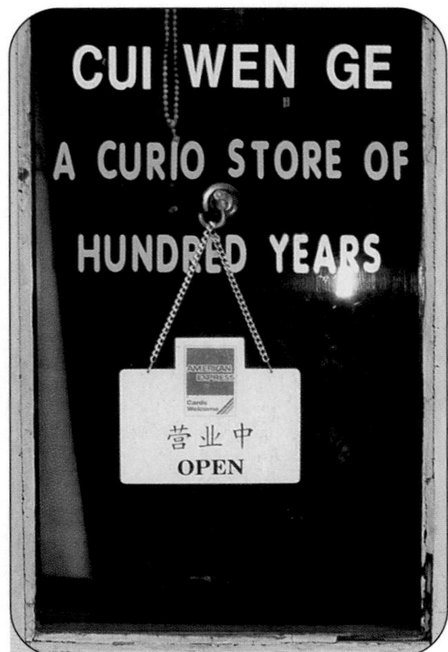

The global economy. This purveyor of souvenirs and antiques is located in Beijing. It welcomes American Express cards. In China and other parts of the world, you can use your U.S. credit card or debit card in local cash machines to obtain the currency of your host country. You will see the amount deducted, in dollars, from your credit-card or bank account when you get home.

global economy. **The *global economy* refers to the increasing tendency of the economies of the world to interact with one another as one market instead of many national markets.**

The economies of the world have never been more entangled. As Kevin Maney writes in *USA Today,* "They're tied together by instantaneous information arriving via everything from currency trading databases to websites to CNN broadcasts. Capital—the money used to build businesses—moves globally and moves in a matter of keystrokes."[15]

Positive Effects

Is a global economy really good for the United States? U.S. exports, international trade, and U.S. workers are connected, points out Nancy Birdsall, executive vice president of the Inter-American Development Bank in Washington, D.C. "As consumers in other regions of the world see their income go up, they are going to be more interested in U.S. products," she said in 1995. "The bottom line is that growth of jobs and income in other countries will mean growth of jobs and income in [the United States]. It's a win-win situation."[16]

Negative Effects

However, global economic interdependency can also turn into a lose-lose situation. Its double-edged nature was shown when, following the devaluation of Thailand's currency in July 1997, the previously fast-growing "Asian Tiger" economies—Thailand, Indonesia, South Korea, Japan—became the "Asian crisis." (*Devaluation* means that a nation's currency is lowered relative to other countries' currencies.) The economic catastrophes of the Pacific Rim began affecting the economies of emerging nations from Latin America to Eastern Europe, eventually hurting Australia, Canada, and certain sectors of the United States.[17] National governments were powerless to stop the flight of capital from weakened economies to stronger ones. U.S. stock markets reacted, for a time losing one-fifth of their value.

Another negative effect is the movement, or outsourcing (discussed in Section 4.3), of formerly well-paying jobs overseas as companies seek cheaper labor costs. Two decades ago, the loss was in American manufacturing jobs; more recently, many service jobs have moved offshore.

But the global economy isn't going to go away just because we don't like some of its destabilizing aspects. "The process is irreversible, if only because of the information technology and communications revolutions," says Claude Smadja, managing director of the World Economic Forum in Switzerland. "The problem also is that, contrary to some illusions, one cannot pick and choose in the package. . . . The new globality means a tremendous emphasis on speed, flexibility, versatility, and permanent change—in some respects, insecurity."[18]

Cross-Border Business: The Rise of Both Megamergers & Minifirms Worldwide

The global market driven by electronic information "forces things to get bigger and smaller at the same time," suggests technology philosopher Nicholas Negroponte. "And that's so ironic, when things want to do both but not stay in the middle. There will be an increasing absence of things that aren't either very local or very global."[19]

If Negroponte is correct, this means we will see more and more of two opposite kinds of businesses: mergers of huge companies into even larger companies, and small, fast-moving startup companies.

Megamergers Operating Worldwide

Exxon + Mobil. British Petroleum + Amoco. Bell Atlantic + GTE. DaimlerBenz + Chrysler. Ford + Volvo. Volkswagen + Rolls-Royce. Travelers Group + Citicorp. Glaxco Wellcome + SmithKline Beecham.

The late 1990s were megamerger time, "corporations on steroids," in one writer's phrase.[20] Oil, telecommunications, automobiles, financial services, and pharmaceuticals aren't suited to being midsize, let alone small and local, so companies in these industries are trying to become bigger and cross-border. The means for doing so is to merge with other big companies. In telecommunications, for instance, Bell Atlantic and GTE teamed up in what's called a "size and scope" deal so that they could deliver worldwide voice, video, data, wireless, Internet, and the like, and be able to compete with other giant companies that are also getting bigger.[21]

Minifirms Operating Worldwide

The Internet and the World Wide Web allow almost anyone to be global, which Kevin Maney points out has two important results:

1 Small Companies Can Get Started More Easily Because anyone can put goods or services on a website and sell worldwide, this wipes out the former competitive advantages of distribution and scope that large companies used to have.

2 Small Companies Can Maneuver Faster Little companies can change direction faster, which gives them an advantage in terms of time and distance over large companies.

The most famous example of these two phenomena is Amazon.com, which has scared major retail store chains. But many small firms, such as online auction companies, have also come from nowhere to collapse time and distance. For instance, so-called "Bay-traders" make a living selling things on eBay, the online auction company. Bay traders find they get higher prices at Internet auctions than at swap meets or collectibles shows because bidding generates excitement and because the Internet's worldwide reach makes multiple bids more likely. Ray and Ann Geeck used to sell antique dolls at shows or at their Lake Panasoffkee, Fla., store, but they started auctioning online and now stick just with that. "We were getting $300 and $400 on eBay for things we couldn't sell for $125 at the shows," says Geeck.[22] ◆

Daimler-Benz+Chrysler. The 1998 $41 billion merger of Germany's Daimler-Benz, maker of Mercedes-Benz cars and trucks, and the U.S.A.'s Chrysler Corp. created a global automotive giant, DaimlerChrysler. Dieter Zetsche, shown here, is the president and CEO of Chrysler USA. Unfortunately, while rival carmakers such as BMW, Toyota, and Nissan all managed to increase sales and market share worldwide in 2003, DaimlerChrysler posted a $527 million loss. Do you think cross-border megamergers are good for the United States?

major question

Why learn about international management, and what characterizes the successful international manager?

The Big Picture

Studying international management prepares you to work with foreign customers or suppliers, for a foreign firm in the United States or for a U.S. firm overseas. Successful international managers aren't ethnocentric or polycentric but geocentric.

Part of the action. If "all of the action in business is international," as one expert says, what role do you think you might play in it? Do you think cultural bias against women in some foreign countries contributes to the low percentage of U.S. female executives working abroad?

Working overseas "is an advantage to your career," says Lyric Merrie Hughes, head of a Chicago international marketing firm. "All of the action in business is international."[23]

This is true for managers of both genders, but women especially may benefit by taking overseas assignments, whether for a few weeks or a year. Only about 15% of the American executives working outside the United States are women, in one estimate, and few of them are married or have children.[24]

This presents an opportunity, although it means breaking through some male executives' stereotypes about women. Research has found that male top managers believe that women don't want to work overseas because it disrupts their and their families' personal lives. They also were skeptical that women would be accepted in foreign cultures.[25] Nevertheless, gender barriers are crumbling, and there are ways for women to demonstrate their value overseas.

Hughes goes to Europe and Asia every two weeks, relying on a nanny and "a good support system" to care for her three children. "Just do it," she says, in urging women to accept overseas assignments. "It's going to enrich you and your family and enhance your career. Get on the plane!"

Why Learn about International Management?

International management is management that oversees the conduct of operations in or with organizations in foreign countries, whether it's through a multinational corporation or a multinational organization.

- **A *multinational corporation,* or multinational enterprise, is a business firm with operations in several countries.** Our publisher, McGraw-Hill, is one such "multinational" (see the 17 foreign cities listed on our book's title page). In terms of revenue, the real behemoths in multinational corporations include the American firms Wal-Mart, Exxon Mobil, General Motors, Ford Motor Co., General Electric, and Citigroup. The largest foreign companies are BP (Britain), Royal Dutch/Shell (Netherlands/Britain), DaimlerChrysler (Germany/USA), and Toyota (Japan).
- **A *multinational organization* is a nonprofit organization with operations in several countries.** Examples are the World Health Organization, the International Red Cross, the Church of Latter Day Saints.

practical action

What You Can Do to Prepare for Overseas Assignments That Will Boost Your Career

What do you need to do to prepare for a career overseas that can advance your career? This is a question for readers of both sexes but particularly for women, who make up only 15% of the American overseas workforce.

Some skills to develop are mentioned in the box.

Skills Most Lacking for Managers Overseas[26]

	For men	For women
Foreign language	31%	27%
Interpersonal skills	14%	7%
Administrative	11%	5%
Management	8%	8%
Technical	8%	15%
Basic computer	7%	9%
Problem solving	5%	6%

Some other suggestions:

Persuade Your Boss That You Can Handle Overseas Duty & That the Organization Will Benefit

First be sure your family supports you. Then let your boss know you want to work overseas at some point and that you can handle all family responsibilities. If you're female, suggest that being a woman can even be an advantage in some cultures, especially in Asia and Latin America, which place strong emphasis on the family.[27]

Study Up on Your Host Country

Study up on the host country's cultural landmarks and shrines, painters, writers, and other outstanding personalities to show you respect their cultural heritage.

Before you go, "Spend at least 10% of preparation time on interpersonal skills," suggests executive coach Arlene B. Isaacs.[28]

Learn rituals of respect, including exchange of business cards. Understand that shaking hands is always permissible, but social kissing may not be.

Learn (perhaps from the hotel concierge) the art of gift giving. You don't want to give a gift that's inappropriate or too pricey and risk bribery charges.

Know how to dress professionally. For women, this means no heavy makeup, no flashy jewelry, no short skirts or sleeveless blouses (particularly in Islamic countries).

Whether male or female, if you learn to adapt appropriate behavior—finesse, consideration, tact, awareness of standards of behavior and cultural values—"you will be perceived as respectful and worthy of a relationship," says Isaacs.

Know Your Field

If you know your field and behave with courtesy and assurance, Asian colleagues will respect your authority, whatever your gender. "They assume you've proven to other people that you deserve respect," says Lorne Walker, who represented a health-care organization in Singapore, "and so they give it to you."[29]

For Women: Realize When You Can't Be One of the Boys

Gender equality is often not a reality overseas. While you may be respected at work, after-hours socialization may remain a males-only prerogative. For instance, if you're single, don't invite your male host to dinner, which can be viewed as being in very bad taste.

"Women can conduct business successfully, but they shouldn't expect to be treated like one of the guys," says Sanjyot Dunung, author of *Doing Business in Asia: The Complete Guide*.[30] In other words, don't expect to be invited out to any karaoke bars. If anything, you may have the advantage in doing business the next day because you can go back to your hotel and rest up while the men are whooping it up into the late hours.

Become Skilled in the Language

Whatever foreign country you're in, at the very least you should learn a few key phrases, such as "hello," "please," and "thank you," in your host country's language.

However, successful international managers have learned there is no adequate substitute for knowing the local language. Indeed, half the top executives in one survey say that among the skills most needed "to maintain a competitive edge" that they find lacking in employees, the one most deficient is knowledge of a foreign language.[31]

In conclusion: Want to know how to really prepare for an overseas job? *Learn a foreign language.*

Even if in the coming years you never travel to the wider world outside North America—an unlikely proposition, we think—the world will assuredly come to you. That, in a nutshell, is why you need to learn about international management.

More specifically, consider yourself in the following situations:

You May Deal with Foreign Customers or Partners

While working for a U.S. company you have to deal with foreign customers. Or you have to work with a foreign company in some sort of joint venture. The people you're dealing with may be outside the United States or visitors to it. Either way you would hate to blow a deal—and maybe all future deals—because you were ignorant of some cultural aspects you could have known about.

A typical scenario is that described by *Fortune* columnist Anne Fisher: "You, a hotshot of either sex, show up alone in Tokyo to meet with the head honchos of a prospective joint-venture partner. You don't know how to say 'hello' or 'thank you' in Japanese, you don't have a proper business card, and you plop yourself down in any old seat at the conference table. Pretty soon your counterparts won't look you in the eye, and before you know it, you're on the plane home and the deal is off."[32] All because you didn't know some details of the culture.

You May Deal with Foreign Suppliers

While working for an American company you have to purchase important components, raw materials, or services from a foreign supplier. And you never know where foreign practices may diverge from what you're accustomed to.

It is estimated, for example, that about 5% of U.S. information technology jobs, such as writing software, have been taken over by suppliers in India, New Zealand, and Eastern Europe, and that by 2007 this figure will rise to 23%. Many U.S. software companies—Microsoft, IBM, Oracle, Motorola, Novell, Hewlett-Packard, and Texas Instruments—have opened offices in India to take advantage of high-quality labor.[33]

You May Work for a Foreign Firm in the United States

You may sometime take a job with a foreign firm doing business in the United States, such as an electronics, pharmaceutical, or car company. And you'll have to deal with managers above and below you whose outlook is different from yours. For instance, Japanese companies, with their emphasis on correctness and face saving, operate in significantly different ways from American companies.

Sometimes it is even hard to know that an ostensibly U.S. company actually has foreign ownership. For example, many American book publishers (though not McGraw-Hill) are British, German, or Canadian owned.

The challenge of interacting successfully with foreign customers. Beyond speaking the language of your host country, what *cultural* skills and awareness might help you gain an advantage over your international competitors?

You May Work for an American Firm Outside the United States

You might easily find yourself working abroad in the foreign operation of a U.S. company. Most big American corporations have overseas subsidiaries or divisions. For example, General Motors has plants in Mexico. Yahoo! has operations in the United Kingdom and many Asian countries.

The Successful International Manager: Geocentric, Not Ethnocentric or Polycentric

Maybe you don't really care that you don't have much understanding of the foreign culture you're dealing with. "What's the point?" you may think. "The main thing is to get the job done." Certainly there are international firms with managers who have this perspective. They are called *ethnocentric,* one of three primary attitudes among international managers, the other two being *polycentric* and *geocentric.*[34]

Ethnocentric Managers—"We Know Best"

Ethnocentric managers **believe that their native country, culture, language, and behavior are superior to all others.** Ethnocentric managers tend to believe that they can export the managers and practices of their home countries to anywhere in the world and that they will be more capable and reliable. Often the ethnocentric viewpoint is less attributable to prejudice than it is to ignorance, since such managers obviously know more about their home environment than the foreign environment.

Is ethnocentrism bad for business? It seems so. A survey of 918 companies with home offices in the United States, Japan, and Europe found that ethnocentric policies were linked to such problems as recruiting difficulties, high turnover rates, and lawsuits over personnel policies.[35]

Polycentric Managers—"They Know Best"

Polycentric managers **take the view that native managers in the foreign offices best understand native personnel and practices, and so the home office should leave them alone.** Thus, the attitude of polycentric managers is nearly the opposite of that of ethnocentric managers.

Geocentric Managers—"What's Best Is What's Effective, Regardless of Origin"

Geocentric managers **accept that there are differences and similarities between home and foreign personnel and practices and that they should use whatever techniques are most effective.** Clearly, being an ethno- or polycentric manager takes less work. But the payoff for being a geocentric manager can be far greater.

The lessons seem clear. If you become an ***expatriate manager*** **—a manager living or working in a foreign country**—it's imperative that you try to learn everything you can about the local culture so that you can deal effectively with it and avoid being beaten by your competitors. ◆

Exports. These American cereal products are being sold in a convenience store in Dublin, Ireland. With 6.3 billion people in the world, the global market contains over 6.3 billion potential customers for goods and services. Almost any good or service used in the United States can be used in other countries as well, although sometimes adapting products to specific global markets can be difficult. However, competition overseas may not be nearly as strong as it is in the U.S. An additional benefit of exporting is that it can help the American economy: According to the U.S. Department of Commerce, every $1 billion in U.S. exports generates 25,000 jobs at home. Can you visualize how one of these jobs might be yours?

major question

Why do companies expand internationally, and how do they do it?

The Big Picture

Multinationals expand to take advantage of availability of supplies, new markets, lower labor costs, access to finance capital, or avoidance of tariffs and import quotas. Five ways they do so are by global outsourcing; importing, exporting, and countertrading; licensing and franchising; joint ventures; and wholly owned subsidiaries.

In Austria, Indonesia, and South Korea, you can find Big Macs in the McDonald's franchises just like in the United States. However, there are also variations for the locals. In Vienna, "McCafés" offer coffee blended for local tastes. In Jakarta, you can get rice as well as French fries. And in Seoul, you can get roast pork on a bun with a garlicky soy sauce.

There's an important lesson here. Says a *New York Times* writer, "That combination of a globally recognized brand with a flexible menu that caters to local palates has helped McDonald's navigate the global economic turbulence that has knocked most of the other big corporations operating around the world way off course."[36]

Clearly, we could all benefit from learning why the McDonald's international division accounts for nearly 60% of the burger chain's profits. Let us consider why and how companies expand overseas.

Why Companies Expand Internationally

Many a company has made the deliberate decision to restrict selling its product or service to just its own country. Is anything wrong with that?

The answer is: It depends. It would probably have been a serious mistake for NEC, Sony, or Hitachi to have limited their markets solely to Japan during the 1990s, a time when the country was in an economic slump and Japanese consumers weren't consuming. During that same period, however, some American banks might have been better off not making loans abroad, when the U.S. economy was booming but foreign economies were not. Going international or not going international—it can be risky either way.

Why, then, do companies expand internationally? There are at least five reasons, all of which have to do with making or saving money.

Where is this? Since 1979, home-improvement retailer Home Depot has grown from four stores in Atlanta to more than 1,500 across North America. The store shown here is in Laual, Quebec, Canada. Why do you think Home Depot probably felt it had to expand internationally?

just consumers, then converted them from U.S.-style left-hand drive to right-hand drive, as required in parts of Africa.

5 Wholly-Owned Subsidiaries

A *wholly-owned subsidiary* is a foreign subsidiary that is totally owned and controlled by an organization. The foreign subsidiary may be an existing company that is purchased outright. **A *greenfield venture* is a foreign subsidiary that the owning organization has built from scratch.**

General Motors owns Adam Opel AG in Germany, Vauxhall Motor Cars Ltd. in the United Kingdom, Holden's in Australia, and half of Saab Automobile AB in Sweden. ◆

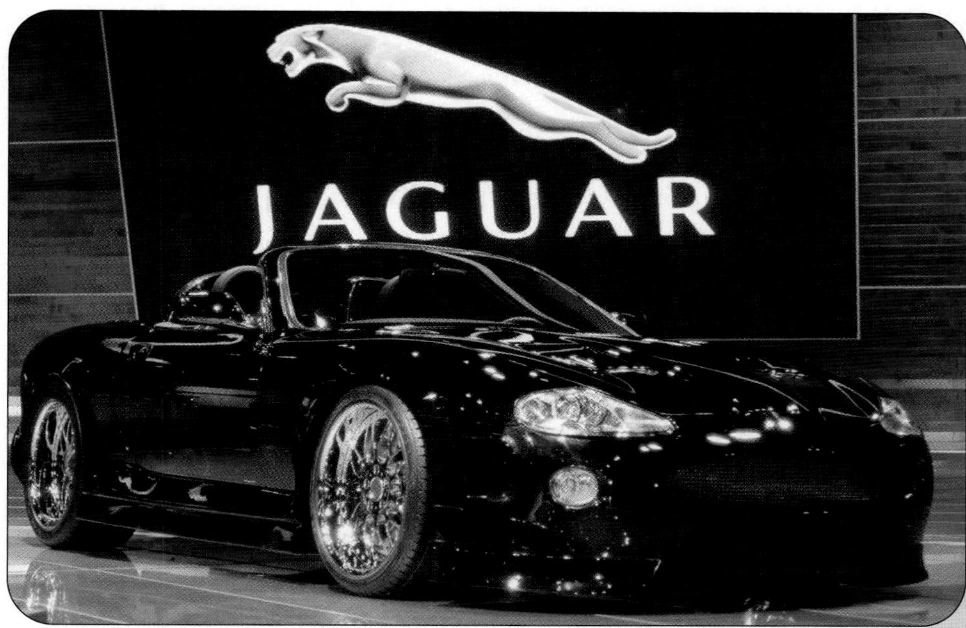

Jaguar. A number of formerly British-owned carmakers have gone over to foreign ownership. Jaguar is a subsidiary of Ford Motor Co., as is Land Rover. Ford also has provided the financial assistance to keep Aston-Martin going. Vauxhall is owned by General Motors. The rights to make Rolls-Royce cars (but not aircraft engines) are now held by German automaker Volkswagen, but Volkswagen's German rival BMW holds the rights to the name and the "RR" marque. Volkswagen owns the Rolls-Royce sister Bentley brand. Do you think the American companies General Motors and Ford could ever wind up under foreign ownership?

major question

How may foreign countries differ in their economic, political, and legal characteristics?

The Big Picture

Countries' economies vary among free-market, command, and mixed economies, as well as in infrastructure and resources and currency exchange rates. Political systems may vary between democratic versus totalitarian, in political risk, and in laws and regulations.

India. This New Delhi street scene suggests India's greatest challenge: raising living standards for 1 billion people. Is its mixed economy the way to accomplish this?

As an international manager, you might well have to operate amid many complexities. What should you be on the lookout for? First let us consider (1) *economic differences,* then (2) *political-legal differences*.

Economic Differences: Adjusting to Other Countries' Economies

How will you, as an international manager, adjust to economic changes? Let's discuss the following important topics: *economic systems, economic development, infrastructure and resources,* and *currency exchange rates*.

Principal Economic Systems: Free Market, Command, & Mixed Economies

How is doing business in Taiwan different from doing business in China? One is a *free-market economy,* the other traditionally a *command economy* (but changing). These are two of the three principal types of economic system around the globe, the third being a *mixed economy.*

1 Free-Market Economy

This is the kind of economy found, for example, in the United States and in Great Britain. **In a *free-market economy,* the production of goods and services are controlled by private enterprise and the interaction of the forces of supply and demand, rather than by the government.** As a manager you may prefer dealing with countries with this kind of system because there will be fewer hassles with government regulators. Moreover, in general the citizens of such countries may have higher incomes, which means there may be more markets for your product or service.

2 Command Economy

This is the kind of economy found in the old communist countries in and around the former Soviet Union. It is still found in Cuba and North Korea and, to a certain extent, in China and Vietnam. **In a *command economy,* or *central-planning economy,* the government owns most businesses and regulates the amounts, types, and prices of goods and services.** The failure of communism in Europe is largely because such economies proved to be unworkable. Other communist countries (Cuba, North Korea) have experienced great economic difficulties, and still others (China, Vietnam) have begun moving away from command economies.

3 Mixed Economy

This type of economy is found in many countries of Europe. **In a *mixed economy,* most of the important industries are owned by the government, but others are controlled by private enterprise.** This used to be the case in Britain, where the government once owned the railroads, airlines, steel, telecommunications, and health industries. However, most of these industries underwent ***privatization*** **—that is, state-owned businesses were sold off to private enterprise.** Russia, too, has been moving away from state ownership of big utilities and other sectors of the economy.

Whatever the type of economy, some countries have *indigenization laws,* which require that citizens within the host country must own a majority of whatever company is operating within that country.

Developed versus Less Developed Countries It used to be that the United States, Canada, western Europe, Australia, New Zealand, and Japan were known as "first-world" countries. The communist nations were called "second-world" countries. Pretty much all the rest, especially those in the southern hemisphere, were known as "third-world" or developing countries. With the end of the Cold War, the world now seems to be divided between *developed countries* and *less-developed countries.*

- **Developed countries:** These are the first-world countries: the United States, Canada, most European countries, Australia, New Zealand, and Japan. ***Developed countries*** **are those with a high level of economic development and generally high average level of income among their citizens.**

  Most international organizations, whether International Paper Co. or the International Red Cross, Royal Dutch/Shell or the World Health Organization, are headquartered in developed countries. Also, about three-quarters of foreign investment has been directed toward developed countries.[53]

- **Less-developed countries:** These are the third-world countries, such as Brazil, China, Haiti, Mexico, and Zambia, to name just a handful of the scores of nations in this category.

  Less-developed countries, **also known as *developing countries,* consist of nations with low economic development and low average incomes.** They also are usually characterized by high birth rates.

  Today the five largest countries in population size are China, India, the United States, Indonesia, and Brazil. By the middle of the 21st century, because of population growth (most of it owing to birth rates, not immigration), the five largest will be India, China, the United States, Indonesia, and Nigeria (today's No. 9).[54]

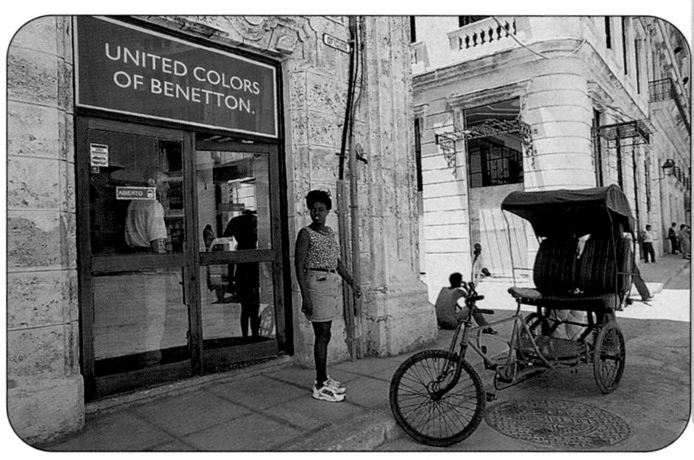

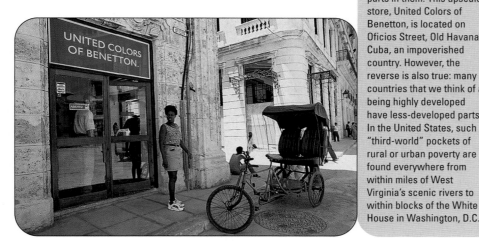

First world or third world? Many "third-world" or less-developed countries have "first-world" or developed parts in them. This upscale store, United Colors of Benetton, is located on Oficios Street, Old Havana, Cuba, an impoverished country. However, the reverse is also true: many countries that we think of as being highly developed have less-developed parts. In the United States, such "third-world" pockets of rural or urban poverty are found everywhere from within miles of West Virginia's scenic rivers to within blocks of the White House in Washington, D.C.

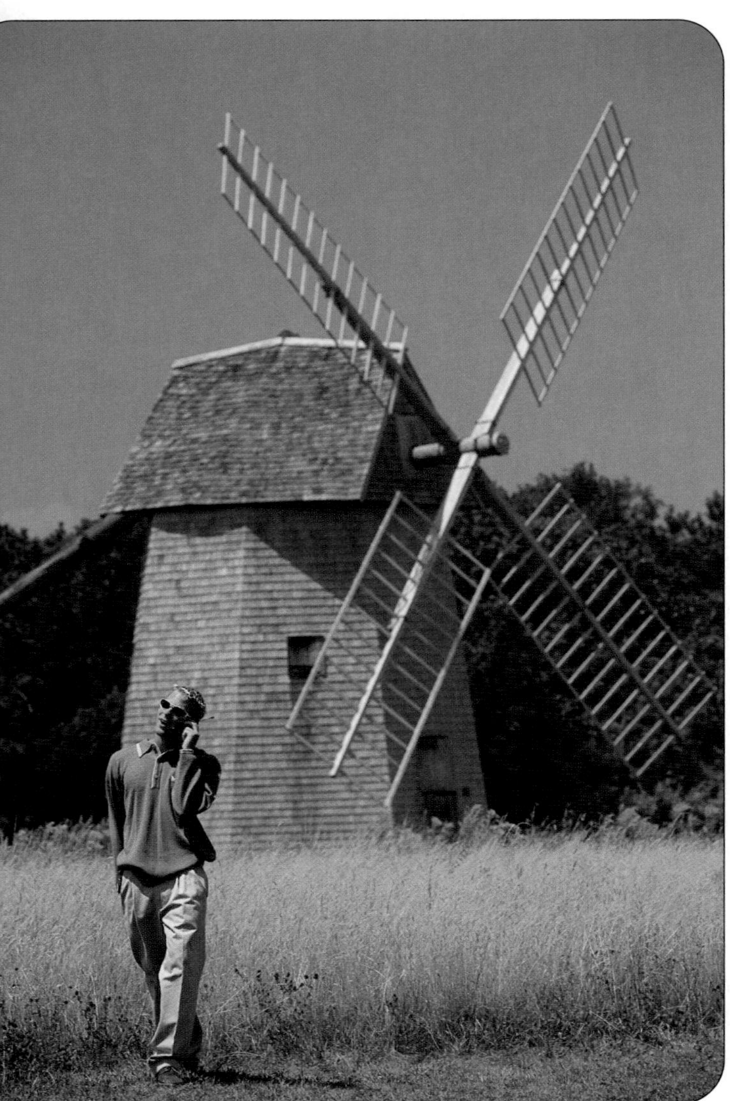

"I need to wind this up." The cellphone represents a boon to less-developed countries because the kind of telephone infrastructure does not entail the costly process of installing miles of telephone poles and land lines.

Infrastructure & Resources

In the United States, Canada, and much of Europe, we pretty much take the phone system for granted. In less-developed countries, getting a phone installed may take weeks, even months, and then it may still be inefficient. The significance of the cellphone is that countries with underdeveloped wired telephone systems can use cellular phones as a fast way of installing better communications, giving Pakistan, China, Nigeria, and others a chance of joining the world economy.

Telephone networks are an essential part of a country's infrastructure, especially since they are important to the development of information technology. **A country's *infrastructure* consists of the physical facilities that form the basis for its level of economic development.** Examples are schools, roads, airports, railroads, harbors, utilities, hospitals, and telecommunications systems. Before you as a manager begin getting involved in major projects in a particular foreign country, you need to be aware of any drawbacks in its infrastructure.

In addition, you'll need to be concerned about resources. If you've set up an apparel plant in Mexico, for example, you need to think about where the fabric and the sewing equipment are going to come from—whether you'll be able to get them from suppliers in that country or you'll have to import them.

Currency Exchange Rates **The *exchange rate* is the rate at which one country's currency can be exchanged for another country's currency.** International managers have to keep a close eye on currency exchange rates because a change of just a few percentage points can have major implications. For example, if one year the American dollar is worth 1.10 Canadian dollars and the next year it is worth 1.34 Canadian dollars, this means that U.S. goods have become more expensive for Canadians, so they are apt to buy less. If the American dollar drops to the equivalent of 1.00 Canadian dollars, they will probably buy more.

Political-Legal Differences: Adjusting to Other Countries' Governments & Laws

When in the early 1990s McDonald's opened an outlet in Belgrade in the former Yugoslavia, should it have tried to anticipate the possibility that the restaurant might someday be wrecked by angry crowds of Serbs (as happened following air strikes by American and other NATO bombers on Serbia in 1999)? Perhaps someone was foresighted enough to take out political risk insurance, which is available for corporations investing in unstable areas.[55]

Such is one of the considerations of a company hoping to develop new markets overseas. A star international manager needs to always be aware of political-legal differences, including different government systems, political risks, and unfamiliar laws and regulations, as we discuss.

Governmental Systems: Democratic versus Totalitarian

No doubt you will have to deal with unfamiliar political systems. There are two extremes:

- **Democratic:** ***Democratic governments*** **rely on free elections and representative assemblies.** The government is supposed to represent the society as a whole, or at least the majority of its citizens.

  From the standpoint of ease in doing business, democratic systems of government, such as those in western Europe, generally seem more familiar to an American international manager. Nevertheless, different national attitudes toward bureaucracy, monopolies, and the acceptance of "gratuities" can make it difficult to do business.

- **Totalitarian:** ***Totalitarian governments*** **are ruled by a dictator, a single political party, or a special-membership group,** such as a handful of ruling families or a military junta (such as Cuba under Fidel Castro or Indonesia under Sukarno). The risk for you as an international manager is that the political tides may change, and through no fault of your own you may find yourself somehow on the wrong side.

  Some governments fall in between democratic and totalitarian. Mexico, for example, regularly features free elections, but for decades it was ruled by a single political party.

Political Risk

It's possible that a democratic country in which your company has started up an overseas operation could overnight become a totalitarian country, accompanied by a sudden change in all the rules. Thus, every firm contemplating establishing itself abroad must calculate its ***political risk*** **—the risk that political changes will cause loss of a company's assets or impair its foreign operations.** Two political risks an organization planning to do business abroad might anticipate are these:

- **Instability:** Even in a developed country a company may be victimized by political instability, such as riots or civil disorders, as happened during the 1989 Rodney King riots in Los Angeles. Overseas an international company may also have to try to anticipate revolutions or changes in government. Italy, for example, has had more than 60 governments since World War II.
- **Expropriation:** ***Expropriation*** **is defined as a government's seizure of a foreign company's assets.** After Fidel Castro overthrew the Batista government in Cuba in 1959, he expropriated millions of dollars worth of assets of American companies. Early in the 20th century, Mexico expropriated American-owned oil fields and production facilities.

Laws & Regulations

"Ignorance of the law is no excuse," one hears. That assumes you're supposed to keep up with the important laws in your own country, which can be complicated enough. Now try keeping up with the laws in another country.

International companies have to work with numerous laws and regulations on subjects ranging from labor to libel to labeling. The United States, for instance, has legislation under the ***Foreign Corrupt Practices Act*** **of 1977, which makes it illegal for employees of U.S. companies to bribe political decision makers in foreign nations,** an acceptable practice in many countries.

Many of the laws and regulations have to do with tariffs, import quotas, and the like, as we discuss in the next section. ◆

major question

What are barriers to free trade, and what major organizations and trading blocs promote trade?

The Big Picture

Barriers to free trade are tariffs, import quotas, and embargoes. Organizations promoting international trade are the World Trade Organization, the World Bank, and the International Monetary Fund. Major trading blocs are NAFTA, the EU, ASEAN, and Mercosur.

If you live in the United States, you see foreign products on a daily basis—cars, appliances, clothes, foods, beers, wines, and so on. Based on what you see every day, which countries would you think are our most important trading partners? Japan? Germany? England? South Korea? France?

These five countries do indeed appear among the top ten leading U.S. trading partners (measured in terms of imports and exports added together). Interestingly, however, our No. 1 and No. 2 trading partners are our immediate neighbors—Canada and Mexico, whose products may not be quite so visible. (Others at the top: 3. China; 4. Japan; 5. Germany; 6. United Kingdom; 7. South Korea; 8. Taiwan; 9. France; 10. Italy.)

Let's begin to consider ***free trade,*** **the movement of goods and services among nations without political or economic obstruction.**

Barriers to International Trade

Countries often use ***trade protectionism*** **—the use of government regulations to limit the import of goods and services**—to protect their domestic industries against foreign competition. The justification they often use is that this saves jobs. Actually, protectionism is not considered beneficial, mainly because of what it does to the overall trading atmosphere.

The three devices by which countries try to exert protectionism consist of *tariffs, import quotas,* and *embargoes.*

Going bananas. Stevedores unload Chiquita bananas from a ship in Antwerp harbor. The Netherlands is a member of the European Union, which had imposed a duty on bananas, including those grown by Cincinnati-based Chiquita Brands Inc. The reason for the duty was that Chiquita's bananas undercut those of the EU's longstanding suppliers. For retaliation, Chiquita successfully lobbied the U.S. government to place duties on European goods (such as paper products) imported into the United States. Such activities among governments are known as a "trade war."

1 Tariffs

A *tariff* is a trade barrier in the form of a customs duty, or tax, levied mainly on imports. At one time, for instance, to protect the American shoe industry, the United States imposed a tariff on Italian shoes.

Actually, there are two types of tariffs: One is designed simply to raise money for the government (revenue tariff). The other, which concerns us more, is to raise the price of imported goods to make the prices of domestic products more competitive (protective tariff). For example, in 2001 President George W. Bush called for tariffs on imported steel, following influxes in imported foreign steel in the previous two years. Although the tariffs gave the U.S. domestic steel industry a chance to regroup and better compete with foreign steelmakers, the tariffs were lifted after the World Trade Organization (discussed below) ruled in 2003 that they were illegal.[56]

Tea from China. The experience of drinking Dragon Well, a variety of Chinese green tea, "is very intense," says one tea fancier, "completely entrancing and entirely unpredictable. I've had the same tea come out one time sweet and gentle, and another time roaring and full of dense, dark, beautiful bitterness." China has had thousands of years to perfect the process of making tea, and experts rate the country's green teas as among the best in the world. Most of it is laboriously dried and processed by hand, one reason why only government officials and the new business class can afford it in China. In the U.S., however, it costs $50–$150 a pound—only a dollar a cup at the most expensive. Why is it so much more affordable to us?

2 Import Quotas

An *import quota* is a trade barrier in the form of a limit on the numbers of a product that can be imported. Its intent is to protect domestic industry by restricting the availability of foreign products.

Effective January 2005, China agreed (as a condition of being allowed into the World Trade Organization) to cancel car import quotas, which it had used to protect its domestic car manufacturing industry against imported vehicles from the United States, Japan, and Germany.[57]

Quotas are designed to prevent ***dumping,* the practice of a foreign company's exporting products abroad at a lower price than the price in the home market—or even below the costs of production—in order to drive down the price of the domestic product.**

3 Embargoes

Ever had a Cuban cigar? They're difficult for Americans to get, since they're embargoed. **An *embargo* is a complete ban on the import or export of certain products.** It has been years since anyone was allowed to import Cuban cigars and sugar into the United States or for an American firm to do business in Cuba. The U.S. government also tries to embargo the export of certain supercomputers and other high-tech equipment with possible military uses to countries such as China.

Organizations Promoting International Trade

In the 1920s, the institution of tariff barriers did not so much protect jobs as depress the demand for goods and services, thereby leading to the loss of jobs anyway—and the massive unemployment of the Great Depression of the 1930s.[58] As a result of this lesson, after World War II the advanced nations of the world began to realize that if all countries could freely exchange the products that each could produce most efficiently, this would lead to lower prices all around. Thus began the removal of barriers to free trade.

The three principal organizations designed to facilitate international trade are the *World Trade Organization,* the *World Bank,* and the *International Monetary Fund.*

1 The World Trade Organization (WTO)

Consisting of 146 member countries, the ***World Trade Organization (WTO)* is designed to monitor and enforce trade agreements.** The agreements are based on the *General Agreement on Tariffs and Trade (GATT),* an international accord first signed by 23 nations in 1947, which helped to reduce worldwide tariffs and other barriers. Out of GATT came a series of "rounds," or negotiations, that resulted in the lowering of barriers; for instance, the Uruguay Round, implemented in 1996, cut tariffs by one-third.

Founded in 1995 and headquartered in Geneva, Switzerland, WTO succeeded GATT as the world forum for trade negotiations and has the formal legal structure for deciding trade disputes. WTO also encompasses areas not previously covered by GATT, such as services and intellectual property rights. A particularly interesting area of responsibility covers telecommunications—cellphones, pagers, data transmission, satellite communications, and the like—with half of the WTO members agreeing in 1998 to open their markets to foreign telecommunications companies.[59]

2 The World Bank

The World Bank was founded after World War II to help European countries rebuild. Today the purpose of the ***World Bank*** **is to provide low-interest loans to developing nations for improving transportation, education, health, and telecommunications.** The bank has 184 member nations, with most contributions coming from the United States, Europe, and Japan.

Most recently, the bank has concentrated on bringing the Internet to less-developed and developing countries, such as those in Africa, in hopes that it will attract more companies to those areas and lead to more rapid economic development.[60]

In recent years, the World Bank has been the target of demonstrations in Seattle, Washington, D.C., Ottawa, and elsewhere. Some protestors believe it finances projects that could damage the ecosystem, such as the Three Gorges Dam on China's Yangtze River. Others complain it supports countries that permit low-paying sweatshops or that suppress religious freedom. Still others think it has dragged its feet on getting affordable AIDS drugs to less-developed countries in Africa. Many of the same protests were leveled against the International Monetary Fund, discussed next. The World Bank has responded by trying to support projects that are not harmful to the environment and that are aimed at helping lift people out of poverty.

3 The International Monetary Fund

Founded in 1945 and now affiliated with the United Nations, the International Monetary Fund is the second pillar supporting the international financial community. Consisting of 182 member nations, **the *International Monetary Fund (IMF)* is designed to assist in smoothing the flow of money between nations.** The IMF operates as a last-resort lender that makes short-term loans to countries suffering from unfavorable balance of payments (roughly the difference between money coming into a country and money leaving the country, because of imports, exports, and other matters).

For example, during the late 1990s' "Asian crisis," the value of Thailand's currency dropped until at the end of 1997 it was worth half what it was at the start of the year. Because Thailand owed other countries, they, too, were affected: Indonesia's currency dropped 70% and South Korea's 45%. In response to pleas for help, the IMF loaned Asian countries billions of dollars—$57 billion to South Korea alone in 1997.

Major Trading Blocs: NAFTA, EU, ASEAN, & Mercosur

A *trading bloc,* also known as an *economic community,* is a group of nations within a geographical region that have agreed to remove trade barriers with one another. The four major trading blocs are the *NAFTA nations,* the *European Union,* the *ASEAN countries,* and the *Mercosur.*

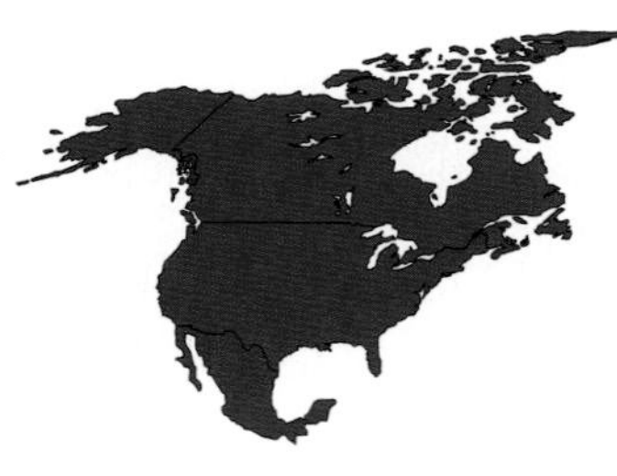

1 NAFTA—the Three Countries of the North American Free Trade Agreement

Formed in 1994, **the *North American Free Trade Agreement (NAFTA)* is a trading bloc consisting of the United States, Canada, and Mexico,** encompassing 421 million people. The agreement is supposed to eliminate 99% of the tariffs and quotas among these countries, allowing for freer flow of goods, services, and capital in North America. Since 1994, trade with Canada and Mexico now accounts for one-third of the U.S. total, up from one-quarter in 1989. Exports to Mexico and Canada rose from $12 billion in 1993 to $26 billion in 2002.[61]

Is NAFTA a job killer, as some have complained? In Mexico, it has failed to generate substantial job growth and has hurt hundreds of thousands of subsistence farmers, so that illegal immigration to the U.S. continues to grow. As for the United States, nearly 525,000 workers, mostly in manufacturing, have been certified by the U.S. government as having lost their jobs or had their hours or wages reduced because of NAFTA's shifting of jobs south of the border. It's also spurred a $418 billion trade deficit.[62] However, supporters insist NAFTA ultimately will result in more jobs and a higher standard of living among all trading partners.

2 The EU—the 25 Countries of the European Union

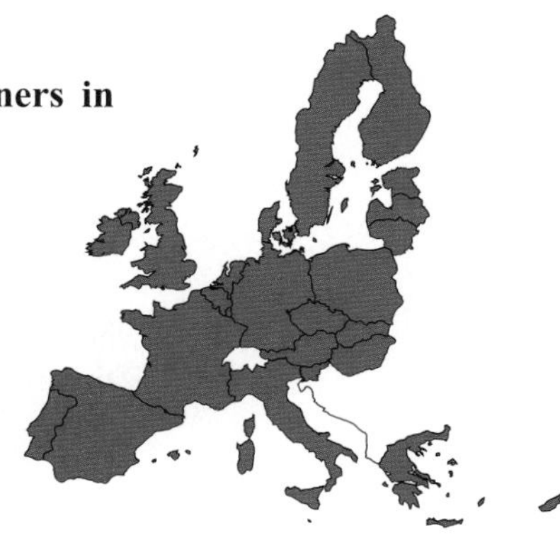

Formed in 1957, **the *European Union (EU)* consists of 25 trading partners in Europe,** covering 455 million consumers.

Nearly all internal trade barriers have been eliminated (including movement of labor between countries), making the EU a union of borderless neighbors and the world's largest free market.

By 2002, such national symbols as the franc, the mark, the lira, the peseta, and the guilder had been replaced with the EU currency, the euro.[63] There has even been speculation that someday the euro could replace the dollar as the dominant world currency.[64] On May 1, 2004, the EU swelled to 25 countries with the addition of eight former Communist states from Eastern Europe and two Mediterranean islands; Bulgaria and Romania hope to join by 2007.

3 ASEAN—Ten Countries of the Association of Southeast Asian Nations

Members of this group were once known as the "Asian tigers," although, as mentioned, in the late 1990s their situation degenerated into the "Asian crisis." **The *Association of Southeast Asian Nations (ASEAN)* is a trading bloc consisting of 10 countries in Asia:** Brunei, Cambodia, Indonesia, Laos, Malaysia, Myanmar (Burma), Philippines, Singapore, Thailand, and Vietnam. Like other trading blocs, ASEAN is working on reducing trade barriers among member countries, promoting the role of private investment, stimulating the free flow of capital, and assisting in access to technology.

4 Mercosur—Six Countries of Latin America

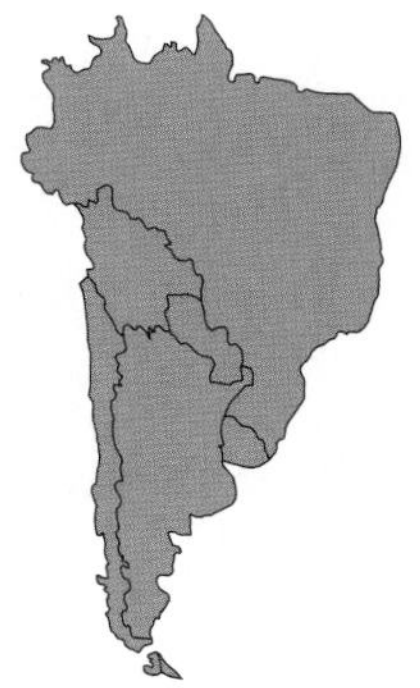

The *Mercosur* is the largest trade bloc in Latin America and has four core members—Argentina, Brazil, Paraguay, and Uruguay—and two associate members, Chile and Bolivia. Besides reducing tariffs by 75%, Mercosur nations are striving for full economic integration, and the alliance is also negotiating trade agreements with NAFTA, the EU, and Japan.

Most Favored Nation Trading Status

Besides joining together in trade blocs, countries will also extend special, "most favored nation" trading privileges to one another. ***Most favored nation* trading status describes a condition in which a country grants other countries favorable trading treatment such as the reduction of import duties.** The purpose is to promote stronger and more stable ties between companies in the two countries. ◆

major question

What are the principal areas of cultural differences?

The Big Picture

Managers trying to understand other cultures need to understand four basic cultural perceptions embodied in language, nonverbal communication, time orientation, and religion.

Americans living near San Jose, Calif., didn't like it when an Australian company acquired the local Valley Fair shopping center and renamed it Shoppingtown.[65]

"The first time I saw the word Shoppingtown, I nearly choked," complained one letter writer to the local paper. "The more I see it, the more it annoys me."

"We aren't the penny-pinchers this name indicates we are," said another. "What happened to that survey about Valley Fair customers having the area's most upscale lifestyle and money to back it up?"

Said a third: "These are the same people—Australians—who did not get [the U.S. television comedy] *Seinfeld*; the show failed miserably there. 'Shoppingtown' is a brand name in Australia. They are trying too hard to accomplish the same thing here in the U.S. Do you really care that your mall is a 'brand'. . . ? They have not done their homework, and do not understand Americans just yet."

Don't Australians and Americans speak the same language? Could a shopping center risk failing simply because of a name change? And if there can be such misperceptions in English, what might it be like in trying to communicate in a different language? *Training* magazine offers some blunt advice: "The lesson for those [managers] plying foreign markets or hosting business visitors is: Slow down. Shut up. Listen."[66]

Would you shop at "Shoppingtown"? That was the name new Australian owners gave to a California shopping center known as Valley Fair.

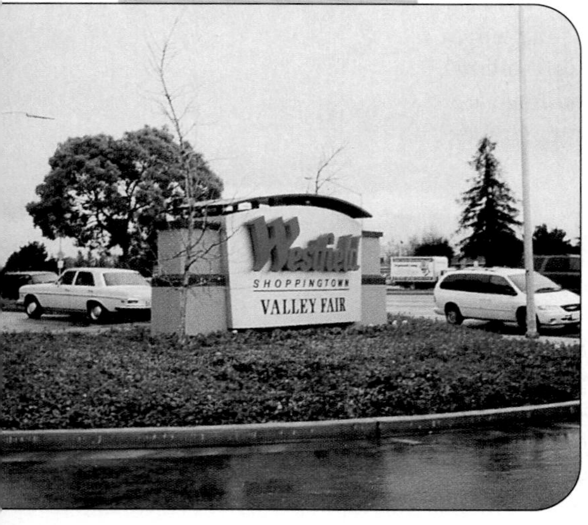

The Importance of National Culture

Some of the problems resulting from the experiences of companies such as that described above are the result of cultural differences. A nation's ***culture*** **is the shared set of beliefs, values, knowledge, and patterns of behavior common to a group of people.**

We begin learning our culture starting at an early age through everyday interaction with people around us. This is why, from the outside looking in, a nation's culture can seem so intangible and perplexing. As cultural anthropologist Edward T. Hall puts it, "Since much of culture operates outside our awareness, frequently we don't even know what we know. . . . We unconsciously learn what to notice and what not to notice, how to divide time and space, how to walk and talk and use our bodies, how to behave as men or women, how to relate to other people, how to handle responsibility. . . ."[67] Indeed, says Hall, what we think of as "mind" is really internalized culture.

And because a culture is made up of so many nuances, this is why visitors to another culture may experience culture shock—the feelings of discomfort and disorientation associated with being in an unfamiliar culture. According to anthropologists, culture shock involves anxiety and doubt caused by an overload of unfamiliar expectations and social cues.[68]

What Are Different Cultural Perceptions of Language, Nonverbal Communication, Time Orientation, & Religion?

How do you go about bridging cross-cultural gaps? It begins with understanding. Let's consider variations in four basic cultural areas: (1) *language,* (2) *nonverbal communication,* (3) *time orientation,* and (4) *religion.*[69]

Note, however, that such cultural differences are to be viewed as *tendencies* rather than absolutes. We all need to be aware that the *individuals* we are dealing with may be exceptions to the cultural rule. After all, there *are* talkative and aggressive Japanese, just as there are quiet and deferential Americans, stereotypes notwithstanding.[70]

1 Language

More than 3,000 different languages are spoken throughout the world. However, even if you are operating in the English language, there are nuances between cultures that can lead to misperceptions. For instance, in Asia, a 'yes' answer to a question "simply means the question is understood," says a well-traveled writer. "It's the beginning of negotiations."[71]

In trying to communicate across cultures you have three options:

- **Speak your own language:** The average American believes that about half the world can speak English, when actually it's about 20%.[72] No doubt you would prefer speaking English, but doing so will put you at a considerable competitive disadvantage.
- **Use a translator:** Live translations, translations of written documents and advertisements, and computer e-mail translations are helpful but plagued by accuracy problems.[73] If you do use a translator, try to get one that will be loyal to you rather than to your overseas hosts.
- **Learn the local language:** When you don't know the language, you miss such subtle yet crucial meanings, risk unintentionally insulting people, and jeopardize your business transactions.

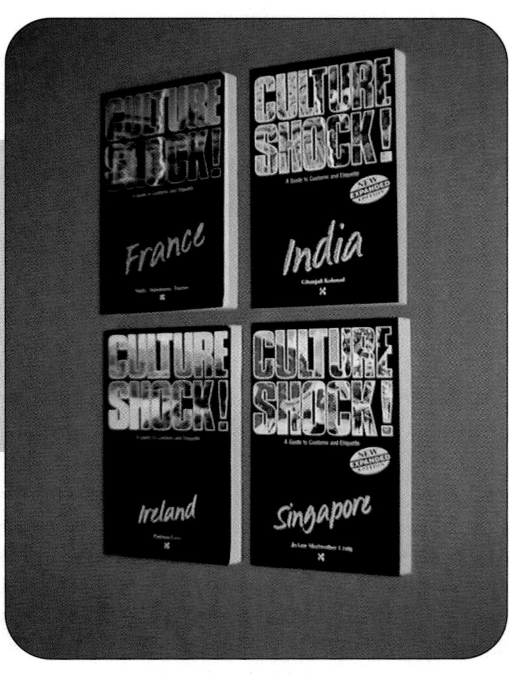

Culture shock. The "Culture Shock!" line of books (there's even one on the USA) offers readers guidance on understanding people in foreign countries. For instance, among the dos and don'ts for France, the guidebook suggests: "DON'T speak or laugh loudly in public places" and "DO return a compliment or praise with an expression of admiration for that person's judgment." Based on your upbringing, would you have guessed that these were nuances of good behavior in France?

2 Nonverbal Communication

***Nonverbal communication* consists of messages sent outside the written or spoken word.** Says one writer, it includes such factors as "use of time and space, distance between persons when conversing, use of color dress, walking behavior, standing, positioning, seating arrangement, office locations, and furnishings."[74] Nonverbal communication is responsible for perhaps as much as 60% of a message being communicated.[75]

Five ways in which nonverbal communication is expressed are through *interpersonal space, eye contact, facial expressions, body movements and gestures,* and *touch*. A sample of different international norms for nonverbal communications is shown below.[76] *(See Figure 4.2.)*

■ China
Hugging or taking someone's arm is considered inappropriate.
Winking or beckoning with one's index finger is considered rude.

■ Indonesia
Handshaking and head noddings are customary greetings.

■ Japan
Business cards are exchanged before bowing or handshaking.
A weak handshake is common.
Lengthy or frequent eye contact is considered impolite.

■ Malaysia
Touching someone casually, especially on the top of the head (even a child's), is considered impolite.
It's best to use your right hand to eat and to touch people and things.

■ The Philippines
Handshaking and a pat on the back are common greetings.

■ South Korea
Men bow slightly and shake hands, sometimes with two hands. Women refrain from shaking hands.
It is considered polite to cover your mouth when laughing.

■ Thailand
Public displays of temper or affection are frowned on.
It is considered impolite to point at anything using your foot or to show the soles of your feet.

FIGURE 4.2 **Different norms.** Variations in meaning of different types of nonverbal communication around the world.

- **Interpersonal space:** People of different cultures have different ideas about what is acceptable interpersonal space—that is, how close or far away one should be when communicating with another person. For instance, the people of North America and Northern Europe tend to conduct business conversations at a range of 3–4 feet. For people in Latin American and Asian cultures, the range is about 1 foot. For Arabs, it is even closer.

  This can lead to cross-cultural misunderstandings. "Arabs tend to get very close and breathe on you," says anthropologist Hall. "The American on the receiving end can't identify all the sources of his discomfort but feels that the Arab is pushy. The Arab comes close, the American backs up. The Arab follows, because he can interact only at certain distances."[77] However, once the American understands that Arabs handle interpersonal space differently and that "breathing on people is a form of communication," says Hall, the situation can sometimes be redefined so that the American feels more comfortable.

- **Eye contact:** Eye contact serves four functions in communication:

  (1) It signals the beginning and end of a conversation; there is a tendency to look away from others when beginning to speak and to look at them when done.

  (2) It expresses emotion; for instance, most people tend to avoid eye contact when conveying bad news or negative feedback.

  (3) Gazing monitors feedback because it reflects interest and attention.

  (4) Depending on the culture, gazing also expresses the type of relationship between the people communicating. For instance, Westerners are taught at an

early age to look at their parents when spoken to. However, Asians are taught to avoid eye contact with a parent or superior to show obedience and subservience.[78]

- **Facial expressions:** Probably you're accustomed to thinking that smiling represents warmth, happiness, or friendship, whereas frowning represents dissatisfaction or anger. But these interpretations of facial expressions don't apply across all cultures.[79] A smile, for example, doesn't convey the same emotions in different countries.
- **Body movements and gestures:** An example of a body movement is leaning forward; an example of a gesture is pointing. Open body positions, such as leaning backward, express openness, warmth, closeness, and availability for communication. Closed body positions, such as folding one's arms or crossing one's legs, represent defensiveness.

  Some body movements and gestures are associated more with one sex than the other, according to communication researcher Judith Hall. For instance, women nod their heads and move their hands more than men do. Men exhibit large body shifts and foot and leg movements more than women do.[80]

  We need to point out, however, that interpretations of body language are subjective, hence easily misinterpreted, and highly dependent on the context and cross-cultural differences.[81] Be careful when trying to interpret body movements, especially when you're operating in a different culture.
- **Touch:** Norms for touching vary significantly around the world. In the Middle East, for example, it is normal for two males who are friends to walk together holding hands—not commonplace behavior in the United States.

  People tend to touch those they like, and women tend to do more touching during conversations than men do.[82] It needs to be noted, however, that men and women interpret touching differently, and in the United States, at least, sexual harassment claims might be reduced by keeping this perceptual difference in mind.

  Still, women clearly have the advantage here, at least in the U.S. One study found that, whereas men are "largely boxed into the formality of a handshake," women are freer to emphasize a point with a brief (nonsexual) touch to the forearm of a man or a woman, give a playful mock push to a man's shoulder, and even place a firm hand on a man's shoulder to signal, if necessary, who is in charge. The risk of touching for a woman, however, is that she may appear flirtatious.[83]

Got your back. In the future, international managers will need to work cooperatively with overseas counterparts.

3 Time Orientation

Time orientation is different in many cultures. Anthropologist Hall makes a useful distinction between monochronic time and polychronic time:

- **Monochronic time:** This kind of time is standard American business practice. That is, ***monochronic time*** **is a preference for doing one thing at a time.** In this perception, time is viewed as being limited, precisely segmented, and schedule driven. This perception of time prevails, for example, when you schedule a meeting with someone and then give the visitor your undivided attention during the allotted time.[84]

  Indeed, you probably practice monochronic time when you're in a job interview. You work hard at listening to what the interviewer says. You may well take careful notes. You certainly don't answer your cellphone or gaze repeatedly out the window.
- **Polychronic time:** This outlook on time is the kind that prevails in Mediterranean, Latin American, and especially Arab cultures. ***Polychronic time*** **is a preference for doing more than one thing at a time.** Here time is viewed as being flexible and multidimensional.

  This perception of time prevails when you visit a Latin American client, find yourself sitting in the waiting room for 45 minutes, and then find in the meeting that the client is dealing with three other people at the same time. (The American variant these days is referred to as "multitasking," as when you talk on the phone while simultaneously watching television and doing a crossword puzzle.)

As a manager, you will probably have to reset your mental clock when doing business across cultures.

Example

Cultural Differences in Time: A Garment Factory in Mexico

Harry Mehserjian and his brothers own a garment factory near Los Angeles, and they still do the high-fashion work there. However, the T-shirts and other low-budget knitware are sent deep into Mexico, to a factory in a suburb of Guadalajara, where wages are one-seventh those in Los Angeles.[85]

"I never wanted to go to Mexico," Harry says. But since NAFTA removed quotas limiting how much clothing could be brought in from Mexico, that country has shot from sixth place to first place (passing China) in exporting garments to the U.S. The changes caused by NAFTA, along with a rise in minimum wage in California, aggressive unionization, and more regulations, made it difficult for the Mehserjians to continue doing all their business in the United States.

One of the challenges to the Mehserjians is to change their workers' attitudes about time. "If they come on Monday, they're out on Tuesday. If they come on Tuesday, they're out on Wednesday," says a plant manager. To try to overcome absenteeism, the Mehserjians offer a 10% bonus to those who come to work faithfully for the entire week. Even so, their factory is still plagued by absenteeism and turnover. The workplace culture in the interior of Mexico is looser than in the United States—or even in northern Mexico, such as Juarez.

Says one UCLA expert, "These workers don't necessarily see their lives revolving around a job. There's a great deal of informality that they have come to expect from factory employment. You work hard during certain periods of time, and relax during others."[86]

4 Religion

Are you a Protestant doing business in a predominantly Catholic country? Or a Muslim in a Buddhist country? How, then, does religion influence the work-related values of the people you're dealing with?

A study of 484 international students at a Midwestern university uncovered wide variations in the work-related values for different religious affiliations.[87] For example, among Catholics, the primary work-related value was found to be consideration. For Protestants, it was employer effectiveness; for Buddhists, social responsibility; for Muslims, continuity. There was, in fact, virtually *no agreement* among religions as to what is the most important work-related value. This led the researchers to conclude: "Employers might be wise to consider the impact that religious differences (and more broadly, cultural factors) appear to have on the values of employee groups."

Current Followers of the Major World Religions	
Christianity	2 billion
Islam	1.3 billion
Hinduism	900 million
Buddhism	360 million
Judaism	14 million
Chinese traditional religions	225 million

After what some World War II veterans have been through, one can sympathize with their outrage over drivers who fly American flags from cars made by their former enemies—Toyotas, Mitsubishis, BMWs, Porsches, and other Japanese and German cars. "I drive all-American," boasts one vet.

But just what *is* an American car nowadays? "Is it a Honda Accord built by Americans in the Midwest," asks a newspaper reader, "or is it a Chrysler built in Mexico with parts from Canada by a company owned by Daimler-Benz?"[88] Perhaps the lesson is this: In a global economy, cultural arrogance is a luxury we can no longer afford. ◆

Who made this car? The assembly line producing these Mercedes-Benz SUVs is located in Alabama, but these days an automobile plant may be located nearly anywhere.

Key Terms Used in This Chapter

Association of Southeast Asian Nations (ASEAN), 123
command economy, 116
countertrading, 112
culture, 124
democratic governments, 119
developed countries, 117
dumping, 121
e-commerce, 103
embargo, 121
ethnocentric managers, 109
European Union (EU), 123
exchange rate, 118
expatriate manager, 109
exporting, 112
expropriation, 119
Foreign Corrupt Practices Act, 119
franchising, 114
free-market economy, 116
free trade, 120
geocentric managers, 109
global economy, 104
global outsourcing, 112
global village, 102
globalization, 102
greenfield venture, 115
import quota, 121
importing, 112
infrastructure, 118
International Monetary Fund (IMF), 122
joint venture, 114
less-developed countries, 117
licensing, 114
maquiladoras, 111
Mercosur, 123
mixed economy, 117
monochronic time, 128
most favored nation, 123
multinational corporation, 106
multinational organization, 106
nonverbal communication, 126
North American Free Trade Agreement (NAFTA), 122
outsourcing, 112
political risk, 119
polycentric managers, 109
polychronic time, 128
privatization, 117
tariff, 121
totalitarian governments, 119
trade protectionism, 120
trading bloc, 122
wholly-owned subsidiary, 115
World Bank, 122
World Trade Organization (WTO), 121

Summary

4.1 Globalization: The Collapse of Time & Distance

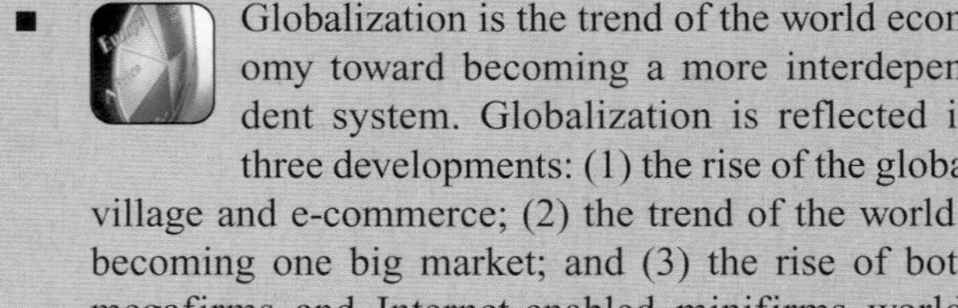

- Globalization is the trend of the world economy toward becoming a more interdependent system. Globalization is reflected in three developments: (1) the rise of the global village and e-commerce; (2) the trend of the world's becoming one big market; and (3) the rise of both megafirms and Internet-enabled minifirms worldwide.
- The rise of the "global village" refers to the "shrinking" of time and space as air travel and the electronic media have made global communication easier. The Internet and the World Wide Web have led to e-commerce, the buying and selling of products and services through computer networks.
- The global economy is the increasing tendency of the economies of the nations of the world to interact with one another as one market instead of many national markets.
- The rise of cross-border business has led to the rise of megamergers, as giant firms have joined forces, and of minifirms, small companies in which managers can use the Internet and other technologies to get enterprises started more easily and to maneuver faster.

4.2 You & International Management

- Studying international management prepares you to work with foreign customers or partners, with foreign suppliers, for a foreign firm in the U.S., or for a U.S. firm overseas. International management is management that oversees the conduct of operations in or with organizations in foreign countries.
- The successful international manager is not ethnocentric or polycentric but geocentric. Ethnocentric managers believe that their native country, culture, language, and behavior are superior to all others. Polycentric managers take the view that native managers in the foreign offices best understand native personnel and practices. Geocentric managers accept

that there are differences and similarities between home and foreign personnel and practices, and they should use whatever techniques are most effective.

4.3 Why & How Companies Expand Internationally

- Companies expand internationally for at least five reasons, all of which have to do with making or saving money. They seek (1) cheaper or more plentiful supplies, (2) new markets, (3) lower labor costs, (4) access to finance capital, and (5) avoidance of tariffs on imported goods or import quotas.
- There are five ways in which companies expand internationally. (1) They engage in global outsourcing, using suppliers outside the company and the U.S. to provide goods and services. (2) They engage in importing, exporting, and countertrading (bartering for goods). (3) They engage in licensing (allow a foreign company to pay a fee to make or distribute the company's product or service) and franchising (allow a foreign company to pay a fee and a share of the profit in return for using the first company's brand name and a package of materials and services). (4) They engage in joint ventures, a strategic alliance with a foreign company to share the risks and rewards of starting a new enterprise together in a foreign country. (5) They become wholly-owned subsidiaries, or foreign subsidiaries that are totally owned and controlled by an organization.

4.4 Economic & Political-Legal Differences

- 
  Among the differences with which international managers must cope are (1) economic differences and (2) political-legal differences.
- Four economic differences that managers must deal with include (1) different economic systems, (2) economic development, (3) infrastructure and resources, and (4) currency exchange rates.
- The principal economic systems are free market, command, and mixed economies. (1) In a free-market economy, the production of goods and services are controlled by private enterprise and the interaction of the forces of supply and demand, rather than by the government. (2) In a command economy, or central-planning economy, the government owns most businesses and regulates the amounts, types, and prices of goods and services. (3) In a mixed economy, most of the important industries are owned by the government, but others are controlled by private enterprise.
- Countries may be divided between developed countries (those with a high level of economic development and generally high average level income) and less-developed countries (nations with low economic development and low average incomes).
- International companies are concerned about a foreign country's infrastructure (the physical facilities that form the basis for its level of economic development, such as roads and schools) and resources (labor and equipment).
- Companies operating internationally also have to be concerned about currency exchange rates. The exchange rate is the rate at which one country's currency can be exchanged for another country's currency.
- Managers operating internationally also need to be concerned about three kinds of political-legal differences: (1) democratic versus totalitarian political systems, (2) political risk, and (3) laws and regulations.
- Governmental systems may be democratic or totalitarian. Democratic governments rely on free elections and representative assemblies. Totalitarian governments are ruled by a dictator, a single political party, or a special-membership group.
- Political risk is defined as the risk that political changes will cause loss of a company's assets or impair its foreign operations. Two political risks a company doing business abroad might anticipate are instability, such as riots or civil disorders, and expropriation, defined as a government's seizure of a foreign company's assets.
- International companies have to work with numerous laws and regulations. The United States has legislation under the Foreign Corrupt Practices Act of 1977 that makes it illegal for employees of U.S. companies to bribe decision makers in foreign nations.

4.5 The World of Free Trade: Regional Economic Cooperation

- 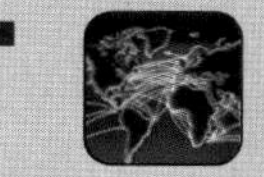
  Free trade is the movement of goods and services among nations without political or economic obstructions.
- Countries often use trade protectionism—the use of government regulations to limit the import of goods and services—to protect their domestic industries against foreign competition. Three barriers to free trade, or devices by which countries try to exert protectionism, are tariffs, import quotas, and embargoes. (1) A tariff is a trade barrier in the form of a customs duty, or tax, levied mainly on imports. (2) An import quota is a trade barrier in the form of a limit on the numbers of a product that can be imported. (3) An embargo is a complete ban on the import or export of certain products.
- Three principal organizations exist that are designed to facilitate international trade. (1) The World Trade Organization is designed to monitor and enforce trade

agreements. (2) The World Bank is designed to provide low-interest loans to developing nations for improving transportation, education, health, and telecommunications. (3) The International Monetary Fund is designed to assist in smoothing the flow of money between nations.

- A trading bloc is a group of nations within a geographical region that have agreed to remove trade barriers. There are four major trading blocs: (1) North American Free Trade Agreement (NAFTA) (U.S., Canada, and Mexico); (2) European Union (EU) (25 trading partners in Europe); (3) Association of Southeast Asian Nations (ASEAN) (10 countries in Asia); (4) Mercosur (Argentina, Brazil, Paraguay, Uruguay, Chile, and Bolivia).
- Besides joining together in trade blocs, countries also extend special, "most favored nation" trading privileges—that is, grant other countries favorable trading treatment such as the reduction of import duties.

4.6 The Importance of Understanding Cultural Differences

-  A nation's culture is the shared set of beliefs, values, knowledge, and patterns of behavior common to a group of people. Visitors to another culture may experience culture shock—feelings of discomfort and disorientation. Managers trying to understand other cultures need to understand four basic cultural perceptions embodied in (1) language, (2) nonverbal communication, (3) time orientation, and (4) religion.
- Regarding language, when you are trying to communicate across cultures you have three options: speak your own language (if others can understand you), use a translator, or learn the local language.
- Nonverbal communication consists of messages sent by means other than the written or the spoken word, and these nonverbal messages can vary according to culture. Five ways in which nonverbal communication is expressed are through interpersonal space, eye contact, facial expressions, body movements and gestures, and touch.
- Time orientation of a culture may be either monochronic (preference for doing one thing at a time) or polychronic (preference for doing more than one thing at a time).
- Managers need to consider the effect of religious differences. In order of size (population), the major world religions are Christianity, Islam, Hinduism, Buddhism, Chinese traditional religion, and Judaism.

Management in Action

ValiCert Learns Important Lessons about Transferring Jobs Overseas

Excerpted from Scott Thurm, "Tough Shift—Lesson in India: Not Every Job Translates Overseas—ValiCert Learned Key Roles Must Remain in U.S. for Outsourcing to Work," The Wall Street Journal, *March 3, 2004, pp. A1, A10. Copyright © 2004, Dow Jones & Company, Inc.*

When sales of their security software slowed in 2001, executives at ValiCert Inc. began laying off engineers in Silicon Valley to hire replacements in India for $7,000 a year.

ValiCert expected to save millions annually while cranking out new software for banks, insurers and government agencies. Senior Vice President David Jevans recalls optimistic predictions that the company would "cut the budget by half here and hire twice as many people there." Colleagues would swap work across the globe every 12 hours, helping ValiCert "put more people on it and get it done sooner," he says.

The reality was different. The Indian engineers, who knew little about ValiCert's software or how it was used, omitted features Americans considered intuitive. U.S. programmers, accustomed to quick chats over cubicle walls, spent months writing detailed instructions for overseas assignments, delaying new products. Fear and distrust thrived as ValiCert's finances deteriorated, and coworkers, 14 times zones apart, traded curt e-mails. In the fall of 2002, executives brought back to the U.S. a key project that had been assigned to India, irritating some Indian employees.

"At times, we were thinking, 'What have we done here?'" recalls John Vigouroux, who joined ValiCert in July 2002 and became chief executive three months later.

Shifting work to India eventually did help cut ValiCert's engineering costs by two-thirds, keeping the company and its major products alive—and saving 65 positions which remained in the U.S. But not before ValiCert experienced a harrowing period of instability and doubt, and only after its executives significantly refined the company's global division of labor.

The successful formula that emerged was to assign the India team bigger projects, rather than tasks requiring continual interaction with U.S. counterparts. The crucial jobs of crafting new products and features stayed in Silicon Valley. In the end, exporting some jobs ultimately led to adding a small but important number of new, higher-level positions in the U.S. . . .

ValiCert's experience offers important insights into the debate over the movement of service jobs to lower-cost countries, such as India. Such shifts can save companies money and hurt U.S. workers. But the process is difficult, and the savings typically aren't as great as a simple wage comparison suggests. Some jobs cannot easily or profitably be exported, and trying to do so can risk a customer backlash. . . .

India was a natural choice because of its large pool of software engineers. Moreover, both Mr. Krishnan [ValiCert's founder] and ValiCert's then-head of engineering grew up in India and were familiar with large tech-outsourcing firms.

Some, including Mr. Jevans, harbored doubts. The Apple Computer Inc. veteran says he preferred "small teams of awesome people" working closely together. Nonetheless, that summer, ValiCert hired Infosys Technologies Ltd., an Indian specialist in contract software-programming, to supply about 15 people in India to review software for bugs, and to update two older products.

With no manager in India, ValiCert employees in the U.S. managed the Infosys workers directly, often late at night or early in the morning because of the time difference. ValiCert also frequently changed the tasks assigned to Infosys, prompting Infosys to shuffle the employees and frustrating ValiCert's efforts to build a team there.

Within a few months, ValiCert abandoned Infosys and created its own Indian subsidiary, with as many as 60 employees. Most employees would be paid less than $10,000 a year. Even after accounting for benefits, office operating costs and communications links back to the U.S., ValiCert estimated the annual cost of an Indian worker at roughly $30,000. That's about half what ValiCert was paying Infosys per worker, and less than one-sixth of the $200,000 comparable annual cost in Silicon Valley.

To run the new office in India, ValiCert hired Sridhar Vutukuri, an outspoken 38-year-old engineer who had headed a similar operation for another Silicon Valley start-up. He set up shop in January 2002 in a ground-floor office in bustling Bangalore, the tech hub of southern India. The office looked much like ValiCert's California home, except for the smaller cubicles and Indian designs on the partitions. There were no savings on the rent. At $1 a square foot, it matched what ValiCert paid for its Mountain View, Calif., home offices, amid a Silicon Valley office glut.

Misunderstandings started right away. U.S. executives wanted programmers with eight to 10 years of experience, typical of ValiCert's U.S. employees. But such "career programmers" are rare in India, where the average age of engineers is 26. Most seek management jobs after four or five years. Expertise in security technology, key to ValiCert's products, was even rarer.

By contrast, Mr. Vutukuri quickly assembled a group to test ValiCert's software for bugs, tapping a large pool of Indian engineers that had long performed this mundane work.

But the Indian manager heading that group ran into resistance. It was ValiCert's first use of code-checkers who didn't report to the same managers who wrote the programs. Those U.S. managers fumed when the team in India recommended in June 2002 delaying a new product's release because it had too many bugs.

By midsummer, when Mr. Vutukuri had enough programmers for ValiCert to begin sending bigger assignments to India, U.S. managers quickly overwhelmed the India team by sending a half-dozen projects at once.

Accustomed to working closely with veteran engineers familiar with ValiCert's products, the U.S. managers offered only vague outlines for each assignment. The less-experienced Indian engineers didn't include elements in the programs that were considered standard among U.S. customers. U.S. programmers rewrote the software, delaying its release by months.

In India, engineers grew frustrated with long silences, punctuated by rejection. Suresh Marur, the head of one programming team, worked on five projects during 2002. All were either cancelled or delayed. Programmers who had worked around the clock for days on one project quit for new jobs in Bangalore's vibrant market. Of nine people on Mr. Marur's team in mid-2002, only three still work for ValiCert. . . .

Executives knew they could save more money by exporting more jobs. But they were developing a keener sense of how critical it was to keep core managers in the U.S. who knew ValiCert, its products, and how they were used by customers. "Even if you could find someone with the right skills in India," says Mr. Krishnan, the ValiCert founder, "it wouldn't make business sense to move the job."

Frustrations came to a head in September 2002, when a prospective customer discovered problems with the log-on feature of a ValiCert program. The anticipated purchase was delayed, causing ValiCert to miss third-quarter financial targets. The India team had recently modified the program, and the glitch prompted U.S. managers to question ValiCert's entire offshore strategy. . . .

For Discussion

1. Why did ValiCert transfer jobs overseas?
2. What were the key sources of conflict between ValiCert's employees in California and in India?
3. Assuming you were Mr. John Vigouroux, what would you have done differently during the process of transferring jobs overseas? Explain.
4. Why is it so difficult to transfer technical work such as software development to an overseas location?

Self-Assessment

How Well Am I Suited to Becoming a Global Manager?*

Objectives

1. To see if you are ready to be a global manager.
2. To help you assess your comfort level with other cultures.

Introduction

As our business world becomes increasingly globalized, U.S. companies need more managers to work in other countries. This usually means vast adjustments for the manager and her or his family during this job assignment. Flexibility is critical as is the ability to adjust to new ways, new people, new foods, different nonverbal communication, a new language, and a host of other new things.

Before agreeing to such an assignment, you need to know more about yourself and how you function in such situations.

Instructions

Are you prepared to be a global manager? Rate the extent to which you agree with each of the following 14 items by circling your response on the rating scale shown below. If you do not have direct experience with a particular situation (for example, working with people from other cultures), respond by circling how you *think* you would feel.

1 = Very strongly disagree
2 = Strongly disagree
3 = Disagree
4 = Neither agree nor disagree
5 = Agree
6 = Strongly agree
7 = Very strongly agree

1. When working with people from other cultures, I work hard to understand their perspectives.	1	2	3	4	5	6	7
2. I have a solid understanding of my organization's products and services.	1	2	3	4	5	6	7
3. I am willing to take a stand on issues.	1	2	3	4	5	6	7
4. I have a special talent for dealing with people.	1	2	3	4	5	6	7
5. I can be depended on to tell the truth regardless of circumstances.	1	2	3	4	5	6	7
6. I am good at identifying the most important part of a complex problem or issue.	1	2	3	4	5	6	7
7. I clearly demonstrate commitment to seeing the organization succeed.	1	2	3	4	5	6	7
8. I take personal as well as business risks.	1	2	3	4	5	6	7
9. I have changed as a result of feedback from others.	1	2	3	4	5	6	7
10. I enjoy the challenge of working in countries other than my own.	1	2	3	4	5	6	7
11. I take advantage of opportunities to do new things.	1	2	3	4	5	6	7
12. I find criticism hard to take.	1	2	3	4	5	6	7

the manager's toolbox

How Do Exceptional Managers Make Their Own Luck?

Risk and luck are two aspects of life that can't be ignored. But planning can improve your odds.

Many people think what happens to them is the result of fickle fate. However, with knowledge and planning, you can better learn what's risky and what's not.

What determines the way people perceive risk? The context in which the risk occurs is often important.[1] For example, you may tend to view something as more risky if you're not in control (as when traveling on an airplane). Another factor is trust: When a company or agency has a shady record, people conclude it can't be trusted and view what it's doing as more risky.

As a manager, you need to be aware of such outside factors when making plans about new endeavors involving some risk. You also need to be aware of how you yourself think about your luck.

Bad luck is when a flaming meteor hits you on the head. But failed business deals, lost promotions, and the like can't be blamed on just bad luck. "We're responsible for a good deal more of what happens to us than we realize," says research psychologist William F. Vitulli.[2]

People who are prone to bad luck are often impulsive. "They routinely speak before they think, make investments and purchases based on passing whims, and put themselves in dangerous spots by failing to plan ahead," says one writer.[3] Other people have bad luck in just one area (such as relationships) in which they are incapable of seeing life realistically. Still others have self-expectations that they will fail, and so they generally do. Or they exaggerate their setbacks to gain sympathy.

How do you improve your luck? Some steps:[4]

- **Make a list and consider your motives:** If you think you could be the victim of self-induced misfortune, make a written list of specific examples in which you contributed to your own bad luck. Then fight it by putting Post-it® reminders (such as the word "Impulse?") on your phone, computer monitor, dashboard, and so on.
- **Cultivate optimism and confidence:** Can you actually *will* yourself to be in control of your life? The chances are that if you act like the person you want to become, you will become that person. Indeed, you are more apt to ACT your way into a new way of thinking than to THINK your way into it.[5] Thus, try to cultivate optimism. Don't automatically expect the worst in any situation.
- **Ask for help:** Many of us can't see ourselves objectively. If you have trouble figuring out a pattern of bad luck, the best solution is to talk to a counselor.

forecast

What's Ahead in This Chapter

In this chapter, we describe planning, the first of the four management functions. We consider the benefits of planning and how it helps you deal with uncertainty. We deal with the fundamentals of planning, including the mission and vision statements and the three types of planning—strategic, tactical, and operational. We consider goals and action plans, SMART goals, the planning/control cycle, and management by objectives (MBO). We then consider project planning.

major question

How do I tend to deal with uncertainty, and how can planning help?

The Big Picture

Planning, the first of four functions in the management process, involves setting goals and deciding how to achieve them. Planning helps you check your progress, coordinate activities, think ahead, and cope with uncertainty. Uncertainty is of three types—state, effect, and response. Organizations respond to uncertainty in various ways.

What is known as the *management process,* you'll recall (from Chapter 1, p. 12), involves the four management functions of *planning, organizing, leading,* and *controlling,* which form four of the part divisions of this book. In this and the next two chapters we discuss ***planning,*** **which we previously defined as setting goals and deciding how to achieve them. Another definition: *Planning* is coping with uncertainty by formulating future courses of action to achieve specified results.**[6] When you make a plan, you make a blueprint for action that describes what you need to do to realize your goals.

Why Not Plan?

On the face of it, planning would seem to be a good idea—otherwise we would not be devoting three chapters to the subject. But there are two cautions to be aware of:

1 Planning Requires You to Set Aside the Time to Do It

Time-starved managers may be quite resentful when superiors order them to prepare a five-year plan for their work unit.

"What?" they may grouse. "They expect me to do that and *still* find time to meet this year's goals?" Somehow, though, that time for planning must be found. Otherwise, managers are mainly just reacting to events.

Planning means that you must involve the subordinates you manage to determine resources, opportunities, and goals. During the process, you may need to go outside the work unit for information about products, competitors, markets, and the like.

2 You May Have to Make Some Decisions without a Lot of Time to Plan

In our time of Internet connections and speedy-access computer databases, can't nearly anyone lay hands on facts quickly to make an intelligent decision? Not always. A competitor may quickly enter your market with a highly desirable product. A change in buying habits may occur. A consumer boycott may suddenly surface. An important supplier may let you down. The caliber of employees you need may not be immediately available at the salary level you're willing to pay. And in any one of these you won't have the time to plan a decision based on all the facts.

Nevertheless, a plan need not be perfect to be executable. While you shouldn't shoot from the hip in making decisions, often you may have to "go with what you've got" and make a decision based on a plan that is perhaps only three-quarters complete.

How Planning Helps You: Four Benefits

You can always hope you'll luck out or muddle through the next time a hurricane, earthquake, tornado, or other natural disaster strikes your area. Or you can plan for it by stocking up on flashlight batteries and canned food. Which is better? The same consideration applies when you're a manager. Some day, after you've dealt with some crisis, you will be very happy that you had a plan for handling it. The benefits of planning are fourfold:

1 Planning Helps You Check on Your Progress

The preprinted score card that golfers use when playing 18 holes of golf isn't blank. For each hole, the card lists the standard number of strokes ("par"), such as three or five, that a good player should take to hit the ball from the tee to the cup. The score card is the plan for the game, with objectives for each hole. After you play the hole, you write your own score in a blank space. At the end of the 18 holes, you add all your scores to see how you performed compared to the standard for the course.

How well is your work going in an organization? You won't know unless you have some way of checking your progress. That's why, like a golfer, you need to have some expectations of what you're supposed to do—in other words, a plan.

2 Planning Helps You Coordinate Activities

"The right hand doesn't know what the left hand is doing!"

We may hear that expression used, for example, when a crisis occurs and an organization's public relations department, legal department, and CEO's office all give the press separate, contradictory statements. Obviously, such an embarrassment can be avoided if the organization has a plan for dealing with the media during emergencies. A plan defines the responsibilities of various departments and coordinates their activities for the achievement of common goals—such as, at minimum, making an organization not look confused and disorganized.

3 Planning Helps You Think Ahead

Founder and former CEO Michael Dell, of Dell Computer, which makes personal computers, says, "In my business, the life cycle of a product is six months, and so there are two types of people: the quick and the dead."[7] Dell is always trying to look into the future to try to plan for what might be the next big change in microcomputer products.

Similarly, as we describe under product life cycle (Chapter 6), the service or product with which you're engaged will probably at some point reach maturity, and sales will begin to falter. Thus, you need to look ahead, beyond your present phase of work, to try to be sure you'll be one of the quick rather than one of the dead.

Thinking ahead. Planning helps companies anticipate new competitive developments. This McDonald's franchise wasn't clowning around when it installed WiFi—"wireless fidelity" technology that allows portable computer users to easily make through-the-air Internet connections—in hopes of luring customers away from rivals.

4 Above All, Planning Helps You Cope with Uncertainty

You don't care for unpleasant surprises? Most people don't. (Pleasant surprises, of course, are invariably welcome.) That's why trying to plan for unpleasant contingencies is necessary (as we'll describe in Chapter 6). Planning helps you deal with uncertainty, as we discuss next.

Three Types of Uncertainty: State, Effect, & Response

Experts tend to classify uncertainty as being of three types—*state, effect,* and *response*:[8]

State Uncertainty—"What Possible Harmful Event Could Occur?"

On a summer day, you're setting out for a hike in the mountains. You scan the skies. Could it rain? Are you at a high enough elevation, and is it cold enough that it could even snow? This is an example of ***state uncertainty,*** **when the environment is considered unpredictable.**

Effect Uncertainty—"What Possible Harmful Effect Might an Environmental Change Have?"

An unexpected rainstorm in the mountains could be just a slight inconvenience, forcing you to take cover until it passes. However, a snowstorm could cause you to lose the trail and perhaps risk freezing and hypothermia. This is an example of ***effect uncertainty,*** **when the effects of environmental changes are unpredictable.**

Response Uncertainty—"What Possible Harmful Consequence Might a Decision Have?"

Which would be better to have in a mountain snowstorm, warm clothes or a cellphone? The clothes would help you survive the weather. The cellphone could help summon emergency aid—if anyone could receive your call from a wilderness area. This is an example of ***response uncertainty,*** **when the consequences of a decision are uncertain.**

Example

Planning for Uncertainty: What Should Cellphone Makers Do?

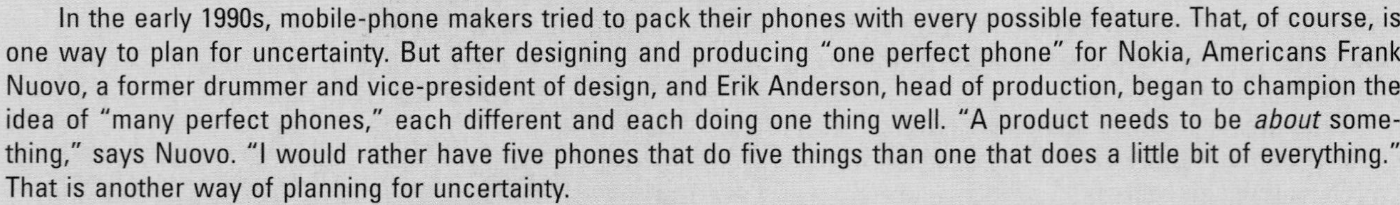

In 1993, Motorola dominated the mobile-phone market, but at the start of the 21st century it was succeeded by Finland-based Nokia. In early 2004, however, Nokia faltered—primarily because it failed to deliver the right mix and price of phones, particularly in Europe—and it was Motorola that surged ahead, in part because its highly anticipated color-camera phones found their market. Motorola "created a set of products that are highly desirable and well priced," said one analyst, so that they had "the most fully featured phones on the market at the lowest price point."[9] But the world may be about to change drastically for both cellphone makers.

In the early 1990s, mobile-phone makers tried to pack their phones with every possible feature. That, of course, is one way to plan for uncertainty. But after designing and producing "one perfect phone" for Nokia, Americans Frank Nuovo, a former drummer and vice-president of design, and Erik Anderson, head of production, began to champion the idea of "many perfect phones," each different and each doing one thing well. "A product needs to be *about* something," says Nuovo. "I would rather have five phones that do five things than one that does a little bit of everything." That is another way of planning for uncertainty.

Not that this planning is easy. "If you make too many phones you go bankrupt," observes Anderson. "If you make lots of products but none are the best in their class, you will go bankrupt. If you make one good product, you might do really well with it, but there won't be enough profit, so you'll go bankrupt. In the end, it all really comes back to balance."[10]

Consumers used to seek out the handsets of Nokia and Motorola, but cellphone brands aren't what they used to be. Now cellphone service providers—Verizon, Sprint PCS, AT&T, and other carriers—are playing up their own brand names on handsets. And they are calling the shots on everything from look and functions to price so that equipment providers are being beaten down. This is good news for consumers but bad news for Motorola and Nokia—especially since Asian competitors such as Samsung, LG, and NEC are willing to downplay their brands and customize their phones to carrier preferences. If Nokia and Motorola don't adapt to the new power shift, they could find themselves out in the cold.[11]

Greater challenges lie ahead. Wireless Internet—and Internet phone—technology, such as Wi-Fi, WiMax, Mobile-Fi, ZigBee, and Ultrawideband, could push wireless networking into all aspects of life, from cars and homes to offices and factories.[12] How should Nokia and Motorola plan for this uncertainty?

How Organizations Respond to Uncertainty

How do you personally respond to uncertainty? Do you react slowly? conservatively? proactively? Do you watch to see what others do? Organizations act in similar ways.

Four Basic Strategy Types

Scholars **Raymond E. Miles** and **Charles C. Snow** suggest that organizations adapt one of four approaches when responding to uncertainty in their environment. They become *Defenders, Prospectors, Analyzers,* or *Reactors.*[13]

GarageBand. Apple Computer introduced this software in early 2004 to turn Mac computers into "digital recording studios," allowing pros and novices alike to perform, record, and create music. Here musician John Mayer (left) and Apple CEO Steve Jobs demonstrate GarageBand at the 2004 Macworld Conference & Expo in San Francisco. Which response would you say Apple is taking to uncertainty?

Defenders—"Let's Stick with What We Do Best, Avoid Other Involvements" Whenever you hear an organization's leader say that "We're sticking with the basics" or "We're getting back to our core business," that's the hallmark of a Defender organization. ***Defenders* are expert at producing and selling narrowly defined products or services.** Often they are old-line successful enterprises—such as Harley-Davidson motorcycles or Brooks Brothers clothiers—with a narrow focus. They do not tend to seek opportunities outside their present markets. They devote most of their attention to making refinements in their existing operations.

Prospectors—"Let's Create Our Own Opportunities, Not Wait for Them to Happen" A company described as "aggressive" is often a Prospector organization. ***Prospectors* focus on developing new products or services and in seeking out new markets, rather than waiting for things to happen.** Like 19th-century gold miners, these companies are "prospecting" for new ways of doing things. The continual product and market innovation has a price: Such companies may suffer a loss of efficiency. Nevertheless, their focus on change can put fear in the hearts of competitors.

Analyzers—"Let Others Take the Risks of Innovating, & We'll Imitate What Works Best" Analyzers take a "me too" response to the world. By and large, you won't find them called "trendsetters." Rather, ***Analyzers* let other organizations take the risks of product development and marketing and then imitate (or perhaps slightly improve on) what seems to work best.**

Reactors—"Let's Wait Until There's a Crisis, Then We'll React" Whereas the Prospector is aggressive and proactive, the Reactor is the opposite—passive and reactive. ***Reactors* make adjustments only when finally forced to by environmental pressures.** In the worst cases, they are so incapable of responding fast enough that they suffer massive sales losses and are even driven out of business. Schwinn bicycles, for instance, failed to respond quickly enough to the sudden popularity of mountain bikes and lost its stature as the leading manufacturer of bicycles.

The Adaptive Cycle

Miles and Snow also introduced the idea of the *adaptive cycle,* which portrays businesses as continuously cycling through decisions about three kinds of business problems: (1) *entrepreneurial* (selecting and making adjustments of products and markets), (2) *engineering* (producing and delivering the products), and (3) *administrative* (establishing roles, relationships, and organizational processes).

Thus, a business that makes decisions in the entrepreneurial area that take it in the direction of being a Prospector will in a short time also begin making Prospector-oriented decisions in the engineering area, then the administrative area, and then even more so in the entrepreneurial area, and so on. Thus, as one scholar points out, "With enough cycles and insight, a given business becomes a very good, comprehensively aligned Prospector, Analyzer, or Defender. If a business lacks insight, or if it fails to take advantage of alignment opportunities afforded by the adaptive cycle, it will be an incongruent, poorly performing Reactor."[14] ◆

major question

What are mission and vision statements, three types of planning and goals, and SMART goals?

The Big Picture

Planning consists of translating an organization's mission into objectives. The organization's purpose is expressed as a mission statement, and what it becomes is expressed as a vision statement. From these are derived strategic planning, then tactical planning, then operational planning. Each kind specifies goals and action plans for accomplishing the goals, which should be S-M-A-R-T.

"Everyone wants a clear reason to get up in the morning," writes journalist Dick Leider. "As humans we hunger for meaning and purpose in our lives."[15]

And what is that purpose? "Life never lacks purpose," says Leider. "Purpose is innate—but it is up to each of us individually to discover or rediscover it."

An organization has a purpose, too—a mission. And managers must have an idea of where they want the organization to go—a vision. The approach to planning can be summarized in the following diagram, which shows how an organization's mission becomes translated into objectives. *(See Figure 5.1.)*

FIGURE 5.1

Making plans. An organization's reason for being is expressed in a *mission statement.* What the organization wishes to become is expressed in a *vision statement.* From these are derived *strategic planning,* then *tactical planning,* and finally *operational planning.* The purpose of each kind of planning is to specify *goals* and *action plans* for accomplishing those goals.

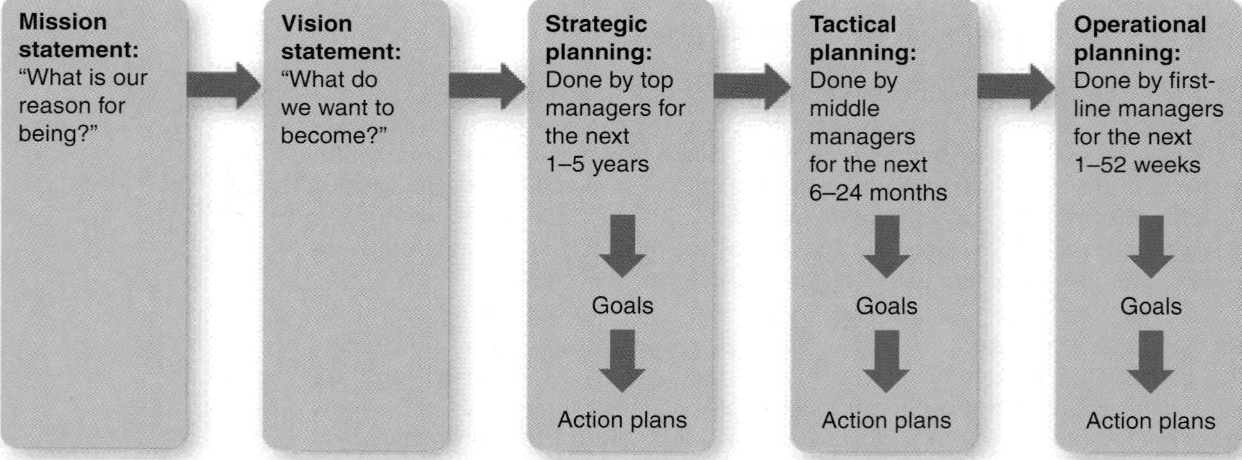
Mission statement: "What is our reason for being?"
Vision statement: "What do we want to become?"
Strategic planning: Done by top managers for the next 1–5 years
Goals
Action plans
Tactical planning: Done by middle managers for the next 6–24 months
Goals
Action plans
Operational planning: Done by first-line managers for the next 1–52 weeks
Goals
Action plans

Measurable

Whenever possible, goals should be *measurable,* or quantifiable (as in "90% of planes should arrive within 15 minutes . . ."). That is, there should be some way to measure the degree to which a goal has been reached.

Of course, some goals—such as those concerned with improving quality—are not precisely quantifiable. In that case, something on the order of "Improve the quality of customer relations by instituting 10 follow-up telephone calls every week" will do. You can certainly quantify how many follow-up phone calls were made.

Attainable

Goals should be challenging, of course, but above all they should be realistic and *attainable*. It may be best to set goals that are quite ambitious so as to challenge people to meet high standards. Always, however, the goals should be achievable within the scope of the time, equipment, and financial support available. *(See Figure 5.3.)*

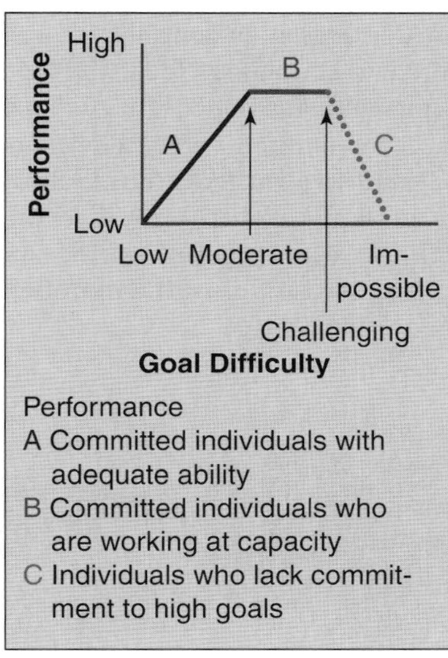

FIGURE 5.3
Relationship between goal difficulty and performance [*Source:* Adapted from E. A. Locke and G. P. Latham, *A Theory of Goal Setting and Task Performance* (Englewood Cliffs, NJ: Prentice Hall, 1990).]

If too easy (as in "half the flights should arrive on time"), goals won't impel people to make much effort. If impossible ("all flights must arrive on time, regardless of weather"), employees won't even bother trying. Or they will try and continually fail, which will end up hurting morale.

Results-Oriented

Only a few goals should be chosen—say, five for any work unit. And they should be *results-oriented*—they should support the organization's vision.

In writing out the goals, start with the word "To" and follow it with action-oriented verbs—"complete," "acquire," "increase" ("to decrease by 10% the time to get passengers settled in their seats before departure").

Some verbs should not be used in your goal statement because they imply activities—the tactics used to accomplish goals (such as having baggage handlers waiting). For example, you should not use "to develop," "to conduct," "to implement."

Target Dates

Goals should specify the *target dates* or deadline dates when they are to be attained. For example, it's unrealistic to expect an airline to improve its on-time arrivals by 10% overnight. However, you could set a target date—three to six months away, say—by which this goal is to be achieved. That allows enough time for lower-level managers and employees to revamp their systems and work habits and gives them a clear time frame in which they know what they are expected to do. ◆

major question How does the planning/control cycle help keep a manager's plans headed in the right direction?

The Big Picture

The four-step planning/control cycle helps you keep in control, to make sure you're headed in the right direction.

Once you've made plans, how do you stay in control to make sure you're headed in the right direction? Actually, there is a continuous feedback loop known as the planning/control cycle. (The "organizing" and "leading" steps within the Planning-Organizing-Leading-Controlling sequence are implied here.) **The *planning/control cycle* has two planning steps (1 and 2) and two control steps (3 and 4), as follows: (1) Make the plan. (2) Carry out the plan. (3) Control the direction by comparing results with the plan. (4) Control the direction by taking corrective action in two ways—namely, (a) by correcting deviations in the plan being carried out, or (b) by improving future plans.** *(See Figure 5.4.)*

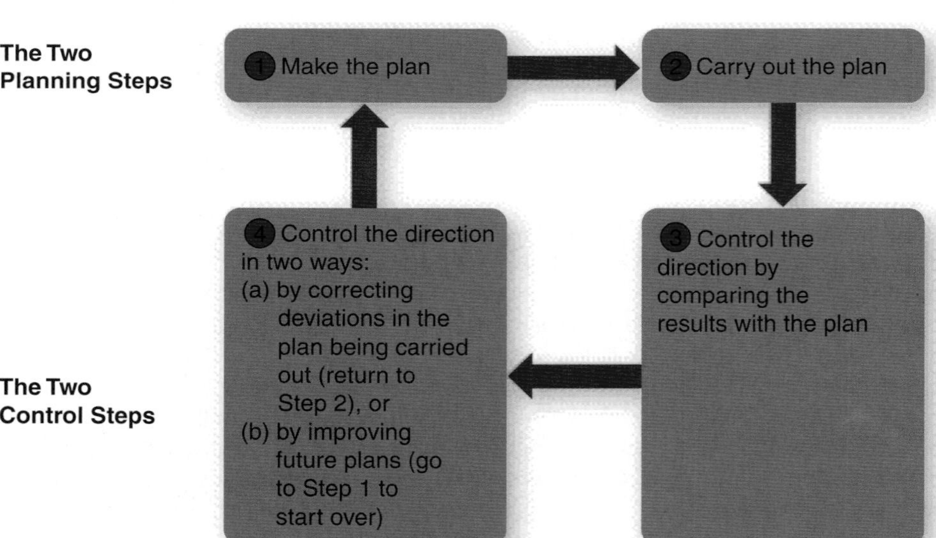

FIGURE 5.4
The planning/control cycle. This describes a constant feedback loop designed to ensure plans stay headed in the right direction. [*Source:* Adapted from R. Kreitner, *Management,* 8th ed. (Boston: Houghton Mifflin, 2001), p. 177, Fig. 6.4.]

The planning/control cycle loop exists for each level of planning—strategic, tactical, and operational. The corrective action in Step 4 of the cycle (a) can get a project back on track before it's too late or (b) if it's too late, can provide data for improving future plans. ◆

A Faulty Planning/Control Cycle: The Golden Books Path to Bankruptcy[33]

Richard Snyder was one of the most well-known figures in book publishing—he had built Simon & Schuster into the largest U.S. publisher—when in May 1996 he became chairman and CEO of Golden Books, a publisher since 1942 of children's classics such as *Scruffy the Tugboat* and Mickey Mouse stories. However, in less than three years, the $400 million company was on the brink of bankruptcy.

What happened? **First,** there was the faulty plan. Probably the plan should have been just to stick with and improve the core business, children's books—at least at the beginning. But simply as a children's book company, says writer Michael Shnayerson, Golden held little interest for Snyder. He dreamed of taking Golden, the brand, and making an empire. Not just Golden Books for kids but also Golden books on parenting, Golden family videos, Golden play centers, even Golden theme parks.

Second, there was the faulty carrying out of the plan. While at Simon & Schuster, Snyder had published award-winning children's books that sold for $16 and up in regular bookstores. But Golden's largest customer was Wal-Mart, which treated the $1.29 books like any other class of discount consumer goods. ("We made books for the children of the masses, not the classes," said one Golden executive. "We sold tonnage.") Snyder learned a new term: fill rate—the rate at which a publisher is able to keep store shelves filled. Wal-Mart told Snyder it would be just as happy if Golden pulled out for good, since the publisher was so disorganized that it couldn't keep store shelves filled with successful books or take away those that didn't sell.

Blowing a Golden opportunity?

Third, there was flawed control of the execution of the plan (or what should have been the plan—to improve customer service with the children's books). Snyder found out that, remarkably, Golden Books had no sales reports at all. It knew how many books went out but not what happened to them. But Snyder compounded the problem by firing virtually all Golden's managers because he felt they were stuck in their ways, thereby eliminating the very mass-market children's-books veterans who might have helped him. Meanwhile, for two years, he was "flying blind," as he later admitted, because the company was without a good financial system.

Fourth, there seems to have been a lack of corrective action. Instead of concentrating on finding a quick and simple approach to the sales-report and fill-rate problems, Snyder ordered up a whole new integrated financial system that was later found to be too complex and too expensive for the company's needs. In addition, he pursued his larger brand-extending ideas for Golden. He started an adult Golden Books line (and also paid $40 million for a brand-new printing plant). He paid $81 million for a video company. He looked into Golden theme parks and Golden play centers. He moved the company's headquarters at great expense from Racine, Wisc., to New York City.

"Unfortunately," says Shnayerson, "all the empire-building schemes sapped cash—eventually $300 million. And though millions of Golden books were selling, the margin of profit on each was very, very small. Much money out, very little in; quarter by quarter, the losses grew." Finally, in 1998, the company went bankrupt. When it emerged from Chapter 11 bankruptcy in early 2000, it was a considerably smaller and less powerful company than it had been five years earlier. A year later, the Golden Books assets (and liabilities) were acquired by Random House and Classic Media for $84.4 million.

major question

What is MBO, and how can it be implemented successfully to achieve results?

The Big Picture

A technique for setting goals, management by objectives (MBO) is a four-step process for motivating employees.

Do you perform better when you set goals or when you don't? What about when you set difficult goals rather than easy ones?

Research shows that if goals are made more difficult ("increase study time 30%"), people may achieve them less often than they would easy goals ("increase study time 5%"), but they nevertheless perform at a higher level. People also do better when the objectives are specific ("increase study time 10 hours a week") rather than general ("do more studying this semester").[34]

These are the kinds of matters addressed in the activity known as *management by objectives.* First suggested by **Peter Drucker** in 1954, MBO has spread largely because of the appeal of its emphasis on converting general objectives into specific ones for all members of an organization.[35]

TABLE 5.1
Three types of objectives used in MBO

Improvement objectives
Purpose Express performance to be accomplished in a specific way for a specific area **Examples** "Increase sport-utility sales by 10%." "Reduce food spoilage by 15%."
Personal development objectives
Purpose Express personal goals to be realized **Examples** "Attend five days of leadership training." "Learn basics of Microsoft Office software by June 1."
Maintenance objectives
Purpose Express the intention to maintain performance at previously established levels **Examples** "Continue to meet the increased sales goals specified last quarter." "Produce another 60,000 cases of wine this month."

What Is MBO? The Four-Step Process for Motivating Employees

Management by objectives (MBO) **is a four-step process in which (1) managers and employees jointly set objectives for the employee, (2) managers develop action plans, (3) managers and employees periodically review the employee's performance, and (4) the manager makes a performance appraisal and rewards the employee according to results.** The purpose of MBO is to *motivate* rather than control subordinates. Let's consider the four steps.

1 Jointly Set Objectives

You sit down with your manager and the two of you jointly set objectives for you to attain. Later you do the same with each of your own subordinates. Joint manager/subordinate participation is important to the program. It's probably best if the objectives aren't simply imposed from above ("Here are the objectives I want you to meet"). Managers also should not simply approve the employee's objectives ("Whatever you aim for is okay with me"). It's necessary to have back-and-forth negotiation to make the objectives practicable. One result of joint participation, research shows, is that it impels people to set more difficult goals—to raise the level of their aspirations—which may have a positive effect on their performance.[36] The objectives should be expressed in writing and should be SMART. There are three types of objectives, shown at left. *(See Table 5.1 at left.)*

2 Develop Action Plan

Once objectives are set, managers at each level should prepare an action plan for attaining them. Action plans may be prepared for both individuals and for work units, such as departments.

3 Periodically Review Performance

You and your manager should meet reasonably often—either informally as needed or formally every three months—to review progress, as should you and your subordinates. Indeed, frequent communication is necessary so that everyone will know how well he or she is doing in meeting the objectives.

During each meeting, managers should give employees feedback, and objectives should be updated or revised as necessary to reflect new realities. If you were managing a painting or landscaping business, for example, changes in the weather, loss of key employees, or a financial downturn affecting customer spending could force you to reconsider your objectives.

4 Give Performance Appraisal & Rewards, If Any

At the end of 6 or 12 months, you and your subordinate should meet to discuss results, comparing performance with initial objectives. *Deal with results,* not personalities, emotional issues, or excuses.

Because the purpose of MBO is to *motivate* employees, performance that meets the objectives should be rewarded—with compliments, raises, bonuses, promotions, or other suitable benefits. Failure can be addressed by redefining the objectives for the next 6- or 12-month period, or even by taking stronger measures, such as demotion. Basically, however, MBO is viewed as being a learning process. After Step 4, the MBO cycle begins anew.

Cascading Objectives: MBO from the Top Down

For MBO to be successful, three things have to happen:

1 The Commitment of Top Management Is Essential

"When top-management commitment [to MBO] was high," said one review, "the average gain in productivity was 56%. When commitment was low, the average gain in productivity was only 6%."[37]

2 It Must Be Applied Organizationwide

The program has to be put in place throughout the entire organization. That is, it cannot be applied in just some divisions and departments; it has to be done in all of them.

3 Objectives Must "Cascade"

MBO works by ***cascading*** **objectives down through the organization; that is, objectives are structured in a *unified hierarchy,* becoming more specific at lower levels of the organization.** Top managers set general *organizational* objectives, which are translated into *divisional* objectives, which are translated into *departmental* objectives. The hierarchy ends in *individual* objectives set by each employee. ◆

Example

Setting Objectives: Microsoft's "The List"

Although Microsoft Corp. is the most profitable company in the technology industry, as it turns 30 it finds that its old businesses (such as its Windows operating system software and Office applications software) are growing only at the rate of the overall software industry, so it is having to focus much more on innovation. To achieve this innovation, chairman Bill Gates has put together what is called "The List."

The List is a priority ranking of 50 or so initiatives that, in one description, "cut across product lines and are critical to making the next generation of products successful—everything from security software and the user interface to Web search and telephony." The List is so important that each of the items is assigned to one top executive, who is responsible for following through on it throughout the company. "We're using a lot of IQ to go after these things," says Gates.[38]

major question

What is project planning, why is it important, and what is the project life cyle?

The Big Picture

Project planning, designed to prepare single-use plans called projects, consists of a four-stage project life cycle: definition, planning, execution, and closing.

When you write a term paper, is that a *task,* a *work assignment,* a *program,* or a *project*—or are they all the same thing? Actually, they're different.[39]

Task or Work Assignment

This is the simplest plan—it is something you (or you and others) might do using a simple "to-do" list. A term paper is a task or a work assignment.

In your management career, you will direct many task/work assignments. To a contractor building a house, pouring concrete for the foundation is one example. Doing the framing is another. Installing the plumbing is another. Putting on the roof is another. And so on.

Program

A program is the most complex plan—a large-scale endeavor that includes many projects. More specifically, a ***program*** **is defined as a single-use plan encompassing a range of projects or activities.**

For example, the U.S. government space *program* has several *projects,* including the *Challenger* project and the Hubble Telescope project. When Disney built Walt Disney World and Eurodisney, each of those were programs that included several projects (the various rides, for instance).

Project

A project is in between a task and a program. **A *project* is defined as a single-use plan of less scope and complexity than a program.**

A project is unique—it is a one-time set of events. It includes numerous complex, goal-oriented, sequenced activities aimed at delivering a product or a service. It has a start date and an end date. It has limited resources and budget. It involves many people, usually drawn from different areas of the organization.

For example, prior to the Sydney, Australia, 2000 Olympics, the government launched a project to clean up rivers, beaches, and waterways within three years before the event. One unique detail was to build 20 kilometers of tunnel under affluent areas north of Sydney Harbour, without any previous specification of methods, machinery, and environmental conditions through detailed prior planning.[40]

Why Project Planning Is Important Today

Project planning **is the preparation of single-use plans, or projects.** Planning is followed by ***project management,*** **achieving a set of goals through planning, scheduling, and maintaining progress of the activities that comprise the project.**[41] The purpose of project planning and project management is to lower the risk of uncertainty in the execution of a project. As we will see, the heart of project planning is the four-stage project life cycle.

Why care about project planning? Because more and more, this is becoming the fastest way of getting things done. Technology has speeded everything up, including the process of getting a new product or service to market.[42] The age of terrorism has also changed the way strategic planners must look at their companies' futures.[43] To complete specific projects quickly, companies will now draw together people with different skills to work together on a temporary basis, then disband once the job is done. Since project management works outside an organization's usual chain of command, project managers need to be adept at people skills, able to communicate, motivate, and negotiate (as we discuss in later chapters).

Project management has long been a standard way of operating for movie production companies, which will pull together a talented team of people to make a film, then disband when the picture is "wrapped." It's also a familiar approach for professional sports teams, construction companies, and even some types of legal teams. However, it is just beginning to be employed by other for-profit organizations, such as manufacturers and insurance companies, as well as nonprofit organizations, such as those in health care and education.

An example of project planning is the ***skunkworks***, **the term given to a project team whose members are separated from the normal operation of an organization and asked to produce a new, innovative product.**

Example

Project Planning: Google's Skunkworks Idea

In the old *Li'l Abner* comic strip about hillbillies, the Skonk Works was the site of the bootleg brewing operation for moonshine (called Kickapoo Joy Juice). In a skunkworks, says futurist Alvin Toffler, "a team is handed a loosely specified problem or goal, given resources, and allowed to operate outside the normal company rules. The skunkworks group thus ignores both the cubbyholes and the official channels—that is, the specialization and hierarchy of the existing corporate bureaucracy."[44]

In the 1960s through 1980s, Clarence "Kelly" Johnson managed Lockheed Aircraft's super-secret Advanced Development Projects Division facility—known as the Skunk Works—in Burbank, Calif., where under strict security some of the nation's most sophisticated aircraft, including the superfast Mach 3 SR-71 Blackbird, were developed. Among Johnson's basic operating rules were "The Skunk Works manager must be delegated practically complete control of his program in all respects" and "There must be a minimum number of reports required, but important work must be recorded thoroughly."

Giggling at Google. Are these people serious?

The computer industry has been particularly creative in employing the concept of the skunkworks. Racing to catch up with Apple Computer, which had been launched in 1976, International Business Machines launched its own version of the microcomputer, the IBM Personal Computer in 1981.[45] To get its PC to market quickly (it took only 12 months), it decided to abandon its traditional slow, methodical development process and instead gave the development of the PC to a nearly autonomous group in Boca Raton, Fla., whose members were reviewed quarterly by corporate headquarters but otherwise permitted to operate as they wished.

Google, the Mountain View, Calif., search-engine company, has extended the notion of skunkworks from protected place to protected idea. Google's managers keep a "Top 100" priorities list (which actually now numbers 240 items). An "S" next to the project stands for "skunkworks" and protects it from premature reviews and criticism. Engineers are rarely told what projects to work on. Instead they are allowed to gravitate to those that interest them, forming fluid work groups that can last weeks or months. They also spend a day a week working on their own personal research projects. "We're encouraging creativity and tolerating chaos," says Google's vice-president for engineering. "We turn that dial all the way over to loud."[46]

The Project Life Cycle: The Predictable Evolution of a Project

Being a project manager is a challenging job if for no other reason than that you have to be attentive both to the big picture *and* to the details. Let us therefore look at the big picture—the four-stage project life cycle that any project goes through, whether it's developing an online magazine or staging an AIDS in Africa music benefit.

***The project life cycle* has four stages from start to finish: definition, planning, execution, and closing.** *(See Figure 5.5.)* As we will see, the graph of the rise and fall of the *project* life cycle resembles that for the *product* life cycle, which we discuss in Chapter 6.

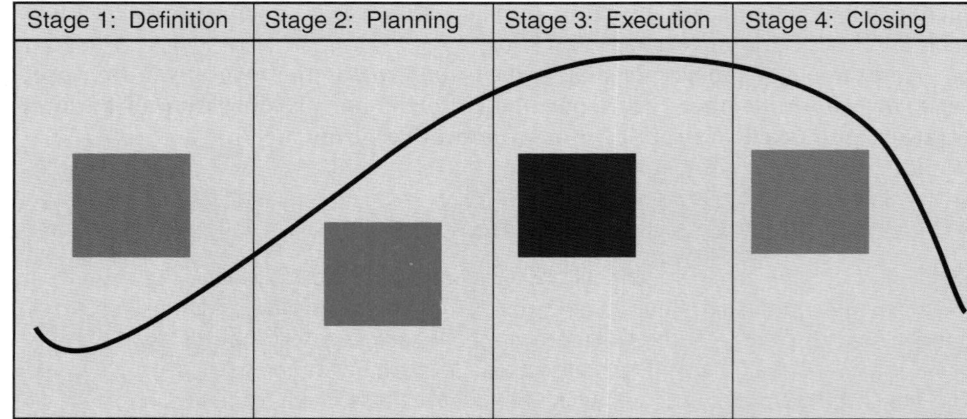

FIGURE 5.5
The project life cycle
[*Source:* Adapted from J. W. Weiss and R. K. Wysocki, *5-Phase Project Management* (Reading, MA: Addison-Wesley, 1992) and J. K. Pinto and O. P. Kharbanda, *Successful Project Manager: Leading Your Team to Success* (New York: Van Nostrand Reinhold, 1995), pp. 17–21.]

Stage 1 Definition

In the *definition* stage, you look at the big picture. You state the problem, look at the assumptions and risks, identify the project's goals and objectives, and determine the budget and schedule. You may also write a project proposal.

Stage 2 Planning

In the *planning* stage, you consider the details needed to make the big picture happen. You identify the facilities and equipment, the people and their duties, and the schedule and coordination efforts needed.

Technology and project planning. On the one hand, information technology is becoming cheaper and more manageable, which means that it is no longer a competitive advantage, as it was for companies willing to invest in it back when computers were expensive and difficult (the mainframe era). With the Internet and online databases, for instance, much of today's project planning can be accomplished quickly and easily. On the other hand, we may be standing at the threshold of a period of "technological overdrive," featuring such advances as tiny wireless sensors (smart dust) to monitor the environment, PCs that become indistinguishable from televisions, open source software (free software that started with Linux), universal connectivity (anywhere, anytime wireless communication), and the convergence of atom-sized machines (nanotechnology) and biotechnology with accelerated computing—all resulting in societal and economic change so fast as to be unimaginable. What do you think this merger of technology and nature would mean for project planning?

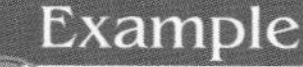

Project Life Cycle: Writing a Research Paper

An example of a project is the approach recommended by one college-success book for producing a research paper.[47]

Stage 1: Definition In the definition stage, you concentrate on picking a topic. That is, you set a deadline for when you will have decided on the topic, by which time you will have picked three alternative topics that are important to the instructor and interesting to you. You next refine the three proposed topics into three questions that your paper will be designed to answer. You then check the topic ideas with your instructor to see if he or she considers them satisfactory in importance and in scope.

Stage 2: Planning When writing a term paper, in your planning stage you do initial research online and in the library to see if there is enough material available to you so that you can adequately research your paper. You then develop a rough outline so that you know the direction your paper will take.

Stage 3: Execution When you're developing a research paper, the execution stage is the longest and most labor-intensive stage. This is when you do extensive research, sort your research notes, revise the outline to reflect changes suggested by your research, write a first draft, and then write and proofread your final draft.

Stage 4: Closing The closing stage for your research paper occurs when you hand in your paper to your "client"—your instructor.

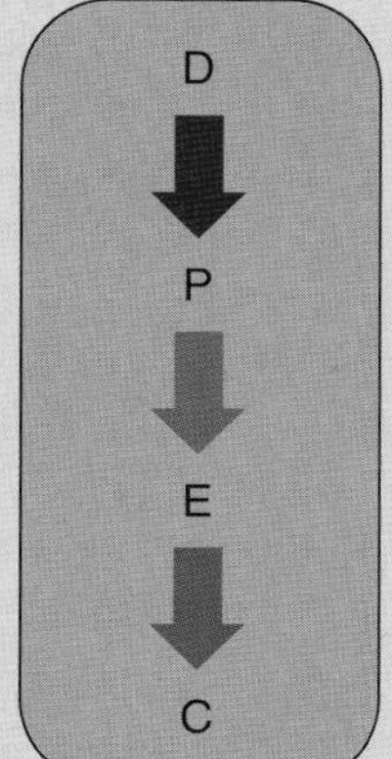

Stage 3 Execution

The *execution* stage is the actual work stage. You define the management style and establish the control tools. You will need to monitor progress, review the project schedule, issue change orders, and prepare status reports to the "client" (boss or customer) for whom the work is being done.

Your main focus is to complete the project on time and under budget while trying to meet the client's expectations.

Stage 4 Closing

The *closing* stage occurs when the project is accepted by the client. This stage can be abrupt but could be gradual, as when you're required to install deliverables (such as a complete computer system) and carry out training.

You may also be required to write a report about the project in which you document everything that happened.

Staying on track. In between an organization's mission statement and an operational action plan there are plenty of opportunities for slips, miscommunications, and errors. If you were leading this meeting in the first stage of a project life cycle, what would be your initial words after "Good morning"?

The Importance of Project Deadlines

There's no question that college is a pressure cooker for many students. The reason, of course, is the seemingly never-ending deadlines. But consider: Would you do all the course work you're doing—and realize the education you're getting—if you *didn't* have deadlines?

As we saw under the "T" in SMART ("has Target date"), deadlines are as essential to project planning as they are to your college career. Because the whole purpose of a planned project is to deliver to a client specified results within a specified period of time, deadlines become a great motivator, both for you and for the people working for you.

It's possible, of course, to let deadlines mislead you into focusing too much on immediate results and thereby ignore project planning—just as students will focus too much on preparing for a test in one course while neglecting others. In general, however, deadlines can help you keep your eye on the "big picture" while simultaneously paying attention to the details that will help you realize the big picture. Deadlines can help concentrate the mind, so that you make quick decisions rather than put them off.

Deadlines help you ignore extraneous matters (such as cleaning up a messy desk) in favor of focusing on what's important—achieving the project on time and on budget. Deadlines provide a mechanism for giving ourselves feedback. ◆

Sam Walton. The Wal-Mart founder could see both the big picture ("Everyday low prices") and the small picture (greeters at store entrances, overtime pay for Sunday work, open-door management policy). No wonder Wal-Mart became the largest private employer in the U.S., with 1 million employees.

practical action

Detail Thinkers versus Strategic Thinkers: Are You One or the Other?

When it comes to planning, are you a "big picture" person or a believer that "the importance is in the details"?

"Those with a natural inclination for either detail orientation or strategic thinking often choose jobs that allow them to rely on their preferred skills," says Intel Corp. senior manager Cheryl Shavers.

"It's no coincidence," she continues, "that manufacturing engineers have an ability to pay acute attention to detail—process flow, documentation, data—whereas technology licensing experts are likely to be strategic thinkers, focusing on long-term benefits and ramifications."[48]

So what happens when a person who is good at seeing the forest but not the trees meets up with a person who can see the trees but not the forest?

Someone told Shavers that he had been asked to work with a colleague to fix their flawed departmental approval process. However, the coworker was "so process driven" that he was not very open to considering anything but an improved version of the old system, whereas the other wanted to explore a more innovative approach.

While most people with the necessary skills can, with practice, learn to move from detail orientation to strategic thinking (or the reverse), there are those who are inflexible because of fears of "not getting things right" or an inability to deal with ambiguity. Or they may get so wrapped up in a new idea they often fall short on implementation.

When detail and strategic thinkers meet, suggests Shavers, it may help to strike a balance by doing the following:

- **Use a visual to focus the discussion:** Developing a flowchart or other visual can help focus the discussion on how old processes may be stretched before new approaches are introduced.
- **Consider implementation:** The practicalities of implementation should be considered before new solutions are adopted.
- **Have mutual respect:** Both parties should respect the fact that neither approach is right or wrong, only different.

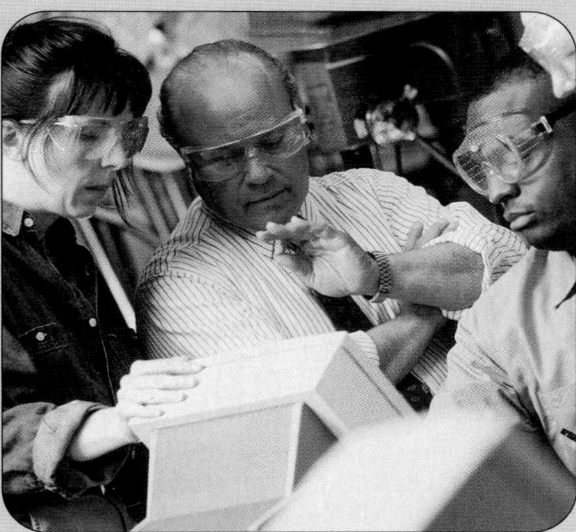

Key Terms Used in This Chapter

analyzers, 143
cascading, 153
defenders, 143
effect uncertainty, 142
management by objectives (MBO), 152
means-end chain, 147
mission, 145
mission statement, 145
operational goals, 147
operational planning, 146
planning, 140
planning/control cycle, 150
program, 154
project, 154
project life cycle, 156
project management, 154
project planning, 154
prospectors, 143
reactors, 143
response uncertainty, 142
skunkworks, 155
SMART goal, 148
state uncertainty, 142
strategic goals, 147
strategic planning, 146
tactical goals, 147
tactical planning, 146
vision, 145
vision statement, 145

Summary

5.1 Planning & Uncertainty

- Planning is defined as setting goals and deciding how to achieve them. It is also defined as coping with uncertainty by formulating future courses of action to achieve specified results.
- Planning has four benefits. (1) It helps you check your progress. (2) It helps you coordinate activities. (3) It helps you think ahead. (4) Above all, it helps you cope with uncertainty.
- Uncertainty is of three types. (1) State uncertainty is when the environment is considered unpredictable. (2) Effect uncertainty is when the effects of environmental changes are unpredictable. (3) Response uncertainty is when the consequences of a decision are uncertain.
- Organizations respond to uncertainty in one of four ways. (1) Defenders are expert at producing and selling narrowly defined products or services. (2) Prospectors focus on developing new products or services and in seeking out new markets, rather than waiting for things to happen. (3) Analyzers let other organizations take the risks of product development and marketing and then imitate (or perhaps slightly improve on) what seems to work best. (4) Reactors make adjustments only when finally forced to by environmental pressures.

5.2 Fundamentals of Planning

- An organization's reason for being is expressed in a mission statement. What the organization wishes to become and where it wants to go strategically—that is, its clear sense of the future and the actions needed to get there—are expressed in a vision statement.
- From these are derived strategic planning, then tactical planning, then operational planning. In strategic planning, managers determine what the organization's long-term goals should be for the next 1–10 years. In tactical planning, managers determine what contributions their departments or similar work units can make during the next 6–24 months. In operational planning, they determine how to accomplish specific tasks with available resources within the next 1–52 weeks.
- Whatever its type—strategic, tactical, or operational—the purpose of planning is to achieve a goal. A goal, also known as an objective, is a specific commitment to achieve a measurable result within a stated period of time. The goal should be followed by an action plan, which defines the course of action needed to achieve the stated goal. As with planning, goals are of the same three types—strategic, tactical, and operational.
- Strategic goals are set by and for top management and focus on objectives for the organization as a whole. Tactical goals are set by and for middle managers and focus on the actions needed to achieve strategic goals. Operational goals are set by and for first-line managers and are concerned with short-term matters associated with realizing tactical goals.
- The five characteristics of a good goal are represented by the acronym SMART. A SMART goal is one that is Specific, Measurable, Attainable, Results oriented, and has Target dates.

5.3 The Planning/Control Cycle

-  Once plans are made, managers must stay in control using the planning/control cycle, which has two planning steps (1 and 2) and two control steps (3 and 4), as follows: (1) Make the plan. (2) Carry out the plan. (3) Control the direction by comparing results with the plan. (4) Control the direction by taking corrective action in two ways—namely, (a) by correcting deviations in the plan being carried out, or (b) by improving future plans.

5.4 Promoting Goal Setting: Management by Objectives

-  Management by objectives (MBO) is a four-step process in which (1) managers and employees jointly set objectives for the employee, (2) managers develop action plans, (3) managers and employees periodically review the employee's performance, and (4) the manager makes a performance appraisal and rewards the employee according to results. The purpose of MBO is to *motivate* rather than control subordinates.
- For MBO to be successful three things have to happen. (1) The commitment of top management is essential. (2) The program must be applied organizationwide. (3) Objectives must cascade—becoming more specific at lower levels of the organization.

5.5 Project Planning

-  Tasks (work assignments) must be distinguished from programs and from projects. A task is simply something one does. A program is a single-use plan encompassing a range of projects or activities. A project, which appears between a task and a program, is a single-use plan of less scope and complexity than a program; it is a one-time set of events.
- Project planning is becoming the fastest way of getting things done. Project management works outside an organization's usual chain of command. An example of project planning is the skunkworks.
- A project evolves through a project life cycle involving four stages: (1) In the definition stage, a project manager looks at the big picture, stating the problem, identifying the project's goals and objectives, and determining the budget and schedule. (2) In the planning stage, managers consider the details needed to make the big picture happen, such as identifying equipment, people, and coordination efforts needed. (3) In the execution stage, the actual work stage, managers define the management style and establish the control tools, then ensure the work is being done on time and under budget. (4) In the closing stage, the project is accepted by the client.
- Deadlines are essential to project planning because they become great motivators both for the manager and for subordinates.

Management in Action

Companies Strive to Cascade Corporate Goals Down Their Organizations

Excerpted from Joe Mullich, "Get in Line," Workforce Management, *December 2003, pp. 44, 45, 46.*

"Often people in staff groups get assignments that maintain the bureaucracy, and they don't see how what they do on a daily basis affects the longer-range corporate goals," says [Robert] Coon, now vice president of human resources at Menlo Worldwide Logistics, a $4.9 billion supply-chain services firm in Redwood City, Calif. "By definition, the vision that the CEO has on top is never carried forward because people don't see that it affects their daily life." . . .

Experts agree that the best corporate messages and goals are clear and simple. "A company needs clear, elevating goals that people at all levels of the organization can understand and relate to," [Tony] Rucci says. [Rucci is executive vice president and chief administrative officer for Cardinal Health, Inc., of Dublin, Ohio.] "Whether a person is a CEO or a forklift operator in Detroit, they need to understand how what they do for their eight hours at work relates to that clear, elevating vision."

Cardinal Health's simple message revolves around four main goals: growth, operational excellence, leadership development, and customer focus. When employees put together their management-by-objective goals at the beginning of the year, they are each asked to identify at least one performance objective that supports each of those four main corporate goals. More important, managers are evaluated, rated, and given feedback on how they performed against those four strategic goals.

In addition, the managers are measured through a 360-degree survey, in which employees answer questions designed to rate their individual manager's performance in relation to the company's four core values as well as to a set of 10 core leadership competencies. The manager's scores on the 360-degree surveys are matched with the employee-satisfaction scores from the 13-question surveys. By combining the information from these surveys, Cardinal can show how management practices aimed at achieving the company's strategic goals lead to employee satisfaction and profits.

Experts agree that the goals must become more specific as they filter down from uppermost management to lower levels of the company. Employees at the functional levels need measurable feedback on a regular basis, even if it's a simple bar chart on what the department did that month. "The board of directors wouldn't accept the president's telling them, 'I think we're making progress, but I'll give you some details in a couple of months.' The board wants to see the numbers," Coon says. "However, it's just as important that the people at the functional levels see the numbers."

When Coon was corporate director of human resources for Conway Transportation, a $2 billion freight company in Ann Arbor, Mich., this kind of information was provided to every driver. The entire company was on a bonus plan based on profitability. The drivers were shown how their individual work—in terms of accidents, productivity, cost per shipment, time to delivery, damaged goods, and absenteeism—affected the company's goals and profits. "When a driver continued to be late with deliveries, his brethren asked what the problem was because it was affecting their bonuses," Coon says. In part because of this process of driving down vision, Conway Transportation became the most profitable company of its kind in America, and the largest non-union trucking company. . . .

Instilling the corporate vision takes a lot of work and even some proselytizing. Cardinal Health conducted a series of small "town hall meetings" with all of its 55,000 employees throughout the world to address the competitive environment in health care, the company's specific goals, and its financial and profit model. "Everything about how we communicate with people is designed to show how we create shareholder value, customer value, and employee value," Rucci says. At these meetings, employees were allowed to talk about what they thought were the core values of the company. This ensured that the employees truly believe in the corporate values, rather than think the company was artificially trying to promote a corporate culture that really didn't exist.

Menlo Logistics maintains a website where employees and customers are invited to send in stories about how the workers uphold the company's core values. Often these stories are related to employees' innovative solutions to customer problems. The website is fun to read, and everyone throughout the organization can see how workers are contributing to the company's goals.

"When you believe you have communicated the vision and goals sufficiently, you need to triple your efforts," Coon says. "You need to triple what your intuition tells you is enough, and only then do you get close to sending out the message."

And sometimes, managers simply have to get tough. Cardinal Health's Rucci says that every company will generally have three groups of employees: those who enthusiastically support the corporate goals, those who comply, and those who actively resist. "I spent the first 28 years of my 32-year management career trying to convert the bottom third," he says. "I wasted 28 years because rarely, if ever, do those people become committed. In retrospect, I should have spent 99% of my time with the people who get it, because they are the ones who drive change and innovation." He'd hold the bottom group more accountable sooner. "I'd tell them, 'Here's where we're going; you have six months to achieve this set of objectives. Either get on the bus or get off.'"

For Discussion

1. Why would goals become more specific as they are cascaded down an organization? Explain.
2. To what extent did Menlo Worldwide Logistics and Cardinal Health use the four-step MBO process?
3. Why do Robert Coon and Tony Rucci place so much importance on ensuring that employees understand their respective organizations' vision statements?
4. Use Figure 5.3 to explain why the goal-setting process at Conway Transportation worked so effectively.

Self-Assessment

Holland Personality Types & You: Matching Your Personality to the Right Work Environment & Occupation*

Objectives

1. To understand the need to plan for your career.
2. To try to match your personality with an occupation.

Introduction

What do you want to be when you grow up? Some people seem to know early in life. Others come to a realization in college. Still others may be forced to such awareness by a crisis in later life, such as being dismissed from a job. Of course, most of us make some sort of plans for our careers. But in doing so we may not always be knowledgeable about how to match our personalities with the choices available.

Instructions

There are four parts to this exercise.

First, select a number from the list of six personality types.

Second, match that choice with the personality you think that type would have.

Third, select the work environment you think would be best for that personality type and personality.

Fourth, based on the preceding three choices, select which occupation would fit best. (For example, if you selected #1, C, and f, the best fit for an occupation would be artist, musical conductor, and other related occupations.)

Try to connect each of the four parts and then check the key to see if your pairings are correct. After that, go through the list again, identifying what you think your personality type is, what your personality is, the work environment you like or think you would like best, and then the occupation that you would or do like best. See if there is an alignment by using the scoring guidelines and interpretation shown below; if there is such an alignment, this suggests you may be on your way to a successful career.

Personality Type

1. Artistic
2. Conventional
3. Realistic
4. Enterprising
5. Social
6. Investigative

Personality

A. Prefers to work with things; is present-oriented, athletic, and mechanical.

B. Is analytical, a problem solver, scientific, and original.

C. Relies on feelings and imagination, is expressive, is intuitive, and values esthetics.

D. Sensitive to needs of others, enjoys interpersonal gatherings, and values educational and social issues.

E. Adventurous, has leadership qualities, persuasive, and values political and economic matters.

F. Structured, accurate, detail-oriented, and loyal follower.

Work Environments

a. Technical/mechanical and industrial.

b. Traditional and rewards conformity and dependability.

c. Cooperative and rewards personal growth.

d. Managerial role in organizations and rewards monetary gains and achievements.

e. Rewards high academic achievement and uses technical abilities to complete tasks.

f. Unstructured and allows nonconformity and rewards creativity.

Occupations

7. Chemist/biological scientist, computer analyst, and emergency medical technician.
8. Lawyer, flight attendant, sales representative, reporter.
9. Accountant, bank teller, medical record technician.
10. Cook, drywall installer, auto mechanic.
11. Artist/commercial artist, musical director, architect, writer/editor.
12. Teacher, clergy, nurse, counselor, librarian.

Scoring Guidelines & Interpretation

Scoring is as follows:

1. 1-C-f-11
2. 2-F-b-9
3. 3-A-a-10
4. 4-E-d-8
5. 5-D-c-12
6. 6-B-e-7

The purpose of this type of exercise is to see how personality type, personality, work environment, and occupation can best fit together. When the elements mesh, you will usually feel more competent and more satisfied with your work conditions and occupation. When these elements or factors are mismatched, one can be very frustrated, feel incompetent, or not be good at one's job.

If you wish to know more about career planning, you can avail yourself of a much more in-depth planning process at *www.soice.state.nc.us/sociss/planning/jh-types.htm*.

Questions for Discussion

1. Does your assessment suggest that your career choice is best for your personality type? How do you feel about this assessment?

2. What do you think the management challenges are for those who are mismatched in their work? Explain.
3. Can you see and describe yourself more clearly in terms of personality type, personality, work environment, and occupation given the results of your scoring? Explain.

*Developed by Anne C. Cowden, Ph.D., based on the information provided by the website *www.soice.state.nc.us/sociss/planning/jh-types.htm.*

Group Exercise

Trying to Solve an "Electric" Problem in Managerial Planning*

Objectives

1. To assess a specific problem where planning is required.
2. To arrive at a mutual and effective solution as a group, taking into consideration different perspectives and different goals.

Introduction

Increasingly problems are being solved by groups of people, each with a different stake in the outcome. However, for a company to achieve its goals successfully, these problems must be solved without alienating members of the group.

Scenario

The company, a large processing center operating in a highly bureaucratic fashion, was experiencing challenging problems in a major division of its operations. Fifteen months earlier, when an electrical storm caused loss of power in one company building, five of the seven members of the night-shift *service staff* reported strange sensations emanating from their computer terminals causing tingling in their hands. In the following days, other staff members reported similar sensations, as well as numbness, headaches, and nausea. Two weeks later there were almost 100 reports of such "electrical shocks." Union representatives requested immediate action on the problems. The issues of workplace health and safety at the company became a hot topic in the local media. Various health and government agencies began to investigate.

Reports of the shocks continued sporadically for the next nine months, then began to rise significantly. During a 10-week period, there were more than 150 reports, many from people working in other parts of the company. The ensuing uproar produced a walkout lasting three days, costing the company an estimated $1 million in lost revenue. The problem didn't seem to be solvable simply by top managers' exercising their authority and dictating a solution. What could be done to get the company back on the right track?

Instructions

The class should divide into groups of seven people each. Within each group, each person should assume one of the roles described below. Take turns discussing the case from each of the seven perspectives, with each person staying within his or her role, until your group has solved the problem by consensus. The goal of the group is to arrive at a solution that will get the company moving efficiently and effectively again.

Roles: The Perspectives of the Positions Involved

1. **Senior management:** "We don't need this problem. We have to restore normal levels of control and efficiency, based on measured results."
2. **The ergonomists:** "There are some routine ergonomic problems that can be improved through the physical redesign of equipment. But there is no evidence of major health and safety problems."
3. **Labor leaders:** "This mess has got to be cleared up. The health and safety features are critical. Management has to take action, but we don't trust them. We are strong and can apply a lot of pressure if necessary."
4. **The politicians:** "We don't want more media coverage on this one and more charges of mismanagement that consume our time. We don't want the unions asking us to solve their problems."
5. **The service staff:** "We're working with a poor system. We don't want the strain and stress. Management has to sort the situation out. More stress breaks. Safer equipment. Find the 'techies' that are 'zapping us.'"
6. **The human resources people:** "The problem rests with the stressful nature of the work itself. We need to redesign the work process. We also need to deal with the collective stress phenomenon that's emerged."
7. **Line managers:** "The situation has changed on us. We're held accountable, but we don't have the power to deliver. We need to get better informed and to learn new skills for managing in a turbulent world."

Questions for Discussion

1. How did your group resolve the situation? Explain.
2. How did you feel, as you had to stay "in role" and respond from that position's perspective?

3. How difficult do you think it is it for people to see each other's perspectives and manage a situation? Explain.
4. How would you manage people who are in conflict about a situation such as the one presented above? Describe.

*Written by Anne C. Cowden, Ph.D.; adapted from a case in Gareth Morgan, *Imaginization: The Art of Creative Management* (Newbury Park, Calif.: Sage, 1993), Chapter 5.

Ethical Dilemma

Should PricewaterhouseCoopers Pass on Rebates to Its Customers?

Excerpted from Jonathan Weil, "Disputed Discounts: Court Files Offer Inside Look at Pricewaterhouse Billing Clash," The Wall Street Journal, *January 5, 2004, p. A1.*

Assume you are the CEO from PricewaterhouseCoopers, and Neal Roberts brings the following information to your attention.

In early 2000, Neal A. Roberts discovered that his employer, PricewaterhouseCoopers LLP, was pocketing millions of dollars a year from what he considered to be a dubious billing gimmick: the accounting giant obtained large rebates on airline tickets used for client business but didn't pass along the savings to its clients. Travel expenses had become an undisclosed source of profits at PricewaterhouseCoopers, and unknowing clients paid the tab.

Solving the Dilemma

As the CEO of PricewaterhouseCoopers, what would you do?

1. Keep the rebates. Inform all employees of the practice and explain that you support this policy because the rebates offset other administrative costs, such as the cost to run your travel department. Further, if you don't do this, then the company will have to charge clients higher hourly rates.
2. Because it would be impractical and difficult to retroactively refund all your clients, keep the rebates the company has already received but initiate a new policy passing future rebates on to clients.
3. Disclosure is important. Inform your clients of the practice, and explain that the rebates offset other costs (for example, running your travel department) and this practice allows you to bill them at a lower hourly rate.
4. Invent other options. Discuss.

Video Case

The Dale Grey Story

The Dale Grey Story starts in Denver, Colorado. In 1983 Dale started Grey & Associates with two weeks' vacation pay (but no associates). Today, the company has evolved into Communication Services and employs over 100 people in six offices and is one of the top 20 companies in telecommunications infrastructure development.

For 17 years now, Grey has enjoyed being an entrepreneur. A turning point came when, as a young man, Grey's boss asked him to slow down his work production because he was outshining the other employees. Grey soon recognized a personal desire and a passion that he didn't see in other people, and he decided that he needed to build his own company. Almost two decades later, he's still excited to work in an environment that's fun, challenging, and profitable.

Grey's initial goal was to build a million-dollar company. After successfully attaining this goal, he and his employees held an off-site planning retreat to determine the company's future goals and direction. Grey and his team considered a number of factors, including what the company was doing right, necessary changes, and the future of the industry. The group articulated and recorded a company vision and decided they wanted to be a 10-million-dollar company by the year 2005 (which they accomplished early).

Like most entrepreneurs, Grey initially shouldered all the workload himself. However, his proudest accomplishment is being just another member of the team. As the name of the company evolved from "Grey & Associates" to "Grey Communications" and finally to "Communication Services," clients relied less and less on Grey and more on the capable talents of company employees. Thus, Grey became "just part of the team," which suits him just fine.

According to Grey, self-confidence is the most important quality of a successful entrepreneur. Even though there are hundreds of opportunities to fail, an entrepreneur must see only the certainty of success. The most difficult aspect of being an entrepreneur is learning the business skills that do not initially interest one or that one does not feel strong in. For example, in the beginning, the company didn't have a business plan (and wasn't required to create one, since the business grew using internally generated profits). However, as the firm grew larger, it became necessary to create the business plan simply to understand how the organization ran and to meet financial expectations and staffing requirements.

Staffing was a critical element in building a successful company. According to Grey, the key is to find people who have the same passion and energy for the organization as he does. Next, training should be viewed as an investment in both the Communication Services team members and the industry as a whole. Finally, Grey respects the need for a balance between work and home life. Although he expects his employees to work hard in the workplace, he knows that they need time with family and friends to rejuvenate and recharge. After all, Grey and his team are prepared for a marathon, not a short race.

Discussion Questions

1. Experts classify uncertainty as three different types: state, effect, and response. Define each of these types. At the planning retreat held by Grey and his colleagues, the group attempted to predict the direction of the telecommunications industry. Which type of uncertainty does this represent?
2. At the off-site planning retreat, were Grey and his team developing strategic, tactical, or operational goals?
3. According to Dale Grey, what is the most critical quality for a successful entrepreneur? What is the most difficult aspect of being an entrepreneur?

chapter 6

Strategic Management

How Star Managers Realize a Grand Design

MAJOR QUESTIONS YOU SHOULD BE ABLE TO ANSWER

6.1 The Dynamics of Strategic Planning

Major Question: Am I really managing if I don't have a strategy?

6.2 The Strategic-Management Process

Major Question: What's the five-step recipe for the strategic-management process?

6.3 Establishing the Grand Strategy

Major Question: How can SWOT and forecasting help me establish my strategy?

6.4 Formulating Strategy

Major Question: How can two techniques—Porter's competitive strategies and the product life cycle—help me formulate strategy?

6.5 Carrying Out & Controlling Strategy

Major Question: How can two techniques—balanced scorecard and measurement management—help me carry out and control strategy?

the manager's toolbox

What Does the Successful Top Manager Do to Stay Successful?

Management tools and techniques, says Darrell K. Rigby, a director of global business consulting firm Bain & Co., "are to some extent fashion items," becoming popular or unpopular as intellectual and economic currents change.[1]

One year the big buzz words may be *reengineering* or *activity-based costing,* according to Rigby, who prepares Bain's annual Management Tools & Trends survey of the use of and satisfaction with the most popular management tools. Another year may favor *customer relationship management* or *contingency planning.* But "management tools are not silver bullets," says Rigby. "They are more like chain saws—potentially powerful when applied to the right problems but extraordinarily dangerous in the wrong hands."

There seem to be two lessons here:

- **Lesson #1—In an era of management fads, strategic planning is still tops:** Over the years, some tools still retain their popularity. The most recent study found that the most widely used management tools in 2002 were the same as those in 2000 (and to some extent in 1998)—namely, *strategic planning, mission and vision statements,* and *benchmarking.* Each of these three tools was used by more than 80% of the 6,300 executives surveyed in over 60 countries.[2] Strategic planning, discussed in this chapter, is concerned with developing a comprehensive program for long-term success. Mission statements describe the organization's purpose, and vision statements describe its intended long-term goal. Benchmarking is a technique in which a company's performance is compared with that of high-performing organizations.
- **Lesson #2—A manager's most valuable character trait: be willing to make large, painful decisions to suddenly alter strategy:** But there's another lesson. In a world of rapid and discontinuous change, managers must always be prepared to make large, painful decisions and radically alter their business design—the very basis of how the company makes money. Today, say two consultants with Boston's Mercer Management Consulting, "a static business model is death."[3]

Intel, for example, used to make memory chips. When that began to look like a hypercompetitive commodity business (a commodity is a mass-produced, unspecialized product), Intel switched to making processor chips. When processors were threatened with becoming commodities, it began marketing them as branded consumer products ("Intel Inside!").[4] Later it focused on making chips for communications and consumer electronics—the chips that power everything. And recently it has become one of the prime backers of high-speed wireless technologies, including Wi-Fi (which can cover a few hundred feet) and WiMax (which has a range up to 30 miles).[5] Because of fast-spreading world conditions such as the threat of products becoming commodities, rapidly increasing productivity, and global overcapacity, managers must be able to make difficult decisions: "exiting businesses, firing people, admitting you were wrong (or at least not omniscient)," as writer Geoffrey Colvin puts it. "So the future will demand ever more people with the golden trait, the fortitude to accept and even seek psychic pain."[6]

Many managers think they can make painful decisions about things that obviously need doing. But, Colvin points out, "those with the far greater courage to make unpleasant decisions based on what they see that *no one else sees*—these people will dominate." These decisions are at the very heart of strategic management.

forecast

What's Ahead in This Chapter

We describe strategic management and strategic planning and why they're important. We go through the five steps in the strategic-management process. Then we show how grand strategy is developed, using two strategic-planning tools—SWOT analysis and forecasting. Next we show how strategy is formulated, using such techniques as Porter's four competitive strategies, product life cycles, single-product versus diversification strategies, and competitive intelligence. Finally, we show how strategy is carried out and controlled.

major question **Am I really managing if I don't have a strategy?**

The Big Picture

This section distinguishes among strategy, strategic management, and strategic planning. We describe three reasons why strategic management and strategic planning are important and how they may work for both large and small firms.

Is thinking strategically really necessary?

After all, in the 1970s and 1980s, Japanese companies rarely developed strategic positions. Instead, they pioneered in what is known as *operational effectiveness,* which means they learned to perform *similar* activities *better* than rivals performed them. Through such practices as total quality management and continuous improvement, Japanese manufacturers gained substantial cost and quality advantages, and for many years they appeared unstoppable.

But most Japanese companies try to imitate one another, so that competitors match one another's plant designs, employ the same distribution channels, and offer most of the same product features and varieties. In the 1990s, as the gap narrowed in operational effectiveness, these companies found themselves engaged in mutually destructive battles. Now they have had to learn strategic positioning—that is, to perform activities that are *different* from those of their rivals or similar activities that are performed in *different* ways.

In this section, we do the following:

- Define strategy and strategic management,
- Explain why strategic planning is important,
- Discuss strategic management in large versus small firms.

Operational effectiveness, not strategic effectiveness. Japanese makers of television sets have been more apt to imitate one another than do strategic planning. When you buy a TV set made in Japan, do you see any difference among those made by Sony, Toshiba, and Panasonic?

practical action

How to Streamline Meetings

"Beware of designing a planning process that requires 40 hours of meetings if your staff or board cannot realistically make the time commitment," advises Bryan W. Barry. "Frustration and failure can result. Effective strategic planning can be done in 10 to 15 hours of meeting time, with good preparation between meetings."[27]

Meetings are a fact of management life—one study of 299 managers found they spent half their time in meetings.[28] If you're not in a position to call meetings but have to attend them regularly, it is frustrating to have to be a victim of a poorly run meeting.

In one survey, 50% of workers at big companies said they had attended a meeting where at least one participant fell asleep.[29] (At smaller companies, where it is harder to hide, the figure was 26%.) Problem meetings can result from a lack of focus, nobody watching the clock, and no leader to keep the meeting on track.[30] Patrick Lencioni, author of *Death by Meeting,* believes one reason meetings are so ineffective is that top executives discourage conflict.[31] But that tactic backfires, he says, because it makes meetings boring and ignores crucial issues.[32]

As a participant, you can always pull an off-track conversation back by saying, for example, "We were discussing the 2006 budget, but now we seem to be discussing the shortfalls of last year." Or you can try making a summary of a series of comments to prevent others from covering the same ground again. If you're constantly exposed to ineffective meetings, you can also offer your assistance to the meeting leader in creating an agenda, with time frames attached for each item, suggests productivity specialist Odette Pollar. She adds: "Your approach, timing, and tone of voice are important. You must avoid appearing to tell the person what to do."[33]

If you're leading meetings, here are three good ways to streamline them:[34]

Eliminate Unnecessary Meetings & Meeting Attendance Don't call a meeting if the same result can be accomplished in some other way: phone call, e-mail, memo, one-on-one visit, and so on. Invite only people who need to attend, and let them know they need stay for only those parts of the meeting that concern them. Hold the meeting in a place where distractions will be minimal. Consider using telephone conferencing or videoconferencing.

Distribute an Action Agenda in Advance Do your homework about the issues. Prepare a list of meeting objectives, topics to be covered and the number of minutes allowed for discussion, and information participants should bring. Organize the topics with the most important ones first. Distribute this agenda a day or more in advance, if possible. For informal meetings, phone conversations, and one-on-one appointments, make a list of items to cover.

Stay in Control of the Meeting Start on time and stay within the time frame of the agenda items. (Coffee breaks, lunchtime, or quitting time provide built-in limits.) Reserve judgments and conclusions until after discussion so that everyone will feel free to give their input. Don't allow a few members to monopolize the discussion. Encourage silent members to participate. Try to reach a decision or make an assignment for every item. Use two notepads or pieces of paper, one for general notes, the other for tasks and assignments. Summarize the highlights at the end of the meeting. Map out a timetable for actions to be taken.

Do Follow-Up After the meeting, type up tasks and assignments for distribution. Set a date for a follow-up meeting to assess progress.

Virtual meeting. Videoconference rooms are operated by many big companies, but users can also rent these sites at Kinko's. Videoconferencing etiquette may take some getting used to: Introduce yourself with a nod or wave. Sit still (rocking in your chair blurs the video). Don't yell (microphones are sensitive). Don't shuffle papers or whisper (everything gets amplified in a video call). Don't doodle, yawn, or eat pizza (everyone can see you).

major question **How can SWOT and forecasting help me establish my strategy?**

The Big Picture

To develop a grand strategy, you need to gather data and make projections, using the tools of SWOT analysis and forecasting.

The first part in developing a grand strategy, Step 2 of the five-step strategic management process, is intelligence gathering—internally and externally. The next part is to make some projections.

Two kinds of strategic-planning tools and techniques are (1) *SWOT analysis* and (2) *forecasting*—trend analysis and contingency planning.

SWOT Analysis

The starting point in establishing a grand strategy is often a ***SWOT analysis*** **—also known as *a situational analysis*—which is a search for the Strengths, Weaknesses, Opportunities, and Threats affecting the organization.** A SWOT analysis should provide you with a realistic understanding of your organization in relation to its internal and external environments so you can better formulate strategy in pursuit of its mission. *(See Figure 6.2.)*

FIGURE 6.2
SWOT analysis. SWOT stands for Strengths, Weaknesses, Opportunities, Threats.

INSIDE MATTERS—analysis of internal Strengths & Weaknesses

S—Strengths: inside matters
Strengths could be work processes, organization, culture, staff, product quality, production capacity, image, financial resources & requirements, service levels, other internal matters

W—Weaknesses: inside matters
Weaknesses could be in the same categories as stated for Strengths: work processes, organization, culture, etc.

O—Opportunities: outside matters
Opportunities could be market segment analysis, industry & competition analysis, impact of technology on organization, product analysis, governmental impacts, other external matters

T—Threats: outside matters
Threats could be in the same categories as stated for Opportunities: market segment analysis, etc.

OUTSIDE MATTERS—analysis of external Opportunities & Threats

The SWOT analysis is divided into two parts: inside matters and outside matters—that is, an analysis of *internal strengths and weaknesses* and an analysis of *external opportunities and threats.*

Inside Matters: Analysis of Internal Strengths & Weaknesses

Does your organization have a skilled workforce? a superior reputation? strong financing? These are examples of ***organizational strengths*** **—the skills and capabilities that give the organization special competencies and competitive advantages in executing strategies in pursuit of its mission.**

Or does your organization have obsolete technology? outdated facilities? a shaky marketing operation? These are examples of ***organizational weaknesses*** **—the drawbacks that hinder an organization in executing strategies in pursuit of its mission.**

Outside Matters: Analysis of External Opportunities & Threats

Is your organization fortunate to have weak rivals? emerging markets? a booming economy? These are instances of ***organizational opportunities*** **—environmental factors that the organization may exploit for competitive advantage.**

Alternatively, is your organization having to deal with new regulations? a shortage of resources? substitute products? These are some possible ***organizational threats*** **—environmental factors that hinder an organization's achieving a competitive advantage.**

Example

SWOT Analysis: How Would You Analyze Starbucks Coffee?

If you were presently a manager for Starbucks Corp., what would be the kinds of things you would identify in a SWOT analysis?[35]

First, the internal *Strengths:* No small part of the company's success is based on the loyalty of the staff—most of whom are young (average age: 26) and 85% of whom have some education beyond high school—which Starbucks calls "partners." Because the company offers above-average pay for food service, health insurance for all, stock options, and channels such as e-mail for employee feedback, partners feel quite involved with the company, and turnover is half the industry average. Employees receive painstaking training in the art of making a high-quality cup of coffee, handling coffee beans and equipment, and dealing with customers. Following a McDonald's-like strategy, Starbucks has been breaking into new markets, opening retail stores throughout the country and the world, expanding into different retail channels such as supermarkets, bookstores, and airports. The payoff: Starbucks revenues continue to climb at above 20% a year, and the stock went up 3,028% from 1992 to 2003.[36]

Second, the internal *Weaknesses:* To be able to charge $1.75 for a cup instead of 50 cents, Starbucks's focus has been to turn coffee—traditionally an inexpensive commodity-type product—into a premium-placed brand, imitating Coca-Cola's strategy of getting people to think "Coke" versus plain old "cola." But if customers are to continue to pay top dollar for specialty coffee, Starbucks can't slip on quality and service. Thus, complaints about "tepid coffee, gruff employees, long waits" in New York can't be ignored. Nor can press accounts expressing disappointment in the company's new food ventures. In addition, the company can't allow itself to be distracted from its core business. In early 1999, for example, CEO Howard Schultz became infatuated with the Internet and began aggressively pursuing a Web e-commerce strategy; as a result of taking his eye off the ball, the company suffered an earnings shortfall, which caused the price of the stock to drop. *(continued)*

Third, the external *Opportunities:* Other chains—Boston Chicken, Rainforest Café, Planet Hollywood—have found the restaurant business tough sledding. But the fact that Starbucks has extremely loyal customers (another Strength) gives the company an Opportunity. Many of the aforementioned theme restaurants were done in because they couldn't get customers to return after the novelty wore off. Moreover, it's been pointed out that coffee is not a fad but rather "the last socially acceptable addiction." Starbucks is also fortunate to have numerous overseas opportunities such as Asia. Indeed, it is even invading Europe, despite Europe's age-old coffee culture.

Fourth, the external *Threats:* Specialty-coffee companies like Starbucks account for only 12% of the coffee roasted in the United States. Most coffee is bought in supermarkets and is dominated by Folgers, Maxwell House, Taster's Choice, and Hills Bros. In years past, they could have turned coffee into either a special beverage, as Starbucks has done, or a drink with mass appeal, like Coke and Pepsi, but they did neither. Instead, they got into price wars with one another, and to cut costs they gradually reduced the quality of coffee. And in fighting one another, they ignored the biggest threat to their industry: soda pop. The result: the coffee industry lost a generation of consumers, who were wooed away by the aggressive marketing of soft drinks. Starbucks is also a victim of its own success, so that in some areas when it moves into a new neighborhood and displaces existing coffee shops it is viewed as a Darth Vader-like corporate giant. A possible recent threat is the Fair Trade coffee movement.

Threat to Starbucks? Coffee that is Fair Trade Certified tries to guarantee peasant coffee farmers more profit—perhaps three or four times as much—by cutting out several middlemen importers, of which Starbucks is one. This approach appeals to many socially conscious consumers.

Forecasting: Predicting the Future

Once they've analyzed their organization's Strengths, Weaknesses, Opportunities, and Threats, planners need to do forecasting for making long-term strategy. **A *forecast* is a vision or projection of the future.**

Lots of people make predictions, of course—and often they are wrong. In the 1950s, the head of IBM, Thomas J. Watson, estimated that the demand for computers would never exceed more than five for the entire world. In the late 1990s, many computer experts predicted power outages, water problems, transportation disruptions, bank shutdowns, and far worse because of computer glitches (the "Y2K bug") associated with the change from year 1999 to 2000.

Of course, the farther into the future one makes a prediction, the more difficult it is to be accurate, especially in matters of technology. Yet forecasting is a necessary part of planning.

Two types of forecasting are *trend analysis* and *contingency planning.*

Trend Analysis

A *trend analysis* is a hypothetical extension of a past series of events into the future.[37] The basic assumption is that the picture of the present can be projected into the future. This is not a bad assumption, if you have enough historical data, but it is always subject to surprises. And if your data is unreliable, it will produce erroneous trend projections.

An example of trend analysis is a time-series forecast, which predicts future data based on patterns of historical data. Time-series forecasts are used to predict long-term trends, cyclic patterns (as in the up-and-down nature of the business cycle), and seasonal variations (as in Christmas sales versus summer sales).

Contingency Planning: Predicting Alternative Futures

***Contingency planning*—also known *as scenario planning* and *scenario analysis*—is the creation of alternative hypothetical but equally likely future**

conditions. The scenarios present alternative combinations of different factors—different economic pictures, different strategies by competitors, different budgets, and so on.

Because the scenarios try to peer far into the future—perhaps five or more years—they are necessarily written in rather general terms. Nevertheless, the great value of contingency planning is that it not only equips an organization to prepare for emergencies and uncertainty, it also gets managers thinking strategically. ◆

Example

Contingency Planning: Southwest Airlines Uses Hedging to Hold Down Price of Aviation Fuel

In mid-2004, when the price of crude oil hit 20-year highs ($41 a barrel), the cost of jet fuel threatened to take a big bite out of airline profits, which were only beginning to return after a prolonged financial downturn. Jet fuel makes up as much as 15% of an airline's operating costs, the second biggest expense after labor.[38]

Some airlines tried to pass the extra cost along to passengers by raising fares on some routes. Low-cost carriers such as Southwest, JetBlue, and America West, however, were better able to weather the fuel price increase without raising seat prices. Southwest Airlines, for example, is in better shape than many larger competitors because it has done effective contingency planning—by hedging the rise of fuel prices in the futures market. Airlines hedge fuel price increases by locking in contracts that allow them to buy fuel at a fixed price. Southwest and JetBlue are in a better position to buy favorable futures contracts because of their financial strengths: they avoid expensive labor contracts, operate only one or two types of aircraft, and fly high-traffic routes.[39]

Thus, Southwest savings from hedges were expected to be around $240 million in 2004, according to its chief financial officer, Gary Kelly. "You probably wouldn't go without health care insurance, you wouldn't go without liability and collision insurance for your automobile," Kelly said. "We view this the same way."[40]

Fuel proof. Locking in the price of jet fuel with long-term contracts with suppliers, a form of contingency planning, has put low-cost airlines such as Southwest and JetBlue in a competitive position with rivals in controlling costs.

major question

How can two techniques—Porter's competitive strategies and the product life cycle—help me formulate strategy?

The Big Picture

Strategy formulation makes use of several concepts. Here we discuss Porter's four competitive strategies, the four-stage product life cycle, diversification and synergy, and competitive intelligence.

After the grand strategy has been determined (Step 2 in the strategic-management process), it's time to turn to strategy formulation (Step 3). Examples of techniques that can be used to formulate strategy are *Porter's four competitive strategies,* the *product life cycle, diversification and synergy,* and *competitive intelligence.*

Porter's Four Competitive Strategies

Harvard Business School professor **Michael Porter** "is the single most important strategist working today, and maybe of all time," raves Kevin Coyne of consulting firm McKinsey & Co.[41]

Is this high praise deserved? Certainly Porter's status as a leading authority on competitive strategy is unchallenged. The Strategic Management Society, for instance, voted him the most influential living strategist.

Porter's reputation stems from work during the 1980s in which he suggested that five forces affect industry competition. They are (1) threats of new entrants, (2) bargaining power of suppliers, (3) bargaining power of buyers, (4) threats of substitute products or services, and (5) rivalry or jockeying for position among industry firms.[42] An organization should do a good SWOT analysis that examines these five competitive forces, Porter felt. Then it was in a position to formulate effective strategy, using what he identified as four competitive strategies.

Porter's four competitive strategies **(also called *four generic strategies*) are (1) cost-leadership, (2) differentiation, (3) cost-focus, and (4) focused-differentiation.**[43] The first two strategies focus on *wide* markets, the last two on *narrow* markets. *(See Figure 6.3.)* Time Warner, which produces lots of media and publications, serves wide markets around the world. Your neighborhood video store serves a narrow market of just local customers.

FIGURE 6.3
Porter's four competitive strategies

Strategy	Type of market targeted: Wide	Narrow
1. Cost-leadership	√	
2. Differentiation	√	
3. Cost-focus		√
4. Focused-differentiation		√

Let's look at these four strategies.

1 Cost-Leadership Strategy: Keeping Costs & Prices Low for a Wide Market

The *cost-leadership strategy* is to keep the costs, and hence prices, of a product or service below those of competitors and to target a wide market.

This puts the pressure on R&D managers to develop products or services that can be created cheaply, production managers to reduce production costs, and marketing managers to reach a wide variety of customers as inexpensively as possible.

Firms implementing the cost-leadership strategy include computer maker Dell, watch maker Timex, hardware retailer Home Depot, and pen maker Bic.

2 Differentiation Strategy: Offering Unique & Superior Value for a Wide Market

The *differentiation strategy* is to offer products or services that are of unique and superior value compared to those of competitors but to target a wide market.

Because products are expensive, managers may have to spend more on R&D, marketing, and customer service. This is the strategy followed by Ritz-Carlton hotels and the makers of Lexus automobiles.

The strategy is also pursued by companies trying to create *brands* to differentiate themselves from competitors. Although Pepsi may cost only cents more than a supermarket's own house brand of cola, PepsiCo. spends millions on ads.

3 Cost-Focus Strategy: Keeping Costs & Prices Low for a Narrow Market

The *cost-focus strategy* is to keep the costs, and hence prices, of a product or service below those of competitors and to target a narrow market.

This is a strategy you often see executed with low-end products sold in discount stores, such as low-cost beer or cigarettes, or with regional gas stations, such as the Terrible Herbst or Rotten Robbie chains in parts of the West.

Needless to say, the pressure on managers to keep costs down is even more intense than it is with those in cost-leadership companies.

4 Focused-Differentiation Strategy: Offering Unique & Superior Value for a Narrow Market

The *focused-differentiation strategy* is to offer products or services that are of unique and superior value compared to those of competitors and to target a narrow market.

Some luxury cars are so expensive—Rolls-Royce, Ferrari, Lamborghini—that only a few car buyers can afford them. Other companies following the strategy are jeweler Cartier and shirtmaker Turnbull & Asser. Yet focused-differentiation products need not be expensive. The publisher Chelsea Green has found success with niche books, such as *The Straw Bale House.*

Focused differentiation. The auto industry has been rolling out new models of cars at prices unheard of only a few years ago. BMW, Audi, Mercedes, and even Volkswagen now market several models in the $100,000–$200,000 range. This Volkswagen 420-horsepower Phaeton sedan, for instance, retails for $102,000. Unlike Rolls-Royce and Lamborghini, however, these are production-line models, not handmade "super-car" collectibles costing a quarter million dollars. The biggest selling point is power.

The Product Life Cycle: Different Stages Require Different Strategies

In Chapter 5, we described a *project* life cycle. A *product* life cycle has a similar curve (although the end is usually not quite so abrupt). **A *product life cycle* is a model that graphs the four stages that a product or a service goes through during the "life" of its marketability: (1) introduction, (2) growth, (3) maturity, and (4) decline.** *(See Figure 6.4.)*

FIGURE 6.4
The product life cycle. Managers can use this cycle to create strategies appropriate to each stage.

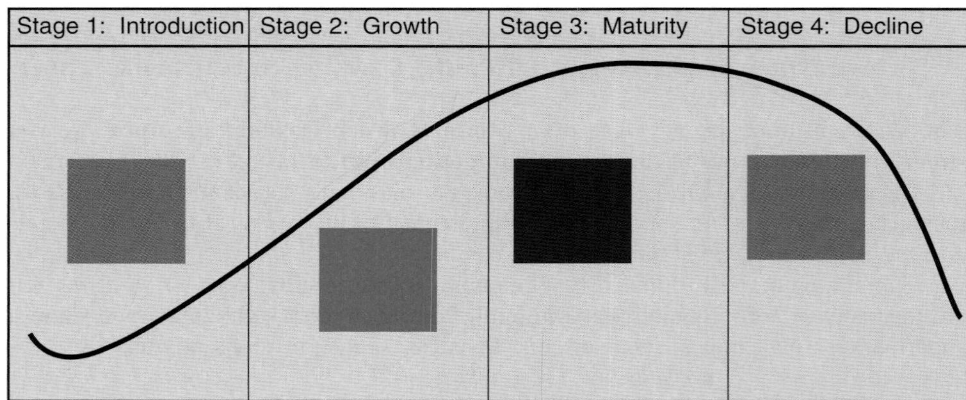

Some products, such as faddish toys or collectibles (for example, Beanie Babies), may have a life cycle of only months or a year or so. Others, such as a shopping center, may have a life cycle equivalent to a human generation (about 30 years) before they begin to decline and need to be redesigned for fresh appeal and modern sensibilities.

For you as a manager it's useful to know about the concept of product life cycle because different strategies—such as those advanced by Michael Porter—can be used to support different products or services in different stages of the cycle. Let's look at these stages.

Stage 1 Introduction—Getting the Product to Market

The *introduction stage* is the stage in the product life cycle in which a new product is introduced into the marketplace.

This is the stage that is heavy on startup costs for production, marketing, and distribution. Managers have to concentrate on building inventory and staff without loss of quality. With sales usually low during this period, the product is probably losing the company money.

There is also the huge risk that the product may be rejected. Following the smashing reception of the original Apple II (and II-Plus) personal computer, for example, Apple Computer introduced the Lisa—which was a good deal less than a resounding success. Fortunately for Apple, the Lisa evolved into the company's best-selling Macintosh.

During the introduction stage, one should, to use a military analogy, follow a strategy of infiltration. A differentiation or a focus (cost-focus or focused-differentiation) strategy may be appropriate.

Stage 2 Growth—Demand Increases

The *growth stage,* which is the most profitable stage, is the period in which customer demand increases, the product's sales grow, and (later) competitors may enter the market.

At the start, the product may have the marketplace to itself and demand for it may be high. Managers need to worry about getting sufficient product into the distribution pipeline, maintaining quality, and expanding the sales and distribution effort.

This phase may go on for years. But all the while, competitors will be scrambling to enter the market. "For 40 years, all we had to do was open restaurants," said McDonald's CEO Jack Greenberg in 1999. "That's not enough anymore."[44] The reason: the competition has become fierce, with other fast-food giants spending millions on promotions.

During the growth stage, managers would advance their attack, probably continuing Stage 1 differentiation or focus strategies.

Stage 3 Maturity—Growth Slows

The *maturity stage* is the period in which the product starts to fall out of favor and sales and profits begin to fall off.

In this phase, sales start to decline as competition makes inroads. At this point, managers need to concentrate on reducing costs and instituting efficiencies to maintain the product's profitability. Sometimes they can extend the life of the product by tinkering with its various features.

McDonald's CEO Greenberg, for instance, put a lid on domestic growth, opening only 92 new restaurants in 1998 compared to 1,130 in 1995, and he laid off 525 employees. He also introduced a $350 million cooking system that allows food to be served fresher and hotter. He increased international expansion, so that 90% of the new stores opened in 1999 were outside the U.S.[45] His successor, James Cantalupo, concentrated on improving the menu (offering entrée salads and McGriddle breakfast sandwiches) and service, trying to draw more diners to existing outlets rather than building more restaurants.[46]

During the maturity stage, managers would become more defensive, perhaps using a cost-leadership or focus strategy.

Stage 4 Decline—Withdrawing from the Market

The *decline stage* is the period in which the product falls out of favor, and the organization withdraws from the marketplace.

In this stage, the product falls out of favor, and managers sound the bugle for retreat, scaling down relevant inventory, supplies, and personnel.

While this phase may mean withdrawal of support for the old product, it doesn't necessarily mean a complete shutdown for the organization. Much of the same expertise will be required to support new products.

Hismanal was a once-promising prescription antihistamine drug for Johnson & Johnson, but the company announced its discontinuation in 1999. "This was a voluntary decision in response to a marketplace crowded with alternatives," said a company spokesman.

Hismanal was one of the first prescription antihistamines that did not cause drowsiness, but later it was found to produce heart problems when taken with other drugs.[47]

What stage in the life cycle? This shopping center clearly has seen better days. Do you think a shopping center could be built that would last 100 years?

Single-Product Strategy versus Diversification Strategy

You might begin to see why, with the birth-to-death stages of the product life cycle, a company needs to think about whether to have a *single-product strategy* or a *diversification strategy*. After all, if you have only one product to sell, what do you do if that product fails?

The Single-Product Strategy: Focused but Vulnerable

In a *single-product strategy,* a company makes and sells only one product within its market. This is the kind of strategy you see all the time as you drive past the small retail businesses in a small town: there may be one shop that sells only flowers, one that sells only security systems, and so on. It's also a strategy used by some bigger companies. For instance, Indian Motorcycle Company, which was once a worthy rival to Harley-Davidson, sold only motorcycles.

The single-product strategy has both positives and negatives:

- **The benefit—focus:** Making just one product allows you to focus your manufacturing and marketing efforts just on that product. This means that your company can become savvy about repairing defects, upgrading production lines, scouting the competition, and doing highly focused advertising and sales. See's Candies, for instance, is a San Francisco–based chain of 200 stores throughout the West that specializes in making boxed chocolates—something it does so well that when it was acquired by Berkshire Hathaway, its corporate owner chose not to tamper with success and runs it with a "hands-off" policy.
- **The risk—vulnerability:** The risk, of course, is that if you do *not* focus on all aspects of the business, if a rival gets the jump on you, or if an act of God intervenes (for a florist, roses suffer a blight right before Mother's Day), your entire business may go under. For instance, in 2003, Gilroy, Calif.–based Indian Motorcycle went bankrupt a second time (it went under in 1953, too) because it was unable to focus on meeting its projected production targets.[48]

The Diversification Strategy: Operating Different Businesses to Spread the Risk

The obvious answer to the risks of a single-product strategy is ***diversification,*** **operating several businesses in order to spread the risk.** You see this at the small retailer level when you drive past a store that sells gas *and* food *and* souvenirs *and* rents videotape and DVD movies. Big companies do it, too: all the major entertainment/media companies, such as Disney, Time Warner, and Sony, run different divisions specializing in television, music, publishing, and the like (a divisional structure we explain further in Chapter 8).

There are two kinds of diversification—*unrelated* and *related.*

Unrelated Diversification: Independent Business Lines If you operate a small shop that sells flowers on one side and computers on the other, you are exercising a strategy of ***unrelated diversification*** **—operating several businesses under one ownership that are not related to one another.** This has been a common big-company strategy in the recent past. General Electric, for instance, which began by making lighting products, diversified into such unrelated areas as plastics, broadcasting, and financial services (a so-called conglomerate structure that we discuss in Chapter 8).

Related Diversification: Related Business Lines In some parts of the world you have to do all your grocery shopping in separate stores—the butcher, the baker, the green grocer, and so on. In most U.S. grocery stores, all these businesses appear under the same roof, an example of the strategy of ***related diversification,*** **in which an organization under one ownership operates separate businesses that are related to one another.** The famous British raincoat maker Burberry, for instance, started by making and marketing outerwear clothing but since then has expanded into related business lines, including accessories such as umbrellas, children's clothing, and even fragrances, which it sells in its own stores.

Related diversification has three advantages:

- **Reduced risk—because more than one product:** Unlike Indian Motorcycles, Burberry is able to reduce its risks. During seasons when rainwear sales are slow, for instance, Burberry's economic risk is reduced by sales of other product lines.
- **Management efficiencies—administration spread over several businesses:** Whatever the business, it usually has certain obligatory administrative costs—accounting, legal, taxes, and so on. Burberry need not have separate versions of these for each business line. Rather, it can actually save money by using the same administrative services for all its businesses.
- **Synergy—the sum is greater than the parts:** When a company has special strengths in one business, it can apply those to its other related businesses—as PepsiCo, for instance, can do in marketing not only Pepsi Cola but also 7-Up and Mountain Dew. This is an example of ***synergy*** **—the economic value of separate, related businesses under one ownership and management is greater together than the businesses are worth separately.**

Competitive Intelligence

Regardless of the kind of diversification (or lack of) a company may have, if it is to survive it must keep track of what its competitors are doing—what is known as competitive intelligence. Practicing ***competitive intelligence*** **means gaining information about one's competitors' activities so that you can anticipate their moves and react appropriately.** If you are a manager, one of your worst nightmares is that a competitor will come out with a service or product—whether it's boutique beer to a major brewer or mountain bikes to a major bicycle maker—that will revolutionize the market and force you to try to play catch-up, if indeed that's even possible.

Gaining competitive intelligence isn't always easy, but there are several avenues—and, surprisingly, most of them are public sources. These include the following:

- **The public prints and advertising:** A product may be worked on in secret for several years, but at some point it becomes subject to announcement—through a press release, advertising piece, news leak, or the like. Much of this is available free through the Internet or by subscription to certain specialized databases, such as Nexus, which contains hundreds of thousands of news stories.
- **Investor information:** Information about new products and services may also be available through the reports filed with the Securities and Exchange Commission and through corporate annual reports.
- **Informal sources:** People in the computer industry every year look forward to major trade shows, as Comdex in Las Vegas has been, when companies roll out their new products. At such times, people also engage in industry-gossip conversation to find out about future directions. Finally, salespeople and marketers, who are out calling on corporate clients, may return with tidbits of information about what competitors are doing. ◆

major question

How can two techniques—balanced scorecard and measurement management—help me carry out and control strategy?

The Big Picture

In carrying out the grand strategy, managers need to do strategic control. Two techniques for this are the balanced scorecard, which provides four indicators for progress, and measurement management.

Stage 1 of the strategic-management process was establishing the mission and the vision. Stage 2 was establishing the grand strategy. Stage 3 was formulating the strategic plans. Now we come to the last two stages—4, carry out the strategy, and 5, control the strategy.

Two techniques used here are the *balanced scorecard* and *measurement management,* matters that even new managers will find useful.

The Balanced Scorecard

Robert Kaplan is a professor of accounting at the Harvard Business School. David Norton is founder and president of Renaissance Strategy Group, a Massachusetts consulting firm. Kaplan and Norton developed what they call the ***balanced scorecard,*** **which gives top managers a fast but comprehensive view of the organization via four indicators: (1) customer satisfaction, (2) internal processes, (3) the organization's innovation and improvement activities, and (4) financial measures.**

"Think of the balanced scorecard as the dials and indicators in an airplane cockpit," write Kaplan and Norton. For a pilot, "Reliance on one instrument can be fatal. Similarly, the complexity of managing an organization today requires that managers be able to view performance in several areas simultaneously."[49] It is not enough, say Kaplan and Norton, to simply measure financial performance, such as sales figures and return on investment. Operational matters, such as customer satisfaction, are equally important.

The balanced scorecard establishes (a) *goals* and (b) *performance measures* according to four "perspectives" or areas—*financial, innovation and learning, customer,* and *internal business. (See Figure 6.5.)*

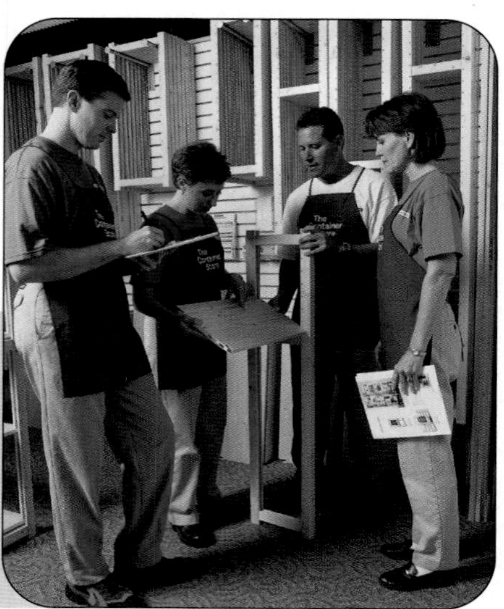

Performance measures. The Container Store, which sells boxes, bins, racks, shelves, and garbage cans, has been in one of the top three places on *Fortune* magazine's list of "100 Best Companies to Work For" for five years in a row. Turnover of full-time salespeople and managers is a fraction of competitors' turnover. What other performance measures would you evaluate to see if The Container Store is truly successful?

FIGURE 6.5

The balanced scorecard. This shows the four perspectives. (Source: Adapted from R. S. Kaplan and D. P. Norton, "The Balanced Scorecard—Measures that Drive Performance," *Harvard Business Review,* January–February 1992, p. 72.)

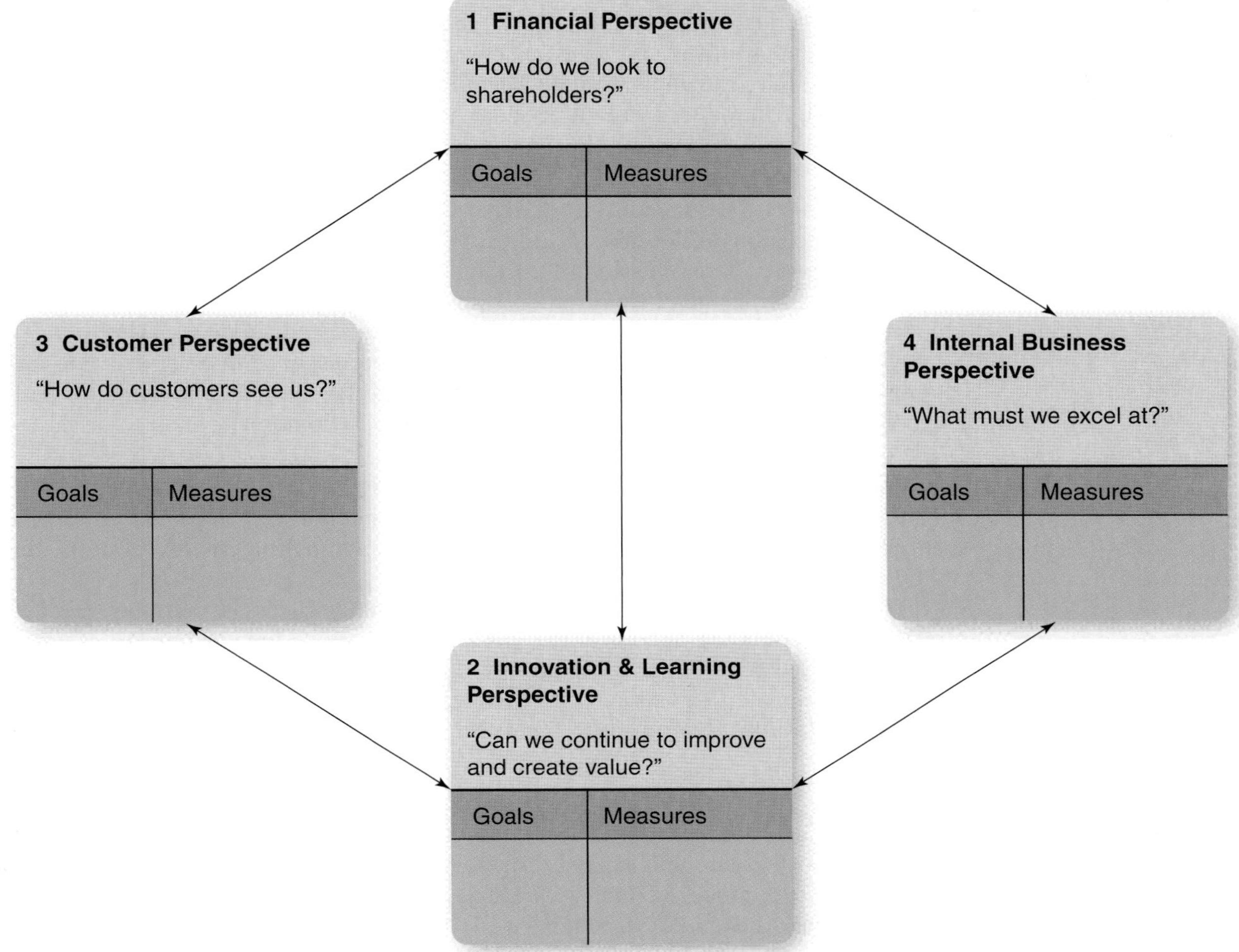

1 Financial Perspective: "How Do We Look to Shareholders?"

Typical financial goals have to do with profitability, growth, and shareholder value. Financial measures such as quarterly sales have been criticized as being short-sighted and not reflecting contemporary value-creating activities. Moreover, critics say that traditional financial measures don't improve customer satisfaction, quality, or employee motivation.

However, making improvements in just the other three operational "perspectives" we will discuss won't *necessarily* translate into financial success. Kaplan and Norton mention the case of an electronics company that made considerable improvements in manufacturing capabilities that did not result in increased profitability.

The hard truth is that "if improved [operational] performance fails to be reflected in the bottom line, executives should reexamine the basic assumptions of their strategy and mission," say Kaplan and Norton. "Not all long-term strategies are profitable strategies. . . . A failure to convert improved operational performance, as measured in the scorecard, into improved financial performance should send executives back to their drawing boards to rethink the company's strategy or its implementation plans."[50]

2 Innovation & Learning Perspective: "Can We Continue to Improve & Create Value?"

Because global competition keeps changing the targets for success, companies (1) must make continual improvements to their existing products and processes and (2) must introduce new products. Thus, an organization must measure its research and development efforts and its efficiencies in manufacturing and delivery.

For example, a company might have a time-to-market measure comparing the time taken for introducing a new product with that of the competition. Or it might measure the percentage of products equal to 80% of the company's sales.

3 Customer Perspective: "How Do Customers See Us?"

Many organizations make taking care of the customer a high priority. The balanced scorecard translates the mission of customer service into specific measures of concerns that really matter to customers—time between placing an order and taking delivery, quality in terms of defect level, performance and service, and cost.

Examples of customer measures are mean-time response to a service call, customer report cards of price and quality compared to the competition, and third-party surveys (such as the J. D. Powers quality survey of automobiles).

4 Internal Business Perspective: "What Must We Excel At?"

This part translates what the company must do internally to meet its customers' expectations. These are business processes such as quality, employee skills, and productivity.

Top management's judgment about key internal processes must be linked to measures of employee actions at the lower levels, such as time to process customer orders, get materials from suppliers, produce products, and deliver them to customers. Computer information systems can help, for example, in identifying late deliveries, tracing the problem to a particular plant.

Measurement Management

"Our need to measure and to apply measurement to strategic analysis and strategic decision-making processes increases every day," says Debra J. Cohen, of the Society for Human Resource Management.[51] "You simply can't manage anything you can't measure," adds Richard Quinn, vice president of quality at the Sears Merchandising Group.[52]

Is this really true? Measurement concepts such as the balanced scorecard seem like good ideas, but how well do they actually work? John Lingle and William Schiemann, principals in a New Jersey consulting firm specializing in strategic assessment, decided to find out.[53]

In a survey of 203 executives in companies of varying size they identified the organizations as being of two types: *measurement-managed* and *nonmeasurement-managed.* The measurement-managed companies were those in which senior management reportedly agreed on measurable criteria for determining strategic success, and management updated and reviewed semiannual performance measures in three or more of six primary performance areas. The six areas were financial performance, operating efficiency, customer satisfaction, employee performance, innovation/change, and community/environment.

The results, concluded Lingle and Schiemann: "A higher percentage of measurement-managed companies were identified as industry leaders, as being financially in the top third of their industry, and as successfully managing their change effort." (The last indicator suggests that measurement-managed companies tend to anticipate the future and are likely to remain in a leadership position in a rapidly changing environment.) "Forget magic," they say. "Industry leaders we surveyed simply have a greater handle on the world around them."

Why Measurement-Managed Firms Succeed

Why do measurement-managed companies outperform those that are less disciplined? The study's data point to four mechanisms that contribute to these companies' success:

- **Top executives agree on strategy:** Most top executives in measurement-managed companies agreed on business strategy, whereas most of those in nonmeasurement-managed companies reported disagreement. Translating strategy into measurable objectives helps make them specific.
- **Communication is clear:** The clear message in turn is translated into good communication, which was characteristic of measurement-managed organizations and not of nonmeasurement-managed ones.
- **There is better focus and alignments:** Measurement-managed companies reported more frequently that unit (division or department) performance measures were linked to strategic company measures and that individual performance measures were linked to unit measures.
- **The organizational culture emphasizes teamwork and allows risk taking:** Managers in measurement-managed companies more frequently reported strong teamwork and cooperation among the management team and more willingness to take risks.

Bellhop. The job of the hotel bellman is like many service-industry jobs, in which, unlike manufacturing jobs, productivity is difficult to measure. What other kinds of jobs can you think of in which "measurement management" is difficult to perform?

The Barriers to Effective Measurement

The four most frequent barriers to effective measurement, according to Lingle and Schiemann, are these:

- **Objectives are fuzzy:** Company objectives are often precise in the financial and operational areas but not in areas of customer satisfaction, employee performance, and rate of change. Managers need to work at making "soft" objectives measurable.
- **Managers put too much trust in informal feedback systems:** Managers tend to overrate feedback mechanisms such as customer complaints or sales-force criticisms about products. But these mechanisms aren't necessarily accurate.
- **Employees resist new measurement systems:** Employees want to see how well measures work before they are willing to tie their financial futures to them. Measurement-managed companies tend to involve the workforce in developing measures.
- **Companies focus too much on measuring activities instead of results:** Too much concern with measurement that is not tied to fine-tuning the organization or spurring it on to achieve results is wasted effort.

The Feedback Loop

Throughout the five-step process, there is a feedback loop (refer to Figure 6.1, p. 175) so that when problems are encountered along the way, managers are directed to return to earlier steps to take corrective action. ◆

Key Terms Used in This Chapter

balanced scorecard, 190
competitive intelligence, 189
contingency planning, 182
cost-focus strategy, 185
cost-leadership strategy, 185
decline stage, 187
defensive strategy, 177
differentiation strategy, 185
diversification, 188
focused-differentiation strategy, 185
forecast, 182
grand strategy, 177
growth stage, 186
growth strategy, 177
introduction stage, 186
maturity stage, 187
organizational opportunities, 181
organizational strengths, 181
organizational threats, 181
organizational weaknesses, 181
Porter's four competitive strategies, 184
product life cycle, 186
related diversification, 189
single-product strategy, 188
stability strategy, 177
strategic control, 178
strategic management, 171
strategy, 171
strategy formulation, 178
strategy implementation, 178
SWOT analysis, 180
synergy, 189
trend analysis, 182
unrelated diversification, 188

Summary

6.1 The Dynamics of Strategic Planning

- Every organization needs to have a "big picture" about where it's going and how to get there. These are matters of strategy, strategic management, and strategic planning. A strategy is a large-scale action plan that sets the direction for an organization. Strategic management involves managers from all parts of the organization in the formulation and implementation of strategies and strategic goals. Strategic planning determines the organization's long-term goals and ways to achieve them.
- There are three reasons why an organization should adopt strategic management and strategic planning. They can (1) provide direction and momentum, (2) encourage new ideas, and above all (3) develop a sustainable competitive advantage. Sustainable competitive advantage occurs when an organization is able to get and stay ahead in four areas: (1) in being responsive to customers, (2) in innovating, (3) in quality, and (4) in effectiveness.

6.2 The Strategic Management Process

- The strategic management process has five steps plus a feedback loop.
- Step 1 is to establish the mission statement and the vision statement. The mission statement expresses the organization's purpose or reason for being. The vision statement describes the organization's long-term direction and strategic intent.
- Step 2 is to translate the broad mission and vision statements into a grand strategy that explains how the organization's mission is to be accomplished. Three common grand strategies are growth, stability, and defensive. (1) A growth strategy involves expansion—as in sales revenues. (2) A stability strategy involves little or no significant change. (3) A defensive strategy involves reduction in the organization's efforts. Among the strategic planning tools and techniques used are (1) SWOT analysis and (2) forecasting, as described in Section 6.3.
- Step 3 is strategy formulation, the translation of the grand strategy into more specific strategic plans, choosing among different strategies and altering them to best fit the organization's needs. Among the techniques used to formulate strategy are Porter's competitive strategies and product life cycles, as described in Section 6.4.
- Step 4 is strategy implementation—putting strategic plans into effect. Step 5 is strategic control, monitoring the execution of strategy and making adjustments.
- Corrective action constitutes a feedback loop in which a problem requires that managers return to an earlier step to rethink policies, budgets, or personnel arrangements.

6.3 Establishing the Grand Strategy

- To develop a grand strategy (Step 2 above), you need to gather data and make projections, using the tools of SWOT analysis and forecasting.

- SWOT analysis is a search for the Strengths, Weaknesses, Opportunities, and Threats affecting the organization. The SWOT analysis is divided into two parts: an analysis of internal strengths and weaknesses and an analysis of external opportunities and threats. Organizational strengths are the skills and capabilities that give the organization special competencies and competitive advantages. Organizational weaknesses are the drawbacks that hinder an organization in executing strategies. Organizational opportunities are environmental factors that the organization may exploit for competitive advantage. Organizational threats are environmental factors that hinder an organization's achieving a competitive advantage.
- Another tool for developing a grand strategy is forecasting—creating a vision or projection of the future. Two types of forecasting are (1) trend analysis, a hypothetical extension of a past series of events into the future; and (2) contingency planning, the creation of alternative hypothetical but equally likely future conditions.

6.4 Formulating Strategy

- 
Strategy formulation (Step 3 in the strategic-management process) makes use of several concepts, two of which are (1) Porter's four competitive strategies and (2) product life cycles.
- Porter's four competitive strategies are as follows: (1) The cost-leadership strategy is to keep the costs, and hence the prices, of a product or service below those of competitors and to target a wide market. (2) The differentiation strategy is to offer products or services that are of unique and superior value compared to those of competitors but to target a wide market. (3) The cost-focus strategy is to keep the costs and hence prices of a product or service below those of competitors and to target a narrow market. (4) The focused-differentiation strategy is to offer products or services that are of unique and superior value compared to those of competitors and to target a narrow market.
- A product life cycle is a model of the four stages a product or service goes through: (1) In the introduction stage, a new product is introduced into the marketplace and is heavy on startup costs for production, marketing, and distribution. (2) In the growth stage, customer demand increases, the product's sales grow, and later competitors may enter the market. (3) In the maturity stage, the product starts to fall out of favor and sales and profits fall off. (4) In the decline stage, the product falls out of favor, and the organization withdraws from the marketplace.

6.5 Carrying Out & Controlling Strategy

- 
In carrying out the grand strategy (Stage 4) and controlling the strategy (Stage 5), managers can avail themselves of two techniques: (1) the balanced scorecard, and (2) measurement management.
- The balanced scorecard gives top managers a fast but comprehensive view of the organization via four indicators. The balanced scorecard establishes (a) goals and (b) performance measures according to four "perspectives" or areas—financial, innovation and learning, customer, and internal business.
- The balanced scorecard is an example of measurement management, in which an organization uses measurable criteria to determine strategic success. Measurement-managed firms succeed because top executives agree on strategy, communication is clear, there is better focus, and the organizational culture emphasizes teamwork and allows risk taking.

Management in Action

Motorola's CEO Is Developing a New Mission, Vision, and Strategies

Excerpted from Adam Lashinsky, "Can Moto Find Its Mojo?" Fortune, *March 21, 2004, pp. 126, 128, 130, 132–133.*

Ed Zander, the loquacious new CEO of Motorola, has devoted his first three months on the job to listening. He's getting an earful. There is, for example, the tongue-lashing he suffered after a brief Hi-I'm-the-new-guy luncheon speech to customers at a wireless conference on the French Riviera in late February. Naguib Sawiris, chairman of Egypt's Orascom Telecom, tardily ambled into a high-ceilinged room at the Carlton hotel in Cannes, overlooking a glittering Mediterranean Sea, and raised his hand. "We have been promised year after year that this company will deliver," began Sawiris, whose wireless licenses span the Middle East, Africa, and India. "And we want to believe [it], perhaps out of some sense of nostalgia. But there's no clarity on the future of this company," he complained—whether the subject is Motorola's commitment to remaining in the wireless infrastructure equipment business or its inability to turn out cellphones on time. "So I want to know, are you the best news?" . . .

Motorola's slide is explained by one flop after another from the mid-1990s on. First it failed to anticipate the worldwide shift to digital cellphones, allowing Nokia to overtake it as the world's No. 1 cellphone maker. Once a leader in wireless infrastructure equipment—the behind-the-scenes gear that makes cellphone systems work—Motorola's market share slid to 10% last year, making it the No. 4 player. In 2000 it bought General Instrument, the market leader in set-top boxes for cable television, for $17 billion. The cable unit's revenues have declined 49% since then as cable companies slowed purchases and Motorola fell behind its competitors in delivering new products. Arguably, Motorola's biggest blunder was the ten-plus years and $2.6 billion it lost in now-bankrupt Iridium, the satellite network famous for its brick-sized phones and dollars-per-minute international calls. The company developed a reputation for owning killer technology that got stuck in its labs. Says Tom Lynch, a General Instrument veteran who now runs Motorola's cellphone business: "There are endless examples of instances where this company has blazed a trail and someone else has reaped the benefits."

If the digital screw-up and the Iridium debacle were embarrassing, more recent flops have established Motorola as the big company that can't shoot straight. "On cellphones they've missed just about every window that's opened," says analyst Berge Ayvazian of the Yankee Group, a market research firm. When color-screen phones became hot in 2002, Motorola couldn't produce them in large volumes, and Samsung came from seemingly nowhere to become the No. 2 cellphone player by revenue. Production glitches last December kept Motorola from delivering camera phones, the holiday season's big seller. Motorola's broadband unit (the former General Instrument), despite being the market leader in set-top boxes, has been slow to release a combination set-top box/digital video recorder, allowing archrival Scientific-Atlanta to sell hundreds of thousands of units essentially unchallenged by Motorola. Its semiconductor unit had a lock on chips for PDAs as recently as three years ago; Intel has snatched that lead. In wireless infrastructure, Motorola has fallen behind in offering products using the latest technologies; that allowed Ericsson, a company with its own financial problems, to stake out a clear No. 1 position in that market.

All those missteps have created big doubts about the company for customers and competitors alike—ones that palliatives from Zander can't quell. Carl-Henric Svanberg, Ericsson's CEO, believes they have what it takes but says, "I haven't really felt that they have yet committed to say, 'This is an area we'll be in.'". . .

As Zander gets his bearings as CEO, it is clear that his mission is nothing less than saving an iconic company that has lost its way. His first task ought to be simple: figuring out what Motorola is. But even that's not straightforward. . . . Critics have come to a simple conclusion: Motorola does too many things—and not enough of them well. Zander grasps that repairing the company's image is his first order of business. "Is Motorola just a collection of disparate standalone businesses?" he asks. He'll judge his success by when critics stop asking that question.

And so Ed Zander is literally searching for a mission statement. He's doing it pretty much nonstop, including over dinner on a brisk February evening in downtown Chicago. A slight man with a long face, an easy smile, and a hairline that receded long ago, Zander speaks plainly, with the occasional flash of Brooklynese from his childhood. He's a natural jokester—one analyst imagines Zander putting whoopee cushions on the chairs at Motorola management meetings to lighten things up—but he's also adept at shifting gears and getting down to business. "The world wants me to come up with this grand vision," he says, "but what I'm hearing from customers right now is 'Execute. Give me the products. Make the company more efficient.' And that's a lot." So while Motorola does indeed need a master plan, simply keeping its promises is an equally urgent concern. . . .

To get a sense of the company, he's doing what any new CEO would do: visiting key employees, hearing out customers, trying to understand his new company's inner workings. Motorola presents a newcomer with special challenges. It's laden with 75 years' worth of stuffiness, as well as acronyms so obscure it takes a glossary to figure out what the heck Motorolans are talking about. . . .

Zander has, however, begun to articulate a vision of the company in terms of its four big end markets: the individual, the home, the auto, and the big organization, including governments. He's picked up on a theme the company had been pursuing before his arrival, seamless mobility, which represents the unrealized opportunity for users to transfer their calls and data easily from office to car to home and back again. It's the kind of commitment he says Motorola needs to make. "If we declare that's the big five-year bet, then everybody in the company's got to get galvanized around it," he says, clearly intending no pun on the founding family's name. Simply getting a once great company to pull in one direction sounds like a modest goal. For Motorola under Ed Zander, it'd be a great start.

For Discussion

1. How would you describe Motorola's grand strategy over the years?
2. At this time, how would you describe Zander's vision for Motorola? Explain.
3. Using Figure 6.2 as a framework, conduct a SWOT analysis of Motorola. What are your conclusions?
4. What type of diversification strategy is Motorola following? Explain.
5. Using the information in Figure 6.5, describe the driving force behind Motorola's decisions.

Core Skills Required in Strategic Planning*

Objectives

1. To assess if you have the skills to be in strategic planning.
2. To see what you think are the important core skill areas in strategic planning.

Introduction

Strategic planning became important as a method of managing the increasing velocity of change. The business environment no longer evolves at a manageable pace but increasingly through a process Charles Handy calls "discontinuous change"—change that radically alters how we think, work, and often behave. The computer, for instance, has completely changed how we communicate, research, write, and work. To meet this challenge, companies have strategic planners and others knowledgeable about their organizations, culture, and environment to shape strategy. Individuals must develop knowledge about their own abilities so that they formulate their own kind of strategic planning.

Instructions

To see whether or not you have the required skills needed to be a strategic planner, truthfully and thoughtfully assess your ability level for the following list of 12 skills. Rate each skill by using a five-point scale in which 1 = exceptional, 2 = very high, 3 = high, 4 = low, and 5 = very low.

1. Ability to synthesize	1	2	3	4	5
2. Analytical skills	1	2	3	4	5
3. Computer skills	1	2	3	4	5
4. Decisiveness	1	2	3	4	5
5. Interpersonal skills	1	2	3	4	5
6. Listening skills	1	2	3	4	5
7. Persuasiveness	1	2	3	4	5
8. Problem-solving skills	1	2	3	4	5
9. Research skills	1	2	3	4	5
10. Team skills	1	2	3	4	5
11. Verbal skills	1	2	3	4	5
12. Written skills	1	2	3	4	5

Scoring & Interpretation

According to research conducted at the Ohio State University College of Business, the core required skills for the 12 skills above rate as follows:

Ability to synthesize	2
Analytical skills	1
Computer skills	3
Decisiveness	3
Interpersonal skills	1
Listening skills	2
Persuasiveness	2
Problem-solving skills	3
Research skills	3
Team skills	2
Verbal skills	2
Written skills	3

If you scored mostly 4s and 5s, strategic planning is probably not for you.
If you scored near the "perfect" score, it may be a possible career path.
If you scored all 1s and 2s, you might do extremely well at this type of work and might want to look into it more.

Questions for Discussion

1. Based on your results, do you think you would like to make a career out of strategic planning? Why or why not?
2. What appeals or does not appeal to you about this career? Explain.
3. How might you enhance your strategic skills? Discuss.

*Developed by Anne C. Cowden, Ph.D.

Group Exercise

Strategizing for Real*

Objectives

1. To help you understand the complexity of the strategic planning process.
2. To more completely familiarize yourself with strategic planning.

Introduction

Social psychologist Kurt Lewin argued that there is nothing as useful as a good theory. The important word here is *good* since bad theories can cause a great deal of trouble. An example of a bad theory was the introduction of the New Coke in 1985 by Coca-Cola, one of the world's most successful companies. Management's "theory" was that customers wanted a New Coke. But its introduction was an enormous fiasco, and furious customers demanded that traditional Coke be brought back. Companies that effectively use strategic planning can try to avoid these blunders.

To have a sense of what function a strategic plan can have, you must (1) look at the theory and (2) apply it to an actual situation that you know. In this way, you can see if you like doing strategic planning, what it entails in terms of complexity and insight, and whether or not you think it is a career area you might like to pursue. Because of transitions in the world economy, the demand for strategists will likely increase. The purpose of this exercise is to provide you the opportunity to create a strategic plan for your college or university.

Instructions

Students should be divided into groups of five each. One person should go to the website for the New Mexico State University Planning Process at *www.nmsu.edu/Strategic/process/fig1.html,* download the chart there, and make copies for everyone. The task of the group is to use this chart as a guide to develop a strategic plan for your college or university. Your first step is to discover if such a document already exists, acquire a copy, and then compare it to your chart, filling in the specifics and trying to improve the process as you go along. This exercise should help make you a better strategic planner of your own education and career.

Questions for Discussion

1. Why is it important for an organization—whether private, public, or not-for-profit—to have a strategic plan? Explain your rationale.
2. Do you think that a strategic plan can ever be totally accurate? Why or why not?
3. Who do you think should be involved in developing and maintaining a strategic plan?
4. How would you grade (A through F) the strategic plan at your college? Explain your rationale.

*Developed by Anne C. Cowden, Ph.D.

Ethical Dilemma

Should I Hire a Qualified Applicant with Questionable Ethics?

Excerpted from Anne Marie Squeo and Andy Pasztor, "Space Case: U.S. Probes Whether Boeing Misused a Rival's Documents," The Wall Street Journal, *May 5, 2003, pp. A1, A8.*

In 1996, Boeing Co. was locked in a fierce competition with Lockheed Martin Corp. to become the government's primary maker of rockets for launching spy, communications and other satellites. With Boeing as the underdog, and the future of its space-launch business at stake, company officials were seeking any advantage they could get over their rival. That's when Kenneth Branch appeared at Boeing's rocket headquarters in Huntington Beach, Calif.

A well-known space engineer and manager with Lockheed's rocket team in Florida, Mr. Branch visited Boeing for a job interview. Toward the end of the meeting, he dug into his briefcase and pulled out and displayed a presentation on Lockheed's rocket project, according to a sworn statement by one of the participants, which later was filed in court. Six months after the interview, in January 1997, Mr. Branch was hired to work on Boeing's rocket program.

What happened during his tenure at Boeing, which ended in 1999 after Boeing bested Lockheed on the contract, is now the focus of criminal and civil investigations by the Justice Department, which is working with the Pentagon's Defense Criminal Investigative Service. An Air Force administrative inquiry also is under way to determine whether to suspend or bar Boeing from certain military work.

At issue is whether Boeing illicitly obtained or used competition-sensitive documents belonging to Lockheed as part of a carefully plotted campaign to win the military contract. Boeing hasn't disclosed the investigations to the Securities and Exchange Commission. . . . E-mails sent by Boeing lawyers to employees, notifying them that they might be contacted by government investigators, show that the company was aware of a probe at least as far back as September 2002, according to one e-mail recipient.

For Boeing, the legal headache threatens more than its largely government-dependent rocket business. The nation's third-largest defense contractor, it saw revenue for its military unit total $25 billion last year. That helped offset a big decline in its commercial-jet business. The investigation also could undermine the company's strategy of becoming the lead contractor on major military programs, including national missile defense that puts together the pieces from other suppliers. In the last few years, Boeing has been trying to cultivate a clean image in an effort to win assignments to supervise other contractors.

The controversy also puts the government in a bind. Industry consolidation during the 1990s left Boeing and Lockheed as the remaining U.S. rocket manufacturers. Punishing Boeing severely could undermine the Pentagon's strategy of maintaining two separate suppliers. Technically, Mr. Branch, now 64 years old, was hired by McDonnell Douglas Corp., to work in its Delta rocket program. At the time, McDonnell Douglas already had agreed to be acquired by Boeing. The deal closed in August 1997, and the personnel in McDonnell Douglas' rocket program became Boeing employees.

Boeing fired Mr. Branch and William Erskine, his former supervisor, after an internal investigation discovered that they possessed several thousand pages of Lockheed proprietary documents, including rocket specifications and detailed cost breakdowns, according to a report of an internal Boeing investigation. At the time of the firings, the company insisted to the Air Force and Lockheed that it had effectively dealt with the transgressions. Investigators now are looking into whether Boeing executives encouraged improper intelligence gathering. They also want to know why Boeing initially returned only two documents to Lockheed, but since has provided thousands of additional pages in piecemeal fashion to its rival, according to people involved in the investigations. . . .

Solving the Dilemma

Suppose you do not have the advantage of hindsight and are one of the hiring managers. What should you do?

1. Hire this applicant because he has all the necessary skills. Do not look over the competitor's documents and make sure they are destroyed to remove any temptation to use them in the future.
2. This applicant's ethics are obviously sub-par, and no matter how skilled he is you pass on hiring him. If he is willing to betray his current employer, what are the odds he won't betray your company in the future?
3. You hire this applicant and pass the documents onto upper management. They can make the decision as to whether or not to use the information. Your job was to simply hire an experienced and skilled engineer, and you feel you have done that.
4. Invent other options. Discuss.

Video Case

JetBlue Airways

David Neeleman, founder and CEO of JetBlue Airways, discusses the debut of his new airline with Matt Lauer of the *Today Show.* The odds are against the survival of any start-up airline. After all, no airline founded since 1996 has endured, and there have been only a few survivors within the last 25 years. So what makes JetBlue different? According to Neeleman, several factors set JetBlue apart. In addition to Neeleman's extensive experience in the airline industry, JetBlue is heavily capitalized. With the extensive capital raised, JetBlue was able to purchase new, technologically advanced plans to operate. The firm has a well-formulated strategic plan prepared by a talented group of top managers. From a passenger's perspective, planes have a wider cabin, wider leather seats, more overhead cargo room, and access to 24 channels of Direct TV for each and every passenger.

JetBlue's pricing strategy incorporates a price range that is narrower than those of its competitors. While matching competitors for advanced purchases, the most expensive JetBlue price will be $159. According to CEO Neeleman, "people will always be able to call JetBlue and get a low fare." For the next several years, the company plans to add a new plane to its fleet every five weeks, until they cover 30 cities throughout the United States.

Travel expert Peter Greenburg thinks JetBlue has several advantages compared to most new airlines. They are capitalized at $130 million and already have 82 planes on order. Unlike most other start-ups, JetBlue is not flying out of a "fortress hub" of a major carrier or based in a location where flying space is already heavily controlled. Instead, JetBlue is based at JFK airport in New York, where there is considerable flexibility for flight allocations. (JFK is slot-controlled only between 3 p.m. and 8 p.m.) Finally, JetBlue is aiming for airports that are either underserved or totally ignored by the major airlines. Greenburg believes these factors give JetBlue a head start over other new carriers.

Even with the most technologically advanced planes in the air, luxurious leather seats, and Direct TV, CEO Neeleman believes that its employees will set JetBlue apart from competitors. The goal is to hire the best people, train them well, and "bring humanity back to air travel." While the planes are nice, it's the people that make the difference.

Discussion Questions

1. A grand strategy explains how the organization's mission is to be accomplished. List each of the three common grand strategies. Which one is evident in the video?
2. Porter's four competitive strategies include cost-leadership, differentiation, cost-focus, and focused-differentiation. Briefly define each of these strategies. Which one is JetBlue using?
3. List some of the factors included in JetBlue's strategic plan. What other advantages bode well for the company's success?

chapter 7

Individual & Group Decision Making

How Managers Make Things Happen

MAJOR QUESTIONS YOU SHOULD BE ABLE TO ANSWER

7.1 The Nature of Decision Making

Major Question: How do I decide to decide?

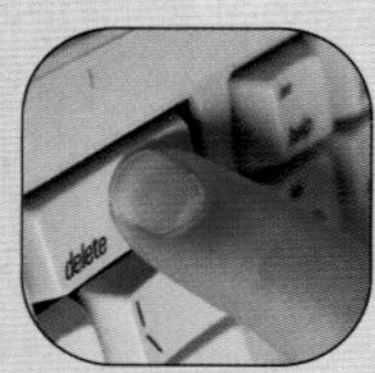

7.2 Two Kinds of Decision Making: Rational & Nonrational

Major Question: How do people know when they're being logical or illogical?

7.3 Making Ethical Decisions

Major Question: What guidelines can I follow to be sure that decisions I make are not just lawful but ethical?

7.4 Group Decision Making: How to Work with Others

Major Question: How do I work with others to make things happen?

7.5 How to Overcome Barriers to Decision Making

Major Question: Trying to be rational isn't always easy. What are the barriers?

the manager's toolbox

How Exceptional Managers Make Decisions

"Failure is a great teacher."

That is one of the life lessons of David Dorman, who at age 45 is the CEO of a $10 billion joint venture between AT&T and British Telecommunications.[1] During his meteoric career, Dorman has had to make many decisions—the subject of this chapter—for which failure is always a possible outcome. But he has learned that that possibility can't stop one from making decisions. And one can probably always learn from the result.

- **When should you make a decision and when should you delay?** Often you want to stay open-minded before making a decision. But sometimes that can just be a cover for procrastination. (After all, *not* making a decision is in itself a kind of decision.) How do you know when you're keeping an open mind or are procrastinating? Ralph L. Keeney, coauthor of *Smart Choices: A Practical Guide to Making Better Decisions*, offers some questions to consider:[2]

  Understanding: Do you have a reasonable grasp of the problem?

  Comfort level about outcome: Would you be satisfied if you chose one of the existing alternatives?

  Future possible alternatives: Would it be unlikely that you could come up with a better alternative if you had more time?

  Seizing the opportunity: Could the best alternatives disappear if you wait?

  If you can answer "yes" to those questions, you almost certainly should decide now, not wait.

- **Making tough choices:** To reach the top, as Dorman has, a manager needs to be able to make tough choices. "On a daily and weekly basis we can be faced with making hundreds of decisions," says management consultant Odette Pollar. "Most of them are small, but the larger ones where more is at stake can be truly painful." Here are some ways she suggests making decision making easier, some of which resemble Keeney's:[3]

  Decide in a timely fashion: "Rarely does waiting significantly improve the quality of the decision," says Pollar. In fact, delay can result in greater unpleasantness in loss of money, time, and peace of mind.

  Don't agonize over minor decisions: Postponing decisions about small problems can mean that they simply turn into large ones later.

  Separate outcome from process: Does a bad outcome mean you made a bad decision? Not necessarily. The main thing is to go through a well-reasoned process of choosing among alternatives, which increases the chances of success. But even then you can't be sure there will always be a positive outcome.

  Learn when to stop gathering facts: "Gather enough information to make a sound decision," suggests Pollar, "but not all the possible information." Taking extra time may mean you'll miss a window of opportunity.

  When overwhelmed, narrow your choices: Sometimes there are many good alternatives, and you need to simplify decision making by eliminating some options.

forecast

What's Ahead in This Chapter

We describe decision making and types of decisions, and we describe the range of decision-making conditions. Next we distinguish between rational and nonrational decision making, and we describe five nonrational models. We then consider four steps in practical decision making. We follow with a discussion of group decision making, including participative management and group problem-solving techniques. We conclude by considering how individuals respond to decision situations and four common decision-making biases.

major question **How do I decide to decide?**

The Big Picture

Decision making, the process of identifying and choosing alternative courses of action, may be programmed or nonprogrammed. The range of decision-making conditions ranges from certainty to risky to uncertainty to confusion.

Ben Swett—former Vassar English major, University of Chicago MBA, TV comedy writer, and Quaker Oats executive—started windowbox.com in 1997 after failing in the seemingly simple task of growing a plant on his balcony in Los Angeles. His mission: to run an online organization that satisfied the needs of urban gardeners, as well as to contribute to the social good.

Selling plants to patio and balcony gardeners, it turns out, is an extremely seasonal business. About half of Swett's annual sales occur at three times: Valentine's Day, Mother's Day, and the two weeks before Christmas. What kinds of decisions do Swett and his managers have to make to scale up and down for such a volatile business?[4]

Decision Making Defined

A *decision* is a choice made from among available alternatives. For example, should your college offer (if it currently does not) computer-based distance learning to better serve students who work odd hours or are homebound and can't easily get to lectures on campus? That question is a decision that the college administrators must make.

***Decision making* is the process of identifying and choosing alternative courses of action.** For example, the college could offer distance learning by televising the lectures of a single professor into several classrooms or to community centers off campus. Or it could offer distance learning interactively over the Internet. It could offer distance learning only for certain subjects (business and education, say) or for selected courses in all majors. It could offer distance learning only during the summer or only during the evenings. It could charge extra for such courses. It could offer them for credit to high school students or to students attending other colleges. Identifying and sorting out these alternatives is the process of decision making.

Success. Basketball coach Larry Brown, surrounded by some of his Detroit Pistons players, is the only coach to win both an NBA championship (the Pistons in 2004) and an NCAA championship (University of Kansas in 1988). As a manager, a coach must make many decisions about what is the right way to success. For Brown, the "right way" is defense, hustle, and teamwork. If you were a coach, what would you do differently?

Types of Decisions: Programmed versus Nonprogrammed

In most day-to-day matters, you automatically know what kind of decision needs to be made and when, who will decide it, who will need to be consulted about it, who should be informed about it. That is, the decisions are *programmed*. However, when you have to stop and think about these matters, then the decisions are *nonprogrammed*.[5]

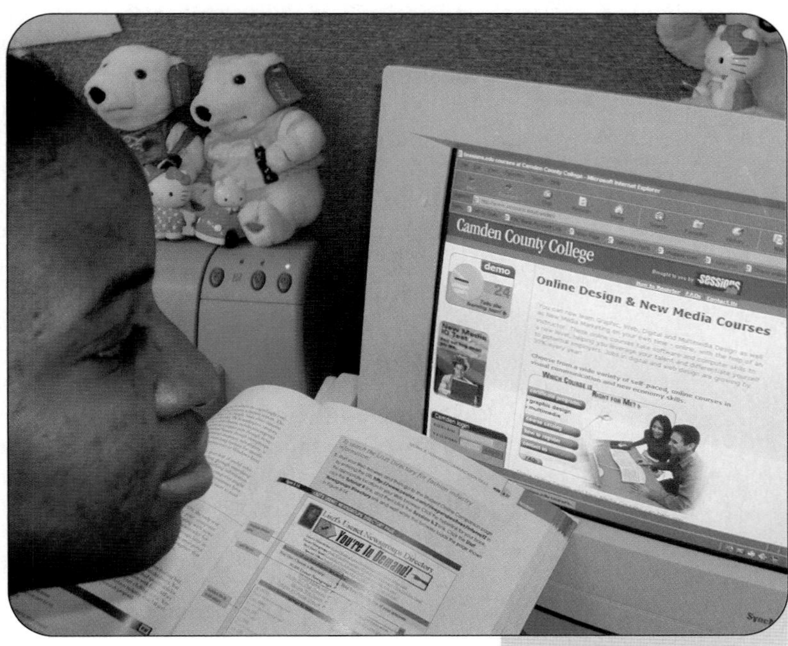

Distance learning. The student is logged on to the distance-learning website at Camden County (New Jersey) College. Today students frequently have the option to take many courses that previously were not available to them. Do you think that the addition of distance-learning courses to a college's course offerings gives you more freedom of choice—or simply more headaches? What must it be like for college administrators?

Let's distinguish further between programmed and nonprogrammed decisions.

Programmed Decisions

***Programmed decisions* are repetitive and routine.** Because they are fairly structured and occur fairly frequently, such decisions tend to follow established rules and so are virtually automatic. This does not mean, however, that the issues are necessarily simple. Even a complicated issue, if its components can be analyzed, may be decided by a programmed decision.

Example: The three-times-a-year peak load times for windowbox.com are predictable. During these periods, plant shipments jump from 2,000 to 32,000, nursery workers go from 8 to 60, and back-office workers triple to 18. Owner Ben Swett taps pools of friends and family, many of whom are used to doing temp work. Even so, says Swett, "I freak out four weeks before the holiday and ask everyone questions like, 'What if the power goes off?'" As a result, a generator is on standby. Thus, says one account, Swett "devises a backup for every problem he can imagine and then is free to focus on those he didn't anticipate."[6]

Nonprogrammed Decisions

***Nonprogrammed decisions* are those that occur under nonroutine, unfamiliar circumstances.** Because they occur in response to unusual, unpredictable opportunities and threats, nonprogrammed decisions are relatively unstructured. Often, too, they tend to involve complex, important situations. The farther you move up the organizational hierarchy, the more important your ability to make nonprogrammed decisions becomes.

Example: Although Ben Swett badgers customers to give their best forecasts, surprises happen anyway. Thus, shortly after moving into an older building with space for plants on the roof, Swett realized that the small elevator would not be able to move all the plants in time for the Mother's Day crunch. Accordingly, he got a nearby tailor to fashion a chute out of canvas, which was used to slide boxed plants down four stories to waiting Federal Express trucks. The lesson, says a *Wall Street Journal* story: "plan for knowable contingencies, be ready to wing the rest."[7]

General Decision-Making Styles: Directive, Analytical, Conceptual, Behavioral

A *decision-making style* reflects the combination of how an individual perceives and responds to information. A team of researchers developed a model of decision-making styles based on the idea that styles vary along two different dimensions: value orientation and tolerance for ambiguity.[8]

Value orientation reflects the extent to which a person focuses on either task and technical concerns or people and social concerns when making decisions. Some people, for instance, are very task focused at work and do not pay much attention to people issues, whereas others are just the opposite.

The second dimension pertains to a person's *tolerance for ambiguity*. This individual difference indicates the extent to which a person has a high need for structure or control in his or her life. Some people desire a lot of structure in their lives (a low tolerance for ambiguity) and find ambiguous situations stressful and psychologically uncomfortable. In contrast, others do not have a high need for structure and can thrive in uncertain situations (a high tolerance for ambiguity). Ambiguous situations can energize people with a high tolerance for ambiguity.

When the dimensions of value orientation and tolerance for ambiguity are combined, they form four styles of decision making: *directive, analytical, conceptual,* and *behavioral*. *(See Figure 7.1.)*

FIGURE 7.1
Decision-making styles

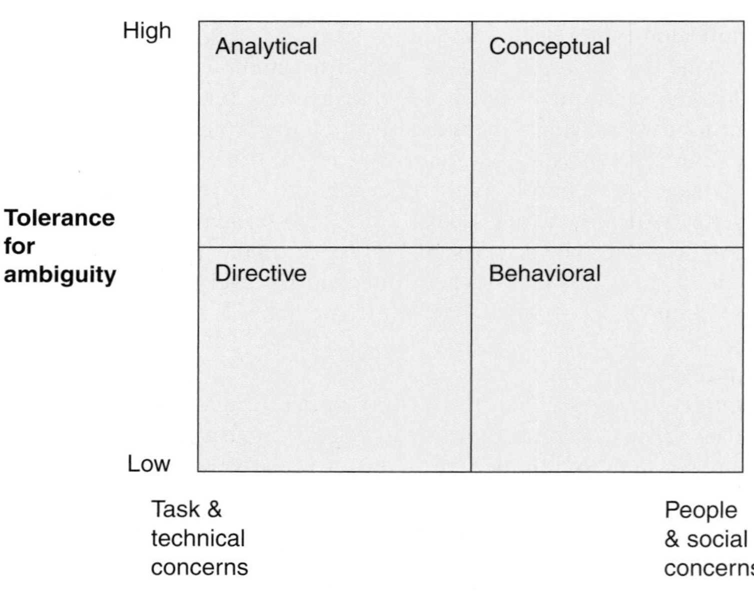

1 Directive

People with a directive style have a low tolerance for ambiguity and are oriented toward task and technical concerns in making decisions. They are efficient, logical, practical, and systematic in their approach to solving problems.

People with this style are action oriented and decisive and like to focus on facts. In their pursuit of speed and results, however, these individuals tend to be autocratic, to exercise power and control, and to focus on the short run.

2 Analytical

This style has a much higher tolerance for ambiguity and is characterized by the tendency to overanalyze a situation. People with this style like to consider more information and alternatives than managers following the directive style.

Analytic individuals are careful decision makers who take longer to make decisions but who also respond well to new or uncertain situations.

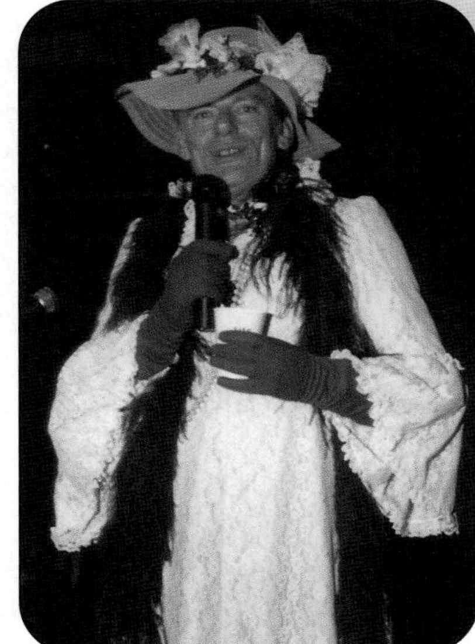

Who is this, er, man? Herb Kelleher, former CEO of highly successful Southwest Airlines, was much beloved by his employees for his humor, informal management style, and extraordinary people orientation. What kind of decision-making styles do you think his successors would try to follow?

3 Conceptual

People with a conceptual style have a high tolerance for ambiguity and tend to focus on the people or social aspects of a work situation. They take a broad perspective to problem solving and like to consider many options and future possibilities.

Conceptual types adopt a long-term perspective and rely on intuition and discussions with others to acquire information. They also are willing to take risks and are good at finding creative solutions to problems. However, a conceptual style can foster an indecisive approach to decision making.

4 Behavioral

This style is the most people oriented of the four styles. People with this style work well with others and enjoy social interactions in which opinions are openly exchanged. Behavioral types are supportive, receptive to suggestions, show warmth, and prefer verbal to written information.

Although they like to hold meetings, people with this style have a tendency to avoid conflict and to be concerned about others. This can lead behavioral types to adopt a wishy-washy approach to decision making and to have a hard time saying no.

Which Style Do You Have?

Research shows that very few people have only one dominant decision-making style. Rather, most managers have characteristics that fall into two or three styles. Studies also show that decision-making styles vary across occupations, job level, and countries.[9] There is not a best decision-making style that applies to all situations.

You can use knowledge of decision-making styles in three ways:

- Knowledge of styles helps you to understand yourself. Awareness of your style assists you in identifying your strengths and weaknesses as a decision maker and facilitates the potential for self-improvement.
- You can increase your ability to influence others by being aware of styles. For example, if you are dealing with an analytical person, you should provide as much information as possible to support your ideas.
- Knowledge of styles gives you an awareness of how people can take the same information and yet arrive at different decisions by using a variety of decision-making strategies. Different decision-making styles represent one likely source of interpersonal conflict at work. ◆

major question

How do people know when they're being logical or illogical?

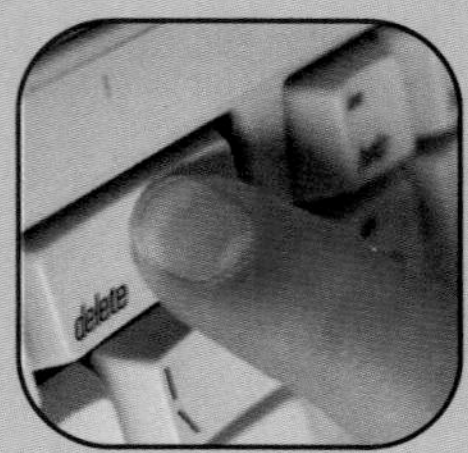

The Big Picture

Decision making may be rational, but often it is nonrational. Four steps in making a rational decision are (1) identify the problem or opportunity, (2) think up alternative solutions, (3) evaluate alternatives and select a solution, and (4) implement and evaluate the solution chosen. Two examples of nonrational models are satisficing and incremental.

Iridium LLC's network of 66 low-orbit satellites was supposed to revolutionize telecommunications by allowing people to make phone calls at any time from anywhere in the world. But nine months after its splashy 1998 launch, the Motorola-led consortium had filed for bankruptcy protection.

What happened? Critics say that Iridium and Motorola became so focused on making the technology work they failed to pay attention to marketing problems. In an era of pocket-size cellphones, the clunky Iridium "space phone" weighed one pound, was the size of a brick, and featured an array of ungainly accessories and adapters. Moreover, because of technology limitations, phone users had to position themselves so nothing blocked the line of sight between the phone's antenna and the satellites overhead. This meant the handset couldn't be used inside buildings, moving cars, or many other locations where the high-powered managers Iridium was targeting tended to make calls. Finally, the phones retailed for $3,000 apiece, and calls ran $2–$8 a minute—at a time when competitors were even giving phones away to induce consumers to subscribe to their low-cost calling plans.[10]

Were Iridium's decisions rational? Let us look at the two approaches managers may take to making decisions: They may follow a *rational model* or various kinds of *nonrational models*.

Rational Decision Making: Managers Should Make Logical & Optimum Decisions

The *rational model of decision making,* also called the *classical model,* explains how managers *should* make decisions; it assumes managers will make logical decisions that will be the optimum in furthering the organization's best interests. Typically there are four stages associated with rational decision making. *(See Figure 7.2.)*

FIGURE 7.2
The four steps in practical decision making

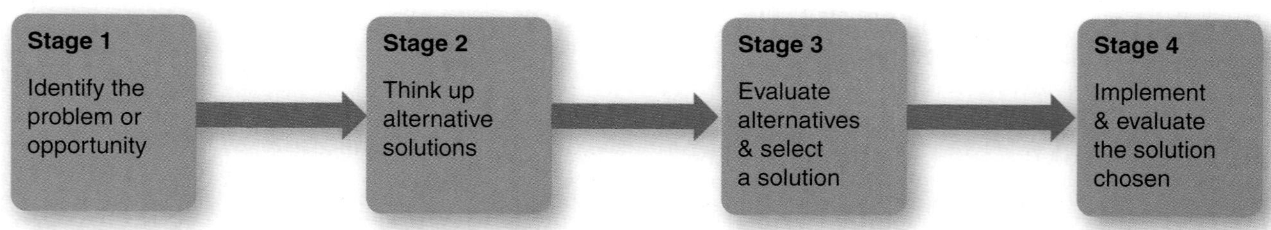
Stage 1
Identify the problem or opportunity
Stage 2
Think up alternative solutions
Stage 3
Evaluate alternatives & select a solution
Stage 4
Implement & evaluate the solution chosen

Stage 1: Identify the Problem or Opportunity—Determining the Actual versus the Desirable

As a manager, you'll probably find no shortage of ***problems,*** **or difficulties that inhibit the achievement of goals.** Customer complaints. Supplier breakdowns. Staff turnover. Sales shortfalls. Competitor innovations.

However, you'll also often find ***opportunities*** **—situations that present possibilities for exceeding existing goals.** It's the farsighted manager, however, who can look past the steady stream of daily problems and seize the moment to actually do *better* than the goals he or she is expected to achieve. When a competitor's top salesperson unexpectedly quits, that creates an opportunity for your company to hire that person away to promote your product more vigorously in that sales territory.

Problems may also be opportunities in disguise. When your top salesperson quits, that may give you the opportunity to reexamine your company culture or system of motivations so that the job can be made more attractive for the next person.

Whether you're confronted with a problem or an opportunity, you're dealing with the difference between the present *actual situation* versus the future *desirable situation*. The decision you're called on to make is how to make *improvements*—how to change conditions from the present to the desirable. This is a matter of ***diagnosis*** **—analyzing the underlying causes.**

Example

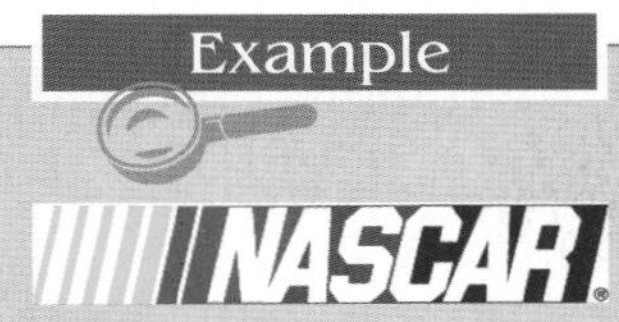

Making a Correct Diagnosis: NASCAR Pit Crew Chief Wins Races

Former NASCAR race car driver Ray Evernham, now boss of a pit crew for famed racer Jeff Gordon, heads a crew of seven who change tires and add fuel during pit stops. Using two-way radio communication with the driver, Evernham makes all the decisions as the race proceeds, such as when to make pit stops, how many tires to change, and how much gas to pump. Thus, if a driver says the car is oversteering or understeering, Evernham must determine what kind of repairs must be made at pit stops, such as adjusting weight bolts on tires. By witnessing how other drivers make their pit stops, Evernham plans his, always trying to save a little time. One day in 1994, for example, Evernham's correct diagnosis shaved crucial seconds off Jeff Gordon's pit stop time, enabling him to overtake Rusty Wallace and win a major race. He watched as Wallace's crew spent 17 seconds changing all four tires. Thus, when Gordon pulled in, Evernham ordered his crew to change just two tires, which took only nine seconds. The eight seconds' difference allowed Gordon to win the race by 2½ seconds.[11]

Stage 2: Think Up Alternative Solutions—Both the Obvious & the Creative

Employees burning with bright ideas are an employer's greatest competitive resource. "Creativity precedes innovation, which is its physical expression," says *Fortune* magazine writer Alan Farnham. "It's the source of all intellectual property."[12]

After you've identified the problem or opportunity and diagnosed its causes, you need to come up with alternative solutions. For a programmed decision, the alternatives will probably be easy and obvious. For nonprogrammed decisions, the more creative and innovative the alternatives, the better.

Stage 3: Evaluate Alternatives & Select a Solution—Ethics, Feasibility, & Effectiveness

In this stage, you need to evaluate each alternative not only according to cost and quality but also according to ethics, feasibility, and effectiveness.

Is It Ethical?

No doubt at times a proposed alternative will seem to be right on nearly all counts. However, if it isn't ethical, you shouldn't give it a second look.

Is It Feasible?

A proposed solution may not be feasible for a variety of reasons: The top decision makers or customers won't accept it. Time is short. Costs are high. Technology isn't available. Company policies don't allow it. The action can't be reversed if there's trouble.

Is It Ultimately Effective?

Satisficing is opting for a course of action because it is "good enough" rather than because it is optimal. For example, managers themselves may continue to operate a business that has been struck by its workers. This may "satisfice" for a while, but the most effective solution is to have the strikers back at work.

Stage 4: Implement & Evaluate the Solution Chosen

With programmed decisions, implementation is usually straightforward (though not necessarily easy—firing employees who steal may be an obvious decision but it can still be emotionally draining). With nonprogrammed decisions, implementation can be quite difficult; when one company acquires another, for instance, it may take months to consolidate the departments, accounting systems, inventories, and so on.

Successful Implementation

For implementation to be successful, you need to do two things:

- **Plan carefully:** Especially if reversing an action will be difficult, you need to make careful plans for implementation. Nonprogrammed decisions may require written plans.
- **Be sensitive to those affected:** You need to consider how the people affected may feel about the change—inconvenienced, insecure, even fearful, all of which can trigger resistance. This is why it helps to give employees and customers latitude during a changeover in business practices or working arrangements.

Example

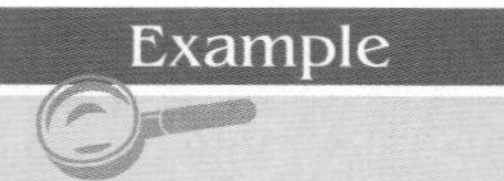

Faulty Implementation: General Motors Has to Rehire Former Workers at Higher Cost

Aggressive cost cutting is a time-honored strategy for improving a manager's bottom line. But reducing expenses through repeated rounds of layoffs and even offering buyout and early retirement packages to workers can be mishandled, leading to negative results.

During the 2001–2003 recession, companies ranging from Procter & Gamble to Lucent Technologies offered voluntary buyout packages to try to shrink their workforces. Instead of using layoffs, companies may see voluntary buyouts as a more compassionate form of cost cutting, allowing employees to walk out on their own. However, the tactic isn't always implemented effectively.

"The thing that doesn't work is just asking for volunteers," says Ron Nicol, a principal at the Boston Consulting Group. "You get the wrong volunteers. Some of your best people will feel they can get a job anywhere. Or you have people who are close to retirement and are a real asset to the company."[13]

In 1994, for example, a General Motors Corp. voluntary early-retirement plan left it shorthanded in plants in Texas and Louisiana. As a result, it was forced to offer GM retirees in California as much as $21,000 in incentives to return to work.

Evaluation

One "law" in economics is the Law of Unintended Consequences—things happen that weren't foreseen. For this reason, you need to follow up and evaluate the results of the decision.

What should you do if the action is not working? Some possibilities:

- **Give it more time:** You need to make sure employees, customers, and so on have had enough time to get used to the new action.
- **Change it slightly:** Maybe the action was correct, but it just needs "tweaking"—a small change of some sort.
- **Try another alternative:** If Plan A doesn't seem to be working, maybe you want to scrap it for another alternative.
- **Start over:** If no alternative seems workable, you need to go back to the drawing board—to Stage 1 of the decision-making process.

What's Wrong with the Rational Model?

The rational model is *prescriptive,* describing how managers ought to make decisions. It doesn't describe how managers *actually* make decisions. Indeed, the rational model makes some highly desirable assumptions—that managers have complete information, are able to make an unemotional analysis, and are able to make the best decision for the organization. *(See Table 7.1.)*

TABLE 7.1
Assumptions of the rational model

• **Complete information, no uncertainty:** You should obtain complete, error-free information about all alternative courses of action and the consequences that would follow from each choice.
• **Logical, unemotional analysis:** Having no prejudices or emotional blind spots, you are able to logically evaluate the alternatives, ranking them from best to worst according to your personal preferences.
• **Best decision for the organization:** Confident of the best future course of action, you coolly choose the alternative that you believe will most benefit the organization.

Evaluation: McDonald's Drops Super Size Menu Option

The McDonald's Super Size french fry and soft drink option generated a lot of attention—and damage to the McDonald's image—so much so that the company decided to phase it out at the end of 2004.

What kind of attention led to this evaluation? First, there was the interest from consumers, with one in 10 requesting the extra-calorie upgrade, so that the term "super sizing" became a pop-culture term for anything oversized. Second, there was the attention from nutritionists and physicians concerned about America's obesity problem. Third, there was attention from lawyers and advocacy groups, who had begun to target fast food as being nearly as damaging as nicotine. Fourth, there was interest from the mass media, including filmmakers (such as Morgan Spurlock, who produced the documentary *Super Size Me*), who had put out a great deal of material on the harm of overeating.

McDonald's downplayed the decision as part of a "menu simplification" process. At the same time, a spokesman said, "It certainly is consistent with and on a parallel path with our ongoing commitment to a balanced lifestyle."[14]

Nonrational Decision Making: Managers Find It Difficult to Make Optimum Decisions

In contrast to models that show how decisions should be made are various models of how decisions actually *are* made. ***Nonrational models of decision making*** **explain how managers do make decisions; they assume that decision making is nearly always uncertain and risky, making it difficult for managers to make optimum decisions.** The nonrational models are *descriptive* rather than prescriptive: They describe how managers *actually* make decisions rather than how they should. Two nonrational models are *satisficing* and *incremental.*

1 Bounded Rationality & the Satisficing Model: "Satisfactory Is Good Enough"

During the 1950s, economist **Herbert Simon**—who later received the Nobel Prize—began to study how managers actually make decisions. From his research he proposed that managers could not act truly logically because their rationality was bounded by so many restrictions.[15] Called ***bounded rationality,*** **the concept suggests that the ability of decision makers to be rational is limited by numerous constraints,** such as complexity, time and money, and their cognitive capacity, values, skills, habits, and unconscious reflexes. *(See Figure 7.3.)*

FIGURE 7.3
Some hindrances to perfectly rational decision making

- **Complexity:** The problems that need solving are often exceedingly complex, beyond understanding.
- **Time and money constraints:** There is not enough time and money to gather all relevant information.
- **Different cognitive capacity, values, skills, habits, and unconscious reflexes:** Managers aren't all built the same way, of course, and all have personal limitations and biases that affect their judgment.
- **Imperfect information:** Managers have imperfect, fragmentary information about the alternatives and their consequences.
- **Information overload:** There is too much information for one person to process.
- **Different priorities:** Some data is considered more important, so certain facts are ignored.
- **Conflicting goals:** Other managers, including colleagues, have conflicting goals.

Because of such constraints, managers don't make an exhaustive search for the best alternative. Instead, they follow what Simon calls the ***satisficing model*** **—that is, managers seek alternatives until they find one that is satisfactory, not optimal.** Iridium's decision to proceed with a clunky one-pound satellite phone instead of waiting to improve the technology is an example of satisficing.

While looking for a solution that is merely "satisficing" might seem to be a weakness, it may well outweigh any advantages gained from delaying making a decision until all information is in and all alternatives weighed. However, making snap decisions can also backfire.

2 The Incremental Model: "The Least That Will Solve the Problem"

Another nonrational decision-making model is the ***incremental model,*** **in which managers take small, short-term steps to alleviate a problem,** rather than steps that will accomplish a long-term solution. Of course, over time a series of short-term steps may move toward a long-term solution. However, the temporary steps may also impede a beneficial long-term solution.

Making Better Decisions through Knowledge Management

No doubt you have made decisions that later you realized you would have made differently if you had had more complete information. The same happens with decision making in organizations. There, however, managers often find that they need information possessed by people working elsewhere in the system. Accordingly, there is now a growing interest in what is known as knowledge management. ***Knowledge management*** **is the development of an organizational culture—and the tools, processes, systems, and structures—that encourages continuous learning and sharing of knowledge and information among employees, for the purpose of making better decisions.**[16]

Science under glass. Columbia University's Biosphere 2, a huge glass and metal ecological research facility located 20 miles north of Tucson, Ariz., is a three-acre test tube meant to mimic Biosphere 1—planet earth. In this kind of model, would decision makers' rationality be less bounded?

The Two Types of Knowledge: Explicit versus Tacit

To begin to comprehend this subject, it helps to understand that there are two types of knowledge—*explicit* and *tacit*.[17]

Explicit Knowledge: "Textbook Knowledge" That Can Be Easily Expressed & Shared. An expert in a certain field (tax lawyer, mortgage broker, whatever) may be said to have surface knowledge or "textbook knowledge." This is ***explicit knowledge,*** **information that can be easily put into words, graphics, and numbers and shared with others.** An example is information about the U.S. tax code that can be looked up.

Tacit Knowledge: "Tricks of the Trade" Learned from Experience & Difficult to Express. An expert of many years' experience also has a lot of deep knowledge or "tricks of the trade." This is ***tacit knowledge,*** **which is individual-based, intuitive, acquired through considerable experience, and hard to express and to share.** Examples are how to swing a golf club, write a speech, or find one-of-a-kind exceptions in the tax code.

Sharing Knowledge to Help Decision Making

Both explicit and tacit knowledge affect decision making. However, it's suggested that it is the sharing of tacit knowledge in particular that creates competitive advantage.[18] Two ways to share knowledge are high-tech solutions and low-tech solutions.[19]

High-Tech Solutions: To Share Explicit Knowledge. As you might expect, information technology—e-mail, intranets, websites, databases—can be of considerable benefit in helping employees learn and share knowledge. This is particularly the case for explicit knowledge.

Low-Tech Solutions: To Share Tacit Knowledge. But technology alone is not enough. As Anne Mulcahy, chair and CEO of Xerox, says, "Technology requires changes in the way humans work, yet companies continue to inject technology without making the necessary changes"—that is, increase learning.[20] Tacit knowledge is best shared directly, as through informal networking, periodic meetings, and interaction with mentors and coaches. Particularly crucial is an organizational culture that encourages the spread of tacit knowledge. ◆

major question

What guidelines can I follow to be sure that decisions I make are not just lawful but ethical?

The Big Picture

A graph known as a decision tree can help one make ethical decisions. In addition, one should be aware of "the magnificent seven" general moral principles for managers.

"Have we saved capitalism from the capitalists?" writes Mortimer Zuckerman, editor-in-chief of *U.S. News & World Report* (and, incidentally, quite a capitalist himself, being a self-made billionaire, mainly through real estate). In the early 2000s, one business scandal followed another, from Enron to WorldCom. "The supposedly 'independent' auditors, directors, accountants, and stock market advisers and accountants were all tarnished," Zuckerman goes on, "the engine of the people's involvement, the mutual fund industry, was shown to be permeated by rip-off artists rigging the system for the benefit of insiders and the rich. To crown it all, the high temple of capitalism, the New York Stock Exchange, was polluted by cronyism and greed."[21]

The images of handcuffed executives has forced the subject of right-minded decision making to the top of the agenda in many organizations. Indeed, many companies now have an ***ethics officer,*** **someone trained about matters of ethics in the workplace, particularly about resolving ethical dilemmas.** More and more companies are also creating values statements to guide employees as to what constitutes desirable business behavior.[22] As a result of this raised consciousness, managers now must try to make sure their decisions are not just lawful but also ethical.

Road Map to Ethical Decision Making: A Decision Tree

One of the greatest pressures—if not *the* greatest pressure—on top executives is to maximize shareholder value, to deliver the greatest return on investment to the owners of their company. But is a decision that is beneficial to shareholders yet harmful to employees—such as forcing them to contribute more to their health benefits, as IBM has done—unethical? Harvard Business School professor Constance Bagley suggests that what is needed is a decision tree to help with ethical decisions.[23] **A *decision tree* is a graph of decisions and their possible consequences; it is used to create a plan to reach a goal.** Decision trees are used to aid in making decisions. Bagley's ethical decision tree is shown opposite. *(See Figure 7.4.)*

When confronted with any proposed action for which a decision is required, a manager should ask the following questions:

1. **Is the Proposed Action Legal?** This may seem an obvious question. But, Bagley observes, "recent [2002–2003] corporate shenanigans suggest that some managers need to be reminded: If the action isn't legal, don't do it."
2. **If "Yes," Does the Proposed Action Maximize Shareholder Value?** If the action is legal, one must next ask whether it will profit the shareholders. If the answer is "yes," should you do it? Not necessarily.
3. **If "Yes," Is the Proposed Action Ethical?** As Bagley, points out, though directors and top managers may believe they are bound by corporate law to

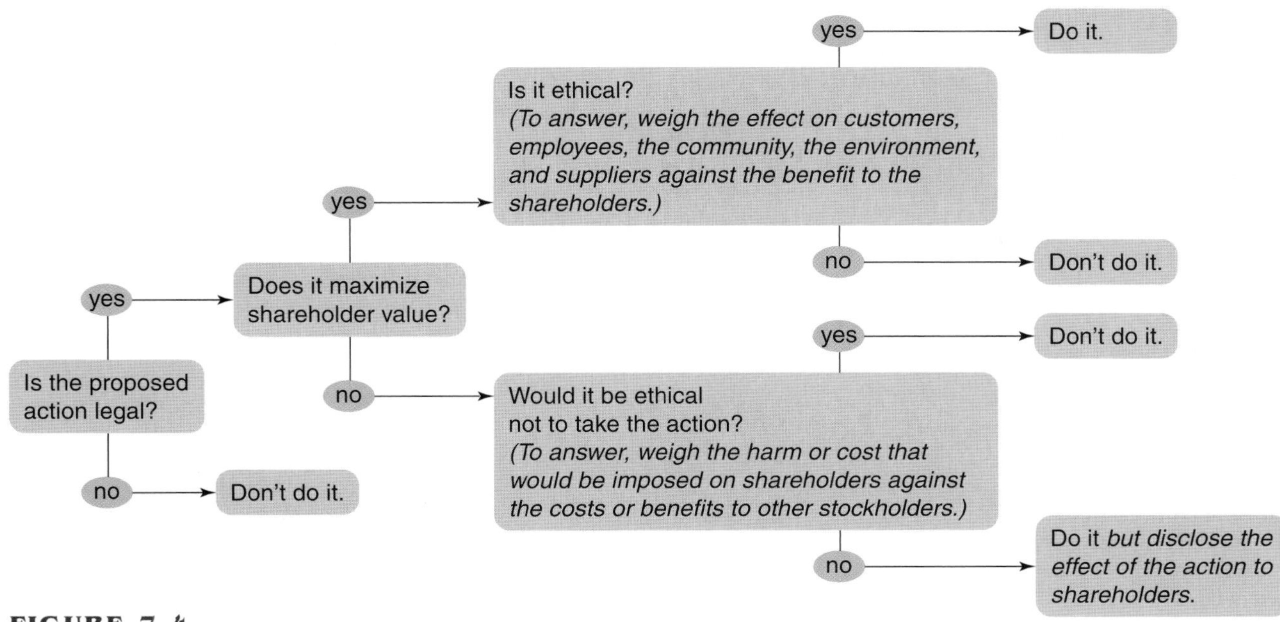

FIGURE 7.4

The ethical decision tree: What's the right thing to do? (Source: C. E. Bagley, "The Ethical Leader's Decision Tree," *Harvard Business Review,* February 2003, p. 19.)

always maximize shareholder value, the courts and many state legislatures have held they are not. Rather, their main obligation is to manage "for the best interests of the corporation," which includes the larger community.

Thus, says Bagley, building a profitable-but-polluting plant in a country overseas may benefit the shareholders but be bad for that country—and for the corporation's relations with that nation. Ethically, then, managers should add pollution-control equipment.

4. **If "No," Would It Be Ethical *Not* to Take the Proposed Action?** If the action would not directly benefit shareholders, might it still be ethical to go ahead with it?

   Not building the overseas plant might be harmful to other stakeholders, such as employees or customers. Thus, the ethical conclusion might be to build the plant with pollution-control equipment but to disclose the effects of the decision to shareholders.

Applying the Ethical Decision Tree

When IBM decided to raise its retirees' health benefit contributions to save the company money, was that an ethical decision? Certainly it created a positive impact on shareholder value. However, at the same it hurt employees, some of whom were not able to easily pay for health-related expenses. For instance, retiree Fran Asbeck, an IBM programmer for 32 years, had to get another job in order to pay for his health insurance. "I'm just going to have to work until I'm in the box and hear the dirt hit the lid," he says.[24] Retirees realize that IBM is covered legally, but they feel betrayed. "We feel that IBM has a social contract with the retirees . . . for which they are now reneging," says a former IBM employee in Vermont.[25]

As a basic guideline to making good ethical decisions on behalf of a corporation, Bagley suggests that directors, managers, and employees need to follow their own individual ideas about right and wrong. There is a lesson, she suggests, in the response of the pension fund manager who, when asked whether she would invest in a company doing business in a country that permits slavery, responded, "Do you mean me, personally, or as a fund manager?" When people feel entitled or compelled to compromise their own personal ethics to advance the interests of a business, "it is an invitation to mischief."[26]

General Moral Principles for Managers

Management consultant and writer Kent Hodgson suggests there are no absolute ethical answers for managerial decision makers. Rather, the goal for managers, he believes, should be to rely on moral principles so that their decisions are *principled, appropriate,* and *defensible.*[27] Accordingly, Hodgson has put forth what he calls "the magnificent seven" general moral principles for managers. *(See Table 7.2)* ◆

TABLE 7.2

The magnificent seven: General moral principles for managers [Source: K. Hodgson, *A Rock and a Hard Place: How to Make Ethical Business Decisions When the Choices Are Tough* (New York: AMACOM, 1992), pp. 69–73. ©1992 Kent Hodgson. Published by AMACOM, a division of the American Management Association. Used with permission.]

1. **Dignity of human life: The lives of people are to be respected.** Human beings, by the fact of their existence, have value and dignity. We may not act in ways that directly intend to harm or kill an innocent person. Human beings have a right to live; we have an obligation to respect that right to life. Human life is to be preserved and treated as sacred.

2. **Autonomy: All persons are intrinsically valuable and have the right to self-determination.** We should act in ways that demonstrate each person's worth, dignity, and right to free choice. We have a right to act in ways that assert our own worth and legitimate needs. We should not use others as mere "things" or only as means to an end. Each person has an equal right to basic human liberty, compatible with a similar liberty for others.

3. **Honesty: The truth should be told to those who have a right to know it.** Honesty is also known as integrity, truth telling, and honor. One should speak and act so as to reflect the reality of the situation. Speaking and acting should mirror the way things really are. There are times when others have the right to hear the truth from us; there are times when they do not.

4. **Loyalty: Promises, contracts, and commitments should be honored.** Loyalty includes fidelity, promise keeping, keeping the public trust, good citizenship, excellence in quality of work, reliability, commitment, and honoring just laws and policies.

5. **Fairness: People should be treated justly.** One has the right to be treated fairly, impartially, and equitably. One has the obligation to treat others fairly and justly. All have the right to the necessities of life—especially those in deep need and the helpless. Justice includes equal, impartial, unbiased treatment. Fairness tolerates diversity and accepts differences in people and their ideas.

6. **Humaneness.** There are two parts: (1) **Our actions ought to accomplish good,** and (2) **we should avoid doing evil.** We should do good to others and to ourselves. We should have concern for the well-being of others; usually, we show this concern in the form of compassion, giving, kindness, serving, and caring.

7. **The common good: Actions should accomplish the "greatest good for the greatest number" of people.** One should act and speak in ways that benefit the welfare of the largest number of people, while trying to protect the rights of individuals.

Example

Deciding to Do Right When It's Difficult: Could You Do What Doug Durand Did?

Do you ever cheat?

David Callahan, founder of the Demos Public Policy Center in New York, is author of *The Cheating Culture: Why More Americans Are Doing Wrong to Get Ahead.*[28] The kind of cheating he's concerned with is not so much with drug use or choices of sexual behavior but, as one book reviewer puts it, with "ordinary people's willingness to deceive others and cut corners purely to make more money or win some prize."[29] Examples are employees who use company time for personal business, doctors who bill for services not delivered, financial advisers who accept payoffs to steer customers toward risky investments—and students who copy test answers or buy term papers.

Consider the last matter: according to one assessment of how well college students learn, 87% of undergraduates say their peers at least "sometimes" copy and paste information from the Web when doing research without citing the source.[30] More and more colleges are therefore signing up for plagiarism-detector websites so that professors can check student papers for originality.[31] Educators have also seen a wave of cheating with camera phones, as when students use their phones in test situations to call up photos of key notes they took back in the dorm.[32] "More students are using cellphones, personal digital assistants, and Internet-connected laptops to cheat during exams," says another article, mostly to exchange notes with fellow exam takers, receive text messages from others outside the testing room, or search the Web for clues to answers.[33] By now, however, most instructors are alert to such practices.

Do people who somehow get away with cheating in college go on to successful careers? No doubt many do—or at least they have in the past and for a certain length of time. Now, however, companies are much more concerned with hiring ethical managers, people who are not bent twigs like, say, WorldCom's chief financial officer Scott Sullivan (who pleaded guilty to fraud and conspiracy) or former Sunbeam CEO Al "Chainsaw" Dunlap (who lied on his résumé about two jobs from which he had been fired). Many organizations have psychological tests and interviewing techniques intended to discover whether job candidates might be inclined to diverge ethically and legally.[34]

Far more valuable are managers like Doug Durand, who after 20 years as a pharmaceutical salesman for Merck & Co. in 1995 joined TAP Pharmaceutical Products Inc. in Lake Forest, Ill., at a salary of $140,000, with the promise of a $50,000 bonus. As a new vice president of sales, Durand was shocked to hear his sales staff in a conference call openly discussing how to bribe urologists (with a 2% "administration fee") for prescribing TAP's prostate cancer drug, Lupron. He also learned that for years TAP reps had encouraged physicians to charge government medical programs full price for Lupron they received for free or at a discount, a tactic designed to help establish Lupron as the prostate treatment of choice. Gradually, Durand learned that TAP, instead of using science to promote its products, relied on kickbacks and freebies—giving big-screen TVs, computers, and golf vacations to cooperating urologists. He also discovered that, though required by federal law, reps could not account for half their Lupron samples. Terrified he might be scapegoated for the illegalities and urged by his wife to get out, he found that other companies that had offered him jobs before TAP had filled their positions.

Eventually, Durand began to secretly document TAP's abuses, sneaking papers home to copy, and finally mailed his material to a friend with close ties to an assistant U.S. attorney specializing in medical fraud. The friend urged him to sue TAP for fraud against the government under the federal whistle-blower program. It wasn't easy for him to do so. "The idea of suing as a whistle-blower intimidated me," Durand said. "Nobody likes a whistle-blower. I thought it could end my career." In the end, however, he found himself believing it was the right thing to do and testifed against former employees and colleagues. The result: The government went after TAP, fined them heavily—and Durand collected $77 million under the federal whistle-blower statute for his efforts.[35]

major question **How do I work with others to make things happen?**

The Big Picture

Group decision making has five potential advantages and four potential disadvantages. There are a number of characteristics of groups that a manager should be aware of, as well as participative management and group problem-solving techniques.

The movies celebrate the lone heroes who, like Clint Eastwood, make their own moves, call their own shots. Most managers, however, work with groups and teams (as we discuss in Chapter 13). Although groups don't make as high-quality decisions as the best individual acting alone, research suggests that groups make better decisions than *most* individuals acting alone.[36] Thus, to be an effective manager, you need to learn about decision making in groups.

Advantages & Disadvantages of Group Decision Making

Because you may often have a choice as to whether to make a decision by yourself or to consult with others, you need to understand the advantages and disadvantages of group-aided decision making.

Advantages

Using a group to make a decision offers five possible advantages.[37] For these benefits to happen, however, the group must be made up of diverse participants, not just people who all think the same way.

- **Greater pool of knowledge:** When several people are making the decision, there is a greater pool of information from which to draw. If one person doesn't have the pertinent knowledge and experience, someone else might.
- **Different perspectives:** Because different people have different perspectives—marketing, production, legal, and so on—they see the problem from different angles.
- **Intellectual stimulation:** A group of people can brainstorm or otherwise bring greater intellectual stimulation and creativity to the decision-making process than is usually possible with one person acting alone.

Different perspectives or groupthink? A diversified team can offer differing points of view, as well as a greater pool of knowledge and intellectual stimulation. Or it can offer groupthink and satisficing. What has been your experience as to the value of decision making in the groups you've been in?

- **Better understanding of decision rationale:** If you participate in making a decision, you are more apt to understand the reasoning behind the decision, including the pros and cons leading up to the final step.
- **Deeper commitment to the decision:** If you've been part of the group that has bought into the final decision, you're more apt to be committed to seeing that the course of action is successfully implemented.

Ford 2005 GT Mustang. Highly motivated work teams depend on open communications and self-management. Ford Motor Co. provided such an atmosphere for its Team Mustang work group, which produced this revamp of the 1969 fastback model. The work team, suppliers, and consumers worked together to make the Mustang a winner in the competitive automobile market.

Disadvantages

The disadvantages of group-aided decision making spring from problems in how members interact.[38]

- **A few people dominate or intimidate:** Sometimes a handful of people will talk the longest and the loudest, and the rest of the group will simply give in. Or one individual, such as a strong leader, will exert disproportional influence, sometimes by intimidation. This cuts down on the variety of ideas.
- **Groupthink:** ***Groupthink* occurs when group members strive to agree for the sake of unanimity and thus avoid accurately assessing the decision situation.** Here the positive team spirit of the group actually works against sound judgment.
- **Satisficing:** Because most people would just as soon cut short a meeting, the tendency is to seek a decision that is "good enough" rather than to push on in pursuit of other possible solutions. Satisficing can occur because groups have limited time, lack the right kind of information, or are unable to handle large amounts of information.[39]
- **Goal displacement:** Although the primary task of the meeting may be to solve a particular problem, other considerations may rise to the fore, such as rivals trying to win an argument. ***Goal displacement* occurs when the primary goal is subsumed by a secondary goal.**

What Managers Need to Know about Groups & Decision Making

If you're a manager deliberating whether to call a meeting for group input, there are four characteristics of groups to be aware of:

1 They Are Less Efficient

Groups take longer to make decisions. Thus, if time is of the essence, you may want to make the decision by yourself. Faced with time pressures or the serious effect of a decision, groups use less information and fewer communication channels, which increases the probability of a bad decision.[40]

2 Their Size Affects Decision Quality

The larger the group, the lower the quality of the decision.[41]

3 They May Be Too Confident

Groups are more confident about their judgments and choices than individuals are. This, of course, can be a liability because it can lead to groupthink.

4 Knowledge Counts

Decision-making accuracy is higher when group members know a good deal about the relevant issues. It is also higher when a group leader has the ability to weight members' opinions.[42] Depending on whether group members know or don't know one another, the kind of knowledge also counts. For example, people who are familiar with one another tend to make better decisions when members have a lot of unique information. However, people who aren't familiar with one another tend to make better decisions when the members have common knowledge.[43]

Some guidelines to using groups are presented below. *(See Figure 7.5.)* Remember that individual decisions are not *necessarily* better than group decisions. As we said at the outset, although groups don't make as high-quality decisions as the *best* individual acting alone, groups generally make better decisions than *most* individuals acting alone.

FIGURE 7.5

When a group can help in decision making: three practical guidelines. The following guidelines may help you as a manager decide whether to include people in a decision-making process and, if so, which people. [Source: Derived from George P. Huber, *Managerial Decision Making* (Glenview, IL: Scott Foresman, 1980), p. 149.]

1 **When it can increase quality:** If additional information would increase the quality of the decision, managers should involve those people who can provide the needed information. Thus, if a type of decision occurs frequently, such as deciding on promotions or who qualifies for a loan, groups should be used because they tend to produce more consistent decisions than individuals do.

2 **When it can increase acceptance:** If acceptance within the organization is important, managers need to involve those individuals whose acceptance and commitment are important.

3 **When it can increase development:** If people can be developed through their participation, managers may want to involve those whose development is most important.

Participative Management: Involving Employees in Decision Making

"Only the most productive companies are going to win," says former General Electric CEO Jack Welch about competition in the world economy. "If you can't sell a top-quality product at the world's lowest price, you're going to be out of the game. In that environment, 6% annual improvement may not be good enough anymore; you may need 8% to 9%."[44]

Welch. The GE CEO was one of the most successful executives in American business history.

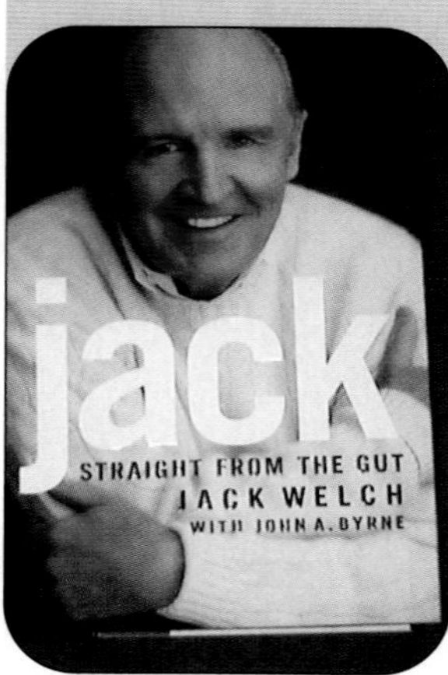

What Is PM?

One technique that has been touted for meeting this productivity challenge is ***participative management (PM),*** **the process of involving employees in (a) setting goals, (b) making decisions, (c) solving problems, and (d) making changes in the organization.**[45] Employees themselves seem to want to participate more in management: in one nationwide survey of 2,408 workers, two-thirds expressed the desire for more influence or decision-making power in their jobs.[46] Thus, participative management is predicted to increase motivation, innovation, and performance because it helps employees fulfill three basic needs: autonomy, meaningfulness of work, and interpersonal contact.[47]

Is PM Really Effective?

Does participative management really work? Certainly it can increase employee job involvement, organizational commitment, and creativity, and it can lower role conflict and ambiguity.[48] Yet it has been shown that, although participation has a significant effect on job performance and job satisfaction, that effect is small—a finding that calls into question the practicality of using PM at all.[49]

So what's a manager to do? In our opinion, PM is not a quick-fix solution for low productivity and motivation. Yet it can probably be effective in certain situations, assuming that managers and employees interact constructively—that is, have the kind of relationship that fosters cooperation and respect rather than competition and defensiveness.[50]

Although participative management doesn't work in all situations, it can be effective if certain factors are present, such as supportive managers and employee trust. *(See Table 7.3.)*

TABLE 7.3
Factors that can help make participative management work

- **Top management is continually involved:** Implementing PM must be monitored and managed by top management.
- **Middle and supervisory managers are supportive:** These managers tend to resist PM because it reduces their authority. Thus, it's important to gain the support and commitment of managers in these ranks.
- **Employees trust managers:** PM is likely to succeed when employees don't trust management.
- **Employees are ready:** PM is more effective when employees are properly trained, prepared, and interested in participating.
- **Employees don't work in interdependent jobs:** Interdependent employees generally don't have a broad understanding of the entire production process, so their PM contribution may actually be counterproductive.
- **PM is implemented with TQM:** A study of Fortune 1000 firms during three different years found employee involvement was more effective when it was implemented as part of a broader total quality management (TQM) program.

Sources: P. E. Tesluk, J. L. Farr, J. E. Matheieu, and R. J. Vance, "Generalization of Employee Involvement Training to the Job Setting: Individual and Situational Effects," *Personnel Psychology,* Autumn 1995, pp. 607–632; R. Rodgers, J. E. Hunter, and D. L. Rogers, "Influence of Top Management Commitment on Management Program Success," *Journal of Applied Psychology,* February 1993, pp. 151–155; and S. A. Mohrman, E. E. Lawler III, and G. E. Ledford Jr., "Organizational Effectiveness and the Impact of Employee Involvement and TQM Programs: Do Employee Involvement and TQM Programs Work?" *Journal for Quality and Participation,* January/February 1996, pp. 6–10.

Group Problem-Solving Techniques: Reaching for Consensus

Using groups to make decisions generally requires that they reach a ***consensus,*** **which occurs when members are able to express their opinions and reach agreement to support the final decision.** More specifically, consensus is reached "when all members can say they either agree with the decision or have had their 'day in court' and were unable to convince the others of their viewpoint," says one expert in decision making. "In the final analysis, everyone agrees to support the outcome."[51] This does not mean, however, that group members agree with the decision, only that they are willing to work toward its success.

Toward consensus. Working to achieve cooperation in a group can tell you a lot about yourself. How well do you handle the negotiation process? What do you do when you're disappointed in a result reached by consensus?

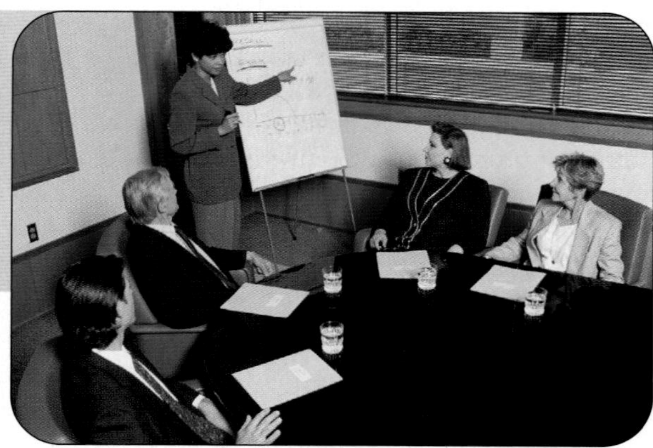

One management expert offers the following dos and don'ts for achieving consensus.[52]

- **Dos:** Use active listening skills. Involve as many members as possible. Seek out the reasons behind arguments. Dig for the facts.
- **Don'ts:** Avoid log rolling and horse trading ("I'll support your pet project if you'll support mine"). Avoid making an agreement simply to keep relations amicable and not rock the boat. Finally, don't try to achieve consensus by putting questions to a vote; this will only split the group into winners and losers, perhaps creating bad feeling among the latter.

More Group Problem-Solving Techniques

Decision-making experts have developed three group-problem-solving techniques to aid in problem solving: (1) *interacting groups,* (2) *nominal groups,* and (3) *Delphi groups*. These may be assisted with (4) *computer-aided decision making.*

1 The Interacting Group: For Open Discussion

The most common decision-making group, the ***interacting group*** **is a group in which members interact and deliberate with one another to reach a consensus.** No doubt you've been in such a group—discussing, arguing, persuading, agreeing, disagreeing until a consensus was achieved.

2 The Nominal Group: For Generating Ideas

Members of a nominal group don't talk to one another—at least in the beginning. Rather, **the purpose of a** ***nominal group*** **is to generate ideas and evaluate solutions, which members do by writing down as many ideas as possible. The ideas are then listed on a blackboard, then discussed, then voted on.**

During the discussion period, there may be a "30-second soapbox" format, in which every participant is allowed 30 seconds to argue for or against any idea listed. After discussion, group members may vote—anonymously—using a weighted voting procedure (for example, first choice = 3 points, second choice = 2 points, third choice = 1 point). The group leader tallies the points to determine the group's choice.[53]

3 The Delphi Group: For Consensus of Experts

The Delphi group technique was originally designed for technological forecasting but now is used as a multipurpose planning tool.[54] **The** ***Delphi group*** **uses physically dispersed experts who fill out questionnaires to anonymously generate ideas; the judgments are combined and in effect averaged to achieve a consensus of expert opinion.**

The Delphi group technique is useful when face-to-face discussions are impractical. It's also practical when disagreement and conflicts are likely to impair communication, when certain individuals might try to dominate group discussions, and when there is a high risk of groupthink.[55]

4 Computer-Aided Decision Making

As in nearly every other aspect of business life, computers have entered the area of decision making, where they are useful not only in collecting information more quickly but also in reducing roadblocks to group consensus.

The two types of computer-aided decision making systems are *chauffeur driven* and *group driven,* as follows:[56]

- **Chauffeur-driven systems—for push-button consensus:** So-called *"chauffeur-driven" computer-aided decision-making systems* ask participants to answer predetermined questions on electronic keypads or dials. These have been used as polling devices, for instance, with audiences on live television shows such as *Who Wants to Be a Millionaire,* allowing responses to be computer-tabulated almost instantly.
- **Group-driven systems—for anonymous networking:** A *group-driven computer-aided decision system* involves a meeting within a room of participants who express their ideas anonymously on a computer network. Instead of talking with one another, participants type their comments, reactions, or evaluations on their individual computer keyboards. The input is projected on a large screen at the front of the room for all to see. Because participation is anonymous and no one person is able to dominate the meeting on the basis of status or personality, everyone feels free to participate, and the roadblocks to consensus are accordingly reduced.

  Compared to the nominal-group technique or traditional brainstorming, group-driven systems have been shown to produce greater quality and quantity of ideas for large groups of people, although there is no advantage with groups of 4–6 people.[57] The technique also produces more ideas as group size increases from 5 to 10 members. ◆

Computer-aided decision making. This photo shows the kind of arrangement that might be set up for group-driven, anonymous networking.

major question

Trying to be rational isn't always easy. What are the barriers?

The Big Picture

Responses to a decision situation may take the form of four ineffective reactions or three effective reactions. Managers should be aware of four common decision-making biases.

Do you make decisions based on how happy or unhappy you think you're going to feel about the outcome? Then here's some interesting news.

It seems that people expect certain life events to have a much greater emotional effect than in fact they do, according to Harvard University psychologist Daniel Gilbert, who has studied individual emotional barometers in decision making. College professors, for example, expect to be quite happy if they are given tenure and quite unhappy if they aren't. However, Gilbert found those who received tenure were happy but not as happy as they themselves had predicted, whereas those denied tenure did not become very unhappy.

The expectation about the level of euphoria or disappointment was also found to be true of big-jackpot lottery winners and of people being tested for HIV infection. That is, people are often right when they describe what outcome will make them feel good or bad, but they are often wrong when asked to predict how strongly they will feel that way and how long the feeling will last. "Even severe life events have a negative impact on people's sense of well-being and satisfaction for no more than three months," says one report, "after which their feelings at least go back to normal."[58]

Perhaps knowing that you have this "immune system" of the mind, which blunts bad feelings and smoothes out euphoric ones, can help make it easier for you to make difficult decisions.

How Do Individuals Respond to a Decision Situation? Ineffective & Effective Responses

What is your typical response when you're suddenly confronted with a challenge in the form of a problem or an opportunity? There are perhaps four ineffective reactions and three effective ones.[59]

Four Ineffective Reactions

Four defective problem-recognition and problem-solving approaches that act as barriers when you must make an important decision in a situation of conflict are the following:

1 Relaxed Avoidance—"There's no point in doing anything; nothing bad's going to happen": **In *relaxed avoidance,* a manager decides to take no action in the belief that there will be no great negative consequences.** This condition, then, is a form of complacency: You either don't see or you disregard the signs of danger (or of opportunity).

For example, you might decide to accept a job offer without checking the financial status of your new employer, even though the company is in an industry being whipsawed by technological change. After his first employer went out of business because of poor money management, programmer Bryan Galdrikian began asking prospective employers more about their finances.[60]

2 Relaxed Change—"Why not just take the easiest way out?": In *relaxed change,* a manager realizes that complete inaction will have negative consequences but opts for the first available alternative that involves low risk. This is, of course, a form of "satisficing"; the manager avoids exploring a variety of alternatives in order to make the best decision.

For example, if you go to the college career center, sign up for one job interview, and are offered and accept a job based on that single interview, you may have no basis for comparison to know that you made the right choice.

3 Defensive Avoidance—"There's no reason for me to explore other solution alternatives": In *defensive avoidance,* a manager can't find a good solution and follows by (a) procrastinating, (b) passing the buck, or (c) denying the risk of any negative consequences. This is a posture of resignation and a denial of responsibility for taking action. By procrastinating, you put off making a decision ("I'll get to this later"). In passing the buck, you let someone else take the consequences of making the decision ("Let George do it"). In denying the risk that there will be any negative consequences, you are engaging in rationalizing ("How bad could it be?").

According to one report, many college students graduating in 2004, following the two-year recession and dismal job prospects, are doing anything but practicing defensive avoidance. Aware of the economy's inherent instability, many have taken steps that will help them find jobs with more security. Thus, when a Ford Motor Co. recruiter visited Ohio State University, he was amazed not to get the usual questions about salaries and vacations from graduating seniors. Armed with Wall Street analysts' reports, the job candidates peppered him with questions about layoff prospects and foreign competition. "They had independent research and were trying to put me on the spot," said the recruiter. "This is a level of inquiry that I didn't use to see from a bachelor of business administration."[61]

4 Panic—"This is so stressful, I've got to do something—anything—to get rid of the problem": This reaction is especially apt to occur in crisis situations. **In *panic,* a manager is so frantic to get rid of the problem that he or she can't deal with the situation realistically.** This is the kind of situation in which the manager has completely forgotten the idea of behaving with "grace under pressure," of staying cool and calm. Troubled by anxiety, irritability, sleeplessness, and even physical illness, if you're experiencing this reaction, your judgment may be so clouded that you won't be able to accept help in dealing with the problem or to realistically evaluate the alternatives.

Panic. Can you think of times in your life when you made a panicky decision? What about situations in which you kept your cool instead of buckling under pressure?

Panic can even be life-threatening. When in 1999 a jetliner skidded off the runway at Little Rock National Airport, passenger Clark Brewster and a flight attendant tried repeatedly to open an exit door that would not budge. "About that time I hear someone say the word 'Fire!'" Brewster said. "The flight attendant bends down and says, 'Please pray with me.'" Fortunately, cooler, quicker-thinking individuals were able to find another way out.[62]

Three Effective Reactions: Deciding to Decide

In *deciding to decide,* a manager agrees that he or she must decide what to do about a problem or opportunity and take effective decision-making steps. Three ways to help you decide whether to decide are to evaluate the following:[63]

1 Importance—"How high priority is this situation?": You need to determine how much priority to give the decision situation. If it's a threat, how extensive might prospective losses or damage be? If it's an opportunity, how beneficial might the possible gains be?

2 Credibility—"How believable is the information about the situation?": You need to evaluate how much is known about the possible threat or opportunity. Is the source of the information trustworthy? Is there credible evidence?

3 Urgency—"How quickly must I act on the information about the situation?": Is the threat immediate? Will the window of opportunity stay open long? Can actions to address the situation be done gradually?

Example

Deciding to Decide: If You Own a Fast Thoroughbred, Should You Even Bother to Race It?

Owning a racehorse, especially one with the potential to win the famed Kentucky Derby, is like owning a million-dollar business. If your objective is to make money, how should you manage such valuable property?

After a horse named Fusaichi Pegasus won the 2000 Kentucky Derby, his owner, Fusao Sekiguchi, had to decide: To make the most money, should he continue to race the horse? Or should he auction it off to a commercial breeder, who would use him to breed with mares to produce a strain of superior thoroughbreds? Because the money involved millions, the answer to his first decision—*Should this be considered a high-priority matter?*—seems obvious.

Sekiguchi decided the facts warranted that he should sell rather than race. The main determinant here was *How believable is the information?* For this decision, research would have shown that the career leader in winning purses, $10 million, was a horse named Cigar, which ran through age 6. Research would also show the stud fees of retired successful race horses ran, per mare, from $5,000 (for Grindstone) to $80,000 (for Charismatic). Finally, recent history showed that breeding had caused horses to be faster but less durable than earlier thoroughbreds, making injury more likely.

The final decision—*How quickly should this information be acted on?*—was affected by the fact that most race horses are finished by age 4, even age 2.

After three more races, Fusaichi Pegasus was sold for $60 million to a stud farm, where he is bred to more than 100 mares a year for a record stud fee of $135,000 a mare.[64]

Four Common Decision-Making Biases: Rules of Thumb, or "Heuristics"

If someone asked you to explain the basis on which you make decisions, could you even say? Perhaps, after some thought, you might come up with some "rules of thumb." Scholars call them ***heuristics*** **(pronounced "hyur-*ris*-tiks")—strategies that simplify the process of making decisions.**

Despite the fact that people use such rules of thumb all the time, that doesn't mean they're reliable. Indeed, some are real barriers to high-quality decision making. Among those that tend to bias how decision makers process information are (1) *availability,* (2) *representativeness,* (3) *anchoring and adjustment,* and (4) *escalation of commitment.*[65]

1 The Availability Bias: Using Only the Information Available

If you had a perfect on-time work attendance record for nine months but then were late for work four days during the last two months because of traffic, shouldn't your boss take into account your entire attendance history when considering you for a raise? Yet managers tend to give more weight to more recent behavior. This is because of the ***availability bias*** **—managers use information readily available from memory to make judgments.**

The bias, of course, is that readily available information may not present a complete picture of a situation. The availability bias may be stoked by the news media, which tends to favor news that is unusual or dramatic. Thus, for example, because of the efforts of interest groups or celebrities, more news coverage may be given to AIDS or to breast cancer than to heart disease, leading people to think the former are the bigger killers when in fact the latter is the biggest killer.

2 The Representativeness Bias: Faulty Generalizing from a Small Sample or a Single Event

As a form of financial planning, playing state lotteries leaves something to be desired. When, for instance, in a recent year the New York jackpot reached $70 million, a New Yorker's chance of winning was one in 12,913,588.[66] (A person would have a greater chance of being struck by lightning.) Nevertheless, millions of people buy lottery tickets because they read or hear about a handful of fellow citizens who have been the fortunate recipients of enormous winnings. This is an example of the ***representativeness bias,*** **the tendency to generalize from a small sample or a single event.**

The bias here is that just because something happens once, that doesn't mean it is representative—that it will happen again or will happen to you. For example, just because you hired an extraordinary sales representative from a particular university, that doesn't mean that same university will provide an equally qualified candidate next time. Yet managers make this kind of hiring decision all the time.

3 The Anchoring & Adjustment Bias: Being Influenced by an Initial Figure

Managers will often give their employees a standard percentage raise in salary, basing the decision on whatever the workers made the preceding year. They may do this even though the raise may be completely out of alignment with what other companies are paying for the same skills. This is an instance of the ***anchoring and adjustment bias,*** **the tendency to make decisions based on an initial figure.**

The bias is that the initial figure may be irrelevant to market realities. This phenomenon is sometimes seen in real estate sales. A homeowner may at first list his or her house at an extremely high (but perhaps randomly chosen) selling price. The seller is then unwilling later to come down substantially to match the kind of buying offers that reflect what the marketplace thinks the house is really worth.

4 The Escalation of Commitment Bias: Feeling Overly Invested in a Decision

If you really hate to admit you're wrong, you need to be aware of the ***escalation of commitment bias,*** **whereby decision makers increase their commitment to a project despite negative information about it.** History is full of examples of heads of state who escalated their commitment to an original decision in the face of overwhelming evidence that it was producing detrimental consequences. A noteworthy example was President Lyndon B. Johnson's pressing on of the Vietnam War despite mounting casualties abroad and political upheavals at home.

The bias is that what was originally made as perhaps a rational decision may continue to be supported for irrational reasons—pride, ego, the spending of enormous sums of money, and being "loss averse." Indeed, scholars have advanced what is known as the *prospect theory,* which suggests that decision makers find the notion of an actual loss more painful than giving up the possibility of a gain.[67] We saw a variant of this when we described the tendency of investors to hold on to their losers but cash in their winners. ◆

Escalation of commitment. Hewlett-Packard Co. CEO Carly Fiorina and Compaq Computer Corp. chief executive Michael Capellas do a friendly bumping of knuckles before an investors meeting. The acquisition of Compaq—a leader in the personal computer revolution in the 1980s and 1990s—by technology leader HP in May 2002 was finally achieved after months of a long and bitter corporate war that threatened to derail the biggest computer merger in history. Many analysts and stockholders were against the merger of these two global corporations—first, because of the enormity of the challenge of integrating the two companies and, second, because of the disastrous track record of past computer-company mergers (as when Compaq acquired DEC). Particularly vociferous in their opposition were descendants of the Hewlett and Packard families, who objected not only to the incredibly risky business strategy but also to the prospect of 15,000 job cuts in what had been an employee-friendly environment. A lawsuit bought by director Walter Hewlett that accused HP of drawing overly optimistic financial targets and of buying shareholder votes to approve the merger was unsuccessful, and stockholders finally approved the merger in a close vote. Since then, in 2004, HP announced a new thrust into consumer electronics, unveiling dozens of products from flat-panel TVs to new digital cameras. Perhaps you're now in a position to judge whether the resulting $87 billion global company fulfilled Fiorina's optimistic predictions. Was there too much of an escalation of commitment bias operating here?

practical action

Being Aware of Your Possible Biases: How Can Your Judgment Be Distorted?

The four common decision-making biases described in the text may be expressed in more specific distortions of judgment. Here are five types of questions that you might ask yourself next time you're poised to make a decision:

"Am I Being Too Cocky?" The Overconfidence Bias If you're making a decision in an area in which you have considerable experience or expertise, you're less likely to be overconfident. Interestingly, however, you're more apt to be overconfident when dealing with questions on subjects you're unfamiliar with or questions with moderate to extreme difficulty.[68]

In addition, many sorts of managers—especially top managers who worked their way up to the top—have a kind of overconfidence that makes them overestimate their ability to control events (the *illusion-of-control bias*).

Recommendation: When dealing with unfamiliar or difficult matters, think how your impending decision might go wrong. Afterward pay close attention to the consequences of your decision for feedback about your judgment.

No New Coke. What kind of biases do you think Coca-Cola's managers might have been operating under when, in 1985, they decided to scrap their successful traditional cola formula in favor of New Coke, which became a marketing disaster?

"Am I Considering the Actual Evidence, or Am I Wedded to My Prior Beliefs?" The Prior-Hypothesis Bias Do you tend to have strong beliefs? When confronted with a choice, decision makers with strong prior beliefs tend to make their decision based on their beliefs—even if evidence show those beliefs are wrong. This is known as the *prior-hypothesis bias.* In addition, people tend to look for evidence to support their beliefs rather than contradict them.[69]

Recommendation: Although it's always more comforting to look for evidence to support your prior beliefs, you need to be tough-minded and weigh the evidence.

"Are Events Really Connected, or Are They Just Chance?" The Ignoring-Randomness Bias Is a rise in sales in athletic shoes because of your company's advertising campaign or because it's the start of the school year? Many managers don't understand the laws of randomness and believe chance events—even multiple chance events—are connected to one another.

Recommendation: Don't attribute trends or connections to a single, random event.

"Is There Enough Data on Which to Make a Decision?" The Unrepresentative Sample Bias If all the secretaries in your office say they prefer dairy creamer to real cream or milk in their coffee, is that enough data on which to launch an ad campaign trumpeting the superiority of dairy creamer? It might if you polled 3,000 secretaries, but not if you asked only 3 or even 30. This is too small a sample to reflect the sentiments of secretaries everywhere.

Recommendation: You need to be attuned to the importance of the size of your sample when making a decision.

"Looking Back, Did I (or Others) Really Know Enough Then to Have Made a Better Decision?" The 20-20 Hindsight Bias Once managers know what the consequences of a decision are, they may begin to think they could have predicted it ahead of time. They can no longer recall how uncertain the circumstances were at the time they made the decision. Instead, they may remember the facts as being a lot clearer than they actually were.[70]

Recommendation: Try to keep in mind—especially when you're evaluating negative outcomes of decisions made by subordinates—that hindsight does not equal foresight.

Key Terms Used in This Chapter

Summary

7.1 The Nature of Decision Making

- A decision is a choice made from among available alternatives. Decision making is the process of identifying and choosing alternative courses of action.
- Decisions are of two types: programmed and nonprogrammed. Programmed decisions are repetitive and routine. They tend to follow established rules and so are virtually automatic. Nonprogrammed decisions are those that occur under nonroutine, unfamiliar circumstances. Because they occur in response to unusual, unpredictable opportunities and threats, nonprogrammed decisions are relatively unstructured.
- A decision-making style reflects the combination of how an individual perceives and responds to information. Decision-making styles may tend to have a value orientation, which reflects the extent to which a person focuses on either task or technical concerns versus people and social concerns when making decisions. Decision-making styles may also reflect a person's tolerance for ambiguity, the extent to which a person has a high or low need for structure or control in his or her life. When the dimensions of value orientation and tolerance for ambiguity are combined, they form four styles of decision making: directive, analytical, conceptual, and behavioral.

7.2 Two Kinds of Decision Making: Rational & Nonrational

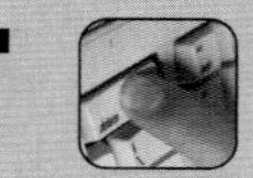

- Two models managers follow in making decisions are rational and nonrational.
- In the rational model, there are four steps in making a decision: Stage 1 is identifying the problem or opportunity. A problem is a difficulty that inhibits the achievement of goals. An opportunity is a situation that presents possibilities for exceeding existing goals. This is a matter of diagnosis—analyzing the underlying causes. Stage 2 is thinking up alternative solutions. For programmed decisions, alternatives will be easy and obvious. For nonprogrammed decisions, the more creative and innovative the alternatives, the better. Stage 3 is evaluating the alternatives and selecting a solution. Alternatives should be evaluated according to cost, quality, ethics, feasibility, and effectiveness. Stage 4 is implementing and evaluating the solution chosen.
- The rational model of decision making assumes managers will make logical decisions that will be the optimum in furthering the organization's best interests. The rational model is prescriptive, describing how managers ought to make decisions. It assumes that managers have complete information and there is no uncertainty, that they can do unemotional analysis, and that they are coolly capable of making the best decision for the organization.

- Nonrational models of decision making assume that decision making is nearly always uncertain and risky, making it difficult for managers to make optimum decisions. Two nonrational models are satisficing and incremental. (1) Satisficing falls under the concept of bounded rationality—that is, that the ability of decision makers to be rational is limited by enormous constraints, such as time and money. These constraints force managers to make decisions according to the satisficing model—that is, managers seek alternatives until they find one that is satisfactory, not optimal. (2) In the incremental model, managers take small, short-term steps to alleviate a problem rather than steps that will accomplish a long-term solution.

7.3 Making Ethical Decisions

- Corporate corruption has made ethics in decision making once again important. Many companies have an ethics officer to resolve ethical dilemmas, and more companies are creating values statements to guide employees as to desirable business behavior.
- To help make ethical decisions, a decision tree—a graph of decisions and their possible consequences—may be helpful. Managers should ask whether a proposed action is legal and, if it is intended to maximize shareholder value, whether it is ethical—and whether it would be ethical *not* to take the proposed action.
- A goal for managers should be to rely on moral principles so that their decisions are principled, appropriate, and defensible, in accordance with "the magnificent seven" general moral principles for managers.

7.4 Group Decision Making: How to Work with Others

- Groups make better decisions than most individuals acting alone, though not as good as the best individual acting alone.
- Using a group to make a decision offers five possible advantages: (1) a greater pool of knowledge; (2) different perspectives; (3) intellectual stimulation; (4) better understanding of the reasoning behind the decision; and (5) deeper commitment to the decision. It also has four disadvantages: (1) a few people may dominate or intimidate; (2) it will produce groupthink, when group members strive for agreement among themselves for the sake of unanimity and so avoid accurately assessing the decision situation; (3) satisficing; and (4) goal displacement, when the primary goal is subsumed to a secondary goal.
- Some characteristics of groups to be aware of are (1) groups are less efficient, (2) their size affects decision quality, (3) they may be too confident, and (4) knowledge counts—decision-making accuracy is higher when group members know a lot about the issues.
- Participative management (PM) is the process of involving employees in setting goals, making decisions, solving problems, and making changes in the organization. PM can increase employee job involvement, organizational commitment, and creativity and can lower role conflict and ambiguity.
- Using groups to make decisions generally requires that they reach a consensus, which occurs when members are able to express their opinions and reach agreement to support the final decision.
- Three group problem-solving techniques aid in problem solving. (1) In interacting groups, members interact and deliberate with one another to reach a consensus. (2) In nominal groups, members generate ideas and evaluate solutions by writing down as many ideas as possible; the ideas are then listed on a blackboard, then discussed, then voted on. (3) In Delphi groups, physically dispersed experts fill out questionnaires to anonymously generate ideas; the judgments are combined and in effect averaged to achieve consensus of expert opinion. These three groups may be assisted by computer-aided decision making, using either chauffeur-driven systems, which ask participants to answer predetermined questions on electronic keypads or dials, or group-driven systems, in which participants in a room express their ideas anonymously on a computer network.

7.5 How to Overcome Barriers to Decision Making

- 

When confronted with a challenge in the form of a problem or an opportunity, individuals may respond in perhaps four ineffective ways and three effective ones.
- The ineffective reactions are as follows: (1) In relaxed avoidance, a manager decides to take no action in the belief that there will be no great negative consequences. (2) In relaxed change, a manager realizes that complete inaction will have negative consequences but opts for the first available alternative that involves low risk. (3) In defensive avoidance, a manager can't find a good solution and follows by procrastinating, passing the buck, or denying the risk of any negative consequences. (4) In panic, a manager is so frantic to get rid of the problem that he or she can't deal with the situation realistically.
- The effective reactions consist of deciding to decide—that is, a manager agrees that he or she must decide what to do about a problem or opportunity and take effective decision-making steps. Three ways to help a manager decide whether to decide are to evaluate (1) importance—how high priority the situation is; (2) credibility—how believable the information about the situation is; and (3) urgency—how quickly the manager must act on the information about the situation.

- Heuristics are rules of thumb or strategies that simplify the process of making decisions. Some heuristics or barriers that tend to bias how decision makers process information are availability, representativeness, anchoring and adjustment, and escalation of commitment. (1) The availability bias means that managers use information readily available from memory to make judgments. (2) The representativeness bias is the tendency to generalize from a small sample or a single event. (3) The anchoring and adjustment bias is the tendency to make decisions based on an initial figure or number. (4) The escalation of commitment bias describes when decision makers increase their commitment to a project despite negative information about it. An example is the prospect theory, which suggests that decision makers find the notion of an actual loss more painful than giving up the possibility of a gain.

Management in Action

IDEO Uses Its Creative Product Design Process to Help Companies Improve Customer Satisfaction

Excerpted from Bruce Nussbaum, "The Power of Design," Business Week, *May 17, 2004, pp. 88, 90–94.*

BusinessWeek From its inception, IDEO has been a force in the world of design. It has designed hundreds of products and won more design awards over the past decade than any other firm. . . . Now, IDEO is transferring its ability to create consumer products into designing consumer experiences in services, from shopping and banking to health care and wireless communication.

Yet by showing global corporations how to change their organizations to focus on the consumer, IDEO is becoming much more than a design company. Indeed, it is now a rival to the traditional purveyors of corporate advice: the management consulting companies such as McKinsey, Boston Consulting, and Bain. . . .

And IDEO works fast. That's because the company requires its clients to participate in virtually all the consumer research, analysis, and decisions that go into developing solutions. When the process is complete, there's no need for a buy-in: Clients already know what to do—and how to do it quickly. Unlike traditional consultants, IDEO shares its innovative process with its customers through projects, workshops, and IDEO U, its customized teaching program. In IDEO-speak this is "open-source innovation." . . .

Corporate execs probably have the most fun simply participating in the IDEO Way, the design firm's disciplined yet wild-and-woolly five-step process that emphasizes empathy with the consumer, anything-is-possible brainstorming, visualizing solutions by creating actual prototypes, using technology to find creative solutions, and doing it all with incredible speed.

Here's how it works: A company goes to IDEO with a problem. It wants a better product, service, or space—no matter. IDEO puts together an eclectic team composed of members from the client company and its own experts who go out to observe and document the consumer experience. Often, IDEO will have top executives play the roles of their own customers. Execs from food and clothing companies shop for their own stuff in different retail stores and on the Web. Health-care managers get care in different hospitals. Wireless providers use their own—and competing—services.

The next stage is brainstorming. IDEO mixes designers, engineers, and social scientists with its clients in a room where they intensely scrutinize a given problem and suggest possible solutions. It is a managed chaos: a dozen or so very smart people examining data, throwing out ideas, writing potential solutions on big Post-its that are ripped off and attached to the wall.

IDEO designers then mock up working models of the best concepts that emerge. Rapid prototyping has always been a hallmark of the company. Seeing ideas in working, tangible form is a far more powerful mode of explanation than simply reading about them off a page. IDEO uses inexpensive prototyping tools—Apple-based iMovies to portray consumer experiences and cheap cardboard to mock up examination rooms or fitting rooms.

Like a law firm, IDEO specializes in different practices. The "TEX"—or technology-enabled experiences—aims to take new high-tech products that first appeal only to early adopters and remake them for mass consumer audience. IDEO's success with the Palm V led AT&T Wireless to call for help on its mMode consumer wireless platform. The company launched mMode in 2002 to allow AT&T Wireless mobile-phone customers to access e-mail and instant messaging, play games, find local restaurants, and connect to sites for news, stocks, weather, and other information. Techies liked mMode, but average consumers were not signing up. "We asked [IDEO] to redesign the interface so someone like my mother who isn't Web savvy can use the phone to navigate how to get the weather or where to shop," says mMode's Hall.

IDEO's GAME PLAN: It immediately sent AT&T Wireless managers on an actual scavenger hunt in San Francisco to see the world from their customers' perspective. They were told to find a CD by a certain Latin singer that was available at only one small music store, find a Walgreen's that sold its own brand of ibuprofen, and get a Pottery Barn catalog. They discovered that it was simply too difficult to find these kinds of things with their mMode service and wound up using the newspaper or the phone directory instead. IDEO and AT&T Wireless teams also went to AT&T Wireless stores and videotaped people using mMode. They saw that consumers couldn't find the sites they wanted. It took too many steps and clicks. "Even teenagers didn't get it," says Duane Bray, leader of the TEX practice at IDEO.

After dozens of brainstorming sessions and many prototypes, IDEO and AT&T Wireless came up with a new mMode wireless service platform. The opening page starts with "My mMode" which is organized like a Web browser's favorites list and can be managed on a Web site. A consumer can make up an individualized selection of sites, such as ESPN or Sony Pictures Entertainment, and ring tones. Nothing is more than two clicks away.

An mMode Guide on the page allows people to list five places—a restaurant, coffee shop, bank, bar, and retail store—that GPS location finders can identify in various cities around the U.S. Another feature spotlights the five nearest movie theatres that still have seats available within the next hour. Yet another, My Locker, lets users store a large number of photos and ring tones with AT&T Wireless. The whole design process took only 17 weeks, "We are thrilled with the results," says Hall. "We talked to frog design, Razorfish, and other design firms, and they thought this was a Web project that needed flashy graphics. IDEO knew it was about making the cell phone experience better."

For Discussion:

1. Was the decision by AT&T Wireless to redesign its wireless platform a programmed or nonprogrammed decision? Explain.
2. To what extent does IDEO use a rational decision-making process?
3. Which of the advantages and disadvantages of group decision making were exhibited in this case? Provide examples.
4. Which of the group problem-solving techniques discussed in this chapter are being used in IDEO's decision-making process?
5. If you owned your own company, would you hire IDEO to help improve customer satisfaction? Explain.

Self-Assessment

What Is Your Decision-Making Style ?*

Objectives

1. To assess your decision-making style.
2. To consider the implications of your decision-making style.

Introduction

This chapter discussed a model of decision-making styles. Decision-making styles are thought to vary according to a person's tolerance for ambiguity and value orientation. In turn, the combination of these two dimensions results in four different decision-making styles (see Figure 7.1). This exercise gives you the opportunity to assess your decision-making style.

Instructions

Following are nine items that pertain to decision making. Read each statement and select the option that best represents your feelings about the issue. Remember, there are no right or wrong answers.

1. I enjoy jobs that
   a. are technical and well defined.
   b. have considerable variety.
   c. allow independent action.
   d. involve people.
2. In my job, I look for
   a. practical results.
   b. the best solutions.
   c. new approaches or ideas.
   d. good working environment.
3. When faced with solving a problem, I
   a. rely on proven approaches.
   b. apply careful analysis.
   c. look for creative approaches.
   d. rely on my feelings.
4. When using information, I prefer
   a. specific facts.
   b. accurate and complete data.
   c. broad coverage of many options.
   d. limited data that are easily understood.

5. I am especially good at
   a. remembering dates and facts.
   b. solving difficult problems.
   c. seeing many possibilities.
   d. interacting with others.
6. When time is important, I
   a. decide and act quickly.
   b. follow plans and priorities.
   c. refuse to be pressured.
   d. seek guidance and support.
7. I work well with those who are
   a. energetic and ambitious.
   b. self-confident.
   c. open-minded.
   d. polite and trusting.
8. Others consider me
   a. aggressive.
   b. disciplined.
   c. imaginative.
   d. supportive.
9. My decisions typically are
   a. realistic and direct.
   b. systematic or abstract.
   c. broad and flexible.
   d. sensitive to the needs of others.

Scoring & Interpretation

Score the exercise by giving yourself one point for every time you selected an A, one point for every B, and so on. Add up your scores for each letter. Your highest score represents your dominant decision-making style. If your highest score was A, you have a directive style; B = analytical; C = conceptual; and D = behavioral. See the related material in this chapter for a thorough description of these four styles.

Questions

1. What are your highest and lowest rated styles?
2. Do the results accurately reflect your self-perceptions? Explain.
3. What are the advantages and disadvantages of your style? Discuss.
4. Which of the other decision-making styles is least consistent with your style? How might you work more effectively with someone who has this style? Discuss.

*Adapted from A. J. Rowe, J. D. Boulgaides, and M. R. McGrath, *Managerial Decision Making* (Chicago: SRA, 1984).

Group Exercise

Ethical Decision Making

Objectives

1. To look at the stages in practical decision making.
2. To gain practice in ethical decision making.

Introduction

In this chapter you learned there are four stages in making practical decisions. The third stage involves evaluating alternatives and selecting a solution. Part of this evaluation entails deciding whether or not the solution is ethical. The purpose of this exercise is to examine the stages in practical decision making and consider the issue of ethical decision making.

Instructions

Break into groups of five or six people and read the following case. As a group discuss the decision made by the company and answer the questions for discussion at the end of the case. Before answering questions 5–6, brainstorm alternative decisions the managers at TELECOMPROS could have made. Finally, the entire class can reconvene and discuss the alternative solutions that were generated.

The Case

For large cellular service providers, maintaining their own customer service call center can be very expensive. Many have found they can save money by outsourcing their customer service calls to outside companies.

TELECOMPROS is one such company. It specializes in cellphone customer service, saving large cellular companies money by eliminating overhead costs associated with building a call center, installing additional telephone lines, and so on. Once TELECOMPROS is hired by large cellular service providers, TELECOMPROS employees are trained on the cellular service providers' systems, policies, and procedures. TELECOMPROS derives its income from charging a per-hour fee for each employee.

Six months ago, TELECOMPROS acquired a contract with Cell2U, a large cellular service provider serving the western United States. At the beginning of the contract, Cell2U was very pleased. As a call center, TELECOMPROS has a computer system in place that monitors the number of calls the center receives and how quickly the calls are answered. When Cell2U received its first report, the system showed that TELECOMPROS was a very productive call center and handled the call volume very well. A month later, however, Cell2U launched a nationwide marketing campaign. Suddenly, the call volume increased and TELECOMPROS customer service reps were unable to keep up. The phone-monitoring system showed that some customers were on hold for 45 minutes or longer, and at any given time throughout the day there were as many as 50 customers on hold. It was clear to Cell2U that the original number of customer service reps they had contracted for was not enough. They renegotiated with upper management at TELECOMPROS and hired additional customer service reps. TELECOMPROS managers were pleased because they were now receiving more money from Cell2U for the extra employees, and Cell2U was happy because the call center volume was no longer overwhelming and its customers were happy with the attentive customer service.

Three months later, though, TELECOMPROS customer service supervisors noticed a decrease in the number of customer service calls. It seemed that the reps had done such a good job that Cell2U customers had fewer problems. There were too many people and not enough calls; with little to do, some reps were playing computer games or surfing the Internet while waiting for calls to come in.

Knowing that if Cell2U analyzed its customer service needs it would want to decrease the number of reps to save money, TELECOMPROS upper management made a decision. Rather than decrease its staff and lose the hourly pay from Cell2U, upper management told customer service supervisors to call the customer service line. Supervisors called in and spent enough time on the phone with reps to ensure that the computer registered the call and the time it took to "resolve" the call. They would then hang up and call the call center again. Thus, TELECOMPROS did not have to decrease its customer service reps, and Cell2U continued to pay for the allotted reps until the end of the contract.

Questions for Discussion

1. Was the decision made by TELECOMPROS an ethical one? Why or why not?
2. What stages in the Practical Decision-Making Process did TELECOMPROS managers skip? Describe and explain.
3. Which of the Nonrational Models of Decision Making did managers at TELECOMPROS follow? Explain.
4. Which of the hindrances to rational decision making listed in Figure 7.3 explain the decision made by TELECOMPROS managers? Explain.
5. What is your recommended solution? Explain why you selected this alternative.
6. How would you implement your preferred solution? Describe in detail.

Ethical Dilemma

Working at a Restaurant: Employees "Eat as They Work"

You work at a large restaurant, which also happens to have a separate employee cafeteria. The restaurant's policy on employee meals is as follows: Employees can eat for free in the employee cafeteria. Alternatively, they can eat meals from the restaurant, but they must pay for them; moreover, they must wait until the end of their shifts before eating. They are not allowed to eat their meals in the kitchen or the customer areas of the restaurant.

You discover that several employees simply "eat as they work." They take food from cooking pots while working. Or they get the cooks to prepare meals without charge. You also discover that several employees are taking butter and other expensive foods from the walk-in fridges, marking them as being past their expiration dates, then eating them in the restaurant or taking them home to eat later. The executive chef is aware of this practice and in fact does the same thing herself.

Solving the Dilemma

As a restaurant employee (not a manager), what would you do?

1. Tell the restaurant manager what is going on, mentioning that the executive chef is also participating in this behavior.
2. Remind your coworkers of the restaurant's policy on employee meals; then, if their behavior doesn't change, report it to the manager.
3. Do as others do—that is, "eat as you work"—with the view that this can be considered ethical behavior so long as the executive chef tolerates it.
4. Invent other options. Discuss.

Video Case

Living Room Café

As the video case opens, partners Jonas Goldberg and Rande Gedaliah exchange greetings. In addition to being business partners, Rande and Jonas are long-time friends. Rande is under increasing stress and doesn't feel that Jonas is "holding up his end" of running the business. Jonas agrees. His spouse is extra busy at work, and he is taking on greater child-care responsibilities. But after all, they always agreed that their families would come first. However, Rande's family life is also affected.

Jonas has missed several meetings. He had "things to do" and felt confident that Rande could handle anything that arose. He twice missed payroll deadlines, delaying salary payments to employees. According to Jonas this is not a significant issue. Jonas feels he can accomplish his normal workload, it just might not be on the tight schedule that Rande is expecting. "It will all get done anyway." However, Rande feels the work is getting done because she is picking up the slack, causing her to be "totally stressed out." Rande senses a lack of concern for both their friendship and the business. She suggests a solution: find a partner to buy Jonas's share of the business. However, at this important juncture Jonas abruptly ends the meeting.

Privately Rande expresses frustration at the tone of the meeting, acknowledging that Jonas is likely frustrated as well. Jonas's goals have changed, and he is no longer taking an active interest in the business. She sees no hope of salvaging the partnership and would rather retain their friendship. Saving both no longer seems possible.

When Rande and Jonas reconvene, Jonas puts forth a proposal. He will "bow out gracefully" and sell his share of the business. For Jonas as well, maintaining their friendship is important. So far, the two partners are in agreement. However, a major point of contention arises. Jonas wants complete control over the choice of buyer, with the intention to sell to the highest bidder. Rande strongly opposes this idea, because the buyer would be her day-to-day partner. She should have total control over that decision and legally has the right of first refusal. Rande has reviewed their contract and consulted with their attorneys, but Jonas is unaware of the legal ramifications. Jonas doesn't want to leave Rande with an undesirable partner but still feels he has the right to sell to whomever he pleases. The discussion becomes heated, and again Jonas must abruptly leave to attend to family business. However, at least the friends have agreed that their partnership can no longer continue.

Privately Rande reflects on Jonas's proposal. With certainty, she states, "we will not be partners." Rande also perceives that the situation has been influenced by their gender differences and that she has been forced into the mother-like role of disciplinarian. Perhaps a female partner would be a better choice, because they would likely have more similar communication and management styles.

Discussion Questions

1. Are Rande and Jonas experiencing functional or dysfunctional conflict? Support your response with evidence from the case.
2. Critique Rande and Jonas's decision-making process thus far. What might they do to improve this process?
3. Jonas is clearly attempting to maintain a comfortable balance between work and family life. Suggest how he might more successfully maintain this balance.
4. Did gender differences play a role in this situation? Support your answer with evidence from the case.

chapter 8

Organizational Culture, Structure, & Design

Building Blocks of the Organization

MAJOR QUESTIONS YOU SHOULD BE ABLE TO ANSWER

8.1 What Kind of Organizational Culture Will You Be Operating In?

Major Question: How do I find out about an organization's "social glue," its normal way of doing business?

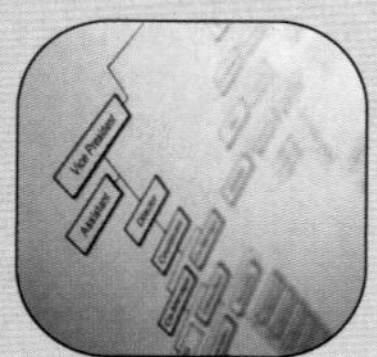

8.2 What Is an Organization?

Major Question: How are for-profit, nonprofit, and mutual-benefit organizations structured?

8.3 The Major Elements of an Organization

Major Question: When I join an organization, what seven elements should I look for?

8.4 Basic Types of Organizational Structures

Major Question: How would one describe the eight organizational structures?

8.5 Contingency Design: Factors in Creating the Best Structure

Major Question: What factors affect the design of an organization's structure?

8.6 Toward Building a Learning Organization

Major Question: Why do organizations resist learning, and what is a new way for employees in an organization to view themselves?

the manager's toolbox

Mentoring: The New Rules

Who's going to help you learn the ropes in a new organization? Maybe you need a mentor.

If you can find an experienced employee to mentor you—to be your organizational sponsor and help you understand and navigate the organization's culture and structure—it can be a great asset to your career. Indeed, mentoring may be especially useful for female and minority managers, for whom there may be fewer role models within their particular organizations.

What's the best advice about acquiring a mentor? Here are some of the new rules.[1]

- **Choose anyone you can learn from, not just someone higher up:** It used to be thought that a mentor should be a seasoned manager higher up in the organization. But a mentor can also be a peer—someone at your own level inside in the organization.
- **Choose more than one mentor:** It might be nice to have a single mentor who can give you lots of one-on-one attention. But everyone's busy, so look around and see if there are two or three people who might be helpful to you. "Diversify your mentor portfolio," goes one piece of advice.
- **Pick your mentors, don't wait to be picked:** Don't wait for organizational veterans to select you to be their protégé. It's up to you to make the first move, to be assertive in a nice way.
- **Do a self-assessment:** Before you begin contacting people to be mentors, assess where you want to go and what skills and knowledge you need to get there, so that you'll know the kind of help you need.
- **Look for someone different from you:** It used to be thought the mentor and mentee should have a lot in common, as in personal chemistry or personal style. But someone who is different from you will challenge you and help you be more objective.
- **Investigate your prospects:** Before approaching prospective mentors, call their administrative assistants, explain your plans, and ask what their bosses are like to work with. Find out the best time to approach them.
- **Show your prospective mentor how you can be helpful:** "Mentoring is a two-way street," says Anne Hayden, senior vice president of Metropolitan Life insurance company. "The person being mentored gets help, advice, and coaching, and the person doing the mentoring generally gets extra effort—someone very committed to working on special projects or on assignments that maybe don't fall within the boxes on the organizational chart."[2]
- **Agree on how your mentoring relationship will work:** In your first meeting, set the ground rules for how frequently you will meet and the type of contact, such as whether it will be in the office, over lunch, or at the gym. A minimum of one meeting a month is recommended, and in between the two of you should keep in touch by phone and e-mail.

forecast

What's Ahead in This Chapter

In this chapter, we consider organizational cultures and why they are important. We then consider the three types of organizations and seven basic characteristics of an organization. We next consider eight types of organizational structures. We look at five factors that should be considered when one is designing the structure of an organization. Finally, we describe the characteristics of a learning organization, why people resist learning, and what a manager can do to help build a learning organization.

major question

How do I find out about an organization's "social glue," its normal way of doing business?

The Big Picture

The study of organizing, the second of the four functions in the management process, begins with a study of organizational culture, which exists on two levels, invisible and visible. An organizational culture has four functions.

As a newcomer to *Fast Company* magazine, Cheryl Dahl wanted to meet new people but found that the office was far too hectic to allow coworkers to give her the kind of time she was looking for. So, she reported, "I nabbed a few minutes whenever I could—walking to the subway station with fellow editors, or popping my head into their offices to say hello." Dahl also wanted to check in frequently with her boss during her first 60 days. Her problem, however, was "How do you set up a meeting in a place that doesn't believe in meetings?" She learned to corner her boss at the coffee pot whenever she just "happened" to stroll by.[3]

People have different behavioral and psychological characteristics. So do organizations—only they're called "cultures." They consist not only of the slightly quirky features that Dahl encountered but also of all an organization's normal way of doing business.

What Is an Organizational Culture?

According to scholar **Edgar Schein, *organizational culture,* sometimes called *corporate culture,* is a system of shared beliefs and values that develops within an organization and guides the behavior of its members.**[4] This is the "social glue" that binds members of the organization together. Just as a human being has a personality—fun-loving, warm, uptight, competitive, or whatever—so an organization has a "personality," too, and that is its culture. For instance, at Pfizer Pharmacy, the Connecticut pharmaceutical company, drug discovery is a high-risk, costly endeavor in which hundreds of scientists screen thousands of chemicals against specific disease targets, but 96% of these compounds are ultimately found to be unworkable. The culture, then, is one of managing failure and disappointment, of helping drug researchers live for the small victories. Thus, says one account, "when a researcher publishes a paper, or when a lab gets some positive results on a new therapy, it's trumpeted throughout the organization."[5] The corporate culture at Houston energy trader Enron was said to have been a "very arrogant place, with a feeling of invincibility," according to whistleblower Sherron Watkins.[6]

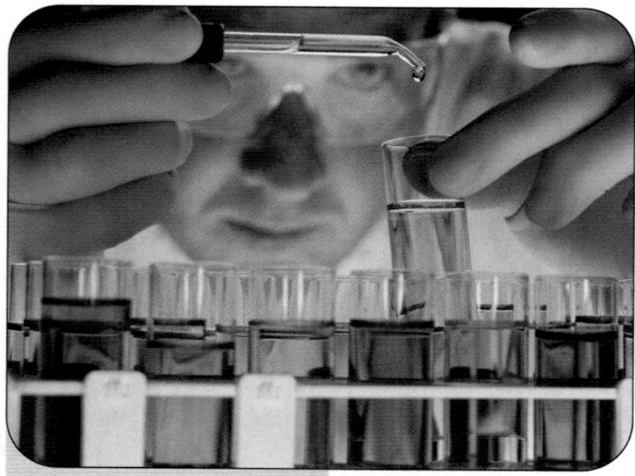

Risky business. In the organizational culture of Pfizer Pharmacy, failure and disappointment are taken for granted.

Culture can vary considerably, with different organizations having differing emphases on risk taking, treatment of employees, teamwork, rules and regulations, conflict and criticism, and rewards. And the sources of these characteristics also vary. They may represent the strong views of the founders, of the reward systems that have been instituted, of the effects of competitors, and so on.

The Idea of Blended Value: Measuring Both Economic & Social Benefits

Jeb Emerson, a former social worker who is now a lecturer at the Stanford Graduate School of Business, has gained some attention by asking this question: what if we did not judge business organizations on profits alone? There is a premise we rarely question, he suggests: "We tend to categorize value as economic or social. You either work for a nonprofit that creates social value or you work for a for-profit that creates economic value."[26] In actuality, however, for-profits create social value: they create jobs (which lead to stable family units), they create products that improve people's lives, and they pay taxes that help build local communities. And, conversely, nonprofits contribute economic value, because they also create jobs and they consume goods and services. (Nonprofits represent 7% of the gross domestic product.)

Example

An Organization That Defies Conventional Wisdom: A For-Profit Cellphone Network Makes Money in a Poor Country

The Asian country of Bangladesh is so poor that the per-capita income is one-hundredth what it is in the United States, "so you need 100 Bangladeshis to provide the buying power of one American," points out Iqbal Z. Quadir, a Bangladesh native who is now a Harvard University professor. Accordingly, when in the early 1990s Quadir was looking for financial backing for his idea for a cellphone network for his homeland, he was turned down by 16 prospective investors, one of whom said, "We're not the Red Cross."

Many Americans have this mindset that only certain kinds of organizations work for certain purposes—that only nonprofit charities can help the poor, that for-profits work only with consumers of a certain affluence. Microsoft's Bill Gates, for instance, has said that places with widespread poverty and unreliable electricity can't support sophisticated technology.

At the end of 2001, however, Quadir had showed how a for-profit venture in a developing country could both provide a service and make a profit. GrameenPhone, the Bangladesh cellphone company he founded, had made $27 million in pretax profits—and after just five years. The company sells phones and airtime to urban customers, and it enables people in rural areas to take out small loans for cellphones and to buy airtime at cost. In fact, GrameenPhone now has more subscribers than Bangladesh's government-owned phone company.[27]

Quadir also used GrameenPhone's infrastructure to support an affiliated nonprofit project called Village Phone, which provides rural women small, no-collateral loans for cellphones, a 50% discount on airtime, and training on how to operate the phone and how to charge users for it. As of October 2003, there were more than 39,000 Village Phones in operation. The women, who use solar panels to power their phones, make $500 a month—a lot more than the Bangladeshi average of $380.[28]

GrameenPhone and Village Phone are examples of what is called *social entrepreneurship,* defined by Gregory Dees of Stanford's Graduate School of Business as the creation of social value through constant innovation and an unrelenting pursuit of new opportunities, without regard for limited resources in order to serve their constituencies.[29] Another example is the Greyston Bakery in Yonkers, N.Y., which employs the chronically unemployed, gives them training and paychecks, and helps them achieve self-sufficiency. Started on a $300,000 loan, the bakery now employs 55 people, generates more than $3.5 million in revenues, and serves as the sole supplier of fudge brownies for Ben & Jerry's ice cream.

The notion of ***blended value,*** **then, is that all investments are understood to operate simultaneously in both economic and social realms.** "There is no 'trade off' between the two but rather a concurrent pursuit of value—both social and financial," Emerson says. "The two operate together, in concert, at all times. They cannot be separated and considered as two distinct propositions, but are one and the same."[30]

Economic and social value (which includes environmental value) may well be all part of a piece, as Emerson proposes. The problem, of course, is that financial performance can be measured by numbers ("econometrics"), whereas measuring social performance is more difficult. However, just as society has been grappling with measuring environmental impacts only for the last 5–10 years, so it may take another 5–50 years to learn how to adequately track and report social value, Emerson believes. "There is increasing pressure on companies to understand, quantify, and measure their social impact," he says. "It's inevitable. Successful companies will be savvy about how understanding the full value proposition can create wider opportunity."

In the future, then, organizations may not be quite so rigorously identified as either for-profit or nonprofit.[31]

The Organization Chart

Whatever the size or type of organization, it can be represented in an organization chart. **An *organization chart* is a box-and-lines illustration showing the formal lines of authority and the organization's official positions or division of labor.** This is the family-tree-like pattern of boxes and lines posted on workplace walls and given to new hires. *(See Figure 8.2.)*

FIGURE 8.2

Organization chart. Example for a hospital

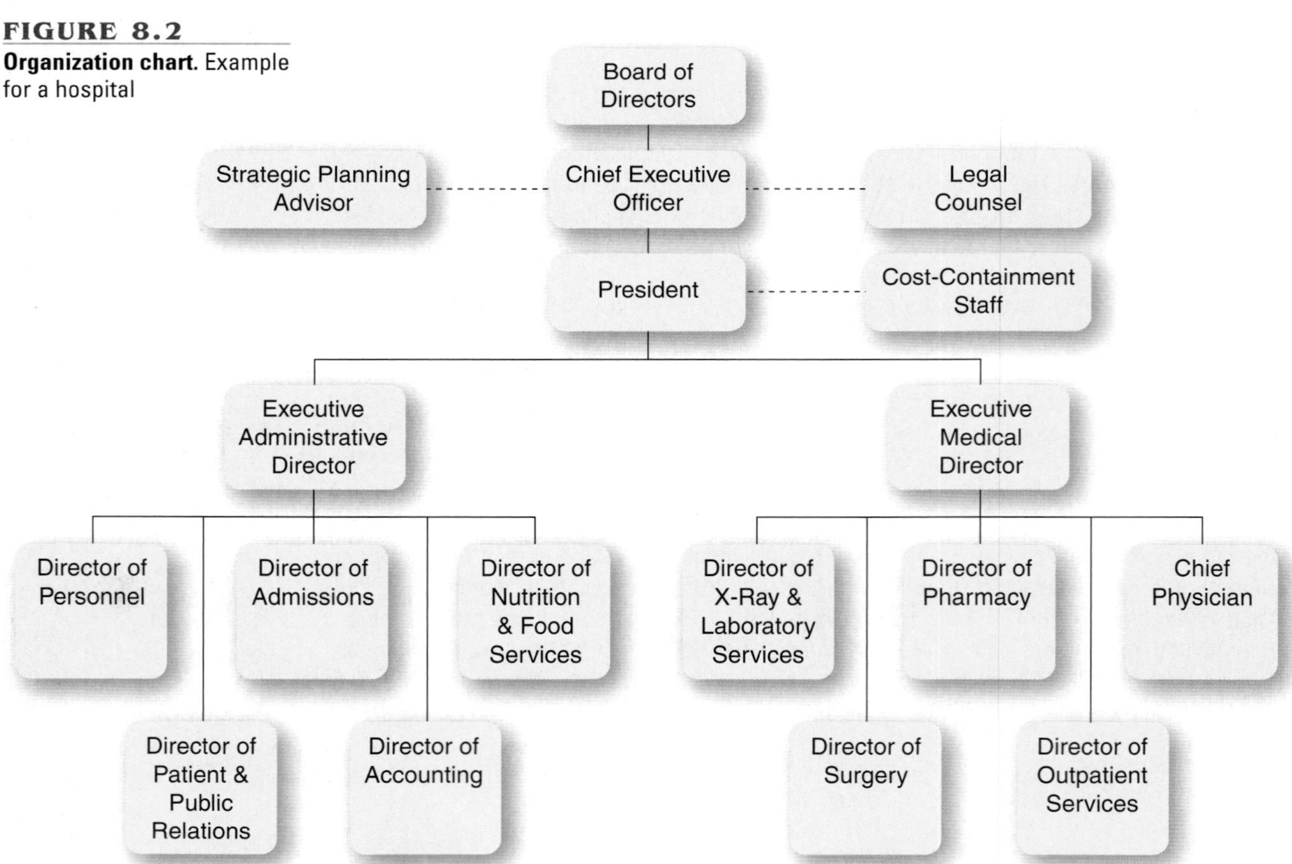

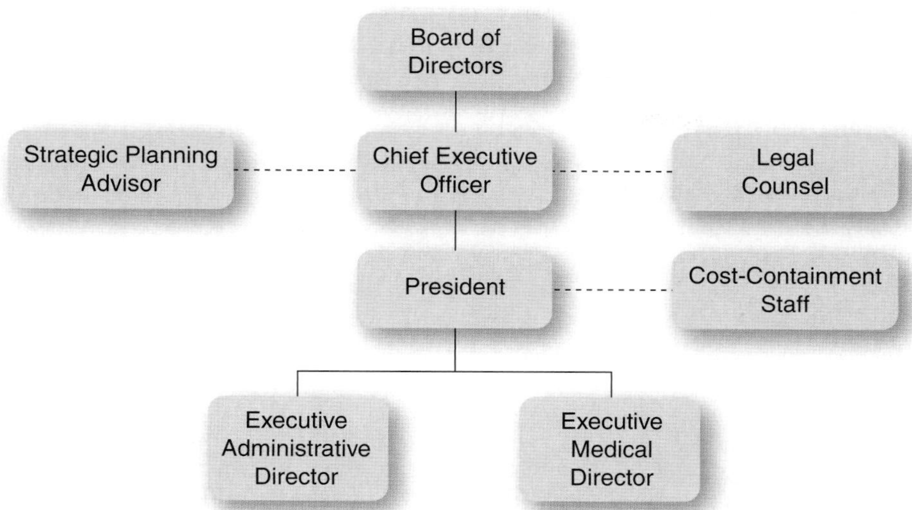

FIGURE 8.4

Line and staff. Line have solid lines, staff have dotted lines.

- **Staff position:** ***Staff personnel*** **have authority functions; they provide advice, recommendations, and research to line managers** (examples: specialists such as legal counsels and special advisors for mergers and acquisitions or strategic planning). Staff positions are indicated on the organization chart by a *dotted line* (usually a horizontal line).

7 Centralization versus Decentralization of Authority

Who makes the important decisions in an organization? That is what the question of centralization versus decentralization of authority is concerned with.

Centralized Authority **With** ***centralized authority,*** **important decisions are made by higher-level managers.** Very small companies tend to be the most centralized, although nearly all organizations have at least some authority concentrated at the top of the hierarchy. Kmart and McDonald's are examples of companies using this kind of authority.

An advantage in using centralized authority is that there is less duplication of work, because fewer employees perform the same task; rather, the task is often performed by a department of specialists. Another advantage of centralization is that procedures are uniform and thus easier to control; all purchasing, for example, may have to be put out to competitive bids.

Decentralized Authority **With** ***decentralized authority,*** **important decisions are made by middle-level and supervisory-level managers.** Here, obviously, power has been delegated throughout the organization. Among the companies using decentralized authority are General Motors and Sears, Roebuck.

An advantage in having decentralized authority is that managers are encouraged to solve their own problems rather than to buck the decision to a higher level. In addition, decisions are made more quickly, which increases the organization's flexibility and efficiency. ◆

major question

How would one describe the eight organizational structures?

The Big Picture

Eight types of organizational structures are simple, functional, divisional, conglomerate, hybrid, matrix, team-based, and network.

Small firm. What type of organizational structure is best suited to a company this size? Should the number of employees influence the decision?

Culture and structure are often intertwined. When in 1997 the Federal Railroad Administration (FRA) sent inspectors to Union Pacific's headquarters in Omaha, Nebraska, to examine why the railroad had had a series of fatal accidents, they learned that the company had a top-down, military-style hierarchy and culture that seemed to discourage teamwork and communication. The antiquated style of management had its roots in the days when railroads' executive ranks were filled with combat-hardened former Civil War officers. "When something happened," said a railroad vice president explaining the attitude of leading by fear, "you pulled out your gun and shot the guy in charge of the territory." Said the head of the FRA of Union Pacific's dysfunctional working arrangements, "They were separated from each other in a way that almost guaranteed problems."[39]

We may categorize the arrangements of organizations into eight types of structures: (1) *simple,* (2) *functional,* (3) *divisional,* (4) *conglomerate,* (5) *hybrid,* (6) *matrix,* (7) *team-based,* and (8) *network.*

1 The Simple Structure: For the Small Firm

The first organizational form is the simple structure. This is the form often found in a firm's very early, entrepreneurial stages, when the organization is apt to reflect the desires and personality of the owner or founder. **An organization with a *simple structure* has authority centralized in a single person, a flat hierarchy, few rules, and low work specialization.** *(See Figure 8.5.)*

There are hundreds of thousands of organizations that are arranged according to a simple structure—for instance, small mom 'n' pop firms running landscaping, construction, insurance sales, and similar businesses. Some of these firms, of course, grow into larger organizations with different kinds of structures. Both Hewlett-Packard and Apple Computer began as two-man garage startups that later became large.

FIGURE 8.5

Simple structure: an example. There is only one hierarchical level of management beneath the owner.

2 The Functional Structure: Grouping by Similar Work Specialties

The second organizational form is the functional structure. **In a *functional structure,* people with similar occupational specialties are put together in formal groups.** This is a quite commonplace structure, seen in all kinds of organizations, for-profit and nonprofit. *(See Figure 8.6.)*

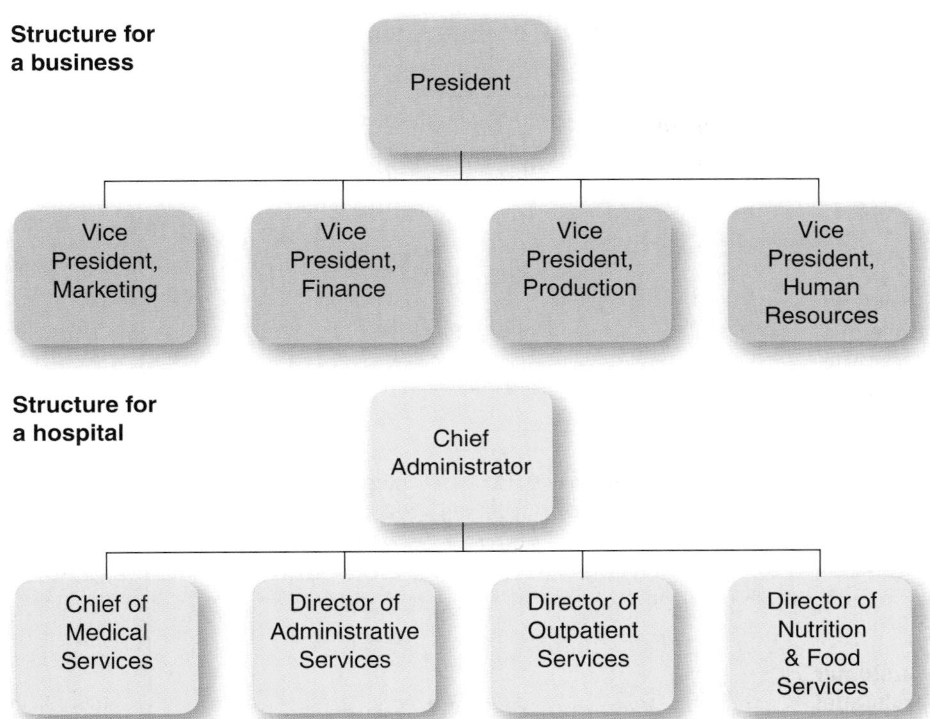

FIGURE 8.6

Functional structure: two examples. This shows the functional structure for a business and for a hospital.

A manufacturing firm, for example, will often group people with similar work skills in a Marketing Department, others in a Production Department, others in Finance, and so on. A nonprofit educational institution might group employees according to work specialty under Faculty, Admissions, Maintenance, and so forth.

How do you like them Apples? When founded in a garage in the late 1970s, Apple Computer was a two-man enterprise consisting of Steve Jobs—shown here in 2004 introducing the iPod mini, as an iPod TV ad plays in the background—and Stephen Wozniak. Do you think the era of garage-based startups in the computer industry is over in the United States?

3 The Divisional Structure: Grouping by Similarity of Purpose

The third organizational form is the divisional structure. **In a *divisional structure*, people with diverse occupational specialties are put together in formal groups by similar products or services, customers or clients, or geographic regions.** *(See Figure 8.7.)*

FIGURE 8.7

Divisional structure: three examples. This shows product, customer, and geographic divisions.

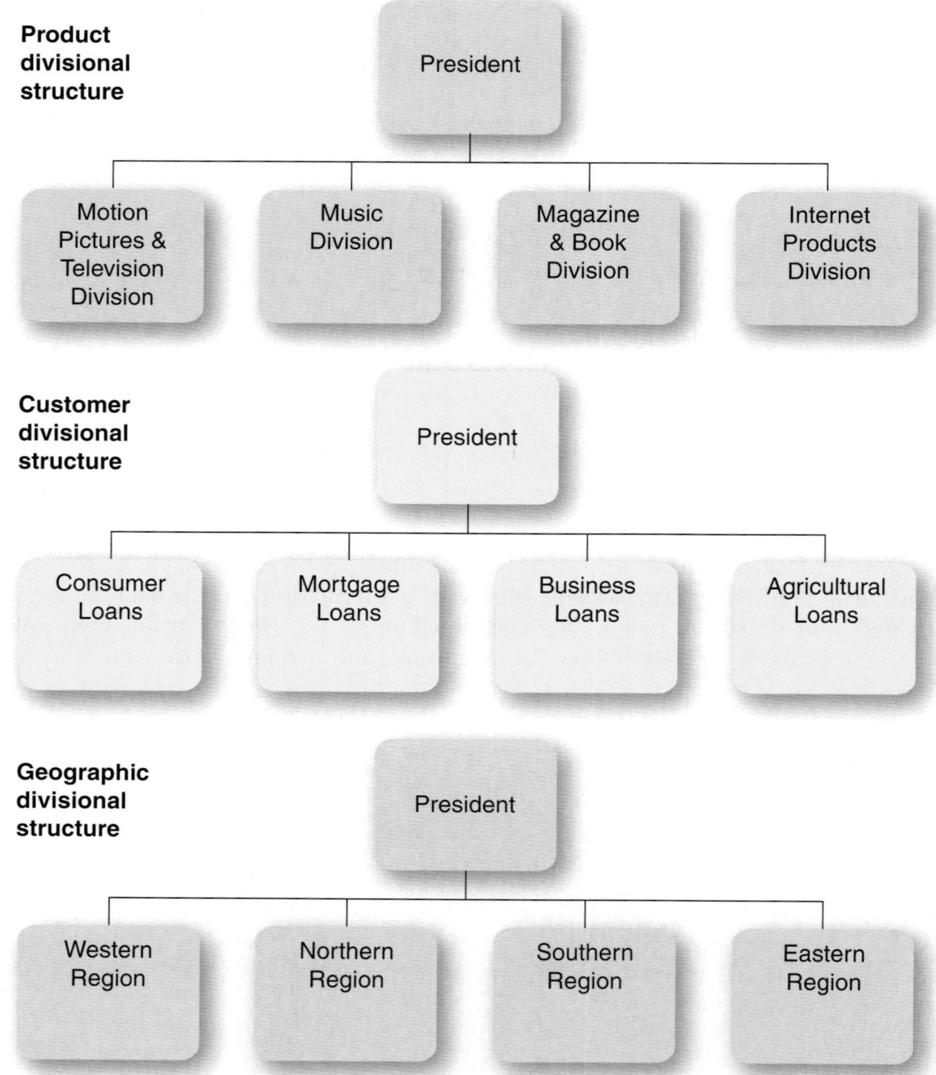

Product Divisions: Grouping by Similar Products or Services

Product divisions **group activities around similar products or services.** For instance, the media giant Time Warner has different divisions for magazines, movies, recordings, cable television, and so on. The $10 billion Warner Bros. part of the empire alone has divisions spanning movies and television, a broadcast network, retail stores, theaters, amusement parks, and music.[40]

Customer Divisions: Grouping by Common Customers or Clients

Customer divisions **tend to group activities around common customers or clients.** For instance, Ford Motor Co. has separate divisions for passenger-car dealers,

How many divisions does Home Depot have? The leading retailer in the home-improvement industry, Atlanta-based Home Depot operates over 1,700 Home Depot stores, which sell building materials and home-improvement and lawn and garden products for do-it-yourself customers. The company also operates EXPO Design Center stores, aimed at professional customers (contractors) interested in interior design and renovation projects. The Maintenance Warehouse subsidiary is a direct marketer of products serving the multifamily housing and lodging facilities management market. The company has also launched The Home Depot Floor Store, which sells only flooring products.

for large trucking customers, and for farm products customers. A savings and loan might be structured with divisions for making consumer loans, mortgage loans, business loans, and agricultural loans.

Geographic Divisions: Grouping by Regional Location

Geographic divisions **group activities around defined regional locations.** This arrangement is frequently used by government agencies. The Federal Reserve Bank, for instance, has twelve separate districts around the United States. The Internal Revenue Service also has several districts.

4 The Conglomerate Structure: Grouping by Industry

A large-scale variant on the divisional structure is the conglomerate structure. A *conglomerate* is a large company that is doing business in different, quite unrelated areas. For example, Tyco International has electronics, fire and security, healthcare, plastics and adhesives, and engineered products and services. **The *conglomerate structure* groups divisions or business units around similar businesses or industries.** *(See Figure 8.8.)*

FIGURE 8.8

Conglomerate structure. This resembles the structure of Tyco International.

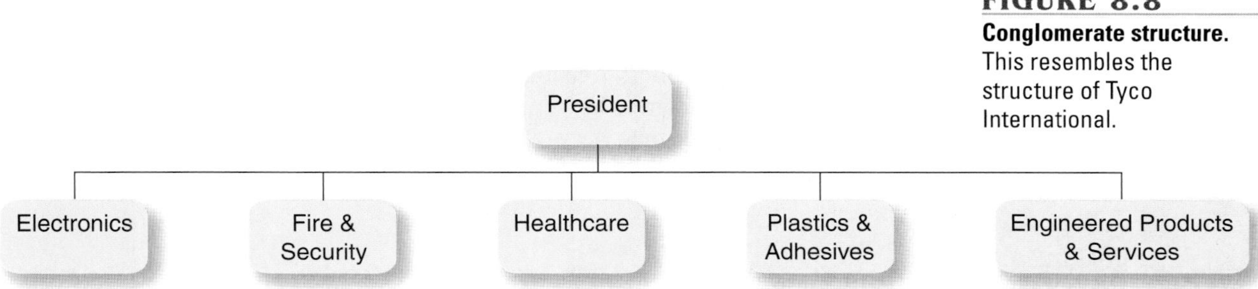

5 The Hybrid Structure: Functional & Divisional Used within the Same Organization

The fifth organizational form is the hybrid structure. **In a *hybrid structure,* an organization uses functional and divisional structures in different parts of the same organization.** *(See Figure 8.9.)*

FIGURE 8.9
Hybrid structure. Hypothetical example of General Motors

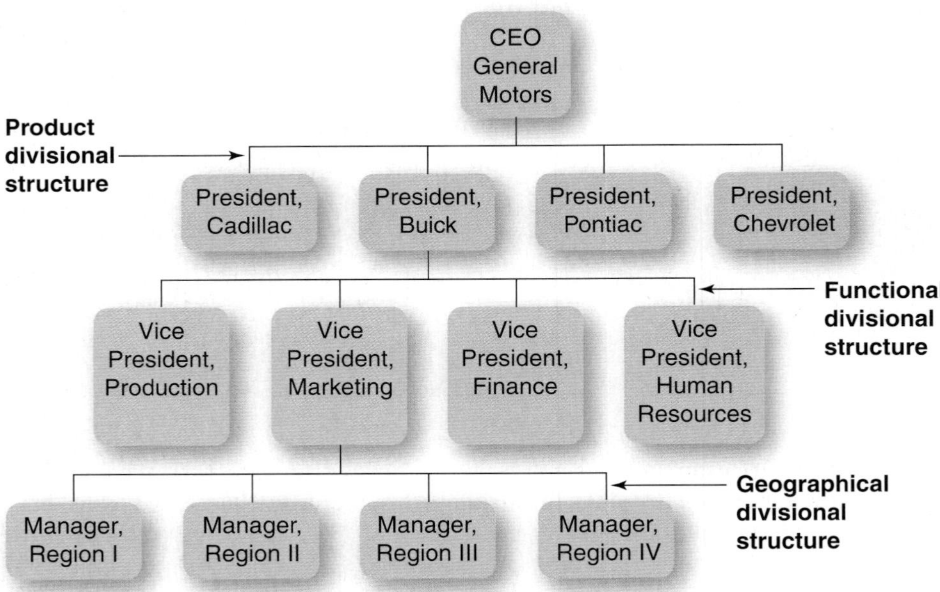

Many different kinds of possible hybrid structures exist. One example is General Motors, which at the top rung of the hierarchy could be organized into product (or customer) divisions: Cadillac, Buick, Pontiac, Chevrolet. (Oldsmobile was recently discontinued.) Within each product division, there could be a functional division according to type of work. Thus, Buick would be organized into Production, Marketing, Finance, Human Resources. Each functional division in turn is organized into a geographical division. Thus, Marketing would be organized into Region I, Region II, Region III, and Region IV.

6 The Matrix Structure: A Grid of Functional & Divisional for Two Chains of Command

The sixth organizational form is the matrix structure. **In a *matrix structure,* an organization combines functional and divisional chains of commands in a grid so that there are two command structures—vertical and horizontal.** The functional structure usually doesn't change—it is the organization's normal departments or divisions, such as Finance, Marketing, Production, and Research & Development. The divisional structure may vary—as by product, brand, customer, or geographic region. *(See Figure 8.10.)*

General Motors' many divisions. Some GM dealers carry all of General Motors' brands, as does Rally Auto Group in Palmdale, Calif.

FIGURE 8.10

Matrix structure. An example of an arrangement that Ford might use.

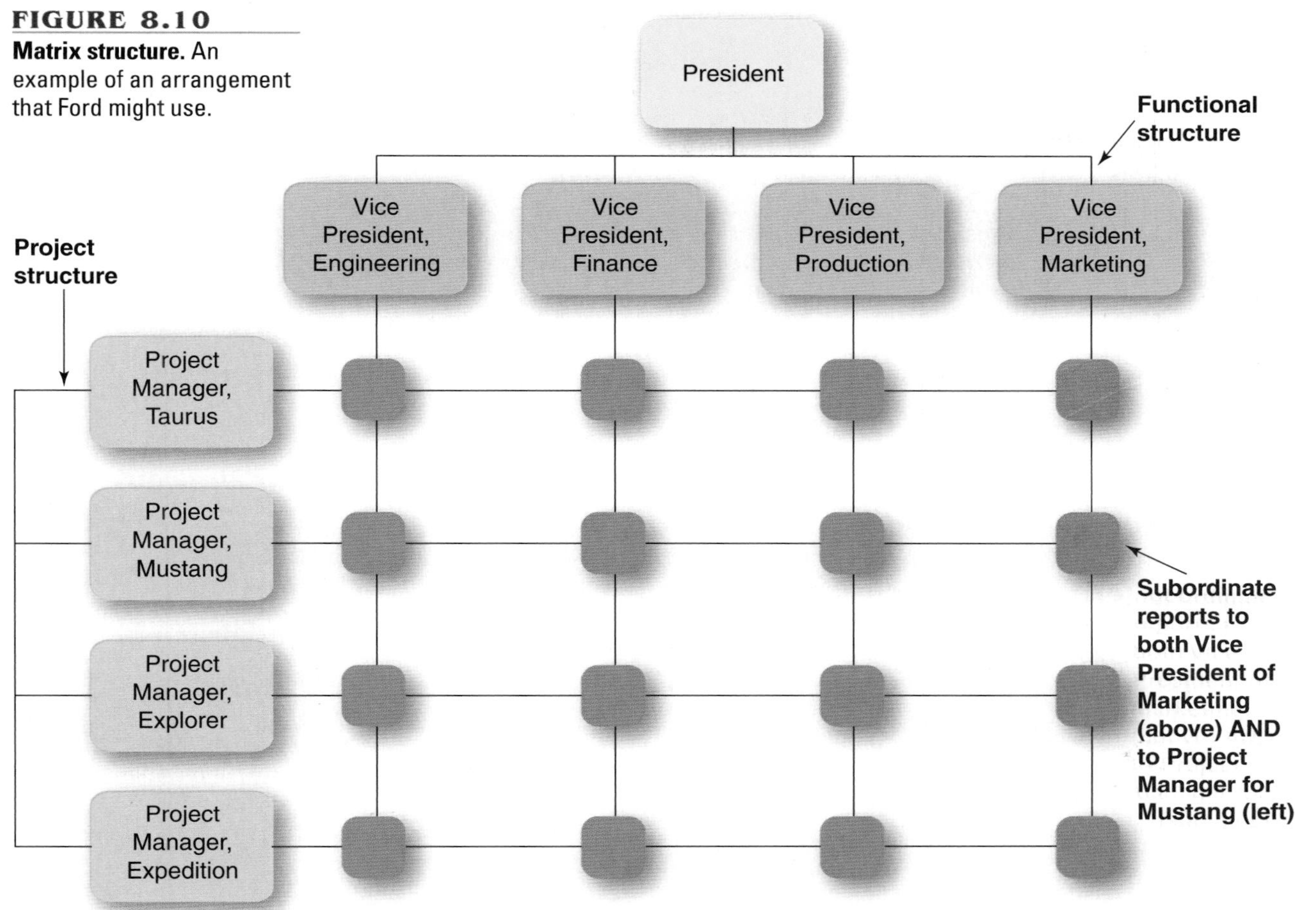

For example, the functional structure might be the departments of Engineering, Finance, Production, and Marketing, each headed by a vice president. Thus, the reporting arrangement is vertical. The divisional structure might be by product (the new models of Taurus, Mustang, Explorer, and Expedition, for example), each headed by a project manager. This reporting arrangement is horizontal. Thus, a marketing person, say, would report to *both* the Vice President of Marketing *and* to the Project Manager for the Ford Mustang. Indeed, Ford Motor Co. used the matrix approach to create the Taurus and a newer version of the Mustang.

7 The Team-Based Structure: Eliminating Functional Barriers to Solve Problems

The seventh organizational form is the team-based structure. **In a *team-based structure,* teams or workgroups, either temporary or permanent, are used to improve horizontal relations and solve problems throughout the organization.**[41] When managers from different functional divisions are brought together in teams—known as cross-functional teams—to solve particular problems, the barriers between the divisions break down. The focus on narrow divisional interests yields to a common interest in solving the problems that brought them together. Yet team members still have their full-time functional work responsibilities and still formally report to their own managers above them in the functional-division hierarchy. *(See Figure 8.11, which follows.)*

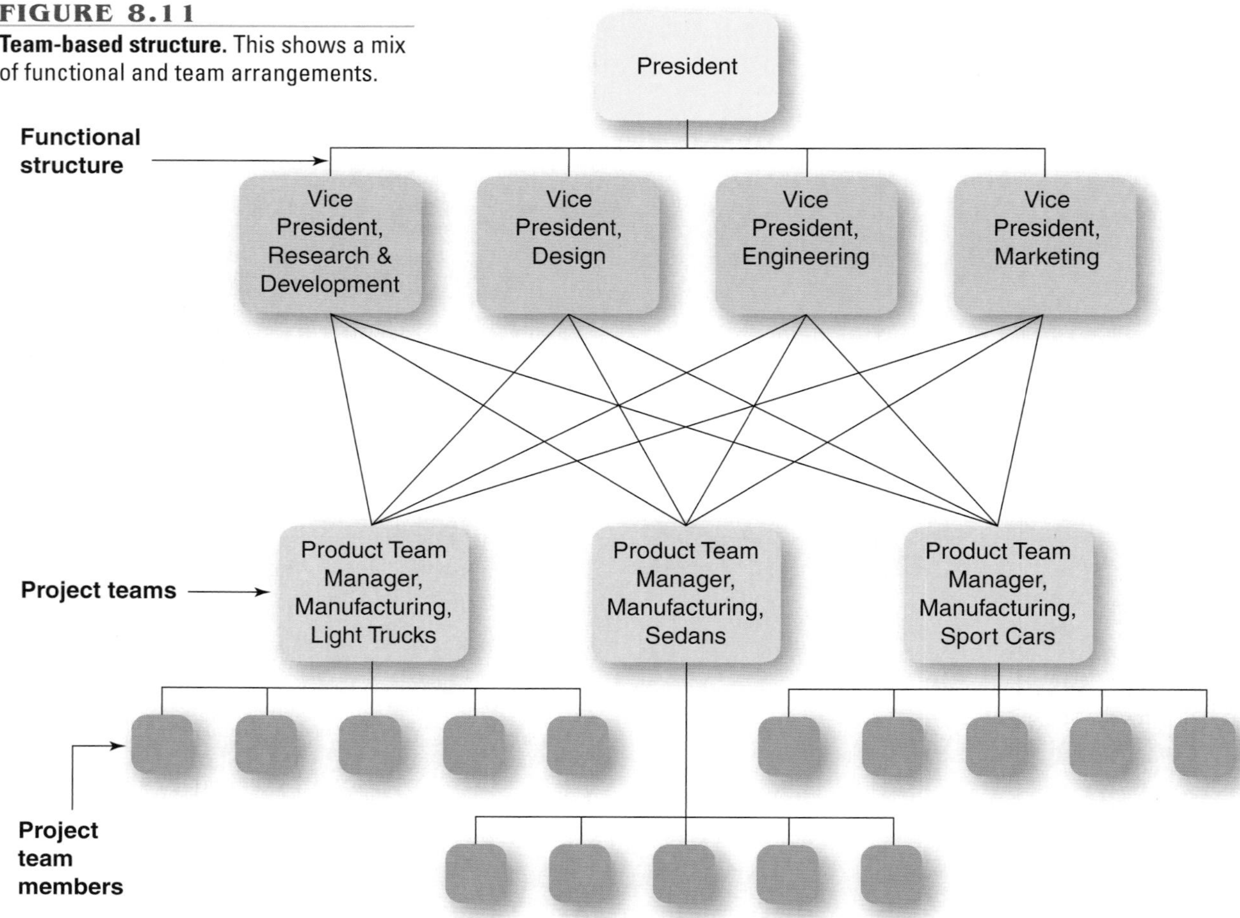

FIGURE 8.11
Team-based structure. This shows a mix of functional and team arrangements.

Example

Use of a Team-Based Structure: Designing the Boeing 777

Many projects require creative problem solving, often drawing on specialized knowledge. To design its 777 jumbo jet, Boeing Aircraft assembled a project team of 8–15 specialists from several areas—engineering, manufacturing, marketing, finance, and customer service—to work together to decide what the product would look like. The team used state-of-the-art computer modeling to develop three-dimensional models of the plane, and design and assembly problems were ironed out in project team meetings before production workers ever started cutting any metal.

This team approach, known as *concurrent engineering* or *integrated product development,* has been found to speed up the design of new products. Contrast this way with the old approach, in which plans and drawings are originated in the engineering department, then are (in the jargon) "thrown over the wall" to be executed by the production department, which then "throws the finished product over the wall" to the marketing department. This can result in inefficiencies and additional expense, as when the engineers design something the production department can't build, and then the plans have to go back and forth between departments until something workable is achieved. Concurrent-engineering teams avoid this problem by in effect having all the specialists together at once.[42]

8 The Network Structure: Connecting a Central Core to Outside Firms by Computer Connections

In the eighth organizational form, ***network structure,*** **the organization has a central core that is linked to outside independent firms by computer connections, which are used to operate as if all were a single organization.** Corporations using this structure are sometimes called *virtual corporations.*[43] *(See Figure 8.12.)*

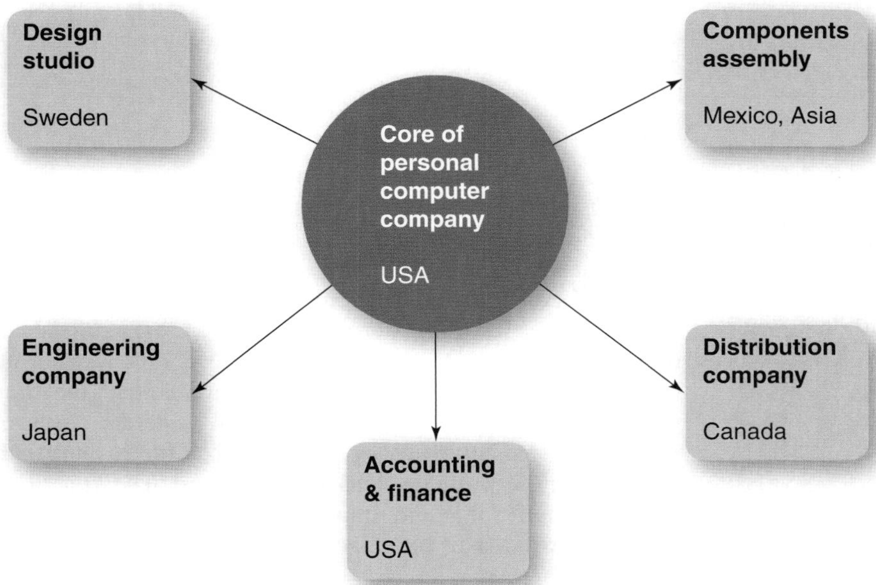

FIGURE 8.12
Network structure. This is an example of a personal computer company.

"The notion of where a corporation starts and stops is going to be very different in the future," said a Hewlett-Packard chief information officer and vice president. "Your expertise might be harvesting timber or processing lumber, but you also need to move your product to the construction industry. Traditionally, we brought all those steps together in a soup-to-nuts operation. Now, given [network structures], someone else can run your truck fleet, but it will still operate like your own fleet."[44]

With a network structure, an organization can operate with extensive, even worldwide operations, yet its basic core can remain small, thus keeping payrolls and overhead down. The glue that holds everything together is information technology, along with strategic alliances and contractual arrangements with supplier companies. ◆

Example

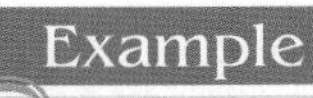

Network Structure: How Weyerhaeuser Makes Doors

Weyerhaeuser Co. upgraded a century-old door-making factory in Marshfield, Wisconsin, by installing an internal communications network (an intranet), then extending the network (as an extranet) to outside suppliers and customers. Doors are actually more complicated to make than you might think—there are millions of design and pricing variations, plus differing building codes requirements in different cities. Under the pre-network system, it could take up to a year to estimate and design a custom odd-size door with exotic veneer, glass peekaboo hole, and brass knobs, say. Now, using a system called DoorBuilder, customers can assemble their own package of doors, frames, veneers, hardware, and stains and tap into suppliers' price lists. Figuring out the options takes minutes rather than months. And the customers can then transmit their orders directly to the Marshfield plant.[45] (Weyerhaeuser has since sold the door operation.)

major question

What factors affect the design of an organization's structure?

The Big Picture

Five factors affecting an organization's structure are whether its environment is mechanistic or organic, whether its environment stresses differentiation or integration, and size, technology, and life cycle.

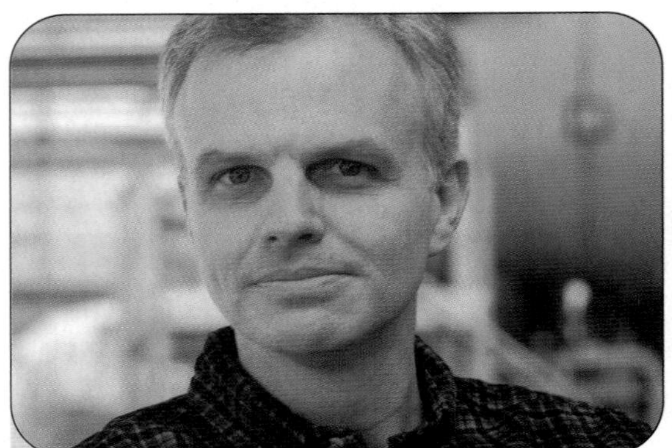

JetBlue CEO David Neeleman. "You don't have to do something grand to be a great company," says the founder of one of the U.S.'s newest airlines, which became profitable only six months after its February 2000 launch. "The ability to focus on customer service is something that applies to every single business you're in." Good customer service also stems from taking good care of employees, who from the first day at JetBlue are given benefits, profit sharing, and double-time overtime pay for hourly workers. The result is a culture in which employees are used to pitching in and helping. "When the plane lands," Neeleman says, "every employee on the plane, be it the CEO or someone from sales, pitches in and helps get the airplane ready. The pilots even come back and do it." What kind of factors affecting JetBlue's structure do you think figure in the company's success?

What is the optimum size for an organization? How big is too big?

"The real growth and innovation in this country," says famed management consultant Peter F. Drucker, "has been in medium-size companies that employ between 200 and 4,000 workers." Despite the informality, smaller than 200 is not necessarily better. "If you are in a small company, you are running all out," says Drucker. "You have neither the time nor the energy to devote to anything but yesterday's crisis." A medium-size company, by contrast, "has the resources to devote to new products and markets, and it's still small enough to be flexible and to move fast. And these companies now have what they once lacked—they've learned how to manage."[46]

When managers are considering what organizational arrangements to choose from, size is one of several factors, or *contingencies,* to consider. Recall from Chapter 2 that the *contingency approach* to management emphasizes that a manager's approach should vary according to—that is, be contingent on—the individual and environmental situation. Thus, the manager following the contingency approach simply asks, "What method is the best to use under these particular circumstances?" **The process of fitting the organization to its environment is called *contingency design.***

Managers taking a contingency approach must consider the following factors in designing the best kind of structure for their particular organization at that particular time:

1. *Environment—mechanistic versus organic*
2. *Environment—differentiation versus integration*
3. *Size*
4. *Technology*
5. *Life cycle*

1 The Environment: Mechanistic versus Organic Organizations—the Burns & Stalker Model

"Here every job is broken down into the smallest of steps, and the whole process is automated," wrote *Business Week* correspondent Kathleen Deveny, reporting about a day she spent working in a McDonald's restaurant. "Anyone could do this, I think."[47]

Actually, Deveny found that she fell behind in, say, bagging French fries, but it was certainly the intention of McDonald's founder Ray Kroc that, in fact, nearly anyone *should* be able to do this—and that a Big Mac should taste the same anywhere. Thus, for example, procedure dictates that a hamburger is always dressed the same way: first the mustard, then the ketchup, then two pickles.

McDonald's is a hugely successful example of what British behavioral scientists **Tom Burns** and **G. M. Stalker** call a *mechanistic organization,* as opposed to an *organic organization.*[48] *(See Table 8.1.)*

Could anyone do this? McDonald's follows the model of a mechanistic organization.

TABLE 8.1
Mechanistic versus organic organizations

Mechanistic Organizations	Organic Organizations
Centralized hierarchy of authority	Decentralized hierarchy of authority
Many rules and procedures	Few rules and procedures
Specialized tasks	Shared tasks
Formalized communication	Informal communication
Few teams or task forces	Many teams or task forces
Narrow span of control, taller structures	Wider span of control, flatter structures

Mechanistic Organizations: When Rigidity & Uniformity Work Best

In a *mechanistic organization,* authority is centralized, tasks and rules are clearly specified, and employees are closely supervised. Mechanistic organizations, then, are bureaucratic, with rigid rules and top-down communication. This kind of structure is effective at McDonald's because the market demands uniform product quality, cleanliness, and fast service.

In general, mechanistic design works best when an organization is operating in a stable environment. Yet new companies that have gone through a rough-and-tumble startup period may decide to change their structures so that they are more mechanistic, with clear lines of authority.

Organic Organizations: When Looseness & Flexibility Work Best

In an *organic organization,* authority is decentralized, there are fewer rules and procedures, and networks of employees are encouraged to cooperate and respond quickly to unexpected tasks. Tom Peters and Robert Waterman called this kind of organization a "loose" structure.[49]

Organic organizations are sometimes termed "adhoc-racies" because they operate on an ad hoc basis, improvising as they go along. As you might expect, information-technology companies such as Motorola favor the organic arrangement because they constantly have to adjust to technological change—yet so also do companies that need to respond to fast-changing consumer tastes, such as clothing retailer The Limited.

2 The Environment: Differentiation versus Integration—the Lawrence & Lorsch Model

Burns and Stalker's ideas were extended in the United States by Harvard University researchers **Paul R. Lawrence** and **Jay W. Lorsch.**[50] Instead of a *mechanistic-organic dimension,* however, they proposed a *differentiation-integration* dimension—forces that impelled the parts of an organization to move apart or to come together. The stability of the environment confronting the parts of the organization, according to Lawrence and Lorsch, determines the degree of differentiation or integration that is appropriate.

Differentiation: When Forces Push the Organization Apart

***Differentiation* is the tendency of the parts of an organization to disperse and fragment.** The more subunits into which an organization breaks down, the more highly differentiated it is.

This impulse toward dispersal arises because of technical specialization and division of labor. As a result, specialists behave in specific, delimited ways, without coordinating with other parts of the organization. For example, a company producing dental floss, deodorants, and other personal-care products might have different product divisions, each with its own production facility and sales staff—a quite differentiated organization.

Integration: When Forces Pull the Organization Together

***Integration* is the tendency of the parts of an organization to draw together to achieve a common purpose.** In a highly integrated organization, the specialists work together to achieve a common goal. The means for achieving this are a formal chain of command, standardization of rules and procedures, and use of cross-functional teams and computer networks so that there is frequent communication and coordination of the parts.

Gather your gladiators. In 1992, John Dooner, president and CEO of McCann-Erickson Advertising Worldwide, watched as the Coca-Cola Co.—his company's major client since the 1950s—gradually handed over nearly all of its advertising business to rival agencies. Instead of pounding on Coke's door and asking to be let back in, Dooner vowed to win back the account by changing everything about his company. Although advertising is staffed by creative geniuses who prefer to work alone, Dooner initiated a strategy of collaboration based on the movie *Gladiator,* in which the preservation-minded gladiators band together. "He tore apart and rebuilt McCann-Erickson into a broad-based shop with blue-chip credentials and a solid creative reputation," says a *Fast Company* account. "He bought 114 agencies that could offer everything from database research to the most cutting-edge video." As a result of the strategic blend, McCann began to attract a number of important clients, such as MasterCard and Microsoft. By the late 1990s, Coke found itself with too many agencies creating too many tag lines and too many treatments for a single brand. When Dooner approached Coke management, it decided to go with McCann's parent group, InterPublic Group of Cos., to ensure that the basic messages about Coca-Cola would "have a foundation of consistency." How does this story fit the Lawrence and Lorsch model of differentiation versus integration?

3 Size: The Larger the Organization, the More Mechanistic

Too big? Mitsubishi headquarters in Tokyo. What do you think the company could do about its size to become more efficient?

Organizational size **is usually measured by the number of full-time employees.** In general, research shows that larger organizations—those with 2,000 or more full-time employees (or the equivalent workload in a mix of full- and part-timers)—tend to have more rules, regulations, and procedures and more job specialization, as well as greater decentralization. That is, larger firms tend to be more mechanistic.[51] Small organizations tend to be more informal, to have fewer rules and regulations, and to have less work specialization. In other words, small firms tend to be more organic.

Economists have long extolled the virtues of economies of scale, suggesting that "bigger is better" because the per-unit cost of production decreases as the organization grows. Opponents, however, contend that "small is beautiful," because large organizations tend to breed apathy, alienation, absenteeism, and turnover. Indeed, bigger is not always better: The world's largest company, Japan's Mitsubishi, with revenues of $176 billion (bigger than those of AT&T, Du Pont, CitiCorp, and Procter & Gamble combined) in a recent year had a puny profit margin of just 0.12%.[52] But the inefficiencies may be related to complexity rather than size.

According to Tom Peters and Robert Waterman, most top-performing organizations keep their division size between $50 million and $100 million, "with a maximum of 1,000 or so employees each. Moreover, they grant their divisions extraordinary independence—and give them the functions and resources to exploit."[53] For example, Parker Hannifin, maker of industrial valves, auto parts, and programmable motion controls, among many other products, has 100 autonomous divisions, with 254 plants in 45 countries. Each division operates only a few plants each in order to keep the company nonunion and the managers close to their customers. "Whenever we get more than 200 people in a plant," says chairman Patrick Parker, "we like to move 50 miles down the road and start another."[54]

4 Technology: Small-Batch, Large-Batch, or Continuous-Process—Woodward's Model

Technology has an important influence on organizational design. ***Technology*** **consists of all the tools and ideas for transforming materials, data, or labor (inputs) into goods or services (outputs).** A hand-cranked ice-cream-making machine, for instance, is the technology that, with your muscle power, transforms cream, ice, sugar, and flavoring into ice cream. This book, the classroom, the blackboard, the instructor's lectures, and so on are the technologies that deliver an education about management.

In a study of 100 manufacturing firms in England, **Joan Woodward** classified firms according to three forms of technology in increasing levels of complexity: *small-batch, large-batch,* and *continuous process.*[55]

Small-Batch Technology: Custom-Made Products Made by Organic Organizations

In *small-batch technology,* often the least complex technology, goods are custom-made to customer specifications in small quantities. The one-of-kind portrait painting, the Saville Row bespoke suit, the *Columbia* space shuttle, the personal stationery you had designed and printed just for you are all examples.

Small-batch organizations, Woodward found, tend to be informal and flexible—that is, organic.

Large-Batch Technology: Mass-Produced Products Made by Mechanized Organizations

So-called ***large-batch technology*** **is mass-production, assembly-line technology.** Large volumes of finished products are made by combining easily available component parts. The clothes you buy at Macy's, Kenmore washers and dryers, Toyota automobiles, and most of the products we purchase on a daily basis fall into this category.

Large-batch organizations tend to have a higher level of specialization and to be more bureaucratic, according to Woodward.

Continuous Process: Highly Routinized Products Made by Organic Organizations

Continuous-process technology **is highly routinized technology in which machines do all the work.** Examples of this kind of technology are found in petroleum refineries, vodka distilleries, nuclear power plants, and steel mills, in which human operators mainly read dials and repair machine breakdowns.

Successful continuous-process organizations, Woodward found, tend to be more organic than mechanistic—less rigid and formal.

5 Life Cycle: Four Stages in the Life of an Organization

Like the four stages of a *project* life cycle (described in Chapter 5) and of a *product* life cycle (Chapter 6), organizations, too, have a life cycle. **The four-stage *organizational life cycle* has a natural sequence of stages: birth, youth, midlife, and maturity.** In general, as an organization moves through these stages, it becomes not only larger but also more mechanistic, specialized, decentralized, and bureaucratic. Each stage offers different managerial challenges and different organizational design issues.[56]

Stage 1 The Birth Stage—Nonbureaucratic

The *birth stage* is the nonbureaucratic stage, the stage in which the organization is created. Here there are no written rules and little if any supporting staff beyond perhaps a secretary.

The founder may be a lone entrepreneur, such as Michael Dell, who began Dell Computers by selling microcomputers out of his University of Texas college dorm room. Or the founders may be pals who got together, as did Apple Computer founders Steven Jobs and Stephen Wozniak, who built the first computer in Wozniak's parents' Palo Alto, California, garage, using the proceeds from the sale of an old Volkswagen.

Stage 2 The Youth Stage—Prebureaucratic

In the *youth stage,* the organization is in a prebureaucratic stage, a stage of growth and expansion.

Now the company has a product that is making headway in the marketplace, people are being added to the payroll (most clerical rather than professional), and some division of labor and setting of rules is being instituted.

For Apple Computer, this stage occurred during the years 1978–1981, with the establishment of the Apple II product line.

Stage 3 The Midlife Stage—Bureaucratic

In the *midlife stage,* the organization becomes bureaucratic, a period of growth evolving into stability.

Now the organization has a formalized bureaucratic structure, staffs of specialists, decentralization of functional divisions, and many rules.

In the 1980s, Apple Computer became a large company with many of these attributes. In 1983, Pepsi-Cola marketer John Scully was hired as a professional manager. Jobs became chairman; Wozniak left.

Stage 4 The Maturity Stage—Very Bureaucratic

In the *maturity stage,* the organization becomes very bureaucratic, large, and mechanistic. The danger at this point is lack of flexibility and innovation.

After Jobs was fired in a boardroom struggle in 1985, Apple entered a period in which it seemed to lose its way, having trouble developing successful products and getting them to market. Scully, who emphasized the wrong technology (a "personal data assistant" called Newton, which failed to establish a following) was followed by two more CEOs who were unable to arrest the company's declining market share.

In 1997, Jobs was brought back as a "temporary" chairman, and Apple's fortunes began to revive.

Employees who were present during birth and youth stages may long for the good old days of informality and fewer rules as the organization moves toward more formalized and bureaucratic structures. Whereas clearly some organizations jump the gun and institute such structures before they are appropriate, some expanding companies in effect never grow up, holding on to the prebureaucratic way of life for too long, hindering their ability to deliver goods or services efficiently in relation to their size. ◆

Pretzel progress. Millions of Auntie Anne's soft pretzels—Glazin' Raisin, Almond, Cinnamon Sugar, and others—are consumed every year by snack-crazed customers throughout the world. The business began in 1988 when Anne Beiler, a housewife in Lancaster, Pa., borrowed $6,000 from her father-in-law to purchase a soft pretzel stand at a local farmer's market. Since then it has expanded to over 800 stores or specialty retail units. Auntie Anne's, Inc. supports stores in 43 states and 12 international territories. It also has expanded into cookies with Cookie Farm in 1999 and into frozen custard with Auntie Anne's Cre-ámo Classic Cones in 2001. Where would you place Auntie Anne's, Inc. in the four-stage organizational life cycle?

major question **Why do organizations resist learning, and what is a new way for employees in an organization to view themselves?**

The Big Picture

Learning organizations are able to modify their behavior to reflect new knowledge. There are three reasons why organizations resist learning. A way to encourage learning is for all employees to view themselves as collaborators, not competitors.

Peter Guber. The director (left), shown here on the set of *Les Miserables* (1997) with actor Liam Neeson, learned from a novice a new way to put together a movie, *Gorillas in the Mist.*

The film *Gorillas in the Mist,* which was being shot in the middle of a jungle in Rwanda and was to use more than 200 animals, had turned into a nightmare, says Peter Guber, who was the producer. In large part, he reports, this was because "the screenplay required the gorillas to do what we wrote—in other words, to 'act.' If they couldn't or wouldn't, we'd have to fall back on a formula that the studio had seen fail before: using dwarfs in gorilla suits on a sound stage."

During an emergency meeting, a young intern had asked, "What if you let the gorillas write the story? . . . . What if you sent a really good cinematographer into the jungle with a ton of film to shoot the gorillas? Then you could write a story around what the gorillas did on the film."

Everyone had laughed and wondered what the intern was doing in a meeting with experienced filmmakers. But ultimately they did exactly what she suggested, and the cinematographer "came back with phenomenal footage that practically wrote the story for us," Guber says. "We shot the film for $20 million—half of the original budget." The moral: the woman's inexperience enabled her to see opportunities where others saw problems."[57]

Guber adopted ideas appropriate to what is known as a *learning organization.* As we said in Chapter 2, a learning organization is an organization that actively creates, acquires, and transfers knowledge within itself and is able to modify its behavior to reflect new knowledge.[58] Learning organizations, says MIT professor **Peter Senge,** who coined the term, are places "where people continually expand their capacity to create the results they truly desire, where new and expansive patterns of thinking are nurtured, where collective aspiration is set free, and where people are continually learning how to learn together."[59]

Why Organizations Might Resist Learning

Like people, organizations must continually learn new things or face obsolescence. A key challenge for managers in today's competitive environment, therefore, is to establish a culture that will enhance their employees' ability to learn. Organizations, like the people in them, do not *consciously* resist learning. But resistance arises anyway, for three reasons.[60] *(See Table 8.2.)*

1. People believe that competition is always better than collaboration.
2. Fragmentation leads to specialized fiefdoms that resist learning.
3. Unless encouraged, people won't take risks, the basis for learning.

TABLE 8.2

Reasons that resistance to learning develops in organizations

1 People Believe Competition Is Always Better Than Collaboration	2 Fragmentation Leads to Specialized Fiefdoms That Resist Learning	3 Unless Encouraged, People Won't Take Risks, the Basis for Learning
One of the most important beliefs (or paradigms—see text) in business is that competition is superior to collaboration. This belief can lead employees within an organization to battle one another when success depends on their cooperation. Overemphasis on competition also makes people—particularly leaders—more concerned about "looking good rather than doing good," hampering learning because they are reluctant to admit ignorance or mistakes. It also makes people hesitate to do tasks they worry they won't perform well. Finally, it makes everyone more concerned about short-term measurable results rather than long-term solutions to root causes of problems.	Today most people are specialists, trained to work in specific areas. This fragmented, piecemeal approach solves some kinds of problems but not those of great significance to society, such as lack of health-care coverage. Nor does it help solve organization-wide problems, such as the effect of new technology on the nature of the enterprise. To address these matters, we need people who have an understanding of systems, who view the world as a whole consisting of interrelated parts. In organizations, fragmentation not only creates specialists working in functional areas, it also erects walls between them, with workers battling one another for power and resources. Left behind on the battlefield are important ideas such as sharing and collaboration and, as a consequence, learning.	Do you resist learning a new word-processing program because you've gotten along just fine with the one you've used so far? Most of us tend to resist change, choosing to stay within our comfort zones, because change can be frustrating, even stressful. However, you no doubt have some areas of great personal interest (video games? cooking? motorcycles?) that inspire your curiosity, imagination, and experimentation—that is, that fuel the drive to learn and take chances. Learning requires taking some risks, as in making mistakes or in revealing your ignorance for all to see. But if our natural tendency to want others' approval is coupled with an organizational climate that favors management by fear and intimidation, people will resist taking risks, and so little learning will take place.

The New Paradigm: "We're All Stakeholders"

Most of us live by certain ***paradigms*****, generally accepted ways of viewing the world.** As stated in Table 8.2, one of the most important in business—and in American society in general—is the paradigm ("*pare*-uh-dime") that competition is superior to collaboration.

Many paradigms have outlived their usefulness, and you need to seriously challenge them if you want to create a learning organization. A principal challenge is to create a climate in which managers and employees stop thinking in terms of "us" versus "them" and start thinking of themselves as mutual stakeholders in the same enterprise.

"This is a company of owners, of partners, of businesspeople," reads one company's mission statement. "We are in business together. . . . No one in this company is just an employee. People have different jobs, make different salaries, have different levels of authority. But all workers will see the same basic information and will have a voice in matters affecting them. And it will be everyone's responsibility to understand how the business operates, to keep track of its results, and to make decisions that contribute to its success in the marketplace."[61]

There could be no better statement of the new managerial paradigm. 

Key Terms Used in This Chapter

accountability, 250
authority, 250
birth stage, 264
blended value, 246
centralized authority, 251
common purpose, 248
conglomerate structure, 255
contingency design, 260
continuous-process technology, 264
coordinated effort, 248
customer divisions, 254
decentralized authority, 251
delegation, 250
differentiation, 262
division of labor, 248
divisional structure, 254
functional structure, 252
geographic divisions, 255
hero, 241
hierarchy of authority, 248
hybrid structure, 256
integration, 262
large-batch technology, 264
line managers, 250
matrix structure, 256
maturity stage, 265
mechanistic organization, 261
midlife stage, 265
network structure, 259
organic organization, 261
organization, 244
organization chart, 246
organizational culture, 240
organizational life cycle, 264
organizational size, 263
paradigms, 267
product divisions, 254
responsibility, 250
rites and rituals, 241
simple structure, 252
small-batch technology, 263
span of control (management), 249
staff personnel, 251
story, 241
symbol, 241
team-based structure, 257
technology, 263
youth stage, 264

Summary

8.1 What Kind of Organizational Culture Will You Be Operating In?

- Organizational culture is a system of shared beliefs and values that develops within an organization and guides the behavior of its members. Culture exists on two levels—invisible and visible. (1) The invisible level is the core culture, which consists of values, beliefs, and assumptions—beliefs and values so widely shared that they are rarely discussed. (2) The visible level is the observable culture, which is expressed in symbols, stories, heroes, and rites and rituals. A symbol is an object, act, quality, or event that conveys meaning to others. A story is a narrative based on true events, which is repeated—and sometimes embellished on—to emphasize a particular value. A hero is a person whose accomplishments embody the values of the organization. Rites and rituals are the activities and ceremonies, planned and unplanned, that celebrate important occasions and accomplishments in the organization's life.
- Culture, which can powerfully shape an organization's success over the long term, has four functions. (1) It gives members an organizational identity. (2) It facilitates collective commitment. (3) It promotes social-system stability. (4) It shapes behavior by helping employees make sense of their surroundings.

8.2 What Is an Organization?

- An organization is a system of consciously coordinated activities or forces of two or more people. There are three types of organizations classified according to the three different purposes for which they are formed: for-profit, nonprofit, and mutual-benefit. It has been proposed that business organizations not be judged on profits alone—that there is blended value, in which all investments are understood to operate simultaneously in both economic and social realms.
- Whatever the size of organization, it can be represented in an organization chart, a boxes-and-lines illustration showing the formal lines of authority and the organization's official positions or division of labor. Two kinds of information that organizations reveal about organizational structure are (1) the vertical hierarchy of authority—who reports to whom, and (2) the horizontal specialization—who specializes in what work.

8.3 The Major Elements of an Organization

- Organizations have seven elements: (1) common purpose, which unifies employees or members and gives everyone an understanding of the organization's reason for being; (2) coordinated effort, the coordination of individual efforts into a group or organization-wide effort; (3) division of labor, having discrete parts of a task done by different people; (4) hierarchy of authority, a control mechanism for making sure the right people do the right things at the right time; (5) span of control, which refers to the number of people reporting directly to a given manager; (6) authority and accountability, responsibility, and delegation. Authority refers to the rights inherent in a managerial position to make decisions, give orders, and utilize resources. Accountability means that managers must report and justify work results to the managers above them. Responsibility is the obligation you have to perform the tasks assigned to you. Delegation is the process of assigning managerial authority and responsibility to managers and employees lower in the hierarchy. Regarding authority and responsibility, the organization chart distinguishes between two positions, line and staff. Line managers have authority to make decisions and usually have people reporting to them. Staff personnel have advisory functions; they provide advice, recommendations, and research to line managers. (7) Centralization versus decentralization of authority. With centralized authority, important decisions are made by higher-level managers. With decentralized authority, important decisions are made by middle-level and supervisory-level managers.

8.4 Basic Types of Organizational Structure

- Organizations may be arranged into eight types of structures. (1) In a simple structure, authority is centralized in a single person; this structure has a flat hierarchy, few rules, and low work specialization. (2) In a functional structure, people with similar occupational specialties are put together in formal groups. (3) In a divisional structure, people with diverse occupational specialties are put together in formal groups by similar products or services, customers or clients, or geographic regions. (4) In a conglomerate structure, divisions are grouped around similar businesses or industries. (5) In a hybrid structure, an organization uses functional and divisional structures in different parts of the same organization. (6) In a matrix structure, an organization combines functional and divisional chains of commands in grids so that there are two command structures—vertical and horizontal. (7) In a team-based structure, teams or workgroups are used to improve horizontal relations and solve problems throughout the organization. (8) In a network structure, the organization has a central core that is linked to outside independent firms by computer connections, which are used to operate as if all were a single organization.

8.5 Contingency Design: Factors in Creating the Best Structure

- The process of fitting the organization to its environment is called contingency design. Managers taking a contingency approach must consider five factors in designing the best kind of structure for their organization at that particular time.
- (1) An organization may be either mechanistic or organic. In a mechanistic organization, authority is centralized, tasks and rules are clearly specified, and employees are closely supervised. In an organic organization, authority is decentralized, there are fewer rules and procedures, and networks of employees are encouraged to cooperate and respond quickly to unexpected tasks.
- (2) An organization may also be characterized by differentiation or integration. Differentiation is the tendency of the parts of an organization to disperse and fragment. Integration is the tendency of the parts of an organization to draw together to achieve a common purpose.
- (3) Organizational size is usually measured by the number of full-time employees. Larger organizations tend to have more rules, regulations, job specialization, and decentralization. Smaller organizations tend to be more informal, have fewer rules, and have less work specialization.
- (4) Technology consists of all the tools and ideas for transforming materials, data or labor (inputs) into goods or services (outputs). Firms may be classified according to three forms of technology in increasing levels of complexity. In small-batch technology, often the least complex technology, goods are custom-made to customer specifications in small quantities. Large-batch technology is mass-production, assembly-line technology. Continuous-process technology is highly routinized technology in which machines do all the work.
- (5) The four-stage organizational life cycle has a natural sequence of stages: birth, youth, midlife, and maturity. The birth stage is the nonbureaucratic stage, the stage in which the organization is created. The youth stage is the prebureaucratic stage, a stage of growth and expansion. In the midlife stage, the organization becomes bureaucratic, a period of growth evolving into stability. In the maturity stage, the organization becomes very bureaucratic, large, and mechanistic.

The danger at this point is lack of flexibility and innovation.

8.6 Toward Building a Learning Organization

- Learning organizations are able to modify their behavior to reflect new knowledge. There are three reasons why organizations resist learning. (1) People believe that competition is always better than collaboration. (2) Fragmentation leads to specialized fiefdoms that resist learning. (3) Unless encouraged, people won't take risks, the basis for learning.
- A way to encourage learning is a new paradigm—namely, for all employees to view themselves as collaborators, not competitors.

Management in Action

Southwest Airlines' Organizational Culture Is a Source of Competitive Advantage

Excerpted from Andy Serwer, "Southwest Airlines: The Hottest Thing in the Sky," Fortune, *March 8, 2004, pp. 86–103.*

It's a little strange how some folks still think about the airline business. There are the big players, they'll tell you, like Delta, United, and American. And then you have the smaller fish. The low-cost carriers, led by that wacky Southwest Airlines, which they mention almost as an afterthought.

Now, hang on a minute. Let's look at those "industry leaders" and ask: big like how? Well, United parent UAL filed the largest bankruptcy in aviation history ($25 billion in assets) in December 2002. That's big. American is weighted down with nearly $18 billion of debt on its books. That's pretty big. And finally, the three large airlines lost a total of some $5.8 billion [in 2003]. That's big too.

Now let's look at Southwest Airlines. [In 2003] the company earned $442 million—more than all the other U.S. airlines combined. Its market capitalization of $11.7 billion is bigger than that of all its competitors combined, too. And [in May 2003], for the first time, Southwest boarded more domestic customers than any other airline, according to the Department of Transportation. Sure, the majors still have more revenue—Southwest, with about $6 billion in sales in 2003, ranks only No. 7 in that department—and they have more planes and carry more passengers when you include their overseas routes. And yes, some analysts question whether Southwest's amazing growth trajectory can continue. But, bottom line: Is there any question which company is the leader of this industry?

No wonder Southwest has landed in the top ten of *Fortune*'s Most Admired Companies in each of the past six years—a distinction shared only by Berkshire Hathaway, General Electric, and Microsoft. Its accomplishments would be estimable in any industry. (Southwest was the nation's best-performing stock from 1972 through 2002, according to *Money* magazine, up a gravity-defying 26% per year.) But that Southwest has achieved this measure of success in the snakebit airline biz is nothing short of astonishing. What's more, Southwest has sustained that success—and its grip on the top ten list—even nearly three years after its eccentric founder, Herb Kelleher, stepped down as CEO (he's still chairman) and after a swarm of upstart airlines, from JetBlue to Ted, have tried to horn in on its formula.

To figure out how, you could do worse than go back to the airline's conception. Southwest famously began 33 years ago when Kelleher (a lawyer by training) and a partner drew up a business plan on a cocktail napkin. Through decades of battling the big airlines, Southwest hasn't really changed its original formula. It enters markets in which traditional airlines hold sway and then blasts them with much lower fares. Southwest flies "point to point" (city to city), ignoring the hub-and-spoke model of most other airlines. It flies only 737s. It serves no meals, only snacks (peanuts, mostly). It charges no fees to change same-fare tickets. It has no assigned seats. It has no electronic entertainment on its planes, relying instead on relentlessly fun flight attendants to amuse passengers. . . .

If competitors are trying so hard to copy Southwest, why in the names of Orville and Wilbur Wright haven't they been able to duplicate its success? "Because they don't get it," says Southwest's idiosyncratic president and COO Colleen Barrett. "What we do is very simple, but it's not simplistic. We really do everything with passion. We scream at each other and we hug each other." There's no question that the other airlines practice the screaming part. They haven't been so good at the hugging. . . .

To truly understand why this company continues to be such a hit with customers, you have to go behind the wall and take a look. Pay a visit to Southwest's headquarters just off Love Field in Dallas, and you'll probably think you've wandered onto the set of *Peewee's Playhouse*. The walls are festooned with more than ten thousand picture frames—no exaggeration—containing photos of employees' pets, of Herb dressed like Elvis or in drag, of stewardesses in miniskirts, of Southwest planes gnawing on competitors' aircraft. Then there are the teddy bears, and jars of pickled hot peppers, and pink flamingos. There is cigarette smoking, and lots of chuckling, and nary a necktie to be seen.

"To me, it's comfortable," says Barrett, who as the ultimate keeper of the culture sits at a desk with a burning scented candle surrounded by the densest zone of bric-a-brac. "This is an open scrapbook. We aren't uptight. We celebrate everything. It's like a fraternity, a sorority, a reunion. We are having a party!" she says, throwing up her hands. I ask Barrett how much her annual picture-frame budget is. "Oh, I couldn't tell you that," she says. "Let's just say that I first gave out the framing work to this hippie fella, and now he has a business with 13 employees."

Okay, but come on. This is a serious business, right? So how does Southwest reconcile this insanity—studied though much of it is—with the fact that it flies 5.5 million people through the air each month? (Southwest—knock on Kelleher's head—has never had a fatal crash.) "Yes, our culture is almost like a religion," says company CFO Gary Kelly, "but it's a dichotomy. In many ways we are conservative. Financially, for instance." Indeed, Southwest is the only airline that maintains an investment-grade rating on its debt—a remarkable accomplishment in that business. And keeping a hawk's eye on costs is just as much a part of the company's culture as its silliness.

Yet lately, even though the airline still has some of the lowest expenses in the industry, costs have been climbing at Southwest. A key metric used in the business is cost per available seat mile (CASM), and in 1995 Southwest's CASM was 7.07 cents. Today it is up to 7.60 cents. . . .

But let's put the cost creep in context. The big carriers all have CASMs of between 9 cents and 13 cents, and they haven't been closing the gap on Southwest. In other words, their costs are increasing at the same rate. (True, JetBlue has been able to achieve costs below Southwest's, but its [expenses] have also been climbing recently—which in part explains why JetBlue's once high-flying stock is off some 50% from its peak.) And Southwest management is working hard to keep a lid on costs. For instance, late last year the company announced it was closing down three call centers to save money—more than $20 million annually—as more of its customers make reservations online. . . .

So what about it, Herb Kelleher? Is the company losing its soul, as some critics have said? "No," says Kelleher, puffing on an early-morning Merit Ultra Light. (I opt for a PayDay candy bar, which he keeps in a jar on his desk—"because I drink," he says.) "It'd better not be, because I'm not going to be around forever," he laughs. "Listen, we have an incredible esprit de corps here. It's like the Marine Corps. The intangibles have always been more important than the tangibles. Plus we run this company to prepare ourselves for the bad times, which always come in the business." . . .

High-stakes jousting with the majors. Squeezing every nickel. All the while keeping the fun level cranked up to the max. That's how Southwest does business. No question, it's a tricky and singular model. And no question it all begins with Herb Kelleher. So what happens when Kelleher finally does depart from the company? Michael Roach of Unisys puts it thus: "I never thought of Southwest as just the Herb Kelleher show. I look at it like Christianity or Islam. It was started by one guy, but it sure keeps on going." Much to the chagrin of its competitors. And much to the delight of its employees, customers, and shareholders.

For Discussion

1. How would you describe the invisible level of culture (that is, values, beliefs, and assumptions) at Southwest Airlines?
2. What symbols, stories, and heroes reflect the organizational culture at Southwest? Explain.
3. How does the organizational culture help Southwest to keep its costs among the lowest in the industry? Explain.
4. Using Table 8.1, describe the extent to which Southwest is mechanistic and organic. Use examples to support your conclusions.

Self-Assessment

Is Your Organization a Learning Organization?

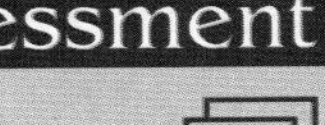

Objectives

1. To gain familiarity with the characteristics of learning organizations.
2. To identify if your organization is a learning organization.

Introduction

As we learned in this chapter, a learning organization is one that actively creates, acquires, and transfers new knowledge. Learning organizations are places in which new ideas and patterns of thinking are nurtured and in which people are allowed to continually expand their abilities to achieve desired results. Most importantly, a learning organization is a place in which the organization and individuals in it are continually learning in order to achieve its goals. The purpose of this exercise is to identify whether or not the organization in which you work is a learning organization.

Instructions

The following survey was created to assess the extent to which an organization follows the principles of a learning organization. If you are currently working, you should answer the questions in regard to this organization. If you are not currently working but have worked in the past, use a past job in completing the survey. If you have never had a job, you can use your school as a reference or use an organization you might be familiar with. For example, you might interview your parents to determine the extent to which the organization they work for follows the principles of a learning organization. Read each statement and use the following scale to indicate which answer most closely matches your response: 1 = strongly disagree; 2 = disagree; 3 = neither agree nor disagree; 4 = agree; 5 = strongly agree.

1. Management uses rewards, praise, and recognition to get what they want done.	1	2	3	4	5
2. The company promotes teamwork.	1	2	3	4	5
3. People are recognized and rewarded on the basis of what they do rather than *who* they know.	1	2	3	4	5
4. I see more examples of optimistic attitudes/behaviors rather than negative and cynical ones.	1	2	3	4	5
5. I have a clear picture of the organization's vision and my role in helping to accomplish it.	1	2	3	4	5
6. This organization relies more on team-based solutions than individual ones.	1	2	3	4	5
7. This organization tends to look at the big picture rather than analyzing problems from a narrow perspective.	1	2	3	4	5
8. People have an open mind when working with others.	1	2	3	4	5
9. This company looks for the root cause of a problem rather than a "quick fix."	1	2	3	4	5
10. I have the skills and knowledge to continuously improve the way I do my job.	1	2	3	4	5

Total ____________________

Scoring

To get your score, add up the numbers that correspond to your responses. The range will be from 10 to 50. Comparative norms for learning organizations are as follows:

Total score of 10–23 = low learning organization
Total score of 24–36 = moderate learning organization
Total score of 37–50 = high learning organization

Group Exercise

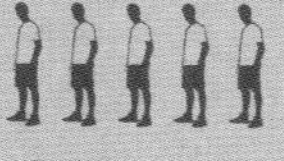

Designing Your Own Organization

Objectives

To learn more about organizational structures.

To consider the relationship between organizational culture and structure.

Introduction

As we learned in this chapter, an organization's culture consists of a system of shared beliefs and values that develops within the organization and guides the behavior of its members. An organization's culture and its structure are closely intertwined. The purpose of this exercise is to examine the relationship between an organization's culture and its structure. To accomplish this, you will design your own company.

Instructions

Break into groups of five or six people. Your first task is to start your own organization. Your organization can be anything from a baseball team to a car company to a bank. Once you have determined what type of organization your group wants to create, the group needs to establish the organizational values that will underlie your organization's culture. Once the values are established, we want you to propose two different organizational structures. Begin by examining the eight types of organizational structures covered in the text. Your first organizational chart should represent your proposed structure at the beginning of your organization's inception. The second organization chart should represent the structure of your organization once it has 300 or more employees.

Questions for Discussion

1. What are your organization's values? Explain why they were chosen.
2. How do the values and culture of your organization correspond to its structure? Explain.
3. How did your organization chart change once your company reached 300 employees? What type of structure does this chart represent? Explain.
4. Do you believe your organization is more mechanistic or organic? Explain.

Ethical Dilemma

Enron's Organizational Culture & Reward System Contribute to Its Problems

Excerpted from John A. Byrne, Mike France, and Wendy Zellner, "The Environment Was Ripe for Abuse," Business Week, *February 25, 2002, pp. 118–120.*

BusinessWeek [Houston energy trader] Enron didn't fail just because of its entrepreneurial culture—the very reason Enron attracted so much attention and acclaim. The unrelenting emphasis on earnings growth and individual initiative, coupled with a shocking absence of the usual corporate checks and balances, tipped the culture from one that rewarded aggressive strategy to one that increasingly relied on unethical corner-cutting. . . .

Central to forging a new Enron culture was an unusual performance review system that [former CEO Jeffrey] Skilling adapted from his days at McKinsey. Under this peer-review process, a select group of 20 people were named to a performance review committee (PRC) to rank more than 400 vice presidents, then all the directors, and finally all of Enron's managers. The stakes were high because all the rewards were linked to ranking decisions by the PRC, which had to unanimously agree on each person. Managers judged "superior"—the top 5%—got bonuses 66% higher than those who got an "excellent" rating, the next 30%. They also got much larger stock option grants. . . .

In practice, the system bred a culture in which people were afraid to get crossways with someone who could screw up their reviews. How did managers ensure they passed muster? "You don't object to anything," says one former Enron executive. "The whole culture at the vice-president level and above just became a yes-man culture."

Several former and current Enron execs say that Andrew S. Fastow, the ex-chief financial officer who is at the center of Enron's partnership controversy, had a reputation for exploiting the review system to get back at people who expressed disagreement or criticism.

Solving the Dilemma

What would you do to the performance evaluation system?

1. Leave it alone because it rewards individual achievement.
2. Keep the basic ranking process but drop the requirement that the PRC must unanimously agree on each person's evaluation. The company might use an average ranking across all raters as the final rating.
3. Drop the entire ranking process because it is too subjective.
4. Invent other options. Discuss.

Video Case

One Smooth Stone

The company name and inspiration come from the story of David and Goliath. David had only one chance to make use of his one smooth stone, and likewise the employees of One Smooth Stone (OSS) have only one shot to tackle each big project. The company provides materials for big corporate events such as sales meetings, client meetings, and product presentations. Most people in the industry have attended many such meetings, so keeping them entertained is a major challenge. That's where OSS comes in. It uses project teams to come up with original and captivating presentations for its customers.

OSS is a fun and interesting place to work, and turnover is low. OSS is structured to be flexible and responsive to its clients. There are no off-the-shelf packages—every presentation is custom designed to meet the needs of each client. OSS utilizes a flat organizational structure. Project managers do supervise employees; however, workers are empowered to make their own decisions, and authority is decentralized. While many organizations are structured around functional areas (for instance, accounting, marketing, and so on), OSS is organized around self-managed project teams. Each team is charged with meeting the needs of an individual client. When needed, the company will utilize freelance professionals who bring the talent and solutions necessary to satisfy clients. Always—the focus is on meeting client needs. OSS also employs staff employees to handle areas such as personnel and legal issues.

The company originally formalized their strategic plans, but they found that the business environment changed so quickly that their plans were soon obsolete. So, the top managers implemented a concept called "strategic improvising": core values and general ground rules provide a template to guide decisions but allow the flexibility to react to a changing business environment. Strategic improvising is an example of how OSS seeks continuous improvement and strives for total quality management.

OSS summarizes its core values in three words: Smart, Fast, and Kind. If OSS can deliver services in a smart way, in a fast way, and in a kind way, clients will keep coming back. For OSS, that's the definition of success. Because of its culture and responsiveness, the company has captured accounts such as Motorola, Sun Microsystems, and International Truck and Engine. Ultimately, the long-run success of the firm is built on its project teams. They carefully listen to what the clients are trying to accomplish and create solutions to their problems. Clearly, OSS has been able to impress the Goliaths of big business.

Discussion Questions

1. Review the basic types of organizational structures. Which type of structure is evident at OSS?
2. Would you characterize OSS as a mechanistic organization or an organic organization? Is this the appropriate structure given the business environment?
3. Technology is classified into three categories: small batch, large batch, and continuous process. Define each. Which type is evident at OSS?

chapter 9

Human Resource Management

Getting the Right People for Managerial Success

MAJOR QUESTIONS YOU SHOULD BE ABLE TO ANSWER

9.1 Strategic Human Resource Management
Major Question: How do star managers view the role of people in their organization's success?

9.2 The Legal Requirements of Human Resource Management
Major Question: To avoid exposure to legal liabilities, what areas of the law do I need to be aware of?

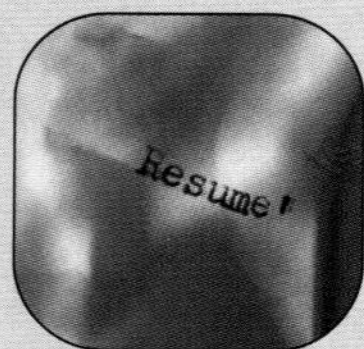

9.3 Recruitment & Selection: Putting the Right People into the Right Jobs
Major Question: How can I reduce mistakes in hiring and find great people who might work for me?

9.4 Orientation, Training, & Development
Major Question: Once people are hired, what's the best way to see that they do what they're supposed to do?

9.5 Performance Appraisal
Major Question: How can I assess employees' performance more accurately and give more effective feedback?

9.6 Managing an Effective Workforce: Compensation & Benefits
Major Question: What are the various forms of compensation?

9.7 Other Concerns in Managing an Effective Workforce
Major Question: How do I manage contemporary workplace problems such as drug abuse and sexual harassment?

the manager's toolbox

Keeping Employees Invested in Their Jobs

"*Get a life!*" everyone says. But what, exactly, is a "life," anyway?

As more and more people have begun asking this question, it has spilled over into organizational life. The result has been a new category of work rewards called *work-life benefits.*

As one definition has it, work-life benefits are programs "used by employers to increase productivity and commitment by removing certain barriers that make it hard for people to strike a balance between their work and personal lives."[1] Examples are nonsalary incentives such as flexible work arrangements, tuition assistance, and paid time off for community service.

Managing human resources, the subject of this chapter, focuses on managing people. You need to be thinking about employees not as "human capital" or "capital assets" but as people who are *investors:* They are investing their time, energy, and intelligence—their lives—in your organization, for which they deserve a return that makes sense to them.[2]

To keep your employees invested in their jobs and performing well, it helps to know what the Gallup Organization discovered in surveying 80,000 managers and 1 million workers over 25 years.[3] Gallup found that in the best workplaces employees gave strong "Yes" answers to the following 12 questions:

1. Do I know what's expected of me?
2. Do I have the right materials and equipment I need to do my work right?
3. Do I have the opportunity to do what I do best every day?
4. In the last seven days, have I received recognition or praise for good work?
5. Does my supervisor, or someone at work, seem to care about me as a person?
6. Is there someone at work who encourages my development?
7. Does my opinion seem to count?
8. Does the mission of my company make me feel like my work is important?
9. Are my coworkers committed to doing quality work?
10. Do I have a best friend at work?
11. In the last six months, have I talked with someone about my progress?
12. Have I had opportunities to learn and grow?

The best managers, Gallup says, meet with workers individually at least every three months, not just once or twice a year. In doing so, they not only discuss performance but also try to find out what employees want to accomplish and how the manager can help. In addition, good managers focus on strengths, rather than weaknesses, allowing employees to devote time to what they do best.

Since *Fortune* magazine began publishing its annual list of "The 100 Best Companies to Work For," managers have been concerned about trying to take better care of their employees. The best organizations, according to a project leader who helps with the *Fortune* list, keep their employees an average of 6 years, as opposed to the nationwide average of 3.6 years. They accomplish this by pushing for employees at all levels to feel involved in the company's success.[4]

forecast

What's Ahead in This Chapter

This chapter considers human resource (HR) management—planning for, attracting, developing, and retaining an effective workforce. We consider how this subject fits in with the overall company strategy, how to evaluate current and future employee needs, and how to recruit and select qualified people. We discuss orientation, training, and development; how to assess employee performance and give feedback; and what HR laws managers should be aware of. Finally, we consider how to manage compensation and benefits, promotions and discipline, and workplace performance problems.

major question

How do star managers view the role of people in their organization's success?

The Big Picture

Human resource management consists of the activities managers perform to plan for, attract, develop, and retain an effective workforce. Planning the human resources needed consists of understanding current employee needs and predicting future employee needs.

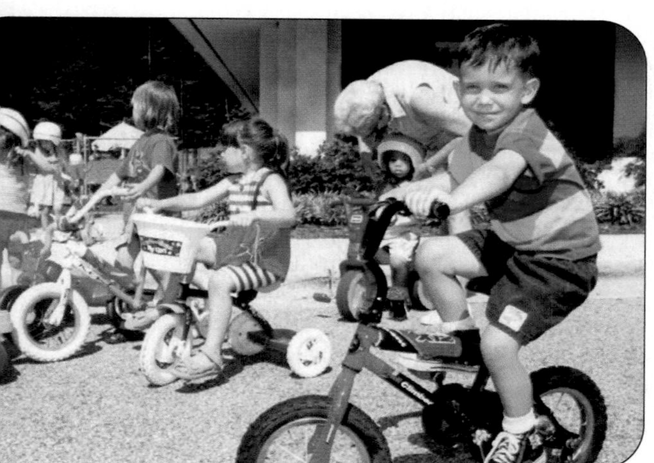

SAS child-care center. If the U.S. Senate can fund itself a child-care center, shouldn't every company have one? Considering how often the working parents of school-age children have to scramble to make special arrangements for their offspring during school closures, wouldn't you find a day-care center at work a special inducement to stay with—and perform well for—a company?

One company that has appeared on *Fortune*'s "The 100 Best Companies to Work For" list (#2 in 2001, #3 in 2002, #8 in 2004) is SAS Institute, a developer of statistical software located on the outskirts of Raleigh, N.C. SAS (pronounced "Sass") "is the closest thing to a workers' utopia in America: on-site child care, health center with physicians and dentists, three different cafeterias, massage therapist, wooded campus, and profit sharing."[5] At least that's according to Robert Levering and Milton Moskowitz, authors of the Best Companies list. SAS also offers flexible work schedules and fills jars all around the company with M&M candies—22.5 tons a year.[6] As a result, SAS has had the lowest employee turnover rate of any company on the list—3%, compared with a software industry average of 25%.

The software has made a billionaire of cofounder James H. Goodnight, whose mansion is on the grounds of the privately held company's country club-like campus. "I like happy people," he says, to explain the perks he lavishes on his employees. The software industry is notorious for inflicting brutal 60- to 80-hour weeks, but SAS workers—more than half of whom are women, drawn to its family-flexible policies—normally work 35 hours a week. Besides providing the free health clinic, two day-care centers, an elder-care program, private offices for everyone, and a pianist in one of the subsidized cafeterias, SAS gives employees an extra week of vacation between Christmas and New Year's, along with a year-end bonus and profit-sharing. Employees also get discounts on memberships in a local country club and tuition breaks for their children at a private school founded by Goodnight.

Too good to be true? SAS can do all these things because it is a privately held company, although it has entertained the idea of going public. (But investors in a public company might ask Goodnight to justify the M&M expense.) However, perhaps the catch, if any, is this: SAS offers benefits that cement employee loyalty while avoiding those that promote autonomy, such as commissions for salespeople, stock options, and tuition reimbursement for further training.[7]

Human Resource Management: Managing an Organization's Most Important Resource

Human resource (HR) management **consists of the activities managers perform to plan for, attract, develop, and retain an effective workforce.** Whether it's McKenzie looking for entry-level business consultants, the U.S. Navy trying to fill its ranks, or churches trying to reverse the declining number of priests and ministers, all organizations must deal with staffing.

Discrimination

Discrimination **occurs when people are hired or promoted—or denied hiring or promotion—for reasons not relevant to the job,** such as skin color or eye shape, gender, religion, national origin, and the like. When an organization is found to have been practicing discrimination, the people discriminated against may sue for back pay and punitive damages.

Affirmative Action

Affirmative action **focuses on achieving equality of opportunity within an organization.** It tries to make up for past discrimination in employment by actively finding, hiring, and developing the talents of people from groups traditionally discriminated against. Steps include active recruitment, elimination of prejudicial questions in interviews, and establishment of minority hiring goals. It's important to note that EEO laws *do not* allow use of hiring quotas.[18] ◆

TABLE 9.1

Some important recent U.S. federal laws and regulations protecting employees

Year	Law or regulation	Provisions
1963	Equal Pay Act	Requires men and women be paid equally for performing equal work
1964	Civil Rights Act, Title VII	Prohibits discrimination on basis of race, color, religion, national origin, or sex
1967, amended 1978 and 1986	Age Discrimination in Employment Act (ADEA)	Prohibits discrimination in employees over 40 years old; restricts mandatory retirement
1970	Occupational Safety & Health Act (OSHA)	Establishes minimum health and safety standards in organizations
1974	Employee Retirement Income Security Act (ERISA)	Sets rules for managing pension plans; provides federal insurance to cover bankrupt plans
1978	Pregnancy Discrimination Act	Broadens discrimination to cover pregnancy, childbirth, and related medical conditions; protects job security during maternity leave
1978	Mandatory Retirement Act	Prohibits forced retirement of employees under 70
1986	Consolidated Omnibus Budget Reconciliation Act (COBRA)	Requires an extension of health insurance benefits after termination
1986	Immigration Reform & Control Act	Prohibits unlawful employment of aliens and unfair immigration-related employment practices
1988	Worker Adjustment and Retraining Notification Act	Requires organizations with 100 or more employees to give 60 days notice for mass layoffs or plant closings
1990	Americans with Disabilities Act (ADA)	Prohibits discrimination against qualified employees with physical or mental disabilities or chronic illness; requires "reasonable accommodation" be provided so they can perform duties
1991	Civil Rights Act	Amends and clarifies Title VII, ADA, and other laws; permits suits against employers for punitive damages in cases of intentional discrimination
1993	Family & Medical Leave Act	Requires employers to provide 12 weeks of unpaid leave for medical and family reasons, including for childbirth, adoption, or family emergency
2003	Sarbanes-Oxley Act	Prohibits employers from demoting or firing employees who raise accusations of fraud to a federal agency

major question

How can I reduce mistakes in hiring and find great people who might work for me?

The Big Picture

Qualified applicants for jobs may be recruited from inside or outside the organization. The task of choosing the best person is enhanced by such tools as reviewing candidates' application forms, résumés, and references; doing interviews, either structured or unstructured; and screening with ability, personality, performance, and other kinds of employment tests.

"Digital résumés, digital employment advertising, digital résumé searches—it's a rebuilding of the [employment] infrastructure," says former Intel chairman Andy Grove.[19]

Companies are using the public Internet with their own internal intranets to revolutionize their human resource departments, going online for everything from listing job openings to conducting new employee orientations. Recruitment efforts have migrated from simple online classified-ad–like job postings to websites that attract candidates with video and audio feeds. Yet as tempting as it is to think that most job-hunting activity has migrated to the Internet, only a minority of job-seekers used the Net in their last job search. *(See Figure 9.2.)*

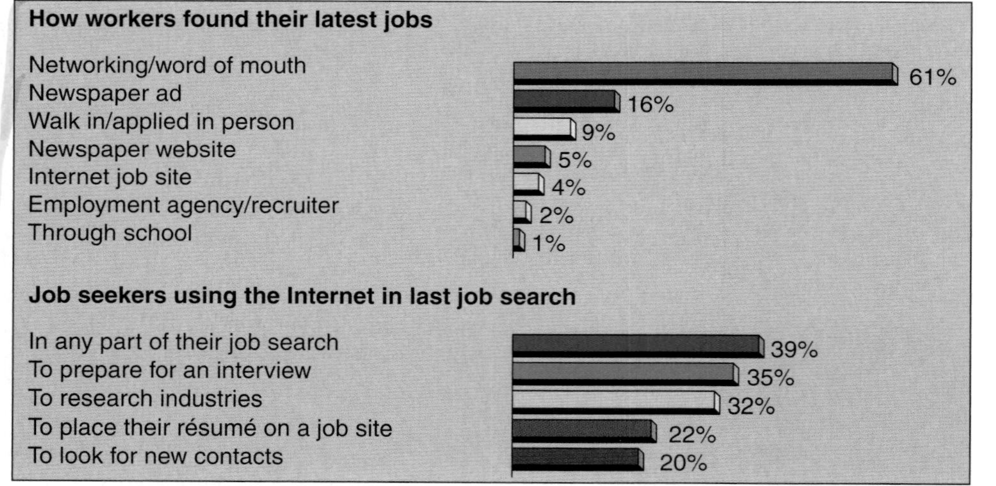

FIGURE 9.2
Job hunting. A survey of 703 Americans released January 2003 produced the following results. (*Sources:* Adapted from The Bernard Haldane Associates Internet Job Report conducted by Taylor Nelson Sofres Intersearch, released January 2003, reported in "How Workers Found Their Latest Jobs," *USA Today,* February 3, 2003, p. 1B, and "Job Hunting the Old-Fashioned Way," *Business Week,* February 17, 2003, p. 10.)

Recruitment: How to Attract Qualified Applicants

At some time nearly every organization has to think about how to find the right kind of people. ***Recruiting*** **is the process of locating and attracting qualified applicants for jobs open in the organization.** The word "qualified" is important: You want to find people whose skills, abilities, and characteristics are best suited to your organization. Recruiting is of two types: *internal* and *external.*

1 Internal Recruiting: Hiring from the Inside

Internal recruiting **means making people already employed by the organization aware of job openings.** Indeed, most vacant positions in organizations are filled through internal recruitment, mainly through ***job posting,*** **placing information about job vacancies and qualifications on bulletin boards, in newsletters, and on the organization's intranet.**

2 External Recruiting: Hiring from the Outside

External recruiting **means attracting job applicants from outside the organization.** Notices of job vacancies are placed through newspapers, employment agencies, executive recruiting firms, union hiring halls, college job-placement offices, technical training schools, and word of mouth through professional associations. Many organizations—and not just high-technology companies—are advertising job openings on the Internet.

Both methods have their advantages and disadvantages. *(See Table 9.2.)*

TABLE 9.2

Internal and external recruiting: advantages and disadvantages

Internal recruiting	
Advantages	Disadvantages
1. Employees tend to be inspired to greater effort and loyalty. Morale is enhanced because they realize that working hard and staying put can result in more opportunities.	1. Internal recruitment restricts the competition for positions and limits the pool of fresh talent and fresh viewpoints.
2. The whole process of advertising, interviewing, and so on is cheaper.	2. It may encourage employees to assume that longevity and seniority will automatically result in promotion.
3. There are fewer risks. Internal candidates are already known and are familiar with the organization.	3. Whenever a job is filled, it creates a vacancy elsewhere in the organization.
External recruiting	
Advantages	Disadvantages
1. Applicants may have specialized knowledge and experience.	1. The recruitment process is more expensive and takes longer.
2. Applicants may have fresh viewpoints.	2. The risks are higher because the persons hired are less well known.

Which External Recruiting Methods Work Best?

Both as a manager trying to hire good candidates and as a job seeker yourself, you'll benefit from knowing which external recruiting sources are most effective in producing superior employees, although these techniques vary by job.

In general, the most effective sources are employee referrals, say human resource professionals, because, to protect their own reputations, employees are fairly careful about whom they recommend and they know the qualifications of both the job and the prospective employee.[20] Other above-average sources are college recruiters and executive search firms, and average sources are professional associations and newspaper ads.

At one time, the Internet seemed to offer the promise of an effective online hiring hall. Although a few companies do a majority of hiring via online systems (J. P. Morgan Chase & Co. in New York said more than three-quarters of its hires in the first half of 2003 started on the corporate website), many jobseekers find their applications simply disappear into a black hole.[21] John Challenger, head of a Chicago outplacement firm, says there's a lot of good information on the Internet, but the popular job sites are simply time wasters.[22]

practical action

Screening Résumés & References

Because it seems to be getting harder to distinguish honest job applicants from the great number of dishonest ones, companies now routinely check résumés or hire companies that do so, such as Illinois-based Credentials LLC, which signs contracts with most major universities to tap into their databases to glean information about their students.

As far as recommendations from previous employers, however, many such employers don't give honest assessments of former employees, for two reasons: (1) They fear that if they say anything negative, they can be sued by the former employee. (2) They fear that if they say anything positive, and the job candidate doesn't pan out, they can be sued by the new employer.

In addition, some companies now resort to computer prescreening, which job seekers must pass before obtaining an in-person interview. Macy's, for instance, requires applicants to undergo an 8- or 10-minute screening, using a phone's keypad to answer multiple-choice questions (such as "If a customer complained to you about the selection of merchandise in a store, what would you do?").[23] Information services firm EDS has an entire website for screening candidates.[24]

Because honest references are so hard to get, candidates are now being scrutinized more carefully for character and candor during the interview process. Indeed, a survey by Robert Half International, a big staffing services firm, found that nearly one-third of executives polled rated honesty and integrity as the most critical qualities in a candidate. "Without such attributes as trustworthiness and integrity, even the most highly skilled and articulate job seeker or employee will have limited success," says Max Messmer, head of Robert Half.[25]

Realistic Job Previews

Often an organization will put on its best face to try to attract the best outside candidates—and then wonder why the new hires leave when the job doesn't turn out to be as rosy as promised.

A better approach is to present what's known as a ***realistic job preview,*** **which gives a candidate a picture of both positive and negative features of the job and the organization before he or she is hired.**[26] People with realistic expectations tend to quit less frequently and be more satisfied than those with unrealistic expectations.

Selection: How to Choose the Best Person for the Job

Whether the recruitment process turns up a handful of job applicants or thousands, now you turn to the ***selection process,*** **the screening of job applicants to hire the best candidate.** Essentially this becomes an exercise in *prediction:* how well will the candidate perform the job and how long will he or she stay?

Three types of selection tools are *background information, interviewing,* and *employment tests.*

1 Background Information: Application Forms, Résumés, & Reference Checks

Application forms and résumés provide basic background information about job applicants, such as citizenship, education, work history, and certifications.

Unfortunately, a lot of résumé information consists of mild puffery and even outrageous fairy tales. According to a 2002 survey of 2.6 million job applicants by Colorado-based Avert Inc., which specializes in background checks, 44% of all résumés contain at least some lies.[27] Lying about education is the most prevalent (such as pretending to hold a college degree or an advanced degree). Automatic Data Processing of Roseland, New Jersey, which has studied employee background veri-

The Desirable Characteristics of Orientation

Like Orientation Week for new college students, the initial socialization period is designed to give new employees the information they need to be effective. In a large organization, orientation may be a formal, established process. In a small organization, it may be so informal that employees find themselves having to make most of the effort themselves.

Following orientation, the employee should emerge with information about three matters (much of which he or she may have acquired during the job-application process):

- **The job routine:** At minimum, the new employee needs to have learned what is required in the job for which he or she was hired, how the work will be evaluated, and who the immediate coworkers and managers are. This is basic.
- **The organization's mission and operations:** Certainly all managers need to know what the organization is about—its purpose, products or services, operations, and history. And it's now understood that low-level employees perform better if they, too, have this knowledge.
- **The organization's work rules and employee benefits:** A public utility's HR department may have a brochure explaining formalized work rules, overtime requirements, grievance procedures, and elaborate employee benefits. A technology startup may be so fluid that many of these matters will have not been established yet. Even so, there are matters of law (such as those pertaining to sexual harassment) affecting work operations that every employee should be made aware of.

Training & Development: Helping People Perform Better

Which business strategy offers the highest returns: (1) downsizing; (2) total quality management, which focuses on work methods and process control; or (3) employee involvement, which focuses on upgrading workers' skills and knowledge? According to a study of 216 big firms, the winner is employee involvement, which had an average return on investment of 19.1% (versus 15.4% for downsizing and 15% for TQM).[47]

In hiring, you always try to get people whose qualifications match the requirements of the job. Quite often, however, there are gaps in what new employees need to know. These gaps are filled by training. The training process involves five steps, as shown below. *(See Figure 9.4.)*

FIGURE 9.4
Five steps in the training process

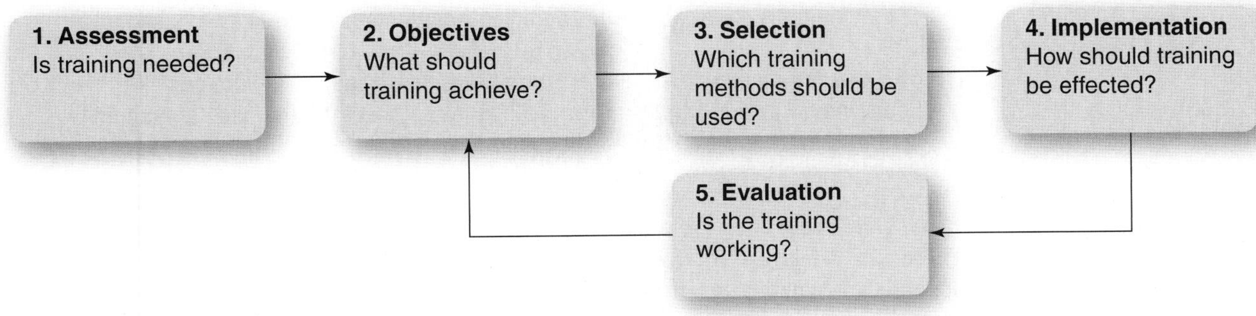

HR professionals distinguish between *training* and *development.*

- **Training—upgrading skills of technical and operational employees:** Electronics technicians, word processors, computer network administrators, and X-ray technicians, among many others, need to be schooled in new knowledge as the requirements of their fields change. ***Training,* then, refers to educating technical and operational employees in how to better do their current jobs.**
- **Development—upgrading skills of professionals and managers:** Accountants, nurses, lawyers, and managers of all levels need to be continually educated in how to do their jobs better not just today but also tomorrow. ***Development* refers to educating professionals and managers in the skills they need to do their jobs in the future.**

Typical areas for which employee training and development are given are shown below. *(See Table 9.3.)*

TABLE 9.3

Typical topics of employee training [*Source:* C. McNamara, "Employee Training and Development: Reasons and Benefits," Free Management Library, located at www.mapnp.org/library; www.managementhelp.org/trng_dev/basics/reasons.htm (accessed August 14, 2004).]

1. ***Communications:*** The increasing diversity of today's workforce brings a wide variety of languages and customs.
2. ***Computer skills:*** Computer skills are becoming a necessity for conducting administrative and office tasks.
3. ***Customer service:*** Increased competition in today's global marketplace makes it critical that employees understand and meet the needs of customers.
4. ***Diversity:*** Diversity training usually includes explanations about how people have different perspectives and views and techniques to value diversity.
5. ***Ethics:*** Today's society has increasing expectations about corporate social responsibility. Also, today's diverse workforce brings a wide variety of values and morals to the workplace.
6. ***Human relations:*** The increased stresses of today's workplace can include misunderstandings and conflict. Training can help people to get along in the workplace.
7. ***Quality initiatives:*** Initiatives such as total quality management, quality circles, and benchmarking require basic training about quality concepts, guidelines and standards for quality, and so on.
8. ***Safety:*** Safety training is critical for people working with heavy equipment, hazardous chemicals, repetitive activities, and so on but can also be useful by providing practical advice for avoiding accidents and the like.
9. ***Sexual harassment:*** Sexual harassment training usually includes careful description of the organization's policies about sexual harassment, especially about what are inappropriate behaviors.

The Different Types of Training or Development

There are all kinds of training and development methods, and their effectiveness depends on whether what is being taught are facts or skills. If people are to learn *facts*—such as work rules or legal matters—lectures, videotapes, and workbooks are effective. If people are to learn *skills*—such as improving interpersonal relations or using new tools—then techniques such as discussion, role playing, and practice work better.

Another way to categorize training methods is to distinguish on-the-job from off-the-job methods. *On-the-job training* takes place in the work setting while employees are performing job-related tasks. Four major training methods are coaching, training positions, job rotation, and planned work activities. *Off-the-job training* consists of classroom programs, videotapes, workbooks, and the like. *(See Table 9.4.)* Lots of off-the-job training consists of ***computer-assisted instruction (CAI),*** **in which computers are used to provide additional help or to reduce instructional time.** ◆

TABLE 9.4

On-the-job and off-the-job training methods [*Source:* "1996 Industry Report," *Training,* October 1996, pp. 37–39 (for off-the-job methods).]

On-the-Job Methods	Off-the-Job Methods (based on survey of 2,833 companies)
1. Coaching—a subordinate is taken under the wing of an experienced employee who points out what's required in the new job. 2. Training positions—trainees are given positions as assistants to experienced managers. 3. Job rotation—employees are given lateral transfers to allow them to work at different jobs, which gives them a broad view of the business. 4. Planned work activities—trainees are given important work assignments (such as heading a task force) to develop their experience.	1. Classroom programs—used by 91% of companies 2. Videotapes—used by 79% 3. Workbooks or manuals—77% 4. Overhead/opaque transparencies—56% 5. Business books—55% 6. Role playing—55% 7. Other: audiotapes, self-testing instruments, case studies, slides

Example

Off-the-Job Training: Practical Courses Through Distance Learning

A college degree isn't the end of the educational road. Between 40 million and 45 million people are taking short-term, practical courses related to their careers, mostly at business schools and continuing-education institutions around the country.[48] Even top managers are brushing up. John Klotsche, 56, chairman of Baker & McKenzie, a global law firm, decided he and his 550 partners didn't know enough about managing a business in today's fast-changing marketplace, so all attorneys in his firm took a two-week executive-education course at Northwestern University.

But while most students are taking classes on campuses, the fastest-growing method of continuing education is via distance learning from videotapes, satellite lectures, or courses offered on the World Wide Web. The benefits of a virtual education are that no transportation is needed and that you can follow a flexible schedule and often work at your own pace. But because of the lack of classroom interaction between students and teachers, the online model of education means that both must assume more responsibility. "If students do not receive adequate teacher feedback and reinforcement," points out one writer, "they will not always know whether they possess an accurate knowledge of the subject matter."[49]

Small company training. How would you expect training in a small company to differ from training in a large company?

9.5 Performance Appraisal

major question **How can I assess employees' performance more accurately and give more effective feedback?**

The Big Picture

Performance appraisal, assessing employee performance and providing them feedback, may be objective or subjective. Appraisals may be by peers, subordinates, customers, oneself. Feedback may be formal or informal.

"Ask most managers the most difficult part of their job, and they'll likely answer having to fire someone," writes Carol Hymowitz in *The Wall Street Journal*. "Ask what they endlessly put off doing, and they'll say advising weak employees that they must improve or risk losing their jobs."[50]

Clearly, it's unfair to underperforming employees to assume that time alone will enable them to shape up. And it's unfair to the organization to allow those employees to continue to stumble along without direction. It's part of your job as a manager to give the people who work for you honest appraisals.

Defining Performance Appraisal

Performance appraisal **consists of (1) assessing an employee's performance and (2) providing him or her with feedback.** Thus, this management task has two purposes: First, performance appraisal helps employees understand how they are doing in relation to objectives and standards; here you must *judge* the employee. Second, it helps in their training and personal development; here you must *counsel* the employee.[51]

Appraisals are of two general types—objective and subjective:

1 Objective Appraisals

Objective appraisals, **also called *results appraisals,* are based on facts and are often numerical.** In these kinds of appraisals, you would keep track of such matters as the numbers of products the employee sold in a month, customer complaints filed against an employee, miles of freight hauled, and the like. The good thing about objective appraisals is that they measure results. It doesn't matter if two appliance salespeople have completely different personal traits (one is formal, reserved, and patient, the other informal, gregarious, and impatient) if each sells the same number of washers and dryers. Human resource professionals point out that, just as in business we measure sales, profits, shareholder value, and other so-called "metrics," so it's important to measure employee performance, benefit costs, and the like as an aid to strategy.[52]

How'm I doing? One of the most important tasks of being a manager is giving employees accurate information about their work performance. Which would you be more comfortable giving—objective appraisals or subjective appraisals?

We discussed an objective approach in Chapter 5 under *management by objectives,* which can encourage employees to feel empowered to adopt behavior that will produce specific results. MBO, you'll recall, is a four-step process in which (1) managers and employees jointly set objectives for the employee, (2) managers develop action plans, (3) managers and employees periodically review the employee's performance, and (4) the manager makes a performance appraisal and rewards the employee according to results. For example, an objective for a copier service technician might be to increase the number of service calls 15% during the next three months.

2 Subjective Appraisals

Few employees can be adequately measured just by objective appraisals—hence the need for ***subjective appraisals,* which are based on a manager's perceptions of an employee's (1) traits or (2) behaviors.**

- **Trait appraisals:** *Trait appraisals* are ratings of such subjective attributes as "attitude," "initiative," and "leadership." Trait evaluations may be easy to create and use, but their validity is questionable because the evaluator's personal bias can affect the ratings.
- **Behavioral appraisals:** Behavioral appraisals measure specific, observable aspects of performance—being on time for work, for instance—although making the evaluation is still somewhat subjective. An example is the ***behaviorally anchored rating scale (BARS),* which rates employee gradations in performance according to scales of specific behaviors.** For example, a five-point BARS rating scale about attendance might go from "Always early for work and has equipment ready to fully assume duties" to "Frequently late and often does not have equipment ready for going to work," with gradations in between.

Who Should Make Performance Appraisals?

As you might expect, most performance appraisals are done by managers. However, to add different perspectives, sometimes appraisal information is provided by other people knowledgeable about particular employees.

Peers, Subordinates, Customers, & Self

Among additional sources of information are coworkers and subordinates, customers and clients, and the employees themselves.

- **Peers and subordinates:** Coworkers, colleagues, and subordinates may well see different aspects of your performance. Such information can be useful for development, although it probably shouldn't be used for evaluation. (Many managers will resist soliciting such information about themselves, of course, fearing negative appraisals.)
- **Customers and clients:** Some organizations, such as restaurants and hotels, ask customers and clients for their appraisals of employees. Publishers ask authors to judge how well they are doing in handling the editing, production, and marketing of their books. Automobile dealerships may send follow-up questionnaires to car buyers.
- **Self-appraisals:** How would you rate your own performance in a job, knowing that it would go into your personnel file? Probably the bias would be toward the favorable. Nevertheless, *self-appraisals* help employees become involved in the whole evaluation process and may make them more receptive to feedback about areas needing improvement.

Example

Self-Appraisal: Workers Review Themselves at International Paper Co.

Passing judgment on everything done by every subordinate is an impossible task, contended P. J. Smoot, former learning and development leader in International Paper Co.'s Memphis, Tennessee, office. The real job of a manager, she suggested, is to listen and learn from employees and then, by asking questions, guide them to a mutually agreed-on performance plan for the coming year.

"Listen for understanding," Smoot advised managers. "And then react honestly and constructively. Focus on the business goals, not on the personality." A manager should then use questions—"What about this?" "Would this be more effective?"—to guide the employee to mutual understanding.

Employees should be asked to describe not what they did during the past review period but what they did that made a difference. In addition, they should be guided to describe something that didn't go right and what they learned from it. This, Smoot suggested, gets across the idea to employees that it's okay not to be perfect.

In addition, Smoot recommended that employees identify other people they work with. Then at review time, the manager can solicit their evaluation of the employee as well.[53]

360-Degree Assessment

We said that performance appraisals may be done by peers, subordinates, customers, and oneself. Sometimes all these may be used, in a technique called 360-degree assessment.

In a "theater in the round," the actors in a dramatic play are watched by an audience on all sides of them—360 degrees. Similarly, as a worker, you have many people watching you from all sides. Thus has arisen the idea of the ***360-degree assessment,*** **or *360-degree feedback appraisal,* in which employees are appraised not only by their managerial superiors but also by peers, subordinates, and sometimes clients,** thus providing several perspectives.

Typically, an employee chooses between six and 12 other people to make evaluations, who then fill out anonymous forms, the results of which are tabulated by computer. The employee then goes over the results with his or her manager and together they put into place a long-term plan for performance goals.

There are advantages and disadvantages to incorporating 360-degree feedback into the performance appraisal process. Most important, managers should not use 360-degree feedback for appraisal decisions unless they can demonstrate the instrument's validity.[54]

Forced Ranking: Grading on a Curve

To increase performance, as many as a quarter of Fortune 500 companies (such as General Electric, Ford, Cisco, and Intel) have instituted performance review systems known as forced ranking (or "rank and yank") systems.[55] **In *forced ranking performance review systems,* all employees within a business unit are ranked against one another and grades are distributed along some sort of bell curve**—just like students being graded in a college course. Top performers (such as the top 20%) are rewarded with bonuses and promotions, the worst performers (such as the bottom 20%) are rehabilitated or dismissed. For instance, every year 10% of GE's managers are assigned the bottom grade, and if they don't improve, they are asked to leave the company.

Proponents of forced ranking say it encourages managers to identify and remove poor performers and also structures a predetermined compensation curve, which enables them to reward top performers. If, however, the system is imposed on an organization overnight without preparation, by pitting employees against one another it can produce shocks to morale, productivity, and loyalty. There may also be legal ramifications, as when employees filed class-action lawsuits alleging that the forced-ranking methods had a disparate effect on particular groups of employees.

Effective Performance Feedback

The whole point of performance appraisal, of course, is to stimulate better job performance. To gather information to feed back to the employee, a manager can use two kinds of appraisals—formal and informal.

1 Formal Appraisals

Formal appraisals **are conducted at specific times throughout the year and are based on performance measures that have been established in advance.** An emergency medical technician might be evaluated twice a year by his or her manager, using objective performance measures such as work attendance time sheets and more subjective measures such as a BARS to indicate the employee's willingness to follow emergency procedures and doctors' and nurses' orders.

As part of the appraisal, the manager should give the employee feedback, describing how he or she is performing well and not so well and giving examples. Managers are sometimes advised to keep diaries about specific incidents so they won't have to rely on their memories (and so that their evaluations will be more lawsuit-resistant). Facts should always be used rather than impressions.

2 Informal Appraisals

Formal appraisals are the equivalent of a student receiving a grade on a midterm test and a grade on a final test—weeks may go by in which you are unaware of how well you're doing in the course. Informal appraisals are the equivalent of occasional unscheduled pop quizzes and short papers or drop-in visits to the professor's office to talk about your work—you have more frequent feedback about your performance. ***Informal appraisals*** **are conducted on an unscheduled basis and consist of less rigorous indications of employee performance.**

You may not feel comfortable about critiquing your employees' performance, especially when you have to convey criticism rather than praise. Nevertheless, giving performance feedback is one of the most important parts of the manager's job. Some suggestions for improvement appear below. *(See Table 9.5.)* ◆

TABLE 9.5

How to give performance feedback to employees. Think of yourself as a coach, as though you were managing a team of athletes.

- *Take a problem-solving approach, avoid criticism, and treat employees with respect:* Recall the worst boss you ever worked for. How did you react to his or her method of giving feedback? Avoid criticism that might be taken personally.

  Example: Don't say "You're picking up that bag of cement wrong" (which criticizes by using the word "wrong"). Say "Instead of bending at the waist, a good way to pick up something heavy is to bend your knees. That'll help save your back."

- *Be specific in describing the employee's present performance and in the improvement you desire:* Describe your subordinate's current performance in specific terms and concentrate on outcomes that are within his or her ability to improve.

  Example: Don't say "You're always late turning in your sales reports." Say "Instead of making calls on Thursday afternoon, why don't you take some of the time to do your sales reports so they'll be ready on Friday along with those of the other sales reps."

- *Get the employee's input:* In determining causes for a problem, listen to the employee and get his or her help in crafting a solution.

  Example: Don't say "You've got to learn to get here at 9:00 every day." Say "What changes do you think could be made so that your station is covered when people start calling at 9:00?"

major question

What are the various forms of compensation?

The Big Picture

Managers must manage for compensation—which includes wages or salaries, incentives, and benefits.

Do we work only for a paycheck? Many people do, of course. But money is only one form of compensation.

Compensation **has three parts: (1) wages or salaries, (2) incentives, and (3) benefits.** In different organizations one part may take on more importance than another. For instance, in some nonprofit organizations (education, government), salaries may not be large, but health and retirement benefits may outweigh that fact. In a high-technology startup, the salary and benefits may actually be somewhat humble, but the promise of a large payoff in incentives, such as stock options or bonuses, may be quite attractive. Let's consider these three parts briefly. (We expand on them in Chapter 12 when we discuss ways to motivate employees.)

Wages or Salaries

Base pay **consists of the basic wage or salary paid employees in exchange for doing their jobs.** The basic compensation is determined by all kinds of economic factors: the prevailing pay levels in a particular industry and location, what competitors are paying, whether the jobs are unionized, if the jobs are hazardous, what the individual's level is in the organization, and how much experience he or she has.

Stock options. Companies like to offer favored employees stock options rather than higher salaries as benefits. Not only do employees place a high value on options, but companies can issue as many as they want without hurting corporate profits because, under present accounting rules, they don't have to count the options' value as an expense.

Incentives

To induce employees to be more productive or to attract and retain top performers, many organizations offer incentives, such as commissions, bonuses, profit-sharing plans, and stock options. We discuss these in detail in Chapter 12.

Benefits

Benefits, **or** ***fringe benefits,*** **are additional nonmonetary forms of compensation** designed to enrich the lives of all employees in the organization, which are paid all or in part by the organization. Examples are many: health insurance, dental insurance, life insurance, disability protection, retirement plans, holidays off, accumulated sick days and vacation days, recreation options, country club or health club memberships, family leave, discounts on company merchandise, counseling, credit unions, legal advice, and education reimbursement. For top executives, there may be "golden parachutes," generous severance pay for those who might be let go in the event the company is taken over by another company.

Benefits are no small part of an organization's costs. According to the U.S. Chamber of Commerce, employee benefit costs were 42.3% of payroll costs in 2002, with medical benefit costs constituting the largest part.[56] ◆

practical action

How to Make Incentive Pay Plans Meet Company Goals: Communicate Them to Employees[57]

There are many incentive compensation plans, ranging from cash awards and gifts to profit sharing and stock ownership, as we discuss in detail in Chapter 12.

Here let's ask the question: Do they work?

A 1998 survey of 139 companies, more than a third of them in the Fortune 500, found that 72% had variable pay plans. But only 22% said their plans had helped them achieve all their business objectives, and 28% said their plans had achieved none of them.

What explains the difference? Good plan design is important but so is good communication and oversight.

According to Ken Abosch, a consultant at Chicago-based Hewett Associates, which conducted the survey, often plans fail to deliver on their intended goals because employees aren't told enough about them and aren't kept up to date on the progress of the plans. Eighty-nine percent of companies that regularly communicated with their employees said their incentive plans met their goals, compared with only 57% of companies that did not discuss them with their employees.

Five keys to a successful incentive-pay plan are the following, according to Abosch:

- **Simplicity:** Does the plan pass the simplicity test? As Abosch puts it, "Can you explain it on an elevator ride?"
- **Clear goals:** Are the goals clear? Are the goals fully supported by management?
- **Realistic goals:** Are the goals realistic—that is, neither too difficult nor too easy to achieve?
- **Consistency with present goals:** Is the plan in line with the organization's present goals? Company goals change. "There are very few organizations that have the same business objective for five to seven years," points out Abosch.
- **Regular communication:** Do managers regularly communicate with employees about the plan? "People want a scorecard," Abosch says.

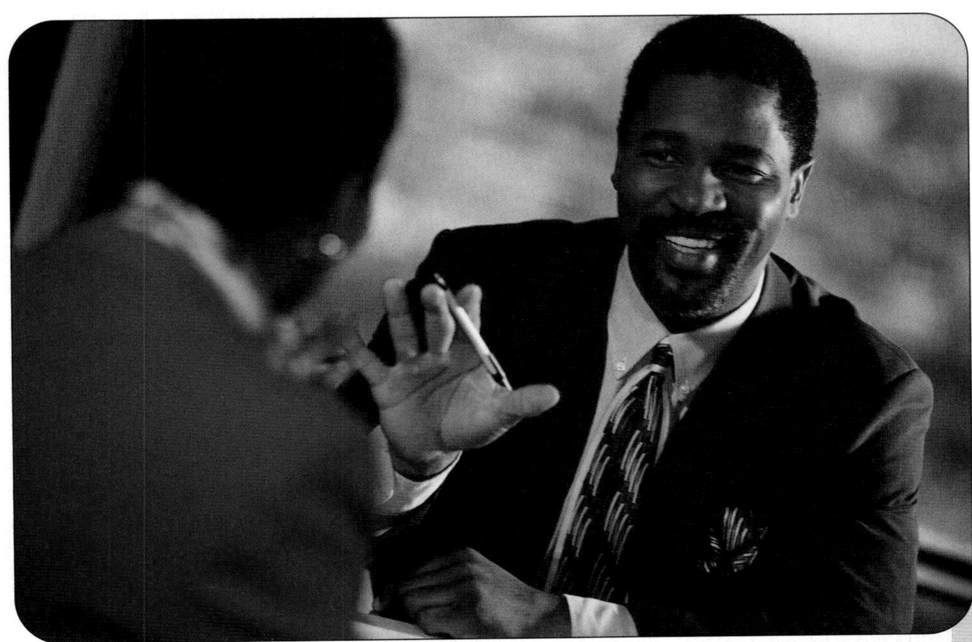

Communication is everything. The questions human resource managers need to keep in mind are: What good does it do a company to have attractive incentive plans if employees don't understand them? Will an employee exert the extra effort in pursuit of rewards if he or she doesn't know what the rewards are?

major question

How do I manage contemporary workplace problems such as drug abuse and sexual harassment?

The Big Picture

Managers must also manage for promotions, transfers, discipline problems, and dismissals, as well as for workplace problems such as drug abuse and sexual harassment.

American society, points out George Washington University sociologist Amitai Etzioni, can be depicted by the term "pluralism within unity." Unlike Europeans, who have great difficulty accepting the idea of diversity—of Turkish-Germans, Algerian-Frenchmen, or Romanian-Austrians, for example—in the United States we pretty much take it for granted that hyphenated Americans can be good workers and citizens.[58]

Indeed, our sense of inclusiveness seems to be gradually growing to embrace not only ethnic and racial diversity but also both genders and different ages, religions, sexual orientation, and physical and mental abilities. And there's more, as roles continue to change. Now more men seek paternity leaves, working parents want flexible hours, employees want to telecommute from home, and questions of "work-life balance" are receiving greater priority.

What this shows is that as a manager you may have quite a complex workforce. Let us see what matters you'll have to deal with.

Managing Promotions, Transfers, Disciplining, & Dismissals

Among the major—and most difficult—decisions you will make as a manager are those about employee movement within an organization: whom should you promote? transfer? discipline? fire? All these matters go under the heading of *employee replacement*. And, incidentally, any time you need to deal with replacing an employee in a job, that's a time to reconsider the job description to see how it might be made more effective for the next person to occupy it.

You'll have to deal with replacement whenever an employee quits, retires, becomes seriously ill, or dies. Or you may initiate the replacement action by promoting, transferring, demoting, laying off, or firing.

1 Promotion

Promotion—moving an employee to a higher-level position—is the most obvious way to recognize that person's superior performance (apart from giving raises and bonuses). Three concerns are these:

- **Fairness:** It's important that promotion be *fair*. The step upward must be deserved. It shouldn't be for reasons of nepotism, cronyism, or other kind of favoritism.
- **Nondiscrimination:** The promotion cannot discriminate on the basis of race, ethnicity, gender, age, or physical ability.
- **Others' resentments:** If someone is promoted, someone else may be resentful about being passed over. As a manager, you may need to counsel the people left behind about their performance and their opportunities in the future.

2 Transfer

Transfer is movement of an employee to a different job with *similar responsibility*. It may or may not mean a change in geographical location (which might be part of a promotion as well).

There are four principal reasons why employees might be transferred. *(See Table 9.6.)*

TABLE 9.6
Reasons why employees are transferred

- **Solve organizational problems:** An organization may order an employee to transfer because it needs his or her skills in solving a particular problem. Example: A manager in a hotel chain who has built a reputation as a good problem solver may be relocated to take over management of a hotel that's having trouble.
- **Broaden managers' experience:** A manager may be transferred to a position with an equal level of responsibility to broaden his or her experience. Example: A manager in the hotel industry may be rotated among different positions in charge of reservations, the front desk, catering, convention sales, and so on.
- **Retain managers' interest and motivation:** Talented managers may feel stultified and bored if they are stuck in one job. Example: A hotel and resort company might move a manager from managing a hotel in Fresno, California, to one in St. Louis, Missouri, then to one in the American Virgin Islands.
- **Solve some employee problems:** Sometimes employees who are unhappy with their current jobs or have personal differences with their bosses will request a job transfer. Or managers may shift poorly performing employees when they can't demote or fire them or are reluctant to do so.

3 Disciplining & Demotion

Poorly performing employees may be given a warning or a reprimand and then disciplined. That is, they may be temporarily removed from their jobs, as when a police officer is placed on suspension or administrative leave—removed from his or her regular job in the field and perhaps given a paperwork job or told to stay away from work.

Alternatively, an employee may be demoted—that is, have his or her current responsibilities, pay, and perquisites taken away, as when a middle manager is demoted to a first-line manager. (Sometimes this may occur when a company is downsized, resulting in fewer higher-level management positions.)

4 Dismissal

Dismissals are of three sorts:

- **Layoffs:** The phrase being *laid off* tends to suggest that a person has been dismissed *temporarily*—as when a car maker doesn't have enough orders to justify keeping its production employees—and may be recalled later when economic conditions improve.
- **Downsizings:** A *downsizing* is a *permanent* dismissal; there is no rehiring later. An auto maker discontinuing a line of cars or on the path to bankruptcy might permanently let go of its production employees.
- **Firings:** The phrase being *fired,* with all its euphemisms and synonyms—being "terminated," "separated," "let go," "canned"—tends to mean that a person was dismissed *permanently "for cause"*: absenteeism, sloppy work habits, failure to perform satisfactorily, breaking the law, and the like.

It used to be that managers could use their discretion about dismissals. Today, however, because of the changing legal climate, steps must be taken to avoid employees suing for "wrongful termination." That is, an employer has to carefully *document* the reasons for dismissals.

The Practical Action box offers some suggestions for handling dismissals.

practical action

The Right Way to Handle a Dismissal

"Employment at will" is the governing principle of employment in the great majority of states, which means that anyone can be dismissed at any time for any reason at all—or for no reason. Exceptions are whistleblowers and people with employment contracts. Civil-rights laws also prohibit organizations' dismissing people for their gender, skin color, or physical or mental disability.[59]

Four suggestions for handling a dismissal follow.

Give the Employee a Chance First If you're dealing with someone who has a problem with absenteeism, alcohol/drug dependency, or the like, articulate to that employee what's wrong with his or her performance, then set up a plan for improvement (which might include counseling). Or if you're dealing with an employee who has a bad cultural or personality fit with the company—a buttoned-down, by-the-book style, say, that's at odds with your flexible, fast-moving organization—have a conversation and give the employee time to find a job elsewhere.[60]

Don't Delay the Dismissal, & Make Sure It's Completely Defensible If improvements aren't forthcoming, don't carry the employee along because you feel sorry for him or her. Your first duty is to the performance of the organization. Make sure, however, that you've *documented* all the steps taken in advance of the dismissal. Also be sure that they follow the law and all important organizational policies.

Be Aware How Devastating a Dismissal Can Be—Both to the Individual & to Those Remaining To the person being let go, the event can be as much of a blow as a divorce or a death in the family. Dismissals can also adversely affect those remaining with the company. This is what psychiatrist Manfred Kets de Vries calls *layoff survivor sickness,* which is characterized by anger, depression, fear, guilt, risk aversion, distrust, vulnerability, powerlessness, and loss of motivation. Indeed, a five-year study by Cigna and the American Management Association found an enormous increase in medical claims, particularly for stress-related illnesses, not only among those dismissed but among continuing employees as well.[61]

Offer Assistance in Finding Another Job Dismissing a long-standing employee with only a few weeks of severance pay not only hurts the person let go but will also hurt the organization itself, as word gets back to the employees who remain. Knowledgeable employers offer assistance in finding another job.

"The best demonstration that a company's values are real," says management scholar Rosabeth Moss Kanter, "is to act on them today even for people who will not be around tomorrow. A company, like a society, can be judged by how it treats its most vulnerable. . . . Bad treatment of departing employees can destroy the commitment of those who stay."[62]

Maintaining Effective Relationships with Employees

Dealing with compensation, promotion, and similar matters would seem to be straightforward if sometimes difficult requirements of the manager's job. But there are other, less straightforward matters as well. We discussed the need to deal with a diversified workforce in Chapter 2 and an international workforce in Chapter 3. There are many, many other sensitive topics that we could discuss (and do so later), but here let us consider just two: (1) alcohol and other drug abuse and (2) sexual harassment.

Alcohol & Other Drug Abuse

Have an employee who's often late? Who frequently calls in sick on Mondays? Whose work is somewhat sloppy? Maybe he or she is afflicted with *alcoholism,* a chronic, progressive, and potentially fatal disease characterized by a growing compulsion to drink. Alcoholics come from every social class, from students to college

to escape religious persecution at home. Most of them settled in Omaha because of its established Sudanese community, affordable housing, plentiful jobs and good schools. "Many employers did not consider other cultures as a viable workforce, but I recognized them as an underutilized market," says Franklin, who also began outreach efforts to the growing Hispanic population. She offered ESL classes, adjusted new-hire training to better reflect the way other cultures learn, and developed presentations for the current workforce and supervisors to promote understanding and empathy among the staff. Today, Sudanese and Hispanic employees make up approximately 25 percent of the workforce at Designer Blinds. Even better, the new diverse workforce results in more employee referrals. "They recruit for us," Franklin says.

The next step was boosting retention. Designer Blinds had developed an unfortunate but well-deserved reputation as a place where "people came in, did a little bit of time and went on their way," Franklin says. To encourage employees to stay put, she implemented a new-hire training program, including classroom and on-the-job learning. She also appointed a "buddy" for new employees—not only to teach things like where the time clock is located, but also to help them socialize, join them for lunch and introduce them around. "No new hire should ever sit in the break room alone," Franklin says.

A new "rolls and roundtable" program was instituted, during which eight employees at a time mix and mingle with senior leadership in an unstructured, casual setting. Those sessions, perhaps more than any other single activity, help employees feel valued and involved in the company, says CEO Lloyd "Woody" Woodworth. "Too often, folks don't feel safe saying what's on their minds," he says. "But in this environment, they say things they wouldn't anywhere else. Whether it's a little thing like needing better lighting or filing cabinets, or something significant, such as a complaint about a manager, they are not afraid to speak up because they've learned it's OK."

Better supervisory training was also key to retention. Before 1998, the company had simply promoted the best technicians to managerial positions—whether or not they were management material. "Our leadership crew was running on autopilot—with no pilot," Woodworth concedes. Realizing that better-trained supervisors were integral to making Designer Blinds a better place to work, the company began a formal management-development program, including both leadership and technical skills. During weekly meetings, supervisors learn about management issues ranging from attitude adjustment to sexual harassment.

"The word is out that Designer Blinds is a good place to work," Franklin says. Thanks to the more stable and experienced workforce, productivity has soared.

For Discussion

1. Using Figure 9.1, how would you evaluate Designer Blinds's strategic human resource management process after Deb Franklin began making changes?
2. What are the advantages and disadvantages of Designer Blinds's current approach toward recruiting? Discuss.
3. What did the company do to improve employee retention?
4. Based on the material covered in this chapter, what advice would you give to Deb Franklin about further improving the human resource function within Designer Blinds? Explain your rationale.

Self-Assessment

HR 101: An Overview*

Objectives

1. To learn that there is more to HR than recruitment and hiring.
2. To assess your skills and determine if a career in HR is right for you.

Introduction

Your chosen career should optimally be based on your interests. The HR field, for example, offers many different career paths that require many different skills. The purpose of this exercise is to help you become familiar with the different career paths available to an HR professional and to see which path best fits your interests. This experience may help you decide if an HR career is right for you.

Among the professionals in the HR field are the following:

The HR generalist: HR generalists take on many different roles, whether negotiating a company's employee benefits package or interviewing a candidate for a director-level position. An HR generalist is supposed to be flexible and able to change gears at a moment's notice.

Compensation professional: Compensation professionals, who are very much in demand, design reward systems that attract, retain, and motivate employees. The job requires not only good technical skills but good people skills as well, a rare combination. It also requires a great deal of number crunching, creativity, and ingenuity, because a compensation package that might work for one employee might not work for another.

HRIS professional: HRIS stands for Human Resource Information Systems. With technology now such a key part of human resources, HRIS products help companies manage their personnel. Because the information systems are now so sophisticated, there is now great demand for experienced HRIS professionals, who must be very detail oriented and, of course, enjoy working with computers. Such professionals are involved in product selection, systems customization, implementation, and ongoing administration.

Benefits professional: This individual is responsible for designing and implementing benefits plans. The job requires strong technical and communication skills.

Training and development professional: This individual is responsible for building environments that foster learning and management and leadership development. People in this field may be involved in distance learning programs as well as on-site, computer-based training programs.

Organizational development professional: Organizational development professionals work with top management to make sure that the organizational design sticks to the company's mission, vision, and goals. Besides doing some training and development, an OD professional must be able to embrace change and work long hours.

Instructions

Ask yourself the following questions and circle whether or not the statement applies to you. Once you have answered all of the questions, use the interpretation guidelines to analyze your responses and determine if a career in HR is right for you.

1.	Do I enjoy changing gears on a moment's notice?	**Yes**	**No**
2.	Am I open to learning about areas in which I currently have no expertise?	**Yes**	**No**
3.	Am I comfortable leaving a project unfinished to handle emergency situations?	**Yes**	**No**
4.	Do I consider myself fairly flexible?	**Yes**	**No**
5.	Am I good at creatively solving problems when resources and instructions are scarce?	**Yes**	**No**
6.	Do I have an aptitude for numbers?	**Yes**	**No**
7.	Am I comfortable seeing other people's salaries?	**Yes**	**No**
8.	Do I have strong communication skills?	**Yes**	**No**
9.	Do I have strong computer skills?	**Yes**	**No**
10.	Am I comfortable working at a computer all day?	**Yes**	**No**
11.	Am I well organized?	**Yes**	**No**
12.	Am I detail oriented?	**Yes**	**No**
13.	Am I comfortable constantly reworking projects I thought were already done?	**Yes**	**No**

14. Am I willing to pay for and donate my free time to professional certifications? **Yes** **No**
15. Am I good at taking complex ideas and making them understandable to the average person? **Yes** **No**
16. Am I good at expressing my ideas and getting people to go along with them? **Yes** **No**
17. Am I a creative person with strong computer skills? **Yes** **No**
18. Am I comfortable in front of an audience? **Yes** **No**
19. Am I comfortable working one very long project instead of lots of small projects? **Yes** **No**
20. Am I passionate about learning and about teaching others? **Yes** **No**
21. Can I handle change? Can I handle it well? **Yes** **No**
22. Do I enjoy pulling together pieces of a puzzle? **Yes** **No**
23. Do I perform well in times of stress? **Yes** **No**
24. Am I a big-picture person? **Yes** **No**

Interpretation

If you answered "yes" to three or more of questions 1–4 (which apply to the HR generalist), three or more of questions 5–8 (compensation professional), three or more of questions 9–12 (HRIS professional), three or more of questions 13–16 (benefits professional), three or more of questions 17–20 (training and development professional), and three or more of questions 21–24 (organizational development professional), then you are well suited for the field of HR.

If you answered "no" to most of the previous 24 questions, the field of HR may not be right for you. (However, since this is only a small sampling of the many aspects of this field, there may still be a place for you in HR.)

Questions for Discussion

1. To what extent did the results fit your interests? Explain.
2. Look at the top two areas of HR for which you tested as being best suited. Look over the descriptions of these fields. What skills do you need to have to be successful? Describe.
3. Even if you do not pursue a career in HR, which skills do you feel you should continue to develop? Explain.

*Adapted from R.C. Matuson, "HR 101: An Overview, Parts I and II," *Monster HR: www.monster.com,* June 2002.

Group Exercise

Choosing the Best Person for the Job*

Objectives

To gain further knowledge of the selection process.

To practice looking for the skills that help HR professionals find the best person for a job.

Introduction

As you learned from this chapter, the recruitment process may turn up a handful of applicants or it may turn up thousands. During the selection process, how do hiring managers make their decisions? What can an applicant do to stand out in the crowd? It is important for applicants to be able to highlight the skills that make them unique. Skills can be looked at in three ways: (1) those gained from past experience, (2) those that can carry through to any job (portable skills), and (3) personal skills. The purpose of this exercise is to enable you to practice looking for skills that help HR professionals find the best person for the job.

Instructions

Break into groups of five to six people. Read the following case about Gina, who has applied for a job at a high-technology company. The company has its own ideas about the ideal applicant, but it hasn't given out much information about them. You are going to try to help Gina get the job. (Remember, she's not the only applicant, so she needs to stand out.) After reading the case:

1. Take a piece of paper and divide it into three columns—the first headed "Past experience," the second "Portable skills" (skills that will carry to any job), and the third "Personality skills." Your group is to identify what skills you think Gina should have based on "Past experience," "Portable skills," and "Personality skills."
2. Using these skills as a guide, brainstorm which of these skills you think Gina has. Make sure you put them in the correct column.
3. Then examine Gina's case again and come up with as many different skills as you can that go *beyond* what the company is looking for. Think about what past skills Gina has besides marketing experience that would make her the perfect candidate.

The Case

After five years, Gina was laid off as a marketing manager for a high-tech company. "Gina hates not having a job," her roommate says. "She always has to have something to do. If not, she'll jump up and start cleaning just to be productive. She's also very organized. For instance, she files all her CDs in alphabetical order."

At her old job, Gina was in charge of marketing the company over the World Wide Web and so she spent a lot of time at the computer. Since being laid off, she has been using the computer to look for another job, as well as searching the Web for art projects to do in her spare time. Her friends describe her as being not only fiercely independent but also very creative. In college, they say, she was always writing. "She used to write short stories," her roommate recalls, "and also worked part time on the college newspaper."

Her friends also say Gina's sense of humor keeps her from feeling unbearably depressed about the layoff, and they believe she will find a new job quickly. Her mother agrees. "Gina is the oldest child," she says, "and she has always been a very good team leader. She's very organized and ever since she was a little girl she's been good at coordinating things." Her father says his daughter has a great head for numbers, and he hoped she would follow in his tracks and become an accountant.

Gina's supervisor at her old job says they hated to see her go. "She was so good at dealing with our customers," he says. "She was also one of the few marketing managers who had a close business relationship with our vendors. In addition, she was very goal oriented: We would tell her what we wanted to achieve and she would dive in head first." Her direct reports state that Gina had a good attitude, a great sense of humor, excellent follow-through, and a superior ability to solve problems. Her colleagues and supervisor all comment on Gina's creativity and her ability to learn things quickly. One coworker noted that Gina was "very flexible" and "always showed good judgment."

Questions for Discussion

1. If you were the HR professional at this high-tech company, would you hire Gina? Do you feel she has the appropriate skills? Why or why not?
2. Are there any skills Gina does not exhibit that you feel she should develop in order to be a more appealing candidate? Discuss.
3. What are some things Gina can do to improve her skills for her future job in marketing? Explain.

*Adapted from "Assessing Your Skills: What Makes You Different from All the Others?" *http://interview.monster.com/rehearsal/assessing,* June 2002.

Ethical Dilemma

More Companies Want the FBI to Screen Employees for Terrorist Connections

Excerpted from Ana Davis, "Companies Want the FBI to Screen Employees for Suspected Terrorists," The Wall Street Journal, *February 6, 2002, pp. B1, B4.*

A wide range of industry groups, from trucking associations to sporting-event organizers, are trying to gain access to the FBI's closely guarded data on suspected terrorists and criminals in an effort to screen their own employees.

The American Trucking Association, for one, is lobbying Congress to give it authority to go directly to the Federal Bureau of Investigation with names and fingerprints of drivers, loading-dock workers, and job applicants of its member companies. . . .

Fueling this push is the supposition that, next time around, terrorists may attack something besides an airplane. But allowing companies to tap into FBI intelligence banks opens a can of worms both for the government and civil liberties advocates. Unions protest that employers could use the system to find old skeletons in people's closets and use them as a pretext for dismissal. . . .

Giving an industry access to the FBI lists typically requires an act of Congress or a new federal regulation. Some industries, such as banking, airlines, and nuclear power plants, already have such access. . . .

Of particular interest to this latest round of companies are the FBI's watch lists of suspected terrorists, including people who may have infiltrated the American workplace years ago as "sleeper" agents. One of these lists, from the State Department, contains 64,000 names from around the world. The FBI keeps its own list and won't say how many people are on it. . . .

Although terrorists typically are trained to avoid detection, at least a few of the Sept. 11 hijackers were on watchlists because their names had popped up in connection with prior attacks: Mohamed Atta had been flagged by the Customs Service, and Khalid al-Midhar was on a CIA list.

FBI background checks should turn up anybody with, among other things, an arrest record, criminal conviction, or protective order filed against them. Not all this information is readily accessible to those outside the agency, and companies are concerned about missing such information in a check on their own. . . .

But truckers and others who want FBI background checks say the pros outweigh the cons. Tony Chrestman, president of the trucking unit of Ruan Transportation Management Systems, says: "Previously, I would never have thought about anyone taking one of our loads of propane and running it into a building. There's got to be improvements to background checks."

Solving the Dilemma

What would you do if you were evaluating the trucking industry's desire for FBI background checks?

1. Allow the trucking industry to obtain FBI background checks.
2. Not allow the trucking industry access to FBI records because such information might adversely affect employment conditions for potential and existing employees.
3. Allow the trucking industry to obtain limited information (that is, only information pertaining to terrorism) about people.
4. Invent other options. Explain.

Video Case

SAS

Jeff Chambers is vice president of human resources at SAS, the world's largest privately owned software company. At SAS, people are truly viewed as key assets. According to Chambers, "we can't produce software, we can't sell software, we can't provide service without good, quality people." Part of Jeff's job is to find and retain such employees. Finding people who want to work at SAS isn't difficult—recently there were about 93,000 applicants for 500 job openings. The challenge is to screen those applications to find the individuals who best fit the SAS model.

As part of this process, the company assesses future labor requirements, prepares job analyses to see what various jobs entail, and first tries to find people within the firm who meet those needs. The organization searches outside the firm to find the necessary skills only if suitable applicants aren't found within the company. At SAS, the strategic plan calls for interviewing, testing, and evaluating prospects. Spending more time in the hiring process means spending less time later trying to replace workers who were not a good fit in the firm. Employee retention is a critical component of SAS's success. At SAS the annual turnover is about 3%, compared to about 25% for the industry average. This differential saves the company 80 to 100 million dollars. These savings fund training and benefits programs that, in turn, keep employees satisfied and loyal.

For example, training programs include inhouse classes for everything from technical skills to "soft" skills, online training, work-life programs, internships, and apprenticeships. Training programs also mean a steady supply of qualified applicants for the company's recruit-from-within policy. Fringe benefits available to SAS workers include free health care, onsite day care and recreation center, and medical insurance benefits to retired workers. SAS tries to accommodate the needs of individual workers as much as possible. Workers can take advantage of telecommuting, flextime, or job-sharing programs. At a company such as SAS, performance evaluations are key. Managers work closely with each employee to make sure he or she understands the company's goals and where he or she fits into those goals. Performance is measured relative to the stated goals.

SAS has a great relationship with its customers. The company spends about 25% of its bottom line on research and development (R&D). Its quality products result in a customer retention rate of about 98%. The company treats its employees with the same care that it treats its customers. With satisfied employees and low turnover rates, the company has more funds to invest in R&D (keeping customers happy) and a generous benefits program for employees (keeping workers happy).

Discussion Questions

1. Describe the recruiting process at SAS. Does the company recruit primarily from internal or external sources? What are the advantages and disadvantages of each?
2. Describe the selection process that applicants face at SAS. Who is responsible for making the final hiring decision? Does the company primarily emphasize the need for technical skills or for people skills?
3. Is it cost effective for SAS to offer such a wide array of perks and benefits for its employees?

chapter 10

Organizational Change & Innovation

Life-Long Challenges for the Exceptional Manager

MAJOR QUESTIONS YOU SHOULD BE ABLE TO ANSWER

10.1 The Nature of Change in Organizations

Major Question: Since change is always with us, what should I understand about it?

10.2 The Threat of Change: Managing Employee Fear & Resistance

Major Question: How are employees threatened by change, and how can I help them adjust?

10.3 Organization Development: What It Is, What It Can Do

Major Question: What are the uses of OD, and how effective is it?

10.4 Promoting Innovation within the Organization

Major Question: What do I need to know to encourage innovation?

the manager's toolbox

Managing for Innovation & Change Takes a Careful Hand

"What I try to do is go out and grab lightning every day."

That's the way Terry Fadem, head of business development at DuPont Co., describes the company's never-ending search for tomorrow's breakthroughs.[1]

Managing for innovation and change takes a careful hand. "Even when their jobs depend on adopting and inventing new maneuvers," says columnist Carol Hymowitz, "most workers hold fast to old ones. The majority either are overwhelmed when asked to do things differently or become entrenched, clinging harder to the past. . . ."[2]

Because the revolution in technology is inflicting what Tom Peters calls Discontinuous Times, or "a brawl with no rules," dealing with change is an ongoing challenge for every manager.[3] "The one constant factor in business today is we live in a perpetual hurricane season," says Mellon Bank Corp. vice chairman Martin McGuinn. "A leader's job is less about getting through the current storm and more about enabling people to navigate the ongoing series of storms."[4]

Some ways to deal with change and innovation:[5]

- **Allow room for failure:** McGuinn won over many Mellon employees when he told them "If everything we try works, we aren't trying enough. And if something isn't working, it is okay to say so."
- **Give one consistent explanation for the change:** When a company is undergoing change, myriad rumors will fly and employees will be uneasy; you and the managers who report to you need to give one consistent explanation. In McGuinn's case, the explanation for overhauling Mellon Bank's retail division was "We want to be the best retailer in financial services."
- **Look for opportunities in unconventional ways:** Most "new" products and services are really knockoffs or marginal variations of the things already on the market and hence are doomed to failure, says Robert Cooper, professor of marketing at Ontario's McMaster University. This doesn't mean, of course, that there isn't room for leveraging existing products with utterly unoriginal ideas. But most people are blinded by the limits of conventional wisdom and their own experience and fail to see huge potential markets in unconventional concepts.
- **Have the courage to follow your ideas:** This may be the hardest job of all—trying to convince others that your ideas for change are feasible, especially if the ideas are radical. This may mean working to gain allies within the organization, standing up to intimidating competitors inside and out, and perhaps being prepared to follow a lonely course for a long time.
- **Allow grieving, then move on:** Managers overseeing change need to give long-term employees a chance to grieve over the loss of the old ways, says McGuinn, who found that staffers were more willing to change after they had a chance to vent their fears.

forecast

What's Ahead in This Chapter

In this chapter, we consider the nature of change in organizations, including the two types of change—reactive and proactive—and the forces for change originating outside and inside the organization. We describe the four areas in which change is often needed: people, technology, structure, and strategy. We then explore the threat of change and how you can manage employee fear and resistance. We next discuss organization development, a set of techniques for implementing planned change. Finally, we discuss how to promote innovation within an organization.

major question **Since change is always with us, what should I understand about it?**

The Big Picture

Two types of change are reactive and proactive. Forces for change may consist of forces outside the organization—demographic characteristics, market changes, technological advancements, and social and political pressures. Or they may be forces inside the organization—employee problems and managers' behavior. Four areas in which change is often needed are people, technology, structure, and strategy.

People are generally uncomfortable about change, even change in apparently minor matters. Philosopher Eric Hoffer told how as a younger man he spent a good part of one year as an agricultural worker picking peas, starting in southern California in January and working his way northward. He picked the last of the peas in June, then moved to another area where, for the first time, he was required to pick string beans. "I still remember," he wrote, "how hesitant I was that first morning as I was about to address myself to the string bean vines. Would I be able to pick string beans? Even the change from peas to string beans had in it elements of fear."

If small changes can cause uneasiness, large changes can cause considerable stress. And as a manager, you will no doubt have to deal with both.

Fundamental Change: What Will You Be Called On to Deal With?

"It is hard to predict, especially the future," physicist Niels Bohr is supposed to have quipped.

But it is possible to identify and prepare for *the future that has already happened,* in the words of management theorist Peter Drucker, by looking at some fundamental changes that are happening now. Declining population in developed countries. More diversity in the workforce. The ascent of knowledge work. Increased globalization. The rise of business-to-business (B2B) technology. Digital long-distance networks. The increase in data storage. The capturing of customer-specific information. The customization of mass goods. Sales in the form of auctions instead of fixed prices.[6] All these trends suggest that organizations should prepare for change.

Clearly, we are all in for an interesting ride.

Two Types of Change: Reactive versus Proactive

As a manager, you will typically have to deal with two types of change: *reactive* and *proactive.*

1 Reactive Change: Responding to Unanticipated Problems & Opportunities

When managers talk about "putting out fires," they are talking about ***reactive change,*** **making changes in response to problems or opportunities as they arise.** When you have to respond to surprises, there is usually less time to get all the information and resources you need to adequately manage the change, and serious mistakes may be made. Nevertheless, some of the best stories in business concern the intelligent management of unanticipated calamities.

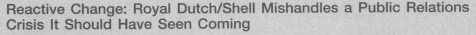

Example

Reactive Change: Royal Dutch/Shell Mishandles a Public Relations Crisis It Should Have Seen Coming

Many companies do not handle crises well. Among the instances: Exxon's handling of the 1989 *Exxon Valdez* oil spill in the Gulf of Alaska, Jack In The Box's management of the 1993 botulism crisis in Washington, TWA's actions on the 1996 crash of Flight 800 off Long Island, and Coca-Cola's reactions to the 1999 illnesses in Europe attributed to bottlers in Belgium and France. Could some of these have been anticipated and managed better?

A prime example of a company that—despite plenty of warning—mishandled a surprise was Royal Dutch/Shell in 1995. On April 29, the oil company learned that a small group of Greenpeace activists had boarded and occupied an obsolete oil-storage platform, the Brent Spar, in the North Sea that Shell was planning to sink. The activists had brought along plenty of members of the media to publicize the occupation of the Spar, which they argued contained low-level radioactive residues in its storage tanks that would harm the environment. Greenpeace also timed the boarding for maximum effect, one month before European Union environmental ministers were to meet to discuss North Sea pollution. As Shell, in full glare of the media, forcibly removed the trespassers from the platform and weeks afterward held off Greenpeace boats with water cannons, opposition to the company's plans—and to Shell itself—rose throughout Europe, with Shell gas stations boycotted and some even firebombed. Criticized by the media and governments, Shell finally announced it was no longer planning to scuttle the Spar.

Shell's "uncoordinated, reactionary, and ultimately futile response to the Greenpeace protest revealed a lack of foresight and planning," point out Harvard Business School professors Michael Watkins and Max Bazerman. Yet there had been many warning signs: Greenpeace had a history of occupying environmentally sensitive structures, Shell's own security advisors had warned of such a scenario—the Spar, after all, was one of the largest such platforms and one of the few with tanks with toxic residues—and other oil companies had protested when Shell had announced its plans. Yet Watkins and Bazerman point out that such clumsy reactions to predictable surprises by companies are all too common. "We have found that organizations' inability to prepare for them can be traced to three kinds of barriers: psychological, organizational, and political."[7]

Shell, however, had had plenty of opportunity to learn from a famous crisis faced down by Johnson & Johnson years before. In 1982, someone in the Chicago area added cyanide to J&J's best-selling Extra-Strength Tylenol packages on store shelves, and seven people died. The company took immediate and unprecedented action, recalling all unsold Tylenol at a cost of $100 million, offering refunds, creating a consumer hotline, introducing tamper-resistant packaging, and making managers (including the CEO) available to the media. The result: three months after the crisis, a poll showed that 93% of the public felt the company had done a good job.[8]

2 Proactive Change: Managing Anticipated Problems & Opportunities

In contrast to reactive change, ***proactive change* or planned change involves making carefully thought-out changes in anticipation of possible or expected problems or opportunities.**[9]

WAL★MART

Proactive Change: Wal-Mart Pushes RFID Tags

The introduction of the product bar-code and scanner system revolutionized retailing. Now it looks like it's all going to change again. Indeed, half of recent productivity gains have occurred in just two sectors, wholesale and retail trade.[10]

Wal-Mart has long been regarded as innovative in finding technology strategies for cutting costs. Indeed, says one analyst, the world's largest discounter is "usually one of the first movers in retail technology. They are the first shot fired, which everybody else follows."[11]

The opening salvo this time, scheduled to begin in early 2005, was the decree by Wal-Mart to its top 100 suppliers that they must tag the pallets and cases of goods that go to certain stores with RFID tags. Short for "radio frequency identification," RFID is a radio-wave tracking technology that's already being used with several million farm animals to aid in tracking health hazards and in about 100 million car keys to prevent theft through key copying.[12]

Wal-Mart, however, expects to use RFID to make its supply-chain and inventory management more efficient. Unlike bar codes, RFID tags contain much more information, such as a product's expiration date, size, shape, quantity, age, and temperature. They can also be scanned from a distance of up to 30 feet, which makes it easier for a retailer to find products in a warehouse.

It won't be easy for suppliers to meet the chain's demands to convert to RFID. But with $256 billion in annual sales and 20 million shoppers in its stores each day, Wal-Mart, in one writer's words, "has greater reach and influence than any retailer in history."[13]

The Forces for Change: Outside & Inside the Organization

How do managers know when their organizations need to change? The answers aren't clear-cut, but you can get clues by monitoring the forces for change—both outside and inside the organization. *(See Figure 10.1, opposite page.)*

Forces Originating Outside the Organization

External forces consist of four types, as follows.

1 Demographic Characteristics Earlier we discussed the demographic changes occurring in the U.S. workforce. We've pointed out that the workforce is now more diverse, and organizations need to effectively manage this diversity.

2 Market Changes As discussed in Chapter 4, the global economy is forcing companies to change the way they do business, with U.S. companies forging new partnerships and alliances with employees, suppliers, and competitors.

3 Technological Advancements Information technology may be one of the greatest forces for productivity in our lifetime. But it can also create headaches.

4 Social & Political Pressures Social events can create great pressures. Changing drinking habits, for example, have led to a rise in wine sales and a decline in whiskey sales.

FIGURE 10.1

Forces for change outside and inside the organization

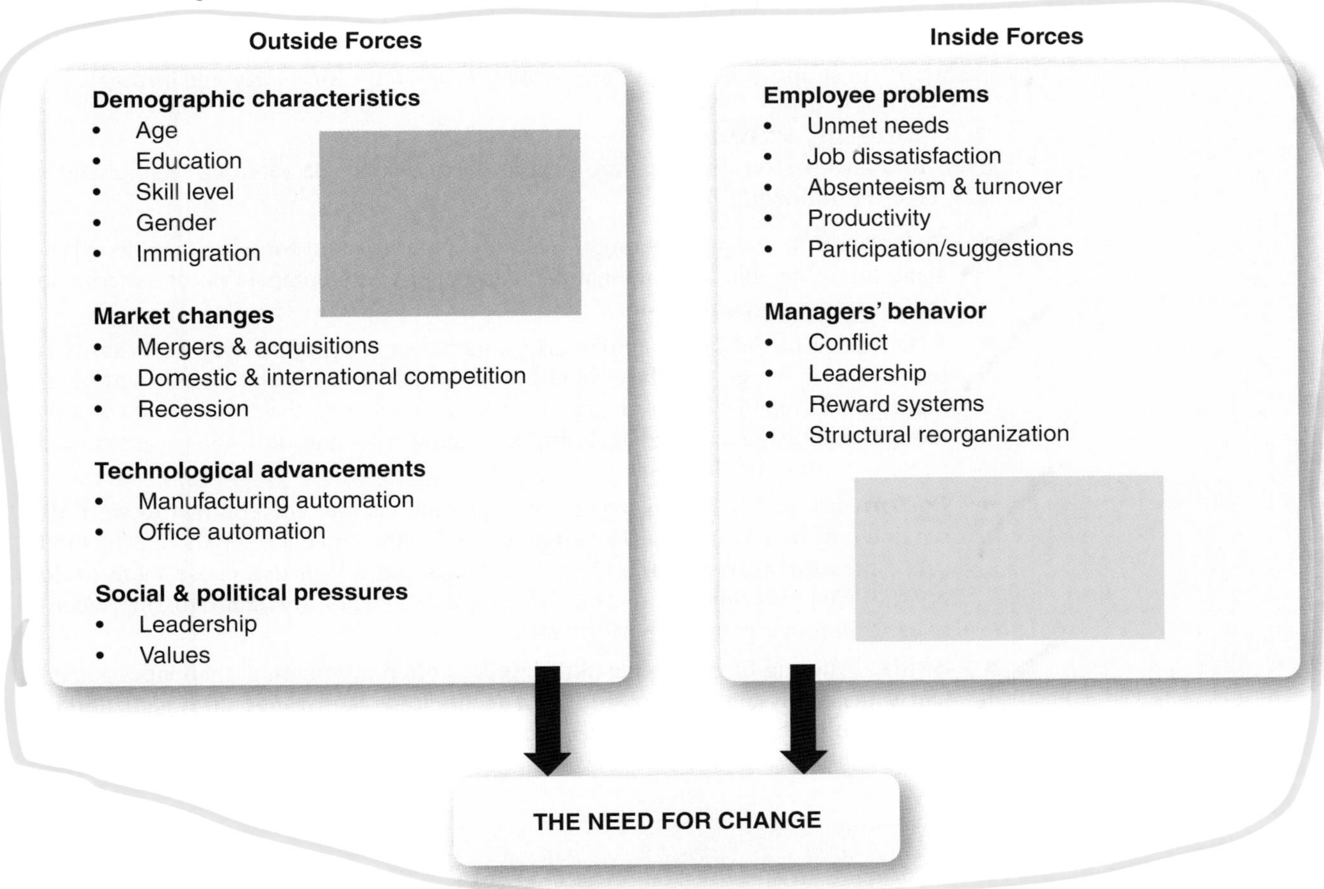

Outside Forces
Demographic characteristics
• Age
• Education
• Skill level
• Gender
• Immigration
Market changes
• Mergers & acquisitions
• Domestic & international competition
• Recession
Technological advancements
• Manufacturing automation
• Office automation
Social & political pressures
• Leadership
• Values
Inside Forces
Employee problems
• Unmet needs
• Job dissatisfaction
• Absenteeism & turnover
• Productivity
• Participation/suggestions
Managers' behavior
• Conflict
• Leadership
• Reward systems
• Structural reorganization
THE NEED FOR CHANGE

Forces Originating Inside the Organization

Internal forces affecting organizations may be subtle, such as low job satisfaction, or more dramatic, such as constant labor-management conflict. Internal forces may be of the two following types.

1 Employee Problems Is there a gap between the employees' needs and desires and the organization's needs and desires? Job dissatisfaction—as expressed through high absenteeism and turnover—can be a major signal of the need for change. Organizations may respond by addressing job design, reducing employees' role conflicts, and dealing with work overload, to mention a few matters.

For instance, when Martin McGuinn was reorganizing the retail division of Mellon Bank, many of the employees who were upset over expanded banking hours were appeased when they were given more freedom to arrange their own schedules.

2 Managers' Behavior Excessive conflict between managers and employees may be another indicator that change is needed. Perhaps there is a personality conflict, so that an employee transfer may be needed. Or perhaps some interpersonal training is required.

Phil Dusenberry, chairman of ad agency BBDO, says that he used to have a gentle way of letting people down because he didn't want to hurt their feelings. Often, however, this would simply confuse people. "They'd go off thinking that I liked their work even if I didn't," he says. "Over time I realized that dealing in terms of black and white wasn't a bad thing. I became much more direct."[14]

Areas in Which Change Is Often Needed: People, Technology, Structure, & Strategy

Change can involve any part of the organization. However, the four areas in which change is most apt to be needed are *people, technology, structure,* and *strategy*.

1 Changing People

Even in a two-person organization, people changes may be required. The changes may take the following forms:

- **Perceptions:** Employees might feel they are underpaid for what they do. Managers might be able to show that pay and benefits are comparable or superior to those offered by competitors.
- **Attitudes:** In old-line manufacturing industries, employees may feel that it is the nature of things that they should be in an adversarial relationship with their managers. It may be up to management to try to change the culture and the attitudes by using educational techniques to show why the old labor wars should become a thing of the past.
- **Performance:** Should an organization pay the people who contract to wash its windows by the hour? by the window? or by the total job? Will one method cause them to work fast and sloppily but cost less? Will one cause them to do pristine windows but cost too much? It's often a major challenge to find incentives to improve people's performance.
- **Skills:** Altering or improving skill levels is often an ongoing challenge, particularly these days, when new forms of technology can change an organization's way of doing business, as we describe next.

Example

Changing Technology: "When the Web Fits into Your Pocket"

Futurist Paul Saffo, director of the think tank Institute for the Future in Menlo Park, Calif., says that new technologies lead to new products. The invention of television, for example, led to TV dinners and TV trays. The invention of the iPod led to the selling of music singles—something that hadn't happened since the 45 rpm record.

In the case of the Internet, he says that, although e-mail has been around since the 1960s and mainframe computers, it didn't mature until it migrated to client-serving computing in the 1980s, which made it easier to provide. In the 1990s, the media expression of client-server was the World Wide Web. "The Web will mature," he suggests, "when we can take it everywhere with us and when we have peer-to-peer systems to manage all the connections [more cheaply and efficiently]. . . . The moment the Web fits into your pocket, you have a whole new set of applications and business opportunities that never existed before."[15]

This process seems to already be well under way. Wi-Fi and other innovative wireless technologies—WiMax, Mobile-Fi, ZigBee, and Ultrawideband—will probably push portable wireless networking into every facet of life.[16] Already, Nestlé has installed hundreds of ice-cream vending machines in France and England with wireless devices that communicate daily reports on sales and notify drivers if they are running low on Maxibon Sandwiches or Extreme cones.[17] Internet phone services are undercutting the traditional telecommunications giants and creating new rivals, making international calls as cheap as local ones.[18] Cellphones and personal digital assistants (PDAs) offer still pictures and videos that can be sent anywhere anytime.[19]

"Each time it gets cheaper to do something," says Saffo, "you get more players. It's irreversibly more complex. You get more than a value chain. You get a value web."

Cellphone power. Camera phones have become commonplace, but the cellphone is still evolving—and rapidly. Movies, for instance, are moving from the big screen to the smallest, and the technology is changing both audience viewing habits and the nature of films themselves. Who wants to watch a 90-minute feature in a 2-inch window with poor screen resolution? But a 2-minute comedy video while stuck in traffic appeals to a lot of people. This forces cellphone filmmakers to rely on more close-ups and more static shots—the opposite of MTV video. In South Korea, where cellphones operate at broadband speeds, giving that country an edge in wireless technology, young commuters on the subway are forsaking print matter and occupying themselves with cellphone news services, videos, and music downloads, as well as e-mail and phone calls. Cellphones there are also doubling as credit cards: a consumer can point his or her phone at an infrared terminal on a store counter, which sends credit-card information straight to the card company. In the future, cellphones might also take the place of driver's licenses and ID cards. When cellphones and accompanying text-messaging features are joined to advanced search engines and huge databases—Amazon.com already has a service that enables users to type in any name or phrase and immediately be told where those words appear in any of several thousand books—the technology will no doubt stand several industries on their heads. Which ones do you think these might be?

2 Changing Technology

Technology is a major area of change for many organizations. ***Technology*** **is not just computer technology; it is any machine or process that enables an organization to gain a competitive advantage in changing materials used to produce a finished product.** Breweries, for example, used to make beer by letting malted cereal grain flavored with hops brew slowly by fermentation; nowadays, the process is often speeded up by the direct injection of carbonation (from carbon dioxide) into the process.

3 Changing Structure

When one organization acquires another, the structure often changes—perhaps from a divisional structure, say, to a matrix structure. The recent trend is toward "flattening the hierarchy," eliminating several middle layers of management, and to using work teams linked by electronic networks.

4 Changing Strategy

Shifts in the marketplace often may lead organizations to have to change their strategy. As a result of the sudden rise in popularity of the Netscape Navigator Web browser, Microsoft Corp. found itself having to shift from a PC-based strategy to an Internet strategy. ◆

major question **How are employees threatened by change, and how can I help them adjust?**

The Big Picture

This section discusses the degree to which employees fear change, from least threatening to most threatening. It also describes Lewin's three-stage change model: unfreezing, changing, and refreezing. Finally, it describes Kotter's eight steps for leading organizational change, which correspond to Lewin's three stages.

As a manager, particularly one working for an American organization, you may be pressured to provide short-term, quick-fix solutions. But when applied to organizational problems, this approach usually doesn't work: quick-fix solutions have little staying power.

What, then, are effective ways to manage organization change and employees' fear and resistance to it? In this section, we discuss the following:

- The extent to which employees fear change
- Lewin's change model
- Kotter's eight stages for leading organizational change

The Degree to Which Employees Fear Change: From Least Threatening to Most Threatening

Whether organizational change is administrative or technological, the degree to which employees feel threatened by it in general depends on whether the change is *adaptive, innovative,* or *radically innovative.*[20]

Least Threatening: Adaptive Change

Adaptive change **is reintroduction of a familiar practice**—the implementation of a kind of change that has already been experienced within the same organization. This form of change is lowest in complexity, cost, and uncertainty. Because it is familiar, it is the least threatening to employees and thus will create the least resistance.

For example, during annual inventory week, a department store may ask its employees to work 12 hours a day instead of the usual 8. During tax-preparation time, the store's accounting department may imitate this same change in work hours. Although accounting employees are in a different department from stockroom and sales employees, it's expected they wouldn't be terribly upset by the temporary change in hours since they've seen it in effect elsewhere in the store.

Somewhat Threatening: Innovative Change

Innovative change **is the introduction of a practice that is new to the organization.** This form of change involves moderate complexity, cost, and uncertainty. It is therefore apt to trigger some fear and resistance among employees.

For example, should a department store decide to adopt a new practice of competitors by staying open 24 hours a day, requiring employees to work flexible schedules, it may be felt as moderately threatening.

Very Threatening: Radically Innovative Change

Radically innovative change **involves introducing a practice that is new to the industry.** Because it is the most complex, costly, and uncertain, it will be felt as extremely threatening to managers' confidence and employees' job security and may well tear at the fabric of the organization.[21]

For example, a department store converting some of its operations to e-commerce—selling its goods on the Internet—may encounter anxiety among its staff, especially those fearing being left behind.

Example

Radically Innovative Change: Kodak Confronts Digital Photography

The title of the book is *The Innovator's Dilemma: When New Technologies Cause Great Firms to Fail.* In it author Clayton M. Christensen, a Harvard Business School professor, argues that when successful companies are confronted with a giant technological leap that transforms their markets, all choices are bad ones.

Kodak

For a century, Rochester, New York–based Eastman Kodak had the film business almost to itself—at least until Fuji Photo Film Co. began to offer strong competition. Then along came the movement toward digital cameras, putting a massive dent in Kodak's so-called "yellow box" or chemical-based film business. Kodak sales hit their peak at $14 billion in 1999, and in 2003 dropped to $13.3 billion. In the fall of 2003, its chairman and CEO, Daniel Carp, declared that the traditional cash cow of the film business was in irreversible decline and announced plans to move into the digital future—"probably," he said, "the biggest turning point in our history."

Now the company is trying to reinvent itself. Although Kodak actually came up with the first digital camera in 1975, only recently has it begun to try to capitalize on this technology. It has quit making big investments in film and is shifting resources toward digital cameras and accessories, digital health-imaging technologies, and inkjet printing and liquid displays.

To make the difficult transition, top executives made some difficult choices. Carp cut the stock dividend by a hefty 72%, which he said would generate $1.3 billion in investable cash over the next three years. The stock, which had been at $27 a share, dropped to $5. Nearly a quarter of the company's 60,000 employees were laid off.

Will the new vision and strategy succeed? The digital business offers much lower profit margins than does film. The workforce has traditionally labored under a complacency that it can introduce one product and then the world will beat a path to its door, something that did not happen when the company introduced a printer dock to make it easy for users to print photos without using a computer—but the dock worked only with a Kodak camera, not other brands. Thus, although the dock's first-year sales topped $100 million, observers believed it could have done better.

Christensen thinks it's very difficult for an existing successful company to take full advantage of a technological breakthrough, such as digitalization, what he calls a "disruptive innovation." Instead, he argues that such a company should set up an entirely separate organization that can operate much like a startup.[22]

Lewin's Change Model: Unfreezing, Changing, & Refreezing

Most theories of organizational change originated with the landmark work of social psychologist **Kurt Lewin.** Lewin developed a model with three stages—*unfreezing, changing,* and *refreezing*—to explain how to initiate, manage, and stabilize planned change.[23]

1 "Unfreezing": Creating the Motivation to Change

In the *unfreezing stage,* managers try to instill in employees the motivation to change, encouraging them to let go of attitudes and behaviors that are resistant to innovation. For this "unfreezing" to take place, employees need to become dissatisfied with the old way of doing things. Managers also need to reduce the barriers to change during this stage.

2 "Changing": Learning New Ways of Doing Things

In the *changing stage,* employees need to be given the tools for change: new information, new perspectives, new models of behavior. Managers can help here by providing benchmarking results, role models, mentors, experts, and training. It's advisable, experts say, to convey the idea that change is a continuous learning process, not just a one-time event.[24]

3 "Refreezing": Making the New Ways Normal

In the *refreezing stage,* employees need to be helped to integrate the changed attitudes and behavior into their normal ways of doing things. Managers can assist by encouraging employees to exhibit the new change and then, through additional coaching and modeling, by reinforcing the employees in the desired change.

One technique used in Stage 1, to help unfreeze organizations, is ***benchmarking,* a process by which a company compares its performance with that of high-performing organizations.**[25] Professional sports teams do this all the time, but so do other kinds of organizations, including nonprofit ones.

For example, one company discovered that their costs to develop a computer system were twice as high as those of the best companies in their industry. They also learned that the time it took to get a new product to market was four times longer than the benchmarked organizations. This data was ultimately used to unfreeze employees' attitudes and motivate people to change the organization's internal processes in order to remain competitive.[26]

Kotter's Eight Steps for Leading Organizational Change

An expert in leadership and change management, **John Kotter** believes that, to be successful, organizational change needs to follow eight steps to avoid the eight common errors senior management usually commits.[27] *(See Table 10.1.)* These correspond with Lewin's unfreezing-changing-refreezing steps.

Lookalikes. One key to the success of Southwest Airlines is that all the planes in its fleet have been the same type, Boeing 737s, which saves on maintenance and training costs. Southwest established its reputation and profitability by being a short-haul, low-fare carrier. In late 2002, the airline decided to enter the long-haul business—nonstop, coast-to-coast flights between Baltimore/Washington International and Los Angeles—invading the domain of bigger airlines such as United. To do so, it added new-generation 737s, which can travel longer distances than the older planes did. Southwest still offers no-frills service—no seat assignments and snacks instead of meals—and competes principally on fare price. In expanding from short routes to long ones, should the company expect to have to undergo any of the steps in Lewin's change model—unfreezing, changing, and refreezing?

TABLE 10.1

Steps to leading organizational change [*Source:* These steps were developed by J. P. Kotter, *Leading Change* (Boston: Harvard Business School Press, 1996).]

Step	Description
1. Establish a sense of urgency.	Unfreeze the organization by creating a compelling reason for why change is needed.
2. Create the guiding coalition.	Create a cross-functional, cross-level group of people with enough power to lead the change.
3. Develop a vision and a strategy.	Create a vision and a strategic plan to guide the change process.
4. Communicate the change vision.	Create and implement a communication strategy that consistently communicates the new vision and strategic plan.
5. Empower broad-based action.	Eliminate barriers to change, and use target elements of change to transform the organization. Encourage risk taking and creative problem solving.
6. Generate short-term wins.	Plan for and create short-term "wins" or improvements. Recognize and reward people who contribute to the wins.
7. Consolidate gains and produce more change.	The guiding coalition uses credibility from short-term wins to create more change. Additional people are brought into the change process as change cascades throughout the organization. Attempts are made to reinvigorate the change process.
8. Anchor new approaches in the culture.	Reinforce the changes by highlighting connections between new behaviors and processes and organizational success. Develop methods to ensure leadership development and succession.

Steps 1–4 represent unfreezing: establish a sense of urgency, create the guiding coalition, develop a vision and strategy, and communicate the change vision.

Steps 5–7 represent the changing stage: empower broad-based action, generate short-term wins, and consolidate gains and produce more change.

Step 8, corresponding to refreezing, is to anchor new approaches in the organization's culture.

The value of Kotter's steps is that they provide specific recommendations about behaviors that managers need to exhibit to successfully lead organizational change. It is important to remember that Kotter's research reveals that it is ineffective to skip steps and that successful organizational change is 70%–90% leadership and only 10%–30% management. Senior managers are thus advised to focus on leading rather than on managing change.[28]

Now let us turn to organization development, which is a systematic way of instituting planned change. ◆

major question **What are the uses of OD, and how effective is it?**

The Big Picture

Organization development (OD) is a set of techniques for implementing change, such as managing conflict, revitalizing organizations, and adapting to mergers. Three characteristics of OD are that it aims for fundamental change; it is process-oriented, not content-oriented; and it is value-loaded. OD has three steps: diagnosis, intervention, and evaluation. Five factors have been found to make OD programs effective.

If you're a bookstore owner, a car dealer, a travel agent, or a stockbroker and aren't worried about the future of your business, you probably haven't been paying attention. The increasing importance of the Internet as a sales and distribution tool gives buyers and sellers the opportunity to link up directly; the middleman is becoming less necessary. Maybe, then, you need to start thinking about how to redesign your business—and soon. Maybe, therefore, you're a candidate for organization development.

Organization development (OD) **is a set of techniques for implementing planned change to make people and organizations more effective.** Note the inclusion of people in this definition. OD focuses specifically on people in the change process. Often OD is put into practice by a person known as a ***change agent,*** **a consultant with a background in behavioral sciences who can be a catalyst in helping organizations deal with old problems in new ways.**

The techniques of OD apply to each of the change models discussed in the preceding section. For example, OD is used during each of Lewin's stages of "unfreezing," "change," and "refreezing."

What Can OD Be Used For?

OD can be used to address the following three matters:

1 Managing Conflict

Conflict is inherent in most organizations. Sometimes an OD expert in the guise of an executive coach will be brought in to help advise an executive on how to improve relationships with others in the organization.

For instance, David Hitz and Michael Malcolm, two cofounders of Network Appliance, a data-storage firm in Sunnyvale, Calif., were feuding with each other. The problem: Malcolm couldn't stick to his decisions, which drove Hitz crazy. An organization behavior specialist began working with the warring executives in separate sessions to solve the problem.

2 Revitalizing Organizations

Information technology is wreaking such change that nearly all organizations these days are placed in the position of having to adapt new behaviors in order to resist decline. OD can help by opening communication, fostering innovation, and dealing with stress.

3 Adapting to Mergers

Mergers and acquisitions are associated with increased anxiety, stress, absenteeism, and turnover and decreased productivity.[29] What is the organizational fit between two disparate organizations, such as AOL and Time Warner? OD experts can help integrate two firms with varying cultures, products, and procedures.

Characteristics of OD

Three identifying characteristics of OD are as follows:[30]

1 OD Aims for Fundamental Change

Managers and consultants using OD aren't looking for temporary improvements. They generally want deep, long-lasting, *fundamental* change. "By fundamental change, as opposed to fixing a problem or improving a procedure," says OD consultant Warner Burke, "I mean that some significant aspect of an organization's culture will never be the same."[31] The emphasis is on changing an organization's *culture,* which, of course, involves people.

2 OD Is Process-Oriented, Not Content-Oriented

You might not understand much of a conversation between product design engineers and marketing managers discussing a new computer chip. But that's all right. The important thing is to focus on the *process*—to coach the two parties to better communicate. In dealing with processes, OD consultants concentrate on such matters as conflict handling, trust, problem solving, power sharing, decision making, and career development.

3 OD Is Value-Loaded

OD consultants prefer cooperation over conflict, self-control over institutional control, and participative management over autocratic management. Thus, OD carries certain values, or biases, rooted in humanistic psychology.[32]

How OD Works

Like physicians, OD managers and consultants follow a medical-like model. They approach the organization as if it were a sick patient, using *diagnosis, intervention,* and *evaluation*—"diagnosing" its ills, "prescribing" treatment or intervention, and "monitoring" or evaluating progress. *(See Figure 10.2, next page.)*

Is small beautiful? With airlines cutting commissions and more travelers ordering tickets off websites, how can a small travel agent compete? In other industries, many large corporations aren't structured to take advantage of the Web because they view it as a mass-marketing medium. However, says the owner of a San Diego Web design firm, "It's very easy for a small business to go out and control an entire niche market. Maybe it's only six to 10,000 users, but that can be enough." Adds the chief strategy officer for a Florida-based online jeweler, "Big companies think they can adapt their environments to them, not adapt to their environments." Whether you work for a big company or small one, do you think you could use OD techniques to help your organization "adapt to its environment"?

FIGURE 10.2
The OD process [*Sources:* Adapted from W. L. French and C. H. Bell Jr., *Organization Development: Behavioral Interventions for Organizational Improvement* (Englewood Cliffs, NJ: Prentice-Hall, 1978); and E. G. Huse and T. G. Cummings, *Organizational Development and Change,* 3rd ed. (St. Paul: West, 1985).]

1. Diagnosis
What is the problem?
2. Intervention
What shall we do about it?
3. Evaluation
How well has the intervention worked?

1 Diagnosis: What Is the Problem?

To carry out the diagnosis, OD consultants or managers use some combination of questionnaires, surveys, interviews, meetings, records, and direct observation to ascertain people's attitudes and to identify problem areas.

2 Intervention: What Shall We Do about It?

"Treatment" or ***intervention*** **is the attempt to correct the diagnosed problems.** Often this is done using the services of an OD consultant who works in conjunction with management teams. Some OD activities for implementing planned change are shown in the box on the page opposite. *(See Table 10.2.)*

3 Evaluation: How Well Has the Intervention Worked?

An OD program needs objective evaluation to see if it has done any good. Answers may lie in hard data about absenteeism, turnover, grievances, and profitability, which should be compared with earlier statistics. The change agent can use questionnaires, surveys, interviews, and the like to assess changes in employee attitudes.

The Effectiveness of OD

Among organizations that have practiced organization development are American Airlines, B.F. Goodrich, General Electric, Honeywell, ITT, Polaroid, Procter & Gamble, Prudential, Texas Instruments, and Westinghouse Canada—companies covering a variety of industries.

Research has found that OD is most apt to be successful under the following circumstances.

1 Multiple Interventions

OD success stories tend to use multiple interventions. Goal setting, feedback, recognition and rewards, training, participation, and challenging job design have had good results in improving performance and satisfaction.[33] Combined interventions have been found to work better than single interventions.[34]

2 Management Support

OD is more likely to succeed when top managers give the OD program their support and are truly committed to the change process and the desired goals of the change program.[35] Also, the expectations for change were not unrealistic.[36]

3 Goals Geared to Both Short- & Long-Term Results

Change programs are more successful when they are oriented toward achieving both short-term and long-term results. Managers should not engage in organizational change for the sake of change. Change efforts should produce positive results.[37]

4 OD Is Affected by Culture

OD effectiveness is affected by cross-cultural considerations. Thus, an OD intervention that worked in one country should not be blindly applied to a similar situation in another country.[38] ◆

TABLE 10.2

Some OD activities for implementing change [*Sources:* D. A. Nadler, *Feedback and Organizational Development: Using Data-Based Methods* (Reading, MA: Addison-Wesley, 1977); G. A. Neuman, J. E. Edwards, and N. S. Raju, "Organizational Development Interventions: A Meta-Analysis of Their Effects on Satisfaction and Other Attitudes," *Personnel Psychology,* August 1989, pp. 461–489; and P. J. Robertson, D. R. Roberts, and J. I. Porras, "Dynamics of Planned Organizational Change: Assessing Empirical Support for a Theoretical Model," *Academy of Management Journal,* June 1993, pp. 619–634.]

- **Survey feedback:** A questionnaire is distributed to employees to ascertain their perceptions and attitudes. The results are then shared with them. The questionnaire may ask about such matters as group cohesion, job satisfaction, and managerial leadership. Once the survey is done, meaningful results can be communicated with employees so that they can then engage in problem solving and constructive changes.

- **Process consultation:** An OD consultant observes the communication process—interpersonal-relations, decision-making, and conflict-handling patterns—occurring in work groups and provides feedback to the members involved. In consulting with employees (particularly managers) about these processes, the change agent hopes to give them the skills to identify and improve group dynamics on their own.

- **Team building:** Work groups are made to become more effective by helping members learn to function as a team. For example, members of a group might be interviewed independently by the OD change agent to establish how they feel about the group, then a meeting may be held away from their usual workplace to discuss the issues. To enhance team cohesiveness, the OD consultant may have members work together on a project such as rock climbing, with the consultant helping with communication and conflict resolution. The objective is for members to see how they can individually contribute to the group's goals and efforts.

- **Intergroup development:** Intergroup development resembles team building in many of its efforts. However, intergroup development attempts to achieve better cohesiveness among several work groups, not just one. During the process, the change agent tries to elicit misperceptions and stereotypes that the groups have for each other so that they can be discussed, leading to better coordination among them.

- **Technostructural activities:** Technostructural activities are interventions concerned with improving the work technology or organizational design with people on the job. An intervention involving a work-technology change might be the introduction of e-mail to improve employee communication. An intervention involving an organizational-design change might be making a company less centralized in its decision making.

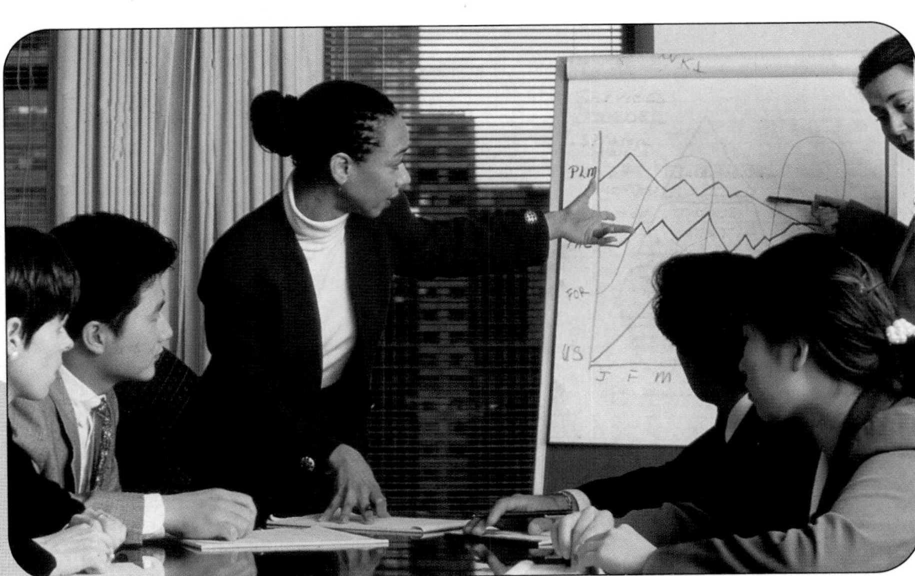

Team building. One technique for implementing change is team building. Teams are often diverse in gender, age, ethnicity, and educational background and experience. Would you prefer to work with a highly diverse team of people?

major question

What do I need to know to encourage innovation?

The Big Picture

Innovation may be a product innovation or a process innovation, an incremental innovation or a radical innovation. Four characteristics of innovation are that it is uncertain, people closest to it know the most about it, it may be controversial, and it may be complex. Three ways to encourage innovation are by providing the organizational culture, the resources, and the reward system. To make innovation happen, you need to recognize problems and opportunities, gain allies, and overcome employee resistance.

Innovation can happen by design or by accident, and it need not come about because of a for-profit orientation. For instance, the computer operating system Linux was written by Finnish programmer Linus Torvalds, who then put his work in the public domain. It is now a free operating system created by hundreds of programmers around the world, who contribute to its "source code," its underlying instructions, which are available to anyone. Indeed, unlike the Microsoft Windows or Macintosh operating systems, Linux is protected by a sort of reverse copyright, called a "copyleft," which prohibits programmers who work on it from taking their versions out of the public domain. "Geeks love Linux because they can lift up the hood of their software and mess around inside, customizing and fixing up what they want," says one report. "The constant tinkering by thousands of coders [programmers] also improves the code, making it ever more sophisticated and crash proof."[39] International Data Corp., a market research organization, predicts that Linux will have 6% of the global desktop market by 2007, doubling its 2.7% share of the market in 2002.[40]

As we've said earlier in the book, innovation is the activity of creating new ideas and converting them into useful applications—specifically new goods and services. The spirit of innovation is essential to keeping an organization vital and in maintaining a competitive advantage. Otherwise, the innovation will come from your competitors, forcing you to scramble to catch up—if you can.

Types of Innovation: Product or Process, Incremental or Radical

Innovations may be of the following two types.

Linus Torvalds, innovator. In 1991, computer programmer Torvalds, then a graduate student in Finland, posted his free Linux operating system on the Internet. Linux is a free version of Unix, and its continual improvements result from the efforts of tens of thousands of volunteer programmers. Can you think of any other innovations that occurred that did not come about because of a for-profit orientation?

Product versus Process Innovations

As a manager, you may need to improve your organization's product or service itself; this is generally a technological innovation. Or you may need to improve the process by which the product or service is created, manufactured, or distributed; this is generally a managerial innovation.

practical action

What Makes a Startup?

Lots of books are written about creativity and innovation in organizational life. In general, the message is the same: "Fire up your companywide brainpower to hatch ideas," as one *Business Week* writer put it, "and make sure the ideas reach the people who can implement them." But it's difficult to come up with a formula for turning companies into prodigious idea factories.[41] As Gina O'Connor, a marketing professor at Rensselaer Polytechnic Institute, points out: "American companies are doing a great job of developing better products. But there's been very little improvement in radical, or 'discontinuous,' innovation."[42]

Interestingly, though, many startups don't begin with radical ideas. According to Amar V. Bhidé, author of *The Origin and Evolution of New Businesses,* successful entrepreneurs start out by making "a small modification in what somebody else is doing."[43] One has only to think of how the notion of disposability has been extended to so many products—phone cards, DVDs, even cellphones.[44]

Most entrepreneurs, he explains, see a small niche opportunity—one in which the company he or she is working for is already involved, or a supplier or customer is involved. "And the person jumps in with very little preparation and analysis," he says, "but with direct firsthand knowledge of the profitability of that opportunity—and pretty much does what somebody else is already doing, but does it better and faster."

And "better and faster" seems to be the main difference. Such entrepreneurs don't have anything in the way of technology or concept that differentiates them from other businesses. "They just work harder, hustle for customers, and know that the opportunity may not last for more than six or eight months," says Bhidé. "But they expect to make a reasonable return on those six to eight months. And along the way they'll figure out something else that will keep the business going."

Another quality of entrepreneurs is "a tolerance for ambiguity," Bhidé says. They are willing to jump into things when it's hard to even imagine what the possible outcomes will be, going ahead in the absence of information, very much capital—or even a very novel idea.

An example of a startup fitting these criteria is Netflix, which rents DVD movies by mail to customers ordering online. This concept does not seem very innovative. The wrinkle, however, which struck founder Reed Hastings when he was charged $40 for returning a movie late to a video rental outfit, is that for a $19.95 monthly subscription, customers can keep three films out at a time. "If you rent five or six a month," says one California retired engineer, "you're ahead compared to what you pay at Blockbuster." (In one month, he watched more than 40 movies.) Another differentiating feature: when you rate the movie you rented, Netflix will recommend other movies you might enjoy that you might not have heard of.

No entrepreneur can afford to rest easily, however. Both Blockbuster and Wal-Mart are also entering the online DVD rental business. And new technology is a big uncertainty, with pay-per-view, TiVo set-top boxes, and digital movie downloads being possible challengers.[45]

More formally, a ***product innovation*** **is a change in the appearance or the performance of a product or a service or the creation of a new one. A *process innovation* is a change in the way a product or service is conceived, manufactured, or disseminated.**

Incremental versus Radical Innovations

An innovation may be small or large. The difference is in modifying versus replacing existing products or services. That is, you might have ***incremental innovations*** **—the creation of products, services, or technologies that modify existing ones.** Or you might have ***radical innovations*** **—the creation of products, services, or technologies that replace existing ones.**

Four Characteristics of Innovation

According to Harvard management scholar Rosabeth Moss Kanter, innovation has four characteristics:[46]

1 Innovating Is an Uncertain Business

Being an innovator means being like the first driver in a line of cars in a snowstorm: You're dealing with the unknown while the less adventurous souls behind you may be carping about your performance. When you're innovating, progress is difficult to predict, and the ultimate success of your endeavor is always somewhat in doubt.

2 People Closest to the Innovation Know the Most about It, at Least Initially

Innovation is knowledge-intensive. The people closest to the development of the idea know the most about it, at least in the early stages. Consequently, it is often difficult for outsiders—such as coworkers or managers who are removed from the process—to understand and appreciate it. This leads to characteristic #3.

3 Innovation May Be Controversial

Whoever is doing the innovating is using the organization's people and funds for that purpose. Since there is always competition for resources, others in the organization may take issue with the way they are being used here—especially since the innovation has not yet shown positive results.

4 Innovation Can Be Complex Because It May Cross Organizational Boundaries

An innovation may involve more than one department or business unit. This, of course, increases the complexity of the process. Thus, you as a manager need to understand not only how the process of innovation works in general but also how it requires special handling to make it successful within different parts of the organization. Shepherding an innovation, therefore, may require you to draw on your finest communication skills—especially because of characteristic #2 above.

Celebrating Failure: Cultural & Other Factors Encouraging Innovation

Innovation doesn't happen as a matter of course. Organizations have to develop ways to make it happen—over and over. Three ways to do so are by providing (1) the right organizational *culture,* (2) the appropriate *resources,* and (3) the correct *reward system*.

1 Culture: Is Innovation Viewed as a Benefit or a Boondoggle?

Although much of American culture seems oriented toward punishing failure, an organizational culture that doesn't just allow but *celebrates* failure is vital toward fostering innovation. Pharmaceutical company Eli Lilly, for example, is said to have "long had a culture that looks at failure as an inevitable part of discovery and encourages scientists to take risks."[47] Most new ideas will fail. Only a few will be successful. But if an organization doesn't encourage this kind of risk taking—if people tend to view experimentation as a boondoggle—that organization won't become a superstar in innovation.

An organizational culture, as we said in Chapter 8, is the "social glue," or system of shared beliefs and values, that binds members together. Among the companies with cultures that strongly encourage innovation are Apple Computer, Corning, Hewlett-Packard, Johnson & Johnson, Merck, Monsanto, Texas Instruments, and 3M.

Achieving Success by Celebrating Failure: 3M's Culture of Innovation

In Chapter 3 we mentioned 3M's Art Fry, inventor of Post-it Notes, as an example of an intrapreneur. But 3M is also famous for having a culture of innovation that celebrates taking chances—which means achieving success by celebrating failure.

A story told around 3M is about an outside inventor, Francis Okie, who in the 1920s wrote 3M for samples of various sandpaper grit. Okie had an idea for a waterproof sandpaper, which he thought might have use in shaving and would reduce the cuts inflicted by razor blades. That idea turned out to be a failure. However, 3M was still interested in the sandpaper, later named Wetordry, and Okie sold them his idea after the company agreed to help bring the product to market. The result was a hugely successful product that became widely used in the automotive market, where previously dry sanding had created clouds of dust and lead-based paint that made people sick. Okie joined 3M in 1921 and became the company's first real inventor.

Only with 20-20 hindsight can people see that a policy of celebrating failure can lead to success. No one can know, when setting out on a new course, whether the effort will yield positive results, and usually, in fact, most such experiments *are* failures. But the *attempts* must be encouraged, or innovation will never happen.

3M builds innovation into its culture. Mistakes are allowed, destructive criticism is forbidden, experimentation is encouraged, and divisions and individuals are allowed to operate with a good deal of autonomy. 3M sets goals decreeing that 25%–30% of annual sales must come from products that are only five years old or less. Investment in research and development is almost double the rate of that of the average American company. In addition, 3M employees are permitted to spend 15% of their time pursuing personal research interests that are not related to current company projects, knowing that if their ideas aren't successful, they will be encouraged to pursue other paths.[48]

2 Resources: Do Managers Put Money Where Their Mouths Are?

An organization's managers may say they encourage innovation, but if they balk at the expense, they aren't putting their money where their mouths are. Innovation doesn't come cheap. Its costs can be measured in all kinds of ways: dollars, time, energy, and focus. For instance, an organization's research and development (R&D) department may need to hire top scientists, whose salaries may be high.

Of course, because there is always competition within an organization for resources, innovation may simply be given short shrift because other concerns seem so urgent—even within a company with a culture encouraging experimentation. But the risk of downgrading innovation in favor of more immediate concerns is that a company may "miss the next wave"—the next big trend, whatever that is.

The culture of innovation. Salespeople are rarely charged with responsibility for innovations in products or services, even though they typically have frequent interaction with customers. Should they be given such a role?

3 Rewards: Is Experimentation Reinforced in Ways That Matter?

Top-performing salespeople are often rewarded with all kinds of incentives, such as commissions, bonuses, and perks. Are R&D people rewarded the same way? Every year Monsanto Corp., for instance, presents a $50,000 award to the scientist or scientists who developed the largest commercial breakthrough.

The converse is also important: People should not be punished when their attempts to innovate don't work out, or else they won't attempt new things in the future. By the nature of experimentation, the end result can't be foreseen. Top managers at 3M, for instance, recognize that three-fifths of the new ideas suggested each year fail in the marketplace. Only when people attempting an innovation are acting half-heartedly, sloppily, or otherwise incompetently should sanctions be used such as the withholding of raises and promotions.

How You Can Foster Innovation: Three Steps

If you're going to not just survive but *prevail* as a manager, you need to know how to make innovation happen within an organization. Here we offer three steps for doing so. *(See Figure 10.3.)*

1. Recognize problems & opportunities & devise solutions
2. Gain allies by communicating your vision
3. Overcome employee resistance, & empower & reward them to achieve progress

FIGURE 10.3
Three steps for fostering innovation [*Source:* Adapted from eight steps in K. M. Bartol and D. C. Martin, *Management,* 3rd ed. (Burr Ridge, IL: Irwin/McGraw-Hill, 1998), pp. 360–363.]

1 Recognize Problems & Opportunities & Devise Solutions

Change may be needed because you recognize a *problem* or recognize an *opportunity*.

- **Recognizing a problem—find a "better way":** Problems, whether competitive threat or employee turnover, tend to seize our attention.

  Sometimes problems lead to new business ideas. When John Decker of Maui, Hawaii, took up classical guitar, he discovered Hawaii's tropical climate was hard on wooden instruments. This led to his forming a company to turn out high-quality classical guitars made of synthetic materials known for their stiffness and durability.[49]

- **Recognizing an opportunity:** Recognition of opportunities may come from long-term employees who regularly expose themselves to new ideas ("technological gate-keepers" in one phrase).[50] Ideas originating at the grassroots level of an organization may be a particularly fruitful source of innovation.[51]

2 Gain Allies by Communicating Your Vision

Once you've decided how you're going to handle the problem or opportunity, you need to start developing and communicating your vision. You need to create a picture of the future and paint in broad strokes how your innovation will be of benefit. That is, you need to start persuading others inside—and perhaps outside—the organization to support you. Having hard data helps. Others will be more persuaded, for example, if you can demonstrate that a similar idea has been successful in another industry. Or if you can take current trends (such as sales or demographics) and project them into the future.

But a great deal of innovation comes about precisely because the future has no resemblance to the past. Thus, you may have to use your imagination to paint the brightest picture you can of the possible payoffs of your innovation.

3 Overcome Employee Resistance, & Empower & Reward Them to Achieve Progress

Once you've persuaded and got the blessing of your managerial superiors, then you need to do the same with the people reporting to you. It's possible, of course, that the idea for innovation came from them and that you already have their support.

Alternatively, you may have to overcome their resistance. Then you'll need to remove obstacles that limit them in executing the vision, such as having to get management to sign off on all aspects of a project. Finally, you'll need to hand out periodic rewards—recognition, celebrations, bonuses—for tasks accomplished. And the rewards should not be withheld until the end of the project, which may be many months away, but given out for the successful accomplishment of short-term phases in order to provide constant encouragement. ◆

Key Terms Used in This Chapter

adaptive change, 322
benchmarking, 324
change agent, 326
incremental innovations, 331
innovative change, 333
intervention, 328
organization development, 326
proactive change, 317
process innovation, 331
product innovation, 331
radical innovations, 331
radically innovative change, 322
reactive change, 316
technology, 321

Summary

10.1 The Nature of Change in Organizations

- Two types of change are reactive and proactive. Reactive change is making changes in response to problems or opportunities as they arise. Proactive change involves making carefully thought-out changes in anticipation of possible or expected problems or opportunities.
- Forces for change may consist of forces outside the organization or inside it. (1) External forces consist of four types: demographic characteristics, market changes, technological advancements, and social and political pressures. (2) Internal forces may be of two types: employee problems and managers' behavior.
- Four areas in which change is most apt to be needed are people, technology, structure, and strategy. (1) People changes may require changes in perceptions, attitudes, performance, or skills. (2) Technology is any machine or process that enables an organization to gain a competitive advantage in changing materials used to produce a finished product. (3) Changing structure may happen when one organization acquires another. (4) Changing strategy may occur because of changes in the marketplace.

10.2 The Threat of Change: Managing Employee Fear & Resistance

- The degree to which employees feel threatened by change depends on whether the change is adaptive, innovative, or radically innovative. Adaptive change, the least threatening, is reintroduction of a familiar practice. Innovative change is the introduction of a practice that is new to the organization. Radically innovative change, the most threatening, involves introducing a practice that is new to the industry.
- Kurt Lewin's change model has three stages—unfreezing, changing, and refreezing—to explain how to initiate, manage, and stabilize planned change. (1) In the unfreezing stage, managers try to instill in employees the motivation to change. One technique used is benchmarking, a process by which a company compares its performance with that of high-performing organizations. (2) In the changing stage, employees need to be given the tools for change, such as new information. (3) In the refreezing stage, employees need to be helped to integrate the changed attitudes and behavior into their normal behavior.
- In a model corresponding with Lewin's, John Kotter's suggests an organization needs to follow eight steps to avoid the eight common errors senior management usually commits. The first four represent unfreezing: establish a sense of urgency, create the guiding coalition, develop a vision and strategy, and communicate the change vision. The next three steps represent the changing stage: empower broad-based action, generate short-term wins, and consolidate gains and produce more change. The last step, corresponding to refreezing, is to anchor new approaches in the organization's culture.

10.3 Organization Development: What It Is, What It Can Do

- 
Organizational development (OD) is a set of techniques for implementing planned change to make people and organizations more effective. Often OD is put into practice by a change agent, a consultant with a background in behavioral sciences who can be a catalyst in helping organizations deal with old problems in new ways. OD can be used to manage conflict, revitalize organizations, and adapt to mergers.
- OD has three identifying characteristics: it aims for fundamental change; it is process-oriented, not content-oriented; and it is value-loaded, preferring cooperation over conflict. The OD process follows a three-step process: (1) Diagnosis attempts to ascertain the problem. (2) Intervention is the attempt to correct the diagnosed problems. (3) Evaluation attempts to find out how well the intervention worked.
- Four factors that make OD work successfully are (1) multiple interventions are used; (2) top managers give the OD program their support; (3) goals are geared to both short- and long-term results; and (4) OD is affected by culture.

10.4 Promoting Innovation within the Organization

- Innovations may be a product innovation or a process innovation. A product innovation is a change in the appearance or performance of a product or service or the creation of a new one. A process innovation is a change in the way a product or service is conceived, manufactured, or disseminated. Innovations may also be an incremental innovation or a radical innovation. An incremental innovation is the creation of a product, service, or technology that modifies an existing one. A radical innovation is the creation of a product, service, or technology that replaces an existing one.
- Four characteristics of innovation are that (1) it is an uncertain business; (2) people closest to the innovation know the most about it, at least initially; (3) it may be controversial; and (4) it can be complex because it may cross organizational boundaries.
- Innovation doesn't happen as a matter of course. Three ways to make it happen are to provide the right organizational culture, so that it is viewed as a benefit rather than as a boondoggle; to provide the resources; and to provide the rewards, so that experimentation is reinforced in ways that matter. Three steps for fostering innovation are as follows. (1) Recognize problems and opportunities and devise solutions. (2) Gain allies by communicating your vision. (3) Overcome employee resistance and empower and reward them to achieve progress.

Management in Action

PepsiCo Continually Innovates Its Products

Excerpted from Diane Brady, "Pepsi's Thousand and One Noshes," Business Week, *June 14, 2004, pp. 54, 56.*

BusinessWeek

Few companies seem as pained by the thought of missing a customer as PepsiCo. Every year, the food and beverage giant adds more than 200 product variations to its vast global portfolio—which ranges from Quaker Soy Crisps to Gatorade Xtremo Thirst Quencher. Steven S. Reinemund, chairman and chief executive officer, believes that constant quest for change, more than even quality and value, is what has driven the Purchase (N.Y.) company to consistent double-digit earnings growth. As Reinemund has put it: "Innovation is what consumers are looking for, particularly in the small, routine things of their life."

What distinguishes PepsiCo from some competitors is an intense lack of sentimentality about its principal brands. Sure, it continues to hawk core products such as Pepsi Cola and Lay's potato chips, adding flavors and doing targeted marketing campaigns every year to jazz up consumer interest. But Reinemund & Co. seem far more obsessed with understanding and catering to changing tastes than in trying to shape them. To capitalize on the growing market for New Age herbally enhanced beverages, for example, the company acquired SoBe Beverages for $370 million in 2001. Since then, the company has extended the brand with such offerings as the energy drink SoBe No Fear, SoBe Synergy targeted at the school-aged market with 50% juice, and SoBe Fuerte, aimed at the Hispanic market.

PepsiCo's huge Frito-Lay division, which dominates 60% of the U.S. chip market and had $9.1 billion in revenues last year, has been equally adept at coming up with products to reflect changing tastes and demographics. Even amid the low-carb craze, it racked up 4% volume growth last year, thanks to new flavors and healthier ingredients. "They have an exceptional ability to face the facts and adapt products to them," says UBS Investment Bank analyst Caroline Levy. Such innovation is a big reason PepsiCo sales jumped 7% last year, to $27 billion, while earnings grew 19%, to $3.6 billion—numbers that rated the No. 44 spot on *Business Week*'s list of the 50 best-performing large public companies.

Just like its parent, Frito-Lay is fanatical about attempting to find opportunity in peril. Worried about obesity? Frito-Lay has come up with several low-fat chips and led the pack in removing all trans fats from its brands, which include Lay's, Ruffles, and Doritos. Looking for healthier snacks? Frito introduced a line of natural and organic chips in 2003, and in June it rolls out low-carb Doritos, Cheetos, and Tostitos. Frito-Lay also caters to ethnic and geographic markets—even hawking a Tastes of Canada chip north of the border, with flavors such as pizza or sea salt and pepper.

In one of its more daring moves, the company reached south of the border two years ago to bring in four popular brands from its $1 billion Mexican subsidiary, Sabritas. The motive was to win over the foreign-born segment of the 46 million-strong Hispanic market that wasn't warming to Latin-flavored versions of Lay's and Doritos chips. . . .

The gamble paid off. Despite no advertising and minimal distribution, U.S. sales of Sabritas brands are expected to exceed $100 million this year—double what they generated in 2002. Sabritas can now be found in markets covering roughly one-third of the U.S. population, up from 10% coverage two years ago. . . .

It's the kind of push that has kept PepsiCo from sinking into a slow-growth pit as its core soda pop and potato chip products age. And the company's continual product and marketing reincarnations seem to have given it a sixth sense for tapping new markets. "They have been early to see trends and aggressive in targeting them," says Robert van Brugge of Sanford C. Bernstein & Co. That means an ever-growing product family that ranges from Wow! low-fat chips to Propel Fitness Water, a flavored vitamin-enhanced water that surpassed $100 million in sales in the year after it launched in 2002.

By defining its mission as serving the customer rather than protecting its venerable brands, PepsiCo is hoping to stave off a stagnant middle age. And if it has to tap its international portfolio for ideas or snap up products in hot new niches to do so, it will. There's nothing more American, after all, than giving consumers what they want.

For Discussion

1. Would you say Steven Reinemund's approach represented reactive change or proactive change? Explain.
2. Using Figure 10.1, identify the external and internal forces of change at PepsiCo.
3. Do you see Lewin's change model exemplified in Reinemund's approach to change? Explain.
4. How does PepsiCo innovate? Discuss.
5. How does the case show the interrelationship among strategy, diversity, and innovation? Explain.

Self-Assessment

How Adaptable Am I?*

Objectives

To assess your adaptability.

To examine how being adaptable can help you cope with organizational change.

Introduction

Ultimately all organizational change passes through an organization's people. People who adapt more easily are better suited to cope with organizational changes and so they clearly are important assets to any organization. The purpose of this exercise is to determine your adaptability.

Instructions

Read the following statements. Using the scale provided, circle the number that indicates the extent to which you agree or disagree with each statement:

1 = strongly disagree
2 = disagree
3 = neither agree nor disagree
4 = agree
5 = strongly agree

1. In emergency situations, I react with clear, focused thinking and maintain emotional control in order to step up to the necessary actions.	1	2	3	4	5
2. In stressful circumstances, I don't overreact to unexpected news. I keep calm, focused, and manage frustration well.	1	2	3	4	5
3. I solve problems creatively by turning them inside out and upside down looking for new approaches to solving them that others may have missed.	1	2	3	4	5
4. I easily change gears in response to uncertain or unexpected events, effectively adjusting my priorities, plans, goals, and actions.	1	2	3	4	5
5. I enjoy learning new ways to do my work and I do what is necessary to keep my knowledge and skills current.	1	2	3	4	5

	1	2	3	4	5
6. I adjust easily to changes in my workplace by participating in assignments or training that prepares me for these changes.	1	2	3	4	5
7. I am flexible and open-minded with others. I listen and consider others' viewpoints, adjusting my own when necessary.	1	2	3	4	5
8. I am open to both negative and positive feedback. I work well in teams.	1	2	3	4	5
9. I take action to learn and understand the values of other groups, organizations, or cultures. I adjust my own behavior to show respect for different customs.	1	2	3	4	5
10. I adjust easily to differing environmental states such as extreme heat, humidity, cold, or dirtiness.	1	2	3	4	5
11. I frequently push myself to complete strenuous or demanding tasks.	1	2	3	4	5
Total	______				

Interpretation

When you are done, add up your responses to get your total score to see how adaptable you are. Arbitrary norms for adaptability:

11–24 = Low adaptability

25–39 = Moderate adaptability

40–55 = High adaptability

Questions for Discussion

1. Were you surprised by your results? Why or why not?
2. Look at the areas where your score was the lowest. What are some skills you can work on or gain to increase your adaptability? Describe and explain.
3. What are some ways being adaptable can improve the way you handle change? Discuss.

*Adapted from S. Arad, M. A. Donovan, K. E. Plamondon, and E. D. Pulakos, "Adaptability in the Workplace: Development of Taxonomy of Adaptive Performance," *Journal of Applied Psychology,* August 2000, pp. 612–624.

Group Exercise

Understanding Resistance to Change*

Objectives

To examine reasons why employees resist change.

To practice using ways to overcome resistance to change.

Introduction

Managers who need to implement planned change find that success depends on how much their employees accept the change. If errors are made in the ways changes are introduced, employee resistance is likely to increase. The purpose of this exercise is to examine ways managers can overcome employee resistance to change.

Instructions

Break into groups of five to six people. Read the following case of the Canadian Furniture Corp. (CFC). Discuss the case with your group and brainstorm, using Lewin's Change Model, and Kotter's Eight Steps for Organizational Change, to find errors in the way managers at CFC implemented change. After your group has identified the errors, compare your notes with other groups. As a class, discuss some managerial strategies that would prevent errors such as the ones at CFC from occurring.

The Case

The Canadian Furniture Corp. is a manufacturer of household furniture located in southern Ontario. It has been in business since the early 1950s and has always experienced steady growth, even in periods of economic downturn. . . . At present, CFC has an assembly plant in 8 of the

10 Canadian provinces. Because of Canada's geography, the unique provincial differences in consumer preferences, and early transportation problems, CFC has traditionally given local assembly plants considerable freedom of action in all aspects of the business. This is especially true in purchasing.

The business was purchased by Centrex, a manufacturer of office furniture headquartered in Toronto, that wanted to expand into household furniture. Shortly after the takeover, Mr. Benton, president of Centrex, decided that CFC's operations should be brought more in line with those of Centrex. These included introducing a new position at CFC—Vice President of Purchasing. To fill this position, Benton selected John Speedman, who had been with Centrex for seven years. Benton assured Speedman that he had authority to make whatever changes he wanted, to bring the CFC operations into line with Centrex. . . . In addition, Benton assigned Bob Hestent as Speedman's assistant. Hestent had been with CFC purchasing group since 1984 and was familiar with the assembly plant managers. The new Purchasing Department was to be located at CFC's Toronto home office.

Speedman decided there was no reason to delay efforts to restructure CFC. As far as he was concerned, this was what Benton and the board of directors at Centrex wanted and that's what they would get. His first move was to centralize the purchasing practices of CFC. All assembly plant purchases over $50,000 would be made through the Toronto office. Speedman thought the coordination of assembly plant purchases would ensure a standard quality of furniture and allow the company to obtain quantity discounts when purchasing high-demand items. He presented his plan to Benton and the Board, and they gave it their complete backing.

At the time Speedman enacted his changes, CFC experienced a major increase in demand for furniture. This was likely to have a major impact on future purchases. Nevertheless, Speedman prepared this letter to be sent to assembly plant managers in order to explain his position:

Dear ___________:

The home office has recently authorized a change in the way CFC obtains its resources. Starting immediately, all purchases over $50,000 will be sent first to my office for approval. This should be done well before the material is actually needed so that quantity purchases can be made where possible. I am sure that you will agree that such a move will improve the quality of CFC's product and help CFC save money. By accomplishing both these objectives, CFC will be better able to compete in what appears to be a very aggressive industry.

Sincerely yours,

(signed) John Speedman

Before mailing the letters, Speedman asked Hestent (his assistant) for his opinion. Hestent thought the letter was good and clearly made its point. However, he suggested that Speedman first meet with some of the assembly plant managers. Speedman was quick to say no because he was too busy, and, as Hestent said, the letter was clear and to the point. There would be no wasteful field trips.

In the weeks that followed, Speedman's office received positive replies from all assembly plant managers. The following is one such response:

Dear Mr. Speedman:

In response to your letter of the 13th, I see no problems in meeting your request. We at South Shore will do our best to inform you of all purchases over $50,000 and will give you the required lead time.

Although the anticipated increase in sales did occur over the next four months and reports from the field indicated a high level of activity, Speedman's office did not receive purchase information from the assembly plant managers.

Questions for Discussion

1. Which steps in Lewin's Change Model did Speedman ignore? Describe and explain.
2. How could Speedman have used these steps to overcome the employees' resistance to change? Discuss in detail.
3. How could Speedman have used Kotter's eight steps to more successfully implement change? Explain.
4. Using Table 10.1 and Figure 10.2 as a guide, describe how Speedman could have used organizational development to implement change. Explain in detail.

*Excerpted from L. W. Mealia and G. P. Latham, "CFC Case Analysis: Understanding Resistance to Change," *Skills for Managerial Success: Theory, Experience, and Practice* (Burr Ridge, IL: Irwin, 1996), pp. 486–488.

Ethical Dilemma

Should Drug Salespeople Be Allowed to Give Doctors Free Drug Samples and Gifts?

Excerpted from D. Lavoie, "Drug Firm Sales Reps Go on Trial," San Francisco Chronicle, *April 13, 2004, pp. C1, C5.*

For years, they've been the standard freebies that drug companies have offered in an attempt to get doctors to prescribe their medications: expensive dinners, golf outings, trips to ski resorts and drug samples. . . .

This week, 11 current and former sales executives from TAP Pharmaceutical Products—a leading drug company—go on trial, accused of conspiring to pay kickbacks to doctors, hospitals, and other customers. The charges focus on efforts to get doctors to prescribe Lupron, the company's prostate cancer drug, as well as Prevacid, its heartburn drug. . . .

Doctors approached by the 11 TAP employees were offered gifts including trips to swanky golf and ski resorts and "educational grants," used to pay for cocktail parties, office Christmas parties and travel, according to prosecutors. Defense lawyers say the sales executives were simply doing their jobs. "As far as I can tell, this is the first time there has ever been a prosecution under the health care statute in which salespeople are being charged with a crime [for things] that they thought were completely within their job descriptions," says Roal Martine, a Chicago attorney who represents Carey Smith, a former TAP executive.

Solving the Dilemma

What is your feeling about drug salespeople giving doctors free drug samples and trips and/or "educational grants" as a way to get doctors to prescribe their products?

1. There is nothing wrong with this practice. Giving drug samples and gifts is simply another form of advertising.
2. Although this practice amounts to bribery, the doctors should not take the gifts. But I think it is all right for doctors to take only free drug samples. Doctors who take trips and "educational grants" for cocktail parties should be punished.
3. The salespeople and TAP should be punished. This practice drives up the costs of drugs, which ultimately are passed along to consumers.
4. Because guidelines established by the American Medical Association are vague, the TAP employees should not be punished. We need clear guidelines that include real penalties for not following them.

Video Case

Louisville Slugger

Hillerich & Bradsby (H&B) is best known for making the Louisville Slugger, the first name in wooden bats. The company now produces aluminum bats as well as golf, hockey, and other sporting good products. But the privately held family company founded in 1857 eventually had to address substantial issues requiring difficult organizational changes.

Coming up with creative and innovative ideas wasn't the problem. Product users, customers, and sales reps provide a wealth of ideas. H&B's role is to take those ideas and synthesize them into forms useful for customers. The company's internal systems, however, weren't running smoothly. Existing computer systems didn't provide up-to-date access to important company information. Departments weren't communicating with one another. Inventory updating was woefully inadequate. Delivery personnel would attempt to ship inventory that wasn't ready or prepare to ship hundreds of items when only dozens were needed. On-time and complete shipping occurred about 30% of the time. Simple communications between production, management, and sales personnel took weeks to complete.

After listening to numerous proposals, H&B decided on an enterprise resource planning system (ERP) and contracted with SAP, a German business solutions software firm. ERP systems are designed to simplify all of the processes of the firm by storing all information in a centralized database and automatically updating information in each stage of the production process. However, even with ample warning from H&B's information systems personnel, CEO John Hillerich underestimated the difficulty of the transition process by "at least ten or a hundred fold." Several years into the implementation process, top management was still debating whether or not to continue. Even though the new ERP system was designed with flexibility in mind, there was an inevitable period of trial and error while the software was customized to the needs of H&B. Implementation can take years, and the transition period is difficult. Employees are forced to abandon the old ways and learn new methods. Productivity sinks as employees struggle to meet demand while operating a completely foreign system. Employee morale slumped during the transition period, as longtime workers struggled to change the way they operated. In fact, several employees chose to retire rather than learn the new system.

But according to H&B top managers, the cost of implementation is worth the savings down the road. Although it took five years before H&B saw quantifiable cost savings from their new ERP system, an estimated 80% of employees are now happy dealing with the new system. Importantly, the company now ships 85% of its orders on time and complete, and customer satisfaction is high. Labor costs were reduced, and employees are free to work more productively.

Discussion Questions

1. Managers have to deal with two types of change: reactive and proactive. Define each of these types. Which type of change occurred at H&B?
2. The forces for change that originate outside the organization include demographic characteristics, market changes, technological advancements, and social and political pressures. Which of these forces is operating at H&B?
3. The degree to which employees feel threatened by change depends on whether the change is adaptive, innovative, or radically innovative. Define each of these levels of change. Which type of change is evident at H&B? Use evidence from the video to support your answer.

chapter 11

Managing Individual Differences & Behavior

MAJOR QUESTIONS YOU SHOULD BE ABLE TO ANSWER

11.1 Values, Attitudes, & Behavior

Major Question: How do the hidden aspects of individuals—their values and attitudes—affect employee behavior?

11.2 Work-Related Attitudes & Behavior Managers Need to Deal With

Major Question: Is it important for managers to pay attention to employee attitudes?

11.3 Personality & Individual Behavior

Major Question: In the hiring process, do employers care about one's personality and individual traits?

11.4 Perception & Individual Behavior

Major Question: What are the distortions in perception that can cloud one's judgment?

11.5 Understanding Stress & Individual Behavior

Major Question: What causes workplace stress, and how can it be reduced?

the manager's toolbox

Leading Younger Workers in Attaining Job Satisfaction

The early 2000s recession was not a good time to be Generation Xers, the 25-to-34-year-olds born roughly 1965–1977, whose unemployment rate was even higher than that for those ages 45 and older.[1] But for Gen Yers, those born 1978–1998, the prospects are considerably brighter. This is because by 2010, the Bureau of Labor Statistics predicts, the United States will have 8 million more jobs than there are workers to do them. This means companies will not only have to do a better job of retaining mature workers. They will also have to learn how to keep younger workers.[2]

"Younger employees want success now, and on their own terms, but paying dues is often a foreign concept. They are less trusting of organizations, institutions, and authority in general."

So writes one management consultant about younger workers. Is it possible for them to find satisfaction in the workplace?

A survey by the Gallup Organization suggests that supposedly discontented twentysomethings may fit into the workplace better than employers previously thought. But managers need to know how to manage for individual and generational differences.[3]

Young people today are much more apt to have had both parents working, or to come from a single-parent family, and are more likely to have been latch-key kids compared to those in previous generations. As a result, they have been left alone to make their own decisions and have had to assume greater responsibility. They are also used to television as entertainment and to a faster pace of life. In the workplace, these translate into a skepticism about rules, policies, and procedures; a requirement for more autonomy; and a need for constant stimulation.[4]

If you're going to be a leader, what should you know about managing this group? Following are some suggestions, some of which may benefit employees of all ages.[5]

- **Make training an obsession:** Just waiting to move up the organizational ladder is no longer good enough. Employer-sponsored training and education is a major attraction for young workers. In the Gallup survey, 84% of those who received at least six days of training within the previous year said they were satisfied. (Only 70% of those who received no training said they were satisfied.) Fifty-eight percent of workers 32 years old and younger said training was useful in preparing them for higher-level jobs. (Among those older, only 42% had the same opinion.)
- **Allow them independent learning while creating bonds with mentors:** The best kind of training for younger workers is not classroom training but forms of independent learning such as internships, work-study programs, and independent study. At the same time, they should be given the chance to create long-term bonds with teaching managers and mentors.
- **Teach people by showing them their results:** Younger workers need to see the daily tangible results of their work. Managers can help by carving a job up into bite-size chunks—as in dividing a sales job into categories such as making cold calls, making second-round calls, meeting in person with hot leads, and so on. A daily checklist helps workers see their results.
- **Provide frequent feedback:** Six-month and 12-month reviews are not as effective with young workers. More important is frequent, timely, and specific feedback each time a task is completed, with concrete suggestions for improvement.
- **Provide frequent rewards for great performance:** Incentives need not always be financial. Such rewards as praise, flex time, telecommuting, and extra responsibility are also recommended. Twentysomethings are likely to want to acquire learning and training opportunities that will make them more marketable, since they have decided to rely on their own abilities, rather than the organization, for security.

forecast

What's Ahead in This Chapter

This first of five chapters on leadership discusses how to manage for individual differences and behaviors. We describe values, attitudes, and behavior; personality dimensions and traits; and specific work-related attitudes and behaviors managers need to be aware of. We next discuss distortions in perception, which can affect managerial judgment. Finally, we consider what stress does to individuals.

major question

How do the hidden aspects of individuals—their values and attitudes—affect employee behavior?

The Big Picture

Organizational behavior (OB) considers how to better understand and manage people at work. In this section, we discuss individual values and attitudes and how they affect people's actions and judgments.

If you look at a company's annual report or at a brochure from its corporate communications department, you are apt to be given a picture of its *formal aspects*: Goals. Policies. Hierarchy. Structure.

Could you exert effective leadership—the subject of this and the next four chapters—if the formal aspects were all you knew about the company? What about the *informal aspects*? Values. Attitudes. Personalities. Perceptions. Conflicts. Culture. Clearly, you need to know about these hidden, "messy" characteristics as well. *(See Figure 11.1.)*

FIGURE 11.1
Formal and informal aspects of an organization

Organizational Behavior: Trying to Explain & Predict Workplace Behavior

The informal aspects are the focus of the interdisciplinary field known as ***organizational behavior (OB),*** **which is dedicated to better understanding and management of people at work.** In particular, OB tries to help managers not only *explain* workplace behavior but also to *predict* it, so that they can better lead and motivate their employees to perform productively. OB looks at two areas:

- **Individual behavior:** This is the subject of this chapter. We discuss such individual attributes as values, attitudes, personality, perception, and learning.
- **Group behavior:** This is the subject of later chapters, particularly Chapter 13, where we discuss norms, roles, and teams.

Let us begin by considering individual values, attitudes, and behavior.

Values: What Are Your Consistent Beliefs & Feelings about *All* Things?

Values **are abstract ideals that guide one's thinking and behavior across all situations.**[6] Lifelong behavior patterns are dictated by values that are fairly well set by the time people are in their early teens. After that, however, one's values can be reshaped by significant life-altering events, such as having a child, undergoing a business failure, or surviving the death of a loved one, a war, or a serious health threat.

From a manager's point of view, it's helpful to know that values are those concepts, principles, things, people, or activities for which a person is willing to work hard—even make sacrifices for. Compensation, recognition, and status are common values in the workplace.[7] Younger people, however, may hold the value that it's best to have balance between work and life. According to the Families and Work Institute, 60% of men and women under the age of 25 with children are willing to make significant sacrifices in money and career to spend more time with their families.[8] With these employees, it helps managers to know there are limits to the inducements they can offer.

Attitudes: What Are Your Consistent Beliefs & Feelings about *Specific* Things?

Values are abstract ideals—global beliefs and feelings—that are directed toward all objects, people, or events.[9] Values tend to be consistent both over time and over related situations. By contrast, attitudes are beliefs and feelings that are directed toward *specific* objects, people, or events. More formally, an ***attitude*** **is defined as a learned predisposition toward a given object.**[10]

Example: If you dislike your present job, will you be happier if you change to a different job? Not necessarily. It depends on your attitude. In one study, researchers found that the attitudes of 5,000 middle-aged male employees toward their jobs were very stable over a five-year period. Men with positive attitudes tended to stay positive, those with negative attitudes tended to stay negative. More revealingly, even those who changed jobs or occupations generally expressed the same attitudes they had previously.[11]

The Three Components of Attitudes: Affective, Cognitive, & Behavioral

Attitudes have three components.[12] *(See Table 11.1.)*

TABLE 11.1
Examples of the three components of attitudes

Affective	"I hate people who talk on cellphones in restaurants." "I hate putting on a suit for work." "I really like working from home." "I like commuting by train because I have time to myself." "I don't like working in office cubicles because they don't have doors and so there's no privacy."
Cognitive	"I can't appoint Herschel because creative people don't make good administrators." "The tallest building in the world is in Chicago." (Actually, it's in Kuala Lumpur.)
Behavioral	"I intend to fill out my expense report tomorrow." "I'm going to turn over a new leaf at New Year's and stop eating junk food." "I'm going to try to avoid John because he's a Democrat." "I'm never going to talk to George because he's a Republican."

- **The affective component—"I feel": The *affective component of an attitude* consists of the feelings or emotions one has about a situation.**
- **The cognitive component—"I believe": The *cognitive component of an attitude* consists of the beliefs and knowledge one has about a situation.**
- **The behavioral component—"I intend": The *behavioral component of an attitude,* also known as the *intentional component,* refers to how one intends or expects to behave toward a situation.**

All three components are often manifested at any given time. For example, if you call a corporation and get one of those telephone-tree menus ("For customer service, press 1 . . .") that never seems to connect you to a human being, you might be so irritated that you would say:

"I hate being given the run-around." [*affective component—your feelings*]

"That company doesn't know how to take care of customers." [*cognitive component—your perceptions*]

"I'll never call them again." [*behavioral component—your intentions*]

major question **Is it important for managers to pay attention to employee attitudes?**

The Big Picture

Attitudes are important because they affect behavior. Managers need to be alert to work-related attitudes having to do with job satisfaction, job involvement, and organizational commitment. Among the types of employee behavior they should attend to are their on-the-job performance and productivity as well as their absenteeism and turnover.

"Keep the employees happy."

It's true that attitudes are important, the reason being that *attitudes affect behavior*. But is keeping employees happy all that managers need to know to get results? We discuss motivation for performance in the next chapter. Here let us consider what managers need to know about work-related attitudes and behaviors.

Work-Related Attitudes: Job Satisfaction, Job Involvement, & Organizational Commitment

Employees will gripe about almost anything. About working in cubicles instead of offices. About not having enough help. About the mediocre cafeteria food. About managers "who don't know anything." They may also say some good things. About the great retirement plan. About flex time. About a product beating competing products. About how cool Manager X is.

Three types of attitudes managers are particularly interested in are (1) *job satisfaction,* (2) *job involvement,* and (3) *organizational commitment.*

1 Job Satisfaction: How Much Do You Like or Dislike Your Job?

***Job satisfaction* is the extent to which you feel positively or negatively about various aspects of your work.** Most people don't like everything about their jobs. Their overall satisfaction depends on how they feel about several components, such as *work, pay, promotions, coworkers,* and *supervision.*[16] Among the key correlates of job satisfaction are stronger motivation, job involvement, organizational commitment, and life satisfaction and less absenteeism, tardiness, turnover, and perceived stress.[17] Job performance seems to be positively correlated with job satisfaction.[18]

2 Job Involvement: How Much Do You Identify with Your Work?

***Job involvement* is the extent to which you identify or are personally involved with your job.** Many people, of course, work simply to put bread on the table; they have no interest in excelling at their jobs. More fortunate are those who actively participate in their jobs and consider their work performance important to their self-worth.

Analysis of nearly 28,000 individuals from 87 different studies demonstrates that job involvement is moderately correlated with job satisfaction.[19] Thus, managers are encouraged to foster satisfying work environments to fuel employees' job involvement.[20]

3 Organizational Commitment

***Organizational commitment* reflects the extent to which an employee identifies with an organization and is committed to its goals.** Research shows a strong relationship between organizational commitment and job satisfaction.[21] Thus, managers are advised to increase job satisfaction to elicit higher levels of commitment. In turn, higher commitment can facilitate higher performance.[22]

Important Workplace Behaviors

Why, as a manager, do you need to learn how to manage individual differences? The answer, as you might expect, is so that you can influence employees to do their best work. Among the types of behavior are (1) performance and productivity and (2) absenteeism and turnover.

Evaluating Behavior When Employees Are Working: Performance & Productivity

Every job has certain expectations, but in some jobs performance and productivity are easier to define than in others. How many contacts should a telemarketing sales rep make in a day? How many sales should he or she close? Often a job of this nature will have a history of accomplishments (from what previous job holders have attained) so that it is possible to quantify performance behavior.

However, an advertising agency account executive handling major clients such as a carmaker or a beverage manufacturer may go months before landing this kind of big account. Or a researcher in a pharmaceutical company may take years to develop a promising new prescription drug.

In short, the method of evaluating performance must match the job being done.

Evaluating Behavior When Employees Are Not Working: Absenteeism & Turnover

Should you be suspicious of every instance of ***absenteeism* —when an employee doesn't show up for work?** Of course, some absences—illness, death in the family, or jury duty, for example—are legitimate. Such no-show behavior is to be expected from time to time. However, absenteeism is related to job dissatisfaction.[23]

You need to make allowances for the employee who is on call all the time, such as a computer network administrator who has to wear a pager and be responsible for keeping the network going in off-hours. Or for a lawyer who puts in evenings and weekends after office hours in order to prepare for trial. Such individuals may be given the flexibility to take "comp time" (compensatory time off) whenever their workload eases.

Absenteeism may be a precursor to ***turnover,* when employees leave their jobs.** Every organization experiences some turnover, as employees leave for reasons of family, better job prospects, or retirement. However, except in low-skill industries, a continual revolving door of new employees is usually not a good sign, since replacement and training is expensive.[24] For instance, one study found the direct and indirect costs of recruiting and training a new mid-level manager—along with lost business to competitors, lost technical knowledge, decreased morale among remaining employees, and the like—came to $64,000.[25] Another study found it costs nearly $108,000 to replace a key worker or a manager.[26] ◆

Performance monitors. These British Airways customer service reps are being monitored by software that keeps track not only of ticket sales and customer-complaint resolutions but also of amount of time spent on breaks and personal phone calls. In tracking employee effectiveness, the technology can count incentive dollars tied to performance and immediately direct them into their nearest paychecks. Do you think these incentive calculators are justified or do you think they intrude too much on employee privacy?

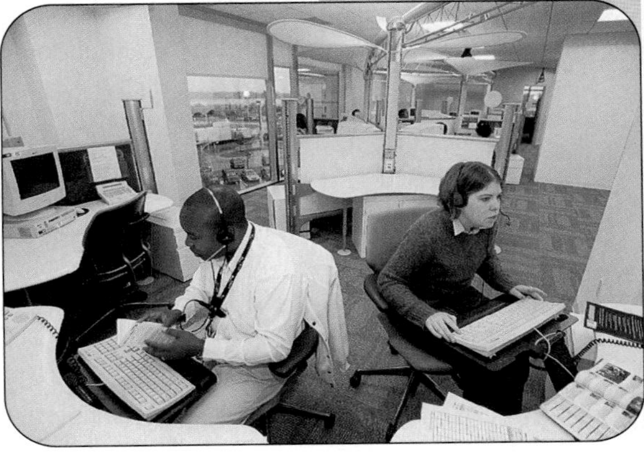

major question

In the hiring process, do employers care about one's personality and individual traits?

The Big Picture

Personality consists of stable psychological and behavioral attributes that give you your identity. We describe five personality dimensions and four personality traits that managers need to be aware of to understand workplace behavior.

How would you describe yourself? Are you outgoing? aggressive? sociable? tense? passive? lazy? quiet? Whatever the combination of traits, which result from the interaction of your genes and your environment, they constitute your personality.

More formally, ***personality*** **consists of the stable psychological traits and behavioral attributes that give a person his or her identity.**[27] As a manager, you need to understand personality attributes because they affect how people perceive and act within the organization.

The Big Five Personality Dimensions

In recent years, the many personality dimensions have been distilled into a list of factors known as the Big Five.[28] **The *Big Five personality dimensions* are (1) extroversion, (2) agreeableness, (3) conscientiousness, (4) emotional stability, and (5) openness to experience.**

- **Extroversion:** How outgoing, talkative, sociable, and assertive a person is.
- **Agreeableness:** How trusting, good-natured, cooperative, and soft-hearted one is.
- **Conscientiousness:** How dependable, responsible, achievement-oriented, and persistent one is.
- **Emotional stability:** How relaxed, secure, and unworried one is.
- **Openness to experience:** How intellectual, imaginative, curious, and broad-minded one is.

Standardized personality tests are used to score people on each dimension to draw a person's personality profile that is supposedly as unique as his or her fingerprints. For example, if you scored low on the first trait, extroversion, you would presumably be prone to shy and withdrawn behavior. If you scored low on emotional stability, you supposedly would be nervous, tense, angry, and worried.

Assertive and sociable. Does it take a certain kind of personality to be a good door-to-door salesperson? Have you ever known people who were quiet, unassuming, even shy but who were nevertheless very persistent and persuasive—that is, good salespeople?

Do Personality Tests Work for the Workplace?

As a manager, you would want to know if the Big Five model in particular and personality testing in general can help predict behavior in the workplace. Is a personality test helpful in predicting a match between personality and job performance? Two findings:

- **Extroversion—the outgoing personality:** As might be expected, extroversion (an outgoing personality) has been associated with success for managers and salespeople. Also, extroversion is a stronger predictor of job performance than agreeableness, across all professions, according to researchers. "It appears that being courteous, trusting, straightforward, and soft-hearted [that is, agreeableness] has a smaller impact on job performance," conclude the researchers, "than being talkative, active, and assertive [that is, extroversion]."[29]

- **Conscientiousness—the dependable personality:** Conscientiousness (strong work ethic) has been found to have the strongest positive correlation with job performance and training performance. According to researchers, "those individuals who exhibit traits associated with a strong sense of purpose, obligation, and persistence generally perform better than those who do not."[30]

The table below presents tips to help managers avoid abuses and discrimination lawsuits when using personality and psychological testing for employment decisions.[31] *(See Table 11.3.)*

TABLE 11.3
Cautions about using personality tests in the workplace

• ***Use professionals:*** Rely on reputable, licensed psychologists for selecting and overseeing the administration, scoring, and interpretation of personality and psychological tests. This is particularly important, since not every psychologist is expert at these kinds of tests.	• ***Don't hire on the basis of personality test results alone:*** Supplement any personality test data with information from reference checks, personal interviews, ability tests, and job performance records. Also avoid hiring people on the basis of specified personality profiles. As a case in point, there is no distinct "managerial personality."	• ***Be alert for gender, racial, and ethnic bias:*** Regularly assess any possible adverse impact of personality tests on the hiring of women and minorities. This is truly a matter of great importance, since you don't want to find your company (or yourself) embroiled in a lawsuit at some point downstream.	• ***Graphology tests don't work, but integrity tests do:*** Personality traits and aptitudes cannot be inferred from samples of people's penmanship, as proponents of graphology tests claim. However, dishonest job applicants can often be screened by integrity tests, since dishonest people are reportedly unable to fake conscientiousness, even on a paper-and-pencil test.

The Proactive Personality

A person who scores well on the Big Five dimension of conscientiousness is probably a good worker. He or she may also be a ***proactive personality,*** **someone who is more apt to take initiative and persevere to influence the environment.**[32] People of this sort identify opportunities and act on them, which makes them associated not only with success—individual, team, and organizational—but also with entrepreneurship.

Four Traits Important in Organizations

Four of the most important personality traits that managers need to be aware of to understand workplace behavior are (1) *locus of control,* (2) *self-efficacy,* (3) *self-esteem,* and (4) *self-monitoring.*

1 Locus of Control: "I Am/Am Not the Captain of My Fate"

As we discussed briefly in Chapter 3, ***locus of control*** **indicates how much people believe they control their fate through their own efforts.** If you have an *internal locus of control,* you believe you control your own destiny. If you have an *external locus of control,* you believe external forces control you.

Research shows internals and externals have important workplace differences. Internals exhibit less anxiety, greater work motivation, and stronger expectations that effort leads to performance. They also obtain higher salaries.[33]

These findings have two important implications for managers:

- **Different degrees of structure and compliance for each type:** Employees with internal locus of control will probably resist close managerial supervision. Hence, they should probably be placed in jobs requiring high initiative and lower compliance. By contrast, employees with external locus of control might do better in highly structured jobs requiring greater compliance.
- **Different reward systems for each type:** Since internals seem to have a greater belief that their actions have a direct effect on the consequences of that action, internals likely would prefer and respond more productively to incentives such as merit pay or sales commissions. (We discuss incentive compensation systems in Chapter 12.)

2 Self-Efficacy: "I Can/Can't Do This Task"

A related trait is ***self-efficacy,*** **belief in one's personal ability to do a task.** Unlike locus of control, this characteristic isn't about how much fate controls events (as in believing whether getting a high grade in a course is determined by you or by outside factors, such as the grade curve or trick questions). Rather, it's about your personal belief that you have what it takes to succeed. (Erik Weihenmayer, 35, is blind but also a self-described "unrealistic optimist," who was the first blind climber to scale Mt. Everest.[34])

Have you noticed that those who are confident about their ability tend to succeed, whereas those preoccupied with failure tend not to? Indeed, high expectations of self-efficacy have been linked with all kinds of positives: not only success in varied physical and mental tasks but also reduced anxiety and increased tolerance for pain.[35] One study found that the sales performance of life-insurance agents was much better among those with high self-efficacy.[36] Low self-efficacy is associated with ***learned helplessness,*** **the debilitating lack of faith in one's ability to control one's environment.**[37]

Among the implications for managers:

- **Job assignments:** Complex, challenging, and autonomous jobs tend to enhance people's perceptions of their self-efficacy. Boring, tedious jobs generally do the opposite.
- **Developing self-efficacy:** Self-efficacy is a quality that can be nurtured. Employees with low self-efficacy need lots of constructive pointers and positive feedback.[38] Goal difficulty needs to match individuals' perceived self-efficacy, but goals can be made more challenging as performance improves.[39] Small successes need to be rewarded. Employees' expectations can be improved through guided experiences, mentoring, and role modeling.[40]

3 Self-Esteem: "I Like/Dislike Myself"

How worthwhile, capable, and acceptable do you think you are? The answer to this question is an indicator of your ***self-esteem,*** **the extent to which people like or dislike themselves, their overall self-evaluation.**[41] Research offers some interesting insights about how high or low self-esteem can affect people and organizations.

- **People with high self-esteem:** Compared to people with low self-esteem, people with high self-esteem are more apt to handle failure better, to emphasize the positive, to take more risks, and to choose more unconventional jobs.[42] However, when faced with pressure situations, high-self-esteem people have been found to become egotistical and boastful.[43] Some have even been associated with aggressive and violent behavior.

- **People with low self-esteem:** Conversely, low-self-esteem people confronted with failure have been found to have focused on their weaknesses and to have had primarily negative thoughts. Moreover, they are more dependent on others and are more apt to be influenced by them and to be less likely to take independent positions.

Can self-esteem be improved? According to one study, "low self-esteem can be raised more by having the person think of *desirable* characteristics *possessed* rather than of undesirable characteristics from which he or she is free."[44] Some ways in which managers can build employee self-esteem are shown below. *(See Table 11.4.)*

TABLE 11.4
Some ways that managers can boost employee self-esteem

• Reinforce employees' positive attributes and skills.
• Provide positive feedback whenever possible.
• Break larger projects into smaller tasks and projects.
• Express confidence in employees' abilities to complete their tasks.
• Provide coaching whenever employees are seen to be struggling to complete tasks.

4 Self-Monitoring: "I'm Fairly Able/Unable to Adapt My Behavior to Others"

As you're rushing to an important meeting, you are stopped by a coworker, who starts to discuss a personal problem. You need to break away, so you glance at your watch.

(a) Does your coworker Get It? Seeing you look at your watch, he says, "Sorry, I see you're busy. Catch you later." Or (b) does he Not Get It? He keeps talking, until you say "I'm late for a big meeting" and start walking away.

The two scenarios show the difference between a high self-monitor and a low self-monitor. ***Self-monitoring*** **is the extent to which people are able to observe their own behavior and adapt it to external situations.** Of course, we would all like to think we are high in self-monitoring—able to regulate our "expressive self-presentation for the sake of desired public appearances," as some experts write, "and thus be highly responsive to social and interpersonal cues" of others.[45] But whereas some high self-monitors are criticized for being chameleons, always able to adapt their self-presentation to their surroundings, low self-monitors are often criticized for being on their own planet and insensitive to others. Instead, their behavior may reflect their own inner states, including their attitudes and feelings.

It might be expected that people in top management are more apt to be high self-monitors able to play different roles—even contradictory roles—to suit different situations. Research shows a positive relationship between high self-monitoring and career success. Among 139 MBA graduates who were tracked for five years, high self-monitors enjoyed more internal and external promotions than did their low self-monitoring classmates.[46] Other research has found that managerial success (in terms of speed of promotions) was tied to political savvy (knowing how to socialize, network, and engage in organizational politics).[47] ◆

major question

What are the distortions in perception that can cloud one's judgment?

The Big Picture

Perception, a four-step process, can be skewed by three types of distortion: selective perception, stereotyping, and the halo effect. We also consider the self-fulfilling prophecy and causal attribution, which can affect our judgment.

If you were a smoker, which warning on a cigarette pack would make you think more about quitting? "Smoking seriously harms you and others around you." A blunt "Smoking kills." Or a stark graphic image showing decaying teeth.

This is the kind of decision public health authorities in various countries are wrestling with. (And a Canadian Cancer Society study in 2000 found that 58% of smokers who saw graphic images thought twice about the health effects of smoking.[48]) These officials, in other words, are trying to decide how *perception* might influence behavior.

The Four Steps in the Perceptual Process

Perception **is the process of interpreting and understanding one's environment.** The process of perception is complex, but it can be boiled down to four steps. *(See Figure 11.2.)*

FIGURE 11.2
The four steps in the perceptual process

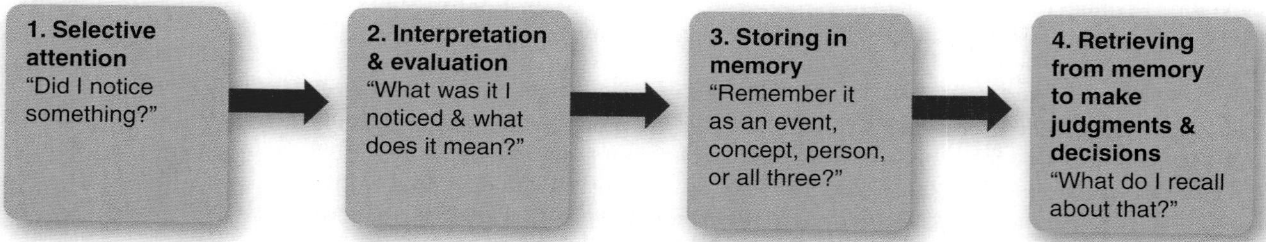
1. Selective attention
"Did I notice something?"
2. Interpretation & evaluation
"What was it I noticed & what does it mean?"
3. Storing in memory
"Remember it as an event, concept, person, or all three?"
4. Retrieving from memory to make judgments & decisions
"What do I recall about that?"

In this book, we are less concerned about the theoretical steps in perception than in how perception is distorted, since this has considerable bearing on the manager's judgment and job. In any one of the four stages of the perception process there is the possibility for misunderstandings or errors in judgment. Perceptual errors can lead to mistakes that can be damaging to yourself, other people, and your organization.

Three Distortions in Perception

Although there are other types of distortion in perception, we will describe the following: (1) *selective perception,* (2) *stereotyping,* and (3) the *halo effect.*

1 Selective Perception: "I Don't Want to Hear about That"

Are there topics that you find especially uncomfortable—your own death, say, or child molestation, or cheating in college—so that you tune out these subjects when people bring them up? For example, many people avoid making a will because they find it too awful to think about their future nonexistence. ***Selective perception*** **is the tendency to filter out information that is discomforting, that seems irrelevant, or that contradicts one's beliefs.**

One classic study found that when executives were asked to determine the key problem in a complex business case, they identified the problem as falling within their particular functional areas of work—they evidently filtered out information about other areas. That is, human resource managers said the principal problem was a people issue, marketing executives said it was a sales issue, and production people said it was a manufacturing issue.[49] This shows how managers can distort problem solving through selective perception.

Marilyn Merlot. Would you be apt to notice—to perceive—this bottle among all the others on a wine-shop shelf? The idea grew out of a home winemaking operation near St. Helena, Calif. The first production, in 1983, under the brand name "Maneater," was a wine labeled "Cannibal Sauvignon." As for the merlot ("mer-*loh*") red wine, what began as a light-hearted appeal to Marilyn Monroe fans is now seriously sought out by wine fanciers.

2 Stereotyping: "Those Sorts of People Are Pretty Much the Same"

If you're a tall African-American man, do people make remarks about basketball players? If you're of Irish descent, do people believe you drink a lot? If you're Jewish, do people think you're money-oriented? If you're a woman, do people think you're automatically nurturing? All these are stereotypes. ***Stereotyping*** **is the tendency to attribute to an individual the characteristics one believes are typical of the group to which that individual belongs.**[50]

Principal areas of stereotyping that should be of concern to you as a manager are (1) *sex-role stereotypes,* (2) *age stereotypes,* and (3) *race/ethnicity stereotypes.*

- **Sex-role stereotypes:** A *sex-role stereotype* is the belief that differing traits and abilities make males and females particularly well suited to different roles.

  A classic study found that women were viewed "as relatively less competent, less independent, less objective, and less logical than men; men are perceived as lacking interpersonal sensitivity, warmth, and expressiveness in comparison to women." Moreover, the study found, "stereotypically masculine traits are more often perceived to be desirable than are stereotypically feminine characteristics."[51]

  Although research shows that men and women do not differ in such a stereotypical manner, the stereotypes still persist.[52] And, unfortunately, promotional decisions may still be affected by sex-role stereotyping. A study of a multinational Fortune 500 company, for example, revealed that men received more favorable evaluations than women in spite of controlling for age, education, organizational tenure, salary grade, and type of job.[53]

- **Age stereotypes:** *Age stereotypes* tend to depict older workers as less involved in their work, less satisfied, less motivated, and less committed than younger workers. But in fact research shows that as employees' age increases, so does their job involvement and satisfaction, work motivation, and organizational commitment.[54]

  Stereotypes also depict older workers as being less productive; however, this is not borne out.[55] Finally, the stereotype that older workers have higher absenteeism is not supported by the research; if anything, managers should focus more attention on absenteeism among younger rather than older workers.[56]

- **Race/ethnicity stereotypes:** *Race/ethnicity stereotypes* don't bear repeating here, but it is noteworthy that there are not a lot of African-American, Hispanic, and Asian managers in the United States. For instance, the Labor Department estimates that women and minorities hold only 5% of senior-level positions—and the majority of those are held by women rather than minorities.[57]

Example

A Women-Friendly Workplace: The Plante & Moran Accounting Firm

Are women somehow motivated differently than men are? Does that explain why women's average pay is 77% of men's compensation today—or more like 44%, if we look at what the typical woman earns over much of her career?[58]

Outright discrimination may account for only about 10 percentage points of the pay gap.[59] The main problem is that most men and women work in largely gender-segregated occupations, with many women stuck in lower-paying jobs.[60] In addition, many family responsibilities typically fall more heavily on women than on men. Finally, while a great many women work just as hard as men, it may be that *most* women don't compete as hard as *most* men, according to Stanford business professor Charles A. O'Reilly III.[61] Indeed, suggests psychiatrist Anna Fels, women don't get the credit they deserve because they tend to deflect praise and understate their achievements.[62] Does this contribute to the stereotype about women being less competent to be managers?

The result in any event is that in most top jobs women are still in the minority (constituting only 15.7% of Fortune 500 corporate officers, for example, and 15.6% of lawyers who make partner). At Southfield, Michigan–based Plante & Moran, however, women constitute 19% of partners. Although only the 11th-largest accounting firm, P&M leads the 15 biggest firms in percentage of female partners. In a field in which human capital is particularly valued and expensive (it costs a year's salary to replace a $75,000 employee), this record has inspired better-known competitors, such as Deloitte & Touche, and KPMG, to be similarly innovative and aggressive in making the workplace women-friendly.

Plante & Moran employees are able to come and go as they please, so long as the work gets done. They also get four weeks of paid time off (five, after five years) and can buy two weeks more. They get a paid four-week sabbatical every seven years. Parents of either sex can get up to six months off for unpaid parental leave. Every mother-to-be is paired with an experienced parent to ease the transition into leave and then back to work.

And on the weekends during tax season before April 15 when CPAs everywhere are expected to work overtime, conference rooms are filled not just with accountants and IRS forms. Some are set aside for sleeping infants and toddlers playing with Fisher-Price toys.[63]

3 The Halo Effect: "One Trait Tells Me All I Need to Know"

Do you think physically attractive people have more desirable traits than unattractive people—that they are happier, kinder, more successful, more socially skilled, more sensitive, more interesting, independent, exciting, sexually warm, even smarter and nicer? All of these traits have been attributed to attractive people.[64] This situation is an example of the ***halo effect,*** **in which we form an impression of an individual based on a single trait.** (The phenomenon is also called the *horn-and-halo effect,* because not only can a single positive trait be generalized into an array of positive traits but the reverse is also true.)

As if we needed additional proof that life is unfair, it has been shown that attractive people generally are treated better than unattractive people. Teachers have higher expectations of them in terms of academic achievement.[65] Potential employers are more apt to view them favorably.[66] Attractive employees are generally paid higher salaries than unattractive ones are.[67] Clearly, however, if a manager fails to look at *all* an individual's traits, he or she has no right to complain if that employee doesn't work out.

Handsomely compensated. Attractive employees are generally paid better than unattractive ones are. Why do you think that is? Do you think it's inevitable?

The Self-Fulfilling Prophecy, or Pygmalion Effect

The *self-fulfilling prophecy,* also known as the *Pygmalion* ("pig-*mail*-yun") *effect,* describes the phenomenon in which people's expectations of themselves or others leads them to behave in ways that make those expectations come true.

Expectations are important. An example is a waiter who expects some poorly dressed customers to be stingy tippers, who therefore gives them poor service and so gets the result he or she expected—a much lower tip than usual. Research has shown that by raising managers' expectations for individuals performing a wide variety of tasks, higher levels of achievement and productivity can be achieved.[68] The lesson for you as a manager is that when you expect employees to perform badly, they probably will, and when you expect them to perform well, they probably will. (In the G. B. Shaw play *Pygmalion,* a speech coach bets he can get a lower-class girl to change her accent and her demeanor so that she can pass herself off as a duchess. In six months, she successfully "passes" in high society, having become a woman of sensitivity and taste.)

practical action

How Can Managers Harness the Pygmalion Effect to Lead Employees?

Does the self-fulfilling prophecy really work? Research in a variety of industries and occupations shows that the effect can be quite strong.[69]

At Microsoft Corp., employees routinely put in 75-hour weeks, especially when trying to meet shipping deadlines for new products. Because Microsoft prides itself on trying to meet its deadlines, positive group-level expectations help create and reinforce an organizational culture of high expectancy for success. This process then excites people about working for the organization, thereby reducing turnover.[70]

This shows the Pygmalion effect at work—that is, managerial expectations powerfully influence employee behavior and performance. Managers can harness this effect by building a hierarchical framework that reinforces positive performance expectations throughout the organization. The foundation of this framework is employee self-expectations. In turn, positive self-expectations improve interpersonal expectations by encouraging people to work toward common goals. This cooperation enhances group-level productivity and promotes positive performance expectations within the work group.

How to Create a Pygmalion Effect

Because positive self-expectations are the foundation for creating an organizationwide Pygmalion effect, let us consider how managers can create positive performance expectations. This task may be accomplished using various combinations of the following:

1. Recognize that everyone has the potential to increase his or her performance.
2. Instill confidence in your staff.
3. Set high performance goals.
4. Positively reinforce employees for a job well done.
5. Provide constructive feedback when necessary.
6. Help employees advance through the organization.
7. Introduce new employees as if they have outstanding potential.
8. Become aware of your personal prejudices and nonverbal messages that may discourage others.
9. Encourage employees to visualize the successful execution of tasks.
10. Help employees master key skills and tasks.[71]

Causal Attributions

***Causal attribution* is the activity of inferring causes for observed behavior.** Rightly or wrongly, we constantly formulate cause-and-effect explanations for our own and others' behavior. Attributional statements such as the following are common: "Joe drinks too much because has no willpower; but I need a few drinks after work because I'm under a lot of pressure."

Even though our causal attributions tend to be self-serving and are often invalid, it's important to understand how people formulate attributions, because they profoundly affect organizational behavior. For example, a supervisor who attributes an employee's poor performance to a lack of effort might reprimand that person. However, training might be deemed necessary if the supervisor attributes the poor performance to a low skill level.

One model of attribution (Kelley's model) proposes that people make causal attributions after they gather information about three dimensions of behavior: *consensus, consistency,* and *distinctiveness.*[72]

- **Consensus—"How does Joe's present behavior compare with others'?"** In *consensus,* you compare an individual's behavior with that of his or her peers. You look to see how much other people in the same situation behave the same way.

  Example: As a restaurant manager on duty during an extremely busy Saturday night, you receive three complaints from customers that Joe, a longtime waiter, was rude to them. There were no complaints about other waitstaffers. (Thus, Joe's behavior had *low consensus* because it varied a lot from the others' performance.)

- **Consistency—"How does Joe's present behavior compare with his past behavior?"** In *consistency,* you look to see whether an individual behaves the same way at different times.

  Example: You might recall that Joe often becomes tense and surly during busy evenings. During the 5 years that you've been his supervisor, his manner has provoked a customer complaint or two on those occasions. (Thus, Joe's performance has *high consistency* because he performs the task the same way time after time.)

- **Distinctiveness—"How does Joe's present behavior compare with his behavior in other situations?"** In *distinctiveness,* you look to see whether an individual behaves the same way in other situations.

  Example: Is Joe sometimes surly and rude when the restaurant is not busy? Or when you're catering special events, such as weddings? Or when he's asked to vacuum the restaurant before it opens? Alas, it does seem to be the case. (Thus, Joe's performance has *low distinctiveness* because he performs the same way on other tasks and under other conditions.)

It's been suggested that people attribute behavior to *personal factors* when they perceive low consensus, high consistency, and low distinctiveness (as with Joe). They attribute behavior to *environmental factors* when they perceive high consensus, low consistency, and high distinctiveness.

As a manager, you need to be alert to two attributional tendencies that can distort one's interpretation of observed behavior—the *fundamental attribution bias* and the *self-serving bias.*

- **Fundamental attribution bias:** In the ***fundamental attribution bias,* people attribute another person's behavior to his or her personal characteristics rather than to situational factors.**

Example: A study of manufacturing employees found that top managers attributed the cause of industrial back pain to individuals, whereas workers attributed it to the environment.[73]

- **Self-serving bias:** In the ***self-serving bias,*** **people tend to take more personal responsibility for success than for failure.**

  Example: The way students typically analyze their performance on exams shows self-serving bias, with "A" students likely to attribute their grade to high ability or hard work and "D" students blaming factors such as bad luck, unclear lectures, and unfair testing.[74] ◆

Why are these people drinking? People tend to equate drinking with relaxation, good times, and fellowship. But some people drink to ease pain and problems. If the people shown here drink more than a couple of drinks, is that necessarily bad, in your opinion? (You should be aware that *binge drinking* is defined as consuming five, for men, or four, for women, or more drinks in a row one or more times in a two-week period.) No doubt you will come up with some explanation—some cause-and-effect reason—as to why particular people drink too much after work. Maybe, you may think, it's because they have no willpower. As for yourself, you may think you need "a few drinks to wind down" at the end of the day because you have such a high-pressure job and need to find some relief. Inferring causes for observed behavior, whether correct or not, is known as causal attribution. We all do it, but it's important to know how it works.

major question **What causes workplace stress, and how can it be reduced?**

The Big Picture

Stress is what people feel when enduring extraordinary demands or opportunities and are not sure how to handle them. Sources of stress are five demands: individual task, individual role, group, organizational, and nonwork. We describe three consequences of stress and three ways to reduce it in the organization.

Although most workers are satisfied with their jobs, 24% say their work is "very stressful," and 43% say it is "moderately stressful."[75] A study by one health plan of 46,000 people working for six large employers found that the employers paid nearly 8% a year of total health care for treatment of what employees characterized as out-of-control stress. Such workers, who suffered from a variety of stress-related illnesses, such as migraines, back pain, and gastrointestinal disorders, had 46% higher health costs.[76]

Work stress can also, as you might guess, put managers at risk. Researchers who interviewed 800 hospital heart-attack patients over a five-year period found that managers run twice the normal risk of heart attack the week after they have had to fire someone or face a high-pressure deadline.[77] Workplace stress is negatively related to job satisfaction, organizational commitment, job performance, and positive emotions.[78]

What Is Stress?

Stress* is the tension people feel when they are facing or enduring extraordinary demands, constraints, or opportunities and are uncertain about their ability to handle them effectively.**[79] Stress is the feeling of tension and pressure; **the source of stress is called a *stressor.

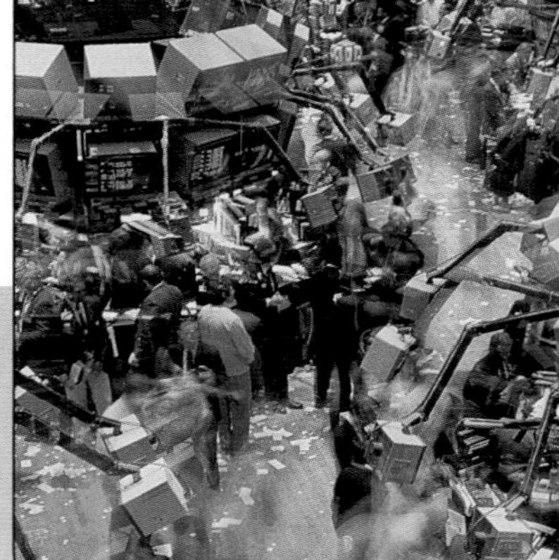

Trading frenzy. Many jobs are stressful, but some are more stressful than others, such as those of traders on the floor of the New York Stock Exchange. What occupations do you think are the most stress-inducing?

Stress has both physical and emotional components. Physically, according to Canadian researcher Hans Selye, considered the father of the modern concept of stress, stress is "the nonspecific response of the body to any demand made upon it."[80] Emotionally, stress has been defined as the feeling of being overwhelmed, "the perception that events or circumstances have challenged, or exceeded, a person's ability to cope."[81]

Stressors can be *hassles,* or simple irritants, such as misplacing or losing things, concerns about one's physical appearance, and having too many things to do.[82] Or they can be *crises,* such as sudden occasions of overwhelming terror—a horrible auto accident, an incident of childhood abuse. Or they can be *strong stressors,* which can dramatically strain a person's ability to adapt—extreme physical discomfort, such as chronic severe back pain.

Stressors can be both *negative and positive*. Selye writes: "It is immaterial whether the agent or situation we face is pleasant or unpleasant; all that counts is the intensity of the demand for adjustment and adaptation."[83]

The Sources of Job-Related Stress: Individual Tasks & Roles, Groups, Organizations, & Nonwork Factors

There are five sources of stress on the job: *individual tasks, individual roles, groups, organizations,* and *nonwork factors.* (See Figure 11.3.)

Individual task demands: stress created by the job itself
Individual role demands: role overload, conflict, & ambiguity
Group demands: stress created by coworkers & managers
Organizational demands: stress created by the environment & culture
Nonwork demands: stress created by forces outside the organization
STRESS!

FIGURE 11.3
Five sources of stress

1 Individual Task Demands: The Stress Created by the Job Itself

Some occupations are more stressful than others. Directing a play is more stressful than selling tickets. Doing brain surgery is more stressful than processing medical claims. Managing employees is more stressful than being a receptionist (usually).

Nevertheless, low-level jobs can be more stressful than high-level jobs because employees often have less control over their lives and thus have less work satisfaction. Being a high-speed word processor or doing telemarketing phone sales, for instance, can be quite stressful.

There is also considerable stress caused by worries over the prospective loss of a job. Recent surveys indicate that employees frequently worry about being laid off.[84] Job security is an important stressor to manage because it can result in reduced job satisfaction, organizational commitment, and performance.[85]

2 Individual Role Demands: The Stress Created by Others' Expectations of You

***Roles* are sets of behaviors that people expect of occupants of a position.**[86] Stress may come about because of *role overload, role conflict,* and *role ambiguity*.

- **Role overload:** Role overload occurs when others' expectations exceed one's ability. Example: If you as a student are carrying a full course load plus working two-thirds time plus trying to have a social life, you know what role overload is—and what stress is. Similar things happen to managers and workers.
- **Role conflict:** Role conflict occurs when one feels torn by the different expectations of important people in one's life. Example: Your supervisor says the company needs you to stay late to meet an important deadline, but your family expects you to be present for your child's birthday party.
- **Role ambiguity:** Role ambiguity occurs when others' expectations are unknown. Example: You find your job description and the criteria for promotion vague, a complaint often voiced by newcomers to an organization.

3 Group Demands: The Stress Created by Coworkers & Managers

Even if you don't particularly care for the work you do but like the people you work with, that can be a great source of satisfaction and prevent stress. When people don't get along, that can be a great stressor.

In addition, managers can create stress for employees in a number of ways: Exhibiting inconsistent behaviors. Failing to provide support. Showing lack of concern. Providing inadequate direction. Creating a demanding, high-productivity environment. Focusing on negatives while ignoring good performance.[87] People who have bad managers are five times more likely to have stress-induced headaches, upset stomachs, and loss of sleep.[88]

4 Organizational Demands: The Stress Created by the Environment & Culture

The physical environments of some jobs are great sources of stress: poultry processing, asbestos removal, coal mining, fire fighting, police work, ambulance driving, and so on. Even white-collar work can take place in a stressful environment, with poor lighting, too much noise, improper placement of furniture, and no privacy.[89] An organizational culture that promotes high-pressure work demands on employees will fuel the stress response.[90] The pace of information technology certainly adds to the stress. Research shows preliminary support for the idea that organizational stress can be reduced by participatory management.[91]

5 Nonwork Demands: The Stresses Created by Forces Outside the Organization

As anyone knows who has had to cope with money problems, divorce, support of elderly relatives, or other serious nonwork concerns, the stresses outside one's work life can have a significant effect on work. And people with lower incomes, education level, and work status are particularly apt to have higher stress.[92] But even people with ordinary lives can find the stress of coping with family life rugged going.

The Consequences of Stress

Positive stress is constructive and can energize you, increasing your effort, creativity, and performance. Negative stress is destructive, resulting in poorer-quality work, dissatisfaction, errors, absenteeism, and turnover.

Negative stress reveals itself in three kinds of symptoms:

- **Physiological signs:** Lesser physiological signs are sweaty palms, restlessness, backaches, headaches, upset stomach, and nausea. More serious signs are hypertension and heart attacks.
- **Psychological signs:** Psychological symptoms include boredom, irritability, nervousness, anger, anxiety, hostility, and depression.
- **Behavioral signs:** Symptoms include sleeplessness, changes in eating habits, and increased smoking/alcohol/drug abuse. Stress may be revealed through reduced performance and job satisfaction.

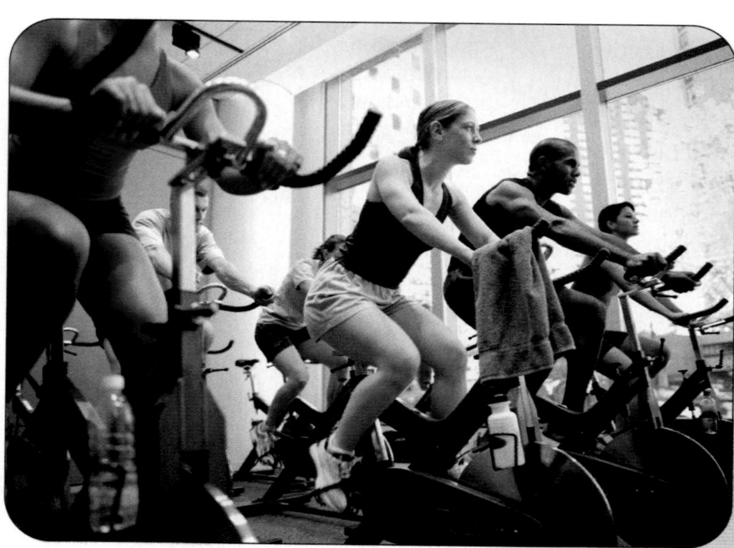

De-stressing. Experts say that exercise can be a tremendous stress reliever. Many companies maintain physical-fitness centers not only as an employee perk but also because they realize that exercise helps to improve stamina and endurance and reduce tension.

Over time, stress may lead to ***burnout,*** **or a state of emotional, mental, and even physical exhaustion,** expressed as listlessness, indifference, or frustration. Clearly, the greatest consequence of negative stress for the organization is reduced productivity. Overstressed employees are apt to call in sick, miss deadlines, take longer lunch breaks, and show indifference to performance. However, some may put in great numbers of hours at work without getting as much accomplished as previously. Mental health experts estimate that 10% of the workforce suffers from depression or high levels of stress that may ultimately affect job performance. In addition, researchers estimate that in a recent year stress caused 11% of all cases of employee absenteeism.[93]

Reducing Stressors in the Organization

There are all kinds of ***buffers,*** **or administrative changes, that managers can make to reduce the stressors that lead to employee burnout.** Examples: Extra staff or equipment at peak periods. Increased freedom to make decisions. Recognition for accomplishments. Time off for rest or personal development. Assignment to a new position.[94] Three- to five-day employee retreats at offsite locations for relaxation and team-building activities. Sabbatical leave programs to replenish employees' energy and desire to work.[95]

Some general organizational strategies for reducing unhealthy stressors are the following:[96]

- **Create a supportive organizational climate:** Job stress often results because organizations have evolved into large, formal, and inflexible bureaucracies. Wherever possible, it's better to try to keep the organizational environment less formal, more personal, and more supportive of employees.
- **Make jobs interesting:** Stress also results when jobs are routinized and boring. Better to try to structure jobs so that they allow employees some freedom.
- **Make career counseling available:** Companies such as IBM make career planning available, which reduces the stress that comes when employees don't know what their career options are and where they're headed. ◆

Key Terms Used in This Chapter

Summary

11.1 Values, Attitudes, & Behavior

- Organizational behavior (OB) is dedicated to better understanding and managing people at work. OB looks at two areas: individual behavior (discussed in this chapter) and group behavior (discussed in later chapters).
- Values must be distinguished from attitudes and from behavior.
  (1)Values are abstract ideals that guide one's thinking and behavior across all situations.
  (2) Attitudes are defined as learned predispositions toward a given object. Attitudes have three components. The affective component consists of the feelings or emotions one has about a situation. The cognitive component consists of the beliefs and knowledge one has about a situation. The behavioral component refers to how one intends or expects to behave toward a situation. When attitudes and reality collide, the result may be cognitive dissonance, the psychological discomfort a person experiences between his or her cognitive attitude and incompatible behavior. Cognitive dissonance depends on three factors: importance, control, and rewards. The ways to reduce cognitive dissonance are to change your attitude and/or your behavior, belittle the importance of the inconsistent behavior, or find consonant elements that outweigh the dissonant ones.
  (3) Together, values and attitudes influence people's workplace behavior—their actions and judgments.

11.2 Work-Related Attitudes & Behaviors Managers Need to Deal With

- Managers need to be alert to work-related attitudes having to do with (1) job satisfaction, the extent to which you feel positively or negatively about various aspects of your work; (2) job involvement, the extent to which you identify or are personally involved with your job; and (3) organizational commitment, reflecting the extent to which an employee identifies with an organization and is committed to its goals.
- Among the types of behavior that managers need to influence are (1) performance and productivity and (2) absenteeism, when an employee doesn't show up for work, and turnover, when employees leave their jobs.

11.3 Personality & Individual Behavior

- Personality consists of the stable psychological traits and behavioral attributes that give a person his or her identity. There are five personality dimensions and four personality traits that managers need to be aware of to understand workplace behavior.
- The Big Five personality dimensions are extroversion, agreeableness, conscientiousness, emotional stability, and openness to experience. Extroversion, an outgoing personality, is associated with success for managers and salespeople. Conscientiousness, or a

dependable personality, is correlated with successful job performance. A person who scores well on conscientiousness may be a proactive personality, someone who is more apt to take initiative and persevere to influence the environment.

- There are four personality traits that managers need to be aware of in order to understand workplace behavior. (1) Locus of control indicates how much people believe they control their fate through their own efforts. (2) Self-efficacy is the belief in one's personal ability to do a task. Low self-efficacy is associated with learned helplessness, the debilitating lack of faith in one's ability to control one's environment. (3) Self-esteem is the extent to which people like or dislike themselves. (4) Self-monitoring is the extent to which people are able to observe their own behavior and adapt it to external situations.

11.4 Perception & Individual Behavior

- Perception is the process of interpreting and understanding one's environment. The process can be boiled down to four steps: selective attention, interpretation and evaluation, storing in memory, and retrieving from memory to make judgments and decisions. Perceptual errors can lead to mistakes that affect management.
- Three types of distortion in perception are (1) selective perception, the tendency to filter out information that is discomforting, that seems irrelevant, or that contradicts one's beliefs; (2) stereotyping, the tendency to attribute to an individual the characteristics one believes are typical of the group to which that individual belongs; and (3) the halo effect, the forming of an impression of an individual based on a single trait.
- The self-fulfilling prophecy (Pygmalion effect) describes the phenomenon in which people's expectations of themselves or others leads them to behave in ways that make those expectations come true.
- Causal attribution is the activity of inferring causes for observed behavior, which may be correct or incorrect. People may make causal attributions after they gather information about three dimensions of behavior: consensus, in which you compare a person's behavior with peer behavior; consistency, in which you look to see if a person behaves the same way at different times; and distinctiveness, in which you look to see if a person behaves the same way in other situations.
- As a manager, you need to be alert to two attributional tendencies that can distort your interpretation of observed behavior. (1) In the fundamental attribution bias, people attribute another person's behavior to his or her personal characteristics rather than to situational factors. (2) In the self-serving bias, people tend to take more personal responsibility for success than for failure.

11.5 Understanding Stress & Individual Behavior

- 
Stress is the tension people feel when they are facing or enduring extraordinary demands, constraints, or opportunities and are uncertain about their ability to handle them effectively. Stress is the feeling of tension and pressure; the source of stress is called a stressor.
- There are five sources of stress on the job: individual tasks, individual roles, groups, organizations, and nonwork factors. (1) Individual task demands are the stresses created by the job itself. (2) Individual role demands are the stresses created by other people's expectations of you. Roles are sets of behaviors that people expect of occupants of a position. Stress may come about because of role overload, role conflict, or role ambiguity. (3) Group demands are the stresses created by coworkers and managers. (4) Organizational demands are the stresses created by the environment and culture of the organization. (5) Nonwork demands are the stresses created by forces outside the organization, such as money problems or divorce.
- Positive stress can be constructive. Negative stress can result in poor-quality work; such stress is revealed through physiological, psychological, or behavioral signs such as burnout, a state of emotional, mental, and even physical exhaustion.
- There are buffers, or administrative changes, that managers can make to reduce the stressors that lead to employee burnout, such as adding extra staff or giving employees more power to make decisions. Some general organizational strategies for reducing unhealthy stressors are to create a supportive organizational climate, make jobs interesting, and make career counseling available.

Management in Action

Are You a Lark or Night Owl?

Excerpted from Jared Sandberg, "Reveille Has Its Fans, but for Late Risers 9-to-5 Days Are a Pain," The Wall Street Journal, *May 12, 2004, p. B1.*

Every morning, Margaret Wong does something that will be heartwarming to some and horrifying to others: She rises and shines at 4:30 a.m., long before the sun comes up in her hometown of Shaker Heights, Ohio.

By 6 a.m., the 53-year-old immigration lawyer has arrived at her office and is sipping coffee, responding to e-mails, reading the paper—any tasks, she says, that don't require interaction. That's because, at that ungodly hour, many of her colleagues are still bunked down.

Eventually, the late sleepers will wobble into work. To accommodate them, Ms. Wong has moved the 8 a.m. staff meeting to 9 a.m. She adjusts, she says, but she doesn't understand the night owls—"I just think they're not disciplined," she confides—any more than they understand a morning lark like her.

Of all the gulfs in understanding at the office, among the most difficult to bridge is that between morning and night people. On the one hand, think bushy-tailed company lawyers who eat lunch at 11 a.m. On the other, consider the bleary-eyed techies for whom the only thing as bad as waking up early is the people who enjoy it so loudly.

The conflict between the morning larks and the night owls would be the office equivalent of the Bloods versus the Crips if, at any given time, one gang weren't so pooped.

But we're not talking about a fair fight here. The 9-to-5 shift overwhelmingly favors larks. When has anyone complained that employees show up too early? Owls, on the other hand, are frequently stigmatized as recalcitrant slugabeds who fritter time and resources on the company's dime.

That stigma is just another sign that shallow emblems of productivity impress American managers more than results. After all, the 9-to-5 shift has become an anachronism in the 24-hour global economy. It fails to take into account the impact of e-mail and other technologies in making traditional work hours less relevant.

It also ignores biology. High schools and colleges have finally woken up to that fact, increasingly delaying the beginning of classes to better suit the biological clocks of students whose sleep cycles naturally slip later into the night. "It is absolutely crazy to expect high-school and college students to learn things at 7 a.m.," says Timothy Monk, director of the Human Chronobiology Research Program at the University of Pittsburgh.

Similarly, he says, "it makes more sense for (employees) to work during hours they are productive than some artificial 9-to-5 schedule."

In fact, staff meetings, which typically start at 9 a.m., would apparently be better 12 hours later. Thomas Wehr, a research psychiatrist at the National Institute of Mental Health, has studied daily sleep cycles, and he has found that almost no one can fall asleep around 9 p.m. "Ironically, the period when we're most alert and at the highest state of arousal is after we leave work," he says. . . .

Night owls are generally more forgiving of larks than the other way around. Novelist Daniel Weiss, who can keep his own hours, retires at 5 a.m. and "rises at the crack of noon," he says. He understands that the 9-to-5 world favors larks, but it does irritate him when people phone at 10:30 in the morning. "Where are these people's manners?" he asks.

Lauren Winer Marrus, president of Chelsea Paper Co., an online stationer in Manhattan, wakes up at 5:30 a.m. She says she gets a cab in no time, slips through a line-less Starbucks and is greeted by a waiting elevator. She is able to get work done that would take a lot longer later in the day, she says, and "I am pretty proud of myself."

Owlish employees can try her patience. Tardiness "has never been the sole reason for letting someone go," she says, but she concedes that "it has been a contributing factor."

For Discussion

1. Are you a lark or a night owl?
2. Which work-related attitudes and behaviors discussed in this chapter would be affected by a night owl working a traditional 9-to-5 schedule? Discuss.
3. What are some possible perceptions/stereotypes that larks might have about night owls, and vice versa? Explain.
4. Is a lark or a night owl likely to experience more stress working a traditional 9-to-5 schedule? Explain.
5. Should organizations accommodate employees' biological clocks? If so, how?

What Is My Emotional Intelligence Score?*

Objectives

To help you assess your emotional intelligence.

To expand your knowledge of the new interpretations of intelligence.

Introduction

Employers have long been guided by one dimension of our personality, our intelligence quotient (IQ). However, a number of researchers and observers of human behavior have been examining components of intelligence that include emotions. Your Emotional Intelligence (EI) includes your abilities to motivate yourself and persist even when you are frustrated, to control your impulses and delay gratification, to regulate your mood and keep distress from overwhelming your thinking ability, to empathize with others, and to hope. The recognition of the emotional dimension to intelligence is vital today in a world of constant change and increased stress. Having a sense of your own EI is fundamental to being successful. The purpose of this exercise is to determine your own EI.

Instructions

Use this scale to indicate the extent to which you agree or disagree with each statement below.

1 = strongly disagree
2 = disagree
3 = neither agree nor disagree
4 = agree
5 = strongly agree

1. I am usually aware—from moment to moment—of my feelings as they change.	1	2	3	4	5
2. I think before I act.	1	2	3	4	5
3. I am impatient when I want something.	1	2	3	4	5
4. I bounce back quickly from life's setbacks.	1	2	3	4	5
5. I can pick up subtle social cues that indicate others' needs or wants.	1	2	3	4	5
6. I'm very good at handling myself in social situations.	1	2	3	4	5
7. I'm persistent in going after the things I want.	1	2	3	4	5
8. When people share their problems with me, I'm good at putting myself in their shoes.	1	2	3	4	5
9. When I'm in a bad mood, I make a strong effort to get out of it.	1	2	3	4	5
10. I can find common ground and build rapport with people from all walks of life.	1	2	3	4	5

Scoring & Interpretation

This questionnaire taps the five basic dimensions of EI: self-awareness (items 1 and 9), self-management (2, 4), self-motivation (3, 7), empathy (5, 8), and social skills (6, 10). Compute your total EI score by adding your responses to all 10 statements. Your total score will fall between 10 and 50. While no definite cutoff scores are available, scores of 40 or higher indicate a high EI. Scores of 20 or less suggest a relatively low EI.

Emotional intelligence is a collection of abilities and competencies that have an effect on a person's capacity to succeed in dealing with demands and pressures. People with high EI have the capacity to correctly perceive, evaluate, articulate, and manage emotions and feelings.

EI may be most predictive of performance in jobs such as sales or management, in which achievement is based as much on interpersonal skills as on technical ability. People with low EI are likely to have trouble managing others, making successful sales presentations, and functioning on teams.

Questions for Discussion

1. Did the results surprise you? Why or why not?
2. Look at the three items on which your score was lowest. What are some skills or attitudes you can work on to improve your EI? Explain.
3. Do you think your EI would help or hinder you when working in a team?

*Based on D. Goleman, *Emotional Intelligence: Why It Can Matter More Than IQ* (New York: Bantam, 1995).

Group Exercise

Identifying Important Values in a Classroom Setting*

Objectives

To identify values important to you in the classroom.

To gain knowledge of others' values in the classroom.

Introduction

Values are abstract ideals that guide one's thinking and behavior across all situations. Your behavior is dictated by values that were instilled in you by the time you were a teenager. As a student, you probably believe that getting a good grade is a very important value. How hard are you willing to work and what sacrifices are you willing to make to get that grade? From a manager's point of view, it's helpful to know what values—concepts, principles, things, people, or activities—employees will work hard for, even make sacrifices for.

The purpose of this exercise is to help you think about what values are important to you in the classroom. Because values differ from person to person, it's beneficial to know which values people are willing to work hard to maintain and which values others feel are less important.

Instructions

Below are 10 different values from the Rokeach Value Survey. Read the list and then rank each value according to which ones you feel are important in the classroom. Rank the values from 1 to 10, with 1 being equal to "most important" and 10 being equal to "least important." Mark your results in the first column.

Once you rank the values, break into teams of five to six people. As a group, compare each of your individual results and discuss them. What do you notice about the differences in rankings? Were the group members' rankings similar to yours, or was there argument as to which values were important? As a team take the average ranking for each value or devise some other method to reach a consensus on which values are important or not important. Mark those results in the second column, again using the scale from 1 to 10, with 1 being equal to "most important" and 10 being equal to "least important." Compare your team's results to the results from the rest of the class.

	My Ranking	Group's Ranking
Broadminded (open-minded)	________	________
Capable (competent, effective)	________	________
Honest (sincere, thoughtful)	________	________
Responsible (dependable, reliable)	________	________
Polite (courteous, well-mannered)	________	________
Sense of accomplishment (lasting contribution)	________	________
Equality (brotherhood, equal opportunity)	________	________
Self-respect (self-esteem)	________	________
Social recognition (respect, admiration)	________	________
True friendship (close companionship)	________	________

Questions for Discussion

1. Were you surprised at how your results differed from the group's? Or were you surprised at how closely your results matched? Why or why not?
2. Imagine you are teaching this course and that your class presented the results of their survey. What are some things you can do to encourage a learning environment that reflects the values your students feel are important? What changes would have to be made? Explain.
3. To what extent do you feel knowing your classmates' values will help you work more effectively with them in teams? Explain.

*The ten values in this exercise were taken from the 36 values listed in the Rokeach Value Survey, 1967, 1982 by M. Rokeach. Reprinted by permission of HALGREN TESTS, NW 1145 Clifford, Pullman, WA 99163; (509) 334-5636.

Ethical Dilemma

Enron Employees Create a Positive Impression for Wall Street Analysts

From Jason Leopold, "En-Ruse? Workers at Enron Say They Posed as Busy Traders to Impress Visitng Analysts," The Wall Street Journal, *February 17, 2002, p. C1.*

Some current and former employees of Enron's retail-energy unit say the company asked them to pose as busy electricity and natural-gas sales representatives one day in 1998 so the unit could impress Wall Street analysts visiting its Houston headquarters.

Enron rushed 75 employees of Enron Energy Services—including secretaries and actual sales representatives—to an empty trading floor and told them to act as if they were trying to sell energy contracts to businesses over the phone, the current and former employees say.

"When we went down to the sixth floor, I remember we had to take the stairs so the analysts wouldn't see us," said Kim Garcia, who at the time was an administrative assistant for Enron Energy Services and was laid off in December [of 2001].

"We brought some of our personal stuff, like pictures, to make it look like the area was lived in," Ms. Garcia said in an interview. "There were a bunch of trading desks on the sixth floor, but the desks were totally empty. Some of the computers didn't even work, so we worked off of our laptops. When the analysts arrived, we had to make believe we were on the phone buying and selling electricity and natural gas. The whole thing took like 10 minutes."

Penny Marksberry—who also worked as an Enron Energy Services administrative assistant in 1998 and was laid off in December—and two employees who still work at the unit also say they were told to act as if they were trying to sell contracts.

"They actually brought in computers and phones, and they told us to act like we were typing or talking on the phone when the analysts were walking through," Ms. Marksberry said. "They told us it was very important for us to make a good impression, and if the analysts saw that the operation was disorganized, they wouldn't give the company a good rating."

Solving the Dilemma

What would you do if you were asked to act busy in front of the analysts?

1. Follow the company's instructions by going to the sixth floor and pretending to be busy for the analysts.
2. Explain to your manager that this behavior is inconsistent with your personal values and that you will not participate.
3. Go to the sixth floor in support of the company's request but not act busy or bring personal artifacts to create a false impression.
4. Invent other options. Explain.

Video Case

TechBox

TechBox produces a specialized computer chip for a large client base. Patrick Bennett is the supervising manager overseeing the production of the main component of the chip. Recently, he and his team began implementing a computerized tracking system to increase quality control and workflow. Historically, the quality control team expended significant time and resources reworking failed chips. This new system is expected to raise quality and productivity levels substantially. This is Patrick's first opportunity to lead a project of this magnitude. Although the new system is costly, it is relatively unproven. Still, expectations are high.

Patrick supervises 50 floor employees. In the two years he's worked at TechBox, he's built a reputation for numerous successes and improvements that have financially benefited the organization. Patrick possesses a unique combination of technical expertise and managerial skill. He is greatly admired by his team and generally well received by top management. At a recent progress meeting, however, Patrick was stunned by the attitudes of top executives. At the meeting were Sam Adelson, Lucinda Bergen, and Morgan Baines.

Sam Adelson is a longtime employee who worked his way up from the mailroom to vice president of operations. He is wary of change and skeptical of computerized system enhancements (which is unusual for someone employed in the high-tech industry). Others perceive him as stodgy, grumpy, and difficult. Lucinda Bergen is director of product management and the sole female executive at TechBox. She is generally perceived as compassionate, understanding, and easygoing. She seems comfortable with change and new ideas. However, she's quick to defend her position within the company and overassert herself when she feels confronted. Morgan Baines is vice president of distribution. He's perceived as the "jokester" of the company. He often speaks without thinking and seems to provide support, to attack, or to withdraw without rhyme or reason. Everyone has the impression that they have his support. Although unconventional, the approach seems to work. He's been at TechBox for years.

Mistakenly, Patrick assumes this to be a routine meeting. Once there, he feels ambushed. In Adelson's opinion, the entire project should be scrapped. He's concerned about the expense and fears that the system won't live up to expectations. Additionally, there are rumors that Patrick's team is intentionally slowing work production. Lucinda Bergen is generally supportive of the project but concerned about the slow rate of progress. Before Patrick can build on her supportive attitude, Adelson sidetracks the issue. Finally, Baines is completely disruptive. He's a total wildcard; Patrick has no clue where Baines stands on the issue. Patrick leaves the meeting frustrated and confused. He'll need to be better prepared for the follow-up meeting, which is scheduled in one week.

Although better informed for the next meeting, Patrick is still nervous. To benefit both the organization and his own career, he must somehow accommodate all three executives so that they will let him complete the project. Adelson's main concerns seem to be effectiveness and general cost. Bergen is focused on the project's conclusion date, and Baines is still the wildcard. Patrick will need to take charge of this meeting and diffuse these volatile personalities. In doing so, he'll have to appeal to the right person on the right issue.

Discussion Questions

1. Does Patrick Bennett have an internal or an external locus of control? Define these terms and provide evidence to support your answer.
2. What is the difference between stress and a stressor? What stressors is Patrick Bennett facing?
3. Managers need to learn about individual differences so that they can influence employees to do their best work. Measuring performance and productivity are ways to evaluate work behaviors. How can the executive team at TechBox evaluate Patrick's work performance?

chapter 12

Motivating Employees
Achieving Superior Performance in the Workplace

MAJOR QUESTIONS YOU SHOULD BE ABLE TO ANSWER

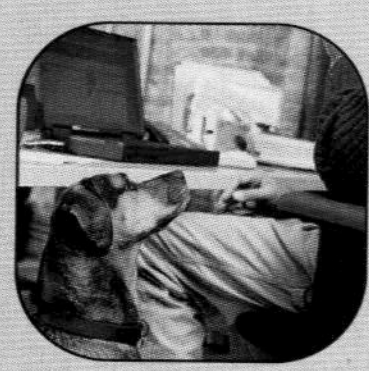

12.1 Motivating for Performance
Major Question: What's the motivation for studying motivation?

12.2 Need-Based Perspectives on Employee Motivation
Major Question: What kinds of needs motivate employees?

12.3 Process Perspectives on Employee Motivation
Major Question: Is a good reward good enough? How do other factors affect motivation?

12.4 Reinforcement Perspectives on Motivation
Major Question: What are the types of incentives I might use to influence employee behavior?

12.5 Motivation Through Job Design
Major Question: What's the best way to design jobs—adapt people to work or work to people?

12.6 Using Compensation & Other Rewards to Motivate
Major Question: How can I use compensation and other rewards to motivate people?

the manager's toolbox

Managing for Motivation: The Flexible Workplace

Can a company slice and dice the 24 hours in a day, the seven days a week, in ways that can better motivate employees?

With the parents of so many two-paycheck families, single parents, and other diverse kinds of employees in the workforce, employers have begun to develop the so-called *flexible workplace* as a way of recruiting, retaining, and motivating employees. Among the types of alternative work schedules available:

- **Part-time work—less than 40 hours:** Part-time work is any work done on a schedule less than the standard 40-hour workweek. Some part-time workers—so-called temporary workers or contingency workers—do want to work 40 hours or more but can't find full-time jobs. Others, however, work part time by choice. Today an organization can hire not only part-time clerical help, for instance, but also part-time programmers, market researchers, lawyers, even part-time top executives.
- **Flextime—flexible working hours:** Flextime, or flexible time, consists of flexible working hours or any schedule that gives one some choices in working hours. If, for example, an organization's normal working hours are 9 A.M. to 5 P.M., a flextime worker might be allowed to start and finish an hour earlier or an hour later—for instance, to work from 8 A.M. to 4 P.M. The main requirement is that the employee be at work during certain "core" hours, so as to be available for meetings, consultations, and so on. By offering flextime hours, organizations can attract and keep employees with special requirements such as the need to take care of children or elderly parents. It also benefits employees who wish to avoid commuting during rush hour.
- **Compressed workweek—40 hours in four days:** In a compressed workweek, employees perform a full-time job in less than five days of standard eight- (or nine-) hour shifts. The most common variation is a 40-hour week performed in four days of 10 hours each, which gives employees three (instead of two) consecutive days off. The benefits are that organizations can offer employees more leisure time and reduced wear and tear and expense from commuting. The disadvantages are possible scheduling problems, unavailability of an employee to coworkers and customers, and fatigue from long workdays.
- **Job sharing—two people split the same job:** In job sharing, two people divide one full-time job. Usually, each person works a half day, although there can be other arrangements (working alternate days or alternate weeks, for example). As with a compressed workweek, job sharing provides employees with more personal or leisure time. The disadvantage is that it can result in communication problems with coworkers or customers.
- **Telecommuting & other work-at-home schedules:** There have always been some employees who have had special full-time or part-time arrangements whereby they are allowed to work at home, keeping in touch with their employers and coworkers by mail and phone. The fax machine, the personal computer, the Internet, and overnight-delivery services have now made work-at-home arrangements much more feasible.

Working at home with telecommunications between office and home is called *telecommuting*. The advantage to employers is increased productivity because telecommuters experience less distraction at home and can work flexible hours.

forecast

What's Ahead in This Chapter

This chapter discusses how to motivate people to perform well. We consider motivation from three perspectives: need-based (covering theories by Maslow, Herzberg, and McClelland); process (covering expectancy, equity, and goal-setting theories); and reinforcement. We also consider how to motivate employees through job design. Finally, we discuss using compensation and other rewards to motivate performance.

major question **What's the motivation for studying motivation?**

The Big Picture

Motivation is defined as the psychological processes that arouse and direct people's goal-directed behavior. The model of how it works is that people have certain needs that motivate them to perform specific behaviors for which they receive rewards, both extrinsic and intrinsic, that feed back and satisfy the original need. The three major perspectives on motivation are need-based, process, and reinforcement.

What would make you rise a half hour earlier than usual to ensure you got to work on time—and to perform your best once there?

A new leased car? Help with college tuition? Bringing your dog to work? Onsite laundry, gym, or childcare? Free lunch? Really nice bosses?

Believe it or not, these are among the perks available to some lucky employees—and not just high-level managers.[1] Especially when employment rates are high, as they were in the late 1990s, companies are desperate to attract, retain, and motivate key people. But even in tough economic times, there are always industries and occupations in which employers feel they need to bend over backward to retain their "human capital."

Motivation: What It Is, Why It's Important

Why do people do the things they do? The answer is this: they are mainly motivated to fulfill their wants, their needs.

What Is Motivation & How Does It Work?

Motivation **may be defined as the psychological processes that arouse and direct goal-directed behavior.**[2] Motivation is difficult to understand because you can't actually see it or know it in another person; it must be *inferred* from one's behavior. Nevertheless, it's imperative that you as a manager understand the process of motivation if you are to guide employees in accomplishing your organization's objectives.

The way motivation works actually is complex. However, in a simple model of motivation, people have certain *needs* that *motivate* them to perform specific *behaviors* for which they receive *rewards* that *feed back* and satisfy the original need. *(See Figure 12.1.)*

FIGURE 12.1
A simple model of motivation

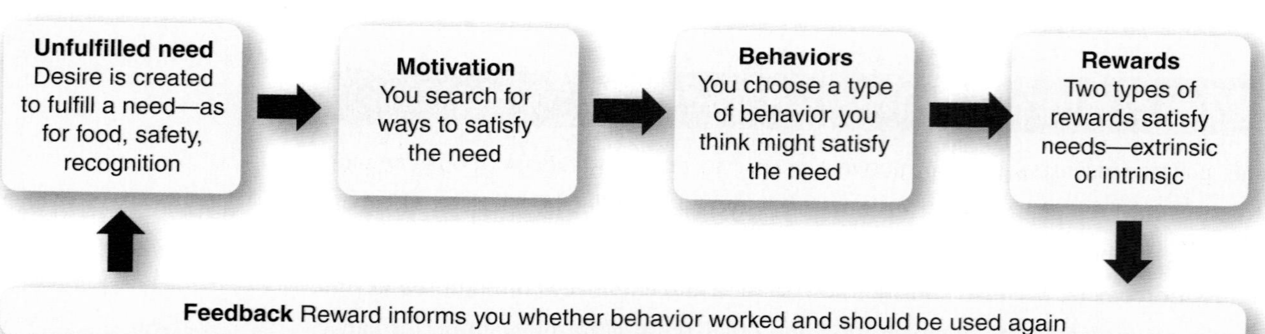
Unfulfilled need
Desire is created to fulfill a need—as for food, safety, recognition
Motivation
You search for ways to satisfy the need
Behaviors
You choose a type of behavior you think might satisfy the need
Rewards
Two types of rewards satisfy needs—extrinsic or intrinsic
Feedback Reward informs you whether behavior worked and should be used again

For example, you find you are hungry (need), which impels you to seek food (motive). You make a sandwich and eat it (behavior), which provides satisfaction (reward) and informs you (feedback loop) that sandwiches will reduce hunger and so should be used in the future. Or as an hourly worker you desire more money (need), which impels you (motivates you) to work more hours (behavior), which provides you with more money (reward) and informs you (feedback loop) that working more hours will fulfill your need for more money in the future.

Rewards (as well as motivation itself) are of two types—*extrinsic* and *intrinsic.*[3] Managers can use both to encourage better work performance.

- **Extrinsic rewards—satisfaction in the payoff from others: An *extrinsic reward* is the payoff, such as money, a person receives from others for performing a particular task.** An extrinsic reward is an external reward; the payoff comes from pleasing others.

  Example: In performing your job as a maker of custom sailboats, you get your principal satisfaction from receiving the great amount of money buyers pay you for a boat—an extrinsic reward.

- **Intrinsic rewards—satisfaction in performing the task itself: An *intrinsic reward* is the satisfaction, such as a feeling of accomplishment, a person receives from performing the particular task itself.** An intrinsic reward is an internal reward; the payoff comes from pleasing yourself.

  Example: In making custom sailboats, you derive satisfaction—warm feelings of accomplishment and heightened self-esteem—from the process of building a sailboat.

Why Is Motivation Important?

It seems obvious that organizations would want to motivate their employees to be more productive. Actually, though, there are five reasons why you as a manager will find knowledge of motivation important.[4] In order of importance, you want to motivate people to . . .

- ***Join your organization:*** You need to instill in talented prospective workers the desire to come to work for you.
- ***Stay with your organization:*** Whether you are in good economic times or bad, you always want to be able to retain good people.
- ***Show up for work at your organization:*** In many organizations, absenteeism and lateness are tremendous problems.[5]
- ***Perform better for your organization:*** Some employees do just enough to avoid being fired.[6] But what you really want is employees who will give you high productivity.
- ***Do extra for your organization:*** You hope your employees will perform extra tasks above and beyond the call of duty (be organizational "good citizens").

The Three Major Perspectives on Motivation: Overview

There is no theory accepted by everyone as to what motivates people. In this chapter, therefore, we present the three principal perspectives. From these, you may be able to select what ideas seem most workable for you. The three perspectives on motivation are (1) *need-based,* (2) *process,* and (3) *reinforcement,* as described in the following three main sections. ◆

major question

What kinds of needs motivate employees?

The Big Picture

Need-based perspectives are theories emphasizing the needs that motivate people. Needs are defined as physiological or psychological deficiencies that arouse behavior. The needs-based perspective includes three theories: Maslow's hierarchy of needs, Herzberg's two-factor theory, and McClelland's acquired needs theory.

Need-based perspectives, **also known as *content perspectives,* are theories that emphasize the needs that motivate people.** Needs theorists ask, "What kind of needs motivate employees in the workplace?" ***Needs*** **are defined as physiological or psychological deficiencies that arouse behavior.** They can be strong or weak, and, because they are influenced by environmental factors, they can vary over time and from place to place.

In addition to McGregor's Theory X/Theory Y (see Chapter 2), needs-based perspectives include three theories:

- Maslow's hierarchy of needs theory
- Herzberg's two-factor theory
- McClelland's acquired needs theory

Maslow's Hierarchy of Needs Theory: Five Levels

In 1943, Brandeis University psychology professor **Abraham Maslow,** one of the first researchers to study motivation, put forth his ***hierarchy of needs theory,*** **which proposes that people are motivated by five levels of needs: (1) physiological, (2) safety, (3) belongingness, (4) esteem, and (5) self-actualization.**[7]

The Five Levels of Needs

In proposing this hierarchy of five needs, ranging from basic to highest level, Maslow suggested that needs are never completely satisfied. That is, our actions are aimed at fulfilling the "deprived" needs, the needs that remain unsatisfied at any point in time. Thus, for example, once you have achieved security, which is the second most basic need, you will then seek to fulfill the third most basic need—belongingness.

In order of ascendance, from bottom to top, the five levels of needs are as follows. *(See Figure 12.2, opposite.)*

Self-actualization. No one has to engage in voluntarism, as this teacher is doing with a young girl at a Garden Grove, California, after-school reading program. But for some people, according to Maslow's theory, it represents the kind of realization of the best life has to offer—after other needs are satisfied. If "you go around only once," as the saying goes, what activity or experience within your lifetime would represent self-fulfillment for you, the best that would realize your potential?

FIGURE 12.2
Maslow's hierarchy of needs

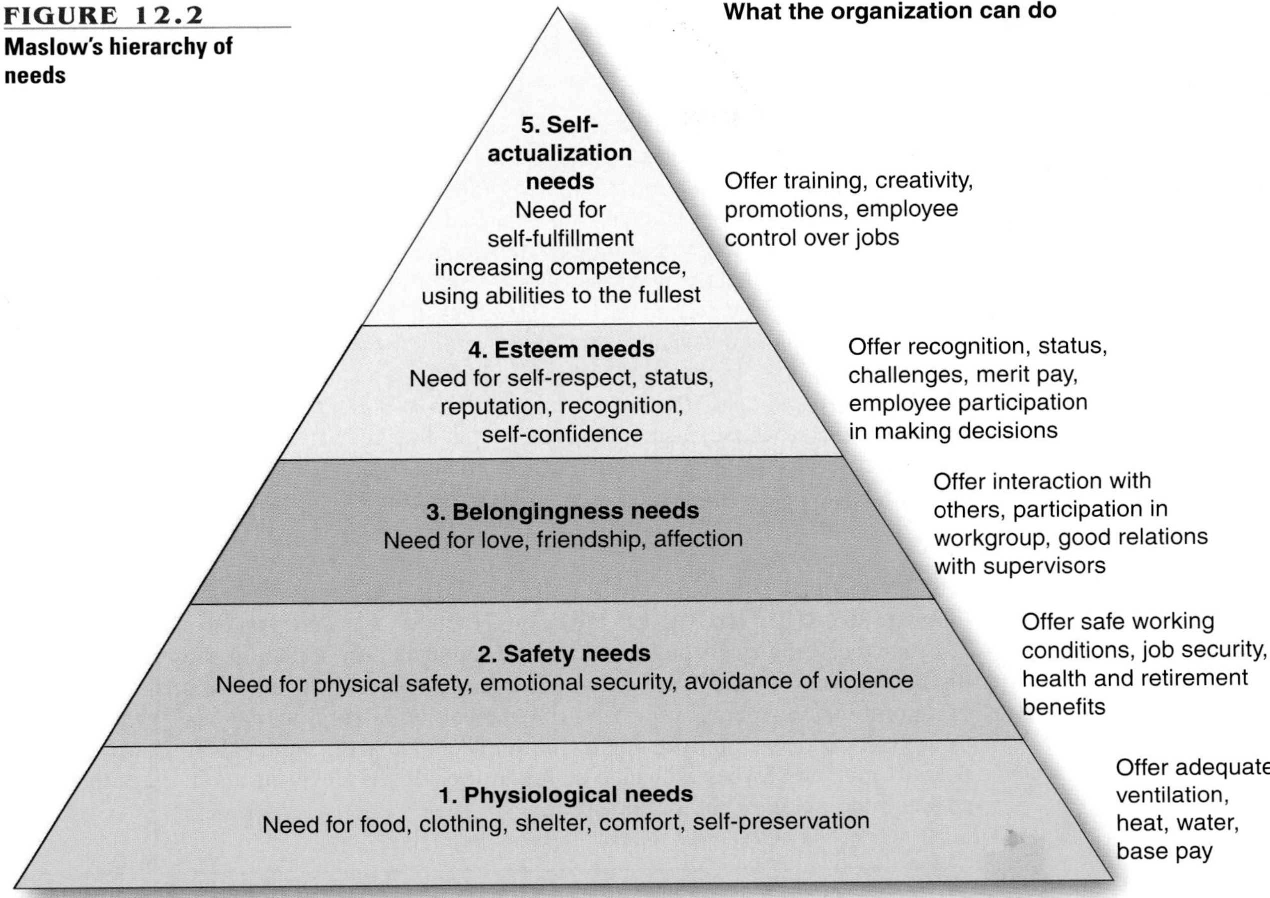
What the organization can do
5. Self-actualization needs
Need for self-fulfillment increasing competence, using abilities to the fullest
Offer training, creativity, promotions, employee control over jobs
4. Esteem needs
Need for self-respect, status, reputation, recognition, self-confidence
Offer recognition, status, challenges, merit pay, employee participation in making decisions
3. Belongingness needs
Need for love, friendship, affection
Offer interaction with others, participation in workgroup, good relations with supervisors
2. Safety needs
Need for physical safety, emotional security, avoidance of violence
Offer safe working conditions, job security, health and retirement benefits
1. Physiological needs
Need for food, clothing, shelter, comfort, self-preservation
Offer adequate ventilation, heat, water, base pay

1 Physiological Needs These are the most basic human physical needs, in which one is concerned with having food, clothing, shelter, and comfort and with self-preservation.

2 Safety Needs These needs are concerned with physical safety and emotional security, so that a person is concerned with avoiding violence and threats.

3 Belongingness Needs Once basic needs and security are taken care of, people look for love, friendship, and affection.

4 Esteem Needs After they meet their social needs, people focus on such matters as self-respect, status, reputation, recognition, and self-confidence.

5 Self-Actualization Needs The highest level of need, self-actualization is self-fulfillment—the need to develop one's fullest potential, to become the best one is capable of being.

Research does not clearly support Maslow's theory, although it remains popular among managers. "There are still very few studies that can legitimately confirm (or refute) it," one scholar writes. "It may be that the dynamics implied by Maslow's theory of needs are too complex to be operationalized and confirmed by scientific research."[8]

Example

Higher-Level Needs: "Tempered Radicals" Strike a Balance between Safety & Higher-Level Needs

Peter Grant is a black executive who for years has worked quietly behind the scenes to recruit thousands of minorities—3,500 at one large financial institution alone. Through the years he asked every person he hired to promise to bring other minorities along. With this strategy of "quiet resistance," he achieved his goal of hiring more people of color without making this a huge issue within his company.

Grant is an example of what Debra Meyerson calls a "tempered radical." In her book *Tempered Radicals: How People Use Difference to Inspire Change at Work,* Meyerson writes that "Tempered radicals want to fit in *and* they want to retain what makes them different. They want to rock the boat, and they want to stay in it."[9]

Tempered radicals, in other words, work to strike a balance between what they believe in and what the system expects. In this way, they fulfill both their safety needs while also striving to fulfill their self-actualization needs.

Using the Hierarchy of Needs Theory to Motivate Employees

For managers, the importance of Maslow's contribution is that he showed that workers have needs beyond that of just earning a paycheck. To the extent the organization permits, managers should first try to meet employees' level 1 and level 2 needs, of course, so that employees won't be preoccupied with them. Then, however, they need to give employees a chance to fulfill their higher-level needs in ways that also advance the goals of the organization.

Herzberg's Two-Factor Theory: From Dissatisfying Factors to Satisfying Factors

Frederick Herzberg arrived at his needs-based theory as a result of a landmark study of 203 accountants and engineers, who were interviewed to determine the factors responsible for job satisfaction and dissatisfaction.[10] Job satisfaction was more frequently associated with achievement, recognition, characteristics of the work, responsibility, and advancement. Job dissatisfaction was more often associated with working conditions, pay and security, company policies, supervisors, and interpersonal relationships. The result was Herzberg's ***two-factor theory,*** **which proposed that work satisfaction and dissatisfaction arise from two different factors—work satisfaction from so-called *motivating factors* and work dissatisfaction from so-called *hygiene factors.***

Hygiene Factors versus Motivating Factors

In Herzberg's theory, the hygiene factors are the lower-level needs, the motivating factors are the higher-level needs. The two areas are separated by a zone in which employees are neither satisfied nor dissatisfied. *(See Figure 12.3, opposite.)*

- **Hygiene factors—"Why are my people dissatisfied?"** The lower-level needs, ***hygiene factors,*** **are factors associated with job *dissatisfaction*—such as salary, working conditions, interpersonal relationships, and company policy—all of which affect the job *context* in which people work.**

  An example of a hygiene factor is the temperature in a factory that's not air-conditioned during the summer. Installing air-conditioning will remove a cause of job dissatisfaction. It will not, however, spur factory workers' motivation and make them greatly satisfied in their work. Because motivating factors are absent,

FIGURE 12.3
Herzberg's two-factor theory: satisfaction versus dissatisfaction

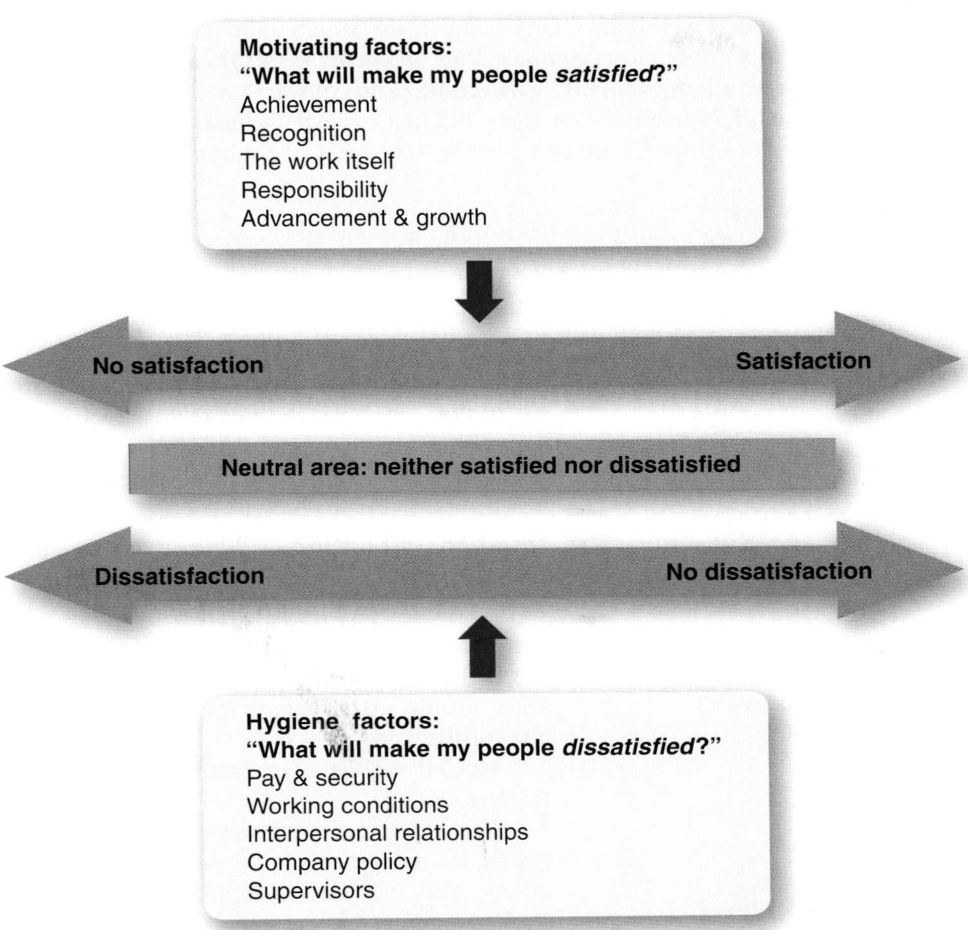

workers become, in Herzberg's view, merely neutral in their attitudes toward work—neither dissatisfied nor satisfied.

- **Motivating factors—"What will make my people satisfied?"** The higher-level needs, ***motivating factors,*** **or simply *motivators,* are factors associated with job *satisfaction*—such as achievement, recognition, responsibility, and advancement—all of which affect the job content or the rewards of work performance.** Motivating factors—challenges, opportunities, recognition—must be instituted, Herzberg believed, to spur superior work performance.

  An example of a motivating factor would be to give factory workers more control over their work. For example, instead of repeating a single task over and over, a worker might join with other workers in a team in which each one does several tasks. This is the approach that Swedish automaker Volvo has taken in building cars.

Using Two-Factor Theory to Motivate Employees

The basic lesson of Herzberg's research is that managers should first eliminate dissatisfaction, making sure that working conditions, pay levels, and company policies are reasonable. They should then concentrate on spurring motivation by providing opportunities for achievement, recognition, responsibility, and personal growth.

McClelland's Acquired Needs Theory: Achievement, Affiliation, & Power

David McClelland, a well-known psychologist, investigated the needs for affiliation and power and as a consequence proposed the ***acquired needs theory,*** **which states that three needs—achievement, affiliation, and power—are major motives determining people's behavior in the workplace.**[11] McClelland believes that we are not born with our needs; rather we learn them from the culture—from our life experiences.

The Three Needs

Managers are encouraged to recognize three needs in themselves and others and to attempt to create work environments that are responsive to them. The three needs, one of which tends to be dominant in each of us, are as follows. *(See Figure 12.4.)*

FIGURE 12.4
McClelland's three needs

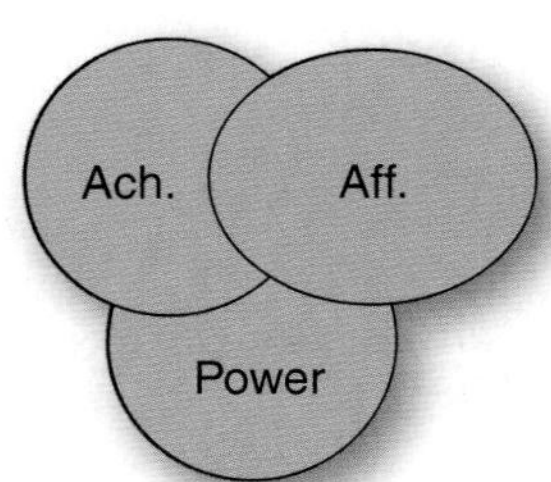

A "well-balanced" individual: achievement, affiliation, and power are of equal size

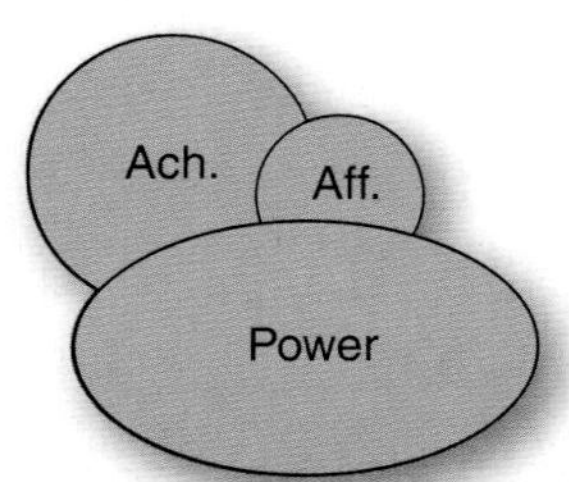

A "control freak" individual: achievement is normal, but affiliation is small and power is large

- **Need for achievement—"I need to excel at tasks":** This is the desire to excel, to do something better or more efficiently, to solve problems, to achieve excellence in challenging tasks.
- **Need for affiliation—"I need close relationships":** This is the desire for friendly and warm relations with other people.
- **Need for power—"I need to control others":** This is the desire to be responsible for other people, to influence their behavior or to control them.[12]

McClelland identifies two forms of the need for power.

The negative kind is the need for *personal power*, as expressed in the desire to dominate others, and involves manipulating people for one's own gratification.

The positive kind, characteristic of top managers and leaders, is the desire for *institutional power,* as expressed in the need to solve problems that further organizational goals.

The three needs theories are compared below. *(See Figure 12.5.)*

FIGURE 12.5
A comparison of needs theories: Maslow, Herzberg, and McClelland. McClelland has no classification for lower-level needs.

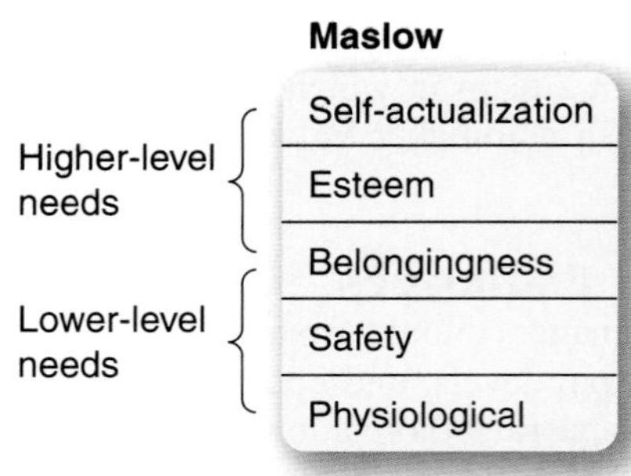

Using Acquired Needs Theory to Motivate Employees

McClelland asssociates the three needs with different sets of work preferences, as follows:[13]

- **Need for achievement:** If you (or an employee) are happy with accomplishment of a task being its own reward, don't mind or even prefer working alone, and are willing to take moderate risks, then you probably have a *high need for achievement*. That being the case, you (or your employee) would probably prefer doing the kind of work that offers feedback on performance, challenging but achievable goals, and individual responsibility for results. People high in need for achievement tend to advance in technical fields requiring creativity and individual skills.[14]
- **Need for power:** If you, like most effective managers, have a *high need for power,* that means you enjoy being in control of people and events and being recognized for this responsibility. Accordingly, your preference would probably be for work that allows you to control or have an effect on people and be publicly recognized for your accomplishments.
- **Need for affiliation:** If you tend to seek social approval and satisfying personal relationships, you may have a *high need for affiliation*. In that case, you may not be the most efficient manager because at times you will have to make decisions that will make people resent you. Instead, you will tend to prefer work, such as sales, that provides for personal relationships and social approval. ◆

Example

Acquired Needs Theory: The Need for Achievement of a Die Engineer at Monroe Auto Equipment

You don't have to be a celebrity or a high-powered executive to display the McClelland feature of high need for achievement (which overlaps with Maslow's higher-order needs of esteem and self-actualization). Consider automotive die engineer Bob Stadler.

When, at age 18, Stadler joined Monroe Auto Equipment, a family-owned company in Monroe, Mich., his one great ambition was to be the best tool and die maker in the world. Throughout his career, Monroe has continued to be his only employer, and he has risen to the position of senior staff engineer. Not widely known outside the company, he is greatly admired within the two-story headquarters of Monroe Auto, where his word is final on whether a product is manufacturable.

"He is the best die engineer I have ever seen in my life," says president Jack Thompson, whose late father also worked with Stadler. "No one [else] even comes close."[15]

major question

Is a good reward good enough? How do other factors affect motivation?

The Big Picture

Process perspectives, which are concerned with the thought processes by which people decide how to act, have three viewpoints: expectancy theory, equity theory, and goal-setting theory.

Process perspectives **are concerned with the thought processes by which people decide how to act**—how employees choose behavior to meet their needs. Whereas need-based perspectives simply try to understand employee needs, process perspectives go further and try to understand why employees have different needs, what behaviors they select to satisfy them, and how they decide if their choices were successful.

In this section we discuss three process perspectives on motivation:

- Expectancy theory
- Equity theory
- Goal-setting theory

Expectancy Theory: How Much Do You Want & How Likely Are You to Get It?

Introduced by **Victor Vroom, *expectancy theory* suggests that people are motivated by two things: (1) how much they want something and (2) how likely they think they are to get it.**[16] In other words, assuming they have choices, people will make the choice that promises them the greatest reward if they think they can get it.

The Three Elements: Expectancy, Instrumentality, Valence

What determines how willing you (or an employee) are to work hard at tasks important to the success of the organization? The answer, says Vroom, is: You will do what you *can* do when you *want* to.

Your motivation, according to expectancy theory, involves the relationship between your *effort,* your *performance,* and the desirability of the *outcomes* (such as pay or recognition) of your performance. These relationships, which are shown in the accompanying drawing, are affected by the three elements of *expectancy, instrumentality,* and *valence. (See Figure 12.6.)*

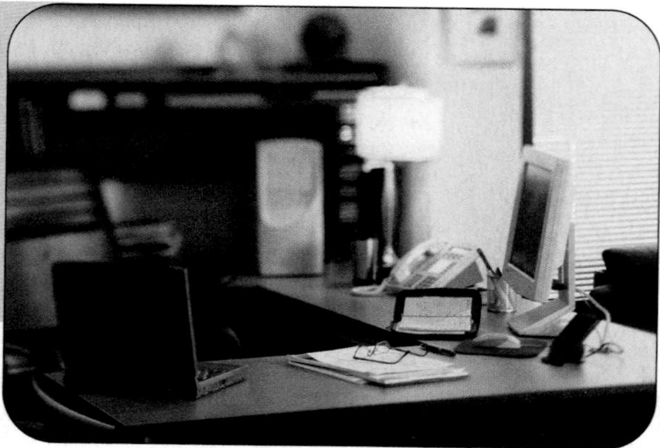

How much do you want? Would a well-appointed office represent the tangible realization of managerial success for you? How likely do you think you are to get it? The answers to these questions represent your important motivations, according to expectancy theory.

FIGURE 12.6
Expectancy theory: The major elements

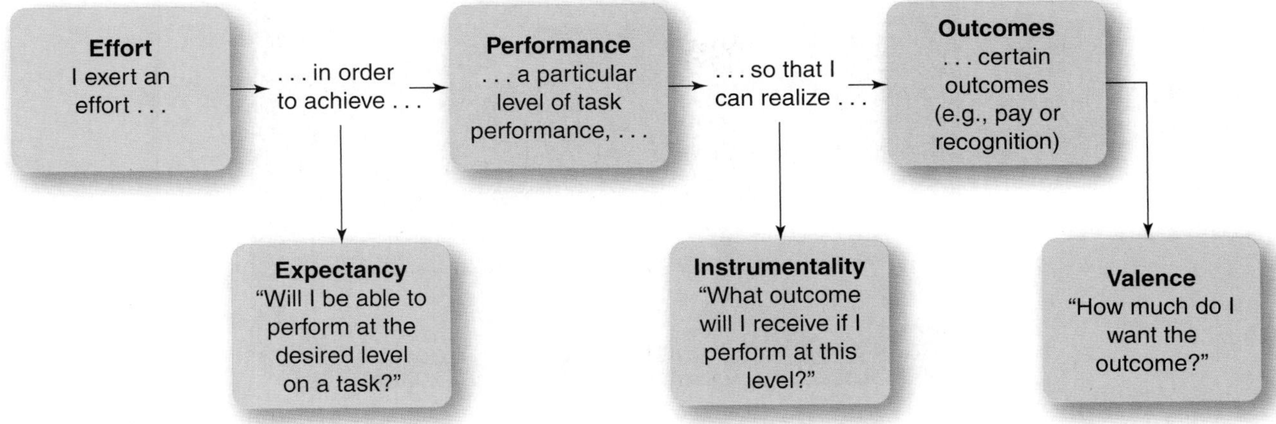
Effort
I exert an effort . . .
. . . in order to achieve . . .
Performance
. . . a particular level of task performance, . . .
. . . so that I can realize . . .
Outcomes
. . . certain outcomes (e.g., pay or recognition)
Expectancy
"Will I be able to perform at the desired level on a task?"
Instrumentality
"What outcome will I receive if I perform at this level?"
Valence
"How much do I want the outcome?"

1 Expectancy—"Will I be able to perform at the desired level on a task?" ***Expectancy*** **is the belief that a particular level of effort will lead to a particular level of performance.** This is called the *effort-to-performance expectancy*.

Example: If you believe that putting in more hours working at Circuit City selling videogame machines will result in higher sales, then you have high effort-to-performance expectancy. That is, you believe that your efforts will matter. You think you have the ability, the product knowledge, and so on so that putting in extra hours of selling can probably raise your sales of videogame machines.

2 Instrumentality—"What outcome will I receive if I perform at this level?" ***Instrumentality*** **is the expectation that successful performance of the task will lead to the outcome desired.** This is called the *performance-to-reward expectancy*.

Example: If you believe that making higher sales will cause Circuit City to give you a bonus, then you have high performance-to-reward expectancy. You believe *if* you can achieve your goals, the outcome will be worthwhile. This element is independent of the previous one—you might decide you don't have the ability to make the extra sales, but if you did, you'll be rewarded.

3 Valence—"How much do I want the outcome?" ***Valence*** **is value, the importance a worker assigns to the possible outcome or reward.**

Example: If you assign a lot of importance or a high value to Circuit City's prospective bonus or pay raise, then your valence is said to be high.

For your motivation to be high, you must be high on all three elements—expectancy, instrumentality, and valence. If any element is low, you will not be motivated. Your effort-to-performance expectancy might be low, for instance, because you doubt making an effort will make a difference (because retail selling has too much competition from Internet sellers). Or your performance-to-reward expectancy might be low because you don't think Circuit City is going to give you a bonus for being a star at selling. Or your valence might be low because you don't think the bonus or raise is going to be high enough to justify working evenings and weekends.

Using Expectancy Theory to Motivate Employees

The principal problem with expectancy theory is that it is complex. Even so, the underlying logic is understandable. When attempting to motivate employees, managers should ask the following questions:

Going for the gold. Athletes at the 2004 Athens Olympics knew what kinds of performance they had to put forth to earn winners' medallions. Do you think the objectives, performance levels, and rewards can be as clear-cut in the business world?

- **What rewards do your employees value?** As a manager, you need to get to know your employees and determine what rewards (outcomes) they value, such as pay raises or recognition.
- **What are the job objectives and the performance level you desire?** You need to clearly define the performance objectives and determine what performance level or behavior you want so that you can tell your employees what they need to do to attain the rewards.
- **Are the rewards linked to performance?** You want to reward high performance, of course. If high-performing employees aren't rewarded, they may leave or slow down and affect the performance of other employees. Thus, employees must be aware that X level of performance within Y period of time will result in Z kinds of rewards.
- **Do employees believe you will deliver the right rewards for the right performance?** Your credibility is on the line here. Your employees must believe that you have the power, the ability, and the will to give them the rewards you promise for the performance you are requesting.

Example

Use of Expectancy Theory: Federal Express Tackles a Problem with Backed-up Packages

At one point, Frederick Smith, founder and chief executive officer of Federal Express Corp., had to deal with a performance problem in which the FedEx planes would all arrive at the package carrier's hub, but the shipments would get backed up during the transfer process because the cargo handlers—who were mostly college students—would allow things to run late. The reason: the more hours they worked, the more money they made.

To fix the problem, FedEx offered the cargo handlers a minimum pay guarantee, then said, in Smith's words, "Look, if you get through before a certain time, just go home, and you will have beat the system." Within 45 days, the problem was solved. In Vroom's model, because the student workers originally had been paid on the basis of hours rather than output, they exerted low effort. By giving the students guaranteed pay and allowing them to go home early if and when they completed their tasks, FedEx prompted high effort.[17]

Equity Theory: How Fairly Do You Think You're Being Treated in Relation to Others?

Fairness—or, perhaps equally important, the *perception* of fairness—can be a big issue in organizations. For example, if you received a 10% bonus from Circuit City for doubling your sales, would that be enough? What if other Circuit City salespeople received 15%?

Equity theory **focuses on employee perceptions as to how fairly they think they are being treated compared to others.** Developed by psychologist **J. Stacy Adams,** equity theory is based on the idea that employees are motivated to see fairness in the rewards they expect for task performance.[18] Clearly, this is an important matter. The U.S. Department of Commerce estimates that employee theft, for example, costs American business about $50 billion a year. This may represent employees' attempts to even the score when they feel that they haven't been treated fairly by their organizations.[19]

The Elements of Equity Theory: Comparing Your Inputs & Outputs with Those of Others

The key elements in equity theory are *inputs, outputs (rewards),* and *comparisons. (See Figure 12.7.)*

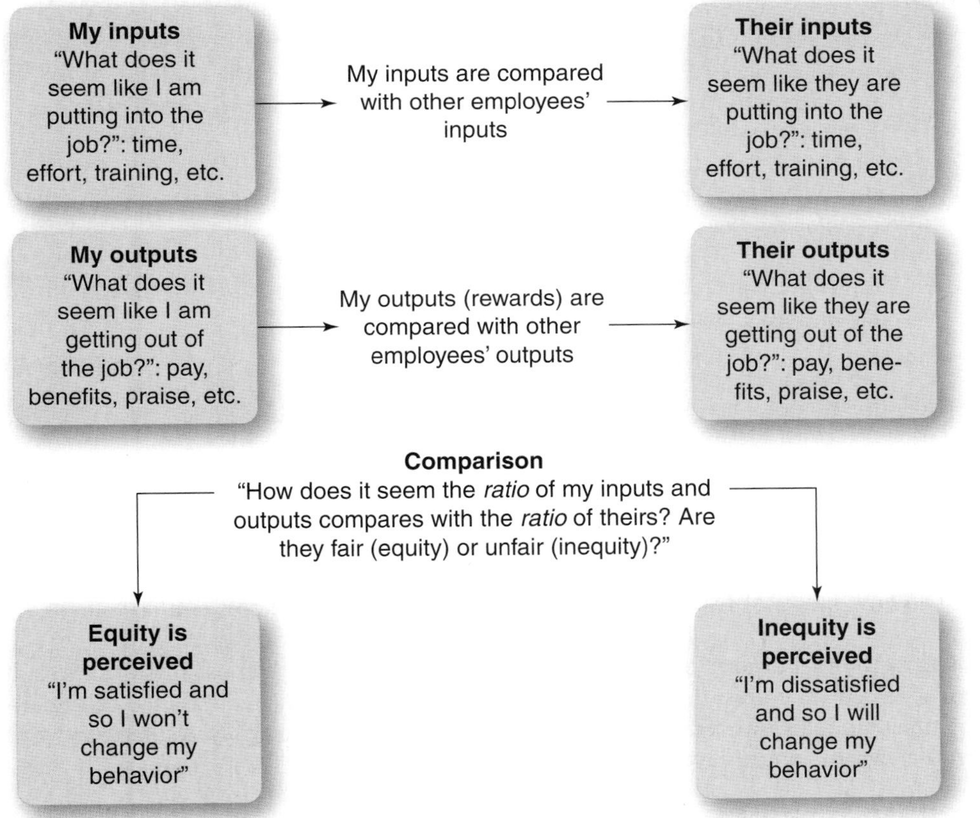
My inputs
"What does it seem like I am putting into the job?": time, effort, training, etc.
My inputs are compared with other employees' inputs
Their inputs
"What does it seem like they are putting into the job?": time, effort, training, etc.
My outputs
"What does it seem like I am getting out of the job?": pay, benefits, praise, etc.
My outputs (rewards) are compared with other employees' outputs
Their outputs
"What does it seem like they are getting out of the job?": pay, benefits, praise, etc.
Comparison
"How does it seem the *ratio* of my inputs and outputs compares with the *ratio* of theirs? Are they fair (equity) or unfair (inequity)?"
Equity is perceived
"I'm satisfied and so I won't change my behavior"
Inequity is perceived
"I'm dissatisfied and so I will change my behavior"

FIGURE 12.7

Equity theory. How people perceive they are being fairly or unfairly rewarded

- **Inputs—"What do you think you're putting in to the job?"** The inputs that people perceive they give to an organization are their time, effort, training, experience, intelligence, creativity, seniority, status, and so on.

- **Outputs or rewards—"What do you think you're getting out of the job?"** The outputs are the rewards that people receive from an organization: pay, benefits, praise, recognition, bonuses, promotions, status perquisites (corner office with a view, say, or private parking space), and so on.
- **Comparison—"How do you think your ratio of inputs and rewards compares with those of others?"** Equity theory suggests that people compare the *ratio* of their own outcomes to inputs against the *ratio* of someone else's outcomes to inputs. When employees compare the ratio of their inputs and outputs (rewards) with those of others—whether coworkers within the organization or even other people in similar jobs outside it—they then make a judgment about fairness. Either they perceive there is *equity*—they are satisfied with the ratio and so they don't change their behavior. Or they perceive there is *inequity*—they feel resentful and act to change the inequity.

Using Equity Theory to Motivate Employees

Adams suggests that employees who feel they are being underrewarded will respond to the perceived inequity in one or more negative ways, as by reducing their inputs, trying to change the outputs or rewards they receive, distorting the inequity, changing the object of comparison, or leaving the situation. *(See Table 12.1.)*

TABLE 12.1
Some ways employees try to reduce inequity.

- **They will reduce their inputs:** They will do less work, take long breaks, call in "sick" on Mondays, leave early on Fridays, and so on.
- **They will try to change the outputs or rewards they receive:** They will lobby the boss for a raise, or they will pilfer company equipment.
- **They will distort the inequity:** They will exaggerate how hard they work so they can complain they're not paid what they're worth.
- **They will change the object of comparison:** They may compare themselves to another person instead of the original one.
- **They will leave the situation:** They will quit, transfer, or shift to another reference group.

By contrast, employees who think they are treated fairly are more likely to support organizational change, more apt to cooperate in group settings, and less apt to turn to arbitration and the courts to remedy real or imagined wrongs.

Three practical lessons that can be drawn from equity theory are as follows.

1 Employee Perceptions Are What Count Probably the most important result of research on equity theory is this: no matter how fair managers think the organization's policies, procedures, and reward system are, each employee's *perception* of those factors is what counts.

2 Employee Participation Helps Managers benefit by allowing employees to participate in important decisions. For example, employees are more satisfied with their performance appraisal when they have a "voice" during their appraisal review.[20]

3 Having an Appeal Process Helps When employees are able to appeal decisions affecting their welfare, it promotes the belief that management treats them fairly. Perceptions of fair treatment promote job satisfaction and commitment and reduce absenteeism and turnover.[21]

Goal-Setting Theory: Objectives Should Be Specific & Challenging but Achievable

Goal-setting theory **suggests that employees can be motivated by goals that are specific and challenging but achievable.** According to psychologists **Edwin Locke** and **Gary Latham,** who developed the theory, it is natural for people to set and strive for goals; however, the goal-setting process is useful only if people *understand* and *accept* the goals. Thus, the best way to motivate performance is to set the right objectives in the right ways.[22]

The benefits of setting goals is that a manager can tailor rewards to the needs of individual employees, clarify what is expected of them, provide regular reinforcement, and maintain equity.

Three Elements of Goal-Setting Theory

A *goal* is defined as an objective that a person is trying to accomplish through his or her efforts. To result in high motivation and performance, according to goal-setting theory, goals must be *specific, challenging,* and *achievable.*

1 Goals Should Be Specific Goals such as "Sell as many cars as you can" or "Be nicer to customers" are too vague and therefore have no effect on motivation. Instead, goals need to be specific—usually meaning *quantitative.* As a manager, for example, you may be asked to boost the revenues of your unit by 25% and to cut absenteeism by 10%, all specific targets.

2 Goals Should Be Challenging Goal theory suggests you not set goals that a lot of people can reach, since this is not very motivational. Rather you should set goals that are challenging, which will impel people to focus their attention in the right place and to apply more effort or inputs toward their jobs—in other words, motivate them toward higher performance.

3 Goals Should Be Achievable Goals can't be unattainable, of course. You might ask data-entry clerks to enter 25% more names and addresses an hour into a database, but if they don't have touch-typing skills, that goal won't be attainable. Thus, managers need to make sure employees have additional training, if necessary, to achieve difficult goals.

Using Goal-Setting Theory to Motivate Employees

When developing employee goals, make sure the goals not only are specific, challenging, and achievable but also are as follows:

1. Set jointly with the employee
2. Are measurable
3. Have a target date for attainment

Finally, make sure that you give feedback so that employees know of their progress—and don't forget to reward people for doing what they set out to do. ◆

Small business. Do employees in small businesses, such as this worker in a hardware store, need the same kind of motivational goals as employees in large corporations? Is setting goals in small businesses, where there's apt to be less specialization, more or less difficult than in large organizations?

major question **What are the types of incentives I might use to influence employee behavior?**

The Big Picture

Reinforcement theory suggests behavior will be repeated if it has positive consequences and won't be if it has negative consequences. There are four types of reinforcement: positive reinforcement, negative reinforcement, extinction, and punishment. This section also describes how to use some reinforcement techniques to modify employee behavior.

Reinforcement evades the issue of people's needs and thinking processes in relation to motivation, as we described under the need-based and process perspectives. Instead, the reinforcement perspective, which was pioneered by **Edward L. Thorndike** and **B. F. Skinner,** is concerned with how the consequences of a certain behavior affect that behavior in the future.[23]

Skinner was the father of *operant conditioning,* the process of controlling behavior by manipulating its consequences. Operant conditioning rests on Thorndike's *law of effect,* which states that behavior that results in a pleasant outcome is likely to be repeated and behavior that results in unpleasant outcomes is not likely to be repeated.

From these underpinnings has come ***reinforcement theory,*** **which attempts to explain behavior change by suggesting that behavior with positive consequences tends to be repeated, whereas behavior with negative consequences tends not to be repeated.** The use of reinforcement theory to change human behavior is called *behavior modification.*

The Four Types of Reinforcement: Positive, Negative, Extinction, & Punishment

Reinforcement **is anything that causes a given behavior to be repeated or inhibited,** whether praising a child for cleaning his or her room or scolding a child for leaving a tricycle in the driveway. There are four types of reinforcement: (1) *positive reinforcement,* (2) *negative reinforcement,* (3) *extinction,* and (4) *punishment. (See Figure 12.8, opposite.)*

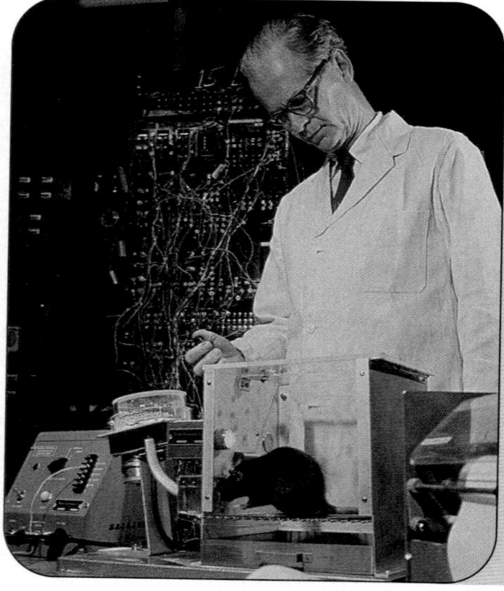

B.F. Skinner and subject. The psychologist known as the father of operant conditioning is shown here in his Harvard University laboratory with a rat in a so-called Skinner box. Besides a lever and food cup, the box contains devices to record every time the animal presses the lever and food pellets are delivered. The goal of the experiment is to condition the rat to press the lever, training it to do so by rewarding it with food every time it does so. A key to operant conditioning is that the reinforcer should immediately follow the desired behavior. Could you use this kind of knowledge to "condition" an employee who is habitually late to show up on time?

FIGURE 12.8

Four types of reinforcement. These are different ways of changing employee behavior.

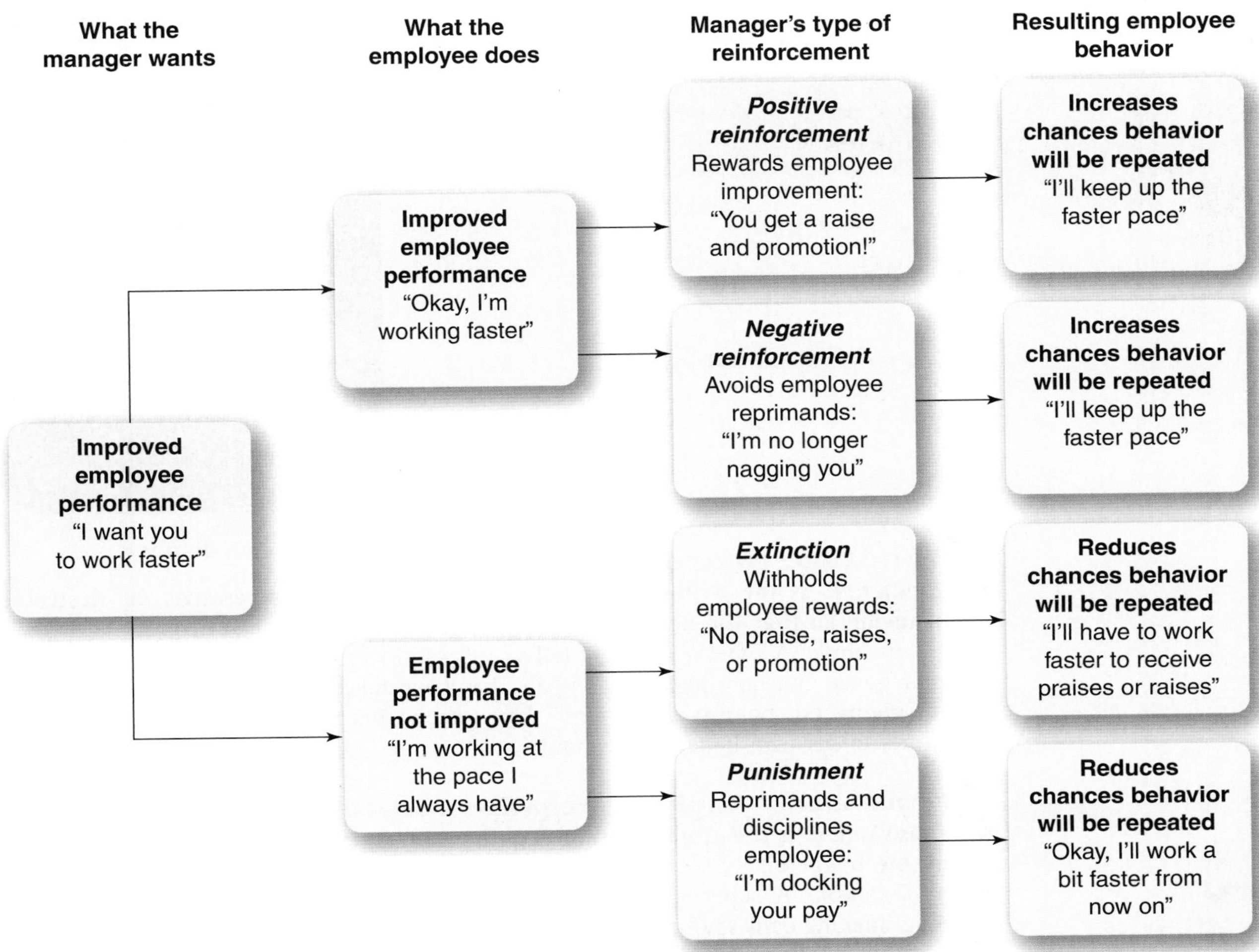

Positive Reinforcement: Giving Rewards

Positive reinforcement **is the use of positive consequences to encourage desirable behavior.**

Example: A supervisor who's asked an insurance salesperson to sell more policies might reward successful performance by saying, "It's great that you exceeded your quota, and you'll get a bonus for it. Maybe next time you'll sell even more and will become a member of the Circle of 100 Top Sellers and win a trip to Paris as well." Note the rewards: praise, more money, recognition, awards. Presumably this will *strengthen* the behavior and the sales rep will work even harder in the coming months.

Negative Reinforcement: Avoiding Unpleasantness

Negative reinforcement **is the removal of unpleasant consequences following a desired behavior.**

Example: A supervisor who has been nagging a salesperson might say, "Well, so you exceeded your quota" and stop the nagging. Note the neutral statement; there is no praise but also no longer any negative statements. This could cause the sales rep to *maintain* his or her existing behavior.

Oh, no! Does getting a wallet-busting traffic ticket (as for parking in a bus zone) change your behavior? What if it happens several times? Looking at the four different kinds of reinforcement, which type is being employed here? Yet consider also other, presumably stronger forms of punishment that are supposed to act as deterrents to bad behavior. Does the existence of the death penalty really deter homicides? Why or why not?

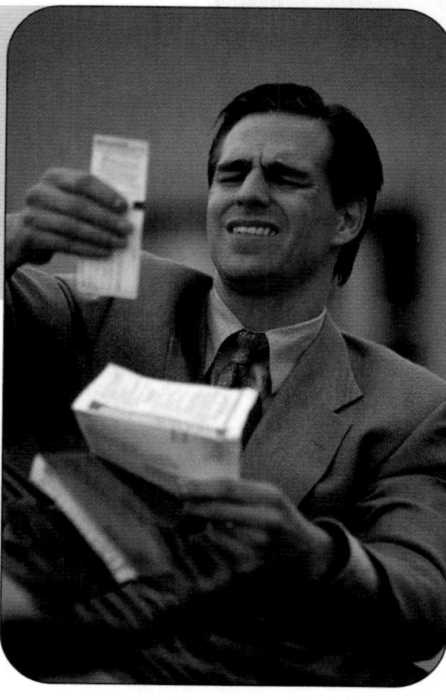

Extinction: Withholding Rewards

Extinction **is the withholding or withdrawal of positive rewards for desirable behavior, so that the behavior is less likely to occur in the future.**

Example: A supervisor might tell a successful salesperson, "I know you exceeded your quota, but now that our company has been taken over by another firm, we're not giving out bonuses any more." Presumably this will *weaken* the salesperson's efforts to perform better in the future.

Punishment: Applying Negative Consequences

Punishment **is the application of negative consequences to stop or change undesirable behavior.**

Example: A supervisor might tell an unsuccessful salesperson who's been lazy about making calls to clients and so didn't make quota, "Well, if this keeps up, you'll probably be let go." This could *inhibit* the salesperson from being so lackadaisical about making calls to clients.

Using Reinforcement to Motivate Employees

The following are some guidelines for using two types of reinforcement—positive reinforcement and punishment.

Positive Reinforcement

There are several aspects of positive reinforcement, which should definitely be part of your toolkit of managerial skills:

- **Reward only desirable behavior:** You should give rewards to your employees only when they show *desirable* behavior. Thus, for example, you should give praise to employees not for showing up for work on time (an expected part of any job) but for showing up early.
- **Give rewards as soon as possible:** You should give a reward as soon as possible after the desirable behavior appears. Thus, you should give praise to an early-arriving employee as soon as he or she arrives, not later in the week.
- **Be clear about what behavior is desired:** Clear communication is everything. You should tell employees exactly what kinds of work behaviors are desirable and you should tell everyone exactly what they must do to earn rewards.

- **Have different rewards and recognize individual differences:** Recognizing that different people respond to different kinds of rewards, you should have different rewards available. Thus, you might give a word of praise verbally to one person, shoot a line or two by e-mail to another person, or send a hand-scrawled note to another.

Punishment

Unquestionably there will be times when you'll need to threaten or administer an unpleasant consequence to stop an employee's undesirable behavior. Sometimes it's best to address a problem by combining punishment with positive reinforcement. Some suggestions for using punishment are as follows.

- **Punish only undesirable behavior:** You should give punishment only when employees show frequent *undesirable* behavior. Otherwise, employees may come to view you negatively as a tyrannical boss. Thus, for example, you should reprimand employees who show up, say, a half hour late for work but not 5 or 10 minutes late.
- **Give reprimands or disciplinary actions as soon as possible:** You should mete out punishment as soon as possible after the undesirable behavior occurs. Thus, you should give a reprimand to a late-arriving employee as soon as he or she arrives.
- **Be clear about what behavior is undesirable:** Tell employees exactly what kinds of work behaviors are undesirable and make any disciplinary action or reprimand match the behavior. A manager should not, for example, dock an hourly employee's pay if he or she is only 5 or 10 minutes late for work.
- **Administer punishment in private:** You would hate to have your boss chew you out in front of your subordinates, and the people who report to you also shouldn't be reprimanded in public, which would lead only to resentments that may have nothing to do with an employee's infractions.
- **Combine punishment and positive reinforcement:** If you're reprimanding an employee, be sure to also say what he or she is doing right and state what rewards the employee might be eligible for. For example, while reprimanding someone for being late, say that a perfect attendance record over the next few months will put that employee in line for a raise or promotion. ◆

Enron revisited. Sherron Watkins, a vice president of Enron, testifies in a hearing before the U.S. Congress, as former CEO Jeffrey Skilling looks on. Watkins testified about her attempts to warn top managers of her fears that the company would "implode" because of irregular financial practices—fears that proved to be well founded. Do you think Enron's managers considered her warnings as undesirable behavior? How common is it for employees to successfully criticize their superiors to other managers?

major question

What's the best way to design jobs—adapt people to work or work to people?

The Big Picture

Job design, the division of an organization's work among employees, applies motivational theories to jobs to increase performance and satisfaction. The traditional approach to job design is to fit people to the jobs; the modern way is to fit the jobs to the people, using job enlargement and enrichment. The job characteristics model offers five job attributes for better work outcomes.

Job design **is (1) the division of an organization's work among its employees and (2) the application of motivational theories to jobs to increase satisfaction and performance.** There are two different approaches to job design, one traditional, one modern, that can be taken in deciding how to design jobs. The traditional way is *fitting people to jobs;* the modern way is *fitting jobs to people.*

Fitting people to jobs is based on the assumption that people will gradually adapt to any work situation. Even so, jobs must still be tailored so that nearly anyone can do them. This is the approach often taken with assembly-line jobs and jobs involving routine tasks. For managers the main challenge becomes *"How can we make the worker most compatible with the work?"*

One technique is ***job simplification,*** **the process of reducing the number of tasks a worker performs.** When a job is stripped down to its simplest elements, it enables a worker to focus on doing more of the same task, thus increasing employee efficiency and productivity. This may be especially useful, for instance, in designing jobs for mentally disadvantaged workers, such as those run by Goodwill Industries. However, research shows that simplified, repetitive jobs lead to job dissatisfaction, poor mental health, and a low sense of accomplishment and personal growth.[24]

Creating Goodwill. Collecting donated clothing and household goods to sell in its 1,900 stores, Goodwill Industries International provides job training and employment services for people with workplace disadvantages and disabilities. The 100-year-old, $1.8 billion nonprofit international organization is a network of 207 community-based member organizations in 25 countries. What kinds of jobs would you guess they provide training for?

Fitting Jobs to People

Fitting jobs to people is based on the assumption that people are underutilized at work and that they want more variety, challenges, and responsibility. This philosophy, an outgrowth of Herzberg's theory, is one of the reasons for the popularity of work teams in the United States. The main challenge for managers is *"How can we make the work most compatible with the worker so as to produce both high performance and high job satisfaction?"* Two techniques for this type of job design include (1) *job enlargement* and (2) *job enrichment.*

Job Enlargement: Putting More Variety into a Job

The opposite of job simplification, ***job enlargement*** **consists of increasing the number of tasks in a job to increase variety and motivation.** For instance, the job of installing television picture tubes could be enlarged to include installation of the circuit boards.

Although proponents claim job enlargement can improve employee satisfaction, motivation, and quality of production, research suggests job enlargement by itself won't have a significant and lasting positive effect on job performance. After all, working at two boring tasks instead of one doesn't add up to a challenging job. Instead, job enlargement is just one tool of many that should be considered in job design.[25]

Job Enrichment: Putting More Responsibility & Other Motivating Factors into a Job

Job enrichment is the practical application of Frederick Herzberg's two-factor motivator-hygiene theory of job satisfaction.[26] Specifically, ***job enrichment* consists of building into a job such motivating factors as responsibility, achievement, recognition, stimulating work, and advancement.**

However, instead of the job-enlargement technique of simply giving employees additional tasks of similar difficulty (known as *horizontal loading*), with job enrichment employees are given more responsibility (known as *vertical loading*). Thus, employees take on chores that would normally be performed by their supervisors. For example, one department store authorized thousands of its sales clerks to handle functions normally reserved for store managers, such as handling merchandise-return problems and approving customers' checks.[27]

The Job Characteristics Model: Five Job Attributes for Better Work Outcomes

Developed by researchers **J. Richard Hackman** and **Greg Oldham,** the job characteristics model of design is an outgrowth of job enrichment.[28] **The *job characteristics model* consists of (a) five core job characteristics that affect (b) three critical psychological states of an employee that in turn affect (c) work outcomes—the employee's motivation, performance, and satisfaction.** The model is illustrated below. *(See Figure 12.9.)*

FIGURE 12.9

The job characteristics model [*Source:* Adapted from J. R. Hackman and G. R. Oldham, *Work Redesign* (Reading, MA: Addison-Wesley, 1980), p. 90.]

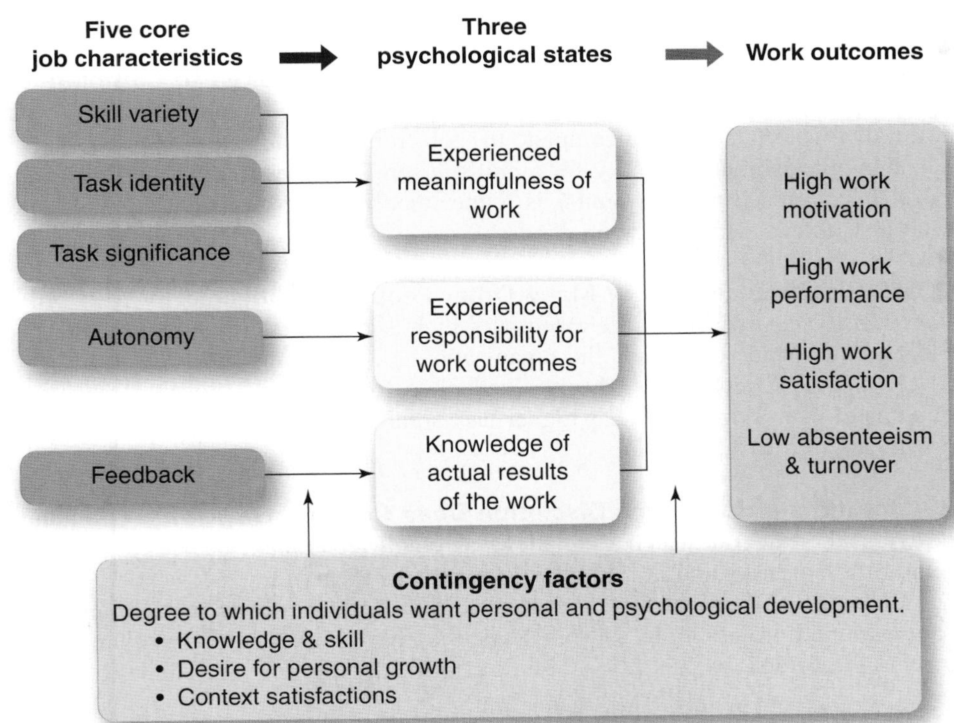

Skill variety. Flying a commercial airliner requires a greater number of skills than, say, driving a truck. Do highly skilled employees typically make good managers? What skills do airline pilots have that would make them effective managers in other industries?

Five Job Characteristics

The five core job characteristics are as follows.

1 Skill Variety—"How Many Different Skills Does Your Job Require?" *Skill variety* describes the extent to which a job requires a person to use a wide range of different skills and abilities.

Example: The skill variety required by a rocket scientist is higher than that for a short-order cook.

2 Task Identity—"How Many Different Tasks Are Required to Complete the Work?" *Task identity* describes the extent to which a job requires a worker to perform all the tasks needed to complete the job from beginning to end.

Example: The task identity for a craftsperson who goes through all the steps to build a hand-made acoustic guitar is higher than it is for an assembly-line worker who just installs windshields on cars.

3 Task Significance—"How Many Other People Are Affected by Your Job?" *Task significance* describes the extent to which a job affects the lives of other people, whether inside or outside the organization.

Example: A technician who is responsible for keeping a hospital's electronic equipment in working order has higher task significance than does a person wiping down cars in a carwash.

4 Autonomy—"How Much Discretion Does Your Job Give You?" *Autonomy* describes the extent to which a job allows an employee to make choices about scheduling different tasks and deciding how to perform them.

Example: College-textbook salespeople have lots of leeway in planning which campuses and professors to call on. Thus, they have higher autonomy than do toll-takers on a bridge, whose actions are determined by the flow of vehicles.

5 Feedback—"How Much Do You Find Out How Well You're Doing?" *Feedback* describes the extent to which workers receive clear, direct information about how well they are performing the job.

Example: Professional basketball players receive immediate feedback on how many of their shots are going into the basket. Engineers working on new weapons systems may go years before learning how effective their performance has been.

How the Model Works

According to the job characteristics model, these five core characteristics affect a worker's motivation because they affect three critical psychological states: *meaningfulness of work, responsibility for results,* and *knowledge of results. (Refer to Figure 12.9 again.)* That is, the more that workers (1) feel that they are doing meaningful work, (2) feel that they are responsible for outcomes of the work, and (3) have knowledge of the actual results of the work and how they affect others, then the more likely they are to have favorable work outcomes: *high motivation, high performance, high satisfaction,* and *low absenteeism and turnover.*

One other element—shown at the bottom of Figure 12.9—needs to be discussed: *contingency factors.* This refers to the degree to which a person wants personal and psychological development. Job enrichment will be more successful for employees with high growth-need strength. Not everyone will respond well to enriched jobs. To be motivated, a person must have three attributes: (1) necessary knowledge and skill, (2) desire for personal growth, and (3) context satisfactions—that is, the right physical working conditions, pay, and supervision.

Applying the Job Characteristics Model

There are three major steps to follow when applying the model.

- **Diagnose the work environment to see if a problem exists:** Hackman and Oldham developed a self-report instrument for managers to use called the *job diagnostic survey.* This will indicate whether an individual's so-called *motivating potential score (MPS)*—the amount of internal work motivation associated with a specific job—is high or low.
- **Determine whether job redesign is appropriate:** If a person's MPS score is low, an attempt should be made to determine which of the core job characteristics is causing the problem. You should next decide whether job redesign is appropriate for a given group of employees. Job design is most likely to work in a participative environment in which employees have the necessary knowledge and skills.
- **Consider how to redesign the job:** Here you try to increase those core job characteristics that are lower than national norms.

  Example: At one time, the 470 workers at Alexander Doll Co. individually produced parts for dolls. Based on input from the workers, owners organized employees into seven- or eight-person teams, each responsible for completing about 300 doll or wardrobe assemblies a day. The result: orders can now be filled in one or two weeks instead of eight.[29] ◆

major question **How can I use compensation and other rewards to motivate people?**

The Big Picture

Compensation, the main motivator of performance, includes pay for performance, bonuses, profit sharing, gain sharing, and stock options, and pay for knowledge. Other nonmonetary incentives address needs that aren't being met, such as work-life balance, growth in skills, and commitment.

Perhaps the first thing that comes to mind when you think about motivating performance is compensation—how much money you or your employees can make. But consider how motivation worked with Mary Morse, a software engineer with a computer-aided design firm, Autodesk, in San Rafael, Calif. During the early 2000s dot-com boom, when talented professionals were scarce, every few weeks another Silicon Valley company would try to lure her away. At least one of them offered a compensation and options package that could have made her rich. Morse turned them all down. The reason: she liked her bosses.[30]

Morse demonstrates the truth of a Gallup Organization poll that found that most workers rate having a caring boss higher than they value monetary benefits.[31] Clearly, then, motivating doesn't just involve dollars.

Motivation & Compensation

Most people are paid an hourly wage or a weekly or monthly salary. Both of these are easy for organizations to administer, of course. But by itself a wage or a salary gives an employee little incentive to work hard. Incentive compensation plans try to do so, although no single plan will boost the performance of all employees.

Characteristics of the Best Incentive Compensation Plans

In accordance with most of the theories of motivation we described earlier, for incentive plans to work, certain criteria are advisable, as follows. (1) Rewards must be linked to performance and be measurable. (2) The rewards must satisfy individual needs. (3) The rewards must be agreed on by manager and employees. (4) The rewards must be perceived as being equitable, believable, and achievable by employees.

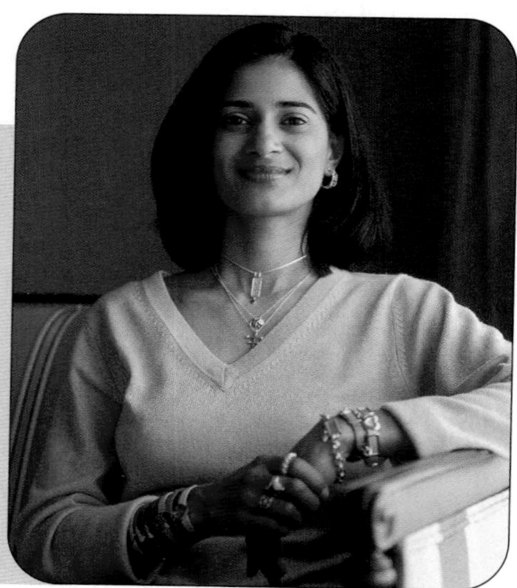

Small-business owner. In 1998, Varsha Rao, 34, co-founded Eve.com, an online cosmetics retailer, which in three years grew to 110 people and $10 million in annual sales. But the company was sold, and then folded, before it ever turned a profit. Rao's newest enterprise, San Francisco–based Zoelle, is a small jewelry company that sells only original designs—what Rao hopes will be a "younger, hipper Tiffany" appealing directly to women. In mid-2004, it was on track to do a half-million dollars in sales. For some people, like Rao, the only way to merge motivation and compensation is to own and manage their own business. What factors or incentives motivate you to work hard?

Popular Incentive Compensation Plans

How would you like to be rewarded for your efforts? Some of the most well-known incentive compensation plans are *pay for performance, bonuses, profit sharing, gainsharing, stock options,* and *pay for knowledge.*

- **Pay for performance:** Also known as *merit pay,* ***pay for performance*** **bases pay on one's results.** Thus, different salaried employees might get different pay raises and other rewards (such as promotions) depending on their overall job performance.

  Examples: One standard pay-for-performance plan, already mentioned, is payment according to a ***piece rate,*** **in which employees are paid according to how much output they produce,** as is often used with farmworkers picking fruit and vegetables. Another is the ***sales commission,*** **in which sales representatives are paid a percentage of the earnings the company made from their sales,** so that the more they sell, the more they are paid.
- **Bonuses:** ***Bonuses*** **are cash awards given to employees who achieve specific performance objectives.**

  Example: Nieman Marcus, the department store, pays its salespeople a percentage of the earnings from the goods they sell.
- **Profit sharing:** ***Profit sharing*** **is the distribution to employees of a percentage of the company's profits.**

  Example: In one T-shirt and sweatshirt manufacturing company, 10% of pretax profits are distributed to employees every month, and more is given out at the end of the year. Distributions are apportioned according to such criteria as performance, attendance, and lateness for individual employees.
- **Gainsharing:** ***Gainsharing*** **is the distribution of savings or "gains" to groups of employees who reduced costs and increased measurable productivity.**

  Example: There are different types of gainsharing plans, but in one known as the *Scanlon plan,* developed in the 1920s by a steel-industry union leader named Joseph Scanlon, a portion of any cost savings, usually 75%, are distributed back to employees; the company keeps the other 25%.[32]
- **Stock options:** With ***stock options,*** **certain employees are given the right to buy stock at a future date for a discounted price.** The motivator here is that employees holding stock options will supposedly work hard to make the company's stock rise so that they can obtain it at a cheaper price. By giving stock options to all employees who work 20 or more hours a week, Starbucks Corp. has been able to hold its annual turnover rate to 60%—in an industry (fast food and restaurants) in which 300% is not unheard of.[33]
- **Pay for knowledge:** Also known as *skill-based pay,* ***pay for knowledge*** **ties employee pay to the number of job-relevant skills or academic degrees they earn.**

  Example: The teaching profession is a time-honored instance of this incentive, in which elementary and secondary teachers are encouraged to increase their salaries by earning further college credit. However, firms such as FedEx also have pay-for-knowledge plans.

Nonmonetary Ways of Motivating Employees

Employees who can behave autonomously, solve problems, and take the initiative are apt to be the very ones who will leave if they find their own needs aren't being met—namely:[34]

- **The need for work-life balance:** A PricewaterhouseCoopers survey of 2,500 university students in 11 countries found that 57% named as their primary career goal "attaining a balance between personal life and career."[35] A 25-year study of values in the United States found that "employees have become less convinced that work should be an important part of one's life or that working hard makes one a better person."[36]
- **The need to expand skills:** Having watched their parents undergo downsizing, younger workers in particular are apt to view a job as a way of gaining skills that will enable them to earn a decent living in the future.
- **The need to matter:** Workers now want to be with an organization that allows them to feel they matter. They want to commit to their profession or fellow team members rather than have to profess a blind loyalty to the corporation.

There is a whole class of nonmonetary incentives to attract, retain, and motivate employees. The foremost example is the *flexible workplace*—including part-time work, flextime, compressed workweek, job sharing, and telecommuting. Other incentives can be expressed simply as *treat employees well,* some examples of which follow.

Thoughtfulness: The Value of Being Nice

A study by Walker Information, an Indianapolis-based research firm, found that employers spend too little time showing workers they matter, as manifested in lack of communication and lack of interest in new ideas and contributions.[37] A majority of employees feel underappreciated, according to a 1999 survey. Forty percent of employees who rated their boss's performance as poor said they were likely to look for a new job; only 11% of those who rated it excellent said they would.[38] "Being nice" to employees means, for example, reducing criticism, becoming more effusive in your praise, and writing thank-you notes to employees for exceptional performance.[39]

The No. 1 reason people quit their jobs, it's believed, is their dissatisfaction with their supervisors, not their paychecks. Thus, industrial psychologist B. Lynn Ware suggests that if you learn valued employees are disgruntled, you should discuss it with them.[40] "It's extraordinary how often it is the small and often banal gestures that are the most meaningful," says another expert. "People will often say things like, 'I'm not really happy, but not yet prepared to jump ship because my boss was really good to me when my mother was sick.'"[41] Employers can promote personal relationships, which most employees are concerned about on the job, by offering breaks or other opportunities in which people can mix and socialize.

Work-Life Benefits

Work-life benefits, according to Kathie Lingle, are programs "used by employers to increase productivity and commitment by removing certain barriers that make it hard for people to strike a balance between their work and personal lives."[42]

Lingle, who is national work-life director for KPMG, an accounting and consulting firm, emphasizes that work-life benefits "are not a reward, but a way of getting work done." After all, some employees are low performers simply because of a lack of life-work balance, with great demands at home. "If you only give these 'rewards' to existing high performers," says Lingle, "you're cutting people off who could, with some support, be high performers."

Besides alternative scheduling, work-life benefits include helping employees with daycare costs or even establishing on-site centers; domestic-partner benefits; job-protected leave for new parents; and provision of technology such as mobile phones and laptops to enable parents to work at home.[43]

Surroundings

The cubicle, according to new research, is stifling the creativity and morale of many workers, and the bias of modern-day office designers for open spaces and neutral colors is leading to employee complaints that their workplaces are too noisy or too bland.

"There is no such thing as something that works for everybody," says Alan Hedge, a professor of environmental analysis at Cornell University.[44] An 8-foot-by-8-foot cubicle may not be a good visual trigger for human brains, and companies wanting to improve creativity and productivity may need to think about giving office employees better things to look at.

Skill-Building & Educational Opportunities

Learning opportunities can take two forms. Managers can see that workers are matched with coworkers that they can learn from, allowing them, for instance, to "shadow" workers in other jobs or be in interdepartmental task forces. There can also be tuition reimbursement for part-time study at a college or university.

Sabbaticals

Intel and Apple understand that in a climate of 80-hour weeks people need to recharge themselves. But even McDonald's offers sabbaticals to longtime employees, giving a month to a year of paid time off in which to travel, learn, and pursue personal projects. The aim, of course, is to enable employees to recharge themselves but also, it is hoped, to cement their loyalty to the organization.[45] ◆

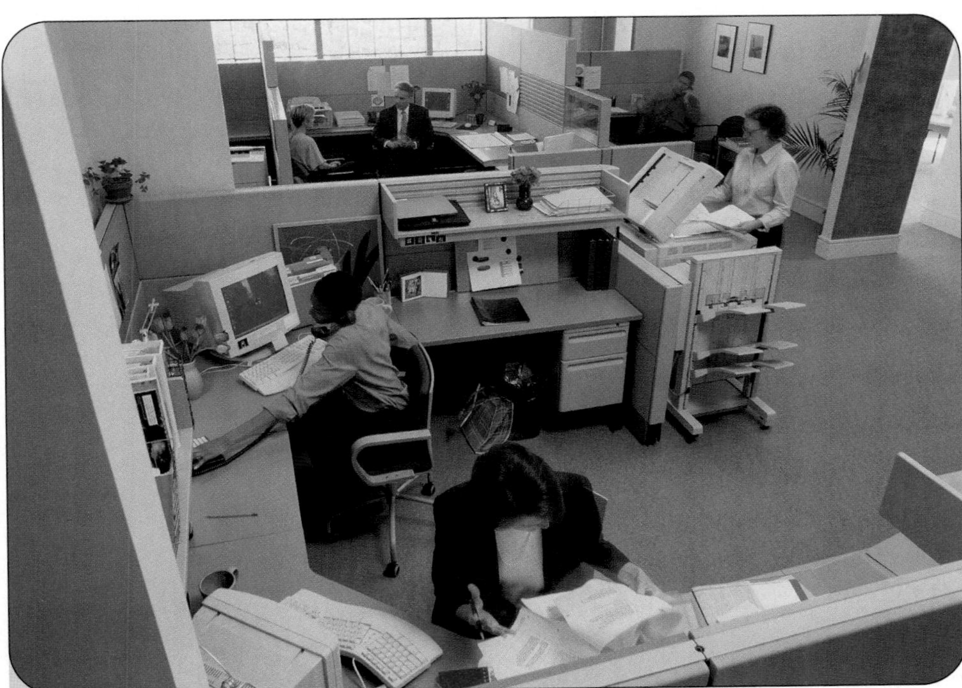

Cubicle culture. It might be too difficult to design a setup in which everyone has an office with a view. But would it be possible to design a layout in which everyone has a private office? Do you think it would motivate employees better?

Key Terms Used in This Chapter

acquired needs theory, 382
bonuses, 399
equity theory, 387
expectancy, 385
expectancy theory, 384
extinction, 392
extrinsic reward, 377
gainsharing, 399
goal-setting theory, 389
hierarchy of needs theory, 378
hygiene factors, 380
instrumentality, 385
intrinsic reward, 377
job characteristics model, 395
job design, 394
job enlargement, 394
job enrichment, 395
job simplification, 394
motivating factors, 381
motivation, 376
need-based perspectives, 378
needs, 378
negative reinforcement, 391
pay for knowledge, 399
pay for performance, 399
piece rate, 399
positive reinforcement, 391
process perspectives, 384
profit sharing, 399
punishment, 392
reinforcement, 390
reinforcement theory, 390
sales commission, 399
stock options, 399
two-factor theory, 380
valence, 385

Summary

12.1 Motivating for Performance

-  Motivation is defined as the psychological processes that arouse and direct goal-directed behavior. In a simple model of motivation, people have certain needs that motivate them to perform specific behaviors for which they receive rewards that feed back and satisfy the original need. Rewards are of two types: extrinsic and intrinsic. An extrinsic reward is the payoff, such as money, a person receives from others for performing a particular task. An intrinsic reward is the satisfaction, such as a feeling of accomplishment, that a person receives from performing the particular task itself.
- As a manager, you want to motivate people to do things that will benefit your organization—join it, stay with it, show up for work at it, perform better for it, and do extra for it.
- Three major perspectives on motivation are (1) need-based, (2) process, and (3) reinforcement.

12.2 Need-Based Perspectives on Employee Motivation

-  Need-based perspectives emphasize the needs that motivate people. Needs are defined as physiological or psychological deficiencies that arouse behavior. Besides the McGregor Theory X/Theory Y (Chapter 1), need-based perspectives include (1) the hierarchy of needs theory, (2) the two-factor theory, and (3) the acquired needs theory.
- The hierarchy of needs theory proposes that people are motivated by five levels of need: physiological, safety, belongingness, esteem, and self-actualization needs.
- The two-factor theory proposes that work satisfaction and dissatisfaction arise from two different factors—work satisfaction from so-called motivating factors, and work dissatisfaction from so-called hygiene factors. Hygiene factors, the lower-level needs, are factors associated with job dissatisfaction—such as salary and working conditions—which affect the environment in which people work. Motivating factors, the higher-level needs, are factors associated with job satisfaction—such as achievement and advancement—which affect the rewards of work performance.
- The acquired-needs theory states that three needs—achievement, affiliation, and power—are major motives determining people's behavior in the workplace.

12.3 Process Perspectives on Employee Motivation

-  Process perspectives are concerned with the thought processes by which people decide how to act. Three process perspectives on motivation are (1) expectancy theory, (2) equity theory, and (3) goal-setting theory.
- Expectancy theory suggests that people are motivated by how much they want something and how likely they think they are to get it. The three elements affecting motivation are expectancy, instrumentality,

and valence. (1) Expectancy is the belief that a particular level of effort will lead to a particular level of performance. (2) Instrumentality is the expectation that successful performance of the task will lead to the outcome desired. (3) Valence is the value, the importance a worker assigns to the possible outcome or reward. When attempting to motivate employees, according to the logic of expectancy theory, managers should ascertain what rewards employees value, what job objectives and performance level they desire, whether there are rewards linked to performance, and whether employees believe managers will deliver the right rewards for the right performance.

- Equity theory focuses on employee perceptions as to how fairly they think they are being treated compared to others. The key elements in equity theory are inputs, outputs (rewards), and comparisons. (1) With inputs, employees consider what they are putting in to the job in time, effort, and so on. (2) With outputs or rewards, employees consider what they think they're getting out of the job in terms of pay, praise, and so on. (3) With comparison, employees compare the ratio of their own outcomes to inputs against the ratio of someone else's outcomes to inputs. Three practical lessons of equity theory are that employee perceptions are what count, employee participation helps, and having an appeal process helps.
- Goal-setting theory suggests that employees can be motivated by goals that are specific and challenging but achievable. Three elements of this theory are that goals must be specific, challenging, and achievable. In addition, the theory suggests that goals should be set jointly with the employee, be measurable, and have a target date for accomplishment and that employees should receive feedback and rewards.

12.4 Reinforcement Perspectives on Motivation

- 
Reinforcement theory attempts to explain behavior change by suggesting that behavior with positive consequences tends to be repeated whereas behavior with negative consequences tends not to be repeated. Reinforcement is anything that causes a given behavior to be repeated or inhibited.
- There are four types of reinforcement. (1) Positive reinforcement is the use of positive consequences to encourage desirable behavior. (2) Negative reinforcement is the removal of unpleasant consequences followed by a desired behavior. (3) Extinction is the withholding or withdrawal of positive rewards for desirable behavior, so that the behavior is less likely to occur in the future. (4) Punishment is the application of negative consequences to stop or change undesirable behavior.
- In using positive reinforcement to motivate employees, managers should reward only desirable behavior, give rewards as soon as possible, be clear about what behavior is desired, and have different rewards and recognize individual differences. In using punishment, managers should punish only undesirable behavior, give reprimands or disciplinary actions as soon as possible, be clear about what behavior is undesirable, administer punishment in private, and combine punishment and positive reinforcement.

12.5 Motivation Through Job Design

- 
Job design is, first, the division of an organization's work among its employees and, second, the application of motivational theories to jobs to increase satisfaction and performance. Two approaches to job design are fitting people to jobs (the traditional approach) and fitting jobs to people.
- Fitting jobs to people assumes people are underutilized and want more variety. Two techniques for this type of job design include job enlargement, (1) increasing the number of tasks in a job to increase variety and motivation, and (2) job enrichment, building into a job such motivating factors as responsibility, achievement, recognition, stimulating work, and advancement.
- An outgrowth of job enrichment is the job characteristics model, which consists of (a) five core job characteristics that affect (b) three critical psychological states of an employee that in turn affect (c) work outcomes—the employee's motivation, performance, and satisfaction. The five core job characteristics are (1) skill variety—how many different skills does a job require; (2) task identity—how many different tasks are required to complete the work; (3) task significance—how many other people are affected by the job; (4) autonomy—how much discretion does the job allow the worker; and (5) feedback—how much do employees find out how well they're doing. These five characteristics affect three critical psychological states: meaningfulness of work, responsibility for results, and knowledge of results. Three major steps to follow when applying the job characteristics model are (1) diagnose the work environment to see if a problem exists, (2) determine whether job redesign is appropriate, and (3) consider how to redesign the job.

12.6 Using Compensation & Other Rewards to Motivate

- 
Compensation is only one form of motivator. For incentive compensation plans for work, rewards must be linked to performance and be measurable; they must satisfy individual

needs; they must be agreed on by manager and employee; and they must be perceived as being equitable, believable, and achievable by employees.

- Popular incentive compensation plans are the following. (1) Pay for performance bases pay on one's results. One kind is payment according to piece rate, in which employees are paid according to how much output they produce. Another is the sales commission, in which sales representatives are paid a percentage of the earnings the company made from their sales. (2) Bonuses are cash awards given to employees who achieve specific performance objectives. (3) Profit sharing is the distribution to employees of a percentage of the company's profits. (4) Gainsharing is the distribution of savings or "gains" to groups of employees who reduced costs and increased measurable productivity. (5) Stock options allow certain employees to buy stock at a future date for a discounted price. (6) Pay for knowledge ties employee pay to the number of job-relevant skills or academic degrees they earn.
- There are also nonmonetary ways of compensating employees. Some employees will leave because they feel the need for work-life balance, the need to expand their skills, and the need to matter. To retain such employees, nonmonetary incentives have been introduced, such as the flexible workplace. Other incentives that keep employees from leaving are thoughtfulness by employees' managers, work-life benefits such as daycare, attractive surroundings, skill-building and educational opportunities, and work sabbaticals.

Management in Action

Saks Fifth Avenue & Roche Diagnostics Use Employee Surveys to Boost Employee Engagement

Excerpted from Steve Bates, "Getting Engaged," HR Magazine, *February 2004, pp. 49–50.*

At Saks Fifth Avenue, the luxury retailer based in New York, executives were looking for ways to boost service to customers in their highly competitive market. Saks officials decided to measure employee engagement and customer engagement at stores, with customer engagement including willingness to make repeat purchases and recommend the store to friends.

"We used both to pinpoint problem spots," says Vice President Jay Redman. Saks found that "there absolutely is a correlation between employee engagement and customer engagement" and that customer engagement creates loyal, repeat customers and increased sales.

"We've seen 20% to 25% improvement in stores with great engagement," he says. But it's not just about higher sales figures. "How you get there is important."

There's been a major change in the nature of the dialog between management and the sales force, says Redman. Saks makes a point about asking employees what they need to do their jobs. Every time there is an initiative resulting from such dialog—for example, a flextime program was implemented recently, and many computers were upgraded—managers make sure to remind workers that this resulted from their suggestions.

"We've probably done 100 things over three years" in response to survey results, says Redman. "Some are as simple as opening a stairwell. People said they used to wait five to 10 minutes to go by elevator between floors" in a store.

A key message from Saks management to employees is that the dialog is intended to be a permanent feature. "The first year everyone thinks that it's a program. It's not a program anymore." . . .

At Roche Diagnostics Corp., a diagnostic systems manufacturer based in Indianapolis, high turnover was a troublesome problem. Company officials did some research and concluded that they needed to define and treat the root cause of the too-frequent departures of key workers.

They had what Patty Ayers, vice president for HR, called "a gut feeling" why turnover was high, but employee engagement surveys pinpointed the reasons. The company discovered, for example, that employees had concerns about career development. They needed better computer resources in the field. They wanted to understand the company's business strategy and where they fit in.

"When you get back hard data, it's no longer HR coming in and saying that we've got some problems over here or there. You now have statistical data to support your observations, and you've got a safe way to open direct conversations with employees. You then really get to the heart of the issues."

Many of the improvements that were implemented probably would have occurred without the engagement surveys, but the company made it clear to workers that certain changes were directly related to the feedback and the company's intent that they succeed. With such a dialog, "people walk away feeling that they are being listened to," says Ayers.

Today, "we are dramatically outperforming our competition," she says. "Having this kind of employee commitment is the reason."

She warns that it takes "a huge commitment in time and energy. But relative to some of the other investments you make, it has a pretty good return." And she notes that anyone doing a survey to gauge employee engagement should "expect to hear bad things. If you're only looking for positive feedback, you're going to be disappointed."

For Discussion

1. What are the pros and cons of using surveys to assess employee motivation or engagement? Explain.
2. How did the use of employee surveys help managers at Saks Fifth Avenue to apply need theory and job design?
3. What unfulfilled needs were causing employee turnover at Roche Diagnostics Corporation? Explain your rationale.
4. How can employee surveys be used to apply expectancy theory?

Questions for Discussion

1. If you were considering a career with Southwest Airlines, would the company's monetary rewards motivate you? Explain.
2. To what extent do you feel Southwest Airlines fills its employees' need for work-life balance? Explain.
3. Judging from the benefits offered at Southwest Airlines, do you feel the company is trying to satisfy a variety of employee needs?

Self-Assessment

What Is Your Reaction to Equity Differences?*

Objectives

Assess your reaction to equity differences.

Gain more insight into yourself.

Introduction

Have you ever noticed that certain people scream "No fair!" whenever they perceive something as unequal? Have you also noticed that other people don't seem bothered by inequity at all? According to researchers, when given the same amount of inequity, people respond differently depending on their individual equity sensitivity. There are varying degrees of equity sensitivity:

Benevolents are individuals who prefer their outcome/input ratios to be less than the others being compared. These are people who don't mind being underrewarded.

Equity Sensitives are individuals who prefer outcome/input ratios to be equal. These people are concerned with obtaining rewards that they perceive to be fair in relation to what others are receiving.

Entitleds are individuals who prefer that their outcome/input ratios go above those of the others being compared. These people aren't worried by inequities and actually prefer situations in which they see themselves as overrewarded.

The purpose of this exercise is to assess your equity sensitivity.

Instructions

The five statements below ask what you would like your relationship to be within any organization. For each question, *divide* 10 points between the two answers (A and B) *by giving the most points to the answer that is most like you and the fewest points to the answer least like you.* You can give an equal number of points to A and B. You can make use of zeros if you like. Just be sure to use all 10 points on each question. (For instance, if statement A is completely appropriate and B is not at all appropriate, give A 10 points and B zero points. If A is somewhat appropriate and B is not completely appropriate, give A 7 points and B 3 points.) Place your points next to each letter.

In any organization where I might work:

1. It would be more important for me to:
   A. Get from the organization ___
   B. Give to the organization ___
2. It would be more important for me to:
   A. Help others ___
   B. Watch out for my own good ___
3. I would be more concerned about:
   A. What I received from the organization ___
   B. What I contributed to the organization ___
4. The hard work I would do should:
   A. Benefit the organization ___
   B. Benefit me ___
5. My personal philosophy in dealing with the organization would be:
   A. If you don't look out for yourself, nobody else will ___
   B. It's better to give than to receive ___

Calculate your total score by adding the points you allocated to the following items: 1B, 2A, 3B, 4A, and 5B. Total score = _______

Analysis & Interpretation

Your total will be between 0 and 50. If you scored less than 29, you are an Entitled; if your score was between 29 and 32, you are Equity Sensitive; and if your score was above 32, you are a Benevolent.

Questions for Discussion

1. To what extent are the results consistent with your self-perception? Explain.
2. Using the survey items as a foundation, how should managers try to motivate Benevolents, Equity Sensitives, and Entitleds? Discuss in detail.

*R. C. Huseman, J. D. Hatfield, and E. W. Miles, "Test for Individual Perceptions of Job Equity: Some Preliminary Findings," *Perceptual and Motor Skills*, vol. 62, 1985, pp. 1055–1064.

Group Exercise

Managing for Motivation

Objectives

To apply aspects from motivation theories covered in this chapter.

To design a motivation plan.

Introduction

As a student, you've probably gone through times in your academic career when you just can't seem to get it together: You miss deadlines, you skip class, your work is of poor quality, you procrastinate, and you just don't put in adequate effort to get your assignments done. Have you ever considered why your performance is problematic? Perhaps you don't feel motivated enough by the assignments. Perhaps your attention and motivation are directed elsewhere: packing for spring break, say, or planning for a weekend party.

Managers frequently encounter performance problems as well. Employees miss deadlines, produce poor-quality work, put in inadequate levels of performance, take excessive time off, display negative attitudes and behaviors, and don't cooperate with their team members. Motivation is part of these performance problems, and managers must learn how to motivate employees to improve their performance. The purpose of this exercise is to give you practice at diagnosing the causes of a performance problem and to propose managerial solutions to fix the problem.

Instructions

Break into groups of five or six people. Read the following case study of Mary Martin. First consider how Herzberg's two-factor theory affects Mary's motivation. Brainstorm with the group to come up with some Hygiene factors that may be affecting Mary's motivation. Next consider Motivating factors—what can Mary's manager do to make her *satisfied*? You can also consider McClelland's Acquired Needs Theory in your discussion. Which of the three needs is Mary most concerned with?

After your group has completed its brainstorming, use the information and solutions you came up with to design a motivation plan for Mary's manager.

The Case*

Mary Martin, 30, received her baccalaureate degree in computer science from a reputable state school in the Midwest, graduating with above-average grades. Mary is currently working in the computer support/analysis department as a programmer for a nationally based firm.

During the past year, Mary has missed 10 days of work. She seems unmotivated and rarely has her assignments completed on time. Usually she is given the harder programs to work on.

Recently, the company turned all hourly positions into salary positions. Some employees have complained that they made more money when they were hourly employees because they were paid for overtime. Mary's pay structure was based on an hourly wage, and she would often work long hours and overtime.

Past records indicate that Mary completes programs classified as "routine" in about 45 hours on average, whereas her coworkers take on average 32 hours for such programs. She finishes programs considered "major problems" on average in about 115 hours, compared with about 100 hours on average for her coworkers.

The company has decided to create a more team-based environment. Many of the programmers who once worked on projects alone are now being given projects to tackle as a team. When Mary has worked in programming teams, her peer performance reviews are generally average or negative. Her male peers say that she is not creative in attacking problems and that she is difficult to work with.

Last year, the company expanded its office and hired 250 new employees. The company moved its offices from a small to a larger building; some employees who worked for the company before the expansion expressed concern that there were not enough resources and tools to go around. Many of the tenured employees also complained to supervisors that new employees were not adequately trained and that it was slowing down production.

Some of the tenured employees expressed concern when some of the newer employees were promoted to supervisory positions; according to e-mail sent to supervisors, many felt that they were overlooked. Others even felt that the criteria for promotion were not based on experience and performance with the company; instead they suspected the supervisors were playing favorites and promoting their friends to supervisory positions.

Along with new employees came new programming demands. However, employees reported to supervisors that they did not feel they had adequate time to learn how to use new software that would make designing new programs easier and more efficient.

The computer department recently sent a questionnaire to all users of its services to evaluate the usefulness and accuracy of data received. The results indicate many departments are not using computer output because they cannot understand the reports. It was also determined that users of output generated from Mary's programs found the output chaotic and not useful for managerial decision making.

Questions for Discussion

1. What are some Hygiene factors associated with Mary's motivation? Describe.
2. How would you correct these Hygiene factors? Discuss.
3. As Mary's manager, how can you use expectancy theory to motivate Mary? Explain the details.
4. If you were Mary's manager, what additional changes would you implement to increase the employees' performance?

*Adapted from R. Kreitner and A. Kinicki, *Organizational Behavior,* 5th ed. (Burr Ridge, IL: McGraw-Hill, 2001), p. 220.

Ethical Dilemma

Would You Fire Someone When You Knew It Might Lead to Divorce as Well as Loss of Income?

From Margaret Popper, "Lost Job, Lost Spouse: Being Fired Can Lead to Divorce," Business Week, *December 17, 2001, p. 26.*

Everyone knows that financial stress can help break up a marriage. But a new study from the National Bureau of Economic Research Inc. shows that some financial problems are more likely than others to lead to divorce.

In particular, the authors of the study, Kerwin Kofi Charles of University of Michigan and Melvin Stephens Jr. of Carnegie Mellon University, find that being fired from a job significantly raises the probability of getting divorced. Married men who are fired have an 18% higher chance of being divorced within the next three years, while women have a 13% higher chance.

But someone losing his or her job because of disability doesn't mean a significantly increased probability of seeing the marriage break up. Similarly, a plant closing that affects a group of people doesn't raise the odds of divorce.

By way of explanation, Charles and Stephens suggest that the character traits that cause a person to be laid off could also make him or her a bad mate. "For example, if a wife can conclude that a husband lost his job because of his repeated irresponsibility or bad temper," they write, "she should conclude both that he is likely to face employment troubles in the future *and* that he may not be a good person with whom to raise children."

By contrast, a plant closing or a sudden disability is viewed as bad luck rather than a deserved punishment for a bad personality. These events are less likely to spark a divorce even though, in the case of disability, the income loss to the couple is generally greater.

Solving the Dilemma

You're supervising an employee, the sole support of his wife and five children, who barely manages to get his work done. Your attempts at using motivational techniques fail to improve his performance. What would you do?

1. Keep him on without expecting too much. After all, everyone has the right to earn a living, and the work does get done.
2. After giving several warnings, fire him, knowing it could lead to considerable hardship in his family. After all, you have to show your bosses you're a productive manager.
3. Fire him, but give him a long time to his termination date and help him with outplacement services, although his continued presence will make you uncomfortable.
4. Invent other options. Discuss.

Video Case

The Container Store

The Container Store was voted "best company to work for in America" twice and was runner-up two additional times. So what's the secret to hiring highly motivated people who believe that their company is America's best? First, you need good products. Employees are motivated when they know that the products they sell are top quality and desired by customers. Second, you have to empower workers to do everything possible to exceed customer expectations (even if that means giving a customer a driving lesson in the parking lot).

One of the cornerstones at the Container Store is "Hire Great People." According to top management, one great person is worth three (or maybe four) good people. In support, they cite famed home-run hitter Babe Ruth, who hit 56 homers in one year; the second-best player hit only 13. The challenge is to find and keep great workers. The Container Store does this by hiring part-time people and then motivating the best of them to stay with the company.

Employees provide astonishing levels of customer service. For example, one worker in Houston loaned her car to a stranded customer! How exactly does the organization encourage this level of outstanding service? By successfully implementing numerous motivational principles. Wages are above the industry standard. Mistakes are tolerated and viewed as learning opportunities. Employees are continually encouraged to go the extra mile to please customers. Throughout the organization, emphasis is placed on a core set of values such as integrity, honesty, and open communication. Outstanding employees are recognized for their contributions, and the social atmosphere is one of "family." The importance of the job environment is recognized, including the quality of coworkers. People like to work with others who are equally motivated and committed.

Employees are cross-trained for a variety of jobs in an effort to prepare them to become managers when openings are available. Stores make use of daily coaching to help employees understand and implement managerial objectives. Through open communication channels, employees learn that good work will be amply rewarded. The communication system includes peer-to-peer communication so that everyone helps everybody else to do the best job possible.

In summary, the Container Store employs a humanistic approach coupled with employee empowerment, strong corporate values, cross-training, and open communication to motivate employees. As a result, employees are committed to one of the best companies to work for in America.

Discussion Questions

1. List Maslow's hierarchy of needs. Does the Container store help satisfy employees' needs in the workplace? Provide evidence to support your response.
2. What are the two factors in Herzberg's two-factor theory? Provide examples of each of these factors at the Container Store.
3. Equity theory focuses on employee perceptions of how fairly they think they are being treated compared to how others are treated. Identify the inputs and the outputs that employees use to determine equity perceptions at the Container Store.

Groups & Teams
From Conflict to Cooperation

MAJOR QUESTIONS YOU SHOULD BE ABLE TO ANSWER

13.1 Managing Conflict
Major Question: Since conflict is a part of life, what should a manager know about it in order to deal successfully with it?

13.2 Teamwork: Cornerstone of Progressive Management
Major Question: If the best managers are usually independent of the herd, why should they cultivate teamwork skills?

13.3 Groups versus Teams
Major Question: How is one collection of workers different from any other?

13.4 Stages of Group & Team Development
Major Question: How does a group evolve into a team?

13.5 Building Effective Teams
Major Question: How can I as a manager build an effective team?

Dealing with Disagreements

Even if you're at the top of your game as a manager, working with groups and teams of people—the subject of this chapter—will now and then put you in the middle of disagreements, sometimes even destructive conflict. How can you deal with it?

There are five conflict-handling styles, or techniques, a manager can use for handling disagreements with individuals, as follows:[1]

- **Avoiding—"Maybe the problem will go away":** *Avoiding* involves ignoring or suppressing a conflict. Avoidance is appropriate for trivial issues, when emotions are high and a cooling-off period is needed, or when the cost of confrontation outweighs the benefits of resolving the conflict. It is not appropriate for difficult or worsening problems.

  The benefit of this approach is that it buys time in unfolding and ambiguous situations. The weakness is that it provides only a temporary fix and sidesteps the underlying problem.
- **Accommodating—"Let's do it your way":** An accommodating manager is also known as a "smoothing" or "obliging" manager. *Accommodating* is allowing the desires of the other party to prevail. As one writer describes it, "An obliging [accommodating] person neglects his or her own concern to satisfy the concern of the other party."[2] Accommodating may be an appropriate conflict-handling strategy when it's possible to eventually get something in return or when the issue isn't important to you. It's not appropriate for complex or worsening problems.

  The advantage of accommodating is that it encourages cooperation. The weakness is that once again it's only a temporary fix that fails to confront the underlying problem.
- **Forcing—"You have to do it my way":** Also known as "dominating," *forcing* is simply ordering an outcome, when a manager relies on his or her formal authority and power to resolve a conflict. Forcing is appropriate when an unpopular solution must be implemented and when it's not important that others be committed to your viewpoint.

  The advantage of forcing is speed: It can get results quickly. The disadvantage is that in the end it doesn't resolve personal conflict—if anything, it aggravates it by breeding hurt feelings and resentments.
- **Compromising—"Let's split the difference":** In *compromising*, both parties give up something in order to gain something. Compromise is appropriate when both sides have opposite goals or possess equal power. But compromise isn't workable when it is used so often that it doesn't achieve results—for example, continual failure to meet production deadlines.

  The benefit of compromise is that it is a democratic process that seems to have no losers. However, since so many people approach compromise situations with a win-lose attitude, they may be disappointed and feel cheated.
- **Collaborating—"Let's cooperate to reach a win-win solution that benefits both of us":** *Collaborating* strives to devise solutions that benefit both parties. Collaboration is appropriate for complex issues plagued by misunderstanding. It is inappropriate for resolving conflicts rooted in opposing value systems.

  The strength of collaborating is its longer lasting effect: it deals with the underlying problem, not just its symptoms. Its weakness is that it's very time-consuming. Nevertheless, collaboration is the best approach for dealing with groups and teams of people.

forecast

What's Ahead in This Chapter

In this chapter, we consider the nature of conflict, both bad and good. We also consider cooperation, as expressed through teamwork. We distinguish groups from teams and discuss different kinds of teams. We discuss how groups evolve into teams, and we describe how managers can build effective teams.

major question

Since conflict is a part of life, what should a manager know about it in order to deal successfully with it?

The Big Picture

Conflict, an enduring feature of the workplace, is a process in which one party perceives that its interests are being opposed or negatively affected by another party. Conflict can be negative (bad) or functional (good). Indeed, either too much or too little conflict can affect performance. This section identifies seven sources of conflict in organizations and also describes four ways to stimulate constructive conflict.

"I've fired many employees through the years," writes a manager to an advice columnist, "but right now I've got a guy who scares me. Maybe there's been one too many postal shootings, but I'm afraid this guy could turn violent."[3]

Firings, of course, generate strong emotions and can easily trigger outbursts, though dismissed workers seldom "go postal"—become violent and start shooting people. (About 20 American workers are murdered on the job every week, but few are by enraged coworkers; around 75% of workplace homicides occur during robberies.[4]) Nevertheless, employee dismissals—along with increased workloads, pressure-cooker deadlines, demands for higher productivity, and other kinds of stress—are among the sources of that enduring feature of the workplace: conflict.

The Nature of Conflict: Disagreement Is Normal

Mention the term *conflict* and many people envision shouting and fighting. But as a manager, during a typical workday you will encounter more subtle, nonviolent types of conflict: opposition, criticism, arguments. Thus, a definition of conflict seems fairly mild: ***Conflict* is a process in which one party perceives that its interests are being opposed or negatively affected by another party.**[5] Conflict is simply disagreement, a perfectly normal state of affairs. Conflicts may take many forms: between individuals, between an individual and a group, between groups, and between an organization and its environment.

While all of us might wish to live lives free of conflict, it is now recognized that certain kinds of conflict can actually be beneficial.[6] Let us therefore distinguish between *negative conflict* (bad) and *constructive conflict* (good).

- **Negative conflict—bad for organizations:** From the standpoint of the organization, ***negative conflict* is conflict that hinders the organization's performance or threatens its interests.** As a manager, you need to do what you can to remove negative conflict, sometimes called *dysfunctional conflict.*
- **Constructive conflict—good for organizations:** The good kind of conflict is ***constructive conflict,* which benefits the main purposes of the organization and serves its interests.**[7] There are some situations in which this kind of conflict—also called *functional conflict* or *cooperative conflict*—is considered advantageous.

Example

Negative & Positive Conflict: Do Abusive or Constructive Bosses Get Better Performance?

There are many examples of bullying, arrogant bosses spreading misery. Fred Ackman, head of Superior Oil, had an abusive temper and tended to treat any kind of disagreement, even simple suggestions, as disloyalty. Michael Eisner, 20-year boss of Walt Disney Co., was famous for chewing out subordinates and once called a former executive a "little midget."[8]

Does such negative conflict get results? Surprisingly, often it does. One study of 173 randomly chosen employees in a wide range of work found that, although some reacted to abusive bosses by doing little or nothing extra, others performed better—in part, it's speculated, to make themselves look good and others look worse.[9] On the other hand, 9 of 13 top executives left within a year after Ackman became chairman. Many Eisner subordinates who couldn't stand his barbs walked out the door, and eventually stockholders voted 43% of Disney shares to withhold support from his reelection to the board.

By contrast, the retired president of General Motors' successful Saturn Corp., Richard (Skip) LeFauve, relied on constructive conflict to energize his organization, which required intense union-management interaction. For example, reported *Business Week,* union members helped pick Saturn's dealers and its advertising agency. Normally this task is a management prerogative, and, as you might guess, there was a certain amount of management-labor disagreement. Still, LeFauve's arrangement prevailed. "A lot of people try to avoid controversy and conflict," he says. But constructive conflict, he contends, often fuels creativity.[10]

Can Too Little or Too Much Conflict Affect Performance?

It's tempting to think that a conflict-free work group is a happy work group, as indeed it may be. But is it a productive group? In the 1970s, social scientists specializing in organizational behavior introduced the revolutionary idea that organizations could suffer from *too little* conflict.

- **Too little conflict—indolence:** Work groups, departments, or organizations that experience too little conflict tend to be plagued by apathy, lack of creativity, indecision, and missed deadlines. The result is that organizational performance suffers.
- **Too much conflict—warfare:** Excessive conflict, on the other hand, can erode organizational performance because of political infighting, dissatisfaction, lack of teamwork, and turnover. Workplace aggression and violence are manifestations of excessive conflict.[11]

On strike. A striker waves an American flag as he pickets SBC Communications offices in San Francisco in May 2004. The Communications Workers of America were striking over health care and job security issues. What issues do you think lead to too much conflict in the workplace?

Thus, it seems that a moderate level of conflict can induce creativity and initiative, thereby raising performance, as shown in the diagram below. *(See Figure 13.1.)* As might be expected, however, the idea as to what constitutes "moderate" will vary among managers.

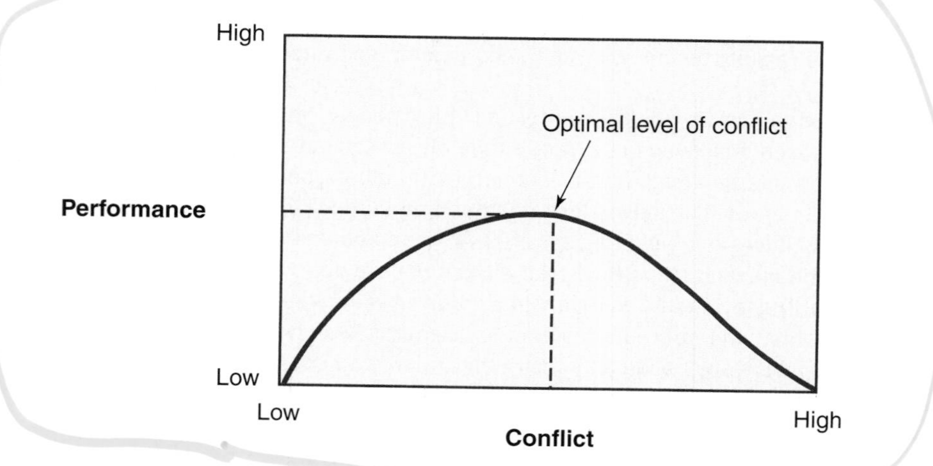

FIGURE 13.1
The relationship between level of conflict and level of performance. Too little conflict or too much conflict causes performance to suffer.

Seven Causes of Conflict

There are a variety of sources of conflict—so-called *conflict triggers*. Seven of the principal ones are listed below. By understanding these, you'll be better able to take charge and manage the conflicts rather than letting the conflicts take you by surprise and manage you.

1 Competition for Scarce Resources: When Two Parties Need the Same Things

Within organizations there is often a scarcity of needed resources—for example, funds, office space, equipment, employees, and money for raises. When resources are scarce, being a manager becomes more difficult and conflict more likely.[12]

Example: There are lots of computer software glitches but not enough programmers to fix them.

2 Time Pressure: When People Believe There Aren't Enough Hours to Do the Work

Setting a deadline is a useful way of inducing people to perform. Or it can be a source of resentment, rage, and conflict if employees think their manager has unrealistic expectations.

Example: If you're in the business of marketing Christmas items to department stores and gift shops, it's imperative that you have your product ready for those important trade shows at which store buyers will appear. But the product-ready deadline for Marketing may be completely unworkable for your company's Production Department, leading to angry conflict.

3 Inconsistent Goals or Reward Systems: When People Pursue Different Objectives

It's natural for people in functional organizations to be pursuing different objectives and to be rewarded accordingly, but this means that conflict is practically built into the system.

Example: The sales manager for a college textbook publisher may be rewarded for achieving exceptional sales of newly introduced titles. But individual salespeople are rewarded for how many books they sell overall, which means they may promote the old tried and true books they know.

4 Ambiguous Jurisdictions: When Job Boundaries Are Unclear

"That's not my job and those aren't my responsibilities." "Those resources belong to me because I need them as part of my job." When task responsibilities are unclear, that can often lead to conflict.

Examples: Is the bartender or the waiter supposed to put the lime in the gin and tonic and the celery in the Bloody Mary? Is management or the union in charge of certain work rules? Is Marketing or Research & Development supposed to be setting up focus groups to explore ideas for new products?

5 Status Differences: When There Are Inconsistencies in Power & Influence

It can happen that people who are lower in status according to the organization chart actually have disproportionate power over those theoretically above them, which can lead to conflicts.

Examples: If a restaurant patron complains his or her steak is not rare enough, the chef is the one who cooked it, but the waiter—who is usually lower in status—is the one who gave the chef the order. Airlines could not hold their schedules without flight crews and ground crews working a certain amount of overtime. But during labor disputes, pilots, flight attendants, and mechanics may simply refuse managers' requests to work overtime.

6 Personality Clashes: When Individual Differences Can't Be Resolved

Personality, values, attitudes, and experience can be so disparate that sometimes the only way to resolve individual differences—personality clashes—is to separate two people.

Example: Are you easygoing, but she's tense and driven? Does he always shade the facts, while you're a stickler for the truth? If you're basically Ms. Straight Arrow and he's Mr. Slippery, do you think you could adapt your personality to fit his? Maybe you should ask for a transfer.

7 Communication Failures: When People Misperceive & Misunderstand

The need for clear communication is a never-ending, ongoing process. Even under the best of circumstances, people misunderstand others, leading to conflict.

Example: Hewlett-Packard hired a consulting firm to explore acquisition of the computer maker Compaq, and at a crucial directors' meeting the consultant gave H-P board members a document about the two companies to discuss. However, an important board member, Walter Hewlett, son of one of the founders, wasn't there. He was playing his cello somewhere—at an annual event he had appeared in for the past three years—and had assumed the board would accommodate him, as it had in the past. But the board plowed ahead, believing Hewlett wouldn't miss such an important session. This turned out to be a crucial misstep for H-P management.[13] The miscommunication ultimately led to a major battle between Hewlett and top H-P officers, including CEO Carleton Fiorina. Heirs of the company's founders, which owned 18% of the stock, were upset at the personal tone Fiorina took in painting Hewlett as a musician and academic who flip-flopped over board decisions.

major question

If the best managers are usually independent of the herd, why should they cultivate teamwork skills?

The Big Picture

Teamwork promises to be a cornerstone of future management. The claims made for teamwork are that it increases productivity, increases speed, reduces costs, improves quality, reduces destructive internal competition, and improves workplace cohesiveness.

"We have this mythology in America about the lone genius," says Tom Kelley, general manager of Ideo, an industrial design company in Palo Alto, Calif., that helped create the Apple mouse and the Palm V handheld computer. "We love to personify things. But Michelangelo didn't paint the Sistine Chapel alone, and Edison didn't invent the light bulb alone."[18]

At Ideo, teamwork is the name of the game—several people "each doing a part but all subordinating personal prominence to the efficiency of the whole," as the dictionary defines it. And the key element of effective teamwork is a commitment to a common purpose.[19]

More Teamwork: The Change Today's Employees Need to Make

The use of teamwork is having substantial impacts on organizations and individuals, and it promises to be a cornerstone of progressive management. According to management guru Peter Drucker, tomorrow's organizations will not only be flatter and information-based but also organized around teamwork.[20] This opinion is bolstered by a survey of human resource executives in which 44% called for *more teamwork* as a change that employees need to make to achieve today's business goals.[21]

When you take a job in an organization, therefore, the chances are you won't be working as a lone genius or even as a lone wolf. You'll be working with others in situations demanding teamwork.

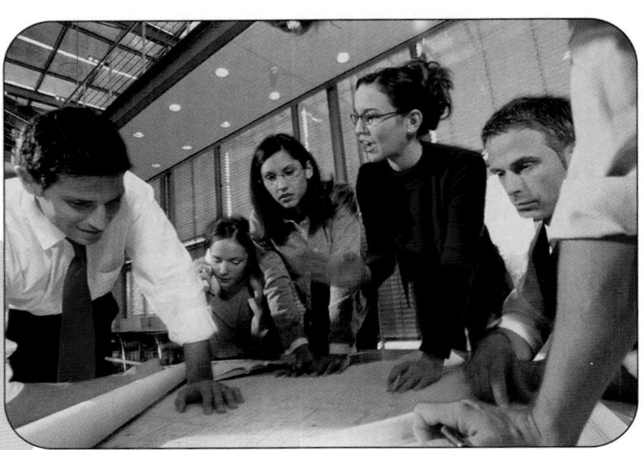

A self-managed team. Employees discuss plans for new construction. Teamwork helps the work get done quickly and efficiently. Not all companies allow employees the necessary independence and responsibility that make effective teams possible. How well do you think you fit into teamwork situations?

Why Teamwork Matters

Plane teamwork. In creating the 777 jetliner, Boeing used new approaches to design and build it. All kinds of specialties—designers, manufacturing representatives, tooling, engineers, finance, suppliers, customers, and others—worked jointly to create the airplane's parts and systems. Design/build teams—238 in all—were linked by mainframe computers in a system that used three-dimensional software allowing designers to see parts as solid images and then simulate the assembly of those parts on screen. As a result of this system, the 777 program exceeded its goal of reducing changes, errors, and rework by 50%. The first 777 aircraft was just .023 of an inch—about the width of a playing card—away from perfect alignment; most airplanes line up to within a half inch.

What are the results that teamwork can achieve? General Electric CEO Jeffrey Immelt offers this concise conclusion: "You lead today by building teams and placing others first. It's not about you."[22]

Some of the claims are as follows.

Increased Productivity

At General Electric's Puerto Rico factory for manufacturing arresters (surge protectors to guard power stations and transmission lines against lightning strikes), use of teamwork resulted in a workforce that was 20% more productive than comparable work units elsewhere in the company. Hourly workers were rotated through different work areas every six months to learn how their jobs affected other workers in the plant.

Increased Speed

Guidant Corp. in Santa Clara, Calif., which makes devices for life-saving medical procedures, used teamwork to create new products and get them to market more quickly—halving the time it took previously.[23] In four years, it also doubled its sales. Finally, it reduced its technical workforce turnover to only 2%–10% annually in an area where typical employee attrition is 20% a year.

Reduced Costs

Boeing used teamwork to develop its latest commercial jetliner, the 777, at costs that were far less than would have been the case with its traditional management techniques.[24]

Improved Quality

Westinghouse used teamwork in its truck and trailer division and within its electronic components division to improve quality performance. In addition, its nuclear fuel division earned one of the first Malcolm Baldrige Quality Awards.

Reduced Destructive Internal Competition

Clothing-store chain Men's Wearhouse actually fired one of its most successful "wardrobe consultants" because he wasn't sharing walk-in customer traffic with other salespeople. After the self-centered salesman was let go, none of his colleagues matched his sales record. But total sales volume for the store nevertheless increased significantly.[25]

Improved Workplace Cohesiveness

In the wake of earnings losses and layoffs following the 2001 collapse of the dot-com economy, Cisco Systems strove to increase productivity gains by increasing teamwork among as many groups as possible. To induce this group cohesiveness, executives were told they would gain or lose 30% of their bonuses based on how well they worked with their peers. Three years later, Cisco was posting record profits.[26]

The basis of teamwork is, as you might guess, an entity called the team. Let us see what this is. ◆

major question

How is one collection of workers different from any other?

The Big Picture

A group typically is management-directed, a team self-directed. Groups may be formal, created to do productive work, or informal, created for friendship. Work teams, which engage in collective work requiring coordinated effort, may be organized according to four basic purposes: advice, production, project, and action. Two types of teams are quality circles and self-managed teams.

Martin Jack Rosenblum is a bearded and long-haired musician and poet who likes to wear snakeskin boots and cowboy shirts to his job as archivist at the Milwaukee headquarters for Harley-Davidson motorcycles. At one time, Rosenblum was an English professor at the University of Wisconsin, but he hated the academic politics and backstabbing. Now, he says, "For the first time in my life, I feel like I'm part of a community. Harley is the University I've always been looking for."[27] The reason: In Harley's team-oriented and more open, goal-directed environment, he found more camaraderie and a sense of accomplishment.

Groups & Teams: How Do They Differ?

Aren't a group of people and a team of people the same thing? By and large, no. One is a collection of people, the other a powerful unit of collective performance. One is typically management-directed, the other self-directed.

Consider the differences.

What a Group Is: Collections of People Performing as Individuals

A *group* is defined as two or more freely interacting individuals who share collective norms, share collective goals, and have a common identity.[28] A group is different from a crowd, a transitory collection of people who don't interact with one another, such as a crowd gathering on a sidewalk to watch a fire. And it is different from an organization, such as a labor union, which is so large that members also don't interact.[29]

An example of a work group would be a collection of, say, 10 employees meeting to exchange information about various companies' policies on wages and hours.

What a Team Is: Collections of People with Common Commitment

McKinsey & Company management consultants Jon R. Katzenbach and Douglas K. Smith say it is a mistake to use the terms *group* and *team* interchangeably. Successful teams, they say, tend to take on a life of their own. Thus, a ***team*** **is defined as a small group of people with complementary skills who are committed to a common purpose, performance goals, and approach for which they hold themselves mutually accountable.**[30] "The essence of a team is common commitment," say Katzenbach and Smith. "Without it, groups perform as individuals; with it, they become a powerful unit of collective performance."[31]

An example of a team would be a collection of 2–10 employees who are studying industry pay scales with the goal of making recommendations for adjusting pay grades within their own company.

Formal versus Informal Groups

Groups may be either formal or informal.

- **Formal groups—created to do productive work: A *formal group* is a group established to do something productive for the organization and is headed by a leader.** A formal group may be a division, a department, a work group, or a committee. It may be permanent or temporary. In general, people are assigned to them according to their skills and the organization's requirements.
- **Informal groups—created for friendship: An *informal group* is a group formed by people seeking friendship and has no officially appointed leader, although a leader may emerge from the membership.** An informal group may be simply a collection of friends who hang out with one another, such as those who take coffee breaks together, or it may be as organized as a prayer breakfast, a bowling team, a service club, or other voluntary organization.

What's important for you as a manager to know is that informal groups can advance or undercut the plans of formal groups. The formal organization may make efforts, say, to speed up the plant assembly line or to institute workplace reforms. But these attempts may be sabotaged through the informal networks of workers who meet and gossip over lunch pails and after-work beers.[32]

However, interestingly, informal groups can also be highly productive—even more so than formal groups.

Example

How Informal Groups Can Be Productive: A Siemens Plant Finds Worker Chitchat "Is Not Goofing Off, It's Training"

To a manager, it may look like goofing off—those quick visits between coworkers, the brief exchanges near the coffeepot. But a two-year $1.6 million study by the Center for Workplace Development showed something more interesting: Workers learn most of what they know on the fly, and often from one another.

Though companies now spend up to $50 billion a year on formal training programs, up to 70% of workplace learning is informal, according to the study, which examined such companies as Motorola, Boeing Commercial Airplane Group, and Siemens Power Transmission and Distribution.[33]

At the Siemens plant in Wendell, N.C., for example, managers had been wondering how to stop workers from gathering so often in the company cafeteria. "The assumption was made that this was chitchat, talking about their golf game," said Barry Blystone, director of training. "But there was a whole lot of work activity."

Following the study, Siemens managers placed overhead projectors and empty pads of paper in the lunchroom to facilitate informal meetings. They also alerted supervisors about the unofficial gatherings. "We tell them, 'Keep an open mind, allow it to go on, and don't get in the way,'" said Blystone.

Work Teams for Four Purposes: Advice, Production, Project, & Action

The names given to different kinds of teams can be bewildering. We have identified some important ones on the top of the next page. *(See Table 13.1.)*

You will probably benefit most by understanding the various types of work teams distinguished according to their purpose. Work teams, which engage in collective work requiring coordinated effort, are of four types, which may be identified according to their basic purpose: *advice, production, project,* or *action.*[34]

TABLE 13.1

Various types of teams. These teams are not mutually exclusive. Work teams, for instance, may also be self-managed, cross-functional, or virtual.

Cross-functional team	Members composed of people from different departments, such as sales and production, pursuing a common objective
Problem-solving team	Knowledgeable workers who meet as a temporary team to solve a specific problem and then disband
Quality circle	Volunteers of workers and supervisors who meet intermittently to discuss workplace and quality-related problems
Self-managed team	Workers are trained to do all or most of the jobs in a work unit, have no direct supervisor, and do their own day-to-day supervision
Top-management team	Members consist of the CEO, president, and top department heads and work to help the organization achieve its mission and goals
Virtual team	Members interact by computer network to collaborate on projects
Work team	Members engage in collective work requiring coordinated effort; purpose of team is advice, production, project, or action *(see text discussion)*

1 Advice Teams

Advice teams are created to broaden the information base for managerial decisions. Examples are committees, review panels, advisory councils, employee involvement groups, and quality circles (as we'll discuss).

2 Production Teams

Production teams are responsible for performing day-to-day operations. Examples are mining teams, flight-attendant crews, maintenance crews, assembly teams, data processing groups, and manufacturing crews.

3 Project Teams

Project teams work to do creative problem solving, often by applying the specialized knowledge of members of a ***cross-functional team,*** **which is staffed with specialists pursuing a common objective.** Examples are task forces, research groups, planning teams, architect teams, engineering teams, and development teams.

4 Action Teams

Action teams work to accomplish tasks that require people with (1) specialized training and (2) a high degree of coordination, as on a baseball team, with specialized athletes acting in coordination. Examples are hospital surgery teams, airline cockpit crews, mountain-climbing expeditions, police SWAT teams, and labor contract negotiating teams.

Two Types of Teams in Action: Quality Circles Compared with Self-Managed Teams

To give you an idea of how teams work, consider two approaches, one of which may evolve into the other: quality circles and self-managed teams. Their differences are summarized on the next page. *(See Table 13.2.)*

TABLE 13.2
Quality circles and self-managed teams compared

Quality Circles	Self-Managed Teams
Advice teams	Production, project, or action teams
Consultation—limited empowerment	Delegation—high empowerment
Voluntary membership	Assigned membership
Outside normal channels of organization's structure	Integrated within organization's structure
Influence low-level operations	Influence possibly all organizational levels

Quality Circles: Organizational Effectiveness through Employee Involvement

***Quality circles,* or *quality control circles,* consist of small groups of volunteers or workers and supervisors who meet intermittently to discuss workplace and quality-related problems.** Typically a group of 10–12 people will meet for 60–90 minutes once or twice a month, with management listening to presentations and the important payoff for members usually being the chance for meaningful participation and skills training.

The movement began when American quality-control experts introduced quality circles to Japanese industry after World War II, then returned to the United States during the 1970s. At its zenith in the 1980s, the quality-circle movement included millions of employee participants and hundreds of U.S. companies and government agencies hoping to duplicate Japan's industrial success, although early enthusiasm frequently gave way to disappointment.[35] Still, quality circles can be more than a management fad. As one pair of researchers states, "quality circles can be an important first step toward organizational effectiveness through employee involvement."[36]

The lifeblood of quality circles is the fact that they are made up of *volunteers*. Thus, management's first hurdle is to sell the idea to suspicious and mistrusting employees as well as to supervisors who may view employee participation as a threat to their authority. Besides training, honesty, and patience, monetary rewards can help, such as a gainsharing formula that will let everyone participate in the benefits of performance improvement.[37]

A quality circle. Employees of Square D, a Palatine, Ill., supplier of electrical industrial controls and automation systems, gather in a circle to discuss workplace and quality-related problems. To be effective, quality circles must be made up of volunteers, people who can see the benefits—both for themselves and for the company—of participating in these monthly or bimonthly events.

Self-Managed Teams: Workers with Own Administrative Oversight

In Malaysia, the quality circles at the Texas Instruments electronics factory near Kuala Lumpur have evolved into a system made up almost entirely of self-managed teams, with routine activities formerly performed by supervisors now performed by team members. "Self-managed" does not, however, mean simply turning workers loose to do their own thing. ***Self-managed teams*** **are defined as groups of workers who are given administrative oversight for their task domains.** Administrative oversight involves delegated activities such as planning, scheduling, monitoring, and staffing. Nearly 70% of *Fortune* 1000 companies have created self-managed work teams.[38]

Self-managed teams are an outgrowth of a blend of behavioral science and management practice.[39] The goal has been to increase productivity and employee quality of work life. The traditional clear-cut distinction between manager and managed is being blurred as nonmanagerial employees are delegated greater authority and granted increased autonomy.

In creating self-managed teams, both technical and organizational redesign are necessary. Self-managed teams may require special technology. Volvo's team-based auto assembly plant, for example, relies on portable assembly platforms rather than traditional assembly lines. Structural redesign of the organization must take place because self-managed teams are an integral part of the organization, not patched onto it, as is the case with quality circles. Personnel and reward systems need to be adapted to encourage teamwork. Staffing decisions may shift from management to team members who hire their own coworkers. Individual bonuses must give way to team bonuses. Supervisory development workshops are needed to teach managers to be facilitators rather than order givers.[40] Finally, extensive team training is required to help team members learn more about technical details, the business as a whole, and how to be team players.[41] ◆

A Volvo plant. This team-based Volvo assembly plant in Torslanda, Sweden, makes cars by using portable assembly platforms rather than a single constantly moving assembly line. Volvo puts the names of team members on every engine they build to instill pride in their work. Although teams have been used since the Egyptians built the pyramids, the idea didn't really gain currency in the workplace until it was promoted by management theorists such as Frederick Taylor and Douglas McGregor. In the 1930s, teams were adopted in factories to streamline manufacturing. In the 1960s, teams gained popularity as ways to improve worker satisfaction. Ironically, Volvo was acquired in 1999 by the company that was instrumental in using the assembly-line concept in manufacturing—Ford Motor Co. Despite Volvo's reputation for building the world's safest cars, it had not been selling well enough to generate the cash needed to develop new models. As an affordable European car, Volvo fits well in Ford's product mix, which includes Mazda, Jaguar, and Aston Martin as well as Ford, Lincoln, and Mercury.

The Challenge of Managing Virtual Teams: Reaching Across Time & Space

Once upon a time, managers subscribed to the so-called Fifty-Foot Rule—namely, "If people are more than 50 feet apart, they are not likely to collaborate." That is no longer true in today's era of virtual teams. Virtual teams are groups of people who use information technology—computers and telecommunications—to collaborate across space, time, and organizational boundaries.[42]

Teams are generally defined as consisting of 2–16 people. But virtual collaborations may be even larger. For instance, NCR Corp. created a virtual "team" (group) of more than 1,000 people working at 17 locations to develop a next-generation computer system. Using a high-bandwidth audio-video-data telecommunications network, members completed the project on budget and ahead of schedule.[43] And Hong Kong-based Cathay Pacific Airlines designed a network, called GalaCXy, appropriate for a company where employees are never in one place for very long but need to be able to communicate intelligently wherever they go. "GalaCXy users can set up meetings with each other without calling to check one another's schedules," says one account. "They can access one another's schedules to see when they're available and then suggest a time by e-mail."[44]

Virtually working. The team members shown on screen could be on the other side of the country or the other side of the world. Virtual meetings like this can save a great deal on costs, time, and travel wear and tear.

As technology has made it easier for workers to function from remote places, it has posed challenges for managers. Following are some suggestions from *Business Week* for managing virtual workers, especially those working at home:[45]

- **Take baby steps:** When trying out virtual arrangements with new employees, take it slow. Let them show they can handle the challenge.
- **State expectations:** Nip problems in the bud by letting virtual workers know what you expect from them. With home-based workers, for example, go over the terms of your virtual arrangement—whether, for example, you want them to carry an office cellphone—and tell them if there are specific ways you want the job done.
- **Write it down:** Record directions, project changes, and updates in writing, by sending an e-mail or fax or using Web-based services that allow for sharing calendars and tracking projects.

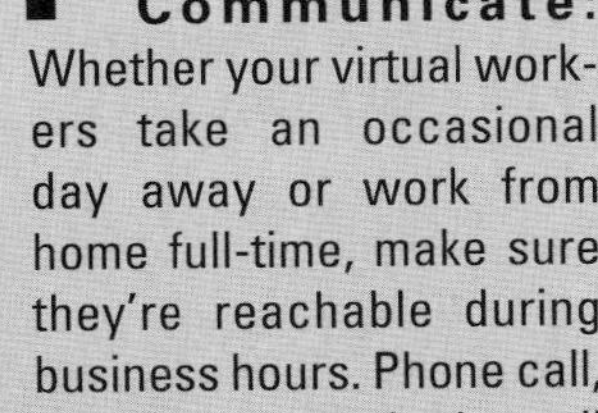

- **Communicate:** Whether your virtual workers take an occasional day away or work from home full-time, make sure they're reachable during business hours. Phone call, e-mail, fax, and chat all work well—but they have to be able to reach you, too.
- **Manage by results:** Focus on what's accomplished, not whether your employee is working from her patio or at 10 P.M. Set interim deadlines on projects and stick to them.
- **Meet regularly:** Human contact still matters. When possible, schedule periodic and regular meetings at which all team members can discuss current projects, and telecommuters can catch up on office gossip. Fly out-of-towners in at least quarterly, so they can develop working friendships with your in-office staff.

major question **How does a group evolve into a team?**

The Big Picture

Groups may evolve into teams by going through five stages of development: forming, storming, norming, performing, and adjourning.

Elsewhere in this book we have described how products and organizations go through stages of development. Groups and teams go through the same thing. One theory proposes five stages of development: *forming, storming, norming, performing, adjourning.*[46] *(See Figure 13.2.)* Let us consider these stages in which groups may evolve into teams—bearing in mind that the stages aren't necessarily of the same duration or intensity.

FIGURE 13.2
Five stages of group and team development

Stage 1: Forming—"Why Are We Here?"

The first stage, ***forming,*** **is the process of getting oriented and getting acquainted.** This stage is characterized by a high degree of uncertainty as members try to break the ice and figure out who is in charge and what the group's goals are. For example, if you were to become part of a team that is to work on a class project, the question for you as an individual would be "How do I fit in here?" For the group, the question is "Why are we here?"

At this point, mutual trust is low, and there is a good deal of holding back to see who takes charge and how. If the formal leader (such as the class instructor or a supervisor) does not assert his or her authority, an emergent leader will eventually step in to fill the group's need for leadership and direction.

What the Leader Should Do

Leaders typically mistake this honeymoon period as a mandate for permanent control, but later problems may force a leadership change. During this stage, leaders should allow time for people to become acquainted and socialize.

Stage 2: Storming—"Why Are We Fighting Over Who Does What & Who's in Charge?"

The second stage, ***storming,*** **is characterized by the emergence of individual personalities and roles and conflicts within the group.** For you as an individual, the question is "What's my role here?" For the group, the issue is "Why are we fighting over who does what and who's in charge?" This stage may be of short duration or painfully long, depending on the goal clarity and the commitment and maturity of the members.

This is a time of testing. Individuals test the leader's policies and assumptions as they try to determine how they fit into the power structure.[47] Subgroups take shape, and subtle forms of rebellion, such as procrastination, occur. Many groups stall in stage 2 because power politics may erupt into open rebellion.

What the Leader Should Do

In this stage, the leader should encourage members to suggest ideas, voice disagreements, and work through their conflicts about tasks and goals.

Stage 3: Norming—"Can We Agree on Roles & Work as a Team?"

In the third stage, ***norming,*** **conflicts are resolved, close relationships develop, and unity and harmony emerge.** For individuals, the main issue is "What do the others expect me to do?" For the group, the issue is "Can we agree on roles and work as a team?" Note, then, that the *group* may now evolve into a *team*.

Teams set guidelines related to what members will do together and how they will do it. The teams consider such matters as attendance at meetings, being late, and missing assignments as well as how members treat one another.

Groups that make it through stage 2 generally do so because a respected member other than the leader challenges the group to resolve its power struggles so something can be accomplished. Questions about authority are resolved through unemotional, matter-of-fact group discussion. A feeling of team spirit is experienced because members believe they have found their proper roles. ***Group cohesiveness,*** **a "we feeling" binding group members together,** is the principal by-product of stage 3. (We discuss cohesiveness next, in Section 13.5.)

What the Leader Should Do

This stage generally does not last long. Here the leader should emphasize unity and help identify team goals and values.

Stage 4: Performing—"Can We Do the Job Properly?"

In ***performing,*** **members concentrate on solving problems and completing the assigned task.** For individuals, the question here is "How can I best perform my role?" For the group/team, the issue is "Can we do the job properly?"

What the Leader Should Do

During this stage, the leader should allow members the empowerment they need to work on tasks.

Stage 5: Adjourning—"Can We Help Members Transition Out?"

In the final stage, ***adjourning,*** **members prepare for disbandment.** Having worked so hard to get along and get something done, many members feel a compelling sense of loss. For the individual, the question now is "What's next?" For the team, the issue is "Can we help members transition out?"

What the Leader Should Do

The leader can help ease the transition by rituals celebrating "the end" and "new beginnings." Parties, award ceremonies, graduations, or mock funerals can provide the needed punctuation at the end of a significant teamwork project. The leader can emphasize valuable lessons learned in group dynamics to prepare everyone for future group and team efforts. ◆

major question

How can I as a manager build an effective team?

The Big Picture

Two types of change are reactive and proactive. Forces for change may consist of forces outside the organization—demographic characteristics, market changes, technological advancements, and social and political pressures. Or they may be forces inside the organization—employee problems and managers' behavior.

Within an organization, you may hear managers loosely (and incorrectly) use the word *team* to describe any collection of people that have been pulled together. But because traditional managers are often reluctant to give up control, no thought is given to providing the "team" (really just a group) with training and support. That is, no attempt is made to sharpen communication skills, reward innovation, or encourage independence without group members running away and losing control.[48]

Thus, as a manager, the first thing you have to realize is that building a high-performance team is going to require some work. But the payoff will be a stronger, better-performing work unit.

The considerations in building a group into an effective team are (1) *performance goals and feedback,* (2) *motivation through mutual accountability,* (3) *size,* (4) *roles,* (5) *norms,* (6) *cohesiveness,* and (7) *groupthink.*

1 Performance Goals & Feedback

As an individual, you no doubt prefer to have measurable goals and to have feedback about your performance. The same is true with teams. Teams are not just collections of individuals. They are individuals organized for a collective purpose. That purpose needs to be defined in terms of specific, measurable performance goals with continual feedback to tell team members how well they are doing.

An obvious example are the teams you see on television at Indianapolis or Daytona Beach during automobile racing. When the driver guides the race car off the track to make a pit stop, a team of people swarm over the wall and quickly jack up the car to change tires, refuel the tank, and clean the windshield—all operating in a matter of seconds. The performance goals are to have the car back on the track as quickly as possible. The number of seconds of elapsed time—and the driver's place among competitors once back in the race—tells them how well they are doing.

Learning teamwork from a NASCAR pit crew. Randy Darcy, chief technical officer for cereal maker General Mills, was given the challenge of cutting $1 billion out of the company's supply chain. Darcy's approach was to adapt lessons in efficiency and high performance learned elsewhere—watching Air Force mechanics fix Stealth bombers, participating in predawn raids with a U.S. Marshals Service SWAT team, and getting time- and money-saving ideas by observing a NASCAR pit crew. Seeing how the pit crew was able to work with blinding speed through better team organization, the cereal company was able to cut the time workers changed a production line for a Betty Crocker product from 4.5 hours to just 12 minutes.

2 Motivation through Mutual Accountability

Do you work harder when you're alone or when you're in a group? When clear performance goals exist, when the work is considered meaningful, when members believe their efforts matter, and when they don't feel they are being exploited by others, this kind of culture supports teamwork.[49] Being mutually accountable to other members of the team rather than to a supervisor makes members feel mutual trust and commitment—a key part in motivating members for team effort. To bring about this team culture, managers often allow teams to do the hiring of new members.

3 Size: Small Teams or Large Teams?

Size, which is often determined by the team's purpose, can be important in affecting members' commitment and performance. Whereas in some flat-organization structures, groups may consist of 30 or more employees, teams seem to range in size from 2 to 16 people, with those of 5 to 12 generally being the most workable. A survey of 400 workplace team members in the United States found that the average team consisted of 10 members, with 8 being the most common size.[50]

Small and large teams have different characteristics, although the number of members is, to be sure, somewhat arbitrary.[51]

Small Teams: 2–9 Members for Better Interaction & Morale

Teams with 9 or fewer members have two advantages:

- **Better interaction:** Members are better able to interact, share information, ask questions of one another, and coordinate activities than are those in larger teams. In particular, teams with five or fewer offer more opportunity for personal discussion and participation.
- **Better morale:** They are better able to see the worth of their individual contributions and thus are more highly committed and satisfied. Members are less apt to feel inhibited in participating. Team leaders are subject to fewer demands and are able to be more informal.[52]

However, small teams also have some disadvantages:

- **Fewer resources:** With fewer hands, there will be fewer resources—less knowledge, experience, skills, and abilities to apply to the team's tasks.
- **Possibly less innovation:** A group that's too small may show less creativity and boldness because of the effect of peer pressure.
- **Unfair work distribution:** Because of fewer resources and less specialization, there may be an uneven distribution of the work among members.

Large Teams: 10–16 Members for More Resources & Division of Labor

Teams with 10–16 members have different advantages over small teams. (Again, the numbers are somewhat arbitrary.)

- **More resources:** Larger teams have more resources to draw on: more knowledge, experience, skills, abilities, and perhaps time. These will give them more leverage to help them realize the team's goals.
- **Division of labor:** In addition, a large team can take advantage of ***division of labor,*** **in which the work is divided into particular tasks that are assigned to particular workers.**

Yet bigness has its disadvantages:

- **Less interaction:** With more members, there is less interaction, sharing of information, and coordinating of activities. Leaders may be more formal and autocratic, since members in teams this size are apt to be more tolerant of autocratic leadership. The larger size may also lead to the formation of cliques.
- **Lower morale:** Because people are less able to see the worth of their individual contributions, they show less commitment and satisfaction and more turnover and absenteeism. They also express more disagreements and turf struggles and make more demands on leaders.
- **Social loafing:** The larger the size, the more likely performance is to drop, owing to the phenomenon known as ***social loafing,*** **the tendency of people to exert less effort when working in groups than when working alone.**[53]

Example

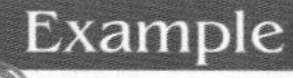

Team Sizes: What's the Optimum Number for a Team?

Various companies have had various ideal sizes for the number of members on a team: Titeflex, 6–10; EDS, 8–12; Johnsonville Foods, 12; DEC, 14–15; Volvo, 20. The general rule is this: small teams make members feel like large contributors. Thus, managers are advised to keep teams small but large enough to accomplish the work needed.

At Microsoft Corp., Nathan Myhrvold, senior vice president for advanced technology, found that the optimum size of a software-development team was 8. Besides keeping members motivated and committed, this number enabled programmers and software engineers to better see the importance of their contributions, interact with one another, share information, and coordinate their efforts.[54]

4 Roles: How Team Members Are Expected to Behave

A *role* is a socially determined expectation of how an individual should behave in a specific position. As a team member, your role is to play a part in helping the team reach its goals. Members develop their roles based on the expectations of the team, of the organization, and of themselves, and they may do different things. You, for instance, might be a team leader. Others might do some of the work tasks. Still others might communicate with other teams.

Two types of team roles are task and maintenance.[55]

Task Roles: Getting the Work Done

A *task role,* or *task-oriented role,* consists of behavior that concentrates on getting the team's tasks done. Task roles keep the team on track and get the work done. If you stand up in a team meeting and say, "What is the real issue here? We don't seem to be getting anywhere," you are performing a task role.

Examples: Coordinators, who pull together ideas and suggestions; orienters, who keep teams headed toward their stated goals; initiators, who suggest new goals or ideas; and energizers, who prod people to move along or accomplish more are all playing task roles.

Maintenance Roles: Keeping the Team Together

A *maintenance role,* or *relationship-oriented role,* consists of behavior that fosters constructive relationships among team members. Maintenance roles focus on keeping team members. If someone at a team meeting says, "Let's hear from those who oppose this plan," he or she is playing a maintenance role.

Examples: Encouragers, who foster group solidarity by praising various viewpoints; standard setters, who evaluate the quality of group processes; harmonizers, who mediate conflict through reconciliation or humor; and compromisers, who help resolve conflict by meeting others "halfway."

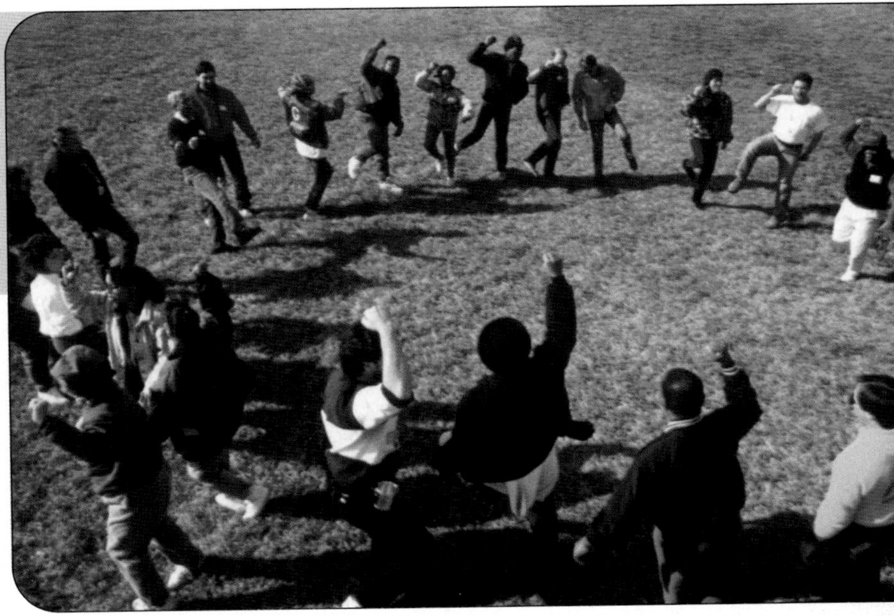

The Saturn cheer. This group of Saturn Corp. employees, builders of the General Motors car, is winding up a team-building exercise, which ends with everyone arranged in a so-called Commitment Circle for closing ceremonies. As a last activity, everyone engages in the Saturn "I Say" cheer: "I say, I say, I say . . . Saturn!" (Some of the Saturn dealers got the idea to do the same cheer for their customers upon buying a car.)

5 Norms: Unwritten Rules for Team Members

Norms are more encompassing than roles. ***Norms*** **are general guidelines or rules of behavior that most group or team members follow.** Norms point up the boundaries between acceptable and unacceptable behavior.[56] Although norms are typically unwritten and seldom discussed openly, they have a powerful influence on group and organizational behavior.[57]

Example

Team Norms: At the Great Little Box Co., "No One Wants to Mess Up"

Established in 1982, the privately owned Great Little Box Company, which makes corrugated boxes and other shipping supplies, has 150 employees in four locations across British Columbia and Washington State. To encourage team norms (and cohesiveness, discussed on the next page), president Robert Meggy, an accountant, sets up what he calls his "BOX" goal. "It stands for Big Outrageous Extravaganza," he says. Every year he sets two budget goals—a realistic one and an extraordinary though attainable one. If employees achieve the BOX goal, they get a reward. In 1998, he took more than 100 of them to Las Vegas.

Meggy says that teamwork improves his bottom line. A few years earlier, Meggy had tracked errors each month and suggested that if they were reduced, employees could earn points redeemable for prizes. That first year, plant errors were reduced 60% and customer service errors by 80%.

"They came up with their own idea of double checking each other's work," he says. "The peer pressure aspect is great. No one wants to mess up."[58]

Why Norms Are Enforced: Four Reasons

Norms tend to be enforced by group or team members for four reasons:[59]

- **To help the group survive—"Don't do anything that will hurt us":** Norms are enforced to help the group, team, or organization survive.

  Example: The manager of your team or group might compliment you because you've made sure it has the right emergency equipment.

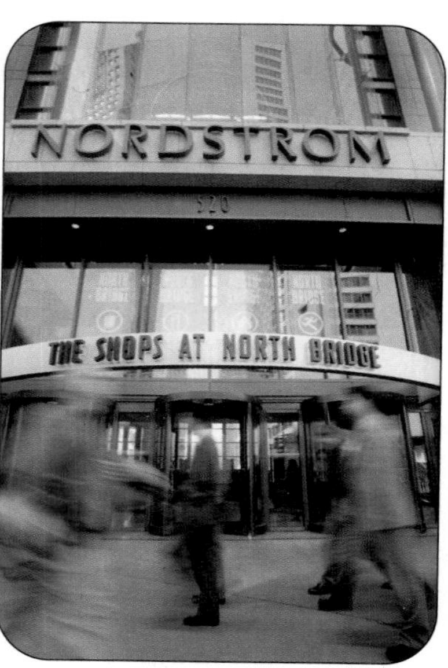

Special norms. Nordstrom gets high marks from shoppers because its employees are instructed to put the customer before the profit line. A customer may return a purchase for any reason, with minimal hassle. As one writer states, "It is hard to find a [non-Nordstrom department] store that actually values the people who keep them in business."

- **To clarify role expectations—"You have to go along to get along":** Norms are also enforced to help clarify or simplify role expectations.

  Example: At one time, new members of Congress wanting to buck the system by which important committee appointments were given to those with the most seniority were advised to "go along to get along"—go along with the rules in order to get along in their congressional careers.

- **To help individuals avoid embarrassing situations—"Don't call attention to yourself":** Norms are enforced to help group or team members avoid embarrassing themselves.

  Examples: You might be ridiculed by fellow team members for dominating the discussion during a report to top management ("Be a team player, not a show-off"). Or you might be told not to discuss religion or politics with customers, whose views might differ from yours.

- **To emphasize the group's important values and identity—"We're known for being special":** Finally, norms are enforced to emphasize the group, team, or organization's central values or to enhance its unique identity.

  Examples: Nordstrom's department store chain emphasizes the great lengths to which it goes in customer service. Every year a college gives an award to the instructor whom students vote best teacher.

6 Cohesiveness: The Importance of Togetherness

Another important characteristic of teams is ***cohesiveness,*** **the tendency of a group or team to stick together.** This is the familiar sense of togetherness or "we-ness" you feel, for example, when you're a member of a volleyball team, a fraternity or a sorority, or a company's sales force. (We gave an example of cohesiveness in the Great Little Box Co. example on the previous page.)

Managers can stimulate cohesiveness by allowing people on work teams to pick their own teammates, allowing off-the-job social events, and urging team members to recognize and appreciate each other's contributions to the team goal.[60] Cohesiveness is also achieved by keeping teams small, making sure performance standards are clear and accepted, and following the tips in the following table. *(See Table 13.3.)*

TABLE 13.3
What managers can do to enhance team cohesiveness

- Keep the team relatively small
- Strive for a favorable public image to increase the status and prestige of belonging
- Encourage interaction and cooperation
- Emphasize members' common characteristics and interests
- Point out environmental threats—e.g., competitors' achievements—to rally the team
- Regularly update and clarify the team's goals
- Give every group member a vital "piece of the action"
- Channel each team member's special talents toward the common goals
- Recognize and equitably reinforce each member's contributions
- Frequently remind group members they need each other to get the job done

7 Groupthink: When Peer Pressure Discourages "Thinking Outside the Box"

Cohesiveness isn't always good. An undesirable by-product that may occur, according to psychologist **Irvin Janis,** is ***groupthink*** **—a cohesive group's blind unwillingness to consider alternatives.** In this phenomenon, group or team members are friendly and tight-knit, but they are unable to think "outside the box." Their "strivings for unanimity override their motivation to realistically appraise alternative courses of action," says Janis.[61]

The word "groupthink" regained some prominence in mid-2004 when the Senate Intelligence Committee said the U.S. invasion of Iraq had occurred because too many people in the government tended to think alike and failed to challenge basic assumptions about Iraq's weapons capability.[62] It cannot be said, however, that group opinion is always risky. Indeed, financial writer James Surowiecki, author of *The Wisdom of Crowds,* argues that "Under the right circumstances, groups are remarkably intelligent, and are often smarter than the smartest people in them."[63] As evidence, he cites how groups have been used to predict the election of the President of the United States, find lost submarines, and correct the spread on a sporting event.

Symptoms of Groupthink

How do you know that you're in a group or team that is suffering from groupthink? Some symptoms:[64]

- **Invulnerability, inherent morality, and stereotyping of opposition:** Because of feelings of invulnerability, group members have the illusion that nothing can go wrong, breeding excessive optimism and risk taking. Members may also be so assured of the rightness of their actions that they ignore the ethical implications of their decisions. These beliefs are helped along by stereotyped views of the opposition, which leads the group to underestimate its opponents.
- **Rationalization and self-censorship:** Rationalizing protects the pet assumptions underlying the group's decisions from critical questions. Self-censorship also stifles critical debate. It is especially hard to argue with success, of course. But if enough key people, such as outside analysts, had challenged the energy giant Enron when it seemed to be flying high, it might not have led to the largest bankruptcy in corporate history.

Example

Groupthink: When Corporate Directors Hate to Be "the Skunk at the Garden Party"

Groupthink can happen anywhere within an organization. Thus, even when the management of a company is performing badly, members of the board of directors—supposedly the top overseers—may be unwilling to take a tough line or rock the boat. Indeed, this unwillingness may be an important reason why top executives at Enron, WorldCom, Tyco, and similar organizations were not reined in.

"No one likes to be the skunk at the garden party," says management consultant Victor Palmieri. "One does not make friends and influence people in the boardroom or elsewhere by raising hard questions that create embarrassment or discomfort for management."[65]

By contrast, Kenneth A. Macke, when he was chairman and CEO of Dayton Hudson Corp., the department store giant, created a groupthink-resistant board by making 12 of its 14 directors outsiders, with one chosen to act as special liaison between the board and Macke. The result was a board of directors so independent that in one year it felt strong enough to withhold CEO Macke's bonus, which was nearly $600,000 the year before.[66]

- **Illusion of unanimity, peer pressure, and mindguards:** The illusion of unanimity is another way of saying that silence by a member is interpreted to mean consent. But if people do disagree, peer pressure leads other members to question the loyalty of the dissenters. In addition, in a groupthink situation there may exist people who might be called *mindguards*—self-appointed protectors against adverse information.
- **Groupthink versus "the wisdom of crowds":** Groupthink is characterized by a pressure to conform that often leads members with different ideas to censor themselves—the opposite of collective wisdom, says James Surowiecki, in which "each person in the group is offering his or her best independent forecast. It's not at all about compromise or consensus."[67]

The Results of Groupthink: Decision-Making Defects

Groups with a moderate amount of cohesiveness tend to produce better decisions than groups with low or high cohesiveness. Members of highly cohesive groups victimized by groupthink make the poorest decisions—even though they show they express great confidence in those decisions.[68]

Among the decision-making defects that can arise from groupthink are the following.

- **Reduction in alternative ideas:** The principal casualty of groupthink is a shrinking universe of ideas. Decisions are made based on few alternatives. Once preferred alternatives are decided on, they are not reexamined, and, of course, rejected alternatives are not reexamined.
- **Limiting of other information:** When a groupthink group has made its decision, others' opinions, even those of experts, are rejected. If new information is considered at all, it is biased toward ideas that fit the group's preconceptions. Thus, no contingency plans are made in case the decision turns out to be faulty.

Preventing Groupthink: Making Criticism & Other Perspectives Permissible

Janis believes it is easier to prevent groupthink than to cure it. As preventive measures, he suggests the following:

- **Allow criticism:** Each member of a team or group should be told to be a critical evaluator, able to actively voice objections and doubts. Subgroups within the group should be allowed to discuss and debate ideas. Once a consensus has been reached, everyone should be encouraged to rethink their position to check for flaws.
- **Allow other perspectives:** Outside experts should be used to introduce fresh perspectives. Different groups with different leaders should explore the same policy questions. Top-level executives should not use policy committees to rubber-stamp decisions that have already been made. When major alternatives are discussed, someone should be made devil's advocate to try to uncover all negative factors. ◆

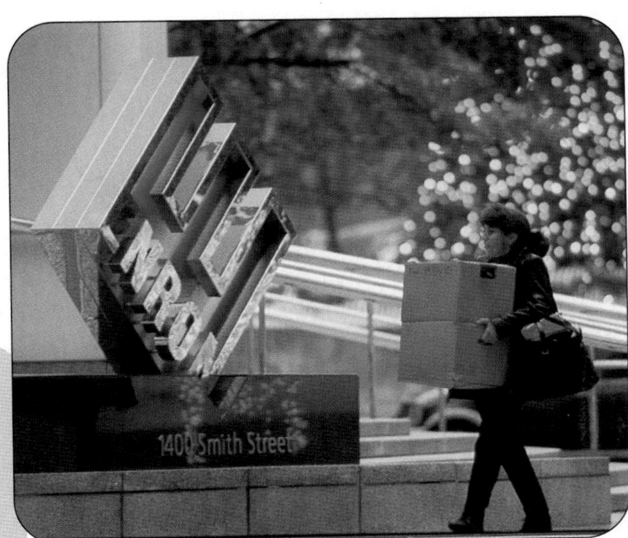

Walking papers. An employee leaves Enron's Houston headquarters. Why did the company go bust? "Start with arrogance," suggested *Fortune* magazine. "Add greed, deceit, and financial chicanery. What do you get? A company that was never what it was cracked up to be." Would you have felt strong enough to try to turn the tide in a culture like this?

Key Terms Used in This Chapter

adjourning, 427
cohesiveness, 432
conflict, 412
constructive conflict, 412
cross-functional team, 422
devil's advocacy, 417
dialectic method, 417
division of labor, 429
formal group, 421
forming, 426
group, 420
group cohesiveness, 427
groupthink, 433
informal group, 421
maintenance role, 430
negative conflict, 412
norming, 427
norms, 431
performing, 427
programmed conflict, 417
quality circles, 423
role, 430
self-managed teams, 424
social loafing, 430
storming, 426
task role, 430
team, 420

Summary

13.1 Managing Conflict

- 
Conflict is a process in which one party perceives that its interests are being opposed or negatively affected by another party. Conflict can be negative. However, constructive, or functional, conflict benefits the main purposes of the organization and serves its interests. Too little conflict can lead to indolence; too much conflict can lead to warfare.
- Seven causes of conflict are (1) competition for scarce resources, (2) time pressure, (3) inconsistent goals or reward systems, (4) ambiguous jurisdictions, (5) status differences, (6) personality clashes, and (7) communication failures.
- Four devices for stimulating constructive conflict are (1) spurring competition among employees, (2) changing the organization's culture and procedures, (3) bringing in outsiders for new perspectives, and (4) using programmed conflict to elicit different opinions without inciting people's personal feelings. Two methods used in programmed conflict are (1) devil's advocacy, in which someone is assigned to play the role of critic to voice possible objections to a proposal, and (2) the dialectic method, in which two people or groups play opposing roles in a debate in order to better understand a proposal.

13.2 Teamwork: Cornerstone of Progressive Management

- 
The claims made for teamwork are that it increases productivity, increases speed, reduces costs, improves quality, reduces destructive internal competition, and improves workplace cohesiveness.

13.3 Groups versus Teams

- 
Groups and teams are different—a group is typically management-directed, a team self-directed. A group is defined as two or more freely interacting individuals who share collective norms, share collective goals, and have a common identity. A team is defined as a small group of people with complementary skills who are committed to a common purpose, performance goals, and approach for which they hold themselves mutually accountable.
- Groups may be either formal, established to do something productive for the organization and headed by a leader, or informal, formed by people seeking friendship with no officially appointed leader.
- Teams are of various types, but one of the most important is the work team, which engages in collective work requiring coordinated effort. Work teams may be of four types, identified according to their basic purpose: advice, production, project, and action. A project team may also be a cross-functional team, staffed with specialists pursuing a common objective.
- Two types of teams worth knowing about are quality circles, consisting of small groups of volunteers or workers and supervisors who meet intermittently to discuss workplace and quality-related problems, and self-managed teams, defined as groups of workers given administrative oversight for their task domains.

13.4 Stages of Group & Team Development

- 
A group may evolve into a team through five stages. (1) Forming is the process of getting oriented and getting acquainted. (2) Storming is characterized by the emergence of

individual personalities and roles and conflicts within the group. (3) In norming, conflicts are resolved, close relationships develop, and unity and harmony emerge. (4) In performing, members concentrate on solving problems and completing the assigned task. (5) In adjourning, members prepare for disbandment.

13.5 Building Effective Teams

■  There are seven considerations managers must take into account in building a group into an effective team.

(1) They must establish measurable goals and have feedback about members' performance.

(2) They must motivate members by making them mutually accountable to one another.

(3) They must consider what size is optimum. Teams with nine or fewer members have better interaction and morale, yet they also have fewer resources, are possibly less innovative, and may have work unevenly distributed among members. Teams of 10–16 members have more resources, and can take advantage of division of labor, yet they may be characterized by less interaction, lower morale, and social loafing.

(4) They must consider the role each team member must play. A role is defined as the socially determined expectation of how an individual should behave in a specific position. Two types of team roles are task and maintenance. A task role consists of behavior that concentrates on getting the team's tasks done. A maintenance role consists of behavior that fosters constructive relationships among team members.

(5) They must consider team norms, the general guidelines or rules of behavior that most group or team members follow. Norms tend to be enforced by group or team members for four reasons: to help the group survive, to clarify role expectations, to help individuals avoid embarrassing situations, and to emphasize the group's important values and identity.

(6) They must consider the team's cohesiveness, the tendency of a group or team to stick together.

(7) They must be aware of groupthink, a cohesive group's blind unwillingness to consider alternatives. Symptoms of groupthink are feelings of invulnerability, certainty of the rightness of their actions, and stereotyped views of the opposition; rationalization and self-censorship; and illusion of unanimity, peer pressure, and the appearance of self-appointed protectors against adverse information. The results of groupthink can be reduction in alternative ideas and limiting of other information. Two ways to prevent groupthink are to allow criticism and to allow other perspectives.

Management in Action

Virtual Teamwork: Using Web-Software Collaboration Tools to Work with Partners

Excerpted from Faith Keenan and Spencer E. Ante, "The New Teamwork," Business Week e.biz, *February 18, 2002, pp. EB12–EB16.*

BusinessWeek

Mark the time and place: October 26, 2001, Lockheed Martin Aeronautics Co. in Fort Worth. On that day, the defense contractor won the first piece of the biggest manufacturing contract ever—$200 billion to build a new family of supersonic stealth fighter planes for the Defense Department. That Friday also marks the kickoff of a new technology era, one that could transform the basic workings of every major corporation.

Lockheed's mega-win will require some intricate teamwork. More than 80 suppliers will be working at 187 locations to design and build components of the Joint Strike Fighter. It's up to the 75-member tech group at Lockheed's Aeronautics division to link them all together, as well as let the U.S. Air Force, Navy and Marines, Britain's Defense Ministry, and eight other U.S. allies track progress and make changes midstream if necessary. All told, people sitting at more than 40,000 computers will be collaborating to get the first plane in the air in just four years—the same amount of time it took to get the much simpler F-16 from contract to delivery in the 1970s.

A project this enormous requires a feat of computing to keep all its moving parts in sync. Lockheed and its partners will be using a system of 90 Web software tools to share designs, track the exchange of documents, and keep an eye on progress against goals. Major partners such as Northrop Grumman Corp. already are hooked up. In about six months, the rest will be on board. "We're getting the best people, applying the best designs, from wherever we need them," says Mark Peden, vice-president for information systems at Lockheed Martin Aeronautics. "It's the true virtual connection."

Management experts have long talked about the so-called virtual corporation: A company that focuses on what it does best and farms out the rest to specialists who can do it better. Now, a new generation of Net-collaboration technologies is making it easier for companies to work hand-in-hand with their partners to bring new products to the market in record time—and on penny-pinching budgets. . . .

These Web tools let people separated by oceans interact with one another as if there were not even a wall between them. They can talk via their computers while looking at shared documents, carry on e-mail chats, and use electronic white boards—where two or more people can draw pictures or charts, in real time, as the others watch and respond. . . .

Tighter relationships between companies also could spur innovation as they tap the best talent from anywhere in the world. Workers might end up identifying less with their company than with their cross-company team—and get bonuses based on the team's performance. . . .

One of the most effective uses of the new collaboration technologies is in the area of product development—everything from designing cars to developing new prescription drugs. This kind of teamwork not only increases efficiency but boosts innovation—the holy grail of companies hoping to produce the Next Big Thing in their industry. General Motors, for one, has chalked up big wins since setting up a collaborative engineering system in 1999 that allows GM employees and external auto parts suppliers to share product design information. . . .

GM's collaboration system serves as a centralized clearinghouse for all the design data. More than 16,000 designers and other workers use the new Web system from Electronic Data Systems Corp. to share 3-D designs and keep track of parts and subassemblies. The system automatically updates the master design when changes are finalized so everyone is on the same page. The result: GM has slashed the time it takes to complete a full mock-up of a car from 12 weeks to two.

For Discussion

1. What kind of work teams would you think are operating here?
2. Do you see a place for self-managed teams in this arrangement?
3. If you never meet your virtual collaborators in the flesh, how do you suppose the stages of group and team development (Section 13.4) take place?
4. How do you think the considerations in building an effective team (Section 13.5) are altered by this Web-based system?

Self-Assessment

What Is Your Conflict-Management Style?*

Objectives

To assess your conflict-management style.

To gain insight on how you manage conflict.

Introduction

Have you ever had a professor whose viewpoints were in conflict with your own? Have you worked in a group with someone who seems to disagree just to cause conflict? How did you react in that situation? In this chapter, you learned that there are five different ways of handling conflict: (1) *avoiding*—this approach is seen in people who wish to suppress conflict or back down from it altogether; (2) *accommodating*—this approach is seen in people who place the other party's interests above their own; (3) *forcing*—this approach is seen when people rely on their authority to solve conflict; (4) *compromising*—this approach is seen in people who are willing to give up something in order to reach a solution; and (5) *collaboration*—this approach is seen in people who desire a win-win situation, striving to address concerns and desires of all the parties involved in the conflict. The purpose of this exercise is to determine your conflict handling style.

Instructions

Read each of the statements below and use the following scale to indicate how often you rely on each tactic.

1 = very rarely
2 = rarely
3 = sometimes
4 = fairly often
5 = very often

1. I work to come out victorious no matter what.	1	2	3	4	5
2. I try to put the needs of others above my own.	1	2	3	4	5
3. I look for a mutually satisfactory solution.	1	2	3	4	5
4. I try to get involved in conflicts.	1	2	3	4	5
5. I strive to investigate and understand the issues involved in the conflict.	1	2	3	4	5
6. I never back away from a good argument.	1	2	3	4	5
7. I strive to foster harmony.	1	2	3	4	5
8. I negotiate to get a portion of what I propose.	1	2	3	4	5
9. I avoid open discussion of controversial subjects.	1	2	3	4	5
10. When I am trying to resolve disagreements, I openly share information.	1	2	3	4	5
11. I would rather win than compromise.	1	2	3	4	5
12. I work through conflict by accepting suggestions of others.	1	2	3	4	5
13. I look for a middle ground to resolve disagreements.	1	2	3	4	5
14. I keep my true opinions to myself to avoid hard feelings.	1	2	3	4	5
15. I encourage the open sharing of concerns and issues.	1	2	3	4	5
16. I am reluctant to admit I am wrong.	1	2	3	4	5
17. I try to save others from embarrassment in a disagreement.	1	2	3	4	5
18. I stress the advantages of give and take.	1	2	3	4	5
19. I give in early on rather than argue about a point.	1	2	3	4	5
20. I state my position and stress that it is the only correct point of view.	1	2	3	4	5

Scoring & Interpretation

Enter your responses, item by item, in the five categories below. Add your responses to get your total for each of the five conflict handling styles. Your primary conflict-handling style will be the area where you scored the highest. Your back-up conflict-handling style will be your second highest score.

Avoiding		**Accommodating**		**Forcing**		**Compromising**		**Collaborating**	
Item	Score	Item	Score	Item	Score	Item	Score	Item	Score
4.	_____	2.	_____	1.	_____	3.	_____	5.	_____
9.	_____	7.	_____	6.	_____	8.	_____	10.	_____
14.	_____	12.	_____	11.	_____	13.	_____	15.	_____
19.	_____	17.	_____	16.	_____	18.	_____	20.	_____
Total =	_____	Total =	_____	Total =	_____	Total =	_____	Total =	_____

Questions for Discussion

1. Were you surprised by the results? Why or why not? Explain.
2. Were the scores for your primary and back-up conflict-handling styles relatively similar, or was there a large gap? What does this imply? Discuss.
3. Is your conflict-handling style one that can be used in many different conflict scenarios? Explain.
4. What are some skills you can work on to become more effective at handling conflict? Describe and explain.

*The survey was developed using conflict-handling styles defined by K. W. Thomas, "Conflict and Conflict Management," in M. Dunnette (ed.), *Handbook of Industrial and Organizational Psychology* (Chicago: Rand McNally, 1976), pp. 889–935.

Group Exercise

Managing Conflict

Objectives

To examine workplace conflict.

To assess ways in which third parties manage conflict.

Introduction

As you learned in this chapter, conflict is not only a way of life but is sometimes necessary to generate new ideas. Conflict can be constructive or dysfunctional. Managers stimulate conflict by spurring competition among employees, changing the organization's culture and procedures, bringing in outsiders for a fresh perspective and sometimes playing devil's advocate, using programmed conflict. However, if there is too much conflict in an organization, it can be very destructive, leading to warfare. The purpose of this exercise is to examine a situation and consider alternative solutions for resolving the conflict.

Instructions

Break into groups of five to six people and read the following case study. Once you have read the case, discuss it with your group by brainstorming ways you could handle the situation if you were senior vice-president of operations at the furniture company. Use the questions for discussion at the end of the case to aid in your discussion.

The Case

Jack Smith is the senior vice-president of operations at a major producer of muscle-car performance accessories. His close personal friend Joe Black reports to him as vice-president and general manager of his largest engine-parts assembly plant. Joe has been with the company for nearly 40 years and will retire soon. Joe worked his way up from the assembly line to his current position and has successfully operated the division for 5 years. Joe is a hard worker and very professional; his staff, however, is rumored to be only marginally competent. Jack always felt that Joe purposely hired only moderately competent people. He agrees with another manager that Joe is threatened by talented assistants.

Last week, Jack went to lunch with another friend, Charles Williams, who happens to be Joe's second in command. Jack has been concerned about Joe's replacement for some time, and Charles seemed to be a good candidate. He is bright and well liked and a business-school graduate. Jack, who has known Charles for some time, also knows that Charles loves muscle cars and spends his free time restoring them. He shows a huge amount of enthusiasm for the company and its operations. At Jack's insistence, Joe hired him at the plant. Jack was relieved because there would finally be someone in the plant with talent and competence.

As Jack ate his lunch, however, he soon learned that Charles and Joe seemed to be engaged in some sort of feud. Jack was disappointed that Joe had not taken to Charles as he had hoped. It seems that Joe is in the process of developing a 5-year plan for his plant. The plan will lead to some major reinvestment and reorganization decisions that will be proposed to Jack and the rest of senior management. However, Joe has not included Charles at all in developing the plan. Because he did not feel like he was part of the team, Charles complained to Jack that he was no longer enthused about his job. Charles told Jack that his dissatisfaction was affecting his performance and that he was not putting forth any effort at managing the plant team. He told Jack he was considering a transfer to another plant or a transfer to a rising competitor's company.

Jack left the restaurant very worried and upset. He did not know the details of Joe's plan; he knew only what he had heard from Charles, but it worried him that Joe was making arbitrary decisions without including the rest of his staff. If Charles did stay at the company, Jack knew that once Joe retired, then Charles would have to live with Joe's plan. Jack was also frustrated because Joe's support is necessary if Charles is to develop as a leader. Jack also felt that Joe ran a good ship, and he did not want to undermine his authority or upset him. Despite some of his hiring choices, Joe had shown really good judgment, and the plant was one of the most successful in the company. Jack didn't know if Joe had a good reason for excluding Charles.

Questions for Discussion

1. Look at pages 414–415. Does this situation fit into one or more of the Seven Sources of Conflict? Which ones? Discuss your rationale.
2. If you were Jack, what would you do to ease the rising conflict between Joe and Charles? Would you intervene? Explain.
3. Why would you take this action? Discuss.
4. If you were Charles, which conflict-handling style would work best to get Joe to include you in developing the plan? Discuss your rationale.

Ethical Dilemma

When Employees Smoke Marijuana Socially: A Manager's Quandary

You are a supervisor at a telephone call center and have very positive relationships with members of your work team and your manager. A friend of yours, Christina, is also a supervisor, and her younger brother, Blake, is a member of her work team.

Christina invites you to her birthday party at her home, and you happily agree to attend. During the party, you walk out to the backyard to get some fresh air and notice that Blake and several other employees of your company are smoking marijuana. You have been told on several occasions by members of your own work team that these same individuals have used marijuana at other social events.

Blake and his friends are not part of your work team, and you never noticed any of them being impaired at work.

Solving the Dilemma

As a supervisor, what would you do?

1. Report the drug users and the incident to the company's human resources department.
2. Mind your own business. The employees are not on your team and don't appear to be impaired at work.
3. Talk to your boss and get her opinion about what should be done.
4. Invent other options. Discuss.

Video Case

Pike Place Fish Market

When John Yokoyama of Pike Place Fish Market took over the business at age 25, he knew only one management style: tyrannical. He watched his employees every second, always vigilant for mistakes, and expected workers to do as they were told. Through his association with Jim Bergquist, owner of Big Features Consulting Company, his style evolved into the highest degree of employee empowerment and trust.

It took Bergquist's idea that a person can "create reality" many meetings to take hold. But one by one, owner and employees began to buy into the idea. According to Bergquist, the only known fact about the future is that it's unknown. This idea makes people feel uncomfortable. We prefer to view the future as predictable because it gives us a sense of comfort and control. However, if we're willing to accept the unknown nature of the future, we then realize that anything's possible. We can create our own reality. It's up to management to create a context in which that can happen.

Several other key concepts guide management philosophies at Pike Place. One such concept is "you have the choice." According to Yokoyama, the power of personal responsibility is vital. We are responsible for all that enters our lives and how we react to it. But most people don't recognize this fact and as a result live as victims of circumstances. As a manager, Yokoyama recognizes that he has a choice when responding to a poorly performing employee. He can choose to pursue his initial negative reaction, or he can choose to recognize a quality employee who needs support in dealing with a problem.

Another founding principle at Pike Place is that employees be "committed to the purpose." When new employees enter the workplace they soon realize that they are not applying for a job opening but rather for the opportunity to try out for the team. Being committed to the purpose is one of the criteria for being on the team. With this committment, the team can "produce outrageous results." Management must allow employees to express their own creativity and empower them to create their own reality. According to Bergquist, the best way to manage that kind of team is to stay out of the way. After all, 15 heads are better than one.

Coaching is key to personal growth and development at Pike Place. Manager Justin Hall explains that everyone, from the newest hire to the owner, has permission to coach one another. Coaching works by recognizing when another person can benefit from your experience and is most powerful when the intention is to empower. If you see someone who needs to be coached, you must speak up, even if it's uncomfortable.

Yokoyama now recognizes that "people aren't numbers" and that managers should relate to employees as human beings and commit to making a difference in their lives. Yokoyama's current management style is best characterized as "management by inspiration." It's his hope that this attitude becomes a widespread movement in the business world.

Discussion Questions

1. Would you characterize the employees of Pike Place Fish Market as a group or a team? Support your answer.
2. Do the employees of Pike Place most closely embody the characteristics of a quality circle or a self-managed team? Support your answer.
3. Explain the phenomenon of groupthink. Do you see any evidence of groupthink at Pike Place? Why or why not?

chapter 14

Power, Influence, & Leadership

From Becoming a Manager to Becoming a Leader

MAJOR QUESTIONS YOU SHOULD BE ABLE TO ANSWER

14.1 The Nature of Leadership: Wielding Influence

Major Question: I don't want to be just a manager; I want to be a leader. What's the difference between the two?

14.2 Trait Approaches: Do Leaders Have Distinctive Personality Characteristics?

Major Question: What does it take to be a successful leader?

14.3 Behavioral Approaches: Do Leaders Show Distinctive Patterns of Behavior?

Major Question: Do effective leaders behave in similar ways?

14.4 Contingency Approaches: Does Leadership Vary with the Situation?

Major Question: How might effective leadership vary according to the situation at hand?

14.5 The Full-Range Approach: Uses of Transactional & Transformational Leadership

Major Question: What does it take to truly inspire people to perform beyond their normal levels?

14.6 Five Additional Perspectives

Major Question: If there are many ways to be a leader, which one would describe me best?

the manager's toolbox

How to Become a Star in the Workplace

People who are stars at work "are made, not born," says Carnegie Mellon professor Robert E. Kelley. "They have a fundamentally different conception of what work is."

Here are nine "star strategies" Kelly has identified, which average performers can adopt to become star performers—even leaders, the subject of this chapter.[1]

- **Initiative:** Initiative, says Kelley, is doing something outside your regular job that makes a difference to the company's core mission—doing something beyond your job description that helps other people. Initiative means you need to see the activity through to the end and you may need to take some risks.
- **Networking:** Star performers use networking to multiply their productivity, to do their current jobs better. "Average performers wait until they need some information, then cold-call someone to get it," Kelley says. "Stars know that you can't get work done today without a knowledge network and that you've got to put it in place beforehand."
- **Self-management:** Stars know how to get ahead of the game instead of waiting for the game to come to them. They look at the big picture and think about managing their whole life at work. They understand who they are and how they work best.
- **Perspective:** Average performers tend to see things just from their own points of view, says Kelley. Star performers try to think how things look through the eyes of their boss, coworkers, clients, and competitors. That depth of perspective can lead to better solutions.
- **Followership:** Stars know not only how to stand out but also how to help out—to be a follower as well as a leader. The idea is that if you help out others, they will later look out for you.
- **Leadership:** Star performers lead by understanding other people's interests and by using persuasion to bring out the best in people. People want leaders who are knowledgeable, who bring energy to a project and create energy in other people, and who pay close attention to the needs of everyone involved in the project.
- **Teamwork:** Stars join only workplace teams in which they think they will make a difference, and they become very good participants. They "make sure, once the team is put together, that it actually gets the job done," says Kelley.
- **Organizational savvy:** Average performers think of office politics as being dirty. Stars avoid getting needlessly involved in office melodramas, but they learn how to manage competing interests to achieve their work goals. They learn that not just one perspective is right, but that there are different perspectives.
- **Show and tell:** In both formal and informal meetings, stars learn how to craft their messages and to time them so that people pay attention. To excel at "show and tell," they learn to match the language of their communication to the language that people speak, then deliver the message in a way that works for them.

The good news is that these nine strategies can be learned. Like improving yourself in a sport, you identify the areas in which you need to improve and then practice those improvements every day. Take a look at yourself, then at the star performers you know. Then become a student of the stars—do what they do.

forecast

What's Ahead in This Chapter

Are there differences between managers and leaders? This chapter considers this question. We discuss the sources of a leader's power and how leaders use persuasion to influence people. We then consider the following approaches to leadership: trait, behavioral, contingency, full-range, and five additional perspectives.

major question

I don't want to be just a manager; I want to be a leader. What's the difference between the two?

The Big Picture

Being a manager and being a leader are not the same. A leader is able to influence employees to voluntarily pursue the organization's goals. Leadership is needed for organizational change. We describe five sources of power leaders may draw on. Leaders use the power of persuasion or influence to get others to follow them. Five approaches to leadership are described in the next five sections.

Leadership. What is it? Is it a skill anyone can develop?

Leadership **is the ability to influence employees to voluntarily pursue organizational goals.**[2] In an effective organization, leadership is present at all levels, say Tom Peters and Nancy Austin in *A Passion for Excellence,* and it represents the sum of many things. Leadership, they say, "means vision, cheerleading, enthusiasm, love, trust, verve, passion, obsession, consistency, the use of symbols, paying attention as illustrated by the content of one's calendar, out-and-out drama (and the management thereof), creating heroes at all levels, coaching, effectively wandering around, and numerous other things."[3]

Managers & Leaders: Not Always the Same

You see the words "manager" and "leader" used interchangeably all the time. However, as one leadership expert has said, "leaders manage and managers lead, but the two activities are not synonymous."[4]

Retired Harvard Business School professor **John Kotter** suggests that one is not better than the other, that in fact they are complementary systems of action. The difference is that . . .

- *Management* is about coping with *complexity,*
- *Leadership* is about coping with *change.*[5]

Let's consider these differences.

Being a Manager: Coping with Complexity

Management is necessary because complex organizations, especially the large ones that so much dominate the economic landscape, tend to become chaotic unless there is good management.

According to Kotter, companies manage complexity in three ways:

- **What needs to be done—planning and budgeting:** Companies manage complexity first by *planning and budgeting*—setting targets or goals for the future, establishing steps for achieving them, and allocating resources to accomplish them.
- **Creating arrangements of people to accomplish an agenda—organizing and staffing:** Management achieves its plan by *organizing and staffing,* Kotter says—creating the organizational structure and hiring qualified individuals to fill the necessary jobs, then devising systems of implementation.
- **Ensuring people do their jobs—controlling and problem solving:** Management ensures the plan is accomplished by *controlling and problem*

solving, says Kotter. That is, managers monitor results versus the plan in some detail by means of reports, meetings, and other tools. They then plan and organize to solve problems as they arise.

Being a Leader: Coping with Change

As the business world has become more competitive and volatile, doing things the same way as last year (or doing it 5% better) is no longer a formula for success. More changes are required for survival—hence the need for leadership.

Leadership copes with change in three ways:

- **What needs to be done—setting a direction:** Instead of dealing with complexity through planning and budgeting, leaders strive for constructive change by *setting a direction*. That is, they develop a vision for the future, along with strategies for realizing the changes.
- **Creating arrangements of people to accomplish an agenda—aligning people:** Instead of organizing and staffing, leaders are concerned with *aligning people,* Kotter says. That is, they communicate the new direction to people in the company who can understand the vision and build coalitions that will realize it.
- **Ensuring people do their jobs—motivating and inspiring:** Instead of controlling and problem solving, leaders try to achieve their vision by *motivating and inspiring*. That is, they appeal to "basic but often untapped human needs, values, and emotions," says Kotter, to keep people moving in the right direction, despite obstacles to change.

Do Kotter's ideas describe real leaders in the real business world? Certainly many participants in a September 2001 seminar convened by *Harvard Business Review* appeared to agree. "The primary task of leadership is to communicate the vision and the values of an organization," Frederick Smith, chairman and CEO of FedEx, told the group. "Second, leaders must win support for the vision and values they articulate. And third, leaders have to reinforce the vision and the values."[6]

Managers have legitimate power (as we'll describe) that derives from the formal authority of the positions to which they have been appointed. This power allows managers to hire and fire, reward and punish. Managers plan, organize, and control, but they don't necessarily have the characteristics to be leaders.

Whereas management is a process that lots of people are able to learn, leadership is more visionary. As we've said, leaders inspire others, provide emotional support, and try to get employees to rally around a common goal. Leaders also play a role in creating a vision and strategic plan for an organization, which managers are then charged with implementing.[7]

Amazing Amazon. Jeffrey Bezos, founder and CEO of online retailer Amazon.com, has done nearly everything Kotter suggests. For instance, Bezos's "culture of divine discontent" permits employees to plunge ahead with new ideas even though they know that most will probably fail.

Five Sources of Power

To really understand leadership, we need to understand the concept of power and authority. ***Authority*** **is the right to perform or command;** it comes with the job. In contrast, ***power*** **is the extent to which a person is able to influence others so they respond to orders.**

People who pursue ***personalized power*** **—power directed at helping oneself—** as a way of enhancing their own selfish ends may give the word power a bad name. However, there is another kind of power, ***socialized power*** **—power directed at helping others.**[8] This is the kind of power you hear in expressions such as "My goal is to have a powerful impact on my community."

Within organizations there are typically five sources of power leaders may draw on: *legitimate, reward, coercive, expert,* and *referent.*

1 Legitimate Power: Influencing Behavior Because of One's Formal Position

Legitimate power, **which all managers have, is power that results from managers' formal positions within the organization.** All managers have legitimate power over their employees, deriving from their position, whether it's a construction supervisor, ad account supervisor, sales manager, or CEO. This power may be exerted both positively or negatively—as praise or as criticism, for example.

2 Reward Power: Influencing Behavior by Promising or Giving Rewards

Reward power, **which all managers have, is power that results from managers' authority to reward their subordinates.** Rewards can range from praise to pay raises, from recognition to promotions.

Example: Lloyd D. Ward, former CEO of Maytag and among the highest-ranking African-Americans in corporate America, skillfully uses praise to reward positive behavior both on and off the job. For instance, while teaching karate moves during a workout with a reporter, he used such phrases as "You got it. Cool!" and "Outstanding! . . . Go! Go, David!"[9]

3 Coercive Power: Influencing Behavior by Threatening or Giving Punishment

Coercive power, **which all managers have, results from managers' authority to punish their subordinates.** Punishment can range from verbal or written reprimands to demotions to terminations. In some lines of work, fines and suspensions may be used. Coercive power has to be used judiciously, of course, since a manager who is seen as being constantly negative will produce a lot of resentments among employees.

4 Expert Power: Influencing Behavior Because of One's Expertise

Expert power **is power resulting from one's specialized information or expertise.** Expertise, or special knowledge, can be mundane, such as knowing the work schedules and assignments of the people who report to you. Or it can be sophisticated, such as having computer or medical knowledge. Secretaries may have expert power because, for example, they have been in a job a long time and know all the necessary contacts. CEOs may have expert power because they have strategic knowledge not shared by many others.

5 Referent Power: Influencing Behavior Because of One's Personal Attraction

Referent power **is power deriving from one's personal attraction.** As we will see later in this chapter (under the discussion of transformational leadership), this kind of power characterizes strong, visionary leaders who are able to persuade their followers by dint of their personality, attitudes, or background. Referent power may be associated with managers, but it is more likely to be characteristic of leaders.

Leadership & Influence: Using Persuasion to Get Your Way at Work

What would you do if you discovered your car stolen from the parking lot? Here's what Doug Dusenberg, a Houston, Texas, businessman, did on noticing his Jeep Cherokee missing. He telephoned the number of his car phone, and when one of the pair of young joyriders answered, he talked them into returning the car in exchange for keeping $20 that was in the glove compartment.[10]

Example

A Strong Leader: Jack Welch, Former CEO of General Electric

Jack Welch (left), with his successor as GE chairman and CEO, Jeffrey R. Immelt.

When John F. (Jack) Welch retired in late 2001, the CEO of General Electric signaled the end of an era. Under Welch, GE went from being a manufacturer with $25 billion in annual sales in 1981 to a $170 billion broad-based conglomerate, with businesses ranging from light bulbs to plastics to aircraft engines to medical-imaging equipment to insurance to financial services. Known as The House That Jack Built, GE is the ninth-biggest and second-most profitable company in the world. And superCEO Welch became one of the most legendary and widely imitated business leaders of all time.[11]

GE's success stemmed from two strategies. First, Welch encouraged diversity in businesses, rather than adherence to a "core" business. Second, he reduced bureaucratic obstructionism by encouraging quick thinking and entrepreneurial action. One tool, for instance, is the WorkOut, a GE-trademarked term, which are meetings that can be called by anyone to address any problem, with no supervisor in the room. When the participants have a plan, they take it to the boss, who must say yes or no on the spot. Says Welch, "Getting a company to be informal is a huge deal, and no one ever talks about it." But the informal just-do-it culture is a key to GE success.

How was Welch's leadership manifested? First was his mastery in motivating people. He personally reviewed the performance of the company's top 3,000 managers every year and personally handed out hundreds of bonuses for good work. In addition, he was a prolific writer of notes to managers and employees, thanking them, suggesting changes, making note of family crises. He also taught at GE's training center, lecturing, cajoling, and listening to the audience of elite managers. Second, he insisted on candor, demanding it from executives and returning it. When managers met goals, Welch showered them with gratitude and monetary rewards. Bad performance, however, was severely punished, often with dismissals. The Welch technique is to use both the carrot and the stick and to insist on a steady flow of information. In an era of management fads, says *Business Week*, the lesson from GE is: personality still counts.[12]

Being a successful leader also depends on having a fair amount of good luck. Welch had hoped to continue GE's success through his carefully chosen successor as chairman and CEO, Jeffrey R. Immelt. However, Immelt's taking the helm was as tumultuous as any leader could have experienced. On his second day on the job, terrorists attacked the World Trade Center, killing two GE employees and inflicting a $600 million hit to the company's insurance business and a slowdown in its aircraft engine operations. That was followed by anthrax attacks at NBC, which is owned by GE. Accounting scandals following in the wake of Enron Corp's. bankruptcy, which diminished stockholders' faith in the financial transparency of American corporations, including that of GE, resulting in a declining stock price. Immelt was to observe, "even Jack's schtick wouldn't work in this environment."

Since then, however, Immelt has become a strong leader in his own right, growing the company through innovation rather than acquisition, expanding into new businesses such as health care, and keeping managers in place longer instead of rotating them in order to build specialists rather than generalists. The result: *Fortune* magazine rated GE as the #4 most profitable company for 2004.[13]

Dusenberg probably would be considered to have leadership skills because of his powers of persuasion, or *influence.* Influence is the ability to get others to follow your wishes. There are nine general tactics for trying to influence others, but some work better than others. In one pair of studies, employees were asked in effect, "How do you get your boss, coworker, or subordinate to do something you want?" The nine answers—ranked from most used to least used tactics—were as follows.[14]

Fashion leader Ralph Lauren. Born Ralph Lifshitz in the Bronx, N.Y., where he shared a bedroom with two brothers, today Lauren has a $1 billion net worth, a classic car collection, a ranch in Colorado, and homes in New York and Jamaica. Following college, two years in the army, and marriage, Lauren worked for a glove maker and a tie manufacturer, then used a $50,000 loan to found Polo Fashions. The company has become a $2.4 billion clothing and home-furnishings business by selling a lifestyle image of sophistication and taste. With his strong design sense, business acumen, perseverance, and innovative mind, Lauren is the kind of visionary leader who has been able to triumph over several business failures and achieve great success. Could you?

1 Rational Persuasion Trying to convince someone by using reason, logic, or facts.

Example: "You know, all the cutting-edge companies use this approach."

2 Inspirational Appeals Trying to build enthusiasm or confidence by appealing to others' emotions, ideals, or values.

Example: "If we do this as a goodwill gesture, customers will love us."

3 Consultation Getting others to participate in a decision or change.

Example: "Wonder if I could get your thoughts about this matter."

4 Ingratiating Tactics Acting humble or friendly or making someone feel good or feel important before making a request.

Example: "I hate to impose on your time, knowing how busy you are, but you're the only one who can help me."

5 Personal Appeals Referring to friendship and loyalty when making a request.

Example: "We've known each other a long time, and I'm sure I can count on you."

6 Exchange Tactics Reminding someone of past favors or offering to trade favors.

Example: "Since I backed you at last month's meeting, maybe you could help me this time around."

7 Coalition Tactics Getting others to support your effort to persuade someone.

Example: "Everyone in the department thinks this is a great idea."

8 Pressure Tactics Using demands, threats, or intimidation to gain compliance.

Example: "If this doesn't happen, you'd better think about cleaning out your desk."

9 Legitimating Tactics Basing a request on one's authority or right, organizational rules or policies, or express or implied support from superiors.

Example: "This has been green-lighted at the highest levels."

These influence tactics are considered *generic* because they are applied in all directions—up, down, and sideways within the organization. The first five influence tactics are considered "soft" tactics because they are considered friendlier than the last four "hard," or pressure, tactics. As it happens, research shows that of the three possible responses to an influence tactic—enthusiastic commitment, grudging compliance, and outright resistance—commitment is most apt to result when the tactics used are consultation, strong rational persuasion, and inspirational appeals.[15]

Knowing this, do you think you have what it takes to be a leader? To answer this, you need to understand what factors produce people of leadership character. We consider these in the rest of the chapter.

Five Approaches to Leadership

The next five sections describe five principal approaches or perspectives on leadership, which have been refined by research. They are (1) *trait,* (2) *behavioral,* (3) *contingency,* (4) *full-range,* and (5) *five additional. (See Table 14.1.)* ◆

TABLE 14.1
Five approaches to leadership

1. **Trait approaches**
   - *Kouzes & Posner's five traits*—honest, competent, forward-looking, inspiring, intelligent
   - *Brossidy*—ability to execute, career runway, team orientation, multiple experiences
   - *Goleman's emotional intelligence*—self-awareness, self-management, social awareness, relationship management
   - *Judge & colleagues*—two meta-analyses: importance of extroversion, conscientiousness, and openness; importance of personality over intelligence
   - *Gender studies*—motivating others, fostering communication, producing high-quality work, and so on
2. **Behavioral approaches**
   - *Michigan model*—two leadership styles: job-centered and employee-centered
   - *Ohio State model*—two dimensions: initiating-structure behavior and consideration behavior
   - *Blake & Mouton's* managerial/leadership grid—concern for production or concern for people
3. **Contingency approaches**
   - *Fiedler's contingency model*—task-oriented style and relationship-oriented style—*and three dimensions of control:* leader-member, task structure, position power
   - *House's path*–goal revised leadership model—clarifying paths for subordinates' goals—and employee characteristics and environmental factors that affect leadership behaviors
   - *Hersey & Blanchard's situational leadership model*—adjusting leadership style to employee readiness
4. **Full-range approach**
   - *Transactional leadership*—clarify employee roles and tasks and provide rewards and punishments
   - *Transformational leadership*—transform employees to pursue organizational goals over self-interests, using inspirational motivation, idealized influence, individualized consideration, intellectual stimulation
5. **Five additional perspectives**
   - *Shared leadership*—mutual influence process in which people share responsibility for leading
   - *Greenleaf's servant leadership model*—providing service to others, not oneself
   - *Loyalty*—Reichheld's six principles: preach what one practices, pay win-win, be picky, keep it simple, reward right results, listen hard and talk straight
   - *Collins's Level 5 Leadership*—leader has humility plus fearless will to succeed, plus four other capabilities
   - *E-Leadership*—using information technology for one-to-one, one-to-many, and between group and collective interactions

14.2 Trait Approaches: Do Leaders Have Distinctive Personality Characteristics?

major question What does it take to be a successful leader?

The Big Picture

Trait approaches attempt to identify distinctive characteristics that account for the effectiveness of leaders. We describe (1) three trait perspectives expressed by Kouzes and Posner, Brossidy, and Goleman; (2) Judge's research on traits; and (3) some results of gender studies.

Consider two high-powered leaders of the late 20th century. Each "personifies the word 'stubborn,'" says a *Fortune* magazine account. Both "are piercingly analytical thinkers who combine hands-on technical smarts with take-no-prisoners business savvy. Both absolutely hate to lose."[16]

Who they are? They are two of the most successful former CEOs in American business—Bill Gates of Microsoft and Andy Grove of Intel. Do they have distinctive personality traits that might teach us something about leadership? Perhaps they do. They would seem to embody the traits of (1) dominance, (2) intelligence, (3) self-confidence, (4) high energy, and (5) task-relevant knowledge.

These are the five traits that researcher **Ralph Stogdill** in 1948 concluded were typical of successful leaders.[17] Stogdill is one of many contributors to ***trait approaches to leadership,*** **which attempt to identify distinctive characteristics that account for the effectiveness of leaders.** Indeed, over the past 70 years, over 300 trait studies have been done.[18]

Trait theory is the successor to what used to be thought of as the "great man" approach to leadership, which held that leaders such as Napoleon Bonaparte and Abraham Lincoln were supposed to have some inborn ability to lead. Trait theorists believed that leadership skills were not innate, that they could be acquired through learning and experience. Today traits still often play a central role in how we perceive leaders, and organizations may find it beneficial to consider selected leadership traits when choosing among candidates for leadership positions. Gender, race, and ethnicity should not be used as any of these traits.

Three Trait Perspectives: Kouzes & Posner, Brossidy, & Goleman

Three examples of trait approaches are those represented in the perspectives presented by Kouzes and Posner, Larry Brossidy, and Daniel Goleman.

Kouzes & Posner's Research: Is Honesty the Top Leadership Trait?

During the 1980s, **James Kouzes** and **Barry Posner** surveyed more than 7,500 managers throughout the United States as to what personal traits they looked for and admired in their superiors.[19] The respondents suggested that a credible leader should have five traits. He or she should be (1) honest, (2) competent, (3) forward-looking, (4) inspiring, and (5) intelligent. The first trait, honesty, was considered particularly important, being selected by 87% of the respondents, suggesting that people want their leaders to be ethical.

Although this research does reveal the traits preferred by employees, it has not, however, been able to predict which people might be successful leaders.

Brossidy's Observations: A Working CEO Tells How to Find & Develop Great Leaders

Larry Brossidy became CEO of AlliedSignal in 1991, when the company was suffering from low everything—morale, stock price, operating margins, and return on equity. Based on his experience of 34 years at General Electric, he realized that AlliedSignal's "inattention to leadership was a major problem."[20] He thereupon began a two-year program of devoting up to 40% of his time to the task of hiring and developing leaders, a successful effort to which he attributes the company's turnaround.

You probably won't find Brossidy's ideas discussed in the scholarly literature about management. Nevertheless, his approach represents the kinds of judgments that working top managers have to practice when they go about the empirical job of finding people who can be groomed into future leaders. The four qualities he looks for when interviewing and evaluating job candidates are (1) the ability to execute, (2) a career runway, (3) a team orientation, and (4) multiple experiences. *(See Table 14.2.)* Brossidy claims a 70% success rate in hiring leaders, and his approach contributed to a ninefold return for AlliedSignal shareholders from 1991 to 1999.

TABLE 14.2
The leadership traits Brossidy looks for in job candidates

1. ***Ability to execute:*** Look for a demonstrated history of real accomplishment and execution. Are you honest?	3. ***A team orientation:*** Someone able to work with other people has better potential than someone who's an individual contributor.
2. ***A career runway:*** Leaders have "plenty of runway" left in their careers, with the perspective to go beyond the present job.	4. ***Multiple experiences:*** People with significant responsibility in two or three different industries or companies have a range of good experience.

Goleman's Concepts of "Emotional Intelligence": Do Moods Make a Leader?

Daniel Goleman, cochairman of the Consortium for Research on Emotional Intelligence in Organizations at Rutgers University, is the author of the popular 1995 book *Emotional Intelligence*. In 1998, he made a contribution to trait theory in an article that argued that the most important attribute in a leader is ***emotional intelligence,*** **the ability to cope, empathize with others, and be self-motivated.**[21] "When I compared star performers with average ones in senior leadership positions," Goleman wrote, "nearly 90% of the difference in their profiles was attributable to emotional intelligence factors rather than cognitive abilities."[22] The traits of emotional intelligence are (1) self-awareness, (2) self-management, (3) social awareness, and (4) relationship management. *(See Table 14.3.)*

TABLE 14.3
The traits of emotional intelligence. The first two concern how we manage ourselves, the last two determine how we manage relationships. [*Source:* Adapted from D. Goleman, R. Royatzis, and A. McKee, "Primal Leadership: The Hidden Driver of Great Performance," *Harvard Business Review,* December 2001, p. 49, and *Primal Leadership: Realizing the Power of Emotional Intelligence* (Boston: Harvard Business School Press, 2002), p. 39.]

1. ***Self-awareness:*** The most essential trait. This is the ability to read your own emotions, gauge your moods and strengths and weaknesses accurately, and have confidence in your self-worth.
2. ***Self-management:*** This is the ability to control your emotions and act with honesty and integrity in reliable and adaptable ways. You can adapt to changing situations, are ready to act on opportunities, and have the drive to improve your performance.
3. ***Social awareness:*** This includes empathy, allowing you to show others that you care, and organizational awareness so you can read the politics and decisions of others.
4. ***Relationship management:*** This is the ability to communicate clearly and convincingly, disarm conflicts, bolster others' abilities through feedback and guidance, and wield a range of tactics for persuasion.

Later Goleman and colleagues expanded on the importance of emotional intelligence in leadership by suggesting that a leader's *mood* plays a key role. "The leader's mood and behaviors drive the behaviors of everyone else," they wrote. "A cranky and ruthless boss creates a toxic organization filled with negative underachievers who ignore opportunities; an inspirational, inclusive leader spawns acolytes for whom any challenge is surmountable."[23]

Good moods can inspire good performance. Still, leaders shouldn't display cheerfulness when sales are down. Indeed, the article suggests, the most effective executives display moods and behaviors that match the situation at hand, with a healthy dose of optimism mixed in. "They respect how other people are feeling—even if it is glum or defeated—but they also model what it looks like to move forward with hope and humor."

Are Goleman's ideas accurate? Preliminary evidence suggests that high emotional intelligence can land you a job. A simulated interview process indicated that interviewers' assessments of an applicant's emotional intelligence were positively associated with their impression of the applicant.[24] However, given the difficulty of measuring emotional intelligence, further research is needed on this leadership trait.[25]

Judge's Research: Is Personality More Important Than Intelligence in Leadership?

Timothy Judge and his colleagues recently published the results of two meta-analyses that bear on the subject of traits and leaderships. **A *meta-analysis* is a statistical pooling technique that permits behavioral scientists to draw general conclusions about certain variables from many different studies.**

The Importance of Extroversion, Conscientiousness, & Openness

The Big Five personality dimensions, you'll recall (from Chapter 11, Section 11.3), are extroversion, agreeableness, conscientiousness, emotional stability, and openness to experience. Judge and his group examined the Big Five personality traits and their relationship to leadership in 94 studies. Their conclusion: extroversion was most consistently and positively related to both leadership emergence and leadership effectiveness. Conscientiousness and openness to experience also were positively related to leadership effectiveness.[26]

The Importance of Personality over Intelligence

In the second meta-analysis, which involved 151 samples, Judge and his colleagues found that intelligence was modestly related to leadership effectiveness. The study concluded that in the selection of leaders personality is more important than intelligence.[27] This conclusion is supported by research that found that managers who were leadership failures showed several personality flaws, including being overly controlling, irritable, exploitative, arrogant, abrasive, selfish, and lacking in emotional intelligence.[28]

Gender Studies: Do Women Have Traits That Make Them Better Leaders?

WOMEN ASPIRE TO BE CHIEF AS MUCH AS MEN DO, declared the headline in *The Wall Street Journal.* A study by a New York research firm found that 55% of women and 57% of men aspire to be CEO, challenging the notion that more women aren't at the top because they don't want to be there.[29] And, in fact, it's possible that women may have traits that make them better managers—indeed, better leaders—than men.

A number of management studies conducted in the United States for companies ranging from high-tech to manufacturing to consumer services were reviewed by *Business Week*.[30] By and large, the magazine reports, the studies showed that "women executives, when rated by their peers, underlings, and bosses, score higher than their male counterparts on a wide variety of measures—from producing high-quality work to goal-setting to mentoring employees." Researchers accidentally stumbled on these findings about gender differences while compiling hundreds of routine performance evaluations and analyzing the results. In one study of 425 high-level executives, women won higher ratings on 42 of the 52 skills measured.[31]

What are the desirable traits in which women excel? Among those traits mentioned are teamwork and partnering, being more collaborative, seeking less personal glory, being motivated less by self-interest than in what they can do for the company, being more stable, and being less turf-conscious. Women were also found to be better at producing quality work, recognizing trends, and generating new ideas and acting on them. A gender comparison of skills is summarized below. *(See Table 14.4.)*

Skill	Men	Women
Motivating others		√√√√√
Fostering communication		√√√√*
Producing high-quality work		√√√√√
Strategic planning	√√	√√*
Listening to others		√√√√√
Analyzing issues	√√	√√*

TABLE 14.4
Where female executives do better: a scorecard. The check mark denotes which group scored higher on the respective studies. The asterisk indicates that in one study women's and men's scores in these categories were statistically even. (*Source:* Data from Hagberg Consulting Group, Management Research Group, Lawrence A. Pfaff, Personnel Decisions International Inc., and Advanced Teamware Inc., in table in R. Sharpe, "As Leaders, Women Rule," *Business Week,* November 20, 2000, p. 75.)

Why, then, aren't more women in positions of leadership? Males and females disagree about this issue. A team of researchers asked this question of 461 executive women holding titles of vice president or higher in Fortune 100 companies and all the male Fortune 100 CEOs. CEOs believed that women are not in senior leadership positions because (1) they lack significant general management experience and (2) women have not been in the executive talent pool long enough to get selected. Women, by contrast, believed that (1) male stereotyping and (2) exclusion from important informal networks are the biggest barriers to promotability.[32]

There are two additional possible explanations. First, as we suggested earlier in the book, there are many women who, though hard working, simply aren't willing to compete as hard as most men are or are not willing to make the required personal sacrifices.[33] (As Jamie Gorelick, former vice chair of Fannie Mae but also mother of two children ages 10 and 15, said when declining to be considered for CEO: "I just don't want that pace in my life."[34]) Second, women have a tendency to be overly modest and to give credit to others rather than taking it for themselves, which can undermine opportunities for promotions and raises.[35] ◆

major question **Do effective leaders behave in similar ways?**

The Big Picture

Behavioral leadership approaches try to determine the distinctive styles used by effective leaders. Three models we describe are the University of Michigan model, the Ohio State model, and the Blake and Mouton Managerial/Leadership Grid.®

Assembly line. Which kind of leadership behavior is appropriate for directing assembly-line workers?

Maybe what's important to know about leaders is not their *personality traits* but rather their *patterns of behavior* or *leadership styles*. This is the line of thought pursued by those interested in ***behavioral leadership approaches,*** **which attempts to determine the distinctive styles used by effective leaders.** By *leadership styles,* we mean the combination of traits, skills, and behaviors that leaders use when interacting with others.

The important models of leadership behavior that we will describe are (1) *the University of Michigan model* and *the Ohio State University model* and (2) the *Blake and Mouton Managerial/Leadership Grid.®*

The University of Michigan Leadership Model & the Ohio State Leadership Model

What all models of leadership behavior have in common is the consideration of *task orientation versus people orientation*. Two classic studies came out of the universities of Michigan and Ohio State.

The University of Michigan Leadership Model

In the late 1940s, researchers at the University of Michigan came up with what came to be known as the **University of Michigan Leadership Model.** A team led by **Rensis Likert** began studying the effects of leader behavior on job performance, interviewing numerous managers and subordinates.[36] The investigators identified two forms of leadership styles: *job-centered* and *employee-centered.*

- **Job-centered behavior—"I'm concerned more with the needs of the job":** In *job-centered behavior,* managers paid more attention to the job and work procedures. Thus, their principal concerns were with achieving production efficiency, keeping costs down, and meeting schedules.
- **Employee-centered behavior—"I'm concerned more with the needs of employees":** In *employee-centered behavior,* managers paid more attention to employee satisfaction and making work groups cohesive. By concentrating on subordinates' needs they hoped to build effective work groups with high-performance goals.

The Ohio State Leadership Model

A second approach to leadership research was begun in 1945 at Ohio State University under **Ralph Stogdill** (mentioned in the last section). Hundreds of dimensions of leadership behavior were studied, resulting in what came to be known as the **Ohio State Leadership Model.**[37] From surveys of leadership behavior, two major dimensions of leader behavior were identified, as follows.

- **Initiating structure—"What do I do to get the job done?"** *Initiating structure* is leadership behavior that organizes and defines what group members should be doing. It consists of the efforts the leader makes to get things organized and get the job done. This is much the same as Likert's "job-centered behavior."

- **Consideration—"What do I do to show consideration for my employees?"** *Consideration* is leadership behavior that expresses concern for employees by establishing a warm, friendly, supportive climate. This behavior, which resembles Likert's "employee-centered behavior," is sensitive to subordinates' ideas and feelings and establishes mutual trust.

All in all, one management expert concluded from the Michigan and Ohio studies that effective leaders (1) tend to have supportive or employee-centered relationships with employees, (2) use group rather than individual methods of supervision, and (3) set high performance goals.[38]

practical action

Transition Problems on Your Way Up: How to Avoid the Pitfalls

Before you can become a good leader you need to become a good manager. Making the leap from individual contributor to a manager of several employees "is one of the most difficult in peoples' careers," suggests *Wall Street Journal* columnist Hal Lancaster.

Although corporations and managements may make noises about training and mentoring support, newly promoted managers may not see any of this and may simply be expected to know what to do. And, as managers move up the ladder, they may encounter other problems that they have not anticipated. How can you avoid some pitfalls as you make your ascent? Some suggestions:[39]

- **Have realistic expectations:** New managers often focus on the rights and privileges of their new jobs and underestimate the duties and obligations.
- **Don't forget to manage upward and sideways as well as downward:** You not only need to manage your subordinates but also the perceptions of your peers and your own managers above you.
- **Stay in touch with managers in other departments:** In addition, you need to have good relationships with managers in other departments—and be perceptive about their needs and priorities—since they have the resources you need to get your job done. Don't make the mistake of thinking your own department is the center of the universe.
- **Think about what kind of manager or leader you want to be:** Make a list of all your previous bosses and their good and bad attributes. This may produce a list of dos and don'ts that can serve you well.
- **Get guidance from other managers:** You may not get advice on how to manage from your own manager, who may have promoted you to help reduce his or her workload, not add to it by expecting some coaching. If this is the case, don't be shy about consulting other managers as well as people in professional organizations.
- **Resist isolation:** If you're promoted beyond supervisor of a small team and you have to manage hundreds rather than dozens, or thousands rather than hundreds, you may find the biggest surprise is isolation. The way to stay in touch is to talk daily with your senior managers, perhaps have "town meetings" with staffers several times a year, and employ "management by walking around"—bringing teams together to talk.

Blake & Mouton's Managerial/Leadership Grid® Model: Concern for Both Production & People

The Michigan and Ohio State studies gave rise to the notion that the ideal leader was both performance-oriented and people-oriented. Perhaps the best-known leadership training model was one devised at the University of Texas by **Robert Blake** and **Jane Mouton** that was first known as the Managerial Grid® and later, when **Anne Adams McCanse** replaced Mouton, as the Leadership Grid®. **The *leadership grid model* identifies the ideal leadership style as having a high concern for (1) production, the job aspects of subordinates' behavior, and (2) people, the human aspects of their behavior.**

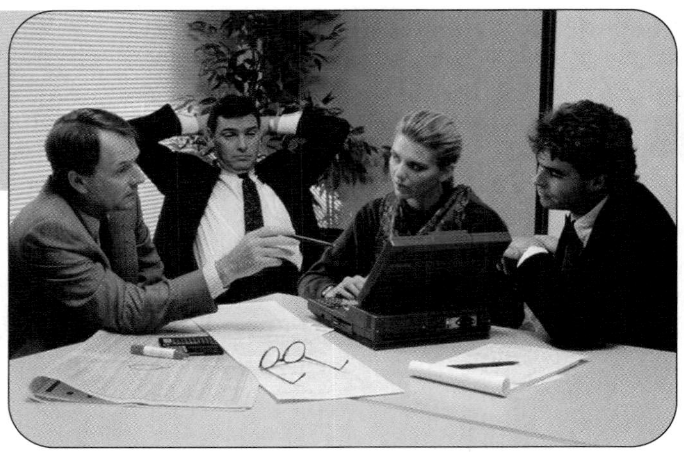

One kind of work. With white-collar workers, such as those shown here, would you be more inclined to be a people-oriented manager?

Five Major Leadership Styles

Using a questionnaire to measure both these concerns on a scale from 1 to 9, the developers identified five major styles, as expressed in the extreme corners and in the middle of the grid, an adaptation of which is shown below.[40] *(See Figure 14.1.)*

FIGURE 14.1

Leadership grid model. This adaptation of the Leadership Grid® identifies the location of the five principal management styles. (*Source:* Adapted from R. R. Blake, J. S. Mouton, L. B. Barnes, and L. E. Greiner, "Breakthrough in Organization Development," *Harvard Business Review,* November–December 1964, p. 136.)

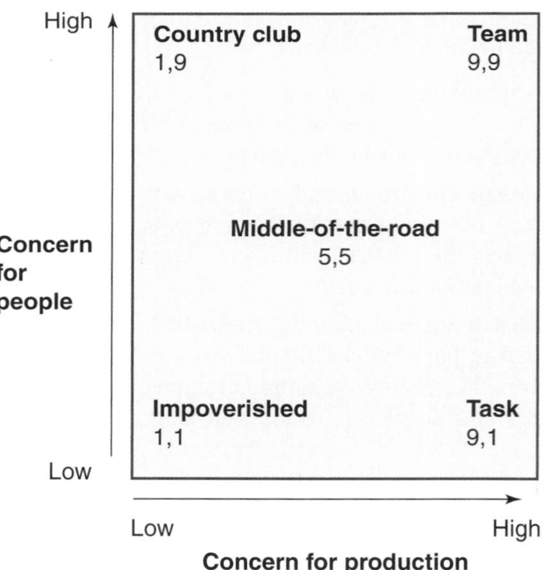

- **(1,1) Impoverished management—"I just want to exert minimal effort":** The impoverished leader, who shows low concern for both people and production, exerts the minimum effort required to stay employed.
- **(9,1) Task management—"I'm mainly focused on getting the job done":** The task-management (or authority-compliance) leader, with high concern for production but low concern for people, is mainly concerned with getting the work done with a minimum of involvement with human elements.

- **(1,9) Country-club management—"I'm mainly focused on keeping my people happy":** The country-club leader is the reverse of the task-management leader. With a low concern for production but a high concern for people, this leader mainly wants to keep people happy in their jobs.
- **(5,5) Middle-of-the-road management—"I want to do the minimum to keep everything balanced":** This leader has balanced concerns for both people and production, but these concerns rank only in the middle of the scale. In other words, this kind of leader is concerned with doing just enough to maintain satisfactory morale to achieve satisfactory production.
- **(9,9) Team management—"I want maximum performance and maximum employee satisfaction":** The team manager is considered most effective because he or she gets the utmost from employees along both dimensions—production and satisfaction.

Which Style Is Most Effective?

As you might expect, behavioral theorists believed that the team-management style would be the most effective. In this style, work is accomplished by having committed people who are linked by having a common stake in the organization's purpose, which in turn generates relationships of trust and respect.

These are high-minded ideas. Unfortunately, the behavioral approach has failed to identify any consistent set of behaviors that leaders should use. Rather, the research shows that effective leaders display different types of behavior in different situations.[41] This conclusion has fueled interest in the contingency approaches, to which we turn next. ◆

Another kind of work. With blue-collar workers, such as construction workers, would you be more inclined to be a production- or a task-oriented manager?

major question

How might effective leadership vary according to the situation at hand?

The Big Picture

Effective leadership behavior depends on the situation at hand, say believers in the three contingency approaches: Fiedler's contingency leadership model, House's path–goal leadership model, and Hersey and Blanchard's situational leadership model.

Perhaps leadership is not characterized by universally important traits or behaviors. Perhaps there is no one best style that will work in all situations. This is the point of view of proponents of the ***contingency approach*** **to leadership, who believe that effective leadership behavior depends on the situation at hand.** That is, as situations change, different styles become appropriate.

Let's consider three contingency approaches: (1) the *contingency leadership model* by Fiedler, (2) the *path-goal leadership model* by House, and (3) the *situational leadership model* by Hersey and Blanchard.

1 The Contingency Leadership Model: Fiedler's Approach

The oldest model of the contingency approach to leadership was developed by **Fred Fiedler** and his associates in 1951.[42] **The *contingency leadership model* determines if a leader's style is (1) task-oriented or (2) relationship-oriented and if that style is effective for the situation at hand.** Fiedler's work was based on 80 studies conducted over 30 years.

Two Leadership Orientations: Tasks versus Relationships

Are you task-oriented or relationship-oriented? That is, are you more concerned with task accomplishment or with people?

To find out, you or your employees would fill out a questionnaire (known as the least preferred coworker, or LPC, scale), in which you think of the coworker you least enjoyed working with and rate him or her according to an eight-point scale of 16 pairs of opposite characteristics (such as friendly/unfriendly, tense/relaxed, efficient/inefficient). The higher the score, the more the relationship-oriented the respondent; the lower the score, the more task-oriented.

Tile style. Do successful entrepreneurs or small-business managers need to be task-oriented, relationship-oriented, or both? What style of leadership model would best suit a small tile manufacturing business in which employees need to work with a great deal of independence?

The Three Dimensions of Situational Control

Once the leadership orientation is known, then you determine *situational control*—how much control and influence a leader has in the immediate work environment.

There are three dimensions of situational control: *leader-member relations, task structure,* and *position power.*

- **Leader-member relations—"Do my subordinates accept me as a leader?"** This dimension, the most important component of situational control, reflects the extent to which a leader has or doesn't have the support, loyalty, and trust of the work group.
- **Task structure—"Do my subordinates perform unambiguous, easily understood tasks?"** This dimension refers to the extent to which tasks are routine, unambiguous, and easily understood. The more structured the jobs, the more influence a leader has.

- **Position power—"Do I have power to reward and punish?"** This dimension refers to how much power a leader has to make work assignments and reward and punish. More power equals more control and influence.

For each dimension, the amount of control can be *high*—the leader's decisions will produce predictable results because he or she has the ability to influence work outcomes. Or it can be *low*—he or she doesn't have that kind of predictability or influence. By combining the three different dimensions with different high/low ratings, we have eight different leadership situations.

Which Style Is Most Effective?

Neither leadership style is effective all the time, Fiedler's research concludes, although each is right in certain situations.

- **When task-oriented style is best:** The task-oriented style works best in either *high-control* or *low-control* situations.

  Example of *high-control* situation (leader decisions produce predictable results because he or she can influence work outcomes): Suppose you were supervising parking-control officers ticketing cars parked illegally in expired meter zones, bus zones, and the like. You have (1) high leader-member relations because your subordinates are highly supportive of you and (2) high task structure because their jobs are clearly defined. (3) You have high position control because you have complete authority to evaluate their performance and dole out punishment and rewards. Thus, a task-oriented style would be best.

  Example of *low-control* situation (leader decisions can't produce predictable results because he or she can't really influence outcomes): Suppose you were a high school principal trying to clean up graffiti on your private-school campus, helped only by students you can find after school. You might have (1) low leader-member relations because many people might not see the need for the goal. (2) The task structure might also be low because people might see many different ways to achieve the goal. And (3) your position power would be low because the committee is voluntary and people are free to leave. In this low-control situation, a task-oriented style would also be best.

- **When relationship-oriented style is best:** The relationship-oriented style works best in situations of *moderate control.*

  Example: Suppose you were working in a government job supervising a group of firefighters fighting wildfires. You might have (1) low leader-member relations if you were promoted over others in the group but (2) high task structure, because the job is fairly well defined. (3) You might have low position power, because the rigidity of the civil-service job prohibits you from doing much in the way of rewarding and punishing. Thus, in this moderate-control situation, relationship-oriented leadership would be most effective.

What do you do if your leadership orientation does not match the situation? Then, says Fiedler, it's better to try to move leaders into suitable situations rather than try to alter their personalities to fit the situations.[43]

2 The Path–Goal Leadership Model: House's Approach

A second contingency approach, advanced by **Robert House** in the 1970s and revised by him in 1996, is the ***path–goal leadership model,*** **which holds that the effective leader makes available to followers desirable rewards in the workplace and increases their motivation by clarifying the *paths,* or behavior, that will help them achieve those *goals* and providing them with support.** A successful leader thus helps followers by tying meaningful rewards to goal accomplishment, reducing barriers, and providing support, so as to increase "the number and kinds of personal payoffs to subordinates for work-goal attainment."[44]

FIGURE 14.2
General representation of House's revised path–goal theory

Numerous studies testing various predictions from House's original path–goal theory provided mixed results.[45] As a consequence, he proposed a new model, a graphical version, shown below. *(See Figure 14.2.)*

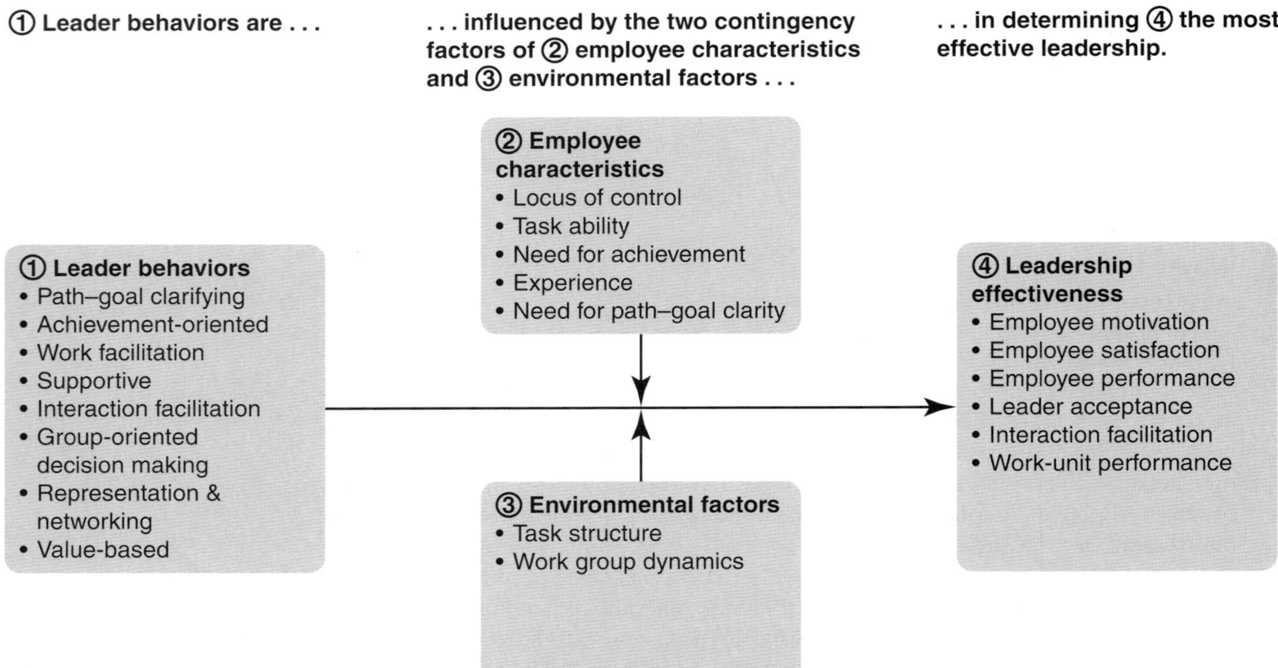

What Determines Leadership Effectiveness: Employee Characteristics & Environmental Factors Affect Leader Behavior

As the drawing indicates, two contingency factors, or variables—*employee characteristics* and *environmental factors*—cause some *leadership behaviors* to be more effective than others.

- **Employee characteristics:** Five employee characteristics are locus of control (described in Chapter 11), task ability, need for achievement, experience, and need for path–goal clarity.
- **Environmental factors:** Two environmental factors are task structure (independent versus interdependent tasks) and work group dynamics.
- **Leader behaviors:** Originally House proposed that there were four leader behaviors, or leadership styles—*directive* ("Here's what's expected of you and here's how to do it"), *supportive* ("I want things to be pleasant, since everyone's about equal here"), *participative* ("I want your suggestions in order to help me make decisions"), and *achievement-oriented* ("I'm confident you can accomplish the following great things"). The revised theory expands the number of leader behaviors from four to eight. *(See Table 14.5, opposite.)*

Thus, for example, employees with an internal locus of control are more likely to prefer achievement-oriented leadership or group-oriented decision making (formerly participative) leadership because they believe they have control over the work environment. The same is true for employees with high task ability and experience.

Employees with an external locus of control, however, tend to view the environment as uncontrollable, so they prefer the structure provided by supportive or path–goal clarifying (formerly directive) leadership. The same is probably true of inexperienced employees.

TABLE 14.5

Eight leadership styles of the revised path–goal theory (*Source:* Adapted from R. J. House, "Path–Goal Theory of Leadership: Lessons, Legacy, and a Reformulated Theory," *Leadership Quarterly,* Autumn 1996, pp. 323–352.)

Style of Leader Behaviors	Description of Behavior toward Employees
1. Path–goal clarifying ("Here's what's expected of you and here's how to do it")	Clarify performance goals. Provide guidance on how employees can complete tasks. Clarify performance standards and expectations. Use positive and negative rewards contingent on performance.
2. Achievement-oriented ("I'm confident you can accomplish the following great things")	Set challenging goals. Emphasize excellence. Demonstrate confidence in employee abilities.
3. Work facilitation ("Here's the goal, and here's what I can do to help you achieve it")	Plan, schedule, organize, and coordinate work. Provide mentoring, coaching, counseling, and feedback to assist employees in developing their skills. Eliminate roadblocks. Provide resources. Empower employees to take actions and make decisions.
4. Supportive ("I want things to be pleasant, since everyone's about equal here")	Treat as equals. Show concern for well-being and needs. Be friendly and approachable.
5. Interaction facilitation ("Let's see how we can all work together to accomplish our goals")	Emphasize collaboration and teamwork. Encourage close employee relationships and sharing of minority opinions. Facilitate communication, resolve disputes.
6. Group-oriented decision making ("I want your suggestions in order to help me make decisions")	Pose problems rather than solutions to work group. Encourage members to participate in decision making. Provide necessary information to the group for analysis. Involve knowledgeable employees in decision making.
7. Representation & networking ("I've got a great bunch of people working for me whom you'll probably want to meet")	Present work group in positive light to others. Maintain positive relationships with influential others. Participate in organization-wide social functions and ceremonies. Do unconditional favors for others.
8. Value-based ("We're destined to accomplish great things")	Establish a vision, display passion for it, and support its accomplishment. Communicate high performance expectations and confidence in others' abilities to meet their goals. Give frequent positive feedback. Demonstrate self-confidence.

Besides expanding the styles of leader behavior from four to eight, House's revision of his theory also puts more emphasis on the need for leaders to foster intrinsic motivation through empowerment. Finally, his revised theory stresses the concept of shared leadership, the idea that employees do not have to be supervisors or managers to engage in leader behavior but rather may share leadership among all employees of the organization.

Does the Revised Path–Goal Theory Work?

There have not been enough direct tests of House's revised path–goal theory using appropriate research methods and statistical procedures to draw overall conclusions. Research on charismatic leadership, however, which is discussed in Section 14.5, is supportive of the revised model.[46]

Although further research is needed on the new model, it offers two important implications for managers:

Cranium's grand poo-bah and chief noodler. Richard Tait (left), responsible for business operations and marketing for the 14-person, Seattle-based game company Cranium, takes the unorthodox title of grand poo-bah. Whit Alexander, who focuses on product development, editorial content, and manufacturing, is called chief noodler. In devising the board game Cranium, the two entrepreneurs decided to adopt the acronym CHIFF—for "clever, high quality, innovative, friendly, and fun"—as the criterion by which all decisions would be guided. "Our survival and success will come from optimizing fun, focus, passion, and profits," says Tait. Which one of the eight path–goal leadership styles would you expect to find dominating this organization?

- ***Use more than one leadership style:*** Effective leaders possess and use more than one style of leadership. Thus, you are encouraged to study the eight styles offered in path–goal theory so that you can try new leader behaviors when a situation calls for them.
- ***Modify leadership style to fit employee and task characteristics:*** A small set of employee characteristics (ability, experience, and need for independence) and environmental factors (task characteristics of autonomy, variety, and significance) are relevant contingency factors, and managers should modify their leadership style to fit them.[47]

3 The Situational Leadership Theory Model: Hersey & Blanchard's Approach

A third contingency approach has been proposed by management writers **Paul Hersey** and **Kenneth Blanchard.**[48] **In their *situational leadership theory,* leadership behavior reflects how leaders should adjust their leadership style according to the readiness of the followers.** The model suggests that managers should be flexible in choosing a leadership behavior style and be sensitive to the readiness level of their employees. ***Readiness*** **is defined as the extent to which a follower possesses the ability and willingness to complete a task.** Subordinates with high readiness (with high ability, skills, and willingness to work) require a different leadership style than do those with low readiness (low ability, training, and willingness).

The appropriate leadership style is found by cross-referencing follower readiness (low–high) with one of four leaderships styles. *(See Figure 14.3, opposite.)*

How the Situational Leadership Model Works

Let's see what the illustration means.

- **Leadership styles—relationship behavior plus task behavior:** The upper part of the drawing shows the leadership style, which is based on the combination of relationship behavior (vertical axis) and task behavior (horizontal axis).

  Relationship behavior is the extent to which leaders maintain personal relationships with their followers, as in providing support and keeping communication open.

  Task behavior is the extent to which leaders organize and explain the role of their followers, which is achieved by explaining what subordinates are to do and how tasks are to be accomplished.
- **Four leadership styles—telling, selling, participating, delegating:** The bell-shaped curve indicates when each of the four leadership styles—telling (S1), selling (S2), participating (S3), and delegating (S4)—should be used.
- **When a leadership style should be used—depends on the readiness of the followers:** How do you know which leadership style to employ? You need to have an understanding of the *readiness* of your followers, as represented by the scale at the bottom of the drawing, where R1 represents low readiness and R4 represents high readiness.

  Let's consider which leadership style to apply when.

  Telling represents the guiding and directing of performance. This leadership style works best for followers with a low level of readiness—that is, subordinates are neither willing nor able to take responsibility.

  Selling is explaining decisions and persuading others to follow a course of action. Because it offers both direction and support, this leadership style is most suitable for followers who are unable but willing to assume task responsibility.

  Participating involves encouraging followers to solve problems on their own. Because it shares decision making, this leadership style encourages subordinates

FIGURE 14.3

Hersey and Blanchard's situational leadership model. [Source: Adapted from P. Hersey, K. H. Blanchard, and D. E. Johnson, *Management of Organizational Behavior: Leading Human Resources,* 8th ed. (Upper Saddle River, NJ: Prentice Hall, 2000). Situational leadership® is a registered trademark of the Center for Leadership Studies, Inc. Copyright © 2002, Center for Leadership Studies, Inc. All rights reserved.]

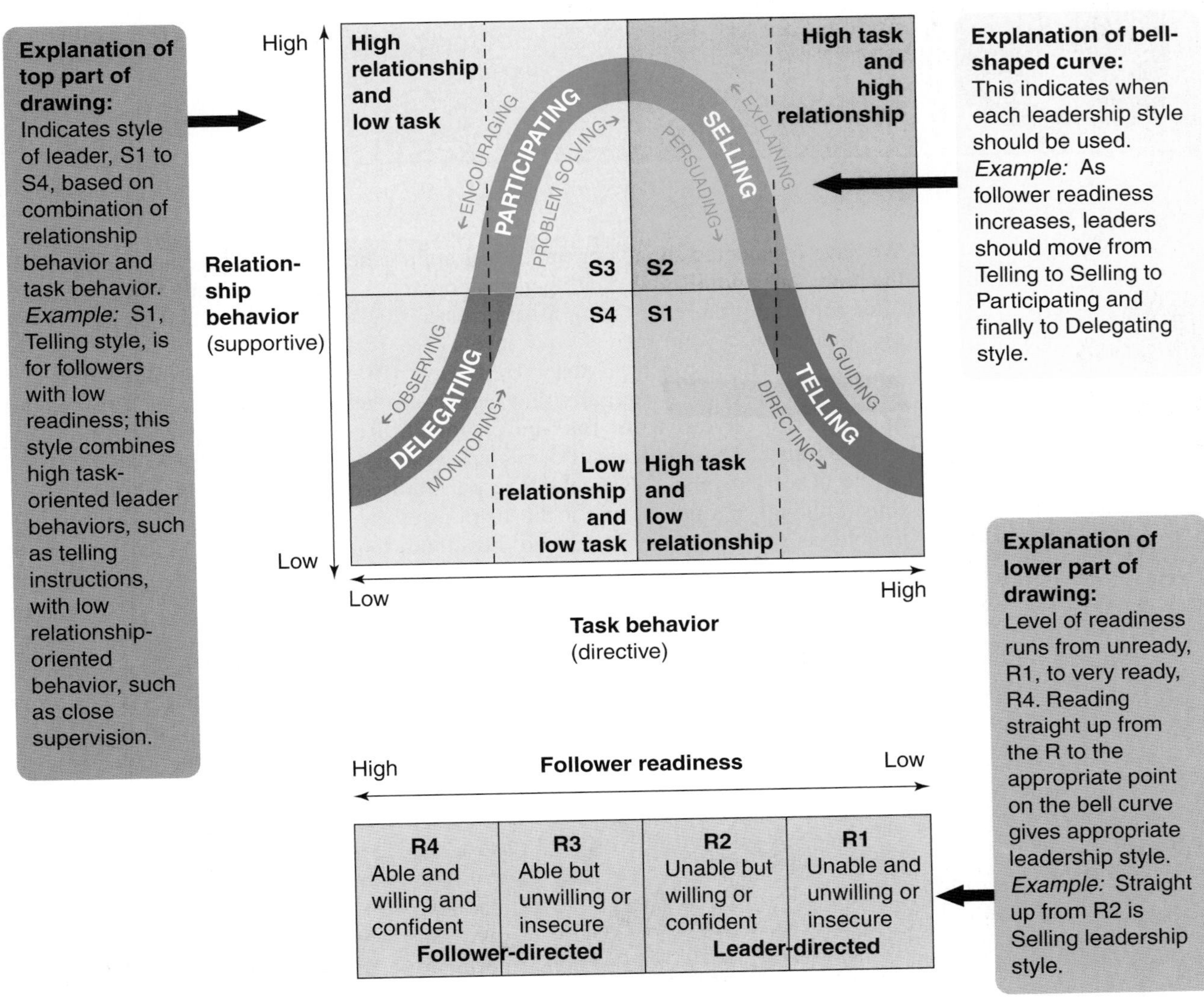

in performing tasks. Thus, it is most appropriate for followers whose readiness is in the moderate to high range.

Delegating is providing subordinates with little support or direction. As such, the leader's role is to observe and monitor. This leadership style is best for followers who have a high level of readiness, both able and willing to perform tasks.

Does the Hersey-Blanchard Model Work?

The situational leadership model is widely used as a training tool, but it is not strongly supported by scientific research. For instance, a study of 459 salespeople found that leadership effectiveness was not attributable to the predicted interaction between follower readiness and leadership style.[49] This is consistent with another study, in which 57 chief nurse executives were found not to delegate in accordance with situational leadership theory.[50] Researchers also have concluded that the self-assessment instrument used to measure leadership style and follower readiness is inaccurate.[51] In sum, managers should exercise discretion when using prescriptions from this model. ◆

major question **What does it take to truly inspire people to perform beyond their normal levels?**

The Big Picture

Full-range leadership describes leadership along a range of styles, with the most effective being transactional/transformational leaders. Four key behaviors of transformational leaders in affecting employees are they inspire motivation, inspire trust, encourage excellence, and stimulate them intellectually.

We have considered the major traditional approaches to understanding leadership—the trait, behavioral, and contingency approaches. But newer approaches seem to offer something more by trying to determine what factors inspire and motivate people to perform beyond their normal levels.

One recent approach proposed by **Bernard Bass and Bruce Avolio,** known as ***full range leadership,*** **suggests that leadership behavior varies along a full range of leadership styles, from take-no-responsibility (*laissez-faire*) "leadership" at one extreme, through transactional leadership, to transformational leadership at the other extreme.**[52] Not taking responsibility can hardly be considered leadership (although it often seems to be manifested by CEOs whose companies got in trouble, as when they say "I had no idea about the criminal behavior of my subordinates"). Transactional and transformational leadership behaviors, however, are both positive aspects of being a good leader.

Transactional versus Transformational Leaders

Jim McNerney, chairman and CEO of 3M, is able to be both a transactional and a transformational leader. Let us consider the differences.

Plans, budgets, schedules. Would you expect management in the construction field to focus more on the nonpeople aspects of work?

Transactional Leadership

As a manager, your power stems from your ability to provide rewards (and threaten reprimands) in exchange for your subordinates' doing the work. When you do this, you are performing ***transactional leadership,*** **focusing on clarifying employees' roles and task requirements and providing rewards and punishments contingent on performance.** Transactional leadership also encompasses the fundamental managerial activities of setting goals and monitoring progress toward their achievement.[53]

"[3M's] McNerney's secret to success is elementary," says a *Business Week* article. "He sets high goals that can be measured, such as business-unit sales or the rate of product introductions, and demands that his managers meet them. Granted, many CEOs do that today. But like a dedicated teacher or coach, McNerney also works with his team day in, day out, to help them make the grade."[54]

We shouldn't think of a transactional leader as being a mediocre leader—indeed, competent transactional leaders are badly needed. But transactional leaders are best in stable situations. What's needed in rapidly changing situations, as is often the case in many organizations today, is a transformational leader.

Transformational Leadership

Transformational leadership **transforms employees to pursue organizational goals over self-interests.** Transformational leaders, in one description, "engender trust, seek to develop leadership in others, exhibit self-sacrifice, and serve as moral agents, focusing themselves and followers on objectives that transcend the more immediate needs of the work group."[55] Whereas transactional leaders try to get people to do *ordinary things,* transformational leaders encourage their people to do *exceptional* things—significantly higher levels of intrinsic motivation, trust, commitment, and loyalty—that can produce significant organizational change and results.

Transformational leaders are influenced by two factors:

- **Individual characteristics:** The personalities of such leaders tend to be more extroverted, agreeable, and proactive than nontransformational leaders. (Female leaders tend to use transformational leadership more than male leaders do.[56])
- **Organizational culture:** Adaptive, flexible organizational cultures are more likely than are rigid, bureaucratic cultures to foster transformational leadership.

The Best Leaders Are Both Transactional & Transformational

It's important to note that transactional leadership is an essential *prerequisite* to effective leadership, and the best leaders learn to display both transactional and transformational styles of leadership to some degree. Indeed, research suggests that transformational leadership leads to superior performance when it "augments" or adds to transactional leadership.[57]

This is apparent in the case of 3M CEO McNerney. "Some people think you either have a demanding, command-and-control management style or you have a nurturing, encouraging style," he says. "I believe you can't have one without the other." *Business Week* points out that McNerney is praised for being an inspirational leader who is comfortable speaking either one-on-one or to large groups. He also is quick to attribute the company's achievements to the entire organization and praises employees for their work ethic.[58]

Four Key Behaviors of Transformational Leaders

Whereas transactional leaders are dispassionate, transformational leaders excite passion, inspiring and empowering people to look beyond their own interests to the interests of the organization. They appeal to their followers' self-concepts—their values and personal identity—to create changes in their goals, values, needs, beliefs, and aspirations.

Transformational leaders have four key kinds of behavior that affect followers.[59]

1 Inspirational Motivation: "Let Me Share a Vision That Transcends Us All"

Transformational leaders have ***charisma*** **("kar-*riz*-muh"), a form of interpersonal attraction that inspires acceptance and support.** Such leaders inspire motivation by offering an agenda, a grand design, an ultimate goal—in short, a *vision,* "a realistic, credible, attractive future" for the organization, as leadership expert Burt Nanus

Sir Branson. One of today's most flamboyant businessmen, Britain's Richard Branson (left) is shown here in May 2003 in Sydney, Australia, with Paul Pester, CEO for the Virgin Money Group Ltd (UK) at the launch of the new Virgin credit card (shown on the screen behind them). Branson left school at 16 to start a 1960s counterculture magazine. By 2002 he was heading a $5 billion empire—the Virgin Group—that included airlines (Virgin Atlantic), entertainment companies (Virgin Records, Virgin Radio), car dealerships, railroads, bridal gowns, soft drinks, and financial services. Knighted in 2000—which entitles him to be called "Sir"—Branson, who is dyslexic, says he is not one for scrutinizing spreadsheets and plotting strategies based on estimates of market share. "In the end," he says, "it is your own gut and your own experience of running businesses." Do you think charismatic business leaders like Sir Branson are able to be more successful than more conventional and conservative managers?

calls it. The right vision unleashes human potential, says Nanus, because it serves as a beacon of hope and common purpose. It does so by attracting commitment, energizing workers, creating meaning in their lives, establishing a standard of excellence, promoting high ideals, and bridging the divide between the organization's problems and its goals and aspirations.[60]

Examples: Civil rights leader Martin Luther King Jr. had a vision—a "dream," as he put it—of racial equality. United Farm Workers leader Cesar Chavez had a vision of better working conditions and pay for agricultural workers. Candy Lightner, founder of Mothers Against Drunk Driving, had a vision of getting rid of alcohol-related car crashes. Apple Computer's Steve Jobs had a vision of developing an "insanely great" desktop computer.

2 Idealized Influence: "We Are Here to Do the Right Thing"

Transformational leaders are able to inspire trust in their followers because they express their integrity by being consistent, single-minded, and persistent in pursuit of their goal. Not only do they display high ethical standards and act as models of desirable values, but they are also able to make sacrifices for the good of the group.

Examples: In 1982, when seven people died consuming cyanide-laced Tylenol capsules, Johnson & Johnson CEO James Burke retained consumer confidence by his actions in taking the drug off the market. Anita Roddick of The Body Shop cosmetics company has been a model for her beliefs in fair trade, environmental awareness, animal protection, and respect for human rights.

3 Individualized Consideration: "You Have the Opportunity Here to Grow & Excel"

Transformational leaders don't just express concern for subordinates' well-being. They actively encourage them to grow and to excel by giving them challenging work, more responsibility, empowerment, and one-on-one mentoring.

Example: Curt "Curre" Linström as head coach of the Finnish national ice hockey team was able to be the caring, fatherly figure to his athletes that enabled them to trust his leadership—and to go from gloomy failure to world championship victory in 1995.

4 Intellectual Stimulation: "Let Me Describe the Great Challenges We Can Conquer Together"

These leaders are gifted at communicating the organization's strengths, weaknesses, opportunities, and threats so that subordinates develop a new sense of purpose. Employees become less apt to view problems as insurmountable or "that's not my department." Instead they learn to view them as personal challenges that they are responsible for overcoming, to question the status quo, and to seek creative solutions.

Example: Ben Cohen, co-founder of Ben & Jerry's, was able to communicate his vision that making ice cream shouldn't be just about profits but also about using some profits for good works.

Implications of Transformational Leadership for Managers

The research shows that transformational leadership yields several positive results. For example, it is positively associated with (1) measures of organizational effectiveness;[61] (2) measures of leadership effectiveness and employee job satisfaction;[62] (3) more employee identification with their leaders and with their immediate work groups;[63] and (4) higher levels of intrinsic motivation, group cohesion, work engagement, and setting of goals consistent with those of the leader.[64]

Besides the fact that, as we mentioned, the best leaders are *both* transactional and transformational, there are three important implications of transformational leadership for managers, as follows.

1 It Can Improve Results for Both Individuals & Groups

You can use the four types of transformational behavior just described to improve results for individuals—such as job satisfaction, organizational commitment, and performance. You can also use them to improve outcomes for groups—an important matter in today's organization, where people tend not to work in isolation but in collaboration with others.

2 It Can Be Used to Train Employees at Any Level

Not just top managers but employees at any level can be trained to be more transactional and transformational.[65] This kind of leadership training among employees should be based on a corporate philosophy, however. Johnson & Johnson, for instance, bases its training on seven principles of leadership development. *(See Table 14.6.)*

1.	Leadership development is a key business strategy.
2.	Leadership excellence is a definable set of standards.
3.	People are responsible for their own development.
4.	Johnson & Johnson executives are accountable for developing leaders.
5.	Leaders are developed primarily on the job.
6.	People are an asset of the corporation; leadership development is a collaborative, corporation-wide process.
7.	Human resources are vital to the success of leadership development.

TABLE 14.6

Seven principles of leadership development. These were developed by Johnson & Johnson. (*Source:* Excerpted from R. M. Fulmer, "Johnson & Johnson: Framework for Leadership," *Organizational Dynamics,* Winter 2001, p. 214.)

3 It Can Be Used by Both Ethical & Unethical Leaders

Ethical transformational leaders help employees to enhance their self-concepts. Unethical leaders may select or produce obedient, dependent, and compliant followers. To better ensure positive results from transformational leadership, top managers should do the following:[66]

- **Code of ethics:** The company should create and enforce a clearly stated code of ethics.
- **Choose the right people:** Recruit, select, and promote people who display ethical behavior.
- **Make performance expectations reflect employee treatment:** Develop performance expectations around the treatment of employees; these expectations can be assessed in the performance-appraisal process.
- **Emphasize value of diversity:** Train employees to value diversity.
- **Reward high moral conduct:** Identify, reward, and publicly praise employees who exemplify high moral conduct. ◆

major question **If there are many ways to be a leader, which one would describe me best?**

The Big Picture

In shared leadership, people share responsibility for leading with others. In servant leadership, leaders provide service to employees and the organization. Loyalty leaders inspire others by their integrity in words and deeds. Level 5 leaders possess the paradoxical qualities of humility and fearless will to succeed. E-leadership involves leader interactions with others via information technology.

Five additional kinds of leadership deserve discussion: (1) *shared leadership,* (2) *servant leadership,* (3) *loyalty leadership,* (4) *Level 5 leadership,* and (5) *e-leadership.*

Shared Leadership

Which is better—leadership in a single chain of command or shared leadership responsibility among two or more individuals? Perhaps, it's suggested, shared leadership is more optimal.[67] ***Shared leadership* is a simultaneous, ongoing, mutual influence process in which people share responsibility for leading.** It is based on the idea that people need to share information and collaborate to get things done. This kind of leadership is most likely to be needed when people work in teams, are involved in complex projects, or are doing knowledge work—work requiring voluntary contributions of intellectual capital by skilled professionals.[68]

Ford Motor Company, for instance, is run by three individuals at the top: CEO Bill Ford, chief operating officer Jim Padilla, and president Nick Scheele. All are at the core of a ten-member group known as the Office of the Chairman and Chief Executive, which meets once a week to review operations. This group is an open forum in which free-flowing discussion is encouraged, although Bill Ford has the last word. "Bill's style is to get a lot of input," says Padilla. "He doesn't like a big meeting with a lot of railbirds. He's not a command-and-control CEO. He's a good listener and manages by consensus."[69] Researchers are beginning to explore the process of shared leadership, and the results are promising. For example, shared leadership in teams has been found to be positively associated with group cohesion, group citizenship, and group effectiveness.[70]

Servant Leadership: Meeting the Goals of Followers & the Organization, Not of Oneself

The term *servant leadership,* coined in 1970 by **Robert Greenleaf,** reflects not only his one-time background as a management researcher for AT&T but also his views as a life-long philosopher and devout Quaker.[71] ***Servant leaders* focus on providing increased service to others—meeting the goals of both followers and the organization—rather than to themselves.**

Former UCLA coach John Wooden, described as "a humble, giving person who wants nothing in return but to see other people succeed," is one such example. Wooden led the university's men's basketball teams to ten national championships.[72] Wal-Mart's Sam Walton believed that leadership consisted of providing employees with the products, training, and support needed to serve customers and then standing back and letting them do their jobs.[73] (Walton, who died in 1992, might be surprised at the unhappiness of many recent Wal-Mart employees, who have complained about being locked in at night and have sued over gender bias in job promotion.[74])

Servant leadership is not a quick-fix approach to leadership. Rather, it is a long-term, transformational approach to life and work. Ten characteristics of the servant leader are shown below. *(See Table 14.7.)* One can hardly go wrong by trying to adopt these characteristics.

TABLE 14.7

Ten characteristics of the servant leader [*Source:* L. C. Spears, "Introduction: Servant-Leadership and the Greenleaf Legacy," in L. C. Spears, ed., *Reflections on Leadership: How Robert K. Greenleaf's Theory of Servant-Leadership Influenced Today's Top Management* (New York: John Wiley & Sons, 1995), pp. 1–14.]

1.	Focus on listening.
2.	Ability to empathize with others' feelings.
3.	Focus on healing suffering.
4.	Self-awareness of strengths and weaknesses.
5.	Use of persuasion rather than positional authority to influence others.
6.	Broad-based conceptual thinking.
7.	Ability to foresee future outcomes.
8.	Belief they are stewards of their employees and resources.
9.	Commitment to the growth of people.
10.	Drive to build community within and outside the organization.

Leading for Loyalty: Six Principles for Generating Faithful Employees, Customers, & Investors

Frederick F. Reichheld, former director of Bain & Company in Boston, is the author of books on loyalty, the latest being *The Loyalty Effect: The Hidden Force Behind Growth, Profits, and Lasting Value.*[75] After a dozen years of research, he has concluded that companies that are most successful in winning and retaining the allegiance of employees, customers, and investors are those that inspire loyalty. And outstanding loyalty, he suggests, "is the direct result of the words and deeds—the decisions and practices—of committed top executives who have personal integrity."[76]

Loyalty leader companies are quite diverse, ranging from Enterprise Rent-A-Car to Harley-Davidson to Northwestern Mutual. But what all have in common, says Reichheld, are six principles designed to engender and retain loyalty—principles that begin with executives at the top of the organization and affect all the relationships within it. Let's consider them.

1 Preach What You Practice

"Many business leaders are vaguely embarrassed by the idea of trumpeting their deepest values," says Reichheld. They feel that their actions should speak louder than their words.

Loyalty leaders realize that more is required—that they need to constantly preach the importance of loyalty in clear, powerful terms to fight beliefs that today loyalty is irrelevant to success. Scott Cook, CEO of personal-finance software maker Intuit, constantly delivers the message to employees that the company's mission is to treat customers right.

2 Play to Win-Win

"In building loyalty, it's not enough that your competitors lose," says Reichheld. "Your partners must win." It is not a good strategy, he suggests, to browbeat employees, unions, and suppliers to make concession after concession or to tolerate dealers who abuse customers, as U.S. carmakers used to do. By treating employees right, loyalty leaders inspire them to deliver superior value to their customers.

Harley-Davidson, for example, has respectful dealings with its unions, and both labor and management have such good relations with customers that many even tattoo the company's logo on their bodies.

3 Be Picky

"Arrogance is thinking your company can be all things to all customers," says Reichheld. "A truly humble company knows it can satisfy only certain customers, and it goes all out to keep them happy." Enterprise Rent-A-Car has become successful by satisfying its existing customer base, not chasing after frequent travelers in every air terminal.

Loyalty leaders are also picky about their employees. Not everyone can get a job with Southwest Airlines, which accepts only 4% of its applicants. As a result, Southwest is known for both service and customer loyalty.

4 Keep It Simple

In a complex world, people need simple rules to guide their decision making, and they work better in small teams that simplify responsibility and accountability. Simplicity also helps companies deal with fast-changing business demands. And small teams help keep customers from getting lost in a faceless bureaucracy.

Northwestern Mutual CEO Jim Ericson piloted the insurance company through a "brutally complex business," Reichheld says, "by keeping his company on one simple rule: Do whatever is in the customer's best interest."

5 Reward the Right Results

Many companies reward the wrong customer or employee, Reichheld points out. For example, they may reward employees who work for short-term profits rather than for long-term value and customer loyalty.

Enterprise Rent-A-Car CEO Andy Taylor devised a pay system that balanced profit inducements with incentives for building long-term employee and customer loyalty, as reflected in a survey measuring customer satisfaction and repeat business.

6 Listen Hard, Talk Straight

"Long-term relationships require honest, two-way communication and learning," writes Reichheld. "True communication promotes trust, which in turn engenders loyalty. Communication also enables businesses to clarify their priorities and coordinate responses to problems and opportunities as they develop."

Dell Computer, for instance, posts all costs on a website, so customers are never confused about prices. It also grades its vendors on a publicly posted online supplier report card, so that suppliers can see how their performance measures against other vendors.

The High Road

"Low-road" companies can survive for some time—maybe even generate impressive financial returns in the short run—by taking advantage of customers, employees, and vendors when they are vulnerable. Ultimately, however, such companies fail to anticipate market shifts or are blindsided by competitors.

Leaders of "high-road" companies realize that high standards of decency and consideration don't diminish profitability. Rather they enable it. Loyalty leaders, says Reichheld, show "they believe that business is not a zero-sum game, that an organization thrives when its partners and customers thrive."

Example

A Strong Loyalty Leader: Pat Croce & Customer Service

Pat Croce is best known as former part owner of the Philadelphia 76ers basketball team and NBC commentator for the 2004 Summer Olympic Games. But before that he owned a company called Sports Physical Therapists (SPT), which he eventually sold for a reported $40 million.

SPT was when his obsession with taking care of the customer really began. When asked later whether he was a marketing or customer-service person, he responded they were both one and the same. "If you want to be a great marketer, you have to fulfill what you're selling with customer service." Acting on an intuition about "how to make people feel great," Croce extended this idea to everyone. "I truly would put myself in the other person's shoes, be it an employee, a customer, a physician, or a season-ticket holder. The vendors, the TV people—I made sure we made it easy for them to do what they do."

Among Croce's Ten Commandments: "Every customer gets a hello and a goodbye." "Listen, listen, listen." "Communicate clearly." "Extend compliments."[77]

Level 5 Leadership

Can a good company become a great company, and, if so, how? That was the question that **Jim Collins** asked, who then proceeded to perform a longitudinal research study to find the answer. The results were summarized in his 2001 bestseller *Good to Great.*[78]

Collins and his team identified a set of companies that shifted from "good" performance to "great" performance, defined as "cumulative stock returns at or below the general stock market for 15 years, punctuated by a transition point, then cumulative returns at least three times the market over the next 15 years."[79] From a sample of 1,435 Fortune 500 companies from 1965 to 1995, 11 good-to-great companies were identified: Abbot, Circuit City, Fannie Mae, Gillette, Kimberly-Clark, Kroger, Nucor, Philip Morris, Pitney Bowes, Walgreens, and Wells Fargo. These companies were then compared with a targeted set of direct-comparison companies to uncover the drivers of the good-to-great transformations. One of the key drivers was that the successful companies had what Collins called Level 5 leadership. Collins' research data revealed "all the good-to-great companies had Level 5 leadership at a time of transition. Furthermore, the absence of Level 5 leadership showed up as a consistent pattern in comparison companies."[80]

Level 5 Leadership: What Is It?

Level 5 leadership **means an organization is led by a person, a Level 5 executive, who possesses the paradoxical characteristics of humility and a fearless will to succeed, as well as the capabilities associated with levels 1–4.** *(See Figure 14.4, top of the next page.)*

An example of a Level 5 executive was President Abraham Lincoln, who, though humble, soft spoken, and shy, possessed great will to keep the American Republic united during the Civil War of 1861–1865, despite a loss of 250,000 Confederate and 360,000 Union soldiers. Like other Level 5 leaders, however, Lincoln also possessed the capabilities of the other four levels of the hierarchy, ranging upward from being a highly capable individual, to a contributing team member, to a competent manager, to an effective leader. Although a Level 5 leader does not move up the hierarchy, he or she must possess the capabilities of levels 1–4 before being able to use the Level 5 characteristics to transform an organization.

Note the resemblances to Level 5 theory and other leadership theories we've discussed. For example, Level 1 is consistent with research on trait theory, which suggests that leaders are intelligent and possess the personality characteristics of extraversion, conscientiousness, and openness to experience. Levels 3 and 4 seem to contain behaviors associated with transactional and transformational leadership. But

FIGURE 14.4
The Level 5 hierarchy
[*Source:* J. Collins, *Good to Great* (New York: Harper Business, 2001), p. 20.]

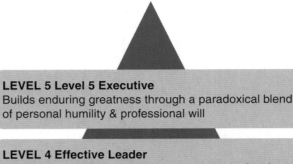

LEVEL 5 Level 5 Executive
Builds enduring greatness through a paradoxical blend of personal humility & professional will
LEVEL 4 Effective Leader
Catalyzes commitment to a vigorous pursuit of a clear & compelling vision, stimulating higher performance
LEVEL 3 Competent Manager
Organizes people & resources toward the effective & efficient pursuit of predetermined objectives
LEVEL 2 Contributing Team Member
Contributes individual capabilities to the achievement of group objectives & works effectively with others in a group setting
LEVEL 1 Highly Capable Individual
Makes productive contributions through talent, knowledge, & good work habits

what is a novel contribution of Level 5 theory is that good-to-great leaders are not only transactional and transformational but, most importantly, are also humble and fiercely determined.

Three Observations about Level 5 Theory

There are three points to keep in mind about Level 5 leadership.

- **Additional drivers:** Collins notes that, besides having a Level 5 leader, additional drivers are required to take a company from good to great.[81] Level 5 leadership, however, enables the implementation of these additional drivers.
- **Further research needed:** To date there has been no additional testing of Collins's conclusions. Future research is clearly needed to confirm the Level 5 hierarchy.
- **Hindrances:** Collins believes that some people will never become Level 5 leaders because their narcissistic and boastful tendencies do not allow them to subdue their own ego and needs to the greater good of others.

E-Leadership: Managing for Global Networks

The Internet and other forms of advanced information technology have led to new possible ways for interacting within and between organizations (e-business) and with customers and suppliers (e-commerce). Leadership within the context of this electronic technology, called ***e-leadership,*** **can involve one-to-one, one-to-many, and within- and between-group and collective interactions via information technology.**[82]

An e-leader doesn't have to be a tech guru, but he or she does have to know enough about information technology to overhaul traditional corporate structures. E-leaders, says one writer, "have a global mind-set that recognizes that the Internet is opening new markets and recharging existing ones. They don't bother fighting mere battles with competitors because they're too busy creating businesses that will surround and destroy them."[83] Harvard Business School professor D. Quinn Mills, author of *E-Leadership,* suggests that individual companies will be replaced by much broader global networks that a single CEO will not be able to manage. Thus, while 20th-century management emphasized competition, he says, future organizations will run on knowledge sharing and open exchange.[84]

These observations suggest that e-leadership means having to deal with quite a number of responsibilities, some of which are suggested below. *(See Table 14.8.)* Some of these responsibilities are developing business opportunities through cooperative relationships, restructuring a company into global networks, decentralizing the company's organization, and energizing the staff.[85] ◆

TABLE 14.8

Six secrets of successful e-leaders. These tips are offered by Don MacRae, president of the Lachlan Group, Toronto. (*Source:* Adapted from D. MacRae, *BusinessWeek online,* September 6, 2001, www.businessweek.com/technology/content/sep2001/tc2001096_619.htm, accessed August 15, 2004.)

1. **Create the future rather than a better status quo.** No matter how successful your business is now, it can be wiped out overnight by the swiftness of the Internet economy. Pay attention to new possibilities rather than simply reacting to today's problems.

2. **Create a "teachable vision."** When Steve Jobs started Apple Computer, his teachable vision was to develop a computer that was as simple to use as a bicycle. Think about how your organization needs to act differently in order to stay at the top of your industry. Have the best and brightest stars in your company investigate how your traditional markets are shifting and what new opportunities might be up for grabs.

3. **Follow a strategy your customers set, not you.** Get over your love affair with your own products and services. What matters most is whether your customers love them. Talk to them about their needs and how you could serve them better. Let them set corporate direction.

4. **Foster a collaborative culture.** E-leaders don't give orders from the top. They let teams form organically in their organizations and encourage people to question the way things are done. Be open to unorthodox strategies.

5. **Think globally.** Technology allows you to build ties with customers, suppliers, and strategic partners all over the world. Don't neglect the opportunity. Be disciplined about finding the best places to do business and seeing opportunities where they exist.

6. **Thrive on information.** This means all kinds of information: overnight sales figures, customer-satisfaction scores, employee turnover, on-time delivery rates, canceled orders, and so on. Technology allows e-leaders to track their companies by every conceivable detail. Without taking a 360-degree view of what's going on in your business—and adjusting your strategy accordingly—you can forget about leading for much longer.

Key Terms Used in This Chapter

authority, 445
behavioral leadership approaches, 454
charisma, 465
contingency approach, 458
contingency leadership model, 458
coercive power, 446
e-leadership, 472
emotional intelligence, 451
expert power, 446
full range leadership, 464
leadership, 444
leadership grid model, 455
legitimate power, 446
Level 5 leadership, 471
meta-analysis, 452
path–goal leadership model, 459
personalized power, 445
power, 445
readiness, 462
referent power, 446
reward power, 446
servant leaders, 468
shared leadership, 468
situational leadership theory, 462
socialized power, 445
trait approaches to leadership, 450
transactional leadership, 464
transformational leadership, 465

Summary

14.1 The Nature of Leadership: Wielding Influence

- Leadership is the ability to influence employees to voluntarily pursue organizational goals. Being a manager and being a leader are not the same. Management is about coping with complexity, whereas leadership is about coping with change. Companies manage complexity by planning and budgeting, organizing and staffing, and controlling and problem solving. Leadership copes with change by setting a direction, aligning people to accomplish an agenda, and motivating and inspiring people.
- To understand leadership, we must understand authority and power. Authority is the right to perform or command; it comes with the manager's job. Power is the extent to which a person is able to influence others so they respond to orders. People may pursue personalized power, power directed at helping oneself, or, better, they may pursue socialized power, power directed at helping others.
- Within an organization there are typically five sources of power leaders may draw on; all managers have the first three. (1) Legitimate power is power that results from managers' formal positions within the organization. (2) Reward power is power that results from managers' authority to reward their subordinates. (3) Coercive power results from managers' authority to punish their subordinates. (4) Expert power is power resulting from one's specialized information or expertise. (5) Referent power is power deriving from one's personal attraction.
- There are nine influence tactics for trying to get others to do something you want, ranging from most used to least used tactics as follows: rational persuasion, inspirational appeals, consultation, ingratiating tactics, personal appeals, exchange tactics, coalition tactics, pressure tactics, and legitimating tactics.
- Four principal approaches or perspectives on leadership, as discussed in the rest of the chapter, are (1) trait, (2) behavioral, (3) contingency, and (4) emerging.

14.2 Trait Approaches: Do Leaders Have Distinctive Personality Characteristics?

- 
Trait approaches to leadership attempt to identify distinctive characteristics that account for the effectiveness of leaders. Representatives of this approach are Kouzes and Posner, Brossidy, Goleman, Judge, and gender studies.

  (1) Kouzes and Posner identified five traits of leaders. A leader should be honest, competent, forward-looking, inspiring, and intelligent.

  (2) Brossidy, a working CEO, identifies four qualities he looks for when assessing prospective leaders: ability to execute, a career runway (ability to go beyond present job), a team orientation, and multiple experiences.

  (3) Goleman argues that the most important attribute in a leader is emotional intelligence—the ability to cope, empathize with others, and be self-motivated—which includes the traits of self-awareness, self-management, social awareness, and relationship management.

  (4) Meta-analyses by Judge and colleagues suggest that the Big Five personality traits of extroversion, as well as conscientiousness and openness, are important to leadership effectiveness and that

personality is more important than intelligence for leadership.

(5) Women may rate higher than men do on producing high-quality work, goal setting, mentoring employees, and other measures. Women excel in such traits as teamwork and partnering, being more collaborative, seeking less personal glory, being motivated less by self-interest than company interest, being more stable, and being less turf-conscious.

14.3 Behavioral Approaches: Do Leaders Show Distinctive Patterns of Behavior?

- Behavioral leadership approaches try to determine the distinctive styles used by effective leaders. Leadership style means the combination of traits, skills, and behaviors that leaders use when interacting with others. We described some important models of leadership behavior.
- In the University of Michigan Leadership Model, researchers identified two forms of leadership styles. In job-centered behavior, managers paid more attention to the job and work procedures. In employee-centered behavior, managers paid more attention to employee satisfaction and making work groups cohesive.
- In the Ohio State Leadership Model, researchers identified two major dimensions of leader behavior: Initiating structure organizes and defines what group members should be doing. Consideration is leadership behavior that expresses concern for employees by establishing a supportive climate.
- One expert concludes from the Michigan and Ohio studies that effective leaders tend to have supportive relationships with employees, use group rather than individual methods of supervision, and set high performance goals.
- The Blake and Moulton (and McCanse) Leadership Grid model identifies the ideal leadership style as having a high concern for production (the job aspects of subordinates' behavior) and people (the human aspects). Five principal management styles were identified: impoverished management, task management, country club management, middle-of-the-road management, and team management. Team management, which gets the utmost from employees along both production and people dimensions, was deemed most effective.

14.4 Contingency Approaches: Does Leadership Vary with the Situation?

- Proponents of the contingency approach to leadership believe that effective leadership behavior depends on the situation at hand—that as situations change, different styles become effective. Three contingency approaches are described.
- The Fiedler contingency leadership model determines if a leader's style is task-oriented or relationship-oriented and if that style is effective for the situation at hand. Once it is determined whether a leader is more oriented toward tasks or toward people, then it's necessary to determine how much control and influence a leader has in the immediate work environment. The three dimensions of situational control are leader-member relations, which reflects the extent to which a leader has the support of the work group; the task structure, which reflects the extent to which tasks are routine and easily understood; and position power, which reflects how much power a leader has to reward and punish and make work assignments. For each dimension, the leader's control may be high or low. A task-oriented style has been found to work best in either high-control or low-control situations; the relationship-oriented style best in situations of moderate control.
- The House path–goal leadership model, in its revised form, holds that the effective leader clarifies paths through which subordinates can achieve goals and provides them with support. Two variables, employee characteristics and environmental factors, cause one or more leadership behaviors—which House expanded to eight from his original four—to be more effective than others.
- Hersey and Blanchard's situational leadership theory suggests that leadership behavior reflects how leaders should adjust their leadership style according to the readiness of the followers. Readiness is defined as the extent to which a follower possesses the ability and willingness to complete a task. The appropriate leadership style is found by cross-referencing follower readiness (low to high) with one of four leadership styles: telling, selling, participating, delegating.

14.5 The Full Range Approach: Uses of Transactional & Transformational Leadership

- Full range leadership describes leadership along a range of styles, with the most effective being transactional/transformational leaders. Transactional leadership focuses on clarifying employees' roles and task requirements and providing rewards and punishments contingent on performance. Transformational leadership transforms employees to pursue goals over self-interests. Transformational leaders are influenced by two factors: (1) Their personalities tend to be more extroverted, agreeable, and proactive. (2) Organizational cultures are more apt to be adaptive and flexible.

- The best leaders are both transactional and transformational. Four key behaviors of transformational leaders in affecting employees are they inspire motivation, inspire trust, encourage excellence, and stimulate them intellectually.
- Transformational leadership has three implications. (1) It can improve results for both individuals and groups. (2) It can be used to train employees at any level. (3) It can be used by both ethical or unethical leaders.

14.6 Five Additional Perspectives

-  Five additional kinds of leadership are (1) shared leadership, (2) servant leadership, (3) loyalty leadership, (4) Level 5 leadership, and (5) e-leadership.
- Shared leadership is a simultaneous, ongoing, mutual influence process in which people share responsibility for leading. It is based on the idea that people need to share information and collaborate to get things done.
- Servant leaders focus on providing increased service to others—meeting the goals of both followers and the organization—rather than to themselves.
- Loyalty leadership is embodied in six principles suggested by Reichheld for generating faithful employees, customers, and investors: preach what you practice, play to win-win, be picky, keep it simple, reward the right results, and listen hard and talk straight.
- Level 5 leadership means an organization is led by a person, a Level 5 executive, who possesses the paradoxical characteristics of humility and a fearless will to succeed, as well as the capabilities associated with levels 1–4: being an effective leader, a competent manager, a contributing team member, and a highly capable individual.
- E-leadership involves leader interactions with others via the Internet and other forms of advanced information technology, which have made possible new ways for interacting within and between organizations (e-business) and with customers and suppliers (e-commerce). E-leadership can involve one-to-one, one-to-many, and within- and between-group and collective interactions via information technology.

Management in Action

Ann Fudge Leaves Early Retirement to Take over the Reins at Young & Rubicam Brands

Excerpted from Diane Brady, "Act II," Business Week, *March 29, 2004, pp. 73–76, 80.*

BusinessWeek

In February, 2001, Ann Fudge did something that has become achingly common among high-powered career women. She quit. After a quarter-century as a rising star in Corporate America and just one year after she had been promoted to run a $5 billion division of Kraft Foods Inc., Fudge walked away. She didn't do it for her two sons, who were already grown and embarked on careers of their own. She didn't do it to accept another turnaround challenge, building on her reputation for reviving brands from Minute Rice to Maxwell House. Like a number of her peers, she simply wanted to define herself by more than her professional status, considerable as it was, and financial rewards, sizable as they were. "It was definitely not dissatisfaction, " says Fudge, now 52. "It was more about life." . . .

About two years into her sojourn, Fudge got a call from Martin Sorrell, chief executive of Britain's advertising conglomerate, WPP Group PLC. He wasn't interested in seeking her reflections on retirement. If anything, he says, "I thought, what a waste." If everybody followed Fudge's lead, he argues, "look at the damage to the economy to have all these talented 50-year-olds out." No, Sorrell called to tempt Fudge back in with an offer to run Young & Rubicam Inc., the distressed advertising and communications giant that he had bought for $4.7 billion in 2000. He thought that Fudge, with her marketing expertise and renowned people skills, could rescue a company that two CEOs in three years couldn't. And he certainly wasn't oblivious to the buzz that hiring a prominent black woman would create. Besides, the notoriously hands-on boss contends, "women are better managers than men."

What an offer, though: Fudge would take over a company with about 40% of the revenues of the unit she ran at Kraft, a company that a former Y&R client calls "distracted and uninspired" in an industry worried about becoming irrelevant. All at a time when Fudge was dreaming of starting her own children's media venture. But here was a chance to make a difference in a hurry. As CEO, she could alter the way that business was done—turning the company from an insular idea factory stymied by its own turf battles to a truly client-focused and efficient operation. Her ideal: a collaborative family in which independent businesses work together to diagnose and solve customers' problems. This was a company where she could put her marketing savvy and management ideas into practice, a company that needed her, a company of her own.

And so in May, 2003, she became chairman and chief executive of what is now called Young & Rubicam Brands, as well as Y&R, its flagship ad agency. . . .

At Young & Rubicam, she has been welcomed with as much skepticism as enthusiasm. Fudge was an unconventional choice as chief executive, and she is taking an unconventional approach—importing a management rigor and an inclusive style rarely associated with advertising. Fudge's leadership could result in dramatic improvements or end in very public failure.

Fudge traded her enlightened early retirement and entrepreneurial plans for a daunting challenge. She has thrust her newly centered self smack in the middle of a company that has endured neglect, executive greed, and a messy merger. . . . Some employees are bitter. And now many are peeved to have a consumer-products executive who espouses management principles like "Lean Six Sigma" at the helm of an ad agency, where a modicum of chaos is thought to be necessary for creativity. To them, it's an awkward match.

The new CEO acknowledges that it'll take time to create goodwill among a group of people who have been so disillusioned for the past few years. . . .

But it is Fudge's vision for how Y&R should operate that really puts her at odds with some of her new colleagues. She brings a client's perspective to the job in a way that is fundamentally different from the usual ad agency ethos. In Fudge's world, creativity is only worthwhile if the client appreciates it. That's practically heresy to some. As an experienced marketing executive, she knows all too well the limits of the traditional 30-second commercial. When clients approach her agency for help selling a product, she believes the response should be to find the best possible combination of services, drawing on all the far-flung units in the empire. To underscore this, she launched the Young & Rubicam Brands name for the group's family of companies. That's a difficult mind shift for a confederation of businesses used to working independently and even competing against one another. Meanwhile, many insiders complain that despite the change in nomenclature, Fudge has failed to give Y&R the dynamic, fresh identity it needs to draw customers and talent back into the fold. Instead, from her open cubicle at Madison Avenue, she has focused on meeting with customers and encouraging her employees to unite in giving them better service. Her goal: more revenue from existing clients, rather than the buzz of new business. Y&R Vice-Chairman Stephanie Kugelman calls the griping "old world adspeak," arguing that marshaling resources for clients trumps fresh slogans. "This is what you have to do these days," says Kugelman. "The whole business has changed."

Fudge may not have won the hearts and minds of all her staffers, but at least some clients are in sync with the kinds of changes she's trying to make. "Too many people add a lot of cost and not a lot of value," says M. Carl Johnson III, chief strategy officer at client Campbell Soup Co. "They have to stop doing stuff that's stupid." Fudge's first big success was Microsoft Corp.'s recent decision to give roughly $250 million of its customer-relationship management business to Y&R. "If it wasn't for her leadership, we wouldn't have been able to close the deal," says John B. Kahan, Microsoft's general manager of corporate customer-relationship management. "Most agencies come to the table with: 'Here's what I did for other customers.' She says: 'What does it take to delight your customer?' " . . .

Such observations underline two obvious characteristics that set Fudge apart: she is female, and she is black. That may account for the preponderance of adjectives like "lovely," "nurturing," and "nice" that get thrown at her. It may also explain why Fudge says she is used to being underestimated. On a recent business trip, someone mixed up Fudge and a junior associate, who is white. "I almost think it's funny," says Fudge, noting that she has experienced racism every day of her life. When her sons were teenagers, she used to tell them not to put their hands in their pockets, in case people thought they were carrying guns. "It's not different for any person who grows up black in this country. You understand who you are. You deal with it." The bigger issue, she says, is "the challenge of being questioned all the time."

For Discussion

1. How many of the five sources of power that leaders draw on is Ann Fudge using? Explain.
2. Which of the eight influence tactics are being used by Fudge?
3. Which of the leadership traits discussed in Section 14.2 are displayed by Fudge?
4. To what extent is Fudge using the full range of leadership? Explain.
5. Evaluate the extent to which Fudge has displayed the components of Level 5 leadership.

Self-Assessment

Do You Have What It Takes to Be a Leader?*

Objectives

To learn more about the skills required for being a leader.

To assess your own leadership ability.

Introduction

Managers cope with complexity: They look at what needs to be done (planning and budgeting), pull together the people needed to get the job done together (organizing and staffing), and ensure that people do their jobs (controlling and problem solving). Leaders, however, cope with change: They look at what needs to be done by setting a direction rather than planning and budgeting, pull people together to do the job through alignment rather than organizing and staffing, and ensure people do their jobs through motivation and inspiration instead of controlling and problem solving. The purpose of this exercise is to assess your skills and determine if you have what it takes to be a leader.

Instructions

Read each of the following statements, and circle the number that best represents your self-perceptions, where 1 = strongly disagree, 2 = disagree, 3 = neither agree nor disagree, 4 = agree, 5 = strongly agree. There is no right or wrong answer.

1.	I can separate my personal life from work/school.	1	2	3	4	5
2.	I'm honest with myself.	1	2	3	4	5
3.	I communicate my ideas clearly.	1	2	3	4	5
4.	I regularly prioritize what I need to get done.	1	2	3	4	5
5.	I am on time for meetings/classes.	1	2	3	4	5
6.	I am positive and upbeat.	1	2	3	4	5
7.	I am solution oriented rather than problem oriented.	1	2	3	4	5
8.	I take responsibility for my actions.	1	2	3	4	5
9.	I do not blame others for my mistakes.	1	2	3	4	5
10.	When working in a group, I work with members to solve and prevent problems.	1	2	3	4	5
11.	I don't have to redo things because my work is thorough and complete.	1	2	3	4	5
12.	I do not procrastinate on projects/tasks.	1	2	3	4	5
13.	I do not get distracted when working on projects/tasks.	1	2	3	4	5
14.	I work well in a group.	1	2	3	4	5
15.	I am people oriented, not just results oriented.	1	2	3	4	5
16.	I listen to others beyond just the words being spoken.	1	2	3	4	5
17.	When working in a group, I am more concerned with the group's success than my own.	1	2	3	4	5
18.	I adjust well to different communication styles.	1	2	3	4	5
19.	I praise others when they are doing a good job.	1	2	3	4	5
20.	I work at getting ahead, but within appropriate boundaries.	1	2	3	4	5
	Total	______				

Scoring & Interpretation

Compute your score by adding the responses for all 20 items. The questions in this survey were designed to give you feedback on your skills in the following areas: (1) personal stability, (2) productivity, (3) self-management, (4) communication, (5) boundary setting, (6) work quality, (7) teamwork. All of these skills are found in good managers, and they represent necessary skills for leaders.

Arbitrary norms for leadership skills:
Excellent leadership skills (95–100)
Good leadership skills (85–90)
Moderate leadership skills (75–80)
Low leadership skills (65–70)
Poor leadership skills (60 and below)

Questions for Discussion

1. Were you surprised by your results? Why or why not?
2. Look at the five questions where you scored the lowest. What can you do to improve or develop your skills represented by these items? Explain.
3. Does the content in the five lowest areas relate to Tables 14.2–14.3? If it does, can you identify additional ways you can improve these skills? Describe and explain.

*Questions for this survey were adapted from Interlink Training and Coaching, "The Leadership Assessment Tool," *www.interlinktc.com/assessment.html.* Interlink Training and Coaching, 3655 W. Anthem Way, Box 315, Anthem, AZ 85086.

Group Exercise

How Do They Do It? Examining the Skills of Famous Leaders

Objectives

To examine the leadership skills of famous leaders.

To further explore different approaches to leadership.

Introduction

In this chapter you learned four different approaches to explaining leadership. We know that leaders possess traits and skills that make them successful. They are effective communicators. They are guided by a vision that is shared by others. They are skillful planners. They are champions for their cause. They are successful at motivating people to voluntarily pursue goals. Leaders can be villains or heroes, trailblazers and visionaries, revolutionaries or college students. The purpose of this exercise is to examine the skills displayed by famous leaders and to determine how you might use this knowledge to improve your leadership skills.

Instructions

Break into groups of five to six people. First, brainstorm a list of famous leaders—CEOs, presidents, politicians, monarchs, or whoever, as long as the group knows something about their skills as leaders. Next, the group needs to pick two leaders to compare and contrast. Try to pick leaders that seem vastly different from one another—for example, Joan of Arc and Mother Teresa. Once you have decided on the two leaders, use the following survey to profile them in terms of their skills and traits. Use the panels and additional material in this chapter to help guide your discussion. Answer the questions for discussion after completing the survey.

Profile Survey	**Leader A** **Name:**		**Leader B** **Name:**	
In terms of power: This person uses/used which sources of power?	Personalized power	_____	Personalized power	_____
	Socialized power	_____	Socialized power	_____
	Legitimate power	_____	Legitimate power	_____
	Reward power	_____	Reward power	_____
	Coercive power	_____	Coercive power	_____
	Expert power	_____	Expert power	_____
	Referent power	_____	Referent power	_____

In terms of influence: What influence tactics does/did this person use?	Consultation	_____	Consultation	_____
	Rational persuasion	_____	Rational persuasion	_____
	Inspirational appeals	_____	Inspirational appeals	_____
	Ingratiating tactics	_____	Ingratiating tactics	_____
	Coalition tactics	_____	Coalition tactics	_____
	Pressure tactics	_____	Pressure tactics	_____
	Upward appeals	_____	Upward appeals	_____
	Exchange tactics	_____	Exchange tactics	_____
In terms of the trait approach to leadership: Which traits does/did this person exhibit?	Honest	_____	Honest	_____
	Competent	_____	Competent	_____
	Forward-looking	_____	Forward-looking	_____
	Inspiring	_____	Inspiring	_____
	Intelligent	_____	Intelligent	_____
	Self awareness	_____	Self awareness	_____
	Self-management	_____	Self-management	_____
	Social awareness	_____	Social awareness	_____
	Relationship management	_____	Relationship management	_____
In terms of behavioral approaches to leadership: Which leadership behaviors did/does this person exhibit?	**U of Michigan Model**		**U of Michigan Model**	
	Job-centered behavior	_____	Job-centered behavior	_____
	Employee-centered behavior	_____	Employee-centered behavior	_____
	Ohio State Model		**Ohio State Model**	
	Initiating structure	_____	Initiating structure	_____
	Consideration	_____	Consideration	_____
	Leadership Grid Model		**Leadership Grid Model**	
	Impoverished leader	_____	Impoverished leader	_____
	Task leader	_____	Task leader	_____
	Country-club leader	_____	Country-club leader	_____
	Middle-of-the-road leader	_____	Middle-of-the-road leader	_____
	Team leader	_____	Team leader	_____
In terms of transactional and charismatic leadership: What general type of leader is/was this person?	Transactional leader	_____	Transactional leader	_____
	Charismatic leader	_____	Charismatic leader	_____
	Servant leader	_____	Servant leader	_____

Questions for Discussion

1. What criteria did your group use to determine which two leaders you would profile? Describe.
2. In what ways are the leadership styles of these leaders similar? In what ways are they different? Explain.
3. After completing this survey, were you surprised at the similarity or dissimilarity between these leaders? Discuss.
4. Which one of these leaders would you want to work for? Explain your rationale.

Ethical Dilemma

Covering for a Laid-Off Friend

You manage a group of software developers for a large organization and several days ago had the difficult task of notifying a friend who works for the company that he is being laid off. Even though he has performed wonderfully in the past and you hate to see him go, your company lost a contract with a major client and thus his position has become obsolete.

The employee wants to build a house, and you're aware that he is 10 days away from closing on a loan for it. He has sold his previous home and now is living with his in-laws. He asks you for a favor: could you extend his employment just 10 more days so that he can qualify for his new home loan? Unfortunately, you don't have the authority to do so, and you tell him you can't help him.

He then tells you that the mortgage company will be calling sometime soon to get a verbal confirmation of his employment. The confirmation is an essential prerequisite if your friend is to obtain the loan for his new home. Would you, he asks, tell the mortgage company that he is still employed?

Solving the Dilemma

As a manager, what would you do?

1. Tell the mortgage company your friend is still employed by the company. Your friend needs a break, and you're confident that he'll find a job in the near future.
2. Refuse to lie. It is unethical to falsify information regarding employment.
3. Simply avoid the mortgage company's phone call.
4. Invent other options. Discuss.

Video Case

Delta Force

Colonel Lee Van Arsdale is a West Point graduate who served 25 years in the Army, 18 of them in Special Operations. Van Arsdale served in Operation Just Cause in Panama and was a member of a Delta Force team in Somalia. According to Van Arsdale, good leadership is good leadership, whether in the Army or in any other organization. He speaks from experience, having managed in both the military and private business. As in business, Special Forces teams have a mission statement. Both businesses and the military provide services and require quality people to carry out the mission. Both need the proper equipment to do the job. Both require enabling personnel through the provision of the education, tools, and training needed to perform. Members of Special Forces are volunteers who are trained to be engineers, communications specialists, weapons specialists, medics, and so on. Teams are trained to operate in various regions of the world, including learning the local language and culture. Those who succeed are self-motivated, mature, and confident. Similarly, businesses operating globally need to train managers to adapt to different countries and cultures.

Special Forces are on call 24/7, 365 days per year. They operate in 60–70 countries and must be prepared to deploy on a moment's notice. This situation creates a strain on both personnel and their families. Because operatives must blend with the peoples of other countries, military dress regulations are relaxed. Personnel are given an assignment, and planning is done from the bottom up. The team, which may consist of up to a dozen individuals, is free to determine how to carry out the mission. Similarly, empowered employees within organizations must determine for themselves how to best accomplish organizational goals.

Leaders must be prepared to adopt several different leadership styles. For example, in battle, a military leader may have to be autocratic and demand the unquestioning obedience of his or her followers. At other times, a military leader may be quite democratic and rely heavily on followers to provide input and suggestions. A good leader has to be a good listener. Working with a dedicated, focused, and fun-loving team develops a camaraderie that holds the team together and allows them to work effectively. These lessons hold true in the military, in sports, and in business.

Discussion Questions

1. In your opinion, would Colonel Lee Van Arsdale more likely subscribe to Fiedler's Contingency Leadership Model or House's Path-Goal Leadership Model. (Hint: Can/should leaders change their leadership style depending on the situation?)
2. Describe the similarities between good military leadership and good business leadership.

chapter 15

Interpersonal & Organizational Communication

MAJOR QUESTIONS YOU SHOULD BE ABLE TO ANSWER

15.1 The Communication Process: What It Is, How It Works

Major Question: What do I need to know about the communication process to be an effective communicator?

15.2 Barriers to Communication

Major Question: What are the important barriers I need to be aware of, so I can improve my communication skills?

15.3 How Managers Fit into the Communication Process

Major Question: How can I use the different channels and patterns of communication to my advantage?

15.4 Communication in the Information Age

Major Question: How do contemporary managers use information technology to communicate more effectively?

15.5 Improving Communication Effectiveness

Major Question: How can I be a better listener, reader, writer, and speaker?

the manager's toolbox

Becoming a Better Communicator: Being Telephone-Savvy

Some communication doesn't matter much (such as small talk with the latte server). Some matters a lot, as when you're using the phone to try to get a job interview. Indeed, despite e-mail, the phone is still the most used business tool, so you need to become skilled at it.

Ever feel that someone you called (whether a prospective date or prospective employer) is ignoring you because they never call back? Maybe the reason is inadequate telephone skills. Following are some suggestions for becoming phone-savvy, which will give you a practical introduction to the subject of communication.[1]

- **Consider the impression you make on the phone:** Watch out for self-defeating telephone behavior. Talking too fast, for instance, makes what you say seem unimportant. Talking too slowly makes you sound tired or uninterested. Talking too softly makes you hard to understand. Talking too loudly grates on others' ears. Talking too much—giving more details than your listener wants—makes people impatient.
- **When you call someone:** When you make a call to someone you don't know, do you speak briefly and above all *clearly*? When leaving a message, do you *slowly* give your name, organization, and phone number (*twice*)? Do you give the date and time you called? If you want a call back, do you specify a *time when you'll be available*? (Don't say: "Uh, I'll be around maybe later.")
- **When someone calls you:** Do you give a favorable first impression, showing the caller that you're helpful and confident? Do you identify yourself? Do you repeat (and *jot down*) the caller's name? (Don't say: "Um, what'd you say your name was again?")
- **Being courteous:** Do you keep your voice interested, attentive, and friendly? Do you say "please" and "thank you"? Do you ask callers if it's okay to put them on hold or if you should call back in a few minutes? Do you say "Thank you for waiting" when you come back on? Do you let the caller hang up first? (Of course, as a time-starved manager you'll sometimes have to politely terminate the conversation first.)
- **Making difficult calls:** When you have to make a difficult telephone call, such as when you're angling for a job interview, are you prepared? Do you have a script that you wrote out beforehand and practiced? Do you get to the point right away? (Attention spans are shorter on the phone.) Do you repeat the other person's name once in a while to make the conversation more personal?
- **Dealing with phone tag:** You phone. Your caller isn't in. That person calls you back. You're not in. That's "phone tag." To deal with it, you need to be aware of the following tricks. (1) Persistence is important. Four or five calls are fine. More than that and the other person may consider you a pest. (2) Don't just use the other person's answering machine or voice mail. If he or she has a secretary or administrative assistant, leave messages with that person as well. (And get to know that person by name and become allies.) (3) Describe your schedule and your availability. (4) If the other person calls back, note the time, which may be when he or she is always at a desk making calls. (5) When you leave a message, make it clear and complete but not overly long.

forecast

What's Ahead in This Chapter

This chapter describes the process of transferring information and understanding from one person to another. It also describes three communications barriers—physical, semantic, and personal. It shows how you can use different channels and patterns of communication, both formal and informal, to your advantage. It discusses how star managers use information technology to communicate more effectively. Finally, we talk about how to be a better listener, talker, writer, and reader.

major question

What do I need to know about the communication process to be an effective communicator?

The Big Picture

Communication is the transfer of information and understanding from one person to another. The process involves sender, message, and receiver; encoding and decoding; the medium; feedback; and dealing with "noise," or interference. Managers need to tailor their communication to the appropriate medium (rich or lean) for the appropriate situation.

"Good writing is one of two key abilities I focus on when hiring," says Richard Todd at the Federal Reserve Bank of Minneapolis; "the other is the ability to read critically. I can train people to do almost anything else, but I don't have time to teach this."[2] In another survey of 300 executives, 71% said they believed written communication skills were a critical competency that needed enhancement via training; 68% said they believed the same about interpersonal communications skills.[3]

Because many students have not had sufficient training of this sort and because today's work environment is so fast-paced, faulty communication has become a real problem in the workplace. According to one survey, executives say 14% of each 40-hour workweek is wasted because of poor communication between staff and managers.[4] That's the equivalent of seven workweeks of lost productivity a year. Thus, there's a hard-headed argument for better communication: It can save money.

Communication Defined: The Transfer of Information & Understanding

***Communication*—the transfer of information and understanding from one person to another**—is an activity that you as a manager will have to do a lot of. Indeed, one study found that 81% of a manager's time in a typical work day is spent communicating.[5]

The fact that managers do a lot of communicating doesn't mean they're necessarily good at it—that is, that they are efficient or effective. You are an *efficient communicator* when you can transmit your message accurately in the least time. You are an *effective communicator* when your intended message is accurately understood by the other person. Thus, you may well be efficient in sending a group of people a reprimand by e-mail. But it may not be effective if it makes them angry so that they can't absorb its meaning.

I hear you. Today some people can work almost anywhere, even more so as the cellphone becomes a more versatile instrument permitting Internet and e-mail access, text messaging, and access to huge databases. Do you think our ability to work outside traditional offices because of today's technology will negatively affect the communication process and employee camaraderie?

From this, you can see why it's important to have an understanding of the communication process.

How the Communication Process Works

Communication has been said to be a process consisting of "a sender transmitting a message through media to a receiver who responds."[6] Let's look at these and other parts of the process.

Sender, Message, & Receiver

The *sender* is the person wanting to share information—called a *message*—and the *receiver* is the person for whom the message is intended, as follows.

Sender → Message → Receiver

Encoding & Decoding

Of course, the process isn't as simple as just sender/message/receiver. If you were sending the message over a telegraph line, you would first have to encode the message, and the receiver would have to decode it. But the same is true if you are sending the message by voice to another person in the same room, when you have to decide what language to speak in and what terms to use.

Encoding **is translating a message into understandable symbols or language.** ***Decoding*** **is interpreting and trying to make sense of the message.** Thus, the communication process is now

Sender **[Encoding]** → Message → **[Decoding]** Receiver

The Medium

The means by which you as a communicator send a message is important, whether it is by typing an e-mail traveling over the Internet, by voice over a telephone line, or by hand-scrawled note. This is the ***medium,*** **the pathway by which a message travels:**

Sender [Encoding] → Message **[Medium]** Message → [Decoding] Receiver

Feedback

"Flight 123, do you copy?" In the movies, that's what you hear the flight controller say when radioing the pilot of a troubled aircraft to see if he or she received ("copied") the previous message. And the pilot may radio back, "Roger, Houston, I copy." This is an example of ***feedback*****—the receiver expresses his or her reaction to the sender's message.**

Sender [Encoding] → Message [Medium] Message → [Decoding] Receiver

[Feedback] Message

Noise

Unfortunately, the entire communication process can be disrupted at several different points by what is called ***noise*****—any disturbance that interferes with the transmission of a message.** The noise can occur in the medium, of course, as when you have static in a radio transmission or fade-out on a cellphone or when there's loud music when you're trying to talk in a noisy restaurant. Or it can occur in the encoding or decoding, as when a pharmacist can't read a prescription because of a doctor's poor handwriting.

Say again? London traffic is only one cause of noise.

Noise also occurs in *nonverbal communication* (discussed in Chapter 4 and again later in this chapter), as when our physical movements send a message that is different from the one we are speaking, or in *cross-cultural communication* (discussed in Chapter 4), as when we make assumptions about other people's messages based on our own culture instead of theirs. We discuss noise further in the next section.)

The communication process is shown below. *(See Figure 15.1.)*

FIGURE 15.1

The communication process. "Noise" is not just noise or loud background sounds but any disturbance that interferes with transmission—static, fadeout, distracting facial expressions, uncomfortable meeting site, competing voices, and so on.

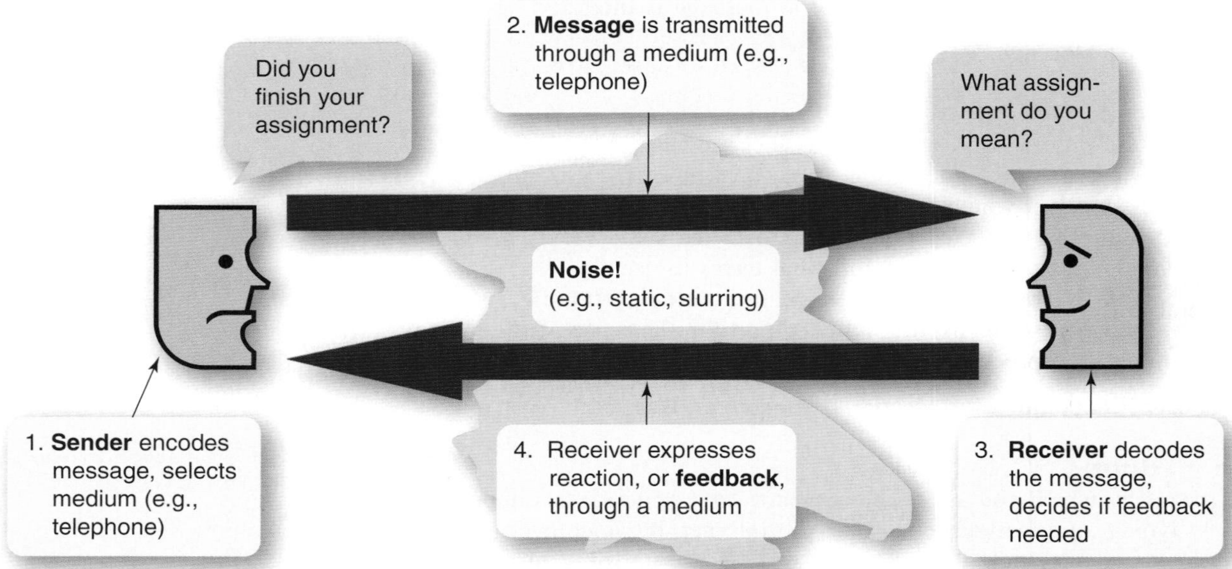
Did you finish your assignment?
2. **Message** is transmitted through a medium (e.g., telephone)
What assignment do you mean?
Noise! (e.g., static, slurring)
1. **Sender** encodes message, selects medium (e.g., telephone)
4. Receiver expresses reaction, or **feedback**, through a medium
3. **Receiver** decodes the message, decides if feedback needed

Selecting the Right Medium for Effective Communication

There are all kinds of communications tools available to managers, ranging from one-to-one face-to-face conversation all the way to use of the mass media. However, managers need to know how to use the right tool for the right condition—when to use e-mail, when to meet face to face, for example. Should you praise an employee by voicing a compliment, sending an e-mail, posting an announcement near the office coffee machine—or all three? How about when carrying out a reprimand?

Is a Medium Rich or Lean in Information?

As a manager, you will have many media to choose from: conversations, meetings, speeches, the telephone, e-mail, memos, letters, bulletin boards, PowerPoint presentations, videoconferencing, printed publications, videos, and so on. Beyond these are the sophisticated communications possibilities of the mass media: public relations, advertising, news reports via print, radio-TV, the Internet.

Media richness **indicates how well a particular medium conveys information and promotes learning.** That is, the "richer" a medium is, the better it is at conveying information. The term *media richness* was proposed by respected organizational theorists Richard Daft and Robert Lengel as part of their contingency model for media selection.[7]

Ranging from high media richness to low media richness, types of media may be positioned along a continuum as follows:

High media richness (Best for nonroutine, ambiguous situations)				**Low media richness** (Best for routine, clear situations)
Face-to-face presence	Video-conferencing	Telephone	Personal written media (e-mail, memos, letters)	Impersonal written media (newsletters, fliers, general reports)

Face-to-face communication, also the most personal form of communication, is the richest. It allows the receiver of the message to observe multiple cues, such as body language and tone of voice. It allows the sender to get immediate feedback, to see how well the receiver comprehended the message. At the other end of the media richness scale, impersonal written media is just the reverse—only one cue and no feedback—making it low in richness.

Matching the Appropriate Medium to the Appropriate Situation

In general, follow these guidelines:

- **Rich medium—best for nonroutine situations and to avoid oversimplification:** A *rich* medium is more effective with nonroutine situations.

  Examples: In what way would you like to learn the facts from your boss of a nonroutine situation such as a major company reorganization, which might affect your job? Via a memo tacked on the bulletin board (a lean medium)? Or via face-to-face meeting or phone call (rich medium)?

  The danger of using a rich medium for routine matters (such as monthly sales reports) is that it results in information *overloading*—more information than necessary.

- **Lean medium—best for routine situations and to avoid overloading:** A *lean* medium is more effective with routine situations.

  Examples: In what manner would you as a sales manager like to get routine monthly sales reports from your 50 sales reps? Via time-consuming phone calls (somewhat rich medium)? Or via written memos or e-mails (somewhat lean medium)? The danger of using a lean medium for nonroutine manners (such as a company reorganization) is that it results in information *oversimplification*—it doesn't provide enough of the information the receiver needs and wants. ◆

Improve or else. How would you like to be reprimanded by your boss? By an e-mail message? Harshly in person? Gently in person?

major question

What are the important barriers I need to be aware of, so I can improve my communication skills?

The Big Picture

We describe three barriers to communication. Physical barriers include sound, time, and space. Semantic barriers include unclear use of words and jargon. Personal barriers include variations in communication skills, trustworthiness and credibility, stereotypes and prejudices, and faulty listening skills.

Stand up and give a speech to a group of coworkers? Connecticut businessman Robert Suhoza would prefer to be trampled by elephants, says a news story. "Make small talk at a cocktail party?" it goes on. "Just go ahead and shoot him. Introduce himself to a room full of strangers? Maybe he'll just come back some other time. . . . Even answering the phone seemed at times an insurmountable task: He knew he should pick up the receiver, but he was paralyzed by not knowing who was on the other end, or what the caller wanted."[8]

Suhoza is 53 years old, but all his life he has suffered from social phobia or social anxiety disorder. In this he has plenty of company: One in every eight Americans apparently meet the diagnostic criteria for social anxiety disorder at some point in their lives, making it the third most common psychiatric condition. More women suffer from it than men, although men are more likely to seek treatment.[9]

Social anxiety disorder is an example (though an extreme one) of a communication *barrier*—a barrier being anything interfering with accurate communication between two people. Some barriers may be thought of as happening within the communication process itself, as the table opposite shows. *(See Table 15.1.)* It's more practical, however, to think of barriers as being of three types: (1) *physical barriers,* (2) *semantic barriers,* and (3) *personal barriers.*

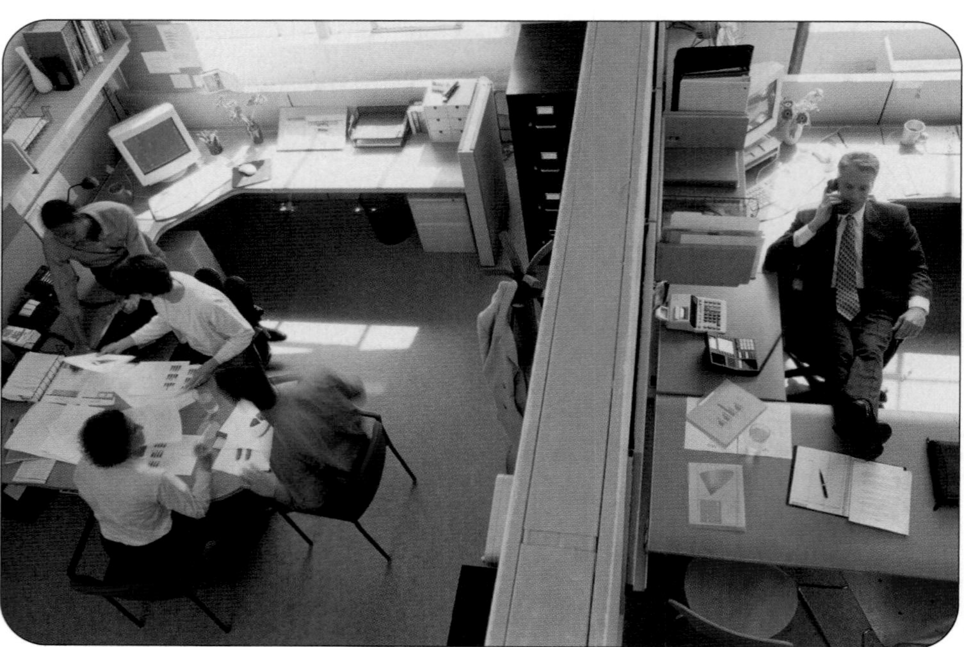

Without walls. Supposedly businesses that have open floor plans with cubicles instead of private offices function better because people can more easily talk across the shoulder-high partitions. But do you think the absence of floor-to-ceiling physical barriers might, in fact, lead to other kinds of barriers—such as others' talking making it hard to hear on the phone?

TABLE 15.1

Some barriers that happen within the communication process. All it takes is one blocked step in the communication process described in the text for communication to fail. Consider the following.

- **Sender barrier—no message gets sent:** Have you ever had an idea but were afraid to voice it because (like Robert Suhoza) you feared criticism? Then obviously no message got sent.

  But the barrier need not be for psychological reasons. Suppose as a new manager you simply didn't realize (because you weren't told) that supervising your subordinates' expense accounts was part of your responsibility. In that case, it may be understandable why you never call them to task about fudging their expense reports—why, in other words, no message got sent.
- **Encoding barrier—the message is not expressed correctly:** No doubt you've sometimes had difficulty trying to think of the correct word to express how you feel about something. If English is not your first language, perhaps, then you may have difficulty expressing to a supervisor, coworker, or subordinate what it is you mean to say.
- **Medium barrier—the communication channel is blocked:** You never get through to someone because his or her phone always has a busy signal. The computer network is down and the e-mail message you sent doesn't go through. These are instances of the communication medium being blocked.
- **Decoding barrier—the recipient doesn't understand the message:** Your boss tells you to "lighten up" or "buckle down," but because English is not your first language, you don't understand what the messages mean. Or perhaps you're afraid to show your ignorance when someone is throwing computer terms at you and says that your computer connection has "a bandwidth problem."
- **Receiver barrier—no message gets received:** Because you were talking to a coworker, you weren't listening when your supervisor announced today's work assignments, and so you have to ask him or her to repeat the announcement.
- **Feedback barrier—the recipient doesn't respond enough:** No doubt you've had the experience of giving someone street directions, but since they only nod their heads and don't repeat the directions back to you, you don't really know whether you were understood. The same thing can happen in many workplace circumstances.

1 Physical Barriers: Sound, Time, Space, & So On

Try shouting at someone on the far side of a construction site—at a distance of several yards over the roar of earth-moving machinery—and you know what physical barriers are. Other such barriers are time-zone differences, telephone-line static, and crashed computers. Office walls can be physical barriers, too, which is one reason for the trend toward open floor plans with cubicles instead of offices in many workplace settings.

2 Semantic Barriers: When Words Matter

When a supervisor tells you, "We need to get this done right away," what does it mean? Does "We" mean just you? You and your coworkers? Or you, your coworkers, and the boss? Does "right away" mean today, tomorrow, or next week? These are examples of semantic barriers. ***Semantics*** **is the study of the meaning of words.**

practical action

Minding Your Manners: Workplace Etiquette Can Be Crucial to Your Career

Even when you're not talking, you're often communicating—nonverbally (as we discuss elsewhere in this chapter). Manners are a big part of this.

Consider: While at lunch with your business clients, do you eat your soup by swiping the spoon from 12 o'clock to 6 o'clock in the bowl? (It should be the reverse.) Do you order a glass of wine with your meal? (Best not to drink alcohol on someone else's clock.) Do you squeeze lemon into your ice tea with a client across the table? (Best not—you might squirt him or her in the eye.) Do you scratch your back with your fork?

We are talking about a form of communication known as *etiquette* or *manners.* Despite the informality (including not just dress-down Fridays but dress-down everydays) of many offices, managers need to learn business etiquette—manners, politeness, appropriate behavior—if they are to achieve career success. Etiquette is more than table manners; it is the expression of being considerate. If you have to take clients out to dinner a couple times a week, you'll be glad if you know which fork to use. MBA candidates at Daniels College of Business at the University of Denver are required to attend an etiquette dinner, and the Massachusetts Institute of Technology also runs a not-for-credit charm school. These and similar courses provide lessons in dining etiquette, pager protocol, cellphone politeness, and the like. "In climbing the slippery ladder of success," says the founder of an etiquette training firm, "people have to recognize that they will never get promoted if their bosses and customers don't see them as looking and acting the part."

Some matters to be aware of:[10]

- **Handshakes:** The proper manner is to clasp firmly at an angle, then give two or three pumps.
- **Introductions:** When your boss is meeting your client, you should start with the person you want to honor—the client. ("Mr. Smith, I'd like you to meet my boss, Janet Jones. Jan, this is Horatio Smith, vice-president of Associated Success Inc.") Also, you should give some information about each person in order to get a conversation started. ("Jan is head of our Far West Division, and she just got back from a rock-climbing vacation.")
- **Thank-you notes:** When someone prepares an all-day or all-week program in which you've participated, send him or her a thank-you note. When the boss entertains you on her boat, send her a thank-you note. When a client gives you a plant tour, send him a note. And ALWAYS send a thank-you note after a job interview.
- **Dining tips and table manners:** Don't order the most expensive item. Don't start eating before your host. Avoid ordering food you think you might have difficulty handling properly because of splattering (such as soup or pasta). Know what to do with your bread. (Take the bread or roll, hold it over your plate—it's the plate on the left—break off a piece of it, and then put butter on it. If you drop a roll on the floor, don't pick it up; point it out to the waiter.) Don't kick your shoes off under the table. Turn off your cellphone so it won't beep. When you leave the table and plan to return, leave your napkin on your chair; when you're leaving for good, leave it on the table. In the U.S., you should keep your elbows off the table, and it's okay to keep your hands beneath it. In European countries, however, the reverse is considered polite.

Such a simple act. Handshakes are an everyday occurrence, but the clasp should be neither too strong nor too weak. After all, first impressions are important.

In addition, we may encounter semantic difficulties when dealing with other cultures (as we discussed in Chapter 4). When talking on the phone with Indians working in call centers in India, for example, we may find their pronunciation unusual. Perhaps that is because, according to one Indian speech-voice consultant, whereas "Americans think in English, we think in our mother tongue and translate it while speaking."[11] As our society becomes more technically oriented, semantic meaning becomes a problem because jargon develops. ***Jargon*** **is terminology specific to a particular profession or group.** (Example: "The HR VP wants the RFP to go out ASAP." Translation: "The Vice President of Human Resources wants the Request For Proposal to go out as soon as possible.") As a manager in a specialized field, you need to remember that what are ordinary terms for you may be mysteries to outsiders.[12]

3 Personal Barriers: Individual Attributes That Hinder Communication

"Is it them or is it me?"

How often have you wondered, when someone has shown a surprising response to something you said, how the miscommunication happened? Let's examine nine personal barriers that contribute to miscommunication.[13]

Variable Skills in Communicating Effectively

As we all know, some people are simply better communicators than others. They have the speaking skills, the vocabulary, the facial expressions, the eye contact, the dramatic ability, the "gift of gab" to express themselves in a superior way. Conversely, other people don't have this quality. But better communication skills can be learned.

Variations in How Information Is Processed & Interpreted

Are you from a working-class or privileged background? Are you from a particular ethnic group? Are you better at math or at language? Are you from a chaotic household filled with alcoholism and fighting, which distracts you at work?

Because people use different frames of reference and experiences to interpret the world around them, they are selective about what things have meaning to them and what don't. All told, these differences affect what we say and what we think we hear.

Variations in Trustworthiness & Credibility

Without trust between you and the other person, communication is apt to be flawed. Instead of communicating, both of you will be concentrating on defensive tactics, not the meaning of the message being exchanged.[14] How will subordinates react to you as a manager if your predecessors in your job lied to them? They may give you the benefit of a doubt, but they may be waiting for the first opportunity to be confirmed in the belief that you will break their trust.

Oversized Egos

Our egos—our pride, our self-esteem, even arrogance—are a fifth barrier. Egos can cause political battles, turf wars, and the passionate pursuit of power, credit, and resources. Egos influence how we treat each other as well as how receptive we are to being influenced by others. Ever had someone take credit for an idea that was yours? Then you know how powerful ego feelings can be.

Faulty Listening Skills

When you go to a party, do people ever ask questions of you and about who you are and what you're doing? Or are they too ready to talk about themselves? And do they seem to be waiting for you to finish talking so that they can then resume saying what they want to say? (But here's a test: Do you actually *listen* when they're talking?)

Tendency to Judge Others' Messages

Suppose another student in this class sees you reading this text and says, "I like the book we're reading." You might say, "I agree." Or you might say, "I disagree—it's boring." The point is that we all have a natural tendency, according to psychologist Carl Rogers, to judge others' statements from our own point of view (especially if we have strong feelings about the issue).[15]

Inability to Listen with Understanding

To really listen with understanding, you have to imagine yourself in the other person's shoes. Or, as Rogers and his coauthor put it, you have to "see the expressed idea and attitude from the other person's point of view, to sense how it feels to him, to achieve his frame of reference in regard to the thing he is talking about."[16] When you listen with understanding, it makes you feel less defensive (even if the message is criticism) and improves your accuracy in perceiving the message.

Stereotypes & Prejudices

A *stereotype* consists of oversimplified beliefs about a certain group of people. There are, for instance, common stereotypes about old people, young people, males, and females. Wouldn't you hate to be categorized according to just a couple of exaggerated attributes—by your age and gender, for example? ("Young men are reckless." "Old women are scolds." Yes, *some* young men and *some* old women are this way, but it's unrealistic and unfair to tar every individual in these groups with the same brush.)

We consider matters of gender communication further on the next page.

Nonverbal Communication

Do your gestures and facial expressions contradict your words? This is the sort of nonverbal communication that you may not even be aware of. We discuss this subject in more detail next.

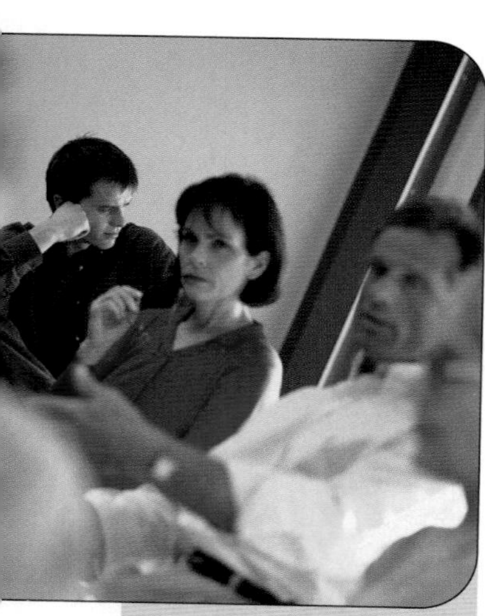

Body language. Who's paying attention and who isn't? If you were a manager speaking at this meeting and you noticed the man at the end of the row looking out the window as you talked, would you continue to speak to those who seem attentive? Or would you try to adjust your remarks—and your own body language—to try to reach the man who is tuning you out?

Nonverbal Communication

You're listening to a sales pitch from the representative of a printing firm who would like to sell your organization a lot of printing business. What do you find yourself responding to? The words? Or the twitching fingers, lack of eye contact, and flat tone of voice?

As we stated in Chapter 4, ***nonverbal communication* consists of messages sent outside the written or spoken word.** Researchers estimate that 90% of every conversation is nonverbal.[17] Given the prevalence of nonverbal communication and its impact on organizational behavior (such as hiring decisions, perceptions of others, and getting one's ideas accepted by others), it is important that you become familiar with the various sources of nonverbal communication.[18] Let us consider some ways in which your nonverbal communication is expressed by your body language, setting, and use of time.[19]

Body Language—Facial Expression, Tone of Voice, Touch, and So On

Body language includes posture, facial expressions, gestures, vocal quality, and touch. What does it mean, for instance, when your listeners cross their arms? Frown? Scratch their heads? Yawn excessively? Speak too quickly? In the culture of the United States, at least, it means that you as the speaker should realize your message is not being received well. *(See Table 15.2.)*

Do	Don't
Maintain eye contact	Look away from the speaker
Lean toward the speaker	Turn away from the speaker
Speak at a moderate rate	Speak too quickly or slowly
Speak in a quiet, reassuring tone	Speak in an unpleasant tone
Smile and show animation	Yawn excessively
Occasionally nod head in agreement	Close your eyes

TABLE 15.2

Toward better nonverbal communication skills. You can practice these skills by watching TV with the sound off and interpreting people's emotions and interactions. (*Source:* Adapted from W. D. St. John, "You Are What You Communicate," *Personnel Journal,* October 1985, p. 43.)

Setting—Arrangement of the Meeting Space

How do you feel when you visit someone who sits behind a big desk and is backlit by a window so her face is obscured? What does it say when someone comes out from behind his desk and invites you to sit with him on his office couch? The location of an office (such as corner office with window versus interior office with no window), its size, and the choice of furniture often express the accessibility of the person in it.

Time—Using Appropriately to Show Interest

When your boss keeps you waiting 45 minutes for an appointment with him, how do you feel? When she simply grunts or makes one-syllable responses to your comments, what does this say about her interest in your concerns? As a manager yourself, you should always give the people who work for you adequate time. You should also talk with them frequently during the meeting so they will understand your interest.

Gender-Related Communication Differences

Men are eight times as likely as women to bargain over starting pay. Indeed, says one account, "Women often are less adroit at winning better salaries, assignments, and jobs—either because they don't ask or because they cave in when they do."[20] In other words, women need to hone their negotiation skills, or else they will fall behind.

A long day, or . . . ? People's behavior doesn't always reflect what's going on around them. It may reflect what's going on *inside* of them. Perhaps this man was up late the night before with a sick child or has been burning the midnight oil for several days to make a project deadline. Even so, when speaking, you need to watch your audience for their reactions. Judging by the looks of the other three in this photo, do you think the speaker is boring?

major question

How can I use the different channels and patterns of communication to my advantage?

The Big Picture

Formal communication channels follow the chain of command, which is of three types—vertical, horizontal, and external. Informal communication channels develop outside the organization's formal structure. One type is gossip and rumor. Another is management by wandering around, in which a manager talks to people across all lines of authority.

If you've ever had a low-level job in nearly any kind of organization, you know that there is generally a hierarchy of management between you and the organization's president, director, or CEO. If you had a suggestion that you wanted him or her to hear, you doubtless had to go up through management channels. That's formal communication.

However, you may have run into that top manager in the elevator. Or in the restroom. Or in a line at the bank. You could have voiced your suggestion casually then. That's informal communication.

Each type of communication requires different kinds of skills. Let's consider how they work.

Formal Communication Channels: Up, Down, Sideways, & Outward

***Formal communication channels* follow the chain of command and are recognized as official.** The organization chart we described in Chapter 8 (page 246) indicates how official communications—memos, letters, reports, announcements—are supposed to be routed.

Formal communication is of three types: (1) *vertical*—meaning upward and downward, (2) *horizontal*—meaning laterally (sideways), and (3) *external*—meaning outside the organization.

How do you communicate with a manager two or three levels above you in the organization's hierarchy? You can send a memo through channels. Or you can watch for when that manager goes to the water cooler or the coffee pot.

1 Vertical Communication: Up & Down the Chain of Command

Vertical communication is the flow of messages up and down the hierarchy within the organization: bosses communicating with subordinates, subordinates communicating with bosses. As you might expect, the more management levels through which a message passes, the more it is prone to distortion.

- **Downward communication—from top to bottom:** ***Downward communication*** **flows from a higher level to a lower level (or levels).** Most downward communication involves one of the following kinds of information:[25]

  (1) Instructions related to particular job tasks. Example (supervisor to subordinate): "The store will close Monday for inventory. All employees are expected to participate."

  (2) Explanations about the relationship between two or more tasks. Example: "While taking inventory, employees need to see what things are missing. Most of that might be attributable to shoplifting."

  (3) Explanations of the organization's procedures and practices. Example: "Start counting things on the high shelves and work your way down."

  (4) A manager's feedback about a subordinate's performance: Example: "It's best not to try to count too fast."

  (5) Attempts to encourage a sense of mission and dedication to the organization's goals. Example: "By keeping tabs on our inventory, we can keep our prices down and maintain our reputation of giving good value."

  In small organizations, top-down communication may be delivered face to face. In larger organizations, it's delivered via meetings, e-mail, official memos, and company publications.

- **Upward communication—from bottom to top:** ***Upward communication*** **flows from lower levels to higher level (or levels).** Often this type of communication is from a subordinate to his or her immediate manager, who in turn will relay it up to the next level, if necessary. Most upward communication involves the following kinds of information:[26]

  (1) Reports of progress on current projects. Example: "We shut down the store yesterday to take inventory."

  (2) Reports of unsolved problems requiring help from people higher up. Example: "We can't make our merchandise count jibe with the stock reports."

  (3) New developments affecting the work unit. Example: "Getting help from the other stores really speeded things up this year."

  (4) Suggestions for improvements. Example: "The stores should loan each other staff every time they take inventory."

  (5) Reports on employee attitudes and efficiency. Example: "The staff likes it when they go to another store and sometimes they pick up some new ways of doing things."

  Effective upward communication depends on an atmosphere of trust. No subordinate is going to want to be the bearer of bad news to a manager who is always negative and bad-tempered.

2 Horizontal Communication: Within & Between Work Units

Horizontal communication **flows within and between work units; its main purpose is coordination.** As a manager, you will spend perhaps as much as a third of your time in this form of communication—consulting with colleagues and coworkers at the same level as you within the organization. In this kind of sideways communication, you will be sharing information, coordinating tasks, solving problems, resolving conflicts, and getting the support of your peers. Horizontal communication is encouraged through the use of committees, task forces, and matrix structures.

Horizontal communication can be impeded in three ways: (1) by specialization that makes people focus just on their jobs alone; (2) by rivalry between workers or work units, which prevents sharing of information; and (3) by lack of encouragement from management.[27]

3 External Communication: Outside the Organization

External communication **flows between people inside and outside the organization.** These are other stakeholders: customers, suppliers, shareholders or other owners, and so on. Companies have given this kind of communication heightened importance, especially with customers or clients, who are the lifeblood of any company.

Informal Communication Channels

Informal communication channels **develop outside the formal structure and do not follow the chain of command**—they skip management levels and cut across lines of authority.

There are two aspects of informal channels that are important to know about: (1) the *grapevine* and (2) *management by wandering around.*

1 The Grapevine: Informal Communication through Gossip & Rumor

The *grapevine* is the unofficial communication system of the informal organization, a network of gossip and rumor of what is called "employee language." One survey found that employees used the grapevine (a term from the Civil War practice of stringing battlefield telegraph lines between trees, resembling hanging grape vines) as their most frequent source of information.[28] Indeed, research shows, (1) the grapevine is faster than formal channels; (2) it is about 75% accurate; (3) people rely on it when they are insecure or faced with organizational changes; and (4) employees use the grapevine to acquire the majority of their on-the-job information.[29]

Two grapevine patterns predominate. In the *gossip chain,* one person seeks out and communicates with several others. In the *cluster pattern,* one person tells the message to three (or more) other people, and then each of them tells three others.[30]

Some gossips are beneficial, consistently passing along important grapevine information to others. Often they are friendly, outgoing people whose jobs allow them to cross departmental lines. Some secretaries, for example, are able to com-

Did you hear? If you were working in a company whose sales have declined recently, would you put more credence in an official from-top-management memo or in some sort of unofficial "employee language" report—that is, gossip and rumor? Why do you think it is that the tidbit you hear from a coworker in passing on the stairs seems so much more believable than the announcement from the CEO at a companywide employee meeting?

municate with all kinds of people up and down the hierarchy, from janitor to top executive.[31] Others, called *moles,* use the grapevine to obtain information, often negative, to enhance their power and status. They secretly report their perceptions about other employees' difficulties or failures to managers in power.[32] Moles can sow conflict, destroy teamwork, and impair productivity.

Since gossip and rumor can't be extinguished, the practical course for managers is to try to *monitor* and *influence* the grapevine by selectively sending information along it. They can talk with individuals important in the gossip chain to make sure information gets spread to people who tend to ignore the formal communications system. They can openly share relevant news, as in providing advance notice of organizational changes.

2 Management by Wandering Around: Informal Communication through Spontaneous Conversations

Can executives manage by staying in their offices? No doubt many do. But many managers—even top executives of, for example, soft-drink maker PepsiCo, oil company ARCO, and hotel chain Marriott—find that getting out from behind the desk helps them get a better feel for their operations.

This kind of informal communication is called ***management by wandering around (MBWA)*** **—a manager literally wanders around his or her organization and talks with people across all lines of authority.**[33] Management by wandering around helps to reduce the problems of distortion that inevitably occur with formal communication flowing up a hierarchy. As telecommunications head Brian Thompson of LCI International puts it, "The problem with being a CEO is that everybody between you and them wants to tell you what you want to hear. So it's really being visible to people, walking around . . ."[34]

MBWA allows managers to listen to employees and learn about their problems. It also enables managers to express to employees what values and goals are important to them. Needless to say, however, if the wandering-around executive is looking for problems for the purpose of disciplining people, the technique won't work.

At Detroit Diesel, which manufactures truck diesel engines, the general manager tours the plant and talks to various employees, listening to them express their concerns. One result is that the company increased its market share significantly as employees were able to voice their suggestions for improvement in quality.[35] ◆

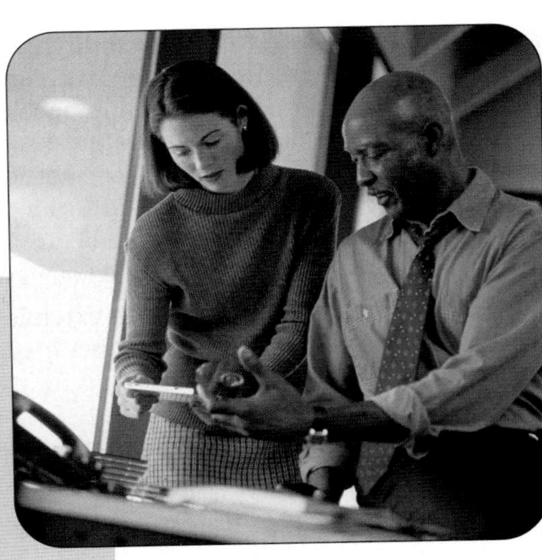

MBWA. Management by wandering around is sort of the reverse of employees exchanging informal views with top managers at the water cooler. That is, by wandering around the organization, top managers can stop and talk to nearly anyone—and thus perhaps learn things that might be screened out by the formal up-the-organization reporting process. If top managers can do MBWA, do you think mid-level managers can as well?

major question

How do contemporary managers use information technology to communicate more effectively?

The Big Picture

We discuss five communications tools of information technology: (1) the Internet and its associated intranets and extranets, (2) e-mail, (3) videoconferencing, (4) collaborative computing, and (5) telecommuting. We also discuss how to deal with information overload.

"I'm dangerous," jokes Gregory Summe between runs at a Utah ski resort, as he pulls out his tiny cellphone and his electronic organizer with its 12,000-name contact list. With this kind of portable information technology, Summe, 42, CEO of EG&G Inc., is able to work anywhere and contact anyone. "There's an expectation for CEOs to be much more in touch with customers, employees, and investors than in the past," he says. "A big part of the reason may be [portable information] technology."[36]

Communications Tools of Information Technology: Offspring of the Internet

Here we explore some of the more important aspects of information technology: (1) the Internet along with intranets and extranets, (2) e-mail, (3) videoconferencing, (4) collaborative computing, and (5) telecommuting.

1 The Internet, Intranets, & Extranets

The Internet, or more simply "the Net," is more than a computer network. As we said in Chapter 1, it is a network of computer networks. The Internet is a global network of independently operating but interconnected computers, linking hundreds of thousands of smaller networks around the world. The Internet connects everything from personal computers to supercomputers in organizations of all kinds.

Two private uses of the Internet are as intranets and extranets.

- **Intranets: An *intranet* is nothing more than an organization's private Internet.** Intranets also have *firewalls* that block outside Internet users from accessing internal information. This is done to protect the privacy and confidentiality of company documents. The top four uses for intranets are information sharing, information publishing, e-mail, and document management.[37] The country with the most numbers of intranets in business in 2002 is reported to be Canada, with 58% of businesses having an intranet, followed by the United Kingdom at 52%, the U.S. at 48%, and Australia at 44% (although these figures may be high).[38]
- **Extranets: An *extranet* is an extended intranet in that it connects internal employees with selected customers, suppliers, and other strategic partners.** Ford Motor Co., for instance, has an extranet that connects its dealers worldwide. Ford's extranet was set up to help support the sales and servicing of cars and to enhance customer satisfaction. Canada also leads with 32% of extranet penetration in businesses in 2002.

No rigorous studies have demonstrated productivity increases from using the Internet, intranets, or extranets. However, research reveals some other organizational benefits. For example, Cisco Systems used the Internet to recruit potential employees, hiring 66% of its people and receiving 81% of its resumes from the Net.[39]

General Mills used to send researchers across country to conduct focus groups or poll consumers on prospective products, but now it conducts 60% of its consumer research online, reducing its costs by half.[40]

2 E-mail

E-mail, short for *electronic mail,* uses the Internet to send computer-generated text and documents between people. In 2002, in the principal industrialized countries, over 90% of firms had Internet access and therefore e-mail access. Irish businesses were most likely to be connected to the Internet (99%), although U.S. businesses tended to have a higher percentage of portable communications technologies (such as cellphones and PDAs) and other, more advanced connectivity.[41]

E-mail has become a major communications medium because of four key benefits: (1) reduced cost of distributing information, (2) increased teamwork, (3) reduced paper costs, and (4) increased flexibility. On the other hand, it has three drawbacks: It can lead to (1) wasted time, as in having to deal with ***spam,*** **or unsolicited jokes and junk mail;** (2) information overload; and (3) neglect of other media. *(See Table 15.4.)* Indeed, the first defect is particularly critical: One study found that companies were expected to receive about 7,500 spam messages per employee in 2004—up from 3,500 in 2003—resulting in an estimated direct cost of $1,934 per employee and an average of 3.1% loss in productivity.[42]

TABLE 15.4

E-mail: benefits, drawbacks, and tips for doing better [*Sources:* R. F. Federico and J. M. Bowley, "The Great E-Mail Debate," *HR Magazine,* January 1996, pp. 67–72; M. S. Thompson and M. S. Feldman, "Electronic Mail and Organizational Communication: Does Saying 'Hi' Really Matter? *Organizational Science,* November–December 1998, pp. 685–698; J. Yaukey, "E-Mail Out of Control for Many," *Reno Gazette-Journal,* May 7, 2001, p. 1E; D. Halpern, "Dr. Manners on E-Mail Dos and Don'ts," *Monitor of Psychology,* April 2004, p. 5; and B. K. Williams and S. C. Sawyer, *Using Information Technology,* 6th ed. (New York: McGraw-Hill Technology Education, 2005), pp. 60–62.]

Benefits

- *Reduced cost of distributing information.* One software developer found that its telephone bill dropped by more than half after its employees and dealers were told to use e-mail instead of the phone.
- *Increased teamwork.* Users can send messages to colleagues anywhere, whether in the office or in the world.
- *Reduced paper costs.* E-mail reduces the costs and time associated with print duplication and paper distribution.
- *Increased flexibility.* Employees with portable computers, PDAs, and cellphones can access their e-mail from anywhere.

Drawbacks

- *Wasted time.* E-mail can distract employees from critical job duties. Employees now average nearly an hour a day managing their e-mail.
- *Information overload.* E-mail users tend to get too much information—in some cases, only 10 of 120 daily inbox messages may be worthwhile.
- *Neglect of other media.* Increased use of e-mail can be found to be associated with decreased face-to-face interactions and decreased overall organizational communication, with lessened cohesion.

Tips for better e-mail handling

- *Treat all e-mail as confidential.* Pretend every message is a postcard that can be read by anyone. (Supervisors may legally read employee e-mail.)
- *Be careful with jokes and informality.* Nonverbal language and other subtleties are lost, so jokes may be taken as insults or criticism.
- *Avoid sloppiness, but avoid criticizing others' sloppiness.* Avoid spelling and grammatical errors, but don't criticize errors in others' messages.
- *When replying, quote only the relevant portion.* Edit long e-mail messages you've received down to the relevant paragraph and put your response immediately following.
- *Not every topic belongs on e-mail.* Complicated topics may be better discussed on the phone or in person to avoid misunderstandings.

3 Videoconferencing

Also known as *teleconferencing, videoconferencing* uses video and audio links along with computers to enable people located at different locations to see, hear, and talk with one another. This enables people from many locations to conduct a meeting without having to travel. Videoconferencing can thus significantly reduce an organization's travel expenses.

Many organizations set up special videoconferencing rooms or booths with specially equipped television cameras. More recent equipment enables people to attach small cameras and microphones to their desks or computer monitors. This enables employees to conduct long-distance meetings and training classes without leaving their office or cubicle.

4 Collaborative Computing

Collaborative computing entails using state-of-the-art computer software and hardware to help people work better together. Collaborative systems enable people to share information without the constraints of time and space. This is accomplished using computer networks to link people across a room or across the globe. Collaborative applications include messaging and e-mail systems, calendar management, videoconferencing, and electronic whiteboards.

Organizations that use full-fledged collaborative systems have the ability to create virtual teams (described in Chapter 13), which tend to use Internet or intranet systems, collaborative software, and videoconferencing to communicate with team members at any time.

5 Telecommuting

Telecommuting involves doing work that is generally performed in the office away from the office, using a variety of information technologies. Employees typically receive and send work from home via phone and fax or by using a modem to link a home computer to an office computer. Among the benefits are (1) reduction of capital costs, because employees work at home; (2) increased flexibility and autonomy for workers; (3) competitive edge in recruiting hard-to-get employees; (4) increased job satisfaction and lower turnover; (5) increased productivity; and (6) ability to tap nontraditional labor pools (such as prison inmates and homebound disabled people).[43]

Telecommuting is more common for jobs that involve computer work, writing, and phone or brain work that requires concentration and limited interruptions. There were an estimated 23.5 million workers telecommuting in the U.S. in 2003, and an additional 23.4 million self-employed people also telecommuted.[44]

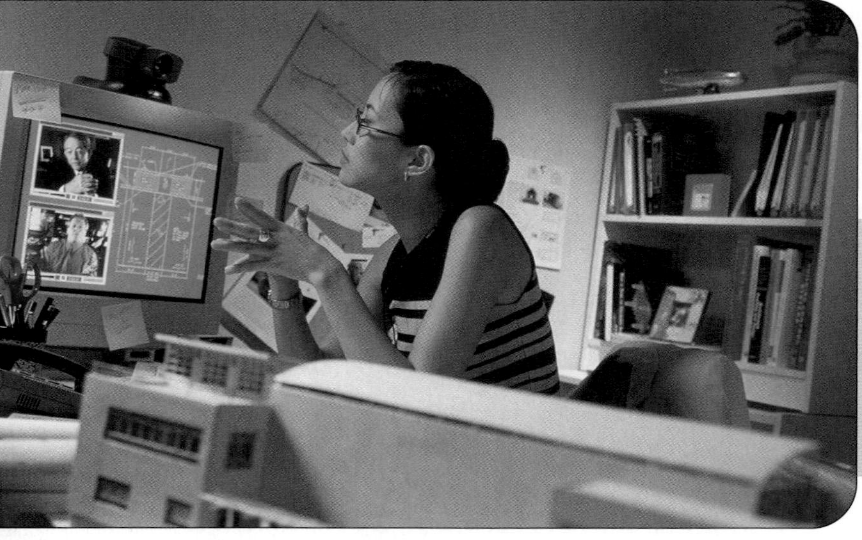

Videoconferencing. In this arrangement three people in different locations can computer-conference—view and interact with one another—while studying a document on screen. Videoconferencing offers considerable savings in time and money over the cost of travel. Do you think you would feel inhibited working with people in this way?

Although telecommuting represents an attempt to accommodate employee needs and desires, it requires adjustments and is not for everybody. People who enjoy the social camaraderie of the office setting, for instance, probably won't like it. Others lack the self-motivation needed to work at home.

Dealing with Information Overload

The primary benefit of the Internet and its variants is that they can enhance employees' ability to find, create, manage, and distribute information. How well they work, however, depends on how well employees know how to deal with the enormous repository of data that the Internet offers. Moreover, the Internet is not the only source of information. According to one study (probably not very reliable, however), the average U.S. employee in 1999 was found to receive 201 messages a day of all kinds.[45] Over half were phone calls and e-mail and voice-mail messages.

Clearly, then, dealing with information overload becomes a critical skill. ***Information overload*** **occurs when the amount of information received exceeds a person's ability to handle or process it.** Chapter 1 offered some suggestions for helping you deal with information overload. A greater information-management strategy, however, is to reduce your information load and increase your information-processing capacity. *(See Table 15.5.)* ◆

TABLE 15.5

Information management strategy. Reducing information load and increasing information-processing capacity (*Sources:* S. G. Thomas, "Online In-Boxes Aim to Simplify Our Harried Lives," *U.S. News & World Report,* March 6, 2000, p. 54; M. Irvine, "You've Got Too Much E-Mail," *San Francisco Chronicle,* July 20, 2000, p. B3; C. Hymowitz, "Flooded with E-Mail? Try Screening, Sorting, or Maybe Just Phoning," *The Wall Street Journal,* September 26, 2000, p. B1; C. Hymowitz, "Taking Time to Focus on the Big Picture Despite the Flood of Data," *The Wall Street Journal,* February 27, 2001, p. B1; R. Strauss, "You've Got Maelstrom," *New York Times,* July 5, 2001, pp. D1, D9; and C. Canabou, "A Message about Managing E-mail," *Fast Company,* August 2001, p. 38.)

Reducing your information load

- *Preview and ignore messages.* When going through your e-mail, quickly glance at the subject line and immediately delete anything that looks like spam or (if you can) messages from people you don't know. Do the same with voice mail or phone slips.
- *Filter messages.* Many e-mail programs have message filtering, so that an urgent message from the boss, for example, will go to the top of your e-mail queue. Spam-killer software is available to help eliminate junk mail. Some executives put all "cc" e-mails in a special file and rarely read them.
- *Organize your e-mail inbox.* Set up a folder for e-mails you want to keep. Don't use your e-mail inbox for general storage.

Increasing your information-processing capacity

- *Use discipline.* Check e-mail only three times a day. Handle every message only once. When an e-mail message arrives, deal with it immediately—read it and then either respond to it, delete it, or file it away in a folder.
- *Get a unified messaging site.* It's possible to get one unified messaging site to which all your e-mails, faxes, and voice mails are delivered. Voice mails arrive as audio files that you can listen to, while e-mails are read to you over the phone by a virtual (robot) assistant.
- *Use your company address for work-related e-mails only.* Have personal messages go to a separate account.

major question

How can I be a better listener, reader, writer, and speaker?

The Big Picture

We describe how you can be a more effective listener, as in learning to concentrate on the content of a message. We also describe how to be an effective reader. We offer four tips for becoming a more effective writer. Finally, we discuss how to be an effective speaker, through three steps.

The principal activities the typical manager does have to do with communication—listening, 40%; talking, 35%; reading, 16%; and writing, 9%.[46] Listening and speaking often take place in meetings (see the Practical Action box in Chapter 5, page 179, "How to Streamline Meetings"), although they are not the only occasions. Regardless of the environment, let's see how you can be more effective at these four essential communication skills.

Being an Effective Listener

Is listening something you're good at? Then you're the exception. Generally, people comprehend only about 35% of a typical verbal message, experts say.[47] Interestingly, the average speaker communicates 125 words per minute, while we can process 500 words per minute. Poor listeners use this information-processing gap to daydream. They think about other things, thus missing the important parts of what's being communicated.[48] Good listeners know how to use these gaps effectively, mentally summarizing the speaker's remarks, weighing the evidence, and listening between the lines.

How do you become the kind of manager who others say is a good listener? Following are some suggestions (you can practice them in your college lectures and seminars).[49]

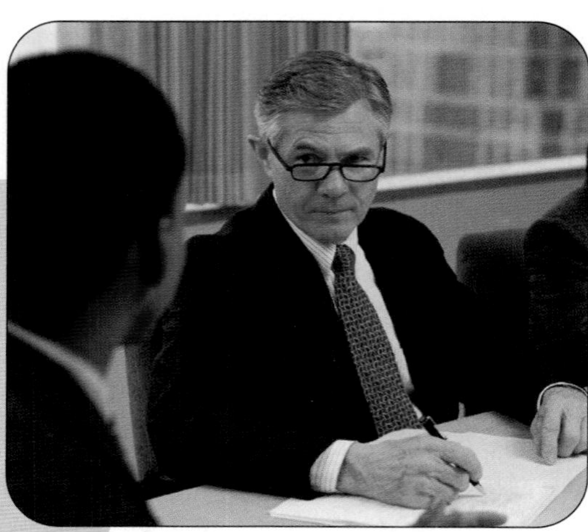

Understand me. What's the recipe for effective listening—for really finding out what someone has to say? Probably it is *listen, watch, write, think, question.* What do you do to fight flagging concentration if you're tired or bored? You suppress negative thoughts, ignore distractions about the speaker's style of delivery or body language, and encourage the speaker with eye contact, an interested expression, and an attentive posture. This will make you more involved and interested in the subject matter.

Concentrate on the Content of the Message

Don't think about what you're going to say until the other person has finished talking.

- **Judge content, not delivery:** Don't tune out someone because of his or her accent, clothing, mannerisms, personality, or speaking style.
- **Ask questions, summarize remarks:** Good listening is hard work. Ask questions to make sure you understand. Recap what the speaker said.
- **Listen for ideas:** Don't get diverted by the details; try to concentrate on the main ideas.
- **Resist distractions, show interest:** Don't get distracted by things other people are doing, paperwork on your desk, things happening outside the window, television or radio, and the like. Show the speaker you're listening, periodically restating in your own words what you've heard.
- **Give a fair hearing:** Don't shut out unfavorable information just because you hear a term—"Republican," "Democrat," "union," "big business," "affirmative action," "corporate welfare"—that suggests ideas you're not comfortable with. Try to correct for your biases.

practical action

Communication by Listening

Often the reason that people act subversively against their employers is that they can't or are afraid to communicate with their managers.

Resistance may take the form of "malicious compliance" (following supervisors' instructions to the letter while ignoring the real goal), withholding crucial data, or sabotaging projects that reflect directly on the manager.

One bookstore employee sabotaged his nonlistening, always-angry boss by going through the store and discreetly pocketing any pens, pencils, even crayons, then hiding them in a backroom cabinet. "My already preternaturally enraged boss," he reported later, "reached glorious heights of apoplexy."[50]

As we discuss in the text, effective communication begins with listening. There is a technique for doing this. "To begin with, listen to people as if you don't know the answer," suggests Meg Price, a Reno, Nev., human resource professional. "This means that you will ask more questions to try to understand the situation from the other person's perspective. When you think you've got it, make a statement to the speaker summarizing what you believe they have told you. Only when they agree that indeed you do 'get it' should you begin to offer potential solutions or answers."[51]

Of course, sometimes there are true disagreements, and no amount of listening on your part is going to change that fact. Here, according to David Stiebel, author of *When Talking Makes Things Worse! Resolving Problems When Communication Fails*, is how to identify the nature of a dispute:

- If you only listened to the other person, would she feel satisfied and stop opposing you?
- If you succeed in explaining yourself, would you really change the other person's mind?
- If the other person explained himself more, would you change your mind?

When true disagreements occur, one person ultimately must be willing to change so that negotiations can begin.[52]

Being an Effective Reader

Reading shares many of the same skills as listening. You need to concentrate on the content of the message, judge the content and not the delivery, and concentrate on the main ideas. But because managers usually have to do so much reading, you also need to learn to apply some other strategies.

Realize That Speed Reading Doesn't Work

Perhaps you've thought that somewhere along the line you could take a course on speed reading. By and large, however, speed reading isn't effective. Psychologists have found that speed reading or skimming may work well with easy or familiar reading material, but it can lead to problems with dense or unfamiliar material. For instance, in one study, when questioned about their reading of difficult material, average readers got half the questions right, while speed readers got only one in three.[53]

Learn to Streamline Reading

Management consultant and UCLA professor Kathryn Alesandrini offers a number of suggestions for streamlining your reading.[54]

- **Be savvy about periodicals and books:** Review your magazine and newspaper subscriptions and eliminate as many as possible. You can subscribe to just a few industry publications, scan and mark interesting material, later read what's marked, and pitch the rest. Read summaries and reviews that condense business books and articles.
- **Transfer your reading load:** With some material you can ask some of your employees to screen or scan it first, then post an action note on each item that needs additional reading by you. You can also ask your staff to read important books and summarize them in four or five pages.
- **Make internal memos and e-mail more efficient:** Ask others to tell you up front in their e-mails, memos, and reports what they want you to do. Instruct them to include a one-page executive summary of a long report. When you communicate with them, give them specific questions you want answered.

Do Top-Down Reading—SQ3R

"The key to better reading is to be a productive rather than a passive reader," writes Alesandrini. "You'll get more out of what you read if you literally produce meaningful connections between what you already know and what you're reading."[55] This leads to what she calls a "top-down" strategy for reading, a variant on the SQ3R (Survey, Question, Read, Recite, Review) method we discussed in the box at the end of Chapter 1, page 24.

The top-down system has five steps:

- **Rate reasons to read:** Rate your reasons for reading ("Why should I read this? Will reading it contribute to my goals?").
- **Question and predict answers:** Formulate specific questions you want the reading to answer. This will give you reasons for reading—to get answers to your questions.
- **Survey the big picture:** Survey the material to be read so you can get a sense of the whole. Take a few minutes to get an overview so that you'll be better able to read with purpose.
- **Skim for main ideas:** Skimming the material is similar to surveying, except it's on a smaller scale. You look for the essence of each subsection or paragraph.

- **Summarize:** Summarize as you skim. Verbally restate or write notes of the main points, using your own words. Visualize or sketch the main points. Answer your initial questions as you skim the material.

Being an Effective Writer

Writing is an essential management skill, all the more so because e-mail has replaced the telephone in so much of business communication. In addition, downsizing has eliminated the administrative assistants who used to edit and correct business correspondence, so even upper-level executives often write their own letters and e-mail now.[56] A lot of students, however, don't get enough practice in writing, which puts them at a career disadvantage. Taking a business writing class can be a real advantage. (Indeed, as a manager, you may have to identify employees who need writing training.)

Following are some tips for writing more effectively. These apply particularly to memos and reports but are also applicable to e-mail messages.

Don't Show Your Ignorance

E-mail correspondence has made people more relaxed about spelling and grammar rules. While this is fine among friends, as a manager you'll need to create a more favorable impression in your writing. Besides using the spelling checkers and grammar checkers built in to most word processing programs, you should reread, indeed proofread, your writing before sending it on.

Understand Your Strategy Before You Write

Following are three strategies for laying out your ideas in writing.

- **Most important to least important:** This is a good strategy when the action you want your reader to take is logical and not highly political.
- **Least controversial to most controversial:** This builds support gradually and is best used when the decision is controversial or your reader is attached to a particular solution other than the one you're proposing.
- **Negative to positive:** This strategy establishes a common ground with your reader and puts the positive argument last, which makes it stronger.[57]

Start with Your Purpose

Often people organize their messages backward, putting their real purpose last, points out Alesandrini. You should *start* your writing by telling your purpose and what you expect of the reader.

Write Simply, Concisely, & Directly

Keep your words simple and use short words, sentences, and phrases. Be direct instead of vague, and use the active voice rather than the passive. (Directness, active voice: "Please call a meeting for Wednesday." Vagueness, passive voice: "It is suggested that a meeting be called for Wednesday.")

Telegraph Your Writing with a Powerful Layout

Make your writing as easy to read as possible, using the tools of highlighting and white space.

- **Highlighting:** Highlighting consists of using **boldface** and *italics* to highlight key concepts and introduce new concepts, and bullets—small circles or squares like the ones in the list you're reading—to emphasize list items. (Don't overuse any of these devices, or they'll lose their effect. And particularly don't use ALL CAPITAL LETTERS for emphasis, except rarely.)

- **White space:** White space, which consists of wide margins and a break between paragraphs, produces a page that is clean and attractive.[58]

Being an Effective Speaker

Speaking or talking covers a range of activities, from one-on-one conversations, to participating in meetings, to giving formal presentations. In terms of personal oral communication, most of the best advice comes under the heading of listening, since effective listening will dictate the appropriate talking you need to do.

However, the ability to talk to a room full of people—to make an oral presentation—is one of the greatest skills you can have. A study conducted by AT&T and Stanford University found that the top predictor of success and professional upward mobility is how much you enjoy public speaking and how effective you are at it.[59]

The biggest problem most people have with public speaking is controlling their nerves. Author and lecturer Gael Lindenfield suggests that you can prepare your nerves by practicing your speech until it's near perfect, visualizing yourself performing with brilliance, getting reassurance from a friend, and getting to the speaking site early and releasing physical tension by doing deep breathing. (And staying away from alcohol and caffeine pick-me-ups before your speech.)[60] As for the content of the speech, some brief and valuable advice is offered by speechwriter Phil Theibert, who says a speech comprises just three simple rules: (1) Tell them what you're going to say. (2) Say it. (3) Tell them what you said.[61]

1 Tell Them What You're Going to Say

The introduction should take 5%–15% of your speaking time, and it should prepare the audience for the rest of the speech. Avoid jokes and such phrases as "I'm honored to be with you here today . . ." Because everything in your speech should be relevant, try to go right to the point. For example:

"Good afternoon. The subject of identity theft may seem far removed from the concerns of most employees. But I intend to describe how our supposedly private credit, health, employment, and other records are vulnerable to theft by so-called identity thieves and how you can protect yourself."

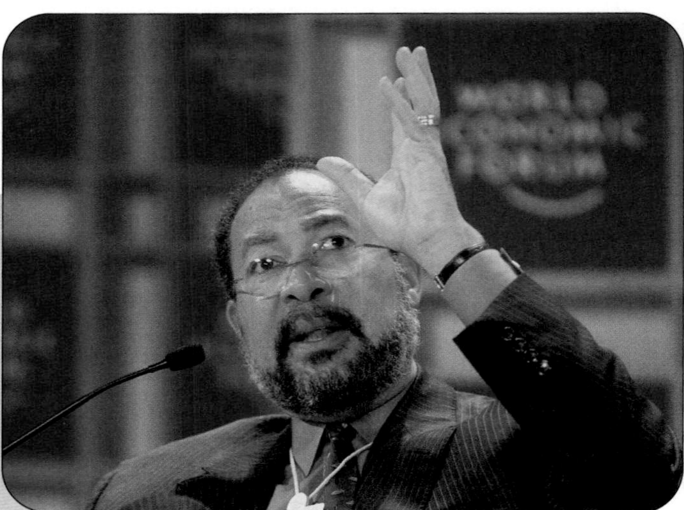

AOL Time Warner's CEO Richard Parsons. When Internet company AOL merged with media goliath Time Warner in 2000, the combination was supposed to be the world's most valuable company, with an enormous market value of $290 billion. Instead, because the merger was accomplished with AOL's overinflated stock during the period known as the "Internet bubble," the empire came crashing down, and in January 2002 the company was worth only $135 billion. Parsons became the new CEO a few months later, with the task of cleaning up the messes left behind by others. How persuasive a speaker is he going to have to be to fix things? He is said to be better than his predecessors at delivering facts rather than exaggerations, but will that be enough?

2 Say It

The main body of the speech takes up 75%–90% of your time. The most important thing to realize is that your audience won't remember more than a few points anyway. Thus, you need to decide which three or four points must be remembered.[62] Then cover them as succinctly as possible.

Be particularly attentive to transitions during the main body of the speech. Listening differs from reading in that the listener has only one chance to get your meaning. Thus, be sure you constantly provide your listeners with guidelines and transitional phrases so they can see where you're going. Example:

"There are five ways the security of your supposedly private files can be compromised. The first way is . . . "

3 Tell Them What You Said

The end might take 5%–10% of your time. Many professional speakers consider the conclusion to be as important as the introduction, so don't drop the ball here. You need a solid, strong, persuasive wrap-up.

Use some sort of signal phrase that cues your listeners that you are heading into your wind-up. Examples:

"Let's review the main points . . . "

"In conclusion, what CAN you do to protect against unauthorized invasion of your private files? I point out five main steps. One . . . "

Give some thought to the last thing you will say. It should be strongly upbeat, a call to action, a thought for the day, a little story, a quotation. Examples:

"I want to leave you with one last thought . . . "

"Finally, let me close by sharing something that happened to me . . ."

"As Albert Einstein said, 'Imagination is more important than knowledge.'"

Then say "Thank you" and stop talking. ◆

Key Terms Used in This Chapter

communication, 484
decoding, 485
downward communication, 497
encoding, 485
external communication, 498
extranet, 500
feedback, 485
formal communication channels, 496
grapevine, 498
horizontal communication, 497
informal communication channels, 498
information overload, 503
intranet, 500
jargon, 491
management by wandering around (MBWA), 499
media richness, 486
medium, 485
message, 485
noise, 485
nonverbal communication, 492
receiver, 485
semantics, 489
sender, 485
spam, 501
stereotype, 492
upward communication, 497

Summary

15.1 The Communication Process: What It Is, How It Works

- 
Communication is the transfer of information and understanding from one person to another. The process involves sender, message, and receiver; encoding and decoding; the medium; feedback; and dealing with "noise." The sender is the person wanting to share information. The information is called a message. The receiver is the person for whom the message is intended. Encoding is translating a message into understandable symbols or language. Decoding is interpreting and trying to make sense of the message. The medium is the pathway by which a message travels. Feedback is the process in which a receiver expresses his or her reaction to the sender's message. The entire communication process can be disrupted at any point by noise, defined as any disturbance that interferes with the transmission of a message.
- For effective communication, a manager must select the right medium. Media richness indicates how well a particular medium conveys information and promotes learning. The richer a medium is, the better it is at conveying information. Face-to-face presence is the richest; an advertising flyer would be one of the lowest. A rich medium is best for nonroutine situations and to avoid oversimplification. A lean medium is best for routine situations and to avoid overloading.

15.2 Barriers to Communication

- 
Barriers to communication are of three types:

  (1) Physical barriers are exemplified by walls, background noise, and time-zone differences.

  (2) Semantics is the study of the meaning of words. Jargon, terminology specific to a particular profession or group, can be a semantic barrier.

  (3) Personal barriers are individual attributes that hinder communication. Nine such barriers are variable skills in communicating effectively, variations in frames of reference and experiences that affect how information is interpreted, variations in trustworthiness and credibility, oversized egos, faulty listening skills, tendency to judge others' messages, inability to listen with understanding, stereotypes (oversimplified beliefs about a certain group of people) and prejudices, and nonverbal communication (messages sent outside of the written or spoken word, including body language).

15.3 How Managers Fit into the Communication Process

- 
Communication channels may be formal or informal.
- Formal communication channels follow the chain of command and are recognized as official. Formal communication is of three types:

  (1) Vertical communication is the flow of messages up and down the organizational hierarchy.

  (2) Horizontal communication flows within and between work units; its main purpose is coordination.

  (3) External communication flows between people inside and outside the organization.
- Informal communication channels develop outside the formal structure and do not follow the chain of command. Two aspects of informal channels that are important to know about are the grapevine and management by walking around.

(1) The grapevine is the unofficial communication system of the informal organization. The grapevine is faster than formal channels, is about 75% accurate, and is used by employees to acquire most on-the-job information. Two grapevine patterns predominate, the gossip chain and the cluster pattern.

(2) In management by wandering around (MBWA), a manager literally wanders around his or her organization and talks with people across all lines of authority; this reduces distortion caused by formal communication.

15.4 Communication in the Information Age

- This section considers five communications tools of information technology:

  (1) The Internet is a global network of independently operating but interconnected computers, linking smaller networks. Two private uses of the Internet are for intranets, organizations' private Internets, and for extranets, extended intranets that connect a company's internal employees with selected customers, suppliers, and other strategic partners.

  (2) E-mail, for electronic mail, uses the Internet to send computer-generated text and documents between people. E-mail has become a major communication medium because it reduces the cost of distributing information, increases teamwork, reduces paper costs, and increases flexibility. However, e-mail has three drawbacks: wasted time; information overload, in part because of spam, or unsolicited jokes and junk mail; and it leads people to neglect other media.

  (3) Videoconferencing uses video and audio links along with computers to enable people located at different locations to see, hear, and talk with one another.

  (4) Collaborative computing entails using state-of-the-art computer software and hardware to help people work better together.

  (5) Telecommuting involves doing work that is generally performed in the office away from the office, using a variety of information technologies.

- A challenge of information technology is that it can produce information overload—the amount of information received exceeds a person's ability to handle or process it.

15.5 Improving Communication Effectiveness

- 
  This section describes how to be more effective at listening, reading, writing, and speaking.
- To become a good listener, you should concentrate on the content of the message. You should judge content, not delivery; ask questions and summarize the speaker's remarks; listen for ideas; resist distractions and show interest; and give the speaker a fair hearing.
- To become a good reader, you need to first realize that speed reading usually doesn't work. You should also be savvy about how you handle periodicals and books, transfer your reading load to some of your employees, and ask others to use e-mails and reports to tell you what they want you to do. A top-down reading system that's a variant on the SQ3R system (survey, question, read, recite, review) is also helpful.
- To become an effective writer, you can follow several suggestions. Use spelling and grammar checkers in word processing software. Use three strategies for laying out your ideas in writing: go from most important topic to least important; go from least controversial topic to most controversial; and go from negative to positive. When organizing your message, start with your purpose. Write simply, concisely, and directly. Telegraph your writing through use of highlighting and white space.
- To become an effective speaker, follow three simple rules. Tell people what you're going to say. Say it. Tell them what you said.

Management in Action

Is Information Technology a Help or a Hindrance?

Excerpted from Carol Hymowitz, "In the Lead: Missing from Work: The Chance to Think, Even to Dream a Little," The Wall Street Journal, *March 23, 2004, p. B1.*

Vickie Farrell had an e-mail account before most people were using desktop computers. Since 1979, when she was a manager at Digital Equipment Corp. in Boston, she has watched e-mail evolve "from an experimental novelty to a significant productivity-improvement tool, to a mainstream work mode enabling people to communicate globally 24/7.

Today, Ms. Farrell, now a vice president at Teradata, a unit of NCR Corp., sees e-mail becoming a counterproductive intrusion in the workplace. She, like other managers, are turning off, or ignoring, their e-mail in an effort to get some work accomplished. They've reached the breaking point, where even attempts to put messages in priority or to use filtering systems to delete junk e-mail aren't helping enough.

Managers complain that the relentless flow of computer messages disrupts thought processes and kills creativity. There is no quiet time available during the workday, or even after office hours, to digest information, to ponder fresh ideas, to concentrate wholeheartedly on a difficult problem, or even to daydream. Instead, the expectation that messages from colleagues, bosses, customers, and suppliers will be answered promptly requires that employees think only in short bursts, moving quickly from one topic to another.

"The messages keep coming and coming," says Ms. Farrell, who recalls how when she first used e-mail she received just three or four messages a day. "Now it has gotten to the point where you can spend your entire day doing nothing but answering e-mail. It's intrusive and disruptive."

It's also juvenile. As children, we had to learn to separate from our parents and become autonomous and independent. We need to go through the same process as adult employees. But BlackBerrys, cellphones, pagers, and other devices demand constant attachment to our workplaces, making it difficult to wean ourselves from the need for immediate response or instant gratification.

As a result, we are losing the ability to initiate work independently and cope with the frustration of not getting answers immediately. The more we are encouraged to remain perpetually logged on, the more we fear separation. We become unable to detach long enough to create a new idea or devise an answer to a complex problem.

Now, Ms. Farrell logs off her e-mail for at least two hours a day to grant herself time to write long memos and reports—and think. She also avoids checking her e-mail when she is working away from the office or at a conference. "Some people think that because I have my laptop with me, I should stay connected, but that would prevent me from meeting potential customers, and defeat the purpose of being at the conference," she says.

Even when she is online, she doesn't read or answer every e-mail. Instead, she tells colleagues to phone her when they send an important e-mail, so that she can quickly handle it.

Jeff Phelps, chief operating officer and senior vice president at ABE Services, Sonoma, Calif., a consulting firm for independent-contractor employment, agrees that the pressure many employees feel to keep up with e-mail traffic undermines their work. "It's like being on a production line and having to plow through the next set of messages, knowing more are coming right behind," he says. "There's no time to think about providing truly thoughtful information."

He understands the value of e-mail when needing to address several people, but he says he is copied on far too many messages. He misses the days when it was acceptable not to respond to an office memo or a letter for at least 24 hours. That interval allowed time to ponder a topic and originate some new ideas.

Mr. Phelps also resents the intrusion of e-mail into his personal life, and refuses to get a BlackBerry. "If I had a BlackBerry, I'd be on line all the time and never get a break or a chance to have another form of engagement," he says.

Many others miss the opportunity for uninterrupted human contact, in person or even on the telephone. To keep up with her e-mail, Cynthia Tsai, founder and head of New York-based Health Expo, which produces consumer health fairs around the country, used to answer e-mail while talking on the phone with clients. This multitasking, however, left her stressed and feeling that she wasn't doing anything very well. She made mistakes—sometimes sending the wrong e-mail to someone or losing track of what someone was saying to her.

Questions for Discussion

1. How can managers increase their time to think while managing the deluge of e-mail messages? Explain.
2. To what extent is e-mail a source of noise in the communication process that exists within work environments?
3. Which of the four barriers to effective communication is affecting Vickie Farrell and Jeff Phelps? Discuss your rationale.
4. Using Table 15.3 as a guide, discuss how men and women might communicate differently with e-mail. Explain your rationale.
5. What advice would you give to Ms. Farrell and Mr. Phelps about managing the manner in which they handle e-mail? Be specific.

Self-Assessment

What Is Your Most Comfortable Learning Style?*

Objectives

To learn about your visual, auditory, and kinesthetic learning/communication style.

To consider how knowledge about learning/communication styles can be used to enhance your communication effectiveness.

Introduction

The purpose of this exercise is to find out what your most prominent learning style is—that is, what forms of communication can you best learn from. You should find the information of value for understanding not only your own style but those of others. Knowing your own style should also allow you to be a much more effective learner.

Instructions

Read the following 36 statements and indicate the extent to which each statement is consistent with your behavior by using the following rating scale: 1 = almost never applies; 2 = applies once in a while; 3 = sometimes applies; 4 = often applies; 5 = almost always applies.

1.	I take lots of notes.	1	2	3	4	5
2.	When talking to others, I have the hardest time handling those who do not maintain good eye contact with me.	1	2	3	4	5
3.	I make lists and notes because I remember things better if I write them down.	1	2	3	4	5
4.	When reading a novel, I pay a lot of attention to passages picturing the clothing, description, scenery, setting, etc.	1	2	3	4	5
5.	I need to write down directions so that I can remember them.	1	2	3	4	5
6.	I need to see the person I am talking to in order to keep my attention focused on the subject.	1	2	3	4	5
7.	When meeting a person for the first time, I initially notice the style of dress, visual characteristics, and neatness.	1	2	3	4	5
8.	When I am at a party, one of the things I love to do is stand back and "people watch."	1	2	3	4	5
9.	When recalling information, I can see it in my mind and remember where I saw it.	1	2	3	4	5
10.	If I had to explain a new procedure or technique, I would prefer to write it out.	1	2	3	4	5
11.	With free time I am most likely to watch television or read.	1	2	3	4	5
12.	If my boss has a message for me, I am most comfortable when he or she sends a memo.	1	2	3	4	5
	Total A (the minimum is 12 and the maximum is 60)	________				
1.	When I read, I read out loud or move my lips to hear the words in my head.	1	2	3	4	5
2.	When talking to someone else, I have the hardest time handling those who do not talk back with me.	1	2	3	4	5
3.	I do not take a lot of notes, but I still remember what was said. Taking notes distracts me from the speaker.	1	2	3	4	5
4.	When reading a novel, I pay a lot of attention to passages involving conversations, talking, speaking, dialogues, etc.	1	2	3	4	5
5.	I like to talk to myself when solving a problem or writing.	1	2	3	4	5

6.	I can understand what a speaker says, even if I am not focused on the speaker.	1	2	3	4	5
7.	I remember things easier by repeating them again and again.	1	2	3	4	5
8.	When I am at a party, one of the things I love to do is have in-depth conversations about a subject that is important to me.	1	2	3	4	5
9.	I would rather receive information from the radio than a newspaper.	1	2	3	4	5
10.	If I had to explain a new procedure or technique, I would prefer telling about it.	1	2	3	4	5
11.	With free time I am most likely to listen to music.	1	2	3	4	5
12.	If my boss has a message for me, I am most comfortable when he or she calls on the phone.	1	2	3	4	5
	Total B (the minimum is 12 and the maximum is 60)	________				
1.	I am not good at reading or listening to directions.	1	2	3	4	5
2.	When talking to someone else, I have the hardest time handling those who do not show any kind of emotional support.	1	2	3	4	5
3.	I take notes and doodle, but I rarely go back and look at them.	1	2	3	4	5
4.	When reading a novel, I pay a lot of attention to passages revealing feelings, moods, action, drama, etc.	1	2	3	4	5
5.	When I am reading, I move my lips.	1	2	3	4	5
6.	I will exchange words and places and use my hands a lot when I can't remember the right thing to say.	1	2	3	4	5
7.	My desk appears disorganized.	1	2	3	4	5
8.	When I am at a party, one of the things I love to do is enjoy activities, such as dancing, games, and totally losing myself.	1	2	3	4	5
9.	I like to move around. I feel trapped when seated at a meeting or desk.	1	2	3	4	5
10.	If I had to explain a new procedure or technique, I would prefer actually demonstrating it.	1	2	3	4	5
11.	With free time, I am most likely to exercise.	1	2	3	4	5
12.	If my boss has a message for me, I am most comfortable when he or she talks to me in person.	1	2	3	4	5
	Total C (the minimum is 12 and the maximum is 60)	________				

Scoring & Interpretation

Total A is your Visual Score ________; Total B is your Auditory Score ________; and Total C is your Kinesthetic Score ________. The area in which you have your highest score represents your "dominant" learning style. You can learn from all three, but typically you learn best using one style. Communication effectiveness is increased when your dominant style is consistent with the communication style used by others. For example, if you are primarily kinesthetic and your boss gives you directions orally, you may have trouble communicating because you do not learn or process communication well by just being told something. You must consider not only how you communicate but also how the people you work with communicate.

Questions for Discussion

1. Do you agree with the assessment? Why or why not? Explain.
2. How valuable is it to know your learning style? Does it help explain why you did well in some learning situations and poorly in others? Describe and explain.
3. How important is it to know the learning style of those you work with? Explain.

*Taken from *www.nwlink.com/~donclark/hrd/vak.html.*

Group Exercise

How Well Does Your Group Swim in a Fishbowl?

Objectives

To see how you communicate in a fishbowl setting.

To assess how you communicate when under pressure.

Introduction

You can learn a great deal about your communication style by receiving feedback from others. Although we communicate all day long, we do not always stop to check if we are actually communicating the intended message. By practicing our communication skills and receiving feedback, this exercise helps you become a more effective communicator. The purpose of this exercise is twofold: to see how you communicate in a group and to see how others communicate—and to learn how to develop your skills from both experiences.

Instructions

The fishbowl technique has been used for many years as a vehicle for providing feedback to individuals or groups. The class should first divide into groups of five or six people. Next these subgroups are formed into teams comprised of two groups of five or six people. Once the groups/teams are formed, one group is selected to be the discussion group, the other group will form the observing group. The seats should be arranged so that members of one group sit in the middle and members in the second group arrange their desks to form a circle around this group. The center group is the discussion group. This group will discuss a topic from the list below for approximately 10 minutes. The group surrounding the center group will observe and take notes on the center group's discussion and interaction with one another.

After time is up, the groups switch—the outer group moves to the center and begins discussion on a topic while the center group moves to the outer circle and begins observing and taking notes.

Once all of the groups have had a chance to observe and discuss, all of the two groups/teams should share their observations with one another. The feedback you receive from the group can be used or discarded by you. It is often hard to hear that we are different than we think we are in terms of how others see and hear us, but this is an opportunity to learn both.

Topics for Discussion

1. Britney Spears and Justin Timberlake should be UN Ambassadors for the United States.
2. The Internet should be regulated.
3. Gnutella and other websites that allow you to download free music should not be regulated, and it is okay to burn CDs with music downloaded from these sites.
4. Chief executive officers who make over $10 million a year are overpaid.
5. The minimum wage should be $10 an hour.
6. All U.S. citizens should be allowed to attend college at the taxpayers' expense.

Observation Guidelines

Use the form shown below to take notes on how the center group communicates. Use the following guidelines.

What personal barriers to communication do you see in this group? That is, do any of the members have a tendency to judge others' messages? Do any of the members exhibit faulty listening skills? What types of communication styles do you see? Do some members appear to be better communicators? Do any members seem to have "the gift of gab"?

How well does this group communicate nonverbally? Do any group members look away from the speaker? Do any of the members speak too quickly or too slowly? Is there a group member that smiles and is animated? Do any of the members yawn excessively?

Questions for Discussion

1. Were you surprised at some of your behavior that your classmates noted? Explain.
2. Based on the feedback from your classmates, what are some things you can do to work on your communication style?
3. During your observation role, did you notice any gender-related communication differences? Explain.
4. Do you think the fishbowl technique is a valuable tool for obtaining feedback on interpersonal skills? Why or why not?

Group One:	**Communication Styles Noted:**
Student Name:	
Student Name:	
Student Name:	
Student Name:	
Student Name:	
Student Name:	

Ethical Dilemma

Are Camera Cellphones Creating Ethical Problems?

Excerpted from Yuri Kageyama, "Cellphones with Cameras Creating Trouble: Concerns Include Voyeurism," The Arizona Republic, *July 10, 2003, p. A18.*

Although camera phones have been broadly available for only a few months in the United States, more than 25 million of the devices are out on the streets of Japan. . . .

Now that the use of cellphones with little digital cameras has spread throughout Asia, so have new brands of misbehavior. Some people are secretly taking photos up women's skirts and down into bathroom stalls. Others are avoiding buying books by snapping free shots of desired pages.

"The problem with a new technology is that society has yet to come up with a common understanding about appropriate behavior," said Mizuko Ito, an expert on mobile phone culture at Keio University Tokyo.

Samsung Electronics is banning their use in semiconductor and research facilities, hoping to stave off industrial espionage. Samsung, a leading maker of cellphones, is taking a low-tech approach, requiring employees and visitors to stick tape over the handset's camera lens.

Solving the Dilemma

You are the manager of a large bookstore. You have seen customers use their camera phones to take pictures of one another in the store. Yesterday, for the first time, you observed a customer taking photos of ten pages of material in a cookbook (and not buying the book). Although you did not say anything to this customer, you wonder what to do in the future. Which of the following options would you select?

1. Place a sign on the door asking customers to mind their "cellphone manners." This way you don't have to prevent people from using their phones; you can rely on common decency.
2. Ask customers to leave their camera cellphones with an employee at the front of the store. The employee will give the customer a claim check, and they can retrieve their phones once they finish shopping.
3. Station an employee at the front of the store who places tape over the lens of camera phones as customers come in.
4. Don't do anything. There is nothing wrong with people taking pictures of materials out of a book.
5. Invent other options. Discuss.

Video Case

Wolinsky & Williams

Wolinsky & Williams, Inc. (W&W) is an international architecture firm employing over 400 individuals in nine countries. They primarily specialize in office parks and corporate high rises. The company has grown quickly over the past eight years—so quickly, in fact, that changes have occurred inefficiently and without proper planning. For instance, new offices were opened without any sense of continuity of process or corporate culture. Each of the offices is using different levels of computerization and different technologies for different tasks. The lack of consistency increases the complexity of all processes, from collaboration and revisions to cost and time management.

Recently, however, business has hit a plateau, and senior management now sees the opportunity to assess practices and make across-the-board improvements.

A committee has been appointed to formulate a proposal for streamlining the antiquated blueprint-generation process. Currently, the committee consists of four account managers. Joe Tanney has been employed at W&W for six years, working his way up from assistant to account manager and has held his current position for one year. Joe is a diligent and motivated worker, eager to move up the corporate ladder. Simon Mahoney has been with the company for over 15 years. Although his job performance is more than adequate, it's clear that he's running on "auto pilot" most of the time. His passion for his job is no longer there. In fact, he seems jaded, tired, and reluctant to step outside his comfortable routine. Cheng Jing has two years' experience as an account manager, but his true passion is designing. He will finish his graduate degree within the next few months and expects to be transferred to a position in the design department. Needless to say, his heart is not in account management. Rosa Denson transferred to her current location from the Dallas office about three years ago. She is known for her enthusiastic attitude and quality work. However, she has a reputation for letting difficulties in her personal life distract her from the work at hand.

For several weeks the team has been trying but unable to agree on a meeting date. In the meantime, all members agreed to individually generate ideas and identify necessary tasks. When the first meeting is finally convened, only Joe Tanney has completed this assignment. In fact, he has created a thorough analysis of the project. All others have come to the first meeting completely unprepared. During this meeting, it is clear that the committee needs to plan a course of action, assign tasks, and set deadlines. Because Simon Mahoney is the most senior manager, everyone, including senior management, assumes that he will assume the role of team leader.

At the second meeting, however, again nobody except Tanney has met a single deadline or shared a single memo. It's clear that Mahoney is not leading the committee; in fact, he's barely even participating. Cheng Jing would like to be more helpful, but committee tasks are still low on his priority list. Rosa Denson realizes the committee will have difficulty meeting deadlines, yet she is willing to work nights and weekends even in the face of continued hardship in her family life.

Discussion Questions

1. It's important to select the right medium for effective communication. Evaluate the richness of the communication media used by the committee. Are these media appropriate for the situation? Why or why not?
2. Identify the three types of barriers to effective communication. Which type is evident in the interactions among committee members?
3. Formal communication comes in three types: vertical, horizontal, and external. Explain each of these types. Which is/are being used by the committee at W&W?

chapter 16

Control

Techniques for Enhancing Organizational Effectiveness

MAJOR QUESTIONS YOU SHOULD BE ABLE TO ANSWER

16.1 Managing for Productivity
Major Question: How do managers influence productivity?

16.2 Control: When Managers Monitor Performance
Major Question: Why is control such an important managerial function?

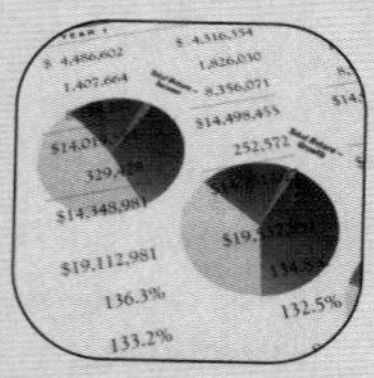

16.3 Levels, Areas, & Styles of Control
Major Question: How do successful companies implement controls?

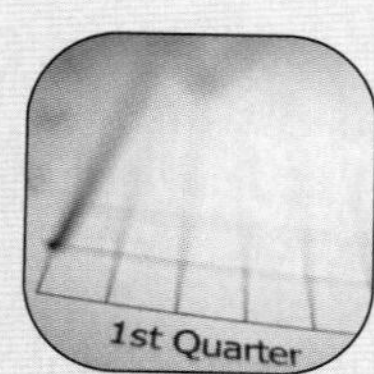

16.4 Some Financial Tools for Control
Major Question: Financial performance is important to most organizations. What are the financial tools I need to know about?

16.5 Total Quality Management
Major Question: How do top companies improve the quality of their products or services?

16.6 Managing Control Effectively
Major Question: What are the keys to successful control, and what are the barriers to control success?

the manager's toolbox

Improving Productivity: Going Beyond Control Techniques to Get the Best Results

How, as a manager, can you increase productivity—get better results with what you have to work with?

In this chapter we discuss control techniques for achieving better results. What are other ways for improving productivity? Following are some suggestions:

- **Establish base points, set goals, and measure results:** To be able to tell whether your work unit is becoming more productive, you need to establish systems of measurement. You can start by establishing the base point, such as the number of customers served per day, quantity of products produced per hour, and the like. You can then set goals to establish new levels that you wish to attain, and institute systems of measurement with which to ascertain progress. Finally, you can measure the results and modify the goals or work processes as necessary.
- **Use new technology:** Clearly, this is a favorite way to enhance productivity. With a word processor, you can produce more typed pages than you can with a typewriter. With a computerized database, you can store and manipulate information better than you can using a box of file cards. Still, computerization is not a panacea; as we have seen, information technology also offers plenty of opportunities for simply wasting time.
- **Improve match between employees and jobs:** You can take steps to ensure the best fit between employees and their jobs, including improving employee selection, paying attention to training, redesigning jobs, and providing financial incentives that are tied to performance.
- **Encourage employee involvement and innovation:** Companies improve productivity by funding research and development (R&D) departments. As a manager, you can encourage your employees, who are closest to the work process, to come up with suggestions for improving their own operations. And, of course, you can give workers a bigger say in doing their jobs, allow employee flextime, and reward people for learning new skills and taking on additional responsibility.
- **Encourage employee diversity:** By hiring people who are diverse in gender, age, race, and ethnicity, you're more likely to have a workforce with different experience, outlooks, values, and skills. By melding their differences, a team can achieve results that exceed the previous standards.
- **Redesign the work process:** Some managers think productivity can be enhanced through cost cutting, but this is not always the case. It may be that the work process can be redesigned to eliminate inessential steps.

forecast

What's Ahead in This Chapter

This final chapter explores the final management function—control. Controlling is monitoring performance, comparing it with goals, and taking corrective action as needed. In the first section, we discuss managing for *productivity,* defining what it is and explaining why it's important. We then discuss *controlling,* identify six reasons it's needed, explain the steps in the control process, and describe three types of control managers use. Next we discuss levels, areas, and styles of control. In the fourth section, we discuss financial tools for control—budgets, financial statements, ratio analysis, and audits. We then discuss total quality management (TQM), identifying its core principles and showing some TQM techniques. We conclude the chapter by describing the four keys to successful control and five barriers to successful control.

major question **How do managers influence productivity?**

The Big Picture

The purpose of a manager is to make decisions about the four management functions—planning, organizing, leading, and controlling—to get people to achieve productivity and realize results. Productivity is defined by the formula of outputs divided by inputs for a specified period of time. Productivity is important because it determines whether the organization will make a profit or even survive.

In Chapter 1, we pointed out that as a manager in the 21st century you will operate in a complex environment in which you will need to deal with six challenges—managing for (1) competitive advantage, (2) diversity, (3) globalization, (4) information technology, (5) ethical standards, and (6) your own happiness and life goals.

Within this dynamic world, you will draw on the practical and theoretical knowledge described in this book to make decisions about the four management functions of planning, organizing, leading, and controlling.

The purpose is to get the people reporting to you *to achieve productivity and realize results.*

This process is diagrammed below. *(See Figure 16.1.)*

FIGURE 16.1
Managing for productivity and results

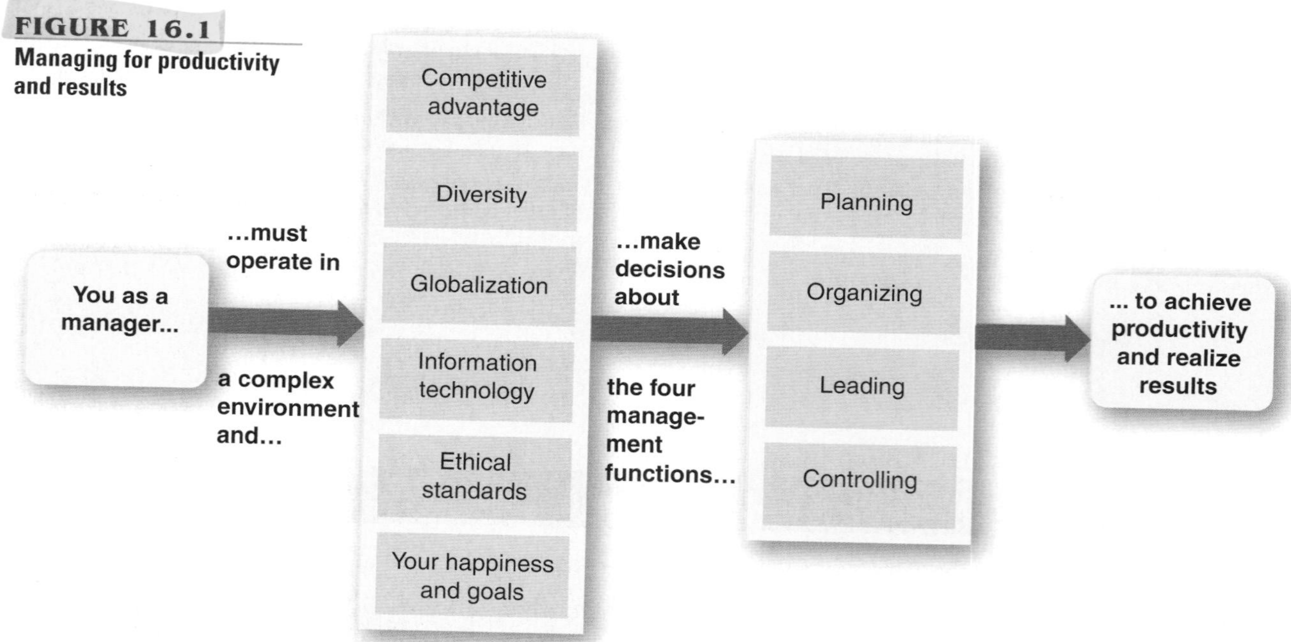

What Is Productivity?

Productivity can be applied at any level, whether for you as an individual, for the work unit you're managing, or for the organization you work for. Productivity is defined by the formula of *outputs divided by inputs* for a specified period of time. Outputs are all the goods and services produced. Inputs are not only labor but also capital, materials, and energy.[1] That is,

$$\text{productivity} = \frac{\text{outputs}}{\text{inputs}} \quad \text{or} \quad \frac{\text{goods} + \text{services}}{\text{labor} + \text{capital} + \text{materials} + \text{energy}}$$

What does this mean to you as a manager? It means that you can increase overall productivity by making substitutions or increasing the efficiency of any one element: labor, capital, materials, energy. For instance, you can increase the efficiency of labor by substituting capital in the form of equipment or machinery, as in employing a bulldozer instead of laborers with shovels to dig a hole. Or you can increase the efficiency of materials inputs by expanding their uses, as when lumber mills discovered they could sell not only boards but also sawdust and wood chips for use in gardens. Or you can increase the efficiency of energy by putting solar panels on a factory roof so the organization won't have to buy so much electrical power from utility companies.

Why Increasing Productivity Is Important

"For a company and for a nation," said former General Electric CEO Jack Welch, "productivity is a matter of survival."[2]

Productivity is important to companies because ultimately it determines whether the organization will make a profit or even survive. But the productivity of the nation is important to us individually and collectively. The more goods and services that are produced and made easily available to us and for export, the higher our standard of living.

During the 1960s, productivity in the United States averaged a spectacular 2.9% a year, then sank to a disappointing 1.5% right up until 1995. Because the decline in productivity no longer allowed the improvement in wages and living standards that had benefited so many Americans in the 1960s, millions of people took second jobs or worked longer hours to keep from falling behind. From 1995 to 2000, however, during the longest economic boom in American history, the productivity rate jumped to 2.5% annually, as the total output of goods and services rose faster than the total hours needed to produce them. The year 2004 was expected to record productivity gains of 3.3%.[3]

Most economists seem to think the recent productivity growth is the result of organizations' huge investment in information technology—computers, the Internet, other telecommunications advances, and computer-guided production line improvements.[4] For example, it used to be thought that service industries are so labor-intensive that productivity improvements are hard to come by. But from 1995 to 2001, labor productivity in services grew at a 2.6% rate, outpacing the 2.3% for goods-producing sectors. The emerging consensus among economists is that information technology played a major role.[5]

Productivity, argues William Lewis, founding director of the McKinsey Global Institute, is produced by product market competition. Although Japan's auto industry, for example, is the most productive in the world—because it is sharpened by bruising global competition—its food-processing industry, which is still dominated by mom-and-pop stores, is only 39% as productive as the U.S. industry (in which Wal-Mart and other retailers have bargained down prices, making wholesalers improve their own operations). As a result, Japanese consumers pay unnecessarily high prices for food.[6]

Maintaining productivity depends on *control.* Let's look at this. ◆

Competing internationally for productivity. This "tank farm"—a cluster of oil storage tanks—represents the continual competition among companies and among nations to achieve productivity—"a matter of survival," as GE's Jack Welch put it. Is the United States doing everything it could to be more productive? What about taking measures to reduce dependence on foreign oil?

major question

Why is control such an important managerial function?

The Big Picture

Controlling is monitoring performance, comparing it with goals, and taking corrective action. This section describes six reasons why control is needed, four steps in the control process, and three types of control.

Control is making something happen the way it was planned to happen. ***Controlling* is defined as monitoring performance, comparing it with goals, and taking corrective action as needed.** Controlling is the fourth management function, along with planning, organizing, and leading, and its purpose is plain: to make sure that performance meets objectives.

- **Planning** is setting goals and deciding how to achieve them.
- **Organizing** is arranging tasks, people, and other resources to accomplish the work.
- **Leading** is motivating people to work hard to achieve the organization's goals.
- **Controlling** is concerned with seeing that the right things happen at the right time in the right way.

All these functions affect one another and in turn affect an organization's productivity. *(See Figure 16.2.)*

FIGURE 16.2
Controlling for productivity. What you as a manager do to get things done, with controlling shown in relation to the three other management functions. (These are not lockstep; all four functions happen concurrently.)

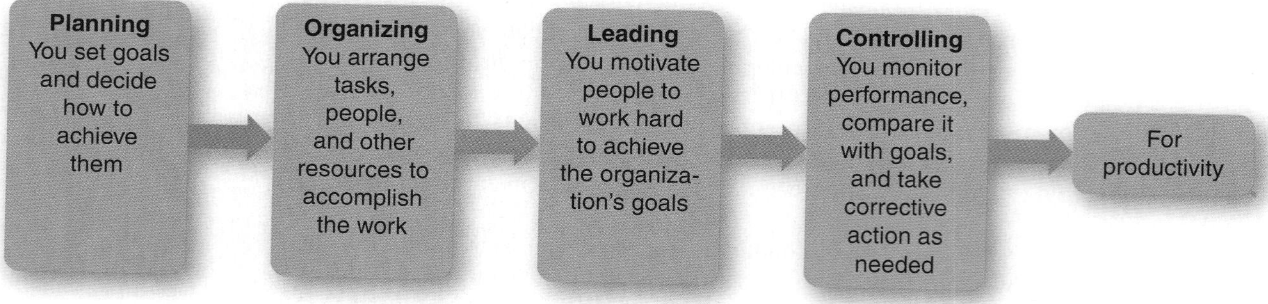

Why Is Control Needed?

There are six reasons why control is needed.

1 To Adapt to Change & Uncertainty

Markets shift. Consumer tastes change. New competitors appear. Technologies are reborn. New materials are invented. Government regulations are altered. All organizations must deal with these kinds of environmental changes and uncertainties. Control systems can help managers anticipate, monitor, and react to these changes.[7]

Example: Until the 1980s, urban department stores had restaurants within the stores (suburban ones did not) but closed them to use the space for merchandise. Now Macy's is reinventing department store dining in an effort to add convenience and induce customers to linger. The new notion: eat while you shop. The offerings, in one description, "can be gobbled while shopping, usually with one hand, leaving the other free to browse." And instead of being restaurants, the new food shops "operate as pit stops amid the merchandise." Of course, this means having to allow for possible food spills and smears on the merchandise. How does management deal with that?[8]

2 To Discover Irregularities & Errors

Small problems can mushroom into big ones. Cost overruns, manufacturing defects, employee turnover, bookkeeping errors, and customer dissatisfaction are all matters that may be tolerable in the short run. But in the long run, they can bring about even the downfall of an organization.

Example: You might not even miss a dollar a month looted from your credit card account. But an Internet hacker who does this with thousands of customers can undermine the confidence of consumers using their credit cards to charge online purchases at Amazon.com, Priceline.com, and other Web retailers. Thus, a computer program that monitors Internet charge accounts for small, unexplained deductions can be a valuable control strategy.

3 To Reduce Costs, Increase Productivity, or Add Value

Control systems can reduce labor costs, eliminate waste, increase output, and increase product delivery cycles. In addition, controls can help add value to a product so that customers will be more inclined to choose them over rival products. For example, as we have discussed early in the book (and will again in this chapter), the use of quality controls among Japanese car manufacturers resulted in cars being produced that were perceived as being better built than American cars.

4 To Detect Opportunities

Hot-selling products. Competitive prices on materials. Changing population trends. New overseas markets. Controls can help alert managers to opportunities that might have otherwise gone unnoticed.

Example: A markdown on certain grocery-store items may result in a rush of customer demand for those products, signaling store management that similar items may also sell faster if they are reduced in price.

5 To Deal with Complexity

Does the right hand know what the left hand is doing? When a company becomes larger or when it merges with another company, it may find it has several product lines, materials-purchasing policies, customer bases, even workers from different cultures. Controls help managers coordinate these various elements.

Example: Following the merger between media conglomerate Time Warner and online giant America Online, the two companies had to learn to deal with two very different cultures—an old-media, lavish-spending culture meshing with a fast-paced, highly reactive, tightwad new-media culture. (Four years after the January 10, 2000, merger, the company was worth about $76 billion—a staggering loss from the pre-merger combined value of about $240 billion.[9])

6 To Decentralize Decision Making & Facilitate Teamwork

Controls allow top management to decentralize decision making at lower levels within the organization and to encourage employees to work together in teams.

Example: At General Motors, former chairman Alfred Sloan set the level of return on investment he expected his divisions to achieve, enabling him to push decision-making authority down to lower levels while still maintaining authority over the sprawling GM organization.[10] Later GM used controls to facilitate the team approach in its joint venture with Toyota at its California plant.

The six reasons are summarized below in Figure 16.3.

FIGURE 16.3
Six reasons why control is needed

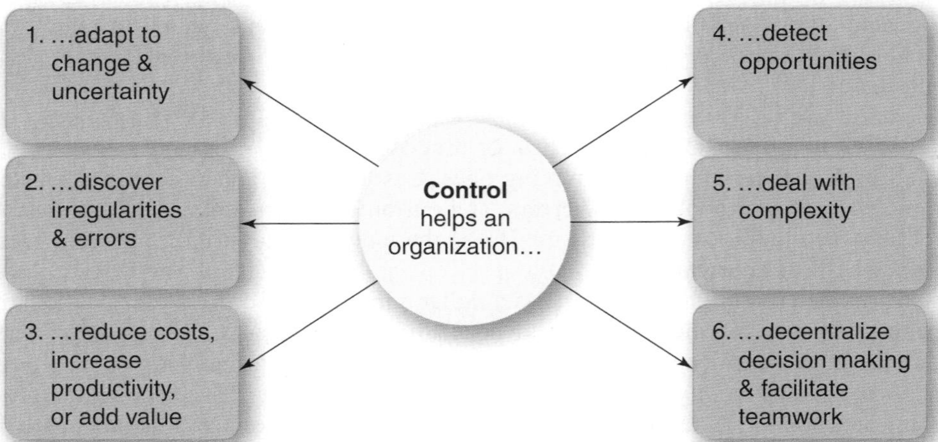
1. ...adapt to change & uncertainty
2. ...discover irregularities & errors
3. ...reduce costs, increase productivity, or add value
Control helps an organization...
4. ...detect opportunities
5. ...deal with complexity
6. ...decentralize decision making & facilitate teamwork

Steps in the Control Process

Control systems may be altered to fit specific situations, but generally they follow the same steps. The four ***control process steps*** **are (1) establish standards; (2) measure performance; (3) compare performance to standards; and (4) take corrective action, if necessary.** *(See Figure 16.4.)*

FIGURE 16.4
Steps in the control process

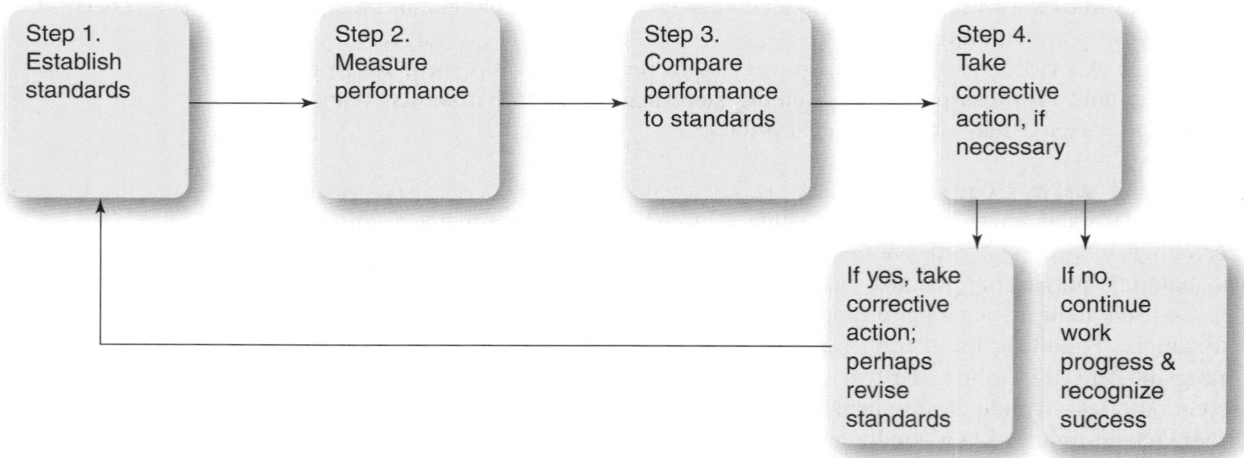
Step 1. Establish standards
Step 2. Measure performance
Step 3. Compare performance to standards
Step 4. Take corrective action, if necessary
If yes, take corrective action; perhaps revise standards
If no, continue work progress & recognize success

Let's consider these six steps.

1 Establish Standards: "What Is the Desired Outcome We Want?"

A *control standard,* or *performance standard* or simply *standard,* is the desired performance level for a given goal. Standards may be narrow or broad, and they can be set for almost anything, although they are best measured when they can be made quantifiable. Nonprofit institutions might have standards for level of charitable contributions, number of students retained, or degree of legal compliance. For-profit organizations might have standards of financial performance, employee hiring, manufacturing defects, percentage increase in market share, percentage reduction in costs, number of customer complaints, and return on investment. More subjective standards, such as level of employee morale, can also be set, although they may have to be expressed more quantifiably as reduced absenteeism and sick days and increased job applications.

Example: United Parcel Service (UPS) establishes certain standards for its drivers that set projections for the number of miles driven, deliveries, and pickups. Because conditions vary depending on whether routes are urban, suburban, or rural, the standards are different for different routes.[11]

2 Measure Performance: "What Is the Actual Outcome We Got?"

The second step in the control process is to measure performance, such as by number of products sold, units produced, or cost per item sold. Less quantifiable activities, such as new products or patents created by a research scientist or scholarly writings produced by a college professor, may be measured by opinions expressed in peer reports.

Performance measures are usually obtained from three sources: (1) written reports, including computerized printouts; (2) oral reports, as in a salesperson's weekly recitation of accomplishments to the sales manager; and (3) personal observation, as when a manager takes a stroll of the factory floor to see what employees are doing.

Example: Every day, UPS managers look at a computer printout showing the miles, deliveries, and pickups a driver attained during his or her shift the previous day.

3 Compare Performance to Standards: "How Do the Desired & Actual Outcomes Differ?"

The third step in the control process is to compare measured performance against the standards established. Most managers are delighted with performance that exceeds standards, which becomes an occasion for handing out bonuses, promotions, and perhaps offices with a view. For performance that is below standards, they need to ask: Is the deviation from performance significant? The greater the difference between desired and actual performance, the greater the need for action.

How much deviation is acceptable? That depends on *the range of variation* built in to the standards in step 1. In voting for political candidates, for instance, there is supposed to be no range of variation; as the expression goes, "every vote counts" (although the 2000 U.S. Presidential election was an eye-opener for many people in this regard). In political polling, however, a range of 3%–4% error is considered an acceptable range of variation. In machining parts for the space shuttle, the range of variation may be a good deal less tolerant than when machining parts for a power lawnmower.

The range of variation is often incorporated in computer systems into a principle called management by exception. ***Management by exception*** **is a control principle that states that managers should be informed of a situation only if data show a significant deviation from standards.**

Example: UPS managers compare the printout of a driver's performance (miles driven and number of pickups and deliveries) with the standards that were set for his or her particular route. A range of variation may be allowed to take into account such matters as winter or summer driving or traffic conditions that slow productivity.

4 Take Corrective Action, If Necessary: "What Changes Should We Make to Obtain Desirable Outcomes?"

There are three possibilities here: (1) Make no changes. (2) Recognize and reinforce positive performance. (3) Take action to correct negative performance.

Small business. How important is it for small businesses to implement all four steps of the control process? Do you think that employees in small companies—such as a restaurant—typically have more or less independence from managerial control than those in large companies do?

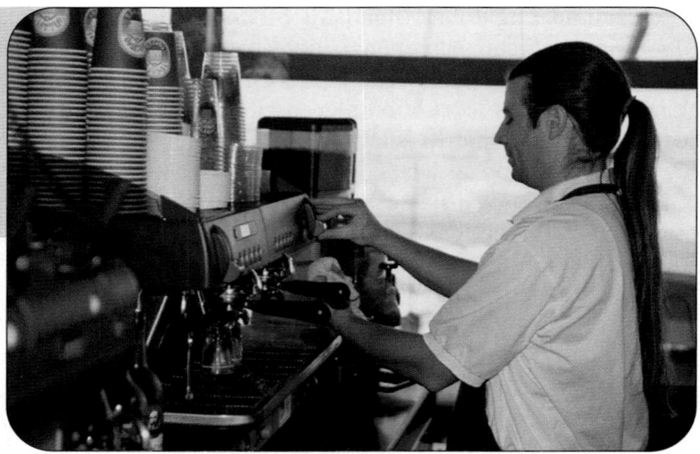

When performance meets or exceeds the standards set, managers should give rewards, ranging from giving a verbal "Job well done" to more substantial payoffs such as raises, bonuses, and promotions to reinforce good behavior.

When performance falls significantly short of the standard, managers should carefully examine the reasons why and take the appropriate action. Sometimes it may turn out the standards themselves were unrealistic, owing to changing conditions, in which case the standards need to be altered. Sometimes it may become apparent that employees haven't been given the resources for achieving the standards. And sometimes the employees may need more attention from management as a way of signaling that they have been insufficient in fulfilling their part of the job bargain.

Example: When a UPS driver fails to perform according to the standards set for him or her, a supervisor then rides along and gives suggestions for improvement. If drivers are unable to improve, they are warned, then suspended, and then dismissed.

Types of Control: Feedforward, Concurrent, & Feedback

Managers use three types of control, which vary according to timing. These controls, which are established *before, during,* or *after* the workflow are known respectively as *feedforward* (future-oriented), *concurrent* (present-oriented), and *feedback* (past-oriented) controls. *(See Figure 16.5.)*

FIGURE 16.5

Three types of control: future, present, and past

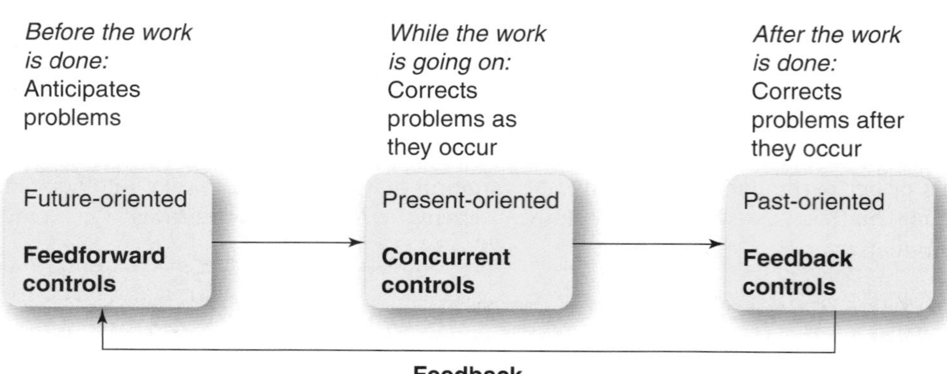
Before the work is done: Anticipates problems
While the work is going on: Corrects problems as they occur
After the work is done: Corrects problems after they occur
Future-oriented
Feedforward controls
Present-oriented
Concurrent controls
Past-oriented
Feedback controls
Feedback

Feedforward—Control for the Future: Before the Work Begins

Feedforward control **takes place before operations begin and is intended to prevent anticipated problems.** An example is a fire drill at school or work.

This future-directed control consist of rules, policies, and procedures intended to ensure that planned performance is carried out properly. The purpose of feedforward control is to keep problems from happening so that managers won't have to fix them afterward. Of course, management may not always have the facts in hand to prevent problems from occurring anyway.

Concurrent—Control for the Present: While the Work Is in Progress

Concurrent control **takes place while operations are going on and is intended to minimize problems as they occur.** An example is a warning light in a car that indicates that the oil level is low.

This present-oriented control consists of directing, monitoring, and fine-tuning activities that can correct problems before they become too difficult or expensive.

Feedback—Control for the Past: After the Work Is Done

Feedback control **takes place after operations are finished and is intended to correct the problems that have already occurred.** An example is a standard performance appraisal review.

This past-oriented control consists of use of information about previous results to correct errors in the standard. The drawback of feedback control is that the damage has already been done. The benefit is that feedback shows how well the planning process worked and tells employees how well they performed, thereby contributing to employee motivation. ◆

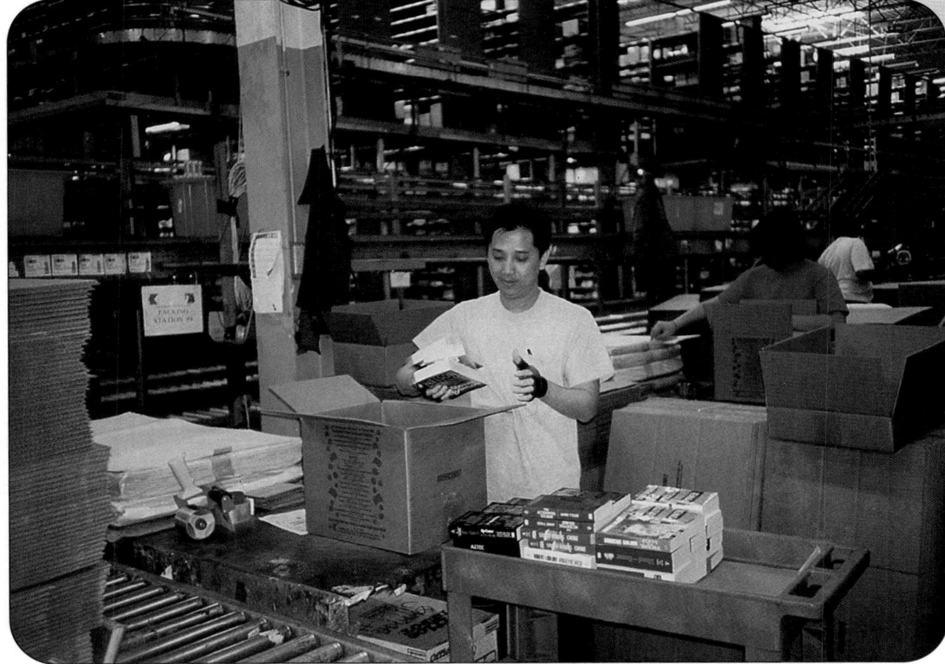

Filling orders. How do you suppose Koen Book Distributors in Moorestown, N.J., uses the three types of control?

major question **How do successful companies implement controls?**

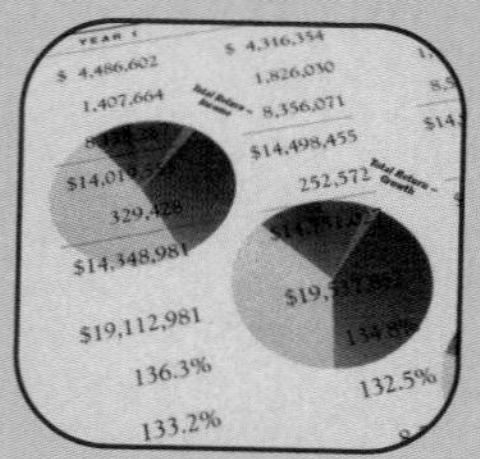

The Big Picture

This section describes three levels of control—strategic, tactical, and operational—and four areas of control—physical, human, informational, and financial resources. We also describe three approaches to implementing controls—bureaucratic, market, and clan.

How are you going to apply the steps and types of control to your own management area? Let's look at this in three ways: First, you need to consider the *level* of management at which you operate—top, middle, or first level. Second, you need to consider the *areas* that you draw on for resources—physical, human, information, and/or financial. Finally, you need to consider the *style* or control philosophy—bureaucratic, market, or clan, as we will explain.

Levels of Control: Strategic, Tactical, & Operational

There are three levels of control, which correspond to the three principal managerial levels: *strategic* planning by top managers, *tactical* planning by middle managers, and *operational* planning by first-line (supervisory) managers.

1 Strategic Control by Top Managers

Strategic control **is monitoring performance to ensure that strategic plans are being implemented and taking corrective action as needed.** Strategic control is mainly performed by top managers, those at the CEO and VP levels, who have an organizational-wide perspective. Monitoring is accomplished by reports issued every 3, 6, 12, or more months, although more frequent reports may be requested if the organization is operating in an uncertain environment.

2 Tactical Control by Middle Managers

Tactical control **is monitoring performance to ensure that tactical plans—those at the divisional or departmental level—are being implemented and taking corrective action as needed.** Tactical control is done mainly by middle managers, those with such titles as "division head," "plant manager," and "branch sales manager." Reporting is done on a weekly or monthly basis.

3 Operational Control by First-Level Managers

Operational control **is monitoring performance to ensure that operational plans—day-to-day goals—are being implemented and taking corrective action as needed.** Operational control is done mainly by first-level managers, those with titles such as "department head," "team leader," or "supervisor." Reporting is done on a daily basis.

Considerable interaction occurs among the three levels, with lower-level managers providing information upward and upper-level managers checking on some of the more critical aspects of plan implementation below them.

Areas of Control: Physical, Human, Informational, & Financial

The four resources that most organizations use are *physical, human, informational,* and *financial*. Different types of controls are used in each area.

1 Physical Resources

Physical resources include buildings, equipment, and tangible products. Thus, for example, there are equipment controls to monitor the use of computers, cars, and other machinery. There are inventory-management controls to keep track of how many products are in stock, how many will be needed, and what their delivery dates are from suppliers. There are quality controls to make sure that products are being built according to certain acceptable standards.

2 Human Resources

The controls used to monitor employees include personality tests and drug testing for hiring, performance tests during training, performance evaluations to measure work productivity, and employee surveys to assess job satisfaction and leadership.

3 Informational Resources

Production schedules. Sales forecasts. Environmental impact statements. Analyses of competition. Public relations briefings. All these are controls on an organization's various information resources.

4 Financial Resources

Are bills being paid on time? How much money is owed by customers? How much money is owed to suppliers? Is there enough cash on hand to meet payroll obligations? What are the debt-repayment schedules? What is the advertising budget? Clearly, the organization's financial controls are important because they can affect the other three types of resources.

Was this man in control? Kenneth Lay, CEO of former energy giant Enron, reads a brief statement in 2002 before Congress. Lay helped create the company in 1985 from the merger of two gas pipelines, but after a few years it was making more than 80% of its earnings by trading natural gas and electricity. It also built new markets for the trading of, for example, weather futures. For six years in a row, it was voted the most innovative of *Fortune* magazine's Most Admired Companies, and by 2000 it was the seventh-largest company in the U.S. By then Enron had also become mostly a pure trading company, an extremely volatile business to be in, although it also made some bad investments in huge overseas projects. In addition, it took equity stakes in all kinds of companies, opaque transactions that were almost impossible to understand and which finally began to adversely affect the Enron balance sheet. When Lay, who had become chairman, took back the role of CEO (relinquished to Jeffrey Skilling, who suddenly quit before things started to sour), he promised to reassure investors by improving the company's disclosure practices. "Did Lay have any idea of what he was talking about?" asks a *Fortune* article. "Or was he as clueless as Enron's shareholders? Most people believe the latter." What do you think? Can a chairman or CEO paid millions of dollars actually not know what ventures his company is engaging in or that it is failing?

Styles of Implementing Controls: Bureaucratic, Market, & Clan

There are three managerial styles or control philosophies: *bureaucratic, market,* and *clan.*[12] *(See Table 16.1.)* Most organizations emphasize either bureaucratic or clan control, with some market control mechanisms added.

TABLE 16.1
Three styles or approaches to implementing controls

Type of approach	Characteristics
Bureaucratic control	Uses rules, regulations, formal authority to elicit employee compliance. Works well in organizations (or situations) where tasks are explicit and certain.
Market control	Uses market mechanisms—pricing, competition, market share—to guide performance. Works well in organizations (or situations) in which there is considerable competition for resources.
Clan control	Uses shared values, beliefs, rituals, and trust emanating from common culture. Works well in organizations (or situations) in which employees are allowed to make their own decisions.

1 Bureaucratic Control: Involves Formal Authority & Rules

***Bureaucratic control* is characterized by use of rules, regulations, and formal authority to guide performance.** This form of control attempts to elicit employee compliance using strict rules, a rigid hierarchy, well-defined job descriptions, and administrative mechanisms such as budgets, performance appraisals, and compensation schemes (external rewards) to get results. The foremost example of use of bureaucratic control is perhaps the traditional military organization.

Bureaucratic control works well in organizations in which the tasks are explicit and certain. While rigid, it can be an effective means of ensuring that performance standards are being met. However, it may not be effective if people are looking for ways to stay out of trouble by simply following the rules, or if they try to beat the system by manipulating performance reports, or if they try to actively resist bureaucratic constraints.

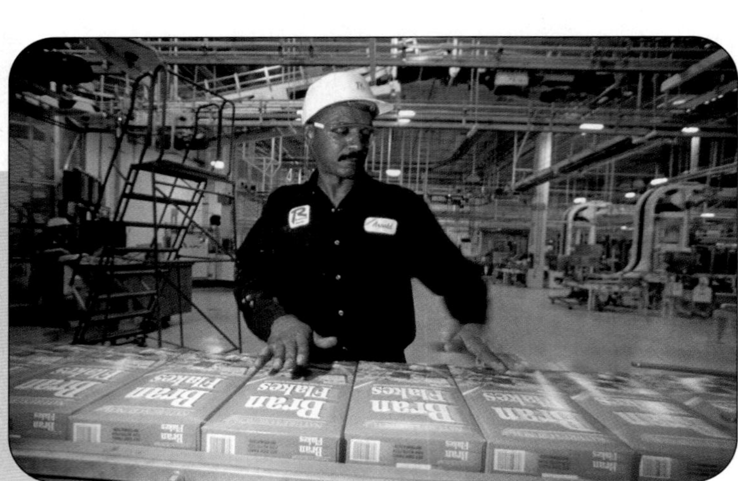

Bureaucratic control. A commercial cereal maker, where employees are expected to perform one task repetitively. A manufacturing firm need not be bureaucratic, especially if it's small.

2 Market Control: Involves Pricing Mechanisms

Market control **is characterized by use of market mechanisms—pricing, competition, market share—to guide performance.** Under this philosophy, managers' performances can be evaluated according to the profit or loss attained by their business units. This approach works well in organizations in which there is considerable competition for resources and the various divisions have distinct products or services. Thus, each division can be gauged as a separate profit center and evaluated according to how well it contributes to the organization's overall profitability. General Electric, for example, has clearly differentiated divisions for different industries, ranging from light bulbs to medical imaging to financial services.

3 Clan Control: Involves Culture & Shared Values

Unlike the bureaucratic and market approaches, clan control does not assume that the organization and its employees have different interests. Rather, ***clan control*** **is characterized by shared values, beliefs, rituals, and trusts emanating from a common culture,** and so formal controls are considered unnecessary. Clan control works best in organizations in which there is no one best way to do a job and in which employees are allowed to make many of their own decisions. Thus, this approach is found in organizations such as Microsoft Corp. or Levi Strauss in which technology or markets are changing rapidly and in which the use of teams is appropriate. ◆

Clan control. Ski resorts, especially small ones, don't have large profit margins. But profit wasn't the main reason why Chuck Shepard (shown here at right) bought Hoodoo Ski Area at Santiam Pass, Ore., in 1999 for $1.6 million. Even though he is an accountant and real-estate investor, "I'm motivated by making something successful," he told a Eugene *Register-Guard* reporter. A central part of Shepard's decision to buy Hoodoo was that he, his wife, and six children are ardent skiers. After looking over the property, he put the proposal to buy it to a family vote, which urged him to go for it. In addition, his oldest child, Tasha, was earning a master's degree in business administration; she became Hoodoo's general manager. The family has done a substantial upgrade of the resort—buying snow-grooming machines, remodeling a 60,000-square-foot day lodge, building a new Hodag quad chairlift, expanding the parking lot, constructing a snow-skate park—in a big push to make Hoodoo appeal to families who like to ski together. Most family, or clan, businesses aren't this large, of course, but do you like the idea of participating in a business in which everyone shares the same values?

major question

Financial performance is important to most organizations. What are the financial tools I need to know about?

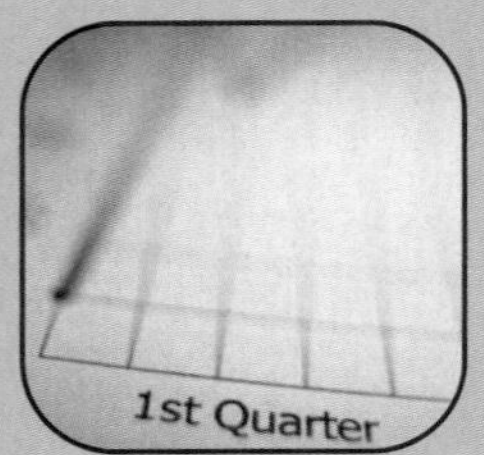

The Big Picture

Financial controls are especially important. These include budgets, financial statements, ratio analysis, and audits.

As you might expect, one of the most important areas for control is in regard to money—financial performance. Just as you need to monitor your personal finances to ensure your survival and avoid catastrophe, so managers need to do likewise with an organization's finances. Whether your organization is for-profit or nonprofit, you need to be sure that revenues are covering costs.

There are a great many kinds of financial controls, but here let us look at the following: *budgets, financial statements, ratio analysis,* and *audits*. (Necessarily this is merely an overview of this topic; financial controls are covered in detail in other business courses.)

Budgets: Formal Financial Projections

A *budget* is a formal financial projection. It states an organization's planned activities for a given period of time in quantitative terms, such as dollars, hours, or number of products. Budgets are prepared not only for the organization as a whole but also for the divisions and departments within it. The point of a budget is to provide a yardstick against which managers can measure performance and make comparisons (as with other departments or previous years).

Two Budget Approaches: Incremental & Zero-Based

Managers can take essentially two budget-planning approaches—*incremental budgeting* and *zero-based budgeting.*

- **Incremental budgeting—using the last budget period as reference point:** Incremental budgets are the traditional form of budget. ***Incremental budgeting* allocates increased or decreased funds to a department by using the last budget period as a reference point; only incremental changes in the budget request are reviewed.**

  One difficulty is that incremental budgets tend to lock departments into stable spending arrangements; they are not flexible in meeting environmental demands. Another difficulty is that a department may engage in many activities—some more important than others—but it's not easy to sort out how well managers performed at the various activities. Thus, the department activities and the yearly budget increases take on lives of their own.

Coca-Cola trucks. The truck fleet represents a huge part of a beverage distributor's capital expenditures budget. What types of data would be needed to justify expansion of this delivery system?

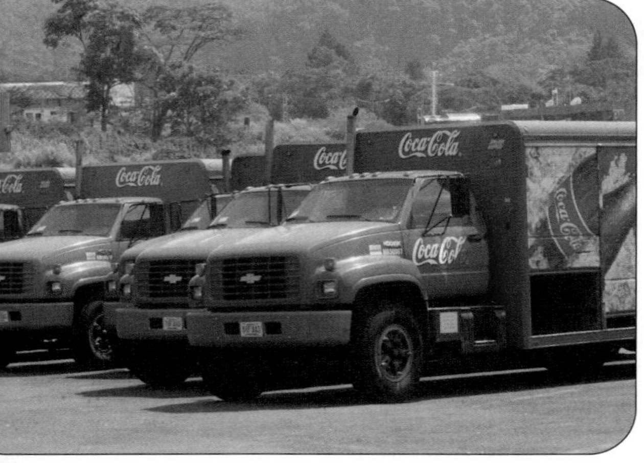

- **Zero-based budgeting—starting over at each budget period:** Developed by the U.S. Department of Agriculture and later adopted by Texas Instruments, ***zero-based budgeting (ZBB)*** **forces each department to start from zero in projecting its funding needs for the coming budget period.** Thus, ZBB forces managers to reexamine their departments' activities and justify their need for funds for the coming budget period based on strategic plans for that period.

  One difficulty with ZBB is that it requires managers to spend more time rationalizing the need for more funds. Another difficulty is that it tends to work better in small work units or departments that are declining in resources.[13]

Azhar's Oriental Rugs. What types of budgeting would best suit a small business like Azhar's? What variables or factors would drive this decision?

Fixed versus Variable Budgets

There are numerous kinds of budgets, and some examples are listed below. *(See Table 16.2.)* In general, however, budgets may be categorized as two types: *fixed* and *variable.*

- **Fixed budgets—where resources are allocated on a single estimate of costs:** Also known as a *static budget,* a ***fixed budget*** **allocates resources on the basis of a single estimate of costs.** That is, there is only one set of expenses; the budget does not allow for adjustment over time. For example, you might have a budget of $50,000 for buying equipment in a given year—no matter how much you may need equipment exceeding that amount.
- **Variable budgets—where resources are varied in proportion with various levels of activity:** Also known as a *flexible budget,* a ***variable budget*** **allows the allocation of resources to vary in proportion with various levels of activity.** That is, the budget can be adjusted over time to accommodate pertinent changes in the environment. For example, you might have a budget that allows you to hire temporary workers or lease temporary equipment if production exceeds certain levels.

TABLE 16.2
Examples of types of budgets

Type of budget	Description
Cash or cashflow budget	Forecasts all sources of cash income and cash expenditures for daily, weekly, or monthly period
Capital expenditures budget	Anticipates investments in major assets such as land, buildings, and major equipment
Sales or revenue budget	Projects future sales, often by month, sales area, or product
Expense budget	Projects expenses (costs) for given activity for given period
Financial budget	Projects organization's source of cash and how it plans to spend it in the forthcoming period
Operating budget	Projects what an organization will create in goods or services, what financial resources are needed, and what income is expected
Nonmonetary budget	Deals with units other than dollars, such as hours of labor or office square footage

Financial Statements: Summarizing the Organization's Financial Status

A *financial statement* is a summary of some aspect of an organization's financial status. The information contained in such a statement is essential in helping managers maintain financial control over the organization.

There are two basic types of financial statements: the *balance sheet* and the *income statement.*

The Balance Sheet: Picture of Organization's Financial Worth for a Specific Point in Time

A *balance sheet* summarizes an organization's overall financial worth—that is, assets and liabilities—at a specific point in time.

Assets are the resources that an organization controls; they consist of current assets and fixed assets. *Current assets* are cash and other assets that are readily convertible to cash within one year's time. Examples are inventory, sales for which payment has not been received (accounts receivable), and U.S. Treasury bills or money market mutual funds. *Fixed assets* are property, buildings, equipment, and the like that have a useful life that exceeds one year but that are usually harder to convert to cash. *Liabilities* are claims, or debts, by suppliers, lenders, and other nonowners of the organization against a company's assets.

The Income Statement: Picture of Organization's Financial Results for a Specified Period of Time

The balance sheet depicts the organization's overall financial worth at a specific point in time. By contrast, the ***income statement* summarizes an organization's financial results—revenues and expenses—over a specified period of time,** such as a quarter or a year.

Revenues are assets resulting from the sale of goods and services. *Expenses* are the costs required to produce those goods and services. The difference between revenues and expenses, called the *bottom line,* represents the profits or losses incurred over the specified period of time.

Ratio Analysis: Indicators of an Organization's Financial Health

The bottom line may be the most important indicator of an organization's financial health, but it isn't the only one. Managers often use ***ratio analysis*—the practice of evaluating financial ratios**—to determine an organization's financial health.

Among the types of financial ratios are those used to calculate liquidity, debt management, asset management, and return. *Liquidity ratios* indicate how easily an organization's assets can be converted into cash (made liquid). *Debt management* ratios indicate the degree to which an organization can meet its long-term financial obligations. *Asset management* ratios indicate how effectively an organization is managing its assets, such as whether it has obsolete or excess inventory on hand. *Return ratios*—often called return on investment, ROI, or return on assets—indicate how effective management is generating a return, or profits, on its assets.

Audits: External versus Internal

When you think of auditors, do you think of grim-faced accountants looking through a company's books to catch embezzlers and other cheats? That's one function of auditing, but besides verifying the accuracy and fairness of financial statements it also is intended to be a tool for management decision making. ***Audits*** **are formal verifications of an organization's financial and operational systems.**

Audits are of two types—*external* and *internal.*

External Audits—Financial Appraisals by Outside Financial Experts

An ***external audit*** **is a formal verification of an organization's financial accounts and statements by outside experts.** The auditors are certified public accountants (CPAs) who work for an accounting firm (such as PricewaterhouseCoopers) that is independent of the organization being audited. Their task is to verify that the organization, in preparing its financial statements and in determining its assets and liabilities, followed generally accepted accounting principles.

Internal Audits—Financial Appraisals by Inside Financial Experts

An ***internal audit*** **is a verification of an organization's financial accounts and statements by the organization's own professional staff.** Their jobs are the same as those of outside experts—to verify the accuracy of the organization's records and operating activities. Internal audits also help uncover inefficiencies and thus help managers evaluate the performance of their control systems. ◆

Accountants at the Academy Awards? No, these clearly are the Oscar-winning Sean Penn, who in 2004 was voted Best Actor (for his role in *Mystic River*), and Charlize Theron, voted Best Actress (for her role in *Monster*). But every year since 1929 the secret ballots for Oscar nominees voted by members of the Academy of Motion Picture Arts and Sciences have been tabulated by accountants from the firm now known as PricewaterhouseCoopers. The accounting firm takes this event very seriously; secrecy is tight, and there is no loose gossip around the office water cooler. Two accountants tally the votes, stuff the winners' names in the envelopes—the ones that will be handed to award presenters during the Academy Awards—and then memorize the winners' names, just in case the envelopes don't make it to the show. The so-called then Big Five accounting firms—PricewaterhouseCoopers, Deloitte & Touche, Ernst & Young, KPMG, and Arthur Andersen—underwent a lot of scrutiny in 2002 after Andersen's document shredding became headline news. Accounting is an important business because investors depend on independent auditors to verify that a company's finances are what they are purported to be.

major question

How do top companies improve the quality of their products or services?

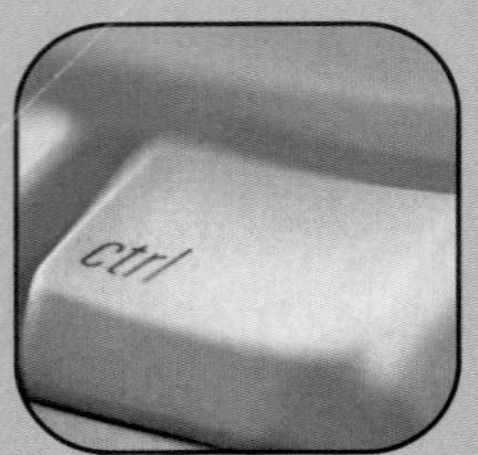

The Big Picture

Total quality management (TQM) is dedicated to continuous quality improvement, training, and customer satisfaction. Two core principles are people orientation and improvement orientation. Some techniques for improving quality are employee involvement, benchmarking, outsourcing, reduced cycle time, and statistical process control.

The Ritz-Carlton Hotel Co., LLC, a luxury chain of 43 hotels that is an independently operated division of Marriott International, puts a premium on doing things right. First-year managers and employees receive 250–310 hours of training. The president meets each employee at a new hotel to ensure he or she understands the Ritz-Carlton standards for service. The chain has also developed a database that records the preferences of more than 1 million customers, so that each hotel can anticipate guests' needs.[14]

Because of this diligence, the Ritz-Carlton has twice been the recipient (in 1992 and in 1999) of the Malcolm Baldrige National Quality Award. (The 2003 awards for service went to Caterpillar Financial Services and to Boeing Aerospace Support.) As we mentioned in Chapter 2, the Baldrige awards were created by Congress in 1987 to be the most prestigious recognition of quality in the United States, which is given annually to U.S. organizations in manufacturing, service, education, health care, and small business.

The Baldrige award is an outgrowth of the realization among U.S. managers in the early 1980s that three-fourths of Americans were telling survey takers that the label "Made in America" no longer represented excellence—that they considered products made overseas, especially Japan, equal or superior in quality to U.S.-made products. As we saw in Chapter 2, much of the impetus for quality improvements in Japanese products came from American consultants W. Edwards Deming and Joseph M. Juran, whose work led to the strategic commitment to quality known as total quality management.

Core TQM Principles: Deliver Customer Value & Strive for Continuous Improvement

Total quality management (TQM) **is defined as a comprehensive approach—led by top management and supported throughout the organization—dedicated to continuous quality improvement, training, and customer satisfaction.**

In Chapter 2 we said there are four components to TQM:

1. Make continuous improvement a priority.
2. Get every employee involved.
3. Listen to and learn from customers and employees.
4. Use accurate standards to identify and eliminate problems.

These may be summarized as ***two core principles of TQM*** **—namely, (1)** ***people orientation*****—everyone involved with the organization should focus on delivering value to customers—and (2)** ***improvement orientation*****—everyone should work on continuously improving the work processes.**[15] Let's look at these further.

1 People Orientation—Focusing Everyone on Delivering Customer Value

Organizations adopting TQM value people as their most important resource—both those who create a product or service and those who receive it. Thus, not only are employees given more decision-making power, so are suppliers and customers.

This people orientation operates under the following assumptions.

- **Delivering customer value is most important:** The purpose of TQM is to focus people, resources, and work processes to deliver products or services that create value for customers.
- **People will focus on quality if given empowerment:** TQM assumes that employees and suppliers will concentrate on making quality improvements if given the decision-making power to do so. Customers can also be a valuable part of the process if they are allowed to express choices.
- **TQM requires training, teamwork, and cross-functional efforts:** Employees and suppliers need to be well trained, and they must work in teams. Teamwork is considered important because many quality problems are spread across functional areas. For example, if car-cellphone design specialists conferred with marketing specialists (as well as customers and suppliers), they would find the real challenge of using a cellphone in a car is not talking on it but pushing 11 tiny buttons to call a phone number while driving 65 miles an hour.

2 Improvement Orientation—Focusing Everyone on Continuously Improving Work Processes

Americans seem to like big schemes, grand designs, and crash programs. While these approaches certainly have their place, the lesson of the quality movement from overseas is that the way to success is through continuous small improvements. ***Continuous improvement* is defined as ongoing small, incremental improvements in all parts of an organization**—all products, services, functional areas, and work processes.

This improvement orientation has the following assumptions.

- **It's less expensive to do it right the first time:** TQM assumes that it's better to do things right the first time than to do costly reworking. To be sure, there are many costs involved in creating quality products and services—training, equipment, and tools, for example. But they are less than the costs of dealing with poor quality—those stemming from lost customers, junked materials, time spent reworking, and frequent inspection, for example.[16]
- **It's better to do small improvements all the time:** This is the assumption that continuous improvement must be an everyday matter, that no improvement is too small, that there must be an ongoing effort to make things better a little bit at a time all the time.

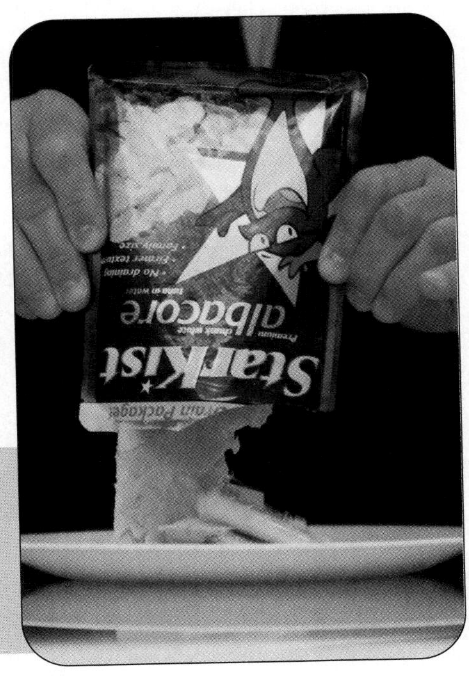

Continuous improvement. When tuna glutted the market so that StarKist Tuna found it couldn't price a can of tuna high enough to be profitable, it turned to developing new forms of packaging, such as this resealable pouch. Not only does the pouch make it easier to save leftovers, there is also no need to drain the tuna, and the product has a firmer texture. Have you noticed other packaging innovations that have increased convenience?

- **Accurate standards must be followed to eliminate small variations:** TQM emphasizes the collection of accurate data throughout every stage of the work process. It also stresses the use of accurate standards (such as benchmarking, as we discuss) to evaluate progress and eliminate small variations, which are the source of many quality defects.
- **There must be strong commitment from top management:** Employees and suppliers won't focus on making small incremental improvements unless managers go beyond lip service to support high-quality work.

Some TQM Techniques

Several techniques are available for improving quality. Here we describe *employee involvement, benchmarking, outsourcing, reduced cycle time,* and *statistical process control.*

Employee Involvement: Quality Circles, Self-Managed Teams, & Special-Purpose Teams

As part of the TQM people orientation, employees (and often suppliers and customers) are given more decision-making power than is typical in non-TQM organizations. The reasoning here is that the people actually involved with the product or service are in the best position to detect opportunities for quality improvements.

Three means for implementing employee involvement are as follows.

- **Quality circles:** *Quality circles,* you'll recall (from Chapter 13), consist of small groups of workers and supervisors who meet intermittently to discuss workplace and quality-related problems. A quality circle may consist of a group of 10–12 people meeting an hour or so once or twice a month, with management listening to presentations. Members of the quality circle attempt to identify and solve problems in production and quality in the work performed in their part of the company.
- **Self-managed teams:** *Self-managed teams,* also described in Chapter 13, are groups of workers who are given administrative oversight of activities such as planning, scheduling, monitoring, and staffing for their task domains. A common feature of self-managed teams is cross-functionalism—that is, a team is made up of technical specialists from different areas.
- **Special-purpose teams:** Quality circles and self-managed teams usually meet on a regular basis. Sometimes, however, an organization needs a ***special-purpose team*** **to meet to solve a special or one-time problem.** The team then disbands after the problem is solved. These teams are often cross-functional, drawing on members from different departments.

One in twelve. Some 19.5 million vehicles in the United States, about one in 12, were recalled in 2003. Among 2004 models, the Dodge Durango was among those recalled, because of a defective instrument cluster circuit board, which could overheat and cause an instrument panel fire. U.S. automakers have fought perceptions of poor quality for decades, but they insist that recent recalls represent a greater commitment to safety.

Benchmarking: Learning from the Best Performers

We discussed benchmarking briefly in Chapter 10. As we stated there, *benchmarking* is a process by which a company compares its performance with that of high-performing organizations. For example, at Xerox Corp., generally thought to be the first American company to use benchmarking, it is defined as, in one description, "the continuous process of measuring products, services, and practices against the toughest competitors or those companies recognized as industry leaders."[17]

Example

Benchmarking: How Xerox Emulated Competitors

THE DOCUMENT COMPANY
XEROX

Southwest Airlines studied auto-racing pit crews to learn how to reduce the turnaround time of its aircraft at each scheduled stop. Toyota managers got the idea for just-in-time inventory deliveries by looking at how U.S. supermarkets replenish their shelves. Ford got ideas from Mazda (in which Ford had ownership) to learn how to create an invoiceless accounts-payable system. Korean automaker Kia looked at Toyota's Avalon and Buick's LeSabre to produce the lush and cushy 2004 Amanti sedan.[18] All these are instances of benchmarking.

One of the most famous examples, however, occurred in 1979, when Xerox found itself up against Japanese photocopiers being sold in the U.S. for prices substantially below even the production costs for Xerox copiers. Xerox managers learned through a Japanese joint-venture partner, Fuji-Xerox, that Xerox's costs were excessive owing to gross inefficiencies in its manufacturing and business practices. As a result, Xerox began a program to benchmark 67 of its key work processes against competitors identified as having the "best practices" in those processes.[19]

Benchmarking isn't everything, however. For several years, Xerox found itself falling behind other technology companies. Its stock, which traded in the $50 range in the late '90s, plummeted to $4 in 2002. More recently, after aggressive cost-cutting under new CEO Anne Mulcahy, the outlook has been more positive.[20]

Outsourcing: Let Outsiders Handle It

Outsourcing (discussed in detail in Chapter 4) is the subcontracting of services and operations to an outside vendor. Usually this is done because the subcontractor vendor can do the job better or cheaper. Or, stated another way, when the services and operations are done in-house, they are not done as efficiently or are keeping personnel from doing more important things. For example, when Eastman Kodak farmed out its computer operations to IBM, it found it got higher-quality computing operations at less cost.[21] And when IBM and other companies outsource components inexpensively for new integrated software systems, says one researcher, offshore programmers make information technology affordable to small and medium-size businesses and others who haven't yet joined the productivity boom.[22]

Outsourcing is also being done by many state and local governments, which, under the banner known as privatization, have subcontracted traditional government services such as fire protection, correctional services, and medical services.

practical action

Outsourcing Public Services: Does Privatization Always Work?

Do public services work better when they're privatized? Privatization has been a popular idea in the last several years. As the term is used in the United States, this means farming out, or outsourcing, to private-sector companies traditional public-sector services such as prison supervision, fire protection, and road maintenance.

The driving force behind privatization is the idea that the for-profit sector is more *motivated* than the nonprofit sector to deliver services in a more customer-friendly, cost-efficient way. However, private companies can also make expensive, bad decisions. One has only to look at the example of Texas-based energy giant Enron, once the seventh-largest company in the U.S., whose off-books investments led it into bankruptcy. Or consider such money-losing private-sector projects as New Coke or the movie *Gigli* or Intel's Itanium processor. As one writer points out, "Is there much difference, after all, between the Defense Department paying $600 for an ordinary toilet seat and a private-sector corporation paying $600 a share for an Internet start-up with no assets, no profits, and no plan for producing either?"[23]

In Elliott Sclar's book *You Don't Always Get What You Pay For: The Economics of Privatization,* the Columbia University economist and urban planning professor points out

(continued)

that privatization alone is not a substitute for good public management.[24] For example, in the 1980s, the Metro-Dade Transit Agency in Florida hired a private company to run 10 of its bus routes, keeping 10 comparable routes in public operation for comparison. The result after 18 months, when the experiment was abandoned: Complaints had more than doubled on the private-sector routes, and ridership had plummeted. Moreover, the 40 new buses that the agency gave the contractor were so poorly maintained that only 10 could be kept in service.

Another example that Sclar gives is that of a mutual-aid pact among several small-town fire departments, in which one town had hired a private corporation to provide fire protection. Responding to its profit motive, the corporation kept smaller crews on each shift than the surrounding nonprofit fire companies did. The effect was to increase the reliance of that department on its public-sector neighbors for reinforcements. And on a day when the reinforcements could not show up, the for-profit department was unable to quell the fire in a $1 million home, which burned to the ground.

The lesson: Municipalities letting out contracts to the private sector have to make sure that the contracts are carefully drawn, that the contractor's performance is adequately monitored, and that the costs are measured against accurate internal costs to protect the public's interest against the company's overzealous pursuit of profit.

In other words, there must be effective *controls*.

Neither fish nor fowl. Is the U.S. Postal Service a government agency? Or now a self-supporting nongovernmental entity? It's neither—it's a creation of Congress, points out the *Atlanta Journal-Constitution.* Thus, it can't close any of its 38,000 post offices—two-thirds of which are not profitable—because voters would howl. Congress also insists on six-day mail delivery to every U.S. address. Do you think UPS or FedEx could operate as well with restraints like these?

The ISO 9000 Series: Meeting Standards of Independent Auditors

If you're a sales representative for Du Pont, the American chemical company, how will your overseas clients know that your products have the quality they are expecting? If you're a purchasing agent for an Ohio-based tire company, how can you tell if the synthetic rubber you're buying overseas is adequate?

At one time, buyers and sellers simply had to rely on a company's past reputation or personal assurances. In 1979, the International Organization for Standardization (ISO), based in Geneva, Switzerland, created a set of quality standards known as the 9000 series—"a kind of Good Housekeeping seal of approval for global business," in one description.[25] **The *ISO 9000 series* consists of quality-control procedures companies must install—from purchasing to manufacturing to inventory to shipping—that can be audited by independent quality-control experts, or "registars."** The goal is to reduce flaws in manufacturing and improve productivity. Companies must document the procedures and train their employees to use them. For instance, DocBase Direct is a Web-delivered document and forms-management system that helps companies comply with key ISO management standards, such as traceable changes and easy reporting.

The ISO 9000 designation is now recognized in 100 countries around the world, and a quarter of the corporations around the globe insist that suppliers have ISO 9000 certification. "You close some expensive doors if you're not certified," says Bill Ekeler, general manager of Overland Products, a Nebraska tool-and-die-stamping firm.[26] In addition, because the ISO process forced him to analyze his company from the top down, he found ways to streamline manufacturing processes that improved his bottom line.

Reduced Cycle Time: Increasing the Speed of Work Processes

Another TQM technique is the emphasis on increasing the speed with which an organization's operations and processes can be performed. This is known as ***reduced cycle time,* or reduction in steps in a work process,** such as fewer authorization steps required to let a contract to a supplier. The point is to improve the organization's performance by eliminating wasteful motions, barriers between departments, unnecessary procedural steps, and the like.

Statistical Process Control: Taking Periodic Random Samples

As the pages of this book were being printed, every now and then a press person would pull a few pages out of the press run and inspect them (under a bright light) to see that the consistency of the color and quality of the ink were holding up. This is an ongoing human visual check for quality control.

All kinds of products require periodic inspection during their manufacture: hamburger meat, breakfast cereal, flashlight batteries, wine, and so on. The tool often used for this is ***statistical process control,*** **a statistical technique that uses periodic random samples from production runs to see if quality is being maintained within a standard range of acceptability.** If quality is not acceptable, production is stopped to allow corrective measures.

Statistical process control is the technique that McDonald's uses, for example, to make sure that the quality of its burgers is always the same, no matter where in the world they are served. Companies such as Intel and Motorola use statistical process control to ensure the reliability and quality of their products.

Six Sigma & Lean Six Sigma: Data-Driven Ways to Eliminate Defects

"The biggest problem with the management technique known as Six Sigma is this: It sounds too good to be true," says a *Fortune* writer. "How would your company like a 20% increase in profit margins within one year, followed by profitability over the long-term that is *ten times* what you're seeing now? How about a 4% (or greater) annual gain in market share?"[27]

What is this name, Six Sigma, which is probably Greek to you, and is it a path to management heaven? The name comes from *sigma,* the Greek letter that statisticians use to define a standard deviation. The higher the sigma, the fewer the deviations from the norm—that is, the fewer the defects. Developed by Motorola in 1985 and since embraced by General Electric, Allied Signal, American Express, and other companies, ***Six Sigma*** **is a rigorous statistical analysis process that reduces defects in manufacturing and service-related processes.** By testing thousands of variables and eliminating guesswork, a company using the technique attempts to improve quality and reduce waste to the point where errors nearly vanish. In everything from product design to manufacturing to billing, the attainment of Six Sigma means there are no more than 3.4 defects per million products or procedures.

"Six Sigma gets people away from thinking that 96% is good, to thinking that 40,000 failures per million is bad," says a vice president of consulting firm A. T. Kearney.[28] Six Sigma means being 99.9997% perfect. By contrast, Three Sigma or Four Sigma means settling for 99% perfect—the equivalent of no electricity for seven hours each month, two short or long landings per day at each major airport, or 5,000 incorrect surgical operations per week.[29]

Six Sigma may also be thought of as a philosophy—to reduce variation in your company's business and make customer-focused, data-driven decisions. The method preaches the use of Define, Measure, Analyze, Improve, and Control (DMAIC). Team leaders may be awarded a Six Sigma "black belt" for applying DMAIC.

More recently, companies are using an approach known as ***lean Six Sigma,*** **which focuses on problem solving and performance improvement—speed with excellence—of a well-defined project.**[30] Xerox Corp., for example, has focused on getting new products to customers faster, which has meant taking steps out of the design process without loss of quality. A high-end, $200,000 machine that can print 100 pages a minute traditionally has taken three to five cycles of design; removing just one of those cycles can shave up to a year off time to market.[31] The grocery chain Albertsons Inc. announced in 2004 that it was going to launch Six Sigma training to reduce customer dissatisfaction and waste to the lowest level possible.[32]

Six Sigma may not be a perfect process, since it cannot compensate for human error or control events outside a company. Still, it lets managers approach problems with the assumption that there's a data-oriented, tangible way to approach problem solving.[33] ◆

major question

What are the keys to successful control, and what are the barriers to control success?

The Big Picture

This section describes four keys to successful control and five barriers to successful control.

How do you as a manager make a control system successful, and how do you identify and deal with barriers to control? We consider these topics next.[34]

The Keys to Successful Control

Successful control systems have a number of common characteristics: (1) They are strategic and results oriented. (2) They are timely, accurate, and objective. (3) They are realistic, positive, and understandable and they encourage self-control. (4) They are flexible.[35]

1 They Are Strategic & Results Oriented

Control systems support strategic plans and are concentrated on significant activities that will make a real difference to the organization. Thus, when managers are developing strategic plans for achieving strategic goals, that is the point at which they should pay attention to developing control standards that will measure how well the plans are being achieved.

Example: "In the 1970s and 1980s, environmental groups did a great job of making people aware that the environment was in trouble," said Marcelo Carvalho de Andrade. "In the [new] millennium, we must direct our efforts toward solutions that don't depend on charity." Solutions, Andrade realized, need money, "and corporations have it." In 1986, the 40-year-old Brazilian mountain climber, former fashion model, and orthopedic surgeon had persuaded enough corporations—including Coca-Cola, Shell, Goodyear, and Christian Dior—to create Pro-Natura. One of its strategic goals is to arrest global warming. One results-oriented project intended to reduce carbon in the rain forest is to plant 10 million trees.[36]

One of 10 million trees. Established in 1986, Pro-Natura is a nongovernmental organization that specializes in sustainable development. The mission of the organization is to conserve biodiversity through integrated sustainable development projects adapted as models that can be replicated at regional levels.

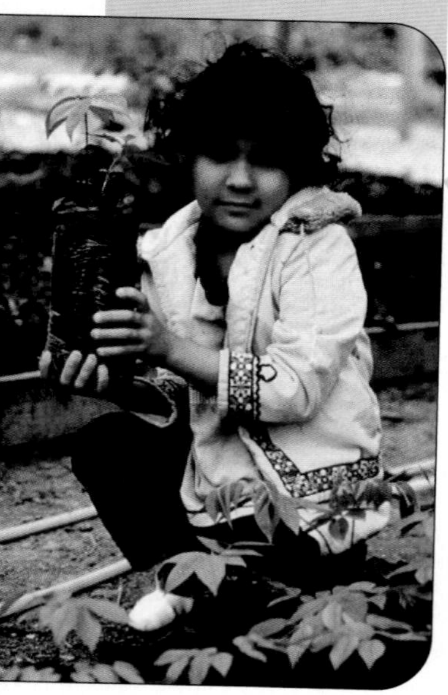

2 They Are Timely, Accurate, & Objective

Good control systems—like good information of any kind—should . . .

- **Be timely—meaning when needed:** The information should not necessarily be delivered quickly, but it should be delivered at an appropriate or specific time, such as every week or every month. And it certainly should be often enough to allow employees and managers to take corrective action for any deviations.
- **Be accurate—meaning correct:** Accuracy is paramount, if decision mistakes are to be avoided. Inaccurate sales figures may lead managers to mistakenly cut or increase sales promotion budgets. Inaccurate production costs may lead to faulty pricing of a product.
- **Be objective—meaning impartial:** Objectivity means control systems are impartial and fair. Although information can be inaccurate for all kinds of rea-

sons (faulty communication, unknown data, and so on), information that is not objective is inaccurate for a special reason: It is biased or prejudiced. Control systems need to be considered unbiased for everyone involved so that they will be respected for their fundamental purpose—enhancing performance.

3 They Are Realistic, Positive, & Understandable & Encourage Self-Control

Control systems have to focus on working for the people who will have to live with them. Thus, they operate best when they are made acceptable to the organization's members who are guided by them. Thus, they should . . .

- **Be realistic:** They should incorporate realistic expectations. If employees feel performance results are too difficult, they are apt to ignore or sabotage the performance system.
- **Be positive:** They should emphasize development and improvement. They should avoid emphasizing punishment and reprimand.
- **Be understandable:** They should fit the people involved, be kept as simple as possible, and present data in understandable terms. They should avoid complicated computer printouts and statistics.
- **Encourage self-control:** They should encourage good communication and mutual participation. They should not be the basis for creating distrust between employees and managers.

4 They Are Flexible

Control systems must leave room for individual judgment, so that they can be modified when necessary to meet new requirements.

Barriers to Control Success

Among the several barriers to a successful control system are the following:[37]

1 Too Much Control

Some organizations, particularly bureaucratic ones, try to exert too much control. They may try to regulate employee behavior in everything from dress code to timing of coffee breaks. Allowing employees too little discretion for analysis and interpretation may lead to employee frustration—particularly among professionals, such as college professors and medical doctors. Their frustration may lead them to ignore or try to sabotage the control process.

2 Too Little Employee Participation

As we've noted elsewhere in the book (Chapter 12), employee participation can enhance productivity. Involving employees in both the planning and execution of control systems can bring legitimacy to the process and heighten employee morale.

3 Overemphasis on Means Instead of Ends

We said that control activities should be strategic and results oriented. They are not ends in themselves but the means to eliminating problems. Too much emphasis on accountability for weekly production quotas, for example, can lead production supervisors to push their workers and equipment too hard, resulting in absenteeism and machine breakdowns. Or it can lead to game playing—"beating the system"—as managers and employees manipulate data to seem to fulfill short-run goals instead of the organization's strategic plan.

4 Overemphasis on Paperwork

A specific kind of misdirection of effort is management emphasis on getting reports done, to the exclusion of other performance activity. Reports are not the be-all and end-all. Undue emphasis on reports can lead to too much focus on quantification of results and even to falsification of data.

Example: A research laboratory decided to use the number of patents the lab obtained as a measure of its effectiveness. The result was an increase in patents filed but a decrease in the number of successful research projects.[38]

5 Overemphasis on One Instead of Multiple Approaches

One control may not be enough. By having multiple control activities and information systems, an organization can have multiple performance indicators, thereby increasing accuracy and objectivity.

Example: An obvious strategic goal for gambling casinos is to prevent employee theft of the cash flowing through their hands. Thus, casinos control card dealers by three means. First, they require they have a dealer's license before they are hired. Second, they put them under constant scrutiny, using direct supervision by on-site pit bosses as well as observation by closed-circuit TV cameras and through overhead one-way mirrors. Third, they require detailed reports at the end of each shift so that transfer of cash and cash equivalents (such as gambling chips) can be audited.[39] ◆

Temptation. Because legal gambling is a heavy cash business, casinos need to institute special controls against employee theft. One of them is the "eye in the sky" over card and craps tables.

Finale: Some Life Lessons

major question

What are four keys to personal managerial success?

The Big Picture

As we end the book, this section describes some life lessons to take away.

We have come to the end of the book, our last chance to offer some suggestions to take with you that we hope will benefit you in the coming years. Following are some life lessons pulled from various sources that can make you a "keeper" in an organization and help you be successful.[40]

- **Initiative is always in short supply:** Many people still hold back in showing initiative because they have the unreasonable fear of getting reprimanded. That may still be possible with short-sighted supervisors, and of course it never hurts to put your boss in the best possible light. But here's a life lesson: "If you set the bar high, even if you don't reach it, you end up in a pretty good place—that is, achieving a pretty high mark."
- **If you have an active desire to learn new things, you'll be ready for the next step:** You should always be learning—whether through classes, on-the-job training, getting tips from a coworker, or reading a book. Learning makes you more valuable to your current employer and gives you more options in the wider work world. Here's a life lesson: "Be brutally honest with yourself about what you know or don't know, and ask what skills you need to take the next step."
- **Think ahead, understand what your obstacles are, and develop a strategy to win:** Ask for the most difficult job, study how to master it, and be willing to be accountable for outcomes. A life lesson: "Remove 'It's not my job' from your vocabulary." And another: "Don't sacrifice understanding for speed."
- **Be flexible, keep your cool, and take yourself lightly:** Things aren't always going to work out your way, so flexibility is important. In addition, the more unflappable you appear in difficult circumstances, the more you'll be admired by your bosses and coworkers. Having a sense of humor helps, since there are enough people spreading gloom and doom in the workplace. Life lesson: "When you're less emotional, you're better able to assess a crisis and develop a workable solution."

We wish you the very best of luck. And we mean it!

Angelo Kinicki
Brian K. Williams

Key Terms Used in This Chapter

audits, 535
balance sheet, 534
budget, 532
bureaucratic control, 530
clan control, 531
concurrent control, 527
continuous improvement, 537
control process steps, 524
control standard, 524
controlling, 522
external audit, 535
feedback control, 527
feedforward control, 527
financial statement, 534
fixed budget, 533
income statement, 534
incremental budgeting, 532
internal audit, 535
ISO 9000 series, 540
lean Six Sigma, 541
management by exception, 525
market control, 531
operational control, 528
ratio analysis, 534
reduced cycle time, 540
Six Sigma, 541
special-purpose team, 538
statistical process control, 541
strategic control, 528
tactical control, 528
total quality management (TQM), 536
two core principles of TQM, 536
variable budget, 533
zero-based budgeting (ZBB), 533

Summary

16.1 Managing for Productivity

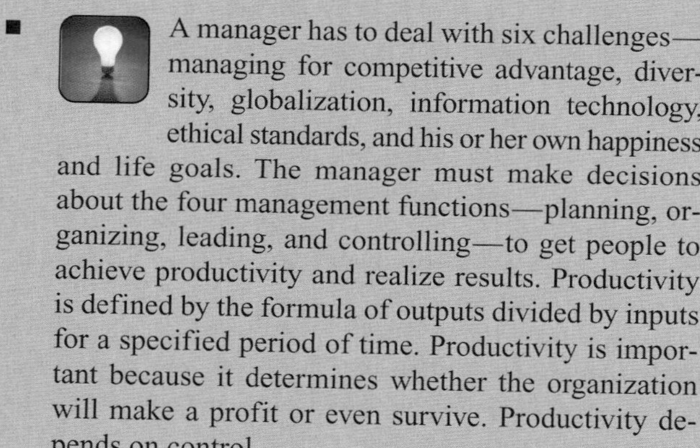

- A manager has to deal with six challenges—managing for competitive advantage, diversity, globalization, information technology, ethical standards, and his or her own happiness and life goals. The manager must make decisions about the four management functions—planning, organizing, leading, and controlling—to get people to achieve productivity and realize results. Productivity is defined by the formula of outputs divided by inputs for a specified period of time. Productivity is important because it determines whether the organization will make a profit or even survive. Productivity depends on control.

16.2 Control: When Managers Monitor Performance

- Controlling is defined as monitoring performance, comparing it with goals, and taking corrective action as needed. There are six reasons why control is needed: (1) to adapt to change and uncertainty; (2) to discover irregularities and errors; (3) to reduce costs, increase productivity, or add value; (4) to detect opportunities; (5) to deal with complexity; and (6) to decentralize decision making and facilitate teamwork.
- There are four control process steps. (1) The first step is to set standards. A control standard is the desired performance level for a given goal. (2) The second step is to measure performance, based on written reports, oral reports, and personal observation. (3) The third step is to compare measured performance against the standards established. (4) The fourth step is to take corrective action, if necessary, if there is negative performance.
- There are three types of control that managers use. (1) Feedforward control takes place before operations begin and is intended to prevent anticipated problems. (2) Concurrent control takes place while operations are going on and is intended to minimize problems as they occur. (3) Feedback control takes place after operations are finished and is intended to correct problems that have already occurred.

16.3 Levels, Areas, & Styles of Control

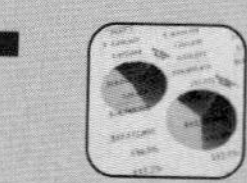

- In applying the steps and types of control, managers need to consider (1) the level of management at which they operate, (2) the areas they can draw on for resources, and (3) the style of control philosophy.
- There are three levels of control, corresponding to the three principal managerial levels. (1) Strategic control, done by top managers, is monitoring performance to ensure that strategic plans are being implemented. (2) Tactical control, done by middle managers, is monitoring performance to ensure that tactical plans are being implemented. (3) Operational control, done by first-level or supervisory managers, is monitoring performance to ensure that day-to-day goals are being implemented.
- Most organization have four areas that they can draw on for resources. (1) Physical resources include buildings,

equipment, and tangible products; these use equipment control, inventory-management controls, and quality controls. (2) Human resources use personality tests, drug tests, performance tests, employee surveys, and the like as controls to monitor people. (3) Information resources use production schedules, sales forecasts, environmental impact statements, and the like to monitor the organization's various resources. (4) Financial resources take various kinds of financial controls, as we discuss in Section 16.4.

- There are three managerial styles or control philosophies. (1) Bureaucratic control is characterized by use of rules, regulations, and formal authority to guide performance. (2) Market control is characterized by use of market mechanisms—pricing, competition, market share—to guide performance. (3) Clan control is characterized by shared values, beliefs, rituals, and trusts emanating from a common culture, and so formal controls are considered unnecessary.

16.4 Some Financial Tools for Control

- 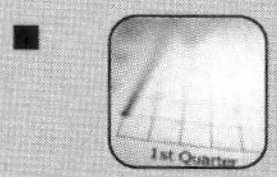
Financial controls include (1) budgets, (2) financial statements, (3) ratio analysis, and (4) audits.

- A budget is a formal financial projection. There are two budget-planning approaches, incremental and zero-based. (1) Incremental budgeting allocates increased or decreased funds to a department by using the last budget period as a reference point; only incremental changes in the budget request are reviewed. (2) Zero-based budgeting (ZBB) forces each department to start from zero in projecting the funding needs for the coming budget period. Whether incremental or zero-based, budgets are either fixed, which allocate resources on the basis of a single estimate of costs, or variable, which allow resource allocation to vary in proportion with various levels of activity.

- A financial statement is a summary of some aspect of an organization's financial status. One type, the balance sheet, summarizes an organization's overall financial worth—assets and liabilities—at a specific point in time. The other type, the income statement, summarizes an organization's financial results—revenues and expenses—over a specified period of time.

- Ratio analysis is the practice of evaluating financial ratios. Managers may use this tool to determine an organization's financial health, such as liquidity ratios, debt management ratios, or return ratios.

- Audits are formal verifications of an organization's financial and operational systems. Audits are of two types. An external audit is formal verification of an organization's financial accounts and statements by outside experts. An internal audit is a verification of an organization's financial accounts and statements by the organization's own professional staff.

16.5 Total Quality Management

- 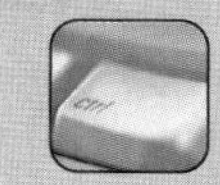
Total quality management (TQM) is defined as a comprehensive approach—led by top management and supported throughout the organization—dedicated to continuous quality improvement, training, and customer satisfaction. The two core principles of TQM are people orientation and improvement orientation.

- In the people orientation, everyone involved with the organization is asked to focus on delivering value to customers, focusing on quality. TQM requires training, teamwork, and cross-functional efforts.

- In the improvement orientation, everyone involved with the organization is supposed to make ongoing small, incremental improvements in all parts of the organization. This orientation assumes that it's less expensive to do things right the first time, to do small improvements all the time, and to follow accurate standards to eliminate small variations.

- Several techniques are available for improving quality. (1) Employee involvement can be implemented through quality circles, self-managed teams, and special-purpose teams—teams that meet to solve a special or one-time problem. (2) Benchmarking is a process by which a company compares its performance with that of high-performing organizations. (3) Outsourcing is the subcontracting of services and operations to an outside vendor. (4) Reduced cycle time consists of reducing the number of steps in a work process. (5) Statistical process control is a statistical technique that uses periodic random samples from production runs to see if quality is being maintained within a standard range of acceptability.

16.6 Managing Control Effectively

- 
Successful control systems have four common characteristics: (1) They are strategic and results oriented. (2) They are timely, accurate, and objective. (3) They are realistic, positive, and understandable and they encourage self-control. (4) They are flexible.

- Among the barriers to a successful control system are the following: (1) Organizations may exert too much control. (2) There may be too little employee participation. (3) The organization may overemphasize means instead of ends. (4) There may be an overemphasis on paperwork. (5) There may be an overemphasis on one approach instead of multiple approaches.

Management in Action

The Pharmaceutical Industry Increases Its Use of Control Techniques

Excerpted from John Carey and Michael Arndt, "Making Pills the Smart Way," Business Week, *May 3, 2004, pp. 102–103.*

BusinessWeek Despite its high-tech image, the pharmaceutical industry is less adept at manufacturing than you might expect. One recent horror story was Schering-Plough Corp.'s slip-up on asthma inhalers. In 1999 and 2000, the company recalled 59 million units because it couldn't prove that the inhalers contained the active ingredient. The Food & Drug Administration, meanwhile, has found hundreds of quality violations at other companies. The woes are a symptom of a deeper problem: factory processes so antiquated that companies typically can't even pinpoint the causes of snafus. "Manufacturing has been the poor stepchild of the pharmaceutical industry," says Jeffrey T. Macher of Georgetown University's McDonough School of Business.

Now, that stepchild is getting the attention it deserves. Macher and his colleague Jackson A. Nickerson of Washington University's Olin School of Business are leading an effort to find and correct flaws in drug-manufacturing practices and in FDA regulations. The FDA itself is altering its rules, hoping to foster more innovation in factories. And companies such as Pfizer Inc. and Abbott Laboratories are spending tens of millions a year to install new technology and processes in plants.

The potential economic gains of a quality boost are huge: "Everyone has said that costs could decline by up to 50%," Nickerson says. That would save scores of billions of dollars. The new approach would also make manufacturing more flexible, making it easier for companies to produce the personalized treatments that are expected to become common in the future.

It won't happen quickly, though. "There is a tremendous cultural change that we all have to go through," says Dr. Janet Woodcock, FDA deputy commissioner. Drug manufacturing has always been more art than science. The traditional approach: figure out by trial and error how to do each of many steps, from mixing to drying to coating tablets. Then, after each step, take samples and test to see if they meet specifications. The testing alone can take days or weeks.

Moreover, there are inevitable variations in the ingredients and in the processes. That causes many drug lots to fail the tests, wasting time and money. Once a batch develops a problem, "the cycle time—which might normally be 30 days—can easily double just doing the investigation. And the lot just sits in inventory," explains Pfizer's manufacturing quality chief, Gerry Migliaccio. And more often than not, the cause of the problems can't be found—or fixed.

Drugmakers are now tackling these issues with new approaches, such as process analytical technology (PAT). Instead of putting a drug lot on hold to test it after each step, the idea is to peer into the process itself and measure what's going on—as it's happening. It is possible, for instance, to shine a laser through a window in a blender. The constituents absorb or reflect the light differently, creating a spectrograph that can tell operators if the ingredients are mixing properly. A host of other technologies, such as Raman spectroscopy and chemical imaging, can help determine the distribution of the active ingredients in a pill or the size of the granules.

Monitoring processes in real time offers the hope of preventing problems in the first place—or coming up with solutions. Quality problems at Abbott were so bad that the FDA hammered the company with a total of $200 million in fines and shut down a Lake County (Ill.) diagnostics plant for four years. Now, with new technology and processes, Abbott can pinpoint the root causes of problems 90% of the time, compared with 50% before, and do so in an average of three months instead of six months to two years. "The biggest bang for the buck has been in investigation improvements, where we figure out what happened and fix it more quickly," says Michael G. Beatrice, vice-president for regulatory and quality sciences.

GlaxoSmithKline PLC recently got approval for a test of microbial contamination that yields results in hours, not 8 to 14 days. And Pfizer is investing more than $10 million a year in PAT. "The magic is increased understanding of the process," says Migliaccio.

The enhanced knowledge also translates into smarter regulation. Instead of being the quality backstop for industry, FDA inspectors can switch to ensuring that companies are running their processes correctly. Plus, the agency can more quickly approve changes in processes.

For Discussion

1. Why is it so difficult to use control techniques when manufacturing drugs? Explain.
2. How does low productivity in the pharmaceutical industry affect the average individual? Discuss.
3. What type of control—feedforward, concurrent, and feedback—is most important for manufacturing drugs? Explain your rationale.
4. Which of the three styles of implementing controls—bureaucratic, market, or clan—is most important to companies such as Abbott and GlaxoSmithKline? Discuss.

Self-Assessment

Do You Have Good Time-Management Skills?*

Objectives

To determine how productive you are.

To look at ways in which you can gain better time-management skills.

Introduction

As we learned in this chapter, productivity is important to companies because it ultimately determines whether or not they make profits and survive. As a student, it is important that you too be productive. Of course there are times when you would rather watch, say, *Jerry Springer* than write your 15-page term paper, and there are definitely times when a few hours at the mall sounds more appealing than a few hours with your Spanish/English dictionary. But establishing good time-management skills now will help you be more productive in all aspects of life. Productive people are important assets to an organization.

The purpose of this exercise is to determine whether or not you have good time-management skills.

Instructions

Read each question and mark your response under the relevant column—"Yes," "No," or "Sometimes." Answer the questions honestly; that is, don't answer as you feel you *should* but rather as you feel you really *would*.

1. Do you make a conscious effort to separate urgent tasks from other ones?	**Yes**	**No**	**Sometimes**
2. Do you take time to think about a situation so you can make the best possible decision?	**Yes**	**No**	**Sometimes**
3. Do you take at least one hour each day for uninterrupted time for thinking, studying, reading, or creative work?	**Yes**	**No**	**Sometimes**
4. Do you spend a lot of time maintaining relationships?	**Yes**	**No**	**Sometimes**
5. Do you work hard to be your best rather than trying to obtain perfection?	**Yes**	**No**	**Sometimes**

Interpretation

If you answered "Yes" to all five questions, your time-management skills are excellent (at least in these areas). If you answered "No" or "Sometimes" to one or more questions, you could definitely benefit by improving your time-management skills.

Questions for Discussion

1. Were you surprised by the results? Why or why not?
2. Even if you answered "Yes" to all these questions, are there some areas where you feel you could improve your time-management skills? Explain.
3. What are some ways you can improve these skills? Discuss.

*Adapted from J. Yager. "Could Your Time Management Skills Use Improvement?" *Creative Time Management for the New Millennium, www.janyager.com/self-quiz-time_management_.htm,* June 2002.

Group Exercise

Objectives

To look at ways in which companies monitor employee productivity.

To look at how monitoring productivity can be used as a control mechanism.

Introduction

In this chapter you learned that monitoring can be an effective tool for managers to identify ways to improve productivity. This control device can help them establish standards, measure performance, compare performance to goals, and assess whether corrective action is needed. The purpose of this exercise is to gain familiarity about ways managers can monitor employee productivity.

Instructions

Break into groups of five or six people. Read the following scenario, which your group is then to role-play. Discuss with your group the concerns listed in the scenario. The group should then decide whether or not your organization should use ProMax software to monitor employee productivity. Once all of the groups in the class have reached their decisions, the various groups should have a class discussion comparing their decisions and their reasoning to those of other groups.

Scenario

Your group is a team of managers for a large organization. Each of you represents a different department. Recently your CEO, who has not been happy with the organization's performance, learned from a golfing friend that the latter's company had spent $1,000 installing a software program—ProMax, made by Replicon Inc.—to monitor employee productivity. Your CEO likes the idea, but he has learned that because your company is bigger, with 2,000 employees, it would cost $20,000 to install the software. Unsure about spending this amount, he has charged all the managers with deciding whether or not the software would work for your company.

He is open to all feedback because he wants to improve the company's productivity, though not at the employees' expense. He wants all of you to do some research and decide whether or not the software would be an effective monitoring tool. He understands that each manager has a different department and that the software might not meet the needs of some of them. Among the concerns he wants you to consider: Will the software really increase productivity? In a company of 2,000 employees, will increased productivity justify the software's cost of $20,000? What are some of the ethical issues involved with using this software? What other concerns should he be made aware of?

Keeping an Eye on Employee Performance

Your group does some research and finds the following article: E. Goodridge, "Replicon Keeps a Close Watch on Employee Performance: ProMax Software Provides Managers with a Reliable Barometer of Worker's Productivity," *Information Week.com*, November 2001. *www.informationweek.com/story/WK20011101S0023,* June 2002.

Measuring the amount of time an employee spends on a job is easy. Measuring employee productivity is another matter, one that poses a challenge for project managers trying to determine accurate time expenditures when billing clients or projects. Workforce-management software supplier Replicon Inc. says it can help with an Internet-based application that tracks employee productivity in real time.

ProMax lets managers set productivity goals for employees, contract workers, projects teams, and departments. When employees enter their billable hours for the day into the software, they can immediately see how their time on the job measures up against expectations set for each individual or project team. Managers receive real-time notifications of employee productivity from the software and can immediately see if a project is running on time and spot potential problems.

While managers may appreciate the hands-on knowledge, the software's ability to measure productivity could raise concerns about employee privacy issues. Replicon CEO John Eddy insists the software will be well received by both managers and employees. "It's a barometer to let an employee know 'where do I stand this month?' and 'where do I need to focus?'" he says. "We've found employees have a natural curiosity to compare their work performance against peers."

ProMax is an application suite from Replicon that tracks and manages time and expense data. FundTech Ltd., a Jersey City, N.J., developer of cash-management infrastructure software, implemented Replicon's Web-TimeSheet 4.0, an application that tracks billable employee and project hours across international time zones and foreign currencies.

FundTech needed the software to manage its international professional services group, which develops software for clients such as Citigroup and Merrill Lynch, says Cenk Ipeker, FundTech's director of information systems and financial analysis.

Installing ProMax "is the natural progression for the company next quarter," Ipeker says. "My job is a hybrid of installing and maintaining systems while tracking project reporting. Having a tool that acts like a scorecard, offering immediate insight to worker productivity, would be helpful."

ProMax will be bundled with TimeSheet software, which is used by major companies such as AT&T, Charles Schwab, Compaq, Kraft, and Sony Music Entertainment. Pricing will range from $1,000 for up to 50 users to $20,000 for up to 2,000 users.

Questions for Discussion

1. Refer to Figure 16.4. Which steps in the control process would use this software? Do you feel this software could make any of these steps easier? How? Discuss and explain.
2. What type of control is this software: feedforward, concurrent, or feedback? Explain.
3. What level of control would this software be most effective in: strategic, tactical, or operational? Explain.
4. Do you feel the ethical concerns with this software outweigh the positive aspects of improving productivity? Why or why not?

Ethical Dilemma

Was Kenneth Lay Acting Ethically When He Bought & Sold Enron Stock?

Excerpted from Paula Dwyer, "The SEC to Top Execs: Read the Fine Print," Business Week, *July 26, 2004, pp. 33–34.*

In 2001, Enron Corp. was quietly lurching from crisis to crisis. Whatever he did or didn't know about Enron's woes at the time, Kenneth L. Lay rarely missed an opportunity to talk up the oil-and-gas trading concern with analysts and Enron employees. The exchairman and CEO even urged workers to follow his lead and buy stock. From August through October, 2001, Lay bought $4 million worth of Enron shares—which he cites as proof that he had faith in the company.

But there's a hitch. Privately, Lay was dumping far more stock than he publicly acquired, according to criminal and civil charges filed against him on July 8 [2004]. In the same three months, he sold $26 million of Enron shares. Altogether in 2001 he unloaded Enron stock for $90 million. But because those shares were sold back to Enron, Lay did not have to disclose the sales until 2002, thanks to a loophole—since closed—in Securities & Exchange Commission rules.

The difference between Lay's public statements and private actions is the foundation of the SEC's civil charges—one of the more aggressive interpretations of insider-trading law in decades.

Solving the Dilemma

What is your opinion about Kenneth Lay's behavior in 2001?

1. He's a crook and should be held liable in the civil suit against him.
2. Although he may have shown bad judgment, give the guy a break. After all, because he was not required to disclose the sale of his stock in 2001, he did not break the law.
3. Regardless of the technicalities about disclosing his stock sales, his behavior is unethical.
4. He is being used as a scapegoat by the SEC.

Video Case

Starbucks

Starbucks has nearly 6,000 outlets in more than 30 countries and annual revenues in excess of $3.3 billion. All this success rides on the back of a very small product: the coffee bean. Three-quarters of the world's coffee supply comes from small farms in the third world, and coffee producers are in the midst of a crisis. Current selling prices are less than the cost of production, and farmers constantly struggle to survive. So how does Starbucks ensure that it will continue to have access to needed products in a market that has the potential to put its suppliers out of business? To start with, Starbucks purchases only specialty coffee at prices that are almost always higher than the prevailing price for commodity-grade coffee. After all, quality comes at a price. Starbucks also negotiates prices with individual growers and co-ops for their products, which can run significantly above market prices. However, the higher prices provide stability for both the growers and the organization. Stability is also enhanced through the use of long-term contracts. Dealing directly with growers delivers more of the purchase price to the farmers. Recently, Starbucks has partnered with Ecologic Enterprise Ventures and Conservation International to provide affordable credit to producers, helping farmers break the cycle of debt plaguing their industry.

Fair Trade coffee is a recent development in the worldwide production of coffee. Coffee producers must belong to democratically run cooperatives and must implement crop management and environmental protection plans. In exchange, they are guaranteed a fair price, long-term relationships with importers, and preharvest financing. Most small farms, however, have difficulty meeting all the requirements for Fair Trade certification. For these farmers, Starbucks still honors long-standing relationships, to the benefit of all involved. Even for those producers who cannot meet the Fair Trade standards, Starbucks is becoming more involved in addressing environmental issues. After all, maintaining a sustainable coffee supply means preserving the environment in which it is grown. At one time, all coffee was grown among shade trees. The trees continually provide mulch and nitrogen to the soil, reducing the likelihood of erosion and the need for fertilizers and herbicides. Recently, however, many farmers have switched to high-yielding plants grown under direct sun. Not only does this practice destroy the forests, but sun-grown coffee requires chemical fertilizers that contaminate water supplies. In contrast, a healthy farm of shade-grown coffee can rival a tropical forest in biodiversity.

Investing in its suppliers has created a number of unexpected results. The financial effect of selling to Starbucks is immense. Farmers and their families who sell to Starbucks have access to better clothing, medicine, and education. Entire communities benefit from a strengthened infrastructure. The growers who work with Starbucks are as committed to the organization as Starbucks is to them. At Starbucks, leaders recognize that being socially aware is good for business.

Discussion Questions

1. Managers use three types of control: feedforward, concurrent, and feedback. Define each of these types. Which type is most prevalent in the relationship between Starbucks and suppliers? Provide evidence from the case to support your answer.
2. There are three levels of control: strategic, tactical, and operational. Define each of these types. Which is most evident in the case?
3. Do you see any evidence of total quality management (TQM) principles at Starbucks? Explain.

appendix

The Project Planner's Toolkit

Flowcharts, Gantt Charts, & Break-Even Analysis

major question

How can you use planning tools to enhance your performance and utmost success?

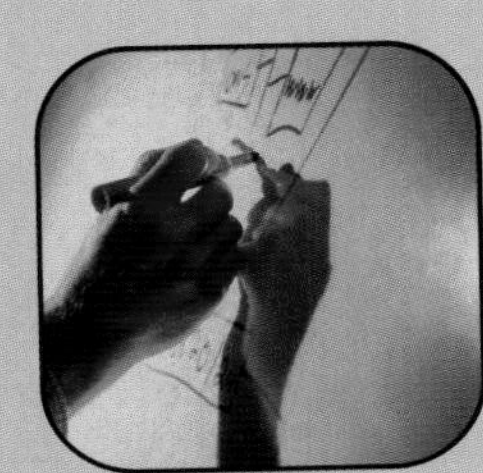

The Big Picture

Three tools used in project planning, which was covered in Chapter 5, are flowcharts, Gantt charts, and break-even analysis.

Project planning may begin (in the definition stage) as a back-of-the-envelope kind of process, but the client will expect a good deal more for the time and money being invested. Fortunately, there are various planning and monitoring tools that give the planning and execution of projects more precision. Three tools in the planner's toolkit are (1) flowcharts, (2) Gantt charts, and break-even analysis.

Tool #1: Flowcharts—for Showing Event Sequences & Alternate Decision Scenarios

A *flowchart* is a useful graphical tool for representing the sequence of events required to complete a project and for laying out "what-if" scenarios. Flowcharts have been used for decades by computer programmers and systems analysts to make a graphical "road map," as it were, of the flow of tasks required. These professionals use their own special symbols (indicating "input/output," "magnetic disk," and the like), but there is no need for you to make the process complicated. Generally, only three symbols are needed: (1) an oval for the "beginning" and "end," (2) a box for a major activity, and (3) a diamond for a "yes or no" decision. *(See Figure A.1, next page.)*

Computer programs such as Micrographix's ABC Flow Charter are available for constructing flowcharts. You can also use the drawing program in word processing programs such as Microsoft Word.

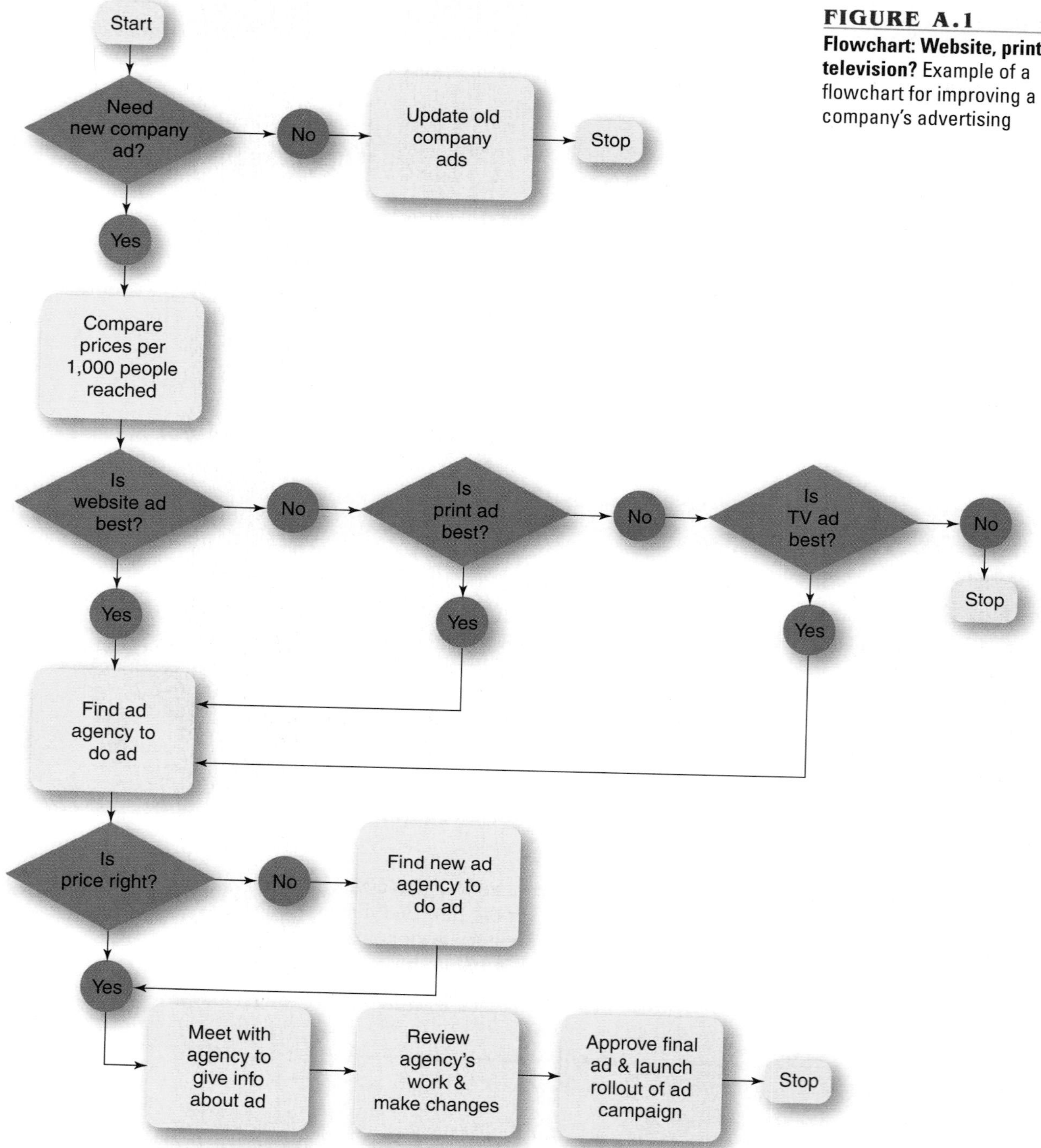

FIGURE A.1
Flowchart: Website, print, or television? Example of a flowchart for improving a company's advertising

Benefits

Flowcharts have two benefits:

- **Planning straightforward activities:** A flowchart can be quite helpful for planning ordinary activities—figuring out the best way to buy textbooks or a car, for example. It is also a straightforward way of indicating the sequence of events in, say, thinking out a new enterprise that you would then turn into a business plan.
- **Depicting alternate scenarios:** A flowchart is also useful for laying out "what-if" scenarios—as in if you answer "yes" to a decision question you should follow Plan A, if you answer "no" you should follow Plan B.

Limitations

Flowcharts have two limitations:

- **No time indication:** They don't show the amounts of time required to accomplish the various activities in a project. In building a house, the foundation might take only a couple of days, but the rough carpentry might take weeks. These time differences can't be represented graphically on a flowchart (although you could make a notation).
- **Not good for complex projects:** They aren't useful for showing projects consisting of several activities that must all be worked on at the same time. An example would be getting ready for football season's opening game, by which time the players have to be trained, the field readied, the programs printed, the band rehearsed, the ticket sellers recruited, and so on. These separate activities might each be represented on their own flowcharts, of course. But to try to express them all together all at once would produce a flowchart that would be unwieldy, even unworkable.

Tool #2: Gantt Charts—Visual Time Schedules for Work Tasks

We have mentioned how important deadlines are to making a project happen. Unlike a flowchart, a Gantt chart can graphically indicate deadlines.

The Gantt chart was developed by **Henry L. Gantt**, a member of the school of scientific management (discussed in Chapter 2).[1] **A *Gantt chart* is a kind of time schedule—a specialized bar chart that shows the relationship between the kind of work tasks planned and their scheduled completion dates.** *(See Figure A.2, next page.)*

A number of software packages can help you create and modify Gantt charts on your computer. Examples are CA-SuperProject, Microsoft Project Manager, SureTrak Project Manager, and TurboProject Professional.

Benefits

There are three benefits to using a Gantt chart:

- **Express time lines visually:** Unlike flowcharts, Gantt charts allow you to indicate visually the time to be spent on each activity.
- **Compare proposed and actual progress:** A Gantt chart may be used to compare planned time to complete a task with actual time taken to complete it, so that you can see how far ahead or behind schedule you are for the entire project. This enables you to make adjustments so as to hold to the final target dates.
- **Simplicity:** There is nothing difficult about creating a Gantt chart. You express the time across the top and the tasks down along the left side. As Figure A.2 shows, you can make use of this device while still in college to help schedule and monitor the work you need to do to meet course requirements and deadlines (for papers, projects, tests).

Limitations

Gantt charts have two limitations:

- **Not useful for large, complex projects:** Although a Gantt chart can express the interrelations among the activities of relatively small projects, it becomes cumbersome and unwieldy when used for large, complex projects. More sophisticated management planning tools may be needed, such as PERT networks.
- **Time assumptions are subjective:** The time assumptions expressed may be purely subjective; there is no range between "optimistic" and "pessimistic" of the time needed to accomplish a given task.

FIGURE A.2

Gantt chart for designing a website. This shows the tasks accomplished and the time planned for remaining tasks to build a company website.

Accomplished: ||||||||||

Planned: \\\\\\\\\\

<table>
<tr><th>Stage of development</th><th>Week 1</th><th>Week 2</th><th>Week 3</th><th>Week 4</th><th>Week 5</th></tr>
<tr><td>1. Examine competitors' websites</td><td>||||||||||||||||||
||||||||||</td><td>||||||||||</td><td></td><td></td><td></td></tr>
<tr><td>2. Get information for your website</td><td>||||||||||||||||||
||||||||||</td><td>||||||||||||||||||
||||||||||</td><td></td><td></td><td></td></tr>
<tr><td>3. Learn web authoring software</td><td></td><td>||||||||||||||||||
||||||||||</td><td>||||||||||||||||||
||||||||||</td><td></td><td></td></tr>
<tr><td>4. Create (design) your website</td><td></td><td></td><td>\\\\\\\\\\</td><td>\\\\\\\\\\\\\\\\\\
\\</td><td>\\\\\</td></tr>
<tr><td>5. "Publish" (put) website online</td><td></td><td></td><td></td><td></td><td>\\\\\\\\\\\\\\\</td></tr>
</table>

Tool #3: Break-Even Analysis—How Many Items Should You Sell to Turn a Profit?

***Break-even analysis* is a way of identifying how much revenue is needed to cover the total costs of developing and selling a product.** Let's walk through the computation of a break-even analysis, referring to the illustration. *(See Figure A.3.)* We assume you are an apparel manufacturer making shirts or blouses. Start in the lower-right corner of the diagram and follow the circled numbers as you read the description on the opposite page.

FIGURE A.3

Break-even analysis

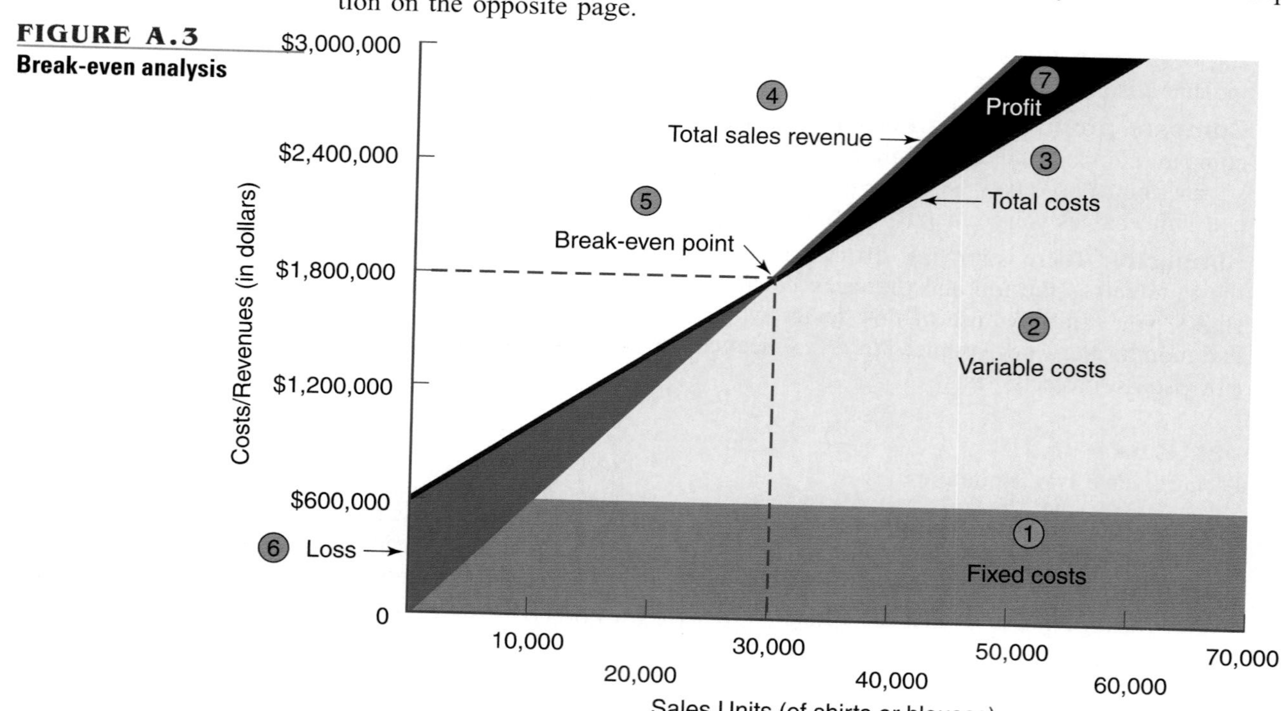

① ***Fixed costs (green area):*** Once you start up a business, whether you sell anything or not, you'll have expenses that won't vary much, such as rent, insurance, taxes, and perhaps salaries. These are called ***fixed costs,* expenses that don't change regardless of your sales or output.** Fixed costs are a function of time—they are expenses you have to pay out on a regular basis, such as weekly, monthly, or yearly. Here the chart shows the fixed costs (green area) are $600,000 per year no matter how many sales units (of shirts or blouses) you sell.

② ***Variable costs (blue area):*** Now suppose you start producing and selling a product, such as blouses or shirts. At this point you'll be paying for materials, supplies, labor, sales commissions, and delivery expenses. These are called ***variable costs,* expenses that vary directly depending on the numbers of the product that you produce and sell.** (After all, making more shirts will cost you more in cloth, for example.) Variable costs, then, are a function of volume—they go up and down depending on the number of products you make or sell. Here the variable costs (blue area) are relatively small if you sell only a few thousand shirts but they go up tremendously if you sell, say, 70,000 shirts.

③ ***Total costs (first right upward-sloping line—green plus blue area added together):*** The sum of the fixed costs and the variable costs equals the total costs (the green and blue areas together). This is indicated by the line that slopes upward to the right from $600,000 to $3,000,000.

④ ***Total sales revenue (second right upward-sloping line):*** This is the total dollars received from the sale of however many units you sell. The sales revenue varies depending on the number of units you sell. Thus, for example, if you sell 30,000 shirts, you'll receive $1,800,000 in revenue. If you sell 40,000 shirts, you'll receive somewhat more than $2,400,000 in revenue.

⑤ ***Break-even point (intersection of dashed lines):*** Finding this point is the purpose of this whole exercise. **The *break-even point* is the amount of sales revenue at which there is no profit but also no loss to your company.** On the graph, this occurs where the "Total sales revenues" line crosses the "Total costs" line, as we've indicated here where the dashed lines meet. This means that you must sell 30,000 shirts and receive $1,800,000 in revenue in order to recoup your total costs (fixed plus variable). Important note: Here is where pricing the shirts becomes important. If you raise the price per shirt, you may be able to make the same amount of money (hit your break-even point) by selling fewer of them—but that may be harder to do because customers may resist buying at the higher price.

⑥ ***Loss (red area):*** If you fail to sell enough shirts at the right price (the break-even point), you will suffer a loss. ***Loss* means your total costs exceed your total sales revenue.** As the chart shows, here you are literally "in the red"—you've lost money.

⑦ ***Profit (black area):*** Here you are literally "in the black"—you've made money. All the shirts you sell beyond the break-even point constitute a profit. ***Profit* is the amount by which total revenue exceeds total costs.** The more shirts you sell, of course, the greater the profit.

The kind of break-even analysis demonstrated here is known as the ***graphic method.*** The same thing can also be done algebraically.

Example

Break-Even Analysis: Why Do Airfares Vary So Much?

Why do some airlines charge four times more than others for a flight of the same distance?

There are several reasons, but break-even analysis enters into it.

United Airlines' average cost for flying a passenger 1 mile in 2003 was 11.7 cents, whereas Southwest's was 7.7 cents. Those are the break-even costs. What they charged beyond that was their profit.

Why the difference? One reason, according to a study by the U.S. Department of Transportation, is that Southwest's expenses are lower. United flies more long routes than short ones, so its costs are stretched out over more miles, making its costs for flying shorter routes higher than Southwest's.

Another factor affecting airfares is the type of passengers flying a particular route—whether they are high-fare-paying business travelers or more price-conscious leisure travelers. Business travelers often don't mind paying a lot (they are reimbursed by their companies), and those routes (such as Chicago to Cincinnati) tend to have more first-class seats, which drives up the average price. Flights to vacation spots (such as Las Vegas) usually have more low-price seats because people aren't willing to pay a lot for pleasure travel. Also, nonstop flight fares often cost more than flights with connections.

Benefits

Break-even analysis has two benefits:

- **For doing future "what-if" alternate scenarios of costs, prices, and sales:** This tool allows you to vary the different possible costs, prices, and sales quantities to do rough "what-if" scenarios to determine possible pricing and sales goals. Since the numbers are interrelated, if you change one, the others will change also.
- **For analyzing the profitability of past projects:** While break-even analysis is usually used as a tool for future projects, it can also be used retroactively to find out whether the goal of profitability was really achieved, since costs may well have changed during the course of the project. In addition, you can use it to determine the impact of cutting costs once profits flow.

Limitations

Break-even analysis is not a cure-all.

- **It oversimplifies:** In the real world, things don't happen as neatly as this model implies. For instance, fixed and variable costs are not always so readily distinguishable. Or fixed costs may change as the number of sales units goes up. And not all customers may pay the same price (some may get discounts).
- **The assumptions may be faulty:** On paper, the formula may work perfectly for identifying a product's profitability. But what if customers find the prices too high? Or what if sales figures are outrageously optimistic? In the marketplace, your price and sales forecasts may really be only good guesses.

Chapter Notes

CHAPTER 1

1. P. Nakache, "Can You Handle the Truth About Your Career?" *Fortune,* July 7, 1997, p. 208.
2. H. Lancaster, "If Your Career Needs More Attention, Maybe You Should Get an Agent," *The Wall Street Journal,* October 20, 1998, p. B1.
3. R. L. Knowdell, "The 10 New Rules for Strategizing Your Career," *The Futurist,* June–July 1998, pp. 19–24.
4. D. Kreneck, quoted in M. W. Thompson, "In the Maelstrom," *American Journalism Review,* December 1998, pp. 38–44.
5. Thompson, 1998.
6. M. P. Follett, quoted in J. F. Stoner and R. E. Freeman, *Management,* 5th ed. (Englewood Cliffs, NJ: Prentice Hall, 1992), p. 6.
7. "Frustrated Bank Customer Lets His Computer Make Complaint," *Los Angeles Times,* October 20, 1993, p. A28.
8. The Gartner Group, cited in Don Oldenburg, Associated Press, "Tired of Automated Phone Menus? Press 1," *Reno Gazette-Journal,* March 15, 2004, p. 3E.
9. Scott Broetzmann, quoted in Oldenburg, 2004.
10. Patrick McGeehan, "Pay Came to $111,000 a Day for Ex-Chief at Citigroup," *New York Times,* March 17, 2004, pp. C1, C13.
11. David R. Francis, "Moves Afoot to Curb CEO Salaries," *The Christian Science Monitor,* July 8, 2003;www.csmonitor.com/2003/0708/p02s02-usec.htm (accessed March 18, 2004).
12. Naween Mangi, "What's Pushing Small-Biz Salaries Sky-High," *Business Week,* August 8, 2000; www.businessweek.com/smallbiz/008/sb00808.htm (accessed March 18, 2004).
13. O. Pollar, "Are You Sure You Want to Be a Manager?" *San Francisco Examiner,* October 4, 1998, p. J-3.
14. M. Csikszentmihalyi, *Flow: The Psychology of Optimal Experience* (New York: HarperCollins, 1990), and *Beyond Boredom and Anxiety* (San Francisco: Jossey-Bass, 1975).
15. Gene J. Koprowski, UPI Technology News, "The Web: The Effect of Illegal Downloading," United Press International, February 18, 2004; www.upi.com/view.cfm?Story ID=200402217-094656-5863r (accessed March 22, 2004). See also Verlyn Klinkenborg, "Tower Records in the Maelstrom of Consumer Desire," *New York Times,* February 15, 2004, Sec. 4 p. 10; Lara Mossa, "Music Dies at Two Stores," *Daily Oakland Press,* February 21, 2004; and Jim Wasserman, "Tower Records Emerges from Bankruptcy," *New York Newsday,* March 15, 2004.
16. U.S. Census Bureau, "U.S. Interim Projections by Age, Sex, Race, and Hispanic Origin," Table 1a, 2004; www.census.gov/ipc/www/usinterimproj (accessed March 18, 2004).
17. W.-T. Kwok, "Online Sensitivity," *San Jose Mercury News,* November 29, 1998, p. 2E.
18. Michael M. Phillips, "More Work Is Outsourced to U.S. Than Away from It, Data Show," *The Wall Street Journal,* March 15, 2004, p. A2.
19. R. D. Hof, "How E-Biz Rose, Fell, and Will Rise Anew," *Business Week,* May 13, 2002, p. 67.
20. M. J. Mandel and R. D. Hof, "Rethinking the Internet," *Business Week,* March 26, 2001, p. 118. See also B. Powell, "The New World Order," *Fortune,* May 14, 2001, pp. 134, 136.
21. Data from "Hurry Up and Decide!" *Business Week,* May 14, 2001.
22. S. Cabot, reported in D. Jones, "Sales Reps Must Watch Step When Rapping Rivals," *USA Today,* June 17, 1997, p. 3B.
23. M. Murray, "A Software Engineer Becomes a Manager, with Many Regrets," *The Wall Street Journal,* May 14, 1997, pp. A1, A14.
24. S. Armour, "Management Loses Its Allure," *USA Today,* October 15, 1997, pp. 1B, 2B.
25. Pollar, 1998.
26. P. Drucker, reported in R. L. Knowdell, "A Model for Managers in the Future Workplace: Symphony Conductor," *The Futurist,* June–July 1998, p. 22.
27. Quentin Hardy, "We Did It," *Forbes,* August 8, 2003; www.forbes.com/forbes/2003/0811/076_print.html (accessed March 18, 2004); Peter Burrows, "Showtime," *Business Week,* February 2, 2004, pp. 56–64.
28. J. Falvey, *After College: The Business of Getting a Job* (Charlotte, VT: Williamson, 1986).
29. B. Karlin, quoted in S. Spring, "Job Titles of the Future: Director of Great People," *Fast Company,* February–March, 1999, p. 46.
30. S. Spring, "Job Titles of the Future: Chief Travel Scientist," *Fast Company,* February–March, 1999, p. 68.
31. C. Sittenfeld, "Hope Is a Weapon," *Fast Company,* February–March, 1999, pp. 179–184.
32. P. M. Blau and W. R. Scott, *Formal Organizations* (San Francisco: Chandler, 1962).
33. H. Mintzberg, *The Nature of Managerial Work* (New York: Harper & Row, 1973).
34. Mintzberg, 1973.
35. J. P. Kotter, "What Effective General Managers Really Do," *Harvard Business Review,* March–April 1999, pp. 145–159.
36. L. Stroh, quoted in A. Muoio, "Balancing Acts," *Fast Company,* February–March 1999, pp. 83–90.
37. S. MacDermid, Purdue University, and M. D. Lee, McGill University, two-year study cited in R. W. Huppke, Associated Press, "Take This Job, and Love It," *San Francisco Chronicle,* January 28, 1999, p. B2.
38. A. Deutschman, "The CEO's Secret of Managing Time," *Fortune,* June 1, 1992, pp. 135–146.
39. D. G. Lepore, quoted in Muio, 1999.
40. H. Lancaster, "Managing Your Time in Real-World Chaos Takes Real Planning," *The Wall Street Journal,* August 19, 1997, p. B1.
41. R. E. Kelley, quoted in S. Shellenbarger, "You Don't Have to Be Chained to Your Desk to Be a Star Performer," *The Wall Street Journal,* August 12, 1998, p. B1.
42. B. Graham, quoted in Shellenbarger, 1998.
43. R. L. Katz, "Skills of an Effective Administrator," *Harvard Business Review,* September–October, 1974, p. 94.
44. Barbara Ross, quoted in Thompson, 1998.
45. C. Cotts, "Press Clips," *Village Voice,* March 29, 2000, ccotts@villagevoice.com.
46. D. Shoemaker, quoted in I. DeBare, "The Incredible Growing Workweek," *San Francisco Chronicle,* February 12, 1999, pp. B1, B2.
47. E. B. Zechmeister and S. E. Nyberg, *Human Memory: An Introduction to Research and Theory* (Pacific Grove, CA: Brooks/Cole, 1982).
48. B. K. Bromage and R. E. Meyer, "Quantitative and Qualitative Effects of Repetition on Learning from Technical Text," *Journal of Educational Psychology,* 1982, vol. 78, pp. 271–278.
49. F. P. Robinson, *Effective Study,* 4th ed. (New York: Harper & Row, 1970).
50. H. C. Lindgren, *The Psychology of College Success: A Dynamic Approach* (New York: Wiley, 1969).
51. R. J. Palkovitz and R. K. Lore, "Note Taking and Note Review: Why Students Fail Questions Based on Lecture Material," *Teaching of Psychology,* 1980, vol. 7, pp. 159–161.
52. J. Langan and J. Nadell, *Doing Well in College: A Concise Guide to Reading, Writing, and Study Skills* (New York: McGraw-Hill, 1980), pp. 93–110.
53. Palkovitz and Lore, 1980, pp. 159–161.

CHAPTER 2

1. E. J. Langer, *The Power of Mindful Learning* (Reading, MA: Addison-Wesley, 1997), p. 4.
2. E. J. Langer, *Mindfulness* (Reading, MA: Addison-Wesley, 1989), pp. 12–13.
3. Langer, 1989, p. 69.
4. A. Webber, "The Best Organization Is No Organization," *USA Today,* March 6, 1997, p. 13A.
5. A. Maslow, "A Theory of Human Motivation," *Psychological Review,* July 1943, pp. 370–396.
6. D. McGregor, *The Human Side of Enterprise* (New York: McGraw-Hill, 1960).
7. See J. T. Delaney, "Workplace Cooperation: Current Problems, New Approaches," *Journal of Labor Research,* Winter 1996, pp. 45–61; H. Mintzberg, D. Dougherty, J. Jorgensen, and F. Westley, "Some Surprising Things About Collaboration—Knowing How People Connect Makes It Work Better," *Organizational Dynamics,* Spring 1996, pp. 60–71; R. Crow, "Institutionalized Competition and Its Effects on Teamwork," *Journal for Quality and Participation,* June 1995, pp. 46–54; K. G. Smith, S. J. Carroll, and S. J. Ashford, "Intra- and Interorganizational Cooperation: Toward a Research Agenda," *Academy of Management Journal,* February 1995, pp. 7–23; M. E. Haskins, J. Liedtka, and J. Rosenblum, "Beyond Teams: Toward an Ethic of Collaboration," *Organizational Dynamics,* Spring 1998, pp. 34–50; and C. C. Chen, X. P. Chen, and J. R. Meindl, "How Can Cooperation Be Fostered? The Cultural Effects of Individualism-Collectivism," *Academy of Management Review,* April 1998, pp. 285–304.
8. A. Kohn, "How to Succeed without Even Vying," *Psychology Today,* September 1986, pp. 27–28. Sports psychologists discuss "cooperative competition" in S. Sleek, "Competition: Who's the Real Opponent?" *APA Monitor,* July 1996, p. 8.
9. D. W. Johnson, G. Maruyama, R. Johnson, D. Nelson, and L. Skon, "Effects of Cooperative, Competitive, and Individualistic Goal Structures on Achievement: A Meta-Analysis," *Psychological Bulletin,* January 1981, pp. 56–57. An alternative interpretation of the foregoing study that emphasizes the influence of situational factors can be found in J. L. Cotton and M. S. Cook, "Meta-Analysis and the Effects of Various Reward Systems: Some Different Conclusions from Johnson et al.," *Psychological Bulletin,* July 1982, pp. 176–183. Also see A. E. Ortiz, D. W. Johnson, and R. T. Johnson, "The Effect of Positive Goal and Resource Interdependence on Individual Performance," *The Journal of Social Psychology,* April 1996, pp. 243–249; and S. L. Gaertner, J. F. Dovidio, M. C. Rust, J. A. Nier, B. S. Banker, C. M. Ward, G. R. Mottola, and M. Houlette, "Reducing Intergroup Bias: Elements of Intergroup Cooperation," *Journal of Personality and Social Psychology,* March 1999, pp. 388–402.
10. E. Perkins, "How to Book Hotel Rooms at Half the Price," *San Francisco Examiner,* December 13, 1998, p. T-2.
11. R. W. Belsky, "Being Hotel Savvy," *The Dollar Stretcher;* www.stretcher.com/stories/00/000515c.cfm (accessed March 25, 2004).
12. S. F. Brown, "Wresting New Wealth from the Supply Chain," *Fortune,* November 9, 1998, pp. 204[C]–204[Z].
13. B. Wysocki Jr., "To Fix Health Care, Hospitals Take Tips from Factory Floor," *The Wall Street Journal,* April 9, 2004, pp. A1, A6.
14. J. Strasburg, "Shaking the Blues," *San Francisco Chronicle,* February 3, 2002, pp. G1, G3; N. Munk, "How Levi's Trashed a Great American Brand," *Fortune,* April 12, 1999, pp. 83–90; and E. Neuborne, K. Kerwin, and bureau reports, "Generation Y," *Business Week,* February 15, 1999, pp. 80–88.
15. N. Klein, *No Logo: Taking Aim at the Brand Bullies* (New York: St. Martin's Press, 1999).
16. J. Strasburg, "Levi's 7th Year of Declining Sales; Company to Economize with Layoffs, Other Trims," *San Francisco Chronicle,* March 2, 2004, p. B-1; and "California; Levi Closes Its Last Two Sewing Plants in U.S.," *Los Angeles Times,* January 9, 2004, p. C-2.
17. J. Schlosser, "Teacher's Bet," *Fortune,* March 8, 2004, pp. 158–164.
18. G. Loveman, "Diamonds in the Data Mine," *Harvard Business Review,* May 2003, pp. 109–113.
19. L. Walker, "Data-Mining Software Digs for Business Leads," *San Francisco Chronicle*, March 8, 2004, p. E6; reprinted from *Washington Post.*
20. J. Case, *Open-Book Management: The Coming Business Revolution* (New York: HarperBusiness, 1996).
21. J. Pfeffer, in A. M. Webber, "Danger: Toxic Company," *Fast Company,* November 1998, pp. 152–161.
22. J. Pfeffer, *The Human Equation: Building Profits by Putting People First* (Cambridge, MA: Harvard Business School Press, 1996).
23. C. Kleiman, "Companies Embracing 'Open-Book' Management," *San Jose Mercury News,* May 18, 1997, pp. PC1, PC2.
24. G. T. Brown, quoted in Kleiman, 1997.
25. K. Carney, "How to Keep Staff in a Boom Economy," *Inc.,* November 1998, p. 110.
26. I. Mochari, "How Motley Fools Talk Back," *Inc.,* June 1999, p. 108.
27. G. Bylinksy, "How to Bring Out Better Products Faster," *Fortune,* November 23, 1998, pp. 238[B]–238[T].
28. P. Senge, *The Fifth Discipline* (New York: Doubleday, 1990), p. 1.
29. R. Hodgetts, F. Luthans, and S. Lee, "New Paradigm Organizations: From Total Quality to Learning to World-Class," *Organizational Dynamics,* Winter 1994, pp. 5–19D; and A. Garvin, "Building a Learning Organization," *Harvard Business Review,* July/August 1993, pp. 78–91.
30. A. S. Miner and S. J. Mezias, "Ugly Duckling No More: Pasts and Futures of Organizational Learning Research," *Organization Science,* January–February 1996, pp. 88–99; and R. P. Mai, *Learning Partnerships: How Leading American Companies Implement Organizational Learning* (Chicago: Irwin, 1996).
31. R. Schultz, quoted in J. Martin "Are You as Good as You Think You Are?" *Fortune,* September 30, 1996, p. 146.
32. D. M. Noer, *Breaking Free: A Prescription for Personal and Organizational Change* (San Francisco: Jossey-Bass, 1996); S. F. Slater, "Learning to Change," *Business Horizons,* November–December 1995, pp. 13–20; and D. Ulrich, T. Jick, and M. Von Glinow, "High-Impact Learning: Building and Diffusing Learning Capability," *Organizational Dynamics,* Autumn 1993, pp. 52–66.
33. Excerpted from J. L. Lunsford, "Lean Times: With Airbus on Its Tail, Boeing Is Rethinking How It Builds Planes," *The Wall Street Journal,* October 5, 2001, pp. A1, A16.
34. P. Burrows, "Show Time," *Business Week,* February 2, 2004, pp. 56–64; N. A. Wishart, J. J. Elam, D. Robey, "Redrawing the Portrait of a Learning Organization: Inside Knight-Ridder, Inc.," *Academy of Management Executive,* February 1996, pp. 7–20; C. Argyris, "Good Communication that Blocks Learning," *Harvard Business Review,* July–August 1994, pp. 77–85; and D. A. Garvin, "Building a Learning Organization," *Harvard Business Review,* July–August 1993, pp. 78–91.

CHAPTER 3

1. Survey by Caliper, Princeton, NJ, 1998. Cited in A. Fisher, "Am I Too Old to Be a Tech Expert?… What Are Employers Really Looking For?" *Fortune,* May 25, 1998, p. 202.
2. O. Pollar, "Keeping Sane in Workplace Full of Change," *San Francisco Examiner,* July 27, 1997, p. J-3.
3. A. Zimmerman, "Costco's Dilemma: Be Kind to Its Workers, or Wall Street?" *The Wall Street Journal,* March 26, 2004, pp. B1, B3; J. Flanigan,

"Costco Sees Value in Higher Pay," *Los Angeles Times,* February 15, 2004, www.latimes.com/business/la-fi-flan15feb15,1,61048 (accessed March 29, 2004); and C. Frey, "Costco's Love of Labor: Employees' Well-being Key to Its Success," *Seattle Post-Intelligencer,* March 29, 2004, http://seattlepi.nwsource.com/business/ 166680_costco29.html (accessed March 29, 2004).

4. J. Useem, "Should We Admire Wal-Mart?" *Fortune,* March 8, 2004, pp. 118–120. See also A. Harrington, "America's Most Admired Companies," *Fortune,* March 8, 2004, pp. 80–82.
5. Zimmerman, 2004, p. B1.
6. Useem, 2004, p. 120.
7. R. B. Reich, "The Company of the Future," *Fast Company,* November 1998, pp. 124–150.
8. M. J. Driver, "Careers: A Review of Personnel and Organizational Research," in C. L. Cooper and I. Robertson, eds., *International Review of Industrial and Organizational Psychology* (New York: Wiley, 1988).
9. Lieber, 1998.
10. Christopher Hart, author of *Extraordinary Guarantees,* quoted in A. Comarow, "Broken? No Problem," *U.S. News & World Report,* January 11, 1999, pp. 68–69.
11. R. Langreth, M. Waldholz, S. D. Moore, "Big Drug Firms Discuss Linking Up to Pursue Disease-Causing Genes," *The Wall Street Journal,* March 4, 1999, pp. A1, A8.
12. S. Greenhouse, "Labor Is Forced to Reassess as Union Leaders Convene," *New York Times,* March 9, 2004, p. A12.
13. R. Pollin, "In Politics: Savvy Organizers Win 'Living Wage' Across U.S.," *San Jose Mercury News,* December 6, 1998, pp. 1P, 6P.
14. L. Atkinson and J. Galaskiewicz, "Stock Ownership and Company Contributions to Charity," *Administrative Science Quarterly,* vol. 33, 1988, pp. 82–100.
15. K. Boo, "The Churn," *The New Yorker,* March 29, 2004, pp. 62–73.
16. J. Madrick, "Economic Scene; As Job Exports Rise, Some Economists Rethink the Mathematics of Free Trade," *New York Times,* March 18, 2004, p. C2.
17. L. Dobbs, "The Imbalance of Trade," *U.S. News & World Report,* April 5, 2004, p. 46.
18. E. Brazil, "300 Protest Gap in S.F.," *San Francisco Examiner,* March 7, 1999, p. A-2.
19. See, for example, J. Blackstone, "Exxon's *Valdez* Fines Still Unpaid," CBS Evening News, March 24, 2004, www.cbsnews.com/stories/2004/03/24/eveningnews/main608520.shtml (accessed March 30, 2004).
20. B. Nussbaum, "Where Are the Jobs?" *Business Week,* March 22, 2004, pp. 36–37.
21. Doug, quoted in C. Sutton, "Designing Women Show Off Their Marks," *San Francisco Examiner,* March 7, 1999, p. W-33.
22. M. Boyle, "Atkins World," *Fortune,* January 12, 2004, pp. 94–104.
23. D. Foote and A. Murr, "Back on the Block," *Newsweek,* May 6, 2002, pp. 42–47.
24. M. Galanter, reported in W. Glaberson, "When the Verdict Is Just a Fantasy," *New York Times,* June 6, 1999, sec. 4 pp. 1, 6.
25. P. Geitner, "Microsoft Says EU Stepping on U.S. Turf," *The Globe & Mail,* March 24, 2004, p. B9.
26. American Council on Education, reported by P. Wingert, "'F' in Global Competence," *Newsweek,* May 20, 2002, p. 11.
27. G. Allred, quoted in S. Armour, "Facing a Tough Choice: Your Ethics or Your Job," *USA Today,* September 21, 1998, p. B1.
28. L. T. Hosmer, *The Ethics of Management* (Homewood, IL: Irwin, 1987).
29. B. Kabanoff, "Equity, Equality, Power, and Conflict," *Academy of Management Review,* April 1991, pp. 416–441.
30. D. Fritzsche and H. Baker, "Linking Management Behavior to Ethical Philosophy: An Empirical Investigation," *Academy of Management Journal,* March 1984, pp. 166–175.
31. S. H. Verhovek, "Northwest Confronts Its Growth: Wild Salmon Called Endangered," *New York Times,* March 16, 1999, pp. A1, A13; Associated Press, "Pacific Salmon to Stay on Endangered List," May 28, 2004, http://msnbc.msn.com/id/5085081, accessed June 12, 2004.
32. American Management Association, reported in M. Jackson, "Most Firms Spy on Employees, Survey Finds," *San Francisco Chronicle,* May 23, 1997, pp. B1, B4; and D. Hawkins, "Who's Watching Now?" *U.S. News & World Report,* September 15, 1997, pp. 55–58.
33. M. C. Gross, quoted in C. Hymowitz, "CEOs Set the Tone for How to Handle Questions of Ethics," *The Wall Street Journal,* December 22, 1998, p. B1.
34. A. Bennett, "Ethics Codes Spread Despite Criticism," *The Wall Street Journal,* July 15, 1988, p. 13.
35. C. Wiley, "The ABC's of Business Ethics: Definitions, Philosophies, and Implementation," *Industrial Management,* January/February 1995, pp. 22–27.
36. T. R. Mitchell, D. Daniels, H. Hopper, J. George-Falvy, and G. R. Ferris, "Perceived Correlates of Illegal Behavior in Organizations," *Journal of Business Ethics,* April 1996, pp. 439–455.
37. R. Pear, "Whistleblowers Likely to Get Stronger Federal Protections," *New York Times,* March 15, 1999, pp. A1, A17.
38. Study by C. C. Masten, inspector general, U.S. Department of Labor, reported in Pear, 1999.
39. F. J. Evans, quoted in C. S. Stewart, "A Question of Ethics: How to Teach Them?" *New York Times,* March 21, 2004, sec. 3, p. 11.
40. C. Andrews, McDonough School of Business, Georgetown University, quoted in Stewart, 2004.
41. S. Seitz, "Richard French Is Doing Good While Doing Well," *The Union Leader,* January 27, 2003, www.theunionleader.com/articles_show.html?article=17708 (accessed April 5, 2004).
42. R. French, quoted in R. D. Schatz and C. Poole, "The Two Bottom Lines: Profits and People," *Business Week,* December 7, 1998, pp. ENT 4, ENT 6.
43. C. MacKerron, quoted in C. Said, "Creating a Corporate Conscience," *San Francisco Chronicle,* March 30, 2004, pp. C1, C6.
44. Roper Starch Worldwide Inc. and Cone Communications 1996 survey, reported in Schatz and Poole, 1998.
45. A. B. Carroll, "The Pyramid of Corporate Responsibility: Toward the Moral Management of Organizational Stakeholders," *Business Horizons,* July/August 1991, p. 42.
46. M. Friedman, *Capitalism and Freedom* (Chicago: University of Chicago Press, 1962).
47. P. Samuelson, "Love that Corporation," *Mountain Bell Magazine,* Spring 1971.
48. A. B. Carroll, *Business & Society: Ethics and Stakeholder Management* (Cincinnati: South-Western, 1989), p. 60.
49. E. Gatewood and A. B. Carroll, "The Anatomy of Corporate Social Response," *Business Horizons,* September–October, 1981, pp. 9–16.
50. D. Eisenberg, "Eyeing the Competition," *Time,* March 22, 1999, pp. 58–59.
51. "Tech Companies to Customers: Privacy Is History" [editorial], *USA Today,* March 12, 1999, p. 14A.
52. J. Collins and J. Porras, *Built to Last: Successful Habits of Visionary Companies* (London: Century Business, 1996).
53. W. Davison, D. Worrell, and C. Lee, "Stock Market Reactions to Announced Corporate Illegalities," *Journal of Business Ethics,* December 1994, pp. 979–988.

54. M. Baucus and D. Baucus, "Paying the Piper: An Empirical Examination of Longer-Term Financial Consequences of Illegal Corporate Behavior," *Academy of Management Journal,* vol. 40, 1997, pp. 129–151.

55. R. Gildea, "Consumer Survey Confirms Corporate Social Action Affects Buying Decisions," *Public Relations Quarterly,* Winter 1994, pp. 20–21.

56. D. Turban and D. Greening, "Corporate Social Performance and Organizational Attractiveness to Prospective Employees," *Academy of Management Journal,* vol. 40, 1997, pp. 658–672.

57. J. Cloud, "Why Coors Went Soft," *Time,* November 2, 1998, p. 70.

58. O. Pollar, "Why Diversity Improves the Bottom Line," *San Francisco Examiner,* November 1, 1998, p. J-1.

59. M. Loden, *Implementing Diversity* (Chicago: Irwin, 1996), pp.14–15.

60. H. Collingwood, "Who Handles a Diverse Work Force Best?" *Working Woman,* February 1996, p. 25.

61. See A. Karr, "Work Week: A Special News Report about Life on the Job—and Trends Taking Shape There," *The Wall Street Journal,* June 1, 1999, p. A1.

62. B. Schlender, "Peter Drucker Takes the Long View," *Fortune,* September 28, 1998, pp. 162–173.

63. R. H. Elliott, "Human Resource Management's Role in the Future Aging of the Workforce," *Public Personnel Administration,* Spring 1995, pp. 5–7.

64. T. G. Exter, "In and Out of Work," *American Demographics,* June 1992, p. 63.

65. B. Cheng, "Gen X Women: Moving Up," *Business Week,* June 14, 2002; www.businessweek.com/print/careers/content/jun2002/ca20020614_3443.htm?bw (accessed April 7, 2004).

66. Study by AFL-CIO and the Institute for Women's Policy Research, reported in T. Lewin, "Union Links Women's Pay to Poverty Among Families," *New York Times,* February 25, 1999, p. A17.

67. Catalyst Inc., reported in Deibel, 1999.

68. Catalyst Inc., reported in L. Tischler, "Where Are the Women?" *Fast Company,* February 2004, pp. 52–60.

69. J. S. Lublin, "Women at the Top Are Still Distant from CEO Jobs," *The Wall Street Journal,* February 28, 1996, pp. B1, B4.

70. R. Sharpe, "As Leaders, Women Rule," *Business Week,* November 20, 2000, pp. 75–84.

71. K. Wisul, "The Bottom Line on Women at the Top," *Business Week,* January 26, 2004; www.businessweek.com/bwdaily/dnflash/jan2004/nf20040126_3378_db035.htm (accessed April 7, 2004).

72. Exter, 1992.

73. U.S. Equal Employment Opportunity Commission, Occupational Employment in Private Industry by Race/Ethnic Group/Sex, and by Industry, United States, 2000; www.eeoc.gov/stats/jobpat/2000/national.html (accessed April 13, 2004).

74. C. Farell, G. DeGeorge, R. A. Melcher, and S. Anderson, "Is Black Progress Set to Stall?" *Business Week,* November 6, 1995, pp. 68, 72, 76.

75. J. I. Sanchez and P. Brock, "Outcomes of Perceived Discrimination among Hispanic Employees: Is Diversity Management a Luxury or a Necessity?" *Academy of Management Journal,* June 1996, pp. 704–719.

76. F. J. Milliken and L. L. Martins, "Searching for Common Threads: Understanding the Multiple Effects of Diversity in Organizational Groups," *Academy of Management Review,* April 1996, pp. 402–433.

77. M. Conlin, "Taking Precautions—or Harassing Workers?" *Business Week,* December 3, 2001, p. 84.

78. B. E. Whitley, Jr., and M. E. Kite, "Sex Differences in Attitudes toward Homosexuality: A Comment on Oliver and Hyde (1993)," *Psychological Bulletin,* January 1995, pp. 146–154.

79. October 1, 2003, study by Harris Interactive Inc. and Witeck Combs Communications Inc., reported in C. Edwards, "Coming Out in Corporate America," *Business Week,* December 15, 2003; www.businessweek.com:/print/magazine/content/03_50/b3862080.htm?bw (accessed April 7, 2004).

80. J. M. Croteau, "Research on the Work Experiences of Lesbian, Gay, and Bisexual People: An Integrative Review of Methodology and Findings," *Journal of Vocational Behavior,* April 1996, pp. 195–209; and L. Badgett, "The Wage Effects of Sexual Orientation Discrimination," *Industrial and Labor Relations Review,* July 1995, pp. 726–739.

81. Edwards, 2003.

82. D. Braddock and L. Bachelder, *The Glass Ceiling and Persons with Disabilities* (Washington, D.C.: Glass Ceiling Commission, U.S. Department of Labor, 1994).

83. K. Springen, "A Boost for Braille," *Newsweek,* May 20, 2002, p. 13.

84. D. L. Stone and A. Colella, "A Model of Factors Affecting the Treatment of Disabled Individuals in Organizations," *Academy of Management Review,* April 1996, pp. 352–401; and G. C. Pati and E. K. Baily, "Empowering People with Disabilities: Strategy and Human Resource Issues in Implementing the ADA," *Organizational Dynamics,* Winter 1995, pp. 52–69.

85. D. C. Feldman and W. H. Turnley, "Underemployment among Recent Business College Graduates," *Journal of Organizational Behavior,* November 1995, pp. 691–706.

86. P. Kaufman, M. N. Alt, and C. Chapman, *Droput Rates in the United States: 2000* (Washington, D.C.: National Center for Education Statistics, 2001).

87. "High School Dropouts by Age, Race, and Hispanic Origin: 1979 to 1993," *Statistical Abstract of the United States,* September 1995, p. 174; and S. Reese, "Illiteracy at Work," *American Demographics,* April 1996, pp. 14–15.

88. T. L. Smith, "The Resource Center: Finding Solutions for Illiteracy," *HRFocus,* February 1995, p. 7. See also A. Bernstein, "The Time Bomb in the Workforce: Illiteracy," *Business Week,* February 25, 2002, p. 122.

89. M. Loden, 1996; E. E. Spragins, "Benchmark: The Diverse Work Force," *Inc.,* January 1993, p. 33.; and A. M. Morrison, *The New Leaders: Guidelines on Leadership Diversity in America* (San Francisco: Jossey-Bass, 1992).

90. G. Dell'Orto, "Special Classes Help 3M Workers Learn How to Get Along," *San Francisco Chronicle,* June 2, 2000, p. B4.

91. S. Shellenbarger, "Please Send Chocolate: Moms Now Face Stress Moving In and Out of Work Force," *The Wall Street Journal,* May 9, 2002, p. D1. See also A. Bernstein, "Too Many Workers? Not for Long," *Business Week,* May 20, 2002, pp. 126–130.

92. D. Roth, "Catch Us If You Can," *Fortune,* February 9, 2004, pp. 65–74.

93. J. Sandred, "Skype's Not Yet Up to All the Hype," *San Francisco Chronicle,* April 5, 2004, pp. D1, D2; and Roth, 2004; and K. Maney, "Kazaa Creators' Latest Invention, Skype, Could Turn Telecom on Its Ear," *USA Today,* April 14, 2004, p.3B.

94. N. Templin, "Boutique-Hotel Group Thrives on Quirks," *The Wall Street Journal,* March 18, 1999, pp. B1, B9.

95. J. M. Higgins, "Innovate or Evaporate: Seven Secrets of Innovative Corporations," *The Futurist,* September–October 1995, pp. 42–43; K.Yakal, "Now You Can Use Your Post-It Notes Electronically," *Computer Shopper,* June 1997, p. 547; and "A Notable Idea," *Selling Power,* May 1998, p. 81.

96. P. F. Drucker, *Innovation and Entrepreneurship* (New York: Harper & Row, 1986), pp. 27–28.
97. Webber, 1998.
98. Bureau of Labor Statistics, cited in Clark, 1998.
99. D. C. McClelland, *The Achieving Society* (New York: Van Nostrand, 1961); D. C. McClelland, *Human Motivation* (Glenview, IL: Scott Foresman, 1985); D. L. Sexton and N. Bowman, "The Entrepreneur: A Capable Executive and More," *Journal of Business Venturing,* vol. 1, 1985, pp. 129–140; D. Hisrich, "Entrepreneurship/Intrapreneurship," *American Psychologist,* February 1990, p. 218; T. Begley and D. P. Boyd, "Psychological Characteristics Associated with Performance in Entrepreneurial Firms and Smaller Businesses," *Journal of Business Venturing,* vol. 2, 1987, pp. 79–93; and C. R. Kuehl and P. A. Lambing, *Small Business: Planning and Management* (Fort Worth, TX: Dryden Press, 19).
100. Global Entrepreneurship Monitor, 2002 study by London Business School and Babson College, reported in J. Bailey, "Desire—More Than Need—Builds a Business," *The Wall Street Journal,* May 21, 2002, p. B4.

CHAPTER 4

1. Survey by the Zimmerman Agency for Residence Inn by Marriott, in "Things You Love to Miss," *USA Today,* March 1, 1999, p. 1B.
2. C. Bowman, "Commuter Flier Is No Longer a Rare Bird," *San Francisco Chronicle,* April 12, 1999, pp. A1, A15.
3. P. Saffo, quoted in G. P. Zachary, "It's a Bird. It's a Plane. It's a Commuter!" *San Francisco Examiner,* September 20, 1998, pp. J-1, J-2; reprinted from *The Wall Street Journal.*
4. V. Schubert-Martin, quoted in S. Armour and K. L. Alexander, 1997.
5. H. Lancaster, "Global Managers Need Boundless Sensitivity, Rugged Constitutions," *The Wall Street Journal,* October 13, 1998, p. B1.
6. These events are described in K. Maney, "Economy Embraces Truly Global Workplace," *USA Today,* December 31, 1998, pp. 1B, 2B.
7. Cellular Telecommunications Industry Association, cited in A. Dunkin, "Smart, Useful—and They Won't Put a Sag in Your Suit," *Business Week,* May 30, 1994, p. 141.
8. Federal Communications Commission, *Annual Report and Analysis of Competitive Market Conditions with Respect to Commercial Mobile Services;* http://hraunfoss.fcc.gov/edocs_public/attachmatch/FCC-03-150A1.pdf (accessed April 19, 2004).
9. Global Reach, "Global Internet Statistics," March 2004; http://global-reach.biz/globstats/index.php3 (accessed April 19, 2004).
10. See J. Quittner, "Tim Berners-Lee," *Time,* March 29, 1999, pp. 193–194.
11. "U.S. Ecommerce Sales on the Up-and-Up," *The Register,* February 24, 2004; www.theregister.com/2004/02/24/us_ecommerce_sales (accessed April 19, 2004).
12. Odyssey, reported in S. Lohr, "Survey Suggests Consumers Are Taking to E-Commerce," *New York Times,* March 22, 1999, p. C4.
13. R. Hof, "Amazon's Stock: Hurts So Good," *Business Week,* January 28, 2004; www.businessweek.com/technology/content/jan2004/tc20040128_3685_tc024.htm (accessed April 19, 2004); and D. Shand, "S&P Raises Credit Ratings for Amazon.com," *Business Week,* April 14, 2004; www.businessweek.com/investor/content/apr2004/pi20040414_3961_pi036.htm (accessed April 19, 2004).
14. R. M. Kantor, quoted in K. Maney, 1998.
15. Maney, 1998.
16. N. Birdsall, quoted in C. Kleiman, "Global Knowledge Helps in Making Career Decisions," *San Jose Mercury News,* September 24, 1995, p. 1PC.
17. K Pennar, "Two Steps Forward, One Step Back," *Business Week,* August 31, 1998, pp. 116–119.
18. C. Smadja, "Living Dangerously," *Time,* February 22, 1999, pp. 94–95.
19. N. Negroponte, quoted in Maney, 1998.
20. A. Sloan, "In the Land of Giants," *Newsweek,* August 10, 1998, pp. 42–43.
21. Sloan, 1998.
22. J. Beckett, "Going, Going, Gone—'Bay Traders' Sold on Auctions," *San Francisco Chronicle,* April 12, 1999, pp. B1, B3.
23. L. M. Hughes, quoted in C. Kleiman, "Women Can Raise Their Visibility by Pursuing Overseas Assignments," *San Jose Mercury News,* November 29, 1998, p. PC1; reprinted from *Chicago Tribune.*
24. Windham International, New York, cited in Kleiman, 1998.
25. L. O. Hallstein, reported in Kleiman, 1998.
26. The Wats House for Select Appointments, North America, in "Skills in Demand," *USA Today,* July 7, 1998, p. 1B.
27. Hallstein, reported in Kleiman, 1998.
28. A. B. Isaacs, "Tact Can Seal a Global Deal . . . ," *New York Times,* July 26, 1998, sec. 3, p. 13.
29. T. L. Speer, "Gender Barriers Crumbling, Traveling Business Women Report," *USA Today,* March 16, 1999, p. 5E.
30. S. Dunung, *Doing Business in Asia: The Complete Guide* (San Francisco: Jossey-Bass, 1998), quoted in Speer, 1999.
31. The Wats House for Select Appointments, North America, 1998.
32. Anne Fisher, "Readers Weigh In on Work and Women Abroad," *Fortune,* March 29, 1999, p. 200.
33. A. Fisher, "Think Globally, Save Your Job Locally," *Fortune,* February 23, 2004, p. 60.
34. D. A. Heenan and H. V. Perlmutter, *Multinational Organization Development* (Reading, MA: Addison-Wesley, 1979).
35. R. Kopp, "International Human Resource Policies and Practices in Japanese, European, and United States Multinationals," *Human Resource Management,* Winter 1994, pp. 581–599.
36. D. Barboza, "Pluralism under Golden Arches," *New York Times,* February 12, 1999, pp. C1, C7.
37. S. McCartney, "Who's Inspecting Your Airplane?" *The Wall Street Journal,* March 3, 2004, pp. D1, D12.
38. Study of government data by Economic Policy Institute, Washington, D. C., cited in R. Keil and L. Arnold, "New Jobs Created at Low End," *San Francisco Chronicle,* April 13, 2004, p. C5.
39. Survey of manufacturing employers by Federal Reserve Bank of Philadelphia, *Business Outlook Survey,* April 2004, www.phil.frb.org/files/bos/bos0404.html (accessed April 22, 2004); see also B. Hagenbaugh, "Good Help Hard to Find for Manufacturers," *USA Today,* April 16, 2004, p. 1B.
40. "Outsourcing Jobs: Is It Bad?" *Business Week,* August 25, 2003, p. 36; "Where Are the Jobs?" *Business Week,* March 22, 2004, p. 37.
41. K. Brown, "Offshore Outsourcing Will Increase, Poll Finds," *The Wall Street Journal,* March 26, 2004, p. B3; and C. Kirby, "Firms Plan to Send More Jobs Abroad," *San Francisco Chronicle,* March 29, 2004, pp. C1, C2.
42. S. Zuckerman, "Some Jobs May Not Return," *San Francisco Chronicle,* February 22, 2004, pp. I-1, I-14; J. Madrick, "As Job Exports Rise, Some Economists Rethink the Mathematics of Free Trade," *New York Times,* March 18, 2004, p. C2; J. C. Cooper, "The Price of Efficiency," *Business Week,* March 22, 2004, pp. 38–42; and J. E. Hilsenrath, "Behind Outsourcing Debate: Surprisingly Few Hard Numbers," *The Wall Street Journal,* April 12, 2004, pp. A1, A7.

43. H. R. Varian, "With Free Trade, What Goes Abroad Usually Finds Its Way Back, to Everyone's Benefit," *New York Times,* March 11, 2004, p. C2.

44. B. Schlender, "Peter Drucker Sets Us Straight," *Fortune,* January 12, 2004, pp. 115–118.

45. Forrester Research, "Losing Our Edge? Estimated Number of High-Skilled U.S. Jobs Moving Offshore," reported in K. Madigan, "Yes: This Is No Longer About a Few Low-Wage or Manufacturing Jobs. Now One Out of Three Jobs Is At Risk," *Business Week,* August 25, 2003, pp. 37–38.

46. J. Thottam, "Is Your Job Going Abroad?" *Time,* March 1, 2004, pp. 26–34.

47. F. Levy, quoted in D. Wessel, "The Future of Jobs: New Ones Arise, Wage Gap Widens," *The Wall Street Journal,* April 2, 2004, pp. A1, A5.

48. K. B. Mitchell, quoted in Fisher, 2004.

49. A. M. Chaker, "Where the Jobs Are," *The Wall Street Journal,* March 18, 2004, pp. D1, D3; J. Shinal, "Which Types of Jobs Will Be in Demand?" *San Francisco Chronicle,* March 25, 2004, pp. C1, C4; and D. Wessel, "The Future of Jobs: New Ones Arise, Wage Gap Widens," *The Wall Street Journal,* April 2, 2004, pp. A1, A5.

50. J. Spohrer, quoted in Shinal, 2004.

51. Drucker, quoted in Schlender, 2004.

52. Wessel, 2004.

53. M. Mendenhall, B. J. Punnett, and D. Ricks, *Global Management* (Cambridge, MA: Blackwell, 1995).

54. U.S. Census Bureau, International Data Base, "Countries Ranked by Population: 2050," updated July 17, 2003; www.census.gov/cgi-bin/ipc/idbrank.pl (accessed April 19, 2004).

55. R. J. Bowman, "Are You Covered?" *World Trade,* March 1995, pp. 100–104.

56. J. Ewinger, "Steel, Tariffs, and Politics Mix at U.S.-Canada Conference," *Cleveland Plain Dealer,* April 18, 2004; www.cleveland.com/news/plaindealer/index.ssf?/base/news/1082282265327050.xml (accessed April 18, 2004).

57. "China to Cancel Car Import Quota in 2005," *China Daily,* February 13, 2004; www.chinadaily.com.cn/english/doc/2004-02/13/content_305954.htm (accessed April 18, 2004).

58. J. Bhagwati, *Protectionism* (Cambridge, MA: MIT Press, 1988).

59. "WTO Telecoms Deal Will Ring in the Changes on 5 February 1998," *World Trade Organization,* January 26, 1998.

60. C. Koch, "It's a Wired, Wired World," *Webmaster,* March 1997, pp. 50–55.

61. E. Iritani, "NAFTA 10 Years Later: U.S. Reaps Bittersweet Fruit of Merger," *Los Angeles Times,* January 19, 2004, p. A1.

62. J. Audley, *Learning Lessons Taught by NAFTA* (Washington, D.C.: Carnegie Endowment for International Peace, 2003); originally published in the *San Diego Union-Tribune,* November 25, 2003; www.ceip.org/files/publications/2003-11-25-sdut.asp (accessed April 20, 2004). See also Iritani, 2004; "Happy Birthday, NAFTA," *Business Week,* December 22, 2003; www.businessweek.com/@@81m9*4cQB0OUSw0A/magazine/content/03_51/b3863147_mz029.htm (accessed April 20, 2004); J. E. Garten, "At 10, NAFTA Is Ready for an Overhaul," *Business Week,* December 22, 2003; www.businessweek.com/@@81m9*4cQB0OUSw0A/magazine/content/03_51/b3863044_mz007.htm (accessed April 20, 2004); and G. Smith and C. Lindblad, "Mexico: Was NAFTA Worth It?" *Business Week,* December 22, 2003; www.businessweek.com/@@81m9*4cQB0OUSw0A/magazine/content/03_51/b3863008.htm (accessed April 20, 2004).

63. F. Vivano, "EU Nations Seek Harmony on Immigrants," *San Francisco Chronicle,* March 5, 1999, p. A10.

64. S. Porjes, "Strengthening Diversity," *International Business,* November 1996, pp. 18–24; and M. Elliott, "Hey, Can You Spare a 'Euro'?" *Newsweek,* February 17, 1997, pp. 48–49.

65. "Fair's Fair" [letters], *West, San Jose Mercury News,* April 4, 1999, pp. 3–4.

66. "Going Global? Stifle Yourself!" *Training,* August 1995, p. 14.

67. "How Cultures Collide," *Psychology Today,* July 1976, p. 69.

68. See P. R. Harris and R. T. Moran, *Managing Cultural Differences,* 4th ed. (Houston: Gulf Publishing, 1996), pp. 223–228; and M. Hilling, "Avoid Expatriate Culture Shock," *HR Magazine,* July 1993, pp. 58–63.

69. This list is based on E. T. Hall, "The Silent Language in Overseas Business," *Harvard Business Review,* May–June 1960, pp. 87–96; and R. Knotts, "Cross-Cultural Management: Transformations and Adaptations," *Business Horizons,* January–February 1989, pp. 29–33.

70. A discussion of Japanese stereotypes in America can be found in L. Smith, "Fear and Loathing of Japan," *Fortune,* February 26, 1990, pp. 50–57.

71. G. A. Michaelson, "Global Gold," *Success,* March 1996, p. 16.

72. Harris Poll, National Foreign Language Center, reported in "Lingua Franca?" *USA Today,* February 23, 1999, p. 1A.

73. Translation services are discussed in D. Pianko, "Smooth Translations," *Management Review,* July 1996, p. 10. CompuServe's online translation service for English, French, Spanish, and German is briefly discussed in L. Alderman, "Step into Cyberspace with an E-mailbox," *Money,* April 1995, p. 174.

74. W. D. St. John, "You Are What You Communicate," *Personnel Journal,* October 1985, p. 40.

75. The importance of nonverbal communication is discussed by D. Arthur, "The Importance of Body Language," *HRFocus,* June 1995, pp. 22–23; and N. M. Grant, "The Silent Shroud: Build Bridges, Not Barriers," *HRFocus,* April 1995, p. 16.

76. Guidelines taken from R. E. Axtell, *Gestures: The Do's and Taboos of Body Language Around the World* (New York: John Wiley & Sons, 1991).

77. "How Cultures Collide," 1976.

78. Norms for cross-cultural eye contact are discussed by C. Engholm, *When Business East Meets Business West: The Guide to Practice and Protocol in the Pacific Rim* (New York: Wiley, 1991).

79. See J. A. Russell, "Facial Expressions of Emotion: What Lies Beyond Minimal Universality?" *Psychological Bulletin,* November 1995, pp. 379–391.

80. Related research is summarized by J. A. Hall, "Male and Female Nonverbal Behavior," in *Multichannel Integrations of Nonverbal Behavior,* eds. A. W. Siegman and S. Feldstein (Hillsdale, NJ: Lawrence Erlbaum, 1985), pp. 195–226.

81. A thorough discussion of cross-cultural differences is provided by Axtell, 1991. Problems with body language analysis also are discussed by C. L. Karrass, "Body Language: Beware the Hype," *Traffic Management,* January 1992, p. 27; and M. Everett and B. Wiesendanger, "What Does Body Language Really Say?" *Sales & Marketing Management,* April 1992, p. 40.

82. Results can be found in Hall, 1985.

83. J. Burgoon, "Types of Touch in Cross-Sex Relationships between Coworkers," *Applied Communication Research,* reported in D. Jones, "Females Bosses Can Touch More Freely," *USA Today,* February 19, 2002, p. 9B.

84. E. T. Hall, *The Hidden Dimension* (New York: Doubleday, 1966).

85. R. W. Moore, "Time, Culture, and Comparative Management: A Review and Future Direction," in *Advances in Comparative Management,* vol. 5. ed. S. B. Prasad (Greenwich, CT: JAI Press, 1990), pp. 7–8.

86. R. Wartzman, "In the Wake of NAFTA, a Family Firm Sees the Business Go South," *The Wall Street Journal,* February 23, 1999, pp. A1, A10.

87. Results adapted from and value definitions quoted from S. R. Safranski and I.-W. Kwon, "Religious Groups and Management Value Systems," in *Advances in International Comparative Management,* vol. 3, eds. R. N. Farner and E. G. McGoun (Greenwich, CT: JAI Press, 1988), pp. 171–183.

88. J. Pohl, "Readers' Views Differ on Buying Japanese," letter to the editor, *Reno Gazette-Journal,* December 5, 2001, p. 9A.

CHAPTER 5

1. P. Sandman, reported in C. J. Farley, "Guarding Against Day-to-Day, Often Deadly Risks," *USA Today,* March 28, 1991, p. 6D.

2. W. F. Vitulli, quoted in R. Bahr, "Stack the Deck," *Men's Health,* August 1991, pp. 82–84.

3. Bahr, 1991.

4. Bahr, 1991.

5. D. G. Myers, *The Pursuit of Happiness: Who Is Happy—and Why* (New York: William Morrow, 1992).

6. R. Kreitner, *Management,* 7th ed. (Boston: Houghton Mifflin, 1998), p. 160.

7. M. Dell, quoted in C. Farkas and P. DeBacker, *Maximum Leadership: The World's Leading CEOs Share Their Five Strategies for Success* (New York: Henry Holt, 1996).

8. Kreitner, 1998, p. 162.

9. R. O. Crockett, "Motorola's Brass Ring," *BusinessWeek Online,* April 21, 2004, www.businessweek.com:/print/technology/content/apr2004/tc20040421_7085_tc024.htm?bw (accessed May 4, 2004).

10. M. Specter, "The Phone Guy," *The New Yorker,* November 26, 2001, pp. 62–72; and J. Guyon, "Nokia Rocks Its Rivals," *Fortune,* March 4, 2002, pp. 115–118.

11. R. O. Crockett, A. Reinhardt, and M. Ihlwan, "Cell Phones: Who's Calling the Shots?" *Business Week,* April 26, 2004, pp. 48–49.

12. R. O. Crockett, S. Rosenbush, and C. Yang, "No Wires, No Rules," *Business Week,* April 26, 2004, pp. 95–102.

13. R. E. Miles and C. C. Snow, *Organizational Strategy, Structure, and Process* (New York: McGraw-Hill, 1978).

14. D. C. Hambrick, "On the Staying Power of Defenders, Analyzers, and Prospectors," *Academy of Management Executive,* November 2003, pp. 115–118. For more about the four basic strategy types, see also D. J. Ketchen Jr., "Introduction: Raymond E. Miles and Charles C. Snow's *Organizational Strategy, Structure, and Process,*" *Academy of Management Executive,* November 2003, pp. 95–96; D. J. Ketchen Jr., "An Interview with Raymond E. Miles and Charles C. Snow," *Academy of Management Executive,* November 2003, pp. 97–104; S. E. Brunk, "From Theory to Practice: Applying Miles and Snow's Ideas to Understand and Improve Firm Performance," *Academy of Management Executive,* November 2003, pp. 105–108; and S. Ghoshal, "Miles and Snow: Enduring Insights for Managers," *Academy of Management Executive,* November 2003, pp. 109–114.

15. D. Leider, "Purposeful Work," *Utne Reader,* July/August 1988, p. 52; excerpted from *On Purpose: A Journal about New Lifestyles & Workstyles,* Winter 1986.

16. P. F. Drucker, *The Practice of Management* (New York: Harper & Row, 1954), p. 122.

17. J. Bezos, "From Zero to 10 Million in Less Than Four Years: Amazon.com to Pass E-Commerce Milestone Today," June 7, 1999, PRNewswire, Amazon.com online press release.

18. Amazon.com Web site, "About Amazon.com: Amazon.com Company Information"; and P. de Jonge, "Riding the Wild, Perilous Waters of Amazon.com," *New York Times Magazine,* March 14, 1999, pp. 36–41, 54, 68, 79–80.

19. Amazon.com 2003 Annual Report, reprinting letter from 1997 Annual Report, http://media.corporate-ir.net/media_files/irol/97/97664/reports/Annual_Report_2003041304.pdf (accessed June 23, 2004).

20. Ford Motor Company, "Vision, Mission, Values," 2003, www.mycareer.ford.com/OURCOMPANY.ASP?CID=23 (accessed June 23, 2004).

21. T. A. Stewart, "A Refreshing Change: Vision Statements That Make Sense," *Fortune,* September 30, 1996, pp. 195–196.

22. Gibney Jr., 1999.

23. de Jonge, 1999.

24. J. Bezos, quoted in D. Eisenberg, "Now It's One Big Market," *Time,* April 5, 1999, pp. 64–65.

25. Amazon.com 1998 Annual Report.

26. Ford Motor Company, 2003.

27. P. J. Below, G. L. Morrisey, and B. L. Acomb, *The Executive Guide to Strategic Planning* (San Francisco: Jossey-Bass, 1987), p. 2.

28. Survey conducted by the Society for Human Resource Management and the Balance Scorecard Collaborative, reported in J. Mullich, "Get in Line," *Workforce Management,* December 2003, pp. 43–44.

29. S. Khan and B. Hansen, "Routes, Type of Fliers Affect Range in Airfare Costs," *USA Today,* May 11, 1999, p. 9B; and B. De Lollis, "Southwest Plans Non-stop, Coast-to-Coast Flights," *USA Today,* May 8, 2002, p. 1B.

30. A. Serwer, "Southwest Airlines: The Hottest Thing in the Sky," *Fortune,* February 23, 2004, www.fortune.com/fortune/subs/article/0,15114,590780,00.html (accessed June 21, 2004).

31. "How Herb Keeps Southwest Hopping," *Money,* June 1999, pp. 61–62.

32. H. Kelleher, quoted in "How Herb Keeps Southwest Hopping," 1999.

33. Adapted from M. Shnayerson, "Dick Snyder's Tarnished Crown," *Vanity Fair,* May 1999, pp. 110–129.

34. See E. A. Locke and G. P. Latham, "Building a Practically Useful Theory of Goal Setting and Task Motivation," *American Psychologist,* September 2002, pp. 705–717.

35. Drucker, 1954.

36. Lock and Latham, 2002.

37. R. Rodgers and J. E. Hunter, "Impact of Management by Objectives on Organizational Productivity," *Journal of Applied Psychology,* April 1991, pp. 322–336.

38. J. Greene, "Microsoft's Midlife Crisis," *Business Week,* April 19, 2004, pp. 88–98.

39. J. W. Weiss and R. K. Wysocki, *5-Phase Project Management* (Reading, MA: Addison-Wesley, 1992), pp. 3–4.

40. T. S. Pitsis, S. R. Clegg, M. Marosszeky, and T. Rura-Polley, "Constructing the Olympic Dream: A Future Perfect Strategy of Project Management," *Organization Science,* September–October 2003, pp. 574–590.

41. TheFreeDictionary.com, 2004, http://encyclopedia.thefreedictionary.com/project%20management (accessed June 23, 2004).

42. R. Gandossy, "The Need for Speed," *Journal of Business Strategy,* January/February 2003, pp. 29–33. See also M. B. Lippitt, "Six Priorities That Make a Great Strategic Decision," *Journal of Business Strategy,* January/February 2003, pp. 21–24.

43. See P. B. Marren, "Business in the Age of Terrorism," *Journal of Business Strategy,* July/August 2002, pp. 19–23.

44. A. Toffler, *Powershift: Knowledge, Wealth, and Violence at the Edge of the 21st Century* (New York: Bantam Books, 1990), pp. 196–197.

45. M. Campbell-Kelly and W. Aspray, *Computer: A History of the Information Machine* (New York: Basic Books, 1996), pp. 253–256.
46. B. Elgin, "Google," *Business Week,* May 3, 2004, pp. 82–90.
47. C. Wahlstrom and B. K. Williams, *Learning Success: Being Your Best at College & Life,* 3rd ed. (Belmont, CA: Wadsworth, 2002).
48. C. Shavers, "Detail vs. Strategic Thinking Can Put Workers at Odds," *San Jose Mercury News,* November 1, 1998, p. 3E.

CHAPTER 6

1. D. K. Rigby, "What's Today's Special at the Consultant's Café?" *Fortune,* September 7, 1998, pp. 162–163.
2. C. Krauss, "Use of Management Tools Leaps 60% as Managers Seek to Navigate Economic Uncertainty," June 2, 2003, Bain & Company press release, www.bain.com/management_tools/pr_detail.asp?id=12197&menu_url=press%5Freleases%2Easp (accessed May 18, 2004).
3. A. J. Slywotzky and D. J. Morrison, quoted in G. Colvin, "The Most Valuable Quality in a Manager," *Fortune,* December 29, 1997, pp. 279–280.
4. John A. Byrne, "Going Where the Money Is," *Business Week,* January 26, 1998, p. 14; review of A. J. Slywotzky and D. J. Morrison, with B. Andelman, *The Profit Zone* (New York: Times Business, 1998).
5. "Intel vs. TI: Guess Who's the Underdog" *BusinessWeek Online,* April 26, 2004, www.businessweek.com/technology/content/apr2004/tc20040426_6980_tc119.htm (accessed May 18, 2004); and H. Green, "Intel's Telecom Weapon: WiMax," *BusinessWeek Online,* April 26, 2004, www.businessweek.com/magazine/ content/04_17/b3880606.htm (accessed May 18, 2004).
6. Colvin, 1997.
7. B. W. Barry, "A Beginner's Guide to Strategic Planning," *The Futurist,* April 1998, pp. 33–36; from B. W. Barry, *Planning Workbook for Nonprofit Organizations* (St. Paul, MN: Amherst H. Wilder Foundation, 1997).
8. A. A. Thompson Jr. and A. J. Strickland III, *Strategic Management: Concepts and Cases,* 6th ed. (Homewood, IL: BPI/Irwin, 1992); and Barry, 1998.
9. N. Byrnes and P. C. Judge, "Internet Anxiety," *Business Week,* June 28, 1999, pp. 79–88.
10. A. Busch III, quoted in interview with G. Hamel, "Turning Your Business Upside Down," *Fortune,* June 23, 1997, pp. 87–88.
11. Barry, 1998.
12. H. Mintzberg, "The Strategy Concept II: Another Look at Why Organizations Need Strategies," *California Management Review,* vol. 30, no.1, 1987, pp. 25–32.
13. G. Hamel, "Killer Strategies That Make Shareholders Rich," *Fortune,* June 23, 1997, pp. 70–84.
14. Byrne, 1998.
15. C. R. Schwenk and C. B. Shrader, "Effects of Formal Strategic Planning on Financial Performance in Small Firms: A Meta-Analysis," *Entrepreneurship Theory and Practice,* Spring 1993, pp. 53–64.
16. "Reputation Renewal," *The Wall Street Journal,* March 30, 2004, pp. B1, B7; adopted from R. J. Alsop, *The 18 Immutable Laws of Corporate Reputation: Creating, Protecting, and Repairing Your Most Valuable Asset* (New York: Free Press, 2004).
17. S. V. Brull, "DVD and Conquer: Why One Technology Prevailed," *Business Week,* July 5, 1999, p. 34; J. Brinkley, "Few Tears Are Shed as DivX Joins the 8-Track," *New York Times,* June 24, 1999, p. D6; M. Fleeman, "Net Flics Soon Will Be Mouse Click Away," *San Francisco Chronicle,* May 31, 1999, pp. E1, E3; and L. Wiener, "New TVs and DVD: Wait or Buy Now?" *U.S. News & World Report,* November 24, 1997, p. 96.
18. P. Svensson, "CDs and DVDs Not So Immortal After All," *The Mercury News* (San Jose, Calif.), May 5, 2004, www.mercurynews.com/mld/mercurynews/8596442.htm?1c (accessed May 18, 2004).
19. M. Snider, "High-Defintion DVD on the Way," *USA Today,* April 27, 2004, www.usatoday.com/tech/news/techinnovations/2003-04-27-hddvd-main_x.htm (accessed May 18, 2004).
20. G. Catapano, quoted in I. Austen, "Dueling Visions of a High-Definition DVD," *New York Times,* April 29, 2004, p. G8.
21. W. Disney, quoted in B. Nanus, *Visionary Leadership: Creating a Compelling Sense of Direction for Your Organization* (San Francisco: Jossey-Bass, 1992), p. 28; reprinted from B. Thomas, *Walt Disney: An American Tradition* (New York: Simon & Schuster, 1976), p. 247.
22. C. A. O'Reilly III and M. L. Tushman, "A Clear Eye for Innovation," *Harvard Business School Working Knowledge,* April 26, 2004; excerpted from "The Ambidextrous Organization," *Harvard Business Review,* April 2004, http://hbswk.hbs.edu/item.jhtml?id=4097&t=leadership&nl=y (accessed May 18, 2004).
23. Nanus, 1992, pp. 28–29.
24. R. Kreitner, *Management,* 7th ed. (Boston: Houghton Mifflin, 1998), p. 206.
25. C. H. Roush Jr. and B. C. Ball Jr., "Controlling the Implementation of Strategy," *Managerial Planning,* November–December 1980, p. 4.
26. Barry, 1998.
27. Barry, 1998, p. 36.
28. Booz, Allen & Hamilton study, cited in S. Winston, *The Organized Executive: New Ways to Manage Time, Paper, People & the Electronic Office,* updated and revised for the nineties (New York: W. W. Norton, 1994), p. 152.
29. K. Maher, "Running Meetings," *The Wall Street Journal,* January 13, 2004, p. B6.
30. C. L. Romero, "Tedious Meetings Top Time-Waster," *Arizona Republic,* April 22, 2003, p. D2.
31. P. M. Lencioni, *Death by Meeting: A Leadership Fable . . . About Solving the Most Painful Problem in Business* (San Francisco: Jossey-Bass, 2004).
32. P. Lencioni, reported in D. Murphy, "Making Sense of Meetings," *San Francisco Chronicle,* April 3, 2004, p. 1C.
33. O. Pollar, "Questions on Peers, Time, and Meetings," *San Francisco Examiner,* June 27, 1999, p. J-3.
34. Winston, 1994, pp. 152–157, 163–164; G. English, "How About a Good Word for Meetings?" *Management Review,* June 1990, pp. 58–60; L. G. McDougle, "Conducting a Successful Meeting," *Personnel Journal,* January 1981.
35. R. Gibson, "Starbucks Holders Wake Up, Smell the Coffee and Sell," *The Wall Street Journal,* July 2, 1999, p. B3; C. Emert, "Why Starbucks Bid for Williams-Sonoma," *San Francisco Chronicle,* June 29, 1999, pp. C1, C7; N. Deogun, "Joe Wakes Up, Smells the Soda," *The Wall Street Journal,* June 8, 1999, pp. B1, B16; C. Burress, "Coffee Heavyweight Rattles Berkeley's 'Gourmet Ghetto,'" *San Francisco Chronicle,* June 1, 1999, p. A12; N. D. Schwartz, "Still Perking After All These Years," *Fortune,* May 24, 1999, pp. 203–210; H. Schultz and D. J. Yan, "Starbucks: Making Values Pay," *Fortune,* September 29, 1997, pp. 261–262; and J. Reese, "Starbucks: Inside the Coffee Cult," *Fortune,* December 9, 1996, pp. 190–200.
36. A. Serwer, "Hot Starbucks to Go," *Fortune,* January 26, 2004, pp. 60–74.
37. Kreitner, 1998, p. 214.
38. J. W. Schoen, "Higher Fuel Prices Threaten Airline Recovery," Business with MSNBC, May 20, 2004, http://msnbc.msn.com/id/5023489 (accessed June 7, 2004).

39. D. Levin, "Hedging Helps Low-Cost Airlines Hold Down Price of Aviation Fuel," *Detroit News,* March 18, 2004, www.detnews.com/2004/business/0403/18/c01-95805.htm (accessed June 7, 2004).

40. G. Kelly, quoted in Reuters, "Rising Fuel Costs Spoil U.S. Profit Outlook," *Airwise News,* March 10, 2004, http://news.airwise.com/stories/2004/03/1078949013.html (accessed June 7, 2004).

41. M. E. Porter, *Competitive Strategy* (New York: The Free Press, 1980).

42. Porter, 1980; and M. E. Porter, *The Competitive Advantage of Nations* (New York: The Free Press, 1990).

43. J. Greenberg, quoted in B. Horovitz, "Restoring the Golden-Arch Shine," *USA Today,* June 16, 1999, p. 3B.

44. Horovitz, 1999.

45. P. Connors, "J&J Decides to Discontinue Its Hismanal," The *Wall Street Journal,* June 22, 1999, p. B9.

46. M. Arndt, "A Tall Order for McDonald's New Chief," *BusinessWeek Online,* April 20, 2004. www.businessweek.com/bwdaily/dnflash/apr2004/nf20040420_7253_db035.htm (accessed May 18, 2004).

47. R. S. Kaplan and D. P. Norton, "The Balanced Scorecard—Measures that Drive Performance," *Harvard Business Review,* January–February 1992, pp. 71–79.

48. "The End Again for Indian Motorcycle Corporation," *American Motorcycle Network,* September 22, 2003, www.americanmotor.com/news.cfm?newsid=2236 (accessed May 20, 2004).

49. R. S. Kaplan and D. P. Norton, *Strategy Maps: Converting Intangible Assets into Tangible Outcomes* (Boston: Harvard Business School Press, 2004).

50. R. Quinn, quoted in J. H. Lingle and W. A. Schiemann, "From Balanced Scorecard to Strategic Gauges: Is Measurement Worth it?" *American Management Association,* March 1996, pp. 56–61.

51. D. J. Cohen, "HR Metrics: A Must," *HR Magazine,* February 2003, p. 136. Regarding the application of measurement to human resources, see also B. Becker and M. Huselid, "Measuring HR? Benchmarking Is *Not* the Answer," *HR Magazine,* December 2003, pp. 57–61.

52. Lingle and Schiemann, 1996.

53. Lingle and Schiemann, 1996.

CHAPTER 7

1. H. Lancaster, "How Life Lessons Have Helped a Successful Manager," *San Francisco Sunday Examiner & Chronicle,* August 15, 1999, p. CL-33; reprinted from *The Wall Street Journal.*

2. R. L. Keeney, reported in D. Murphy, "When to Make Decisions—or Delay Them," *San Francisco Examiner,* December 6, 1998, p. J-2.

3. O. Pollar, "Six Steps for Making Tough Choices," *San Francisco Examiner and Chronicle,* April 4, 1999, p. J-3.

4. P. Thomas, "Be Prepared for Surges of a Volatile Business," *The Wall Street Journal,* May 11, 2004, p. B4; and "Windowbox.com: Making the World a Better Place; Ben Swett—Founder & CEO Biography," www.windowbox.com/contact/pr_benbio.html (accessed May 29, 2004).

5. A. S. Grove, *High Output Management* (New York: Random House, 1983), p. 98.

6. Thomas, 2004.

7. Thomas, 2004.

8. The discussion of styles was based on material contained in A. J. Rowe and R. O. Mason, *Managing with Style: A Guide to Understanding, Assessing and Improving Decision Making* (San Francisco: Jossey-Bass, 1987), pp. 1–17.

9. See Rowe and Mason, 1987; and M. J. Dollinger and W. Danis, "Preferred Decision-Making Styles: A Cross-Cultural Comparison," *Psychological Reports,* 1998, pp. 755–761.

10. Q. Hardy, "Iridium Shares Fall After News of Missed Goals," *The Wall Street Journal,* May 17, 1999, p. B6; D. Barboza, "Motorola Rolls Itself Over," *New York Times,* July 14, 1999, pp. C1, C2; S. Rosenbush, "Iridium Bets on New Structure," *USA Today,* August 4, 1999, p. 3B; L. Cauley, "Iridium's Downfall: The Marketing Took a Back Seat to Science," *The Wall Street Journal,* August 18, 1999, pp. A1, A6; and M. B. Lippitt, "Six Priorities That Make a Great Strategic Decision," *Journal of Business Strategy,* January–February 2003, pp. 21–24.

11. K. Liebeskind, "In the Fast Lane," *Selling Power,* September 1997, pp. 16–17.

12. A. Farnham, "Teaching Creativity Tricks to Buttoned-Down Executives," *Fortune,* January 10, 1994, pp. 94–100.

13. Ron Nichol, quoted in J. E. Hilsenrath, "Adventures in Cost Cutting," *The Wall Street Journal,* May 10, 2004, pp. R1, R3.

14. B. Horovitz, "By Year's End, Regular Size Will Have to Do," *USA Today,* March 4, 2004, p. 3B.

15. H. A. Simon, *Administrative Behavior,* 3rd ed. (New York: Free Press, 1996); and H. A. Simon, "Making Management Decisions: The Role of Intuition and Emotion," *The Academy of Management Executive,* February 1987, pp. 57–63.

16. W. Miller, "Building the Ultimate Resource," *Management Review,* January 1999, pp. 42–45; J. S. Brown and P. Duguid, "Balancing Act: How to Capture Knowledge without Killing It," *Harvard Business Review,* May–June 2000, pp. 73–80; and D. W. De Long and P. Seemann, "Confronting Conceptual Confusion and Conflict in Knowledge Management," *Organizational Dynamics,* Summer 2000, p. 33.

17. S. A. Akhter, "Strategic Planning, Hypercompetition, and Knowledge Management," *Business Horizons,* January–February 2003, pp. 19–24.

18. R. Lubit, "Tacit Knowledge and Knowledge Management: The Keys to Sustainable Competitive Advantage," *Organizational Dynamics,* vol. 29, no. 3, 2001, pp. 164–178.

19. P. Babcock, "Shedding Light on Knowledge Management," *HR Magazine,* May 2004, pp. 47–50.

20. A. Mulcahy, quoted in E. E. Gordon, "Bridging the Gap," *Training,* September 2003, p. 32.

21. M. B. Zuckerman, "Policing the Corporate Suites," *U.S. News & World Report,* January 19, 2004, p. 72.

22. C. McNamara, "Complete Guide to Ethics Management: An Ethics Toolkit for Managers," www.mapnp.org/library/ethics/ethxgde.htm (accessed May 29, 2004).

23. C. E. Bagley, "The Ethical Leader's Decision Tree," *Harvard Business Review,* February 2003, pp. 18–19.

24. A.-M. Cusac, "U.S. Companies Trick Retirees out of Health Benefits," *UNI In Depth,* September 4, 2001, www.union-network.org/uniindep.nsf/0/54491a47e00ad956c1256a2900282ebe?OpenDocument (accessed May 29, 2004).

25. J. Appleby, "More Companies Trim Retiree Health Benefits," *USATODAY.com,* January 14, 2004, www.usatoday.com/money/industries/health/2004-01-15-retiree_x.htm (accessed May 29, 2004).

26. Bagley, 2003, p. 19.

27. K. Hodgson, *A Rock and a Hard Place: How to Make Ethical Business Decisions When the Choices Are Tough* (New York: AMACOM, 1992), pp. 66–77.

28. D. Callahan, *The Cheating Culture: Why More Americans Are Doing Wrong to Get Ahead* (New York: Harcourt, 2004).

29. L. Jennings, "Anything to Get Ahead: The New American Norm?" *The Futurist,* September–October 2004, pp. 60–61.

30. Converting Data into Action: Expanding the Boundaries of Institutional Improvement. National Survey of Student Engagement: The College Student Report, *2003 Annual Report,* sponsored by the

Carnegie Foundation for the Advancement of Teaching, www.iub.edu/~nsse/2003_annual_report/pdf/NSSE_2003_Annual_Report.pdf (accessed September 20, 2004).

31. M. Wong, "New Battlefields to Fight Plagiarism," *San Francisco Chronicle,* April 12, 2004; and S. Hansen, "Dear Plagiarists: You Get What You Pay For," *The New York Times Book Review,* August 22, 2004, p. 11.

32. C. Said, "Are Camera Phones Too Revealing?" *San Francisco Chronicle,* May 165, 2004, pp. A1, A2; M. A. Walker, "High-Tech Crib: Camera Phones Boost Cheating," *The Wall Street Journal,* September 10, 2004, pp. B1, B4; and S. McAndrew, "Cellular Cheating?" *Reno Gazette-Journal,* September 11, 2004, pp. 1E, 8E.

33. B. Read, "Wired for Cheating," *The Chronicle of Higher Education,* July 16, 2004, pp. A27–A28.

34. J. O'Donnell, "How Recruiters Catch a Rascal," *USA Today,* August 26, 2004, p. 3B.

35. C. Haddad and A. Barrett, "A Whistle-Blower Rocks an Industry," *Business Week,* June 24, 2002, pp. 126, 128.

36. G. W. Hill, "Group versus Individual Performance: Are $n + 1$ Heads Better Than 1?" *Psychological Bulletin,* May 1982, pp. 517–539.

37. N. F. R. Maier, "Assets and Liabilities in Group Problem Solving: The Need for Integrative Function," *Psychological Review,* vol. 74, 1967, pp. 239–249.

38. Maier, 1967.

39. Methods for increasing group consensus were investigated by R. L. Priem, D. A. Harrison, and N. K. Muir, "Structured Conflict and Consensus Outcomes in Group Decision Making," *Journal of Management,* December 22, 1995, pp. 691–710.

40. See D. L. Gladstein and N. P. Reilly, "Group Decision Making under Threat: The Tycoon Game," *Academy of Management Journal,* September 1985, pp. 613–627.

41. These conclusions were based on the following studies: J. H. Davis, "Some Compelling Intuitions about Group Consensus Decisions, Theoretical and Empirical Research, and Interpersonal Aggregation Phenomena: Selected Examples, 1950–1990," *Organizational Behavior and Human Decision Processes,* June 1992, pp. 3–38; and J. A. Sniezek, "Groups Under Uncertainty: An Examination of Confidence in Group Decision Making," *Organizational Behavior and Human Decision Processes,* June 1992, pp. 124–155.

42. Supporting results can be found in J. R. Hollenbeck, D. R. Ilgen, D. J. Sego, J. Hedlund, D. A. Major, and J. Phillips, "Multilevel Theory of Team Decision Making: Decision Performance in Teams Incorporating Distributed Expertise," *Journal of Applied Psychology,* April 1995, pp. 292–316.

43. See D. H. Gruenfeld, E. A. Mannix, K. Y. Williams, and M. A. Neale, "Group Composition and Decision Making: How Member Familiarity and Information Distribution Affect Process and Performance," *Organizational Behavior and Human Decision Processes,* July 1996, pp. 1–15.

44. "Jack Welch's Lessons for Success," *Fortune,* January 25, 1993, p. 86.

45. See D. Pojidaeff, "Human Productivity and Pride in Work: The Core Principles of Participative Management," *Journal for Quality and Participation,* December 1995, pp. 44–47; and N. A. Holland, "A Pathway to Global Competitiveness and Total Quality: Participative Management," *Journal for Quality and Participation,* September 1995, pp. 58–62.

46. Results are presented in J. T. Delaney, "Workplace Cooperation: Current Problems, New Approaches," *Journal of Labor Research,* Winter 1996, pp. 45–61.

47. For an extended discussion, see M. Sashkin, "Participative Management Is an Ethical Imperative," *Organizational Dynamics,* Spring 1984, pp. 4–22.

48. Supporting results can be found in C. R. Leana, R. S. Ahlbrandt, and A. J. Murrell, "The Effects of Employee Involvement Programs on Unionized Workers' Attitudes, Perceptions, and Preferences in Decision Making," *Academy of Management Journal,* October 1992, pp. 861–873; and D. Plunkett, "The Creative Organization: An Empirical Investigation of the Importance of Participation in Decision Making," *Journal of Creative Behavior,* Second Quarter 1990, pp. 140–148. Results pertaining to role conflict and ambiguity can be found in C. S. Smith and M. T. Brannick, "A Role Replication and Theoretical Extension," *Journal of Organizational Behavior,* March 1990, pp. 91–104.

49. See J. A. Wagner III, "Participation's Effects on Performance and Satisfaction: A Reconsideration of Research Evidence," *Academy of Management Review,* April 1994, pp. 312–330.

50. A through discussion of this issue is provided by W. A. Randolph, "Navigating the Journey to Empowerment," *Organizational Dynamics,* Spring 1995, pp. 19–32.

51. G. M. Parker, *Team Players and Teamwork: The New Competitive Business Strategy* (San Francisco: Jossey-Bass, 1990).

52. These recommendations were obtained from G. M. Parker, *Team Players and Teamwork.*

53. A complete description of the nominal group technique can be found in A. L. Delbecq, A. H. Van de Ven, and D. H. Gustafson, *Group Techniques for Program Planning: A Guide to Nominal Group and Delphi Processes* (Glenview, IL: Scott Foresman, 1975).

54. See N. C. Dalkey, D. L. Rourke, R. Lewis, and D. Snyder, *Studies in the Quality of Life: Delphi and Decision Making* (Lexington, MA: Lexington Books, 1972).

55. Benefits of the Delphi technique are discussed by N. I. Whitman, "The Committee Meeting Alternative: Using the Delphi Technique," *Journal of Nursing Administration,* July–August 1990, pp. 30–36.

56. A thorough description of computer-aided decision-making systems is provided by M. C. Er and A. C. Ng, "The Anonymity and Proximity Factors in Group Decision Support Systems," *Decision Support Systems,* May 1995, pp. 75–83; and A. LaPlante, "Brainstorming," *Forbes,* October 25, 1993, pp. 45–61.

57. Results can be found in J. S. Valacich and C. Schwenk, "Devils' Advocacy and Dialectical Inquiry Effects on Face-to-Face and Computer-Mediated Group Decision Making," *Organizational Behavior and Human Decision Processes,* August 1995, pp. 158–173; R. B. Gallupe, W. H. Cooper, M. Grise, and L. M. Bastianutti, "Blocking Electronic Brainstorms," *Journal of Applied Psychology,* February 1994, pp. 77–86; and A. R. Dennis and J. S. Valacich, "Computer Brainstorms: More Heads Are Better Than One," *Journal of Applied Psychology,* August 1993, pp. 531–537.

58. A description of the work of Daniel Gilbert appears in P. J. Hilts, "In Forecasting Their Emotions, Most People Flunk Out," *New York Times,* February 16, 1999, p. D2.

59. D. D. Wheeler and I. L. Janis, *A Practical Guide for Making Decisions* (New York: Free Press, 1980), pp. 34–35; and I. L. Janis and L. Mann, *Decision Making: A Psychological Analysis of Conflict, Choice, and Commitment* (New York: The Free Press, 1977).

60. H. Lancaster, "Academics Have to Do Their Own Homework on Job Opportunities," *The Wall Street Journal,* July 13, 1999, p. B1.

61. E. Porter and G. Winter, "'04 Graduates Learned Lesson in Practicality," *New York Times,* May 30, 2004, sec. 1, pp. 1, 18.

62. A. Levin and L. Parker, "Human, Mechanical Flaws Cut Off Path to Survival," *USA Today,* July 12, 1999, pp. 1A, 8A, 9A.

63. Wheeler and Janis, 1980.

64. J. Drape, "For the Best Thoroughbreds, It Quickly Pays Not to Race," *New York Times,* May 2, 2002, pp. A1, C19.

65. D. Kahnemann and A. Tversky, "Judgment under Uncertainty: Heuristics and Biases," *Science,* vol. 185, 1974, pp. 1124–1131; A. Tversky and D. Kahneman, "Availability: A Heuristic for Judging Frequency and Probability," *Cognitive Psychology,* vol. 5, 1975, pp. 207–232; A. Tversky and D. Kahneman, "The Belief in the Law of Numbers," *Psychological Bulletin,* vol. 76, 1971, pp. 105–110; C. R. Schwenk, "Cognitive Simplification Processes in Strategic Decision Making," *Strategic Management Journal,* vol. 5, 1984, pp. 111–128; K. McKean, "Decisions," *Discover,* June 1985, pp. 22–31; J. Rockner, "The Escalation of Commitment to a Failing Course of Action: Toward Theoretical Progress," *Academy of Management Review,* vol. 17, 1980, pp. 39–61; D. R. Bobocel and J. P. Meyer, "Escalating Commitment to a Failing Course of Action: Separating the Roles of Choice and Justification," *Journal of Applied Psychology,* June 1994, pp. 360–363; and B. M. Shaw, "The Escalation of Commitment to a Course of Action," *Academy of Management Review,* October 1981, pp. 577–587.
66. W. Goodman, "How Gambling Makes Strange Bedfellows," *New York Times,* June 10, 1997, p. B3.
67. P. Slovic, "The Construction of a Preference," *American Psychologist,* vol. 50, 1995, pp. 364–371; and K. J. Dunegan, "Framing, Cognitive Roles, and Image Theory: Toward an Understanding of a Glass Half Full," *Journal of Applied Psychology,* vol. 78, 1993, pp. 491–503.
68. M. H. Bazerman, *Judgment in Managerial Decision Making* (New York: Wiley, 1990); D. E. Vell, H. Raiffa, and A. Tversky, *Decision Making* (Cambridge, UK: Cambridge University Press, 1988).
69. H. J. Einhorn and R. M. Hogarth, "Confidence in Judgment: Persistence in the Illusion of Validity," *Psychological Review,* vol. 85, 1978, pp. 395–416.
70. B. Fischoff, "Hindsight ≠ Foresight: The Effect of Outcome Knowledge on Judgment under Uncertainty," *Journal of Experimental Psychology: Human Perception and Performance,* vol. 1, 1975, pp. 288–299.

CHAPTER 8

1. M. Cottle, "Minding Your Mentors," *New York Times,* March 7, 1999, sec. 3, p. 8; C. Dahle, "HP's Mentor Connection," *Fast Company,* November 1998, pp. 78–80; I. Abbott, "If You Want to Be an Effective Mentor, Consider These Tips," *San Francisco Examiner,* October 18, 1998, p. J-3; D. A. Thomas, "The Truth about Mentoring Minorities—Race Matters," *Harvard Business Review,* April 2001, pp. 99–107; J. E. Wallace, "The Benefits of Mentoring for Female Lawyers," *Journal of Vocational Behavior,* June 2001, pp. 366–391; S. A. Mehta, "Best Companies for Minorities: Why Mentoring Works," *Fortune,* July 9, 2001, www.fortune.com/fortune/diversity/articles/0,15114,370475,00.html (accessed July 4, 2004); F. Warner, "Inside Intel's Mentoring Movement," *Fast Company,* April 2002, p. 116; B. Raabe and T. A. Beehr, "Formal Mentoring versus Supervisor and Coworker Relationships: Differences in Perceptions and Impact," *Journal of Organizational Behavior,* vol. 24, 2003, pp. 271–293; and A. Fisher, "A New Kind of Mentor," *Fortune,* July 28, 2004, www.fortune.com/fortune/annie/0,15704,368863,00.html (accessed July 4, 2004).
2. A. E. Hayden, quoted in Cottle, 1999.
3. C. Dahle, "*My* First 60 Days," *Fast Company,* June–July, 1998, p. 190.
4. E. H. Schein, "Organizational Culture," *American Psychologist,* vol. 45, 1990, pp. 109–119; E. H. Schein, *Organizational Culture and Leadership* (San Francisco: Jossey-Bass, 1985); and E. H. Schein, "The Role of the Founder in Creating Organizational Culture," *Organizational Dynamics,* Summer 1983, pp. 13–28.
5. B. Breen, "The Thrill of Defeat," *Fast Company,* June 2004, pp. 76–81.
6. S. S. Watkins, in testimony before the Oversight and Investigations Subcommittee of the House Energy and Commerce Committee, U.S. Congress, February 14, 2002.
7. See C. Ostroff, A. Kinicki, and J. Tamkins, "Organizational Culture and Climate." In W. C. Borman, D. R. Ilgen, and R. J. Klimoski (Eds.). *Handbook of Psychology,* vol. 12 (New York: John Wiley & Sons, 2003), pp. 565–593.
8. P. Burrows, "Carly's Last Stand?" *Business Week,* December 24, 2001, pp. 63–70.
9. T. E. Deal and A. A. Kennedy, *Corporate Cultures: The Rites and Rituals of Corporate Life* (Reading, MA: Addison-Wesley, 1982), p. 22.
10. R. Jacob, "Corporate Reputations: The Winners Chart a Course of Constant Renewal and Work to Sustain Cultures that Produce the Very Best Products and People," *Fortune,* March 6, 1995, pp. 54–64.
11. D. Maraniss, "Lombardi's Way," *Vanity Fair,* September 1999, pp. 206–226, 231–246; excerpted from D. Maraniss, *When Pride Still Mattered: A Life of Vince Lombardi* (New York: Simon & Schuster, 1999).
12. A. Farnham, "Mary Kay's Lessons in Leadership," *Fortune,* September 20, 1993, pp. 68–77.
13. Deal and Kennedy, 1982.
14. Adapted from L. Smircich, "Concepts of Culture and Organizational Analysis," *Administrative Science Quarterly,* September 1983, pp. 339–358.
15. S. McCarney, "Airline Industry's Top-Rated Woman Keeps Southwest's Small-Fry Spirit Alive," *The Wall Street Journal,* November 30, 1996, pp. B1, B11.
16. D. Anfuso, "3M's Staffing Strategy Promotes Productivity and Pride," *Personnel Journal,* February 1995, pp. 28–34.
17. R. J. Blitzer and J. R. Reynolds Rush, *Find the Bathrooms First! Starting Your New Job on the Right Foot* (Menlo Park, CA: Crisp Publications, 1999); D. Ciampa and M. Watkins, *Right from the Start: Taking Charge in a New Leadership Role* (Boston: Harvard Business School Press, 1999); E. Holton, S. Naquin, and E. Holton, *So You're New Again: How to Succeed When You Change Jobs* (San Francisco: Berrett-Koehler Publishers, 2001); and M. Watkins, *The First 90 Days: Critical Success Strategies for New Leaders at All Levels* (Boston: Harvard Business School Press, 2003); "Dip, Before Diving, into That New Job," *BusinessWeek Online,* July 3, 2004, www.businessweek.com/bschools/content/jun2004/bs20040628_9967_bs001.htm (accessed July 4, 2004).
18. L. Seale, quoted in C. Dahle, "Fast Start: Your First 60 Days," *Fast Company,* June–July 1998, pp. 182–190.
19. D. Murphy, "Surviving and Thriving in a First Job," *San Francisco Examiner,* September 13, 1998, p. J-3.
20. Dahle, 1998; Murphy, 1998; and S. Gruner, "Lasting Impressions," *Inc.,* July 1998, p. 126.
21. R. Ailes, in "Your First Seven Seconds," *Fast Company,* June–July 1998, p. 184.
22. L. P. Frankel, in "Your First Impression," *Fast Company,* June–July 1998, p. 188.
23. P. Burrows, "The Hottest Property in the Valley?" *Business Week,* August 30, 1999, pp. 69–74.
24. C. I. Barnard, *The Functions of the Executive* (Cambridge, MA: Harvard University Press, 1938), p. 73.
25. P. M. Blau and W. R. Scott, *Formal Organizations* (San Francisco: Chandler, 1962).
26. Jed Emerson, quoted in C. Dahle, "60 Seconds with Jed Emerson," *Fast Company,* March 2004, p. 42.
27. S. E. Reed, "Helping the Poor, Phone by Phone," *New York Times,* May 26, 2002, sec. 3, p. 2.
28. S. Rahman, "Wireless Environment—an Untapped Avenue," *The Daily Star,* February 18, 2004, www.thedailystar.net/2004/02/18/d402181601113.htm (accessed June 1, 2004).

29. Gregory Dees, cited in T. Backer, "Social Entrepreneurship: Beyond Theory," *onPhilanthropy,* January 30, 2004, www.onphilanthropy.com/tren_comm/tc2004-01-30.html (accessed June 1, 2004).

30. J. Emerson, "The Nature of Returns: A Social Capital Markets Inquiry into Elements of Investment and the Blended Value Proposition," *Social Enterprise Series No. 17* (Boston: Harvard Business School Press, 2000), p. 36.

31. See also A. Argandoña, "Fostering Values in Organizations," *Journal of Business Ethics,* vol. 45, 2003, pp. 15–28.

32. S. Steklow, "Management 101," *The Wall Street Journal,* December 9, 1994, p. B1.

33. O. Pollar, "Don't Overlook the Importance of Delegating," *San Francisco Examiner,* August 8, 1999, p. J-3; D. Anderson, "Supervisors and the Hesitate to Delegate Syndrome," *Supervision,* November 1992, pp. 9–11; and E. Raudsepp, "Why Supervisors Don't Delegate," *Supervision,* May 1979, pp. 12–15.

34. S. Caudron, "Delegate for Results," *Industry Week,* February 6, 1995, pp. 27–30; R. Morgan, "Guidelines for Delegating Effectively," *Supervision,* April 1995, pp. 20–22; J. Ninemeier, "10 Tips for Delegating Tasks," *Hotels,* June 1995, pp. 20–22; Pollar, 1999; R. Wild, "Clone Yourself," *Working Women,* May 2000, pp. 79–80; C. M. Avery, M. A. Walker, and E. O'Toole, *Teamwork Is an Individual Skill: Getting Your Work Done When Sharing Responsibility* (San Francisco: Berrett-Koehler, 2001); S. Gazda, "The Art of Delegating: Effective Delegation Enhances Employee Morale, Manager Productivity, and Organizational Success," *HR Magazine,* January 2002, pp. 75–79; R. Burns, *Making Delegation Happen: A Simple and Effective Guide to Implementing Successful Delegation* (St. Leonards, Australia: Allen & Unwin, 2002); D. M. Genett, *If You Want It Done Right, You Don't Have to Do It Yourself! The Power of Effective Delegation* (Sanger, CA: Quill Driver Books, 2003).

35. E. H. Schein, *Organizational Psychology,* 3rd ed. (Englewood Cliffs, NJ: Prentice-Hall, 1980).

36. For an overview of the span of control concept, see D. D. Van Fleet and A. G. Bedeian, "A History of the Span of Management," *Academy of Management Review,* July 1977, pp. 356–372.

37. T. A. Stewart, "CEOs See Clout Shifting," *Fortune,* November 6, 1989, p. 66.

38. Pollar, 1999.

39. D. Machalaba, "After Crippling Chaos, Union Pacific Can See the Proverbial Light," *The Wall Street Journal,* August 25, 1999, pp. A1, A8.

40. J. Lippman, "In the Wings: Time Warner's Next Generation," *The Wall Street Journal,* July 22, 1999, pp. B1, B12.

41. L. Grant, "New Jewel in the Crown," *U.S. News & World Report,* February 28, 1994, pp. 55–57; H. Rothman, "The Power of Empowerment," *Nation's Business,* June 1993, pp. 49–52; and J. Galbraith, *Designing Complex Organizations* (Reading, MA: Addison-Wesley, 1973).

42. A. Reinhardt and S. Browder, "Boeing," *Business Week,* September 30, 1996, pp. 194–226; and B. Filpczak, "Concurrent Engineering: A Team by Any Other Name?" *Training,* August 1996, pp. 55–56.

43. J. A. Byrne, "The Virtual Corporation," *Business Week,* February 8, 1993, pp. 98–102; G. Lorenzoni and C. Baden-Fuller, "Creating a Strategic Center to Manage a Web of Partners," *California Management Review,* Spring 1995, pp. 146–163.

44. R. Walker, quoted in B. Richards, "The Business Plan," *The Wall Street Journal,* November 18, 1996, pp. R10, R16.

45. B. Richards, "A Total Overhaul," *The Wall Street Journal,* December 7, 1999, p. R30.

46. P. F. Drucker, quoted in J. A. Byrne, "Advice from the Dr. Spock of Business," *Business Week,* September 28, 1987, p. 61.

47. K. Deveny, "Bag Those Fries, Squirt That Ketchup, Fry That Fish," *Business Week,* October 13, 1986, p. 86.

48. T. Burns and G. M. Stalker, *The Management of Innovation* (London: Tavistock, 1961).

49. T. J. Peters and R. H. Waterman, *In Search of Excellence* (New York: Harper & Row, 1982).

50. P. R. Lawrence and J. W. Lorsch, *Organization and Environment* (Homewood, IL: Irwin, 1967).

51. D. S. Pugh and D. J. Hickson, *Organization Structure in Its Context: The Aston Program* (Lexington, MA: D. C. Heath, 1976); and R. Z. Gooding and J. A. Wagner III, "A Meta-Analytic Review of the Relationship between Size and Performance: The Productivity and Efficiency of Organizations and Their Subunits," *Administrative Science Quarterly,* December 1985, pp. 462–481.

52. L. Smith, "Does the World's Biggest Company Have a Future?" *Fortune,* August 7, 1995, p. 124.

53. Peters and Waterman, 1982, pp. 272–273.

54. P. Parker, quoted in C. Palmeri, "A Process that Never Ends," *Forbes,* December 21, 1992, p. 55.

55. J. Woodward, *Industrial Organization: Theory and Practice* (London: Oxford University Press, 1965).

56. J. R. Kimberly, R. H. Miles, and associates, *The Organizational Life Cycle* (San Francisco: Jossey-Bass, 1980).

57. P. Gruber, quoted in A. Muoio, ed., "My Greatest Lesson," *Fast Company,* June–July 1998, pp. 83–92.

58. D. A. Garvin, "Building a Learning Organization," *Harvard Business Review,* July-August 1993, pp. 78–91; and R. Hodgetts, F. Luthans, and S. Lee, "New Paradigm Organizations: From Total Quality to Learning to World-Class," *Organizational Dynamics,* Winter 1994, pp. 5–19.

59. P. Senge, *The Fifth Discipline* (New York: Doubleday, 1990), p. 1.

60. J. B. Keys, R. M. Fulmer, and S. A. Stumpf, "Microworlds and Simuworlds: Practice Fields for the Learning Organization," *Organizational Dynamics,* Spring 1996, pp. 36–49; and F. Kogman and P. M. Senge, "Communities of Commitment: The Heart of Learning Organizations," *Organizational Dynamics,* Autumn 1993, pp. 5–23.

61. J. Case, "A Company of Businesspeople," *Inc.,* April 1993, p. 86.

CHAPTER 9

1. K. Lingle, national work-life director for KPMG, an accounting and consulting firm, quoted in C. Kleiman, "Work-Life Rewards Grow," *San Francisco Examiner,* January 16, 2000, p. J-2; reprinted from *Chicago Tribune.*

2. See H. R. Nalbantian, R. A. Guzzo, D. Kieffer, and J. Doherty, *Play to Your Strengths: Managing Your Internal Labor Markets for Lasting Competitive Advantage* (New York: McGraw-Hill, 2004).

3. M. Buckingham and C. Coffman, *First, Break All the Rules: What the World's Greatest Managers Do Differently* (New York: Simon & Schuster, 1999).

4. Kimberly Scott, project leader for Hewitt Associates, which helps compile the *Fortune* list, reported in D. Murphy, "Can Morale Contribute to Safer Skies?" *San Francisco Examiner,* February 11, 2000, p. J-1.

5. R. Levering and M. Moskowitz, "The 100 Best Companies to Work For," *Fortune,* January 10, 2000, pp. 82–102; *Fortune,* January 8, 2001, pp. 148–168; *Fortune,* January 12, 2004, pp. 56–78.

6. K. Maney, "SAS Gets Off on Right Foot with Workers, but What Does It Do?" *USA Today,* May 23, 2001, p. 3B.

7. T. D. Schellhardt, "An Idyllic Workplace Under a Tycoon's Thumb," *The Wall Street Journal,* November 23, 1998, pp. B1, B4.

8. J. Welch, quoted in N. M. Tichy and S. Herman, *Control Your Destiny or Someone Else Will: How Jack Welch Is Making General Electric the World's Most Competitive Corporation* (New York: Doubleday, 1993), p. 251.
9. P. Capelli and A. Crocker-Hefter, "Distinctive Human Resources Are Firms' Core Competencies," *Organizational Dynamics,* Winter 1996, pp. 7–22.
10. G. Bollander, S. Snell, and A. Sherman, *Managing Human Resources,* 12th ed. (Cincinnati, OH: SouthWestern Publishing, 2001), pp. 13–15; and B. E. Becker, M. A. Huselid, and D. Ulrich, *The HR Scorecard: Linking People, Strategy, and Performance* (Boston: Harvard Business School Press, 2001), p. 4.
11. S. Meisinger, "Taking the Measure of Human Capital," *HR Magazine,* January 2003, p. 10.
12. E. E. Gordon, "Bridging the Gap," *Training,* September 2003, pp. 30–34.
13. J. Mullich, "They Don't Retire Them, They Hire Them," *Workforce Management,* December 2003, pp. 49–54.
14. Inspired by P. S. Adler and S. Kwon, "Social Capital: Prospects for New Concept," *Academy of Management Review,* January 2002, pp. 17–40. See also R. A. Baaron and G. D. Markman, "Beyond Social Capital: How Social Skills Can Enhance Entrepreneurs' Success," *Academy of Management Executive,* February 2000, pp. 106–116.
15. Data from "What Makes a Job Okay," *USA Today,* May 15, 2000, p. 1B.
16. R. Levering and M. Moskowitz, "The 100 Best Companies to Work For," *Fortune,* January 12, 2004, p. 68.
17. R. J. Mirabile, "The Power of Job Analysis," *Training,* April 1990, pp. 70–74; and S. F. Mona, "The Job Description," *Association Management,* February 1991, pp. 33–37.
18. For a thorough discussion of affirmative action, see F. J. Crosby, A. Iyer, S. Clayton, and R. A. Downing, "Affirmative Action," *American Psychologist,* February 2003, pp. 93–115.
19. J. Useem, "For Sale Online: You," *Fortune,* July 5, 1999, pp. 67–78.
20. G. McWilliams, "The Best Way to Find a Job," *The Wall Street Journal,* December 6, 1999, pp. R16, R22.
21. K. Maher, "Online Job Hunting Is Tough. Just Ask Vinnie," *The Wall Street Journal,* June 24, 2003, pp. B1, B10.
22. L. Stern, "New Rules of the Hunt," *Newsweek,* February 17, 2003, p. 67.
23. S. Armour, "Firms Key Up PCs for Job Screening," *USA Today,* October 20, 1997, p. 6B.
24. B. Weinstein, "Prescreened Interviews Are Catching On," *San Francisco Sunday Examiner & Chronicle,* February 21, 1999, p. CL-21.
25. M. Messmer, quoted in "Honesty Counts in Job Interview," *The Futurist,* July–August 1997, p. 49.
26. B. M. Meglino, A. S. DeNisi, S. A. Youngblood, and K. J. Williams, "Effects of Realistic Job Previews: A Comparison Using an Enhancement and a Reduction Preview," *Journal of Applied Psychology,* vol. 73, 198l, pp. 259–266.
27. J. Kluger, "Pumping Up Your Past," *Time,* June 10, 2002, p. 52.
28. Report by Automatic Data Processing, Roseland, NJ, cited in J. L. Seglin, "Lies Can Have a (Long) Life of Their Own," *New York Times,* June 16, 2002, sec. 3, p. 4. See also S. Armour, "Security Checks Worry Workers," *USA Today,* June 19, 2004, p. 1B.
29. J. S. Lublin, "Job Hunters with Gaps in Their Résumés Need to Write Around Them," *The Wall Street Journal,* May 6, 2003, p. B1.
30. M. Conlin, "Don't Hedge Your Age," *Business Week,* October 6, 2003, p. 14.
31. S. McManis, "Little White-Collar Lies," *San Francisco Chronicle,* October 1, 1999, pp. B1, B3.
32. D. Stamps, "Cyberinterviews Combat Turnover," *Training,* August 1995, p. 16.
33. D. S. Chapman, K. L. Uggerslev, and J. Webster, "Applicant Reactions Face-to-Face and Technology-Mediated Interviews: A Field Investigation," *Journal of Applied Psychology,* vol. 88, 2003, pp. 944–953.
34. E. D. Pursell, M. A. Campion, and S. R. Gaylord, "Structured Interviewing: Avoiding Selection Problems," *Personnel Journal,* November 1980.
35. M. C. Blackman, "Personality Judgment and the Utility of the Unstructured Employment Interview," *Basic and Applied Social Psychology,* vol. 24, 2002, pp. 241–250.
36. J. G. Rosse and R. A. Levin, *High-Impact Hiring* (San Francisco: Jossey-Bass, 1997); D. Murphy, "Choice Advice," *San Francisco Examiner,* November 15, 1998, pp. J-1, J-2; "Biggest Interviewing Mistakes," *USA Today,* November 19, 2001, p. 1B; D. Murphy, "Interviewers Just Don't Get the Importance of Failure," *San Francisco Chronicle,* May 19, 2002, pp. J1, J3B; Rosner, "Turning Your Job Interview into a Circus Isn't Always Bad," *San Francisco Chronicle,* June 2, 2002, p. J2; L. Adler, *Hire with Your Head: Using POWER Hiring to Build Great Teams,* 2nd ed. (New York: John Wiley, 2002); and R. W. Wendover, *Smart Hiring: The Complete Guide to Finding and Hiring the Best Employees,* 3rd ed. (Naperville, IL: Sourcebooks, 2002).
37. H. Lancaster, "Making a Good Hire Takes a Little Instinct and a Lot of Research," *The Wall Street Journal,* March 3, 1998, p. B1.
38. L. G. Otting, "Don't Rush to Judgment," *HR Magazine,* January 2004, pp. 95–98.
39. M. P. Cronin, "This Is a Test," *Inc.,* August 1993, pp. 64–68.
40. D. P. Shuit, "At 60, Myers-Briggs Is Still Sorting Out and Identifying People's Types," *Workforce Management,* December 2003, pp. 72–74.
41. S. Adler, "Personality Tests for Salesforce Selection: Worth a Fresh Look," *Review of Business,* Summer/Fall 1994, pp. 27–31.
42. D. Cadrain, "Are Your Employee Drug Tests *Accurate?*" *HR Magazine,* January 2003, pp. 41–45.
43. S. Shellenbarger, "Companies Are Finding It Really Pays to Be Nice to Employees," *The Wall Street Journal,* July 22, 1998, p. B1.
44. Brookings Institution, cited in Shellenbarger, 1998.
45. MCI Communications surveys, reported in Shellenbarger, 1998.
46. G. R. Jones, "Organizational Socialization as Information Processing Activity: A Life History Analysis," *Human Organization,* vol. 42, no. 4, 1983, pp. 314–320.
47. E. Lawler, reported in S. Ross, "Worker Involvement Pays Off," *San Francisco Examiner,* November 15, 1998, p. J-2.
48. L. Koss-Feder, "Brushing Up from the Boardroom to the Back Office," *Time,* July 20, 1998, p. B5.
49. B. Muirhead, "Looking at Net Colleges" [letter], *USA Today,* November 12, 1999, p. 14A.
50. C. Hymowitz, "Why Managers Take Too Long to Fire Employees," *San Francisco Examiner,* February 21, 1999, p. J-2; reprinted from *The Wall Street Journal.*
51. L. B. Combings and D. P. Schwab, *Performance in Organizations: Determinants and Appraisal* (Glenview, IL: Scott Foresman, 1973).
52. D. J. Cohen, "HR Metrics: A Must," *HR Magazine,* February 2003, p. 136.
53. H. Lancaster, "Why Bosses Are Encouraging Workers to Review Themselves," *San Francisco Examiner,* February 28, 1999, p. J-2; reprinted from *The Wall Street Journal.*

54. This issue is thoroughly discussed by G. Toegel and J. A. Conger, "360-Degree Assessment: Time for Reinvention," *Academy of Management Learning and Education,* September 2003, pp. 297–311.

55. M. Boyle, "Performance Reviews: Perilous Curves Ahead," *Fortune,* May 15, 2001, www.fortune.com/fortune/subs/print/0,15935,374010,00.html (accessed June 6, 2004); C. M. Ellis, G. B. Moore, and A. M. Saunier, "Forced Ranking: Not So Fast," *Perspectives,* June 30, 2003, www.imakenews.com/eletra/mod_print_view.cfm?this_id=162170&u=sibson&issue_id=000034313 (accessed June 6, 2004); and A. Meisler, "Dead Man's Curve," *Workforce Management,* July 2003, pp. 45–49.

56. *Employee Benefits Study, 2003* (Washington, D.C.: U.S. Chamber of Commerce, 2004), www.uschamber.com/press/releases/2004/january/04-07.htm (accessed July 5, 2004).

57. Adapted from D. L. McClain, "Tricks for Motivating the Pay to Motivate the Ranks," *New York Times,* November 15, 1998, sec. 3, p. 5.

58. A. Etzioni, "Americans Could Teach Austrians about Diversity," *USA Today,* February 14, 2000, p. 19A.

59. A. Fisher, "Dumping Troublemakers, and Exiting Gracefully," *Fortune,* February 15, 1999, p. 174.

60. Hymowitz, 1999.

61. R. Moss Kanter, "Show Humanity When You Show Employees the Door," *The Wall Street Journal,* September 21, 1997, p. A22.

62. Moss Kanter, 1997.

63. G. Skoning, "Explanations of Sexual Harassment: Are They Viable Defenses?" *HR Magazine,* July 1998, pp. 130–134; D. R. Sandler, "Sexual Harassment Rulings: Less Than Meets the Eye," *HR Magazine,* October 1998, pp. 136–143; M. Maremont, "A Case Puts a Value on Touching and Fondling," *The Wall Street Journal,* May 25, 1999, pp. B1, B4; and R. Ganzel, "What Sexual Harassment Training Really Prevents," *Training,* October 1998, pp. 86–94.

64. "Workplace Drug Use Appears on Decline," *Arizona Republic,* July 7, 2003, p. D1; reprinted from *New York Times.*

65. *Public Health Report,* U.S. Department of Health and Human Services, June 1991, pp. 280–292.

CHAPTER 10

1. T. J. Fadem, quoted in O. Port and J. Carey, "Getting to 'Eureka!'" *Business Week,* November 10, 1997, pp. 72–75.

2. C. Hymowitz, "Task of Managing in Workplace Takes a Careful Hand," *The Wall Street Journal,* July 1, 1997, p. B1.

3. T. Peters, "A Brawl with No Rules," *Forbes ASAP,* February 21, 2000, p. 155.

4. M. McGuinn, quoted in Hymowitz, 1997.

5. G. Kawasaki with M. Moreno, *Rules for Revolutionaries: The Capitalist Manifesto for Creating and Marketing New Products and Services* (New York: HarperBusiness, 1999); P. Carbonara, "What Do You Do with a Great Idea?" *Your Company,* August–September 1998, pp. 26–31; Port and Carey, 1997; and Hymowitz, 1997.

6. L. Jennings and J. Minerd, "Cybertrends Shaping Tomorrow's Marketplace," *The Futurist,* March 1999, pp. 12–14; N. D. Schwartz, "The Tech Boom Will Keep on Rocking," *Fortune,* February 15, 1999, pp. 64–80; and P. Drucker, "The Future that Has Already Happened," *The Futurist,* November 1998, pp. 16–18;

7. M. D. Watkins and M. H. Bazerman, "Predictable Surprises: The Disasters You Should Have Seen Coming," *Harvard Business Review,* March 2003, pp. 72–80.

8. "J&J Is on a Roll," *Fortune,* December 26, 1994, pp. 178–192; S. Siwolop and C. Eklund, "The Capsule Controversy: How Far Should the FDA Go?" *Business Week,* March 3, 1986, p. 37; and "After Its Recovery, New Headaches for Tylenol," *Business Week,* May 14, 1984, p. 137.

9. P. Robertson, D. Roberts, and J. Porras, "Dynamics of Planned Organizational Change: Assessing Empirical Support for a Theoretical Model," *Academy of Management Journal,* vol. 36, no. 3, 1993, pp. 619–634.

10. W. W. Lewis, *The Power of Productivity: Wealth, Power, and the Threat to Global Stability* (New York: W. W. Norton, 2003), reported in D. Brooks, "Scanning for Success," *New York Times,* April 3, 2004, p. A27.

11. G. Alvarez, quoted in "The IT Marksman at Wal-Mart," *BusinessWeek Online,* May 12, 2004, www.businessweek.com/technology/content/may2004/tc20040512_3630_tc147.htm (accessed June 7, 2004).

12. "RFID: On Track for a Rapid Rise," *BusinessWeek Online,* February 4, 2004, www.businessweek.com/technology/content/feb2004/tc2004024_8389_tc165.htm (accessed June 7, 2004); "Like It or Not, RFID Is Coming," *BusinessWeek Online,* March 18, 2004, www.businessweek.com/technology/content/mar2004/tc20040318_7698_tc121.htm (accessed June 7, 2004); and S. Crane, "RFID: Symbol's Growth Engine?" *BusinessWeek Online,* March 19, 2004, www.businessweek.com/investor/content/mar2004/pi20040319_2070_pi044.htm (accessed June 7, 2004).

13. S. Greenhouse, "Wal-Mart, a Nation unto Itself," *New York Times,* April 17, 2004, pp. A15, A17.

14. P. Dusenberry, "The Challenges of Managing Creative People," *USA Today,* November 20, 1997, p. 4B.

15. R. D. Hof, "Online Extra: Trading in a Cloud of Electrons," *BusinessWeek Online,* May 20, 2004, www.businessweek.com/@@TUSaZYUQTmOUSw0A/magazine/content/04_19/b3882621.htm (accessed June 8, 2004).

16. H. Green, "No Wires, No Rules," *Business Week,* April 26, 2004, pp. 95–102.

17. A. Reinhardt, "A Machine-to-Machine 'Internet of Things,'" *Business Week,* April 26, 2004, p. 102.

18. S. Rosenbush, "Telecom Turmoil," *Business Week,* May 10, 2004, p. 84; and K. Belson and M. Richtel, "Ventures Aim to Cut Cost of Overseas Cell Calls to Pennies," *New York Times,* May 17, 2004, p. C6.

19. B. Evangelista, "Cell Phones and PDAs Now Offer Not Just Still Pictures but Action Clips," *San Francisco Chronicle,* May 10, 2004, pp. D1, D3; and C. Said, "Are Camera Phones Too Revealing?" *San Francisco Chronicle,* May 16, 2004, pp. A1, A10.

20. This three-way typology of change was adapted from discussion in P. C. Nutt, "Tactics of Implementation," *Academy of Management Journal,* June 1986, pp. 230–261.

21. Radical organizational change is discussed by T. E. Vollmann, *The Transformational Imperative* (Boston: Harvard Business School Press, 1996); and J. A. Neal and C. L. Tromley, "From Incremental Change to Retrofit: Creating High-Performance Work Systems," *Academy of Management Executive,* February 1995, pp. 42–53.

22. F. Arner and R. Tiplady, "'No Excuse Not to Succeed,'" *Business Week,* May 10, 2004, pp. 96–98; J. Nocera, "The CEO vs. the Gadfly," *Fortune,* December 29, 2003; and C. M. Christensen, *The Innovator's Dilemma: When New Technologies Cause Great Firms to Fail* (Cambridge, MA: Harvard Business School Press, 1997).

23. K. Lewin, *Field Theory in Social Science* (New York: Harper & Row, 1951).

24. The role of learning within organizational change is discussed by C. Hendry, "Understanding and Creating Whole Organizational Change through Learning Theory," *Human Relations,* May 1996, pp. 621–641; and D. Ready, "Mastering Leverage, Leading Change," *Executive Excellence,* March 1995, pp. 18–19.

25. C. Goldwasser, "Benchmarking: People Make the Process," *Management Review,* June 1995, p. 40; and *Cambridge Advanced Learner's Dictionary* (Cambridge: Cambridge University Press, 2004), http://dictionary.cambridge.org/define.asp?key=94109&dict=CALD (accessed July 5, 2004).

26. R. Kreitner and A. Kinicki, *Organizational Behavior,* 4th ed. (Burr Ridge, IL: Irwin/McGraw-Hill, 1998), p. 619.

27. These errors are discussed by J. P. Kotter, "Leading Change: The Eight Steps to Transformation," in J. A. Conger, G. M. Spreitzer, and E. E. Lawler III, eds., *The Leader's Change Handbook* (San Francisco: Jossey-Bass, 1999), pp. 87–99.

28. The type of leadership needed during organizational change is discussed by J. P. Kotter, *Leading Change* (Boston: Harvard Business School Press, 1996); and B. Ettorre, "Making Change," *Management Review,* January 1996, pp. 13–18.

29. M. Fugate, A. Kinicki, and C. L. Scheck, "Coping with an Organizational Merger over Four Stages," *Personnel Psychology,* Winter 2002, pp. 905–928.

30. An historical overview of the field of OD can be found in J. Sanzgiri and J. Z. Gottlieb, "Philosophic and Pragmatic Influences on the Practice of Organization Development, 1950–2000," *Organizational Dynamics,* Autumn 1992, pp. 57–69.

31. W. W. Burke, *Organization Development: A Normative View* (Reading, MA: Addison-Wesley, 1987), p. 9.

32. The role of values and ethics in OD is discussed by M. McKendall, "The Tyranny of Change: Organizational Development Revisited," *Journal of Business Ethics,* February 1993, pp. 93–104.

33. G. A. Neuman, J. E. Edwards, and N. S. Raju, "Organizational Development Interventions: A Meta-Analysis of Their Effects on Satisfaction and Other Attitudes," *Personnel Psychology,* Autumn 1989, pp. 461–490.

34. W. G. Dyer, *Team Building: Current Issues and New Alternatives,* 3rd ed. (Reading, MA: Addison-Wesley, 1995).

35. See R. Rodgers, J. E. Hunter, and D. L. Rogers, "Influence of Top Management Commitment on Management Program Success," *Journal of Applied Psychology,* February 1993, pp. 151–155.

36. R. J. Schaffer and H. A. Thomson, "Successful Change Programs Begin with Results" *Harvard Business Review,* January–February 1992, pp. 80–89.

37. P. J. Robertson, D. R. Roberts, and J. I. Porras, "Dynamics of Planned Organizational Change: Assess Empirical Support for a Theoretical Model," *Academy of Management Journal,* June 1993, pp. 619–634.

38. C.-M. Lau and H.-Y. Ngo, "Organization Development and Firm Performance: A Comparison of Multinational and Local Firms," *Journal of International Business Studies,* First Quarter 2001, pp. 95–114.

39. C. C. Mann, "The SlashDot Effect," *Forbes ASAP,* February 21, 2000, pp. 43–50.

40. W. M. Bulkeley, "Can Linux Take Over the Desktop?" *The Wall Street Journal,* May 24, 2004, pp. R1, R4; and S. Hamm, "Software Shift," *Business Week,* May 10, 2004, p. 90.

41. S. Baker, "How to Keep the Idea Pot Bubbling," *Business Week,* October 20, 1997, pp. 15–18.

42. G. C. O'Connor, quoted in Port and Carey, 1997.

43. A. V. Bhidé, quoted in G. Gendron, "The Origin of the Entrepreneurial Species," *Inc.,* February 2000, pp. 105–114.

44. J. Yaukey, "Disposable Cell Phones Will Reach Retail Soon," *Reno Gazette-Journal,* October 22, 2001, p. 1E; and D. Pogue, "Cellphones for a Song, Just in Case," *New York Times,* September 27, 2001, pp. D1, D7.

45. B. Evangelista, "Movies by Mail: Netflix.com Makes Renting DVDs Easy," *San Francisco Chronicle,* January 26, 2002, p. B1; and V. Kopytoff, "Successful Netflix Faces Competition," *San Francisco Chronicle,* March 8, 2004, pp. E1, E4.

46. R. Moss Kanter, *The Change Masters* (New York: Simon & Schuster, 1983).

47. T. Kuczmarski, "Inspiring and Implementing the Innovation Mind-Set," *Planning Review,* September–October 1994, pp. 37–48; L. K. Gundry, J. R. Kickul, and C. W. Prather, "Building the Creative Organization," *Organizational Dynamics,* Spring 1994, pp. 22–36; and T. M. Burton, "By Learning from Failures, Lilly Keeps Drug Pipeline Full," *The Wall Street Journal,* April 21, 2004, pp. A1, A9.

48. T. J. Martin, "Ten Commandments for Managing Creative People," *Fortune,* January 16, 1995, pp. 135–136; B. Schneider, S. K. Gunnarson, and K. Niles-Jolly, "Creating the Climate and Culture of Success," *Organizational Dynamics,* Spring 1994, pp. 22–36; T. Katauskas, "Follow-Through: 3M's Formula for Success," *R&D,* November 1990; and R. Mitchell, "Masters of Innovation: How 3M Keeps Its New Products Coming," *Business Week,* April 10, 1989, pp. 58–63.

49. Carbonara, 1998.

50. T. J. Allen and S. I. Cohen, "Information Flow in Research and Development Laboratories," *Administrative Science Quarterly,* March 1969, pp. 12–19.

51. Moss Kanter, 1983.

CHAPTER 11

1. M. Conlin, "For Gen X, It's Paradise Lost," *BusinessWeek Online,* June 30, 2003, www.businessweek.com/@@ygqsk4YQtnmUSw0A/magazine/content/03_26/b3839081_mz021.htm (accessed July 12, 2004). See also G. David, "Aren't You Boomers Ever Going Away?" *Fortune,* January 2, 2002, www.fortune.com/fortune/articles/0,15114,373554,00.html (accessed July 12, 2004).

2. Bureau of Labor Statistics, reported in P. O'Connell, "Ready for a Worker Shortage?" *BusinessWeek Online,* March 22, 2004, www.businessweek.com/bwdaily/dnflash/mar2004/nf20040321_5457_db079.htm (accessed July 12, 2004). See also R. E. Herman, T. G. Olivo, and J. L. Gioia, *Impending Crisis: Too Many Jobs, Too Few People* (Winchester, VA: Oakhill Press, 2003); B. Tulgan and C. A. Martin, *Managing Generation Y: Global Citizens Born in the Late Seventies and Early Eighties* (Amherst, MA: Human Resource Development Press, 2001). See also S. Eisner, "Teaching Generation Y—Three Initiatives," *Proceedings in 2004 College Teaching and Learning Conference,* http://phobos.ramapo.edu/~seisner/Teaching.htm (accessed July 12, 2004).

3. Survey by Gallup Organization, reported in S. L. Lynch, "Gen Xers Sharpen Work Skills," *San Francisco Chronicle,* September 7, 1998, p. A2.

4. O. Pollar, "Managing the MTV Generation," *San Francisco Examiner & Chronicle,* June 15, 1997, p. J-3.

5. Tulgan and Martin, 2001. See also S. Baker, "Channeling the Future," *Business Week,* July 12, 2004, pp. 70–71; R. Zemke, C. Raines, and B. Filipczak, *Generations at Work: Managing the Clash of Veterans, Boomers, Xers and Nexters in Your Workplace* (New York: AMACOM, 1999); J. Minerd, "Bringing Out the Best in Generation X," *The Futurist,* January 1999, pp. 6–7; "19 to 33 Years Old," *San Francisco Examiner,* March 7, 1999, special section, pp. W-1–W-34; Lynch, 1998.

6. See M. Rokeach, *Beliefs, Attitudes, and Values* (San Francisco: Jossey-Bass, 1968), p. 168.

7. M. Rokeach, *The Nature of Human Values* (New York: Free Press, 1973).

8. Families and Work Institute, cited in C. Shavers, "Qualities that Make Working with Gen Xers a Special Challenge," *San Jose Mercury News,* December 6, 1998, p. 3E; see also Tulgan and Martin, 2001.

64. See E. Hatfield and S. Sprecher, *Mirror, Mirror . . . The Importance of Looks in Everyday Life* (Albany, NY: State University of New York Press, 1986); K. Dion, "Stereotyping Based on Physical Attractiveness: Issues and Conceptual Perspectives," in *Physical Appearance, Stigma, and Social Behavior: The Ontario Symposium on Personality and Social Psychology,* eds. C. P. Herman, M. P. Zanna, and E. T. Higgins (Hillsdale, NJ: Erlbaum), vol. 3; J. C. Brigham, "Limiting Conditions of the 'Physical Attractiveness Stereotype': Attributions About Divorce," *Journal of Research and Personality,* vol. 14, 1980, pp. 365–375; M. M. Clifford and E. H. Walster, "The Effect of Physical Attractiveness on Teacher Expectation," *Sociology of Education,* vol. 46, 1973; pp. 248–258; and G. R. Adams and T. L. Huston, "Social Perception of Middle-Aged Persons Varying in Physical Attractiveness," *Developmental Psychology,* vol. 11, 1975, pp. 657–658.
65. Clifford and Walster, 1973.
66. T. Cash and L. H. Janda, "The Eye of the Beholder," *Psychology Today,* December 1984, pp. 46–52.
67. R. P. Quinn, "Physical Deviance and Occupational Mistreatment: The Short, The Fat, and the Ugly," master's thesis, University of Michigan Survey Research Center, University of Michigan, Ann Arbor, 1978.
68. See D. Eden and Y. Zuk, "Seasickness as a Self-Fulfilling Prophecy: Raising Self-Efficacy to Boost Performance at Sea," *Journal of Applied Psychology,* October 1995, pp. 628–635. For a thorough review of research on the Pygmalion effect, see D. Eden, *Pygmalion in Management: Productivity as a Self-Fulfilling Prophecy* (Lexington, MA: Lexington Books, 1990), ch. 2.
69. D. B. McNatt, "Ancient Pygmalion Joins Contemporary Management: A Meta-Analysis of the Result," *Journal of Applied Psychology,* April 2000, pp. 314–322.
70. See B. Schlender, "How Bill Gates Keeps the Magic Going," *Fortune,* June 18, 1990, pp. 82–89.
71. These recommendations were adapted from J. Keller, "Have Faith—in You," *Selling Power,* June 1996, pp. 84, 86; and R. W. Goddard, "The Pygmalion Effect," *Personnel Journal,* June 1985, p. 10.
72. H. H. Kelley, "The Processes of Causal Attribution," *American Psychologist,* February 1973, pp. 107–128.
73. S. J. Linton and L.E. Warg, "Attributions (Beliefs) and Job Satisfaction Associated with Back Pain in an Industrial Setting," *Perceptual and Motor Skills,* February 1993, pp. 51–62.
74. W. S. Silver, T. R. Mitchell, and M. E. Gist, "Responses to Successful and Unsuccessful Performance: The Moderating Effect of Self-Efficacy on the Relationship between Performance and Attributions," *Organizational Behavior and Human Decision Processes,* June 1995, pp. 286–299; and D. Dunning, A. Leuenberger, and D. A. Sherman, "A New Look at Motivated Inference: Are Self-Serving Theories of Success a Product of Motivational Forces?" *Journal of Personality and Social Psychology,* July 1995, pp. 58–68.
75. *The Wirthlin Report,* reported in "Job Stress Can Be Satisfying," *USA Today,* April 19, 1999, p. 1B.
76. Study by The Medstat Group appearing in the *American Journal of Health Promotion,* October 3, 2000, reported in K. Fackelmann, "Stress, Unhealthy Habits Costing USA," *USA Today,* October 3, 2000, p. 5A.
77. Study in *Circulation,* March 1998, reported in "Managers at Risk from Work Stress," *San Jose Mercury News,* April 12, 1998, p. 5E; reprinted from *New York Times.*
78. See A. J. Kinicki, F. M. McKee-Ryan, C. A. Schriesheim, and K. P. Carson, "Assessing the Construct Validity of the Job Descriptive Index: A Review and Meta-Analysis," *Journal of Applied Psychology,* February 2002, pp. 14–32; M. A. Cavanaugh, W. R. Boswell, M. V. Roehling, and J. W. Boudreau, "An Empirical Examination of Self-Reported Work Stress among U.S. Managers," *Journal of Applied Psychology,* February 2000, pp. 65–74; and J. R. Edwards and N. P. Rothbard, "Work and Family Stress and Well-Being: An Examination of Person-Environment Fit in the Work and Family Domains," *Organizational Behavior and Human Decision Processes,* February 1999, pp. 85–129.
79. R. S. Schuler, "Definition and Conceptualization of Stress in Organizations," *Organizational Behavior and Human Performance,* April 1980, p. 1980; and R. S. Lazarus, *Psychological Stress and Coping Processes* (New York: McGraw-Hill, 1966).
80. H. Selye, *Stress without Distress* (New York: Lippincott, 1974), p. 27.
81. R. S. Lazarus and S. Folkman, "Coping and Adaptation," in *Handbook of Behavioral Medicine,* ed. W. D. Gentry (New York: Guilford, 1982).
82. R. S. Lazarus, "Little Hassles Can Be Hazardous to Health," *Psychology Today,* July 1981, p. 61.
83. Selye, 1974, pp. 28–29.
84. T. D. Schellhardt, "Company Memo to Stressed-Out Employees: 'Deal with It,'" *The Wall Street Journal,* October 2, 1996, pp. B1, B4; see also L. A. Wah, "An Executive's No. 1 Fear," *American Management Association International,* January 1998, p. 87.
85. J. A. Davy, A. J. Kinicki, and C. L. Scheck, "A Test of Job Security's Direct and Mediated Effects on Withdrawal Cognitions," *Journal of Organizational Behavior,* July 1, 1997, p. 323.
86. G. Graen, "Role-Making Processes within Complex Organizations," in *Handbook of Industrial and Organizational Psychology,* ed. M. D. Dunnette (Chicago: Rand McNally, 1976), p. 1201.
87. T. D. Wall, P. R. Jackson, S. Mullarkey, and S. K. Parker, "The Demands-Control Model of Job Strain: A More Specific Test," *Journal of Occupational and Organizational Psychology,* June 1996, pp. 153–166; and R. C. Barnett and R. T. Brennan, "The Relationship between Job Experiences and Psychological Distress: A Structural Equation Approach," *Journal of Organizational Behavior,* May 1995, pp. 250–276.
88. "Lousiest Bosses," *The Wall Street Journal,* April 4, 1995, p. A1.
89. J. Schaubroeck and D. C. Ganster, "Chronic Demands and Responsivity to Challenge," *Journal of Applied Psychology,* February 1993, pp. 73–85; E. Demerouti, A. B. Bakker, F. Nachreiner, and W. B. Schaufeli, "The Job Demands-Resources Model of Burnout," *Journal of Applied Psychology,* June 2001, pp. 499–512.
90. J. M. Plas, *Person-Centered Leadership: An American Approach to Participatory Management* (Thousand Oaks, CA: Sage, 1996).
91. N. E. Adler, T. Boyce, M. A. Chesney, S. Cohen, S. Folkman, R. L. Kahn, and S. L. Syme, "Socioeconomic Status and Health: The Challenge of the Gradient," *American Psychologist,* January 1994, pp. 15–24.
92. The link between stress and depression is discussed by P. Freiberg, "Work and Well-Being: Experts Urge Changes in Work, Not the Work," *The APA Monthly,* January 1991, p. 23.
93. Absenteeism and stress are discussed by S. Shellenbarger, "Work & Family: Was That 24-Hour Flu That Kept You Home Really Just the Blahs?" *The Wall Street Journal,* July 24, 1996, p. B1.
94. Recommendations for reducing burnout are discussed by M. Wylie, "Preventing Worker Burnout while Supporting the Users," *MacWeek,* October 4, 1993, pp. 12–14; and "How to Avoid Burnout," *Training,* February 1993, pp. 15, 16, 70.
95. These examples and techniques are discussed by R. L. Rose, "Time Out: At the Menninger Clinic, Executives Learn More About Themselves—and Why They're So Unhappy," *The Wall Street Journal,* February 26, 1996, p. R5; and L. Landon, "Pump Up Your Employees," *HR Magazine,* May 1990, pp. 34–37.

96. F. Luthans, *Organizational Behavior* (New York: McGraw-Hill, 1985), pp. 146–148.

CHAPTER 12

1. A. Zipkin, "The Wisdom of Thoughtfulness," *New York Times*, May 31, 2000, pp. C1, C10; L. Brenner, "Perks that Work," *Business Week Frontier*, October 11, 1999, pp. F.22–F30; L. Alderman, "And We'll Even Throw In . . . ," *Business Week Frontier*, October 11, 1999, pp. F.34–F.37; L. Stern, "Talent Trawl: What's the Best Bait?" *Business Week Enterprise*, December 7, 1998, pp. ENT22–ENT24; and S. Schafer, "Battling a Labor Shortage? It's All in Your Imagination," *Inc.*, August 1997, p. 24.
2. Adapted from definition in T. R. Mitchell, "Motivation: New Directions for Theory, Research, and Practice," *Academy of Management Review*, January 1982, p. 81.
3. See R. M. Ryan and E. L. Deci, "Intrinsic and Extrinsic Motivations: Classic Definitions and New Directions," *Contemporary Educational Psychology*, January 2000, pp. 54–67.
4. D. Katz and R. L. Kahn, *The Social Psychology of Organizations* (New York: Wiley, 1966).
5. K. Down and L. Liedtka, "What Corporations Seek in MBA Hires: A Survey," *Selections*, Winter 1994, pp. 34–39; see also S. Armour, "Companies Get Tough on Absent Employees," *Arizona Republic*, February 7, 2003, p. A2; reprinted from *USA Today*.
6. T. Van Tassel, "Productivity Dilemmas," *Executive Excellence*, April 1994, pp. 16–17.
7. A. Maslow, "A Theory of Human Motivation," *Psychological Review*, July 1943, pp. 370–396.
8. C. C. Pinder, *Work Motivation: Theory, Issues, and Applications* (Glenview, IL: Scott Foresman, 1984), p. 52.
9. D. E. Meyerson, quoted in J. N. Lynem, "New Breed Wants to Rock the Boat but Still Stay in It," *San Francisco Chronicle*, "Sunday," November 11, 2001, pp. J1, J3; see also D. E. Meyerson, *Tempered Radicals: How Everyday Leaders Inspire Change at Work* (Boston: Harvard Business School Press, 2003).
10. F. Herzberg, B. Mausner, and B. B. Snyderman, *The Motivation to Work* (New York: Wiley, 1959); and F. Herzberg, "One More Time: How Do You Motivate Employees?" *Harvard Business Review*, January–February 1968, pp. 53–62.
11. D. C. McClelland, *Human Motivation* (Glenview, IL: Scott Foresman, 1985).
12. D. McClelland and H. Burnham, "Power Is the Great Motivator," *Harvard Business Review*, March/April 1976, pp. 100–110.
13. D. C. McClelland and R. E. Boyatsis, "The Leadership Motive Pattern and Long Term Success in Management," *Journal of Applied Psychology*, vol. 67, 1982, pp. 737–743.
14. Recent studies of achievement motivation can be found in H. Grant and C. S. Dweck, "A Goal Analysis of Personality and Personality Coherence," in *The Coherence of Personality*, eds. D. Cervone and Y. Shoda (New York: Guilford Press, 1999), pp. 345–371.
15. C. Ansberry, "Shock Absorber: Bob Stadler Has Lived All the Business Trends of the Past 50 Years," *The Wall Street Journal*, July 11, 1996, p. A1.
16. V. H. Vroom, *Work and Motivation* (New York: Wiley, 1964).
17. "Federal Express's Fred Smith," *Inc.*, October 1986, p. 38.
18. J. S. Adams, "Toward an Understanding of Inequity," *Journal of Abnormal and Social Psychology*, November 1963, pp. 422–436; and J. S. Adams, "Injustice in Social Exchange," in L. Berkowitz, ed., *Advances in Experimental Social Psychology*, 2nd ed. (New York: Academic Press, 1965), pp. 267–300.
19. U.S. Department of Commerce, cited in A. Salkever, "An Easy Antidote to Employee Theft," *BusinessWeek Online*, May 20, 2003, www.businessweek.com/smallbiz/content/may2003/sb20030520_9328_sb018.htm (accessed July 10, 2004). See also J. Greenberg, "Employee Theft as a Reaction to Underpayment Inequity: The Hidden Cost of Pay Cuts," *Journal of Applied Psychology*, vol. 75, 1990, pp. 561–568.
20. See M. A. Korsgaard and L. Roberson, "Procedural Justice in Performance Evaluation: The Role of Instrumental and Non-Instrumental Voice in Performance Appraisal Decisions," *Journal of Management*, 1995, pp. 657–669; the role of voice in justice perceptions was investigated by D. R. Avery and M. A. Quiñones, "Disentangling the Effects of Voice: The Incremental Roles of Opportunity, Behavior, and Instrumentality in Predicting Procedural Fairness," *Journal of Applied Psychology*, February 2002, pp. 81–86.
21. B. J. Tepper, "Health Consequences of Organizational Injustice: Tests of Main and Interactive Effects," *Organizational Behavior and Human Decision Processes*, November 2001, pp. 197–215; and S. Fox, P. E. Spector, and D. Miles, "Counterproductive Work Behavior (CWB) in Response to Job Stressors and Organizational Justice: Some Mediator and Moderator Tests for Autonomy and Emotions," *Journal of Vocational Behavior*, December 2001, pp. 291–309.
22. For a thorough discussion of goal-setting theory and application, see E. A. Locke and G. P. Latham, "Building a Practically Useful Theory of Goal Setting and Task Motivation," *American Psychologist*, September 2002, pp. 705–717.
23. See E. L. Thorndike, *Educational Psychology: The Psychology of Learning, Vol. II* (New York: Columbia University Teachers College, 1913); B. F. Skinner, *Walden Two* (New York: Macmillan, 1948); *Science and Human Behavior* (New York: Macmillan, 1953); and *Contingencies of Reinforcement* (New York: Appleton-Century-Crofts, 1969).
24. B. Melin, U. Lundberg, J. Söderlund, and M. Granqvist, "Psychological and Physiological Stress Reactions of Male and Female Assembly Workers: A Comparison between Two Different Forms of Work Organization," *Journal of Organizational Behavior*, January 1999, pp. 47–61; and S. Melamed, I. Ben-Avi, J. Luz, and M. S. Green, "Objective and Subjective Work Monotony: Effects on Job Satisfaction, Psychological Distress, and Absenteeism in Blue-Collar Workers," *Journal of Applied Psychology*, February 1995, pp. 29–42.
25. M. A. Campion and C. L. McClelland, "Follow-Up and Extension of the Interdisciplinary Costs and Benefits of Enlarged Jobs," *Journal of Applied Psychology*, June 1993, pp. 339–351.
26. Herzberg et al., 1959.
27. S. Phillips and A. Dunkin, "King Customer," *Business Week*, March 12, 1990, p. 91.
28. J. R. Hackman and G. R. Oldham, *Work Redesign* (Reading, MA: Addison-Wesley, 1980).
29. A. Taylor III, "Rally of the Dolls: It Worked for Toyota. Can It Work for Toys?" *Fortune*, January 11, 1999, p. 36.
30. Zipkin, 2000.
31. Gallup Organization study, reported in Zipkin, 2000.
32. B. E. Graham-Moore and T. L. Ross, *Productivity Gainsharing* (Englewood Cliffs, NJ: Prentice-Hall, 1983).
33. "Take Stock of Stock Options," *Human Resource Executive Magazine*, June 3, 2004, workindex.com, www.workindex.com/editorial/hre/hre0406-03.asp (accessed July 12, 2004).
34. Lewis, 2000.
35. PricewaterhouseCoopers survey, reported in S. Shellenbarger, "What Job Candidates Really Want to Know: Will I Have a Life?" *The Wall Street Journal*, November 17, 1999, p. B1.
36. K. W. Smola and C. D. Sutton, "Generational Differences: Revisiting Generational Work Values for the New Millennium," *Journal of Organizational Behavior*, June 2002, p. 379.

37. Walker Information survey, reported in Lewis, 2000.
38. Spherion and Louis Harris Associates 1999 survey, reported in Zipkin, 2000.
39. See P. Falcone, "Doing More with Less: How to Motivate and Reward Your Overworked Staff During Lean Times," *HR Magazine,* February 2003, pp. 101–103; and D. Kehrer, "Here Are Some Keys to Keeping Good Employees," *Reno Gazette-Journal,* March 30, 2004, p. 4D.
40. B. L. Ware, quoted in Zipkin, 2000.
41. B. Moses, quoted in Lewis, 2000.
42. K. Lingle, quoted in C. Kleiman, "Work-Life Rewards Grow," *San Francisco Examiner,* January 16, 2000, p. J-2; reprinted from *Chicago Tribune.*
43. C. Kleiman, "CEO of Family-Friendly Firm Tells Others to 'Just Do It,' " *San Jose Mercury News,* September 19, 1999, p. PC-1; and D. Dallinger, "Battling for a Balanced Life," *San Francisco Chronicle,* November 14, 1999, "Sunday" section, p. 9; see also A. Fisher, "The Rebalancing Act," *Fortune,* October 6, 2003, pp. 110–113; D. Cadrain, "Cash vs. Non-cash Rewards," *HR Magazine,* April 2003, pp. 81–87; and C. Hymowitz, "While Some Women Choose to Stay Home, Others Gain Flexibility," *The Wall Street Journal,* March 30, 2004, p. B1.
44. A. Hedge, quoted in P. Wen, "Drab Cubicles Can Block Workers' Creativity, Productivity," *San Francisco Chronicle,* March 10, 2000, pp. B1, B3; reprinted from *Boston Globe.*
45. J. P. Smith, "Sabbaticals Pervade Business Sector," *Reno Gazette-Journal,* February 22, 2004, p. H1; see also H. Lancaster, "Sabbaticals Can Help You Improve Your Job or Spur a New Career," *The Wall Street Journal,* February 13, 1996, p. B1.

CHAPTER 13

1. K. W. Thomas, "Conflict and Conflict Management," in *Handbook of Industrial and Organizational Psychology,* M. Dunnette, ed. (Chicago: Rand McNally, 1976), pp. 889–935; K. W. Thomas "Toward Multiple Dimensional Values in Teaching: The Example of Conflict Behaviors," *Academy of Management Review,* July 1977, pp. 484–490; and M. A Rahim, "A Strategy for Managing Conflict in Complex Organizations," *Human Relations,* January 1985, p. 84.
2. Rahmin, 1985.
3. B. Rosner, "How to Avoid Violence from a Fired Worker," *San Francisco Sunday Examiner & Chronicle,* November 15, 1998, p. CL-13.
4. D. Loomis, S. H. Wolf, C. W. Runyan, S. W. Marshall, and J. D. Butts, "Homicide on the Job: Workplace and Community Determinants," *American Journal of Epidemiology,* September 1, 2001, pp. 410–417. See also J. Carpenter, "Killer Jobs: New Study Finds Risk in Retail," abcnews.com, August 29, 2001, http://abcnews.go.com/sections/business/DailyNews/workplace_mortality_010829.html (accessed July 12, 2004).
5. J. A. Wall Jr. and R. Robert Callister, "Conflict and Its Management," *Journal of Management,* no. 3, 1995, p. 517.
6. C. Alter, "An Exploratory Study of Conflict and Coordination in Interorganizational Service Delivery Systems," *Academy of Management Journal,* September 1990, pp. 478–502; S. P. Robbins, " 'Conflict Management' and 'Conflict Resolution' Are Not Synonymous Terms," *California Management Review,* Winter 1978, p. 70.
7. Cooperative conflict is discussed in D. Tjosvold, *Learning to Manage Conflict: Getting People to Work Together Productively* (New York: Lexington, 1993); and D. Tjosvold and D. W. Johnson, *Productive Conflict Management Perspectives for Organizations* (New York: Irvington, 1983). See also A. C. Amason, K. R. Thompson, W. A. Hochwarter, and A. W. Harrison, "Conflict: An Important Dimension in Successful Management Teams," *Organizational Dynamics,* Autumn 1995, pp. 20–35; and A. C. Amason, "Distinguishing the Effects of Functional and Dysfunctional Conflict on Strategic Decision Making: Resolving a Paradox for Top Management Teams," *Academy of Management Journal,* February 1996, pp. 123–148.
8. S. Flax, "The Toughest Bosses in America," *Fortune,* August 6, 1984, p. 21; and C. Hymowitz, "Business Leaders Face a Grassroots Demand for a Lot Less Hubris," *The Wall Street Journal,* March 9, 2004, p. B1.
9. Study by B. Tepper, April 2004, reported in B. Carey, "Fear in the Workplace: The Bullying Boss," *The New York Times,* June 22, 2004, pp. D1, D6.
10. J. B. Treece, "Richard LeFauve," *The 1990 Business Week 1000,* April 13, 1990, p. 130. For a Saturn update, see M. Maynard, "Automaker's Influence Takes Orbit," *USA Today,* October 2, 1996, pp. 1B–2B.
11. A. M. O'Leary-Kelly, R. W. Griffin, and D. J. Glew, "Organization-Motivated Aggression: A Research Framework," *Academy of Management Review,* January 1996, pp. 225–253.
12. L. R. Pondy, "Organizational Conflict: Concepts and Models," *Administrative Science Quarterly,* vol. 2, 1967, pp. 296–320.
13. P. Burrows, "Carly's Last Stand?" *Business Week,* December 24, 2001, pp. 63–70. See B. Pimentel, "Heftier HP Is Ready to Forge Ahead," *San Francisco Chronicle,* May 5, 2002, pp. G1, G4.
14. R. A. Cosier and C. R. Schwenk, "Agreement and Thinking Alike: Ingredients for Poor Decisions," *Academy of Management Executive,* February 1990, p. 71. Also see J. P. Kotter, "Kill Complacency," *Fortune,* August 5, 1996, pp. 168–170.
15. See "Facilitators as Devil's Advocates," *Training,* September 1993, p. 10; and C. R. Schwenk, "Devil's Advocacy in Managerial Decision Making," *Journal of Management Studies,* April 1984, pp. 153–168.
16. S. G. Katzenstein, "The Debate on Structured Debate: Toward a Unified Theory," *Organizational Behavior and Human Decision Processes,* June 1996, pp. 316–332.
17. W. Kiechel III, "How to Escape the Echo Chamber," *Fortune,* June 18, 1990, p. 130.
18. T. Kelley, quoted in P. Sinton, "Teamwork the Name of the Game for Ideo," *San Francisco Chronicle,* February 23, 2000, pp. D1, D3.
19. J. Katzenback and D. Smith, "The Discipline of Teams," *The Harvard Business Review,* March–April 1993, pp. 111–120; S. J. Kozlowski and B. S. Bell, "Work Groups and Teams in Organizations," in *Handbook of Psychology,* vol. 12, W. C. Borman, D. R. Ilgen, and R. J. Klimoski, eds. (New York: John Wiley, 2003), pp. 333–375.
20. See P. F. Drucker, "The Coming of the New Organization," *Harvard Business Review,* January–February 1988, pp. 45–53.
21. Data from "HR Data Files," *HR Magazine,* June 1995, p. 65.
22. "Top 10 Leadership Tips from Jeff Immelt," *Fast Company,* April 2004, p. 96.
23. P. Sinton, "The Enemy Within," *San Francisco Chronicle,* February 23, 2000, pp. D1, D3.
24. E. E. Lawler III, *From the Ground Up* (San Francisco: Jossey-Bass, 1996).
25. Sinton, 2000.
26. P. Burrows, "John Chambers: 'We Never Lost Track,' " *BusinessWeek Online,* November 24, 2003, www.businessweek.com/@@UdH6O4YQxnuUSw0A/magazine/content/03_47/b3859015.htm (accessed July 12, 2004).
27. B. Dumaine, "Why Do We Work?" *Fortune,* December 26, 1994, p. 202; see also D. Luhrssen, "Whirling through the Festival Season," *Shepherd Express Metro,* June 15, 2000, www.shepherd-express.com/shepherd/21/25/cover_story.html (accessed July 12, 2004).

28. This definition is based in part on one found in D. Horton Smith, "A Parsimonious Definition of 'Group': Toward Conceptual Clarity and Scientific Utility," *Sociological Inquiry,* Spring 1967, pp. 141–167.

29. E. H. Schein, *Organizational Psychology,* 3rd ed. (Englewood Cliffs, NJ: Prentice-Hall, 1980), p. 145.

30. J. R. Katzenbach and D. K. Smith, *The Wisdom of Teams: Creating the High-Performance Organization* (Boston: Harvard Business School Press, 1993), p. 45.

31. J. R. Katzenbach and D. K. Smith, "The Discipline of Teams," *Harvard Business Review,* March–April 1995, p. 112.

32. D. Krackhardt and J. R. Hanson, "Informal Networks: The Company Behind the Chart," *Harvard Business Review,* July–August 1993, p. 104.

33. Study by Center for Workforce Development, Newton, MA, reported in M. Jackson, "It's Not Chitchat, It's Training," *San Francisco Chronicle,* January 7, 1998, p. D2.

34. E. Sundstrom, K. P. DeMeuse, and D. Futrell, "Work Teams," *American Psychologist,* February 1990, pp. 120–133.

35. See K. Buch and R. Spangler, "The Effects of Quality Circles on Performance and Promotions," *Human Relations,* June 1990, pp. 573–582; and G. R. Ferris and J. A. Wagner III, "Quality Circles in the United States: a Conceptual Reevaluation," *The Journal of Applied Behavioral Science,* no. 2, 1985, pp. 155–167.

36. E. E. Lawler III and S. A. Mohrman, "Quality Circles: After the Honeymoon," *Organizational Dynamics,* Spring 1987, pp. 42–54. Also see E. E. Lawler III, "Total Quality Management and Employee Involvement: Are They Compatible?" *Academy of Management Executive,* February 1994, pp. 68–76.

37. Lawler and Mohrman, 1987.

38. G. L. Stewart and M. R. Barrick, "Team Structure and Performance: Assessing the Mediating Role of Intrateam Process and the Moderating Role of Task," *Academy of Management Journal,* April 2000, p. 135.

39. Good background discussions can be found in P. S. Goodman, R. Devadas, and T. L. Griffith Hughson, "Groups and Productivity: Analyzing the Effectiveness of Self-Managing Teams," in *Productivity in Organizations,* eds. J. P. Campbell, R. J. Campbell and Associates (San Francisco: Jossey-Bass, 1988), pp. 295–327; also see E. G. Rogers, W. Metlay, I. T. Kaplan, and T. Shapiro, "Self-Managing Work Teams: Do They Really Work?" *Human Resource Planning,* no. 2, 1995, pp. 53–57; and V. U. Druskat and S. B. Wolff, "Effects and Timing of Developmental Peer Appraisals in Self-Managing Work Teams," *Journal of Applied Psychology,* February 1999, pp. 58–74.

40. See C. Douglas and W. L. Gardner, "Transition to Self-Directed Work Teams: Implications of Transition Time and Self-Monitoring for Managers' Use of Influence Tactics," *Journal of Organizational Behavior,* vol. 25, 2004, pp. 47–65; and K. Kraiger, "Perspectives on Training and Development," in *Handbook of Psychology,* vol. 12, W. C. Borman, D. R. Ilgen, and R. J. Klimoski, eds. (New York: John Wiley, 2003), pp. 176–177.

41. C. Douglas and W. L. Gardner, "Transition to Self-Directed Work Teams: Implications of Transition Time and Self-Monitoring for Managers' Use of Influence Tactics," *Journal of Organizational Behavior,* vol. 25, 2004, pp. 47–65.

42. See B. S. Bell and S. W. J. Kozlowski, "A Typology of Virtual Teams: Implications for Effective Leadership," *Group & Organization Management,* March 2002, pp. 14–49.

43. Review of J. Lipnack and J. Stamps, *Virtual Teams: Reaching Across Space, Time, and Organization with Technology* (New York: John Wiley, 1997), in "Virtual Teams Transcend Space and Time," *The Futurist,* September–October 1997, p. 59.

44. W. Arnold, "Cathay Pacific Is Lesson in Culture, Computing," *The Wall Street Journal,* November 25, 1998, p. B6.

45. Adapted from "Managing the Challenge of a Virtual Workplace," box in C. Sandlund, "Remote Control," *Business Week Frontier,* March 27, 2000, pp. F.14–F.20; see also C. Joinson, "Managing Virtual Teams," *HR Magazine,* June 2002, p. 71; and A. Salkever, "Home Truths about Meetings," *BusinessWeek Online,* April 24, 2003, www.businessweek.com/smallbiz/content/apr2003/sb20030424_0977_sb010.htm (accessed July 12, 2004).

46. See B. W. Tuckman, "Developmental Sequence in Small Groups," *Psychological Bulletin,* June 1965, pp. 384–399; and B. W. Tuckman and M. A. C. Jensen, "Stages of Small-Group Development Revisited," *Group & Organization Studies,* December 1977, pp. 419–427. An instructive adaptation of the Tuckman model can be found in L. Holpp, "If Empowerment Is So Good, Why Does It Hurt?" *Training,* March 1995, p. 56; see also C. Gersick, "Marking Time: Predictable Transitions in Task Groups,' *Academy of Management Journal,* June 1989, pp. 274–309.

47. Practical advice on handling a dominating group member can be found in M. Finley, "Belling the Bully," *HR Magazine,* March 1992, pp. 82–86; see also B. Carey, "Fear in the Workplace: The Bullying Boss," *New York Times,* June 22, 2004, pp. D1, D6.

48. J. Case, "What the Experts Forgot to Mention," *Inc.,* September 1993, pp. 66–78.

49. M. Erez, "Is Group Productivity Loss the Rule or the Exception? Effects of Culture and Group-based Motivation," *Academy of Management Journal,* vol. 39, 1996, pp. 1513–1537.

50. "A Team's-Eye View of Teams," *Training,* November 1995, p. 16.

51. M. E. Shaw, *Group Dynamics,* 3rd ed. (New York: McGraw-Hill, 1981); G. Manners, "Another Look at Group Size, Group Problem-Solving and Member Consensus," *Academy of Management Journal,* vol. 18, 1975, pp. 715–724.

52. H.-S. Hwang and J. Guynes, "The Effect of Group Size on Group Performance in Computer-Supported Decision Making," *Information & Management,* April 1994, pp. 189–198.

53. S. J. Karau and K. D. Williams, "Social Loafing: Research Findings, Implications, and Future Directions," *Current Directions in Psychological Science,* October 1995, pp. 134–140; S. J. Zacarro, "Social Loafing: The Role of Task Attractiveness," *Personality and Social Psychology Bulletin,* vol. 10, 1984, pp. 99–106; P. W. Mulvey, L. Bowes-Sperry, and H. J. Klein, "The Effects of Perceived Loafing and Defensive Impression Management on Group Effectiveness," *Small Group Research,* June 1998, pp. 394–415; and L. Karakowsky and K. McBey, "Do My Contributions Matter? The Influence of Imputed Expertise on Member Involvement and Self-Evaluations in the Work Group," *Group & Organization Management,* March 2001, pp. 70–92.

54. Deutschman, 1994.

55. K. D. Benne and P. Sheats, "Functional Roles of Group Members," *Journal of Social Issues,* Spring 1948, pp. 41–49.

56. D. C. Feldman, "The Development and Enforcement of Group Norms," *Academy of Management Review,* January 1984, pp. 47–53.

57. D. Kahneman, "Reference Points, Anchors, Norms, and Mixed Feelings," *Organizational Behavior and Human Decision Processes,* March 1992, pp. 296–312.

58. C. V. Haaff, "How to Foster Teamwork in a Small Business," *Business in Vancouver,* 1998, www.biv.com/howto/teamwork.html (accessed July 12, 2004).

59. Feldman, 1984.

60. See, for example, P. Jin, "Work Motivation and Productivity in Voluntarily Formed Work Teams: A Field Study in China," *Organizational Behavior and Human Decision Processes,* vol. 54, no. 1, 1993, pp. 133–155.

61. L Janis, *Groupthink,* 2nd ed. (Boston: Houghton Mifflin, 1982), p. 9.

62. V. Kemper, "Groupthink Viewed as Culprit in Move to War," *Los Angeles Times,* July 10, 2004, www.latimes.com/la-na-groupthink10jul10,1,4397696.story (accessed July 12, 2004).

63. J. Surowiecki, quoted in J. Freeman, "Books," *The Christian Science Monitor,* May 25, 2004, www.csmonitor.com/2004/0525/p15s01-bogn.html (accessed July 12, 2004). Also see J. Surowiecki, *The Wisdom of Crowds: Why the Many Are Smarter Than the Few and How Collective Wisdom Shapes Business, Economies, Societies, and Nations* (New York: Doubleday, 2004).

64. V. H. Palmieri, quoted in L. Baum, "The Job Nobody Wants," *Business Week,* September 8, 1986, p. 60.

65. J. Flynn, "Giving the Board More Clout," *Business Week,* Bonus Issue: Reinventing America, 1992, p. 74.

66. Janis, 1982, pp. 174–175.

67. Surowiecki, quoted in Kemper, 2004.

68. M. R. Callway and J. K. Desser, "Groupthink: Effects of Cohesiveness and Problem-Solving Procedures on Group Decision Making," *Social Behavior and Personality,* no. 2, 1984, pp.157–164.

CHAPTER 14

1. R. E. Kelley, *How to Be a Star at Work: Nine Breakthrough Strategies You Need to Succeed* (New York: Times Books, 1999); A. M. Webber, "Are You a Star at Work?" *Fast Company,* June 1998, p. 114; C. Shavers, "Being a Star at Work Requires Self-Management," *San Jose Mercury News,* December 13, 1998, p. 4E; I. DeBare, "How to Become a Star in the Workplace," *San Francisco Chronicle,* July 20, 1998, p. D2; L. M. Sixel, "So You Want to Be a Star at Your Job," *San Francisco Examiner & Chronicle,* September 13, 1998, p. CL-17; reprinted from *Houston Chronicle;* and C. Smith, "'Star' Traits Aren't Always Obvious Ones," *San Francisco Examiner & Chronicle,* August 15, 1999, p. CL-17.

2. C. A. Schriesheim, J. M. Tolliver, and O. C. Behling, "Leadership Theory: Some Implications for Managers," *MSU Business Topics,* Summer 1978, p. 35. See also G. Yukl, "Managerial Leadership: A Review of Theory and Research," *Journal of Management,* vol. 15, 1989, pp. 251–289.

3. T. Peters and N. Austin, *A Passion for Excellence* (New York: Random House, 1985), pp. 5–6; but see also B. Kellerman, "Leadership—Warts and All," *Harvard Business Review,* January 1, 2004, pp. 40–45.

4. B. M. Bass, *Bass & Stogdill's Handbook of Leadership: Theory, Research, and Managerial Applications,* 3rd ed. (New York: Free Press, 1990), p. 383.

5. J. P. Kotter, "What Leaders Really Do," *Harvard Business Review,* December 2001, pp. 85–96; the role of leadership within organizational change is discussed in J. P. Kotter, *Leading Change* (Boston: Harvard Business School Press, 1996).

6. F. Smith, quoted in "All in a Day's Work," *Harvard Business Review,* December 2001, pp. 54–66.

7. N. Tichy and C. DeRose, "Roger Enrico's Master Class," *Fortune,* November 27, 1995, pp. 105–106.

8. L. H. Chusmir, "Personalized versus Socialized Power Needs among Working Women and Men," *Human Relations,* February 1986, p. 149.

9. D. Leonhardt, "Don't Mess with This Maytag Repairman," *Business Week,* August 9, 1999, p. 70.

10. C. H. Deutsch, "G.E. Taps Successor to the Chief," *New York Times,* November 28, 2000, pp. C1, C14; T. A. Stewart, "See Jack. See Jack Run Europe," *Fortune,* September 27, 1999, pp. 124–136; G. Colvin, "The Ultimate Manager," *Fortune,* November 22, 1999, pp. 185–187; C. H. Deutsch, "GE's Chief Sets a Date to Step Down," *New York Times,* November 3, 1999, pp. C1, C2; M. Allen, "Another Jack Welch Isn't Good Enough," *The Wall Street Journal,* November 22, 1999, p. A22; A. Sloan, "Judging GE's Jack Welch," *Newsweek,* November 15, 1999, p. 67; R. Slater, *Jack Welch and the GE Way* (New York: McGraw-Hill, 1999); and J. A. Byrne, "Jack," *Business Week,* June 8, 1998, pp. 90–106.

11. "Management 101: Motivation Matters" [editorial], *Business Week,* June 8, 1998, p. 130.

12. See J. Useem, "Another Boss, Another Revolution," *Fortune,* April 5, 2004, pp. 112–124; and "The 2004 Global 500: Top Performers," Fortune.com, www.fortune.com/fortune/global500/subs/topperformers/snapshot/0,20850,profit,00.html (accessed July 12, 2004).

13. "Push-Button Age," *Newsweek,* July 9, 1990, p. 57.

14. Based on Table 1 in G. Yukl, C. M. Falbe, and J. Y. Youn, "Patterns of Influence Behavior for Managers," *Group & Organization Management,* March 1993, pp. 5–28.

15. G. Yukl, H. Kim, and C. M. Falbe, "Antecedents of Influence Outcomes," *Journal of Applied Psychology,* June 1996, pp. 309–317.

16. B. Schlender, "A Conversation with the Lords of Wintel," *Fortune,* July 8, 1996, p. 44.

17. R. M. Stogdill, "Personal Factors Associated with Leadership: A Survey of the Literature," *Journal of Psychology,* 1948, pp. 35–71; and R. M. Stogdill, *Handbook of Leadership* (New York: Free Press, 1974).

18. B. Bass, *Stogdill's Handbook of Leadership,* rev. ed. (New York: Free Press, 1981).

19. J. M. Kouzes and B. Z. Posner, "The Credibility Factor: What Followers Expect from Their Leaders," *Business Credit,* July–August 1990, pp. 24–28; J. M. Kouzes and B. Z. Posner, *The Leadership Challenge: How to Get Extraordinary Things Done in Organizations* (San Francisco: Jossey-Bass, 1995); and J. M. Kouzes and B. Z. Posner, *Credibility* (San Francisco: Jossey-Bass, 1993).

20. L. Brossidy, "The Job No CEO Should Delegate," *Harvard Business Review,* March 2001, pp. 47–49.

21. D. Goleman, *Emotional Intelligence: Why It Can Matter More Than IQ* (New York: Bantam Books, 1995).

22. D. Goleman, "What Makes a Leader," *Harvard Business Review,* November–December 1998, pp. 93–102.

23. Goleman, Boyatzis, and McKee, 2001, pp. 42–51.

24. S. Fox and P. E. Spector, "Relations of Emotional Intelligence, Practical Intelligence, General Intelligence, and Trait Affectivity with Interview Outcomes: It's Not All Just 'G,'" *Journal of Organizational Behavior,* March 1, 2000, pp. 203–220.

25. M. D. Davies, L. Stankov, and R. D. Roberts, "Emotional Intelligence: In Search of an Elusive Construct," *Journal of Personality & Social Psychology,* October 1, 1998, pp. 989–1015.

26. Results can be found in T. A. Judge, J. E. Bono, R. Ilies, and M. W. Gerhardt, "Personality and Leadership: A Qualitative and Quantitative Review," *Journal of Applied Psychology,* August 2002, pp. 765–780.

27. See T. A. Judge, A. E. Colbert, and R. Ilies, "Intelligence and Leadership: A Quantitative Review and Test of Theoretical Propositions," *Journal of Applied Psychology,* June 2004, pp. 542–552.

28. A summary of this research is provided by B. J. Avolio, J. J. Soskik, D. I. Jung, and Y. Berson, "Leadership Models, Methods, and Applications," in W. C. Borman, D. R. Ilgen, and R. J. Klimoski, eds., *Handbook of Psychology* (Hoboken, NJ: John Wiley & Sons, 2003), vol. 12, pp. 277–307.

29. Study by Catalyst, New York, reported in J. S. Lublin, "Women Aspire to Be Chief as Much as Men Do," *The Wall Street Journal,* June 28, 2004, p. D2.

30. R. Sharpe, "As Leaders, Women Rule," *Business Week,* November 20, 2000, pp. 75–84.

31. Study by Hagberg Consulting Group, Foster City, Calif., reported in Sharpe, 2000, p. 75.

32. B. R. Ragins, B. Townsend, and M. Mattis, "Gender Gap in the Executive Suite: CEOs and Female Executives Report on Breaking the Glass Ceiling," *Academy of Management Executive,* February 1, 1998, pp. 28–42.

33. L. Tischler, "Where Are the Women?" *Fast Company,* February 2004, pp. 52–60.

34. P. Sellers, "Power: Do Women Really Want It?" *Fortune,* October 13, 2003, p. 88.

35. See M. Conlin, "Self-Deprecating Women," *Business Week,* June 14, 2004, p. 26.

36. R. Likert, *New Patterns of Management* (New York: McGraw-Hill, 1961); and R. Likert, *The Human Organization* (New York: McGraw-Hill, 1967).

37. C. A. Schriesman and B. J. Bird, "Contributions of the Ohio State Studies to the Field of Leadership," *Journal of Management Studies,* vol. 5, 1979, pp. 135–145; and C. L. Shartle, "Early Years of the Ohio State University Leadership Studies," *Journal of Management,* vol. 5, 1979, pp. 126–134.

38. V. H. Vroom, "Leadership," in *Handbook of Industrial and Organizational Psychology,* ed. M. D. Dunnette (Chicago: Rand McNally, 1976).

39. H. Lancaster, "New Managers Get Little Help Tackling Big, Complex Jobs," *The Wall Street Journal,* February 10, 1998; and C. Hymowitz, "New Top Managers Often Find They Miss Close Peers, Counsel," *The Wall Street Journal,* November 25, 1997, p.B1; see also M. Stettner, *Skills for New Managers* (New York: McGraw-Hill, 2000); J. H. Grossman and J. R. Parkinson, *Becoming a Successful Manager: How to Make a Smooth Transition from Managing Yourself to Managing Others* (New York: McGraw-Hill, 2001); and L. A. Hill, *Becoming a Manager: How New Managers Master the Challenges of Leadership,* 2nd ed. (Boston: Harvard Business School Press, 2003).

40. The Leadership Grid® figure is adapted from R. R. Blake, J. S. Mouton, L. B. Barnes, and L. E. Greiner, "Breakthrough in Organization Development," *Harvard Business Review,* November–December 1964, p. 136.

41. P. C. Nystrom, "Managers and the Hi-Hi Leader Myth," *Academy of Management Journal,* June 1978, pp. 325–331; and L. L. Larson, J. G. Hunt, and R. N. Osborn, "The Great Hi-Hi Leader Behavior Myth: A Lesson from Occam's Razor," *Academy of Management Journal,* December 1976, pp. 628–641.

42. F. E. Fiedler, "Assumed Similarity Measures as Predictors of Team Effectiveness," *Journal of Abnormal and Social Psychology,* vol. 49, 1954, pp. 381–388; F. E. Fiedler, *Leader Attitudes and Group Effectiveness* (Urbana, IL: University of Illinois Press, 1958); and F. E. Fiedler, *A Theory of Leadership Effectiveness* (New York: McGraw-Hill, 1967).

43. A recent review of the contingency theory and suggestions for future theoretical development is provided by R. Ayman, M. M. Chemers, and F. Fiedler, "The Contingency Model of Leadership Effectiveness: Its Levels of Analysis," in F. Dansereau and F. J. Yamminrino, eds., *Leadership: The Multiple-Level Approaches* (Stamford, CT: JAI Press, 1998), pp. 73–94.

44. R. J. House, "A Path-Goal Theory of Leader Effectiveness," *Administrative Science Quarterly,* September 1971, pp. 321–338; and R. J. House and T. R. Mitchell, "Path–Goal Theory of Leadership," *Journal of Contemporary Business,* Autumn 1974, pp. 81–97. The most recent version of the theory is found in R. J. House, "Path–Goal Theory of Leadership: Lessons, Legacy, and a Reformulated Theory," *Leadership Quarterly,* Autumn 1996, pp. 323–352.

45. These studies are summarized in House, 1996.

46. Supportive results can be found in D. Charbonneau, J. Barling, and E. K. Kelloway, "Transformational Leadership and Sports Performance: The Mediating Role of Intrinsic Motivation," *Journal of Applied Social Psychology,* July 2001, pp. 1521–1534.

47. Results can be found in P. M. Podsakoff, S. B. MacKenzie, M. Ahearne, and W. H. Bommer, "Searching for a Needle in a Haystack: Trying to Identify the Illusive Moderators of Leadership Behaviors," *Journal of Management,* 1995, pp. 422–470.

48. A thorough discussion is provided by P. Hersey and K. H. Blanchard, *Management of Organizational Behavior: Utilizing Human Resources,* 5th ed. (Englewood Cliffs, NJ: Prentice-Hall, 1988).

49. Results can be found in J. R. Goodson, G. W. McGee, and J. F. Cashman, "Situational Leadership Theory," *Group & Organization Studies,* December 1989, pp. 446–461.

50. C. Adams, "Leadership Behavior of Chief Nurse Executives," *Nursing Management,* August 1990, pp. 36–39.

51. See D. C. Lueder, "Don't Be Misled by LEAD," *Journal of Applied Behavioral Science,* May 1985, pp. 143–154; and C. L. Graeff, "The Situational Leadership Theory: A Critical View," *Academy of Management Review,* April 1983, pp. 285–291.

52. For a complete description of the full range leadership theory, see B. J. Bass and B. J. Avolio, *Revised Manual for the Multi-Factor Leadership Questionnaire* (Palo Alto, CA: Mindgarden, 1997).

53. A definition and description of transactional leadership is provided by J. Antonakis and R. J. House, "The Full-Range Leadership Theory: The Way Forward," in B. J. Avolio and F. J. Yammarino, eds., *Transformational and Charismatic Leadership: The Road Ahead* (New York: JAI Press, 2002), pp. 3–34.

54. M. Arndt, "3M's Rising Star," *Business Week,* April 12, 2004, p. 65.

55. U. R. Dundum, K. B. Lowe, and B. J. Avolio, "A Meta-Analysis of Transformational and Transactional Leadership Correlates of Effectiveness and Satisfaction: An Update and Extension," in B. J. Avolio and F. J. Yammarino, eds., *Transformational and Charismatic Leadership: The Road Ahead* (New York: JAI Press, 2002), p. 38.

56. Supportive results can be found in T. A. Judge and J. E. Bono, "Five-Factor Model of Personality and Transformational Leadership," *Journal of Applied Psychology,* October 2000, pp. 751–765.

57. Supportive research is summarized by Antonakis and House, 2002.

58. Arndt, 2004, p. 65.

59. These definitions are derived from R. Kark, B. Shamir, and C. Chen, "The Two Faces of Transformational Leadership: Empowerment and Dependency," *Journal of Applied Psychology,* April 2003, pp. 246–255.

60. B. Nanus, *Visionary Leadership* (San Francisco: Jossey-Bass, 1992), p. 8.

61. See K. B. Lowe, K. G. Kroeck, and N. Sivasubramaniam, "Effectiveness Correlates of Transformational and Transactional Leadership: A Meta-Analytic Review of the MLQ Literature," *Leadership Quarterly,* 1996, pp. 385–425.

62. Results can be found in Dumdum, Lowe, and Avolia, 2002.

63. See Kark, Shamir, and Chen, 2003.

64. Supportive results can be found in B. M. Bass, B. J. Avolio, D. I. Jung, and Y. Berson, "Predicting Unit Performance by Assessing Transformational and Transactional Leadership," *Journal of Applied Psychology,* April 2003, pp. 207–218; J. E. Bono and T. A. Judge, "Self-Concordance at Work: Toward Understanding the Motivational Effects of Transformational Leaders," *Academy of Management Journal,* October 2003, pp. 554–571; and D. Charbonneau, J. Barling, and E. K. Kelloway, "Transformational Leadership and Sports Performance: The Mediating Role of Intrinsic Motivation," *Journal of Applied Social Psychology,* July 2001, pp. 1521–1534.

65. See A. J. Towler, "Effects of Charismatic Influence Training on Attitudes, Behavior, and Performance," *Personnel Psychology,* Summer 2003, pp. 363–381; and M. Frese and S. Beimel, "Action

Training for Charismatic Leadership: Two Evaluations of Studies of a Commercial Training Module on Inspirational Communication of a Vision," *Personnel Psychology,* Autumn 2003, pp. 671–697.

66. These recommendations were derived from J. M. Howell and B. J. Avolio, "The Ethics of Charismatic Leadership: Submission or Liberation," *The Executive,* May 1992, pp. 43–54.
67. R. J. House and R. N. Aditya, "The Social Scientific Study of Leadership: Quo Vadis?" *Journal of Management,* vol. 23, 1997, pp. 409–473.
68. A thorough discussion of shared leadership is provided by C. L. Pearce, "The Future of Leadership: Combining Vertical and Shared Leadership to Transform Knowledge Work." *Academy of Management Executive,* February 2004, pp. 47–57.
69. A. Taylor III, "Bill's Brand-New Ford," *Fortune,* June 28, 2004, p. 74.
70. This research is summarized in B. J. Avolio, J. J. Soskik, D. I. Jung, and Y. Benson, "Leadership Models, Methods, and Applications," in W. C. Borman, D. R. Ilgen, and R. J. Klimoski, eds. *Handbook of Psychology* (Hoboken, NJ: John Wiley & Sons, 2003), vol. 12, pp. 277–307.
71. An overall summary of servant leadership is provided by L. C. Spears, *Reflections on Leadership: How Robert K. Greenleaf's Theory of Servant-Leadership Influenced Today's Top Management Thinkers* (New York: Wiley, 1995).
72. D. L. Moore, "Wooden's Wizardry Wears Well," *USA Today,* March 29, 1995, pp. 1C, 2C.
73. B. Saporito, "And the Winner Is Still . . . Wal-Mart," *Fortune,* May 2, 1994, pp. 62–70.
74. See W. Zellner, "Analyzing the 'Sins' of Wal-Mart," *BusinessWeek Online,* April 15, 2004, www.businessweek.com/bwdaily/dnflash/apr2004/nf20040415_1545_db017.htm (accessed July 12, 2004).
75. F. F. Reichheld and T. Teal, *The Loyalty Effect: The Hidden Force Behind Growth, Profits, and Lasting Value* (Boston: Harvard Business School Press, 2001); see also F. F. Reichheld, *Loyalty Rules! How Today's Leaders Build Lasting Relationships* (Cambridge, MA: Harvard Business School Press, 2001); and *The Loyalty Effect: The Hidden Force Behind Growth* (Cambridge, MA: Harvard Business School Press, 1996).
76. F. F. Reichheld, "Lead for Loyalty," *Harvard Business Review,* July–August 2001, pp. 76–84.
77. B. L. Clark, "Slavish Devotion to the Cult of Customer Service," *FSB,* November 2001, p. 42.
78. J. Collins, *Good to Great* (New York: Harper Business, 2001).
79. J. Collins, "Level 5 Leadership," *Harvard Business Review,* January 2001, p. 68.
80. Collins, *Good to Great,* 2001, p. 21.
81. See Collins, *Good to Great,* 2001.
82. See B. J. Avolio, J. J. Sosik, D. I. Jung, and Yair Berson, 2003, pp. 295–298.
83. D. MacRae, "Six Secrets of Successful E-Leaders," *BusinessWeek Online,* September 6, 2001, www.businessweek.com/technology/content/sep2001/tc2001096_619.htm (accessed July 23, 2004).
84. D. Q. Mills, *E-Leadership: Guiding Your Business to Success in the New Economy* (Paramus, NJ: Prentice Hall Press, 2001). See also R. Hargrove, *E-Leader: Reinventing Leadership in a Connected Economy* (Boulder, CO: Perseus Books Group, 2001); S. Annunzio, *eLeadership: Bold Solutions for the New Economy* (New York: Simon & Schuster, 2001); and T. M. Siebel, *Taking Care of eBusiness: How Today's Market Leaders Are Increasing Revenue, Productivity, and Customer Satisfaction* (New York: Doubleday, 2001).
85. L. Capotosto, "Millenial Management," *Darwin,* www2.darwinmag.com/connect/books/book.cfm?ID=188 (accessed July 24, 2004).

CHAPTER 15

1. See C. Kanchier, "Telephone Skills Crucial for Success," *San Francisco Examiner,* May 2, 1999, p. J-2; C. Kanchier, "How to Make Effective Phone Calls," *San Francisco Examiner,* September 26, 1999, p. J-3; B. Roserner, "The Right Tone for When You Use the Phone," *San Francisco Examiner & Chronicle,* August 29, 1999, p. CL-13; and O. Pollar, "How to Be a Winner at Phone Tag," *San Francisco Examiner & Chronicle,* May 2, 1999, p. J-3.
2. R. Todd, quoted in A. Fisher, "Readers Speak Out on Illiterate MBAs and More," *Fortune,* March 1, 1999, p. 242.
3. See D. Fenn, "Benchmark: What Drives the Skills Gap?" *Inc.,* May 1996, p. 111.
4. September 1998 survey by Office Team, reported in S. Armour, "Failure to Communicate Costly for Companies," *USA Today,* September 30, 1998, p. B1.
5. J. R. Hinrichs, "Communications Activity of Industrial Research Personnel," *Personnel Psychology,* Summer 1964, pp. 193–204.
6. J. Kotter, "Power, Dependence, and Effective Management," *Harvard Business Review,* vol. 55, 1977, pp. 125–136.
7. R. L. Daft, and R. H. Lengel, "Information Richness: A New Approach to Managerial Behavior and Organizational Design," in *Research in Organizational Behavior,* eds. B. M. Staw and L. L. Cummings (Greenwich, CT: JAI Press, 1984), p. 196; and R. H. Lengel and R. L. Daft, "The Selection of Communication Media as an Executive Skill," *Academy of Management Executive,* August 1988, pp. 225–232.
8. E. Goode, "Old as Society, Social Anxiety Is Yielding Its Secrets," *New York Times,* October 20, 1998, pp. D7, D11.
9. Goode, 1998; for more on social anxiety disorder, see T. J. Bruce and S. A. Saeed, "Social Anxiety Disorder: A Common, Underrecognized Mental Disorder," *American Family Physician,* November 15, 1999, pp. 2311–2320, 2322.
10. M. Brody, "Test Your Etiquette," *Training & Development,* February 2002, pp. 64–66; P. Post and P. Post, *Emily Post's The Etiquette Advantage in* Business (New York: HarperCollins, 2000); J. Flaherty, "Finding Your Manners," *New York Times,* February 13, 1999, pp. B1, B14; E. White, "Lessons in Shaking Hands, Twirling Spaghetti Await Some Workers," *The Wall Street Journal,* December 7, 1999, pp. B1, B16; H. Lancaster, "Workday Etiquette: Know the Right Fork and Watch that Email," *The Wall Street Journal,* April 21, 1998, p. B1; J. Blais, "Mind Your Manners, Even If You're at Work," *USA Today,* January 17, 2000, p. 5B; B. Rosner, "Giving Thanks without Looking Like a Phony," *San Francisco Examiner & Chronicle,* March 7, 1999, p. C1-13; and C. Smith, "How Clean Underwear Aids Your Career," *San Francisco Examiner,* February 28, 1999, p. CL-13.
11. S. Merchant, quoted in S. Srivastava, "Why India Worries about Outsourcing," *San Francisco Chronicle,* March 21, 2004, p. E3.
12. The role of jargon in communication is discussed by R. Spragins, "Don't Talk to Me That Way," *Fortune Small Business,* February 2002, p. 26.
13. Some of these barriers are discussed in J. P. Scully, "People: The Imperfect Communicators," *Quality Progress,* April 1995, pp. 37–39.
14. A. Farnham, "Trust Gap," *Fortune,* December 4, 1989, p. 70.
15. C. R. Rogers and F. J. Roethlisberger, "Barriers and Gateways to Communication," *Harvard Business Review,* July–August 1952, pp. 46–52.
16. Rogers and Roethlisberger, 1952, p. 47.
17. This statistic was provided by A. Fisher, "How Can I Survive a Phone Interview?" *Fortune,* April 10, 2004, p. 54.
18. See N. Morgan, "The Kinesthetic Speaker: Putting Action into Words," *Harvard Business Review,* April 2001, pp. 113–120.

19. Problems with interpreting nonverbal communication are discussed by A. Pihulyk, "Communicate with Clarity: The Key to Understanding and Influencing Others," *The Canadian Manager*, Summer 2003, pp. 12–13.

20. See J. S. Lublin, "Women Fall Behind When They Don't Hone Negotiation Skills," *The Wall Street Journal,* November 4, 2003, p. B1.

21. J. C. Tingley, *Genderflex: Men & Women Speaking Each Other's Language at Work* (New York: American Management Association, 1994), p. 16.

22. D. Tannen, "The Power of Talk: Who Gets Heard and Why," in *Negotiation: Readings, Exercises, and Cases,* 3rd ed., eds. R. J. Lewicki and D. M. Saunders (Burr Ridge, IL: Irwin/McGraw-Hill, 1999), pp. 147–148; research on gender differences in communication can be found in E. L. MacGeorge, A. R. Graves, B. Feng, S. J. Gillihan, and B. R. Burleson, "The Myth of Gender Cultures: Similarities Outweigh Differences in Men's and Women's Provision of Responses to Supportive Communication," *Sex Roles,* vol. 50, 2004, pp. 143–175; and V. N. Giri and H. O. Sharma, "Brain Wiring and Communication Style," *Psychological Studies,* vol. 48, 2003, pp. 59–64.

23. R. Sharpe, "As Leaders, Women Rule," *Business Week,* November 20, 2000, pp. 75–84.

24. D. Jones, "Male Execs Like Female Coaches," *USA Today,* October 24, 2001, p. 3B.

25. D. Katz and R. Kahn, *The Social Psychology of Organizations* (New York: Wiley, 1966).

26. E. Planty and W. Machaver, "Upward Communications: A Project in Executive Development," *Personnel,* vol. 28, 1952, pp. 304–318.

27. G. M. Goldhaber, *Organizational Communication,* 4th ed. (Dubuque, IA: W. C. Brown, 1986).

28. S. J. Modic, "Grapevine Rated Most Believable," *Industry Week,* May 15, 1989, pp. 11, 14.

29. Early research is discussed by K. Davis, "Management Communication and the Grapevine," *Harvard Business Review,* September–October 1953, pp. 43–49; and R. Rowan, "Where Did *That* Rumor Come From?" *Fortune,* August 13, 1979, pp. 130–137. The most recent research is discussed in "Pruning the Company Grapevine," *Supervision,* September 1986, p. 11; and R. Half, "Managing Your Career: 'How Can I Stop the Gossip?'" *Management Accounting,* September 1987, p. 27.

30. K. Davis and J. W. Newstrom, *Human Behavior at Work: Organizational Behavior,* 7th ed. (New York: Mc-Graw-Hill, 1985).

31. H. B. Vickery III, "Tapping into the Employee Grapevine," *Association Management,* January 1984, pp. 59–60.

32. A thorough discussion of organizational moles is provided by J. G. Bruhn and A. P. Chesney, "Organizational Moles: Information Control and the Acquisition of Power and Status," *Health Care Supervisor,* September 1995, pp. 24–31.

33. T. J. Peters and R. H. Waterman Jr., *In Search of Excellence* (New York: Harper & Row, 1982); and T. Peters and N. Austin, *A Passion for Excellence: the Leadership Difference* (New York: Random House, 1985).

34. S. Branch, "The 100 Best Companies to Work for in America," *Fortune,* January 11, 1999, pp. 118–144.

35. J. B. White, "How Detroit Diesel, Out from Under GM, Turned Around Fast," *The Wall Street Journal,* August 16, 1991, p. A1.

36. W. H. Bulkeley, "The View from the Top," *The Wall Street Journal,* June 21, 1999, p. R6.

37. International Data Corp., *U.S. Intranet Usage and User Intentions, 1998–1999,* reported in Michael Pastore, "Companies Expanding Intranet Uses," ClickZ Network, September 3, 1999, www.clickz.com/stats/big_picture/hardware/article.php/192561 (accessed July 30, 2004).

38. Department of Trade and Industry (United Kingdom), *Business in the Information Age: International Benchmarking Study 2003,* a report prepared by Booz Allen Hamilton, www.ukonlineforbusiness.gov.uk/benchmarking2003/index.htm (July 30, 2004).

39. See J. Useem, "For Sale Online: You," *Fortune,* July 5, 1999, pp. 67–78.

40. "Websmart," *Business Week e.biz,* May 14, 2001, p. EB56.

41. International Data Corp., 1999.

42. Nucleus Research, cited in "U.S. Companies Losing the Spam War," eMarketer, June 21, 2004, www.emarketer.com/Article.aspx?1002870 (accessed August 19, 2004).

43. R. Balu, "Work Week: A Special News Report about Life on the Job," *The Wall Street Journal,* July 20, 1999, p. A1; D. E. Baily and N. B. Kurland, "A Review of Telework Research: Findings, New Directions, and Lessons for the Study of Modern Work," *Journal of Organizational Behavior,* June 2002, pp. 383–400; and S. Shellenbarger, "Work and Family: This Time, Firms See Work-Life Plans as Aid During the Downturn," *The Wall Street Journal,* March 28, 2001, p. B1.

44. 2003 American Interactive Consumer Survey conducted by The Dieringer Research Group, cited in International Telework Association and Council, "Home-Based Telework by U.S. Employees Grows 40% Since 2001," www.telecommute.org/news/pr090403.htm, September 4, 2003 (accessed August 19, 2004).

45. D. Clark, "Managing the Mountain," *The Wall Street Journal,* June 21, 1999, p. R4.

46. See M. Burley-Allen, "Listen Up," *HR Magazine,* November 2001, pp. 115–120.

47. Burley-Allen, 2001; see also C. G. Pearce, "How Effective Are We as Listeners?" *Training & Development,* April 1993, pp. 79–80; and R. A. Luke Jr., "Improving Your Listening Ability," *Supervisory Management,* June 1992, p. 7.

48. See the discussion on listening in G. Manning, K. Curtis, and S. McMillen, *Building Community: The Human Side of Work* (Cincinnati, OH: Thomson Executive Press, 1996), pp. 127–154.

49. Derived from G. Manning, K. Curtis, and S. McMillen, *Building the Human Side of Work Community* (Cincinnati, OH: Thomson Executive Press, 1996), pp. 127–154; P. Slizewski, "Tips for Active Listening," *HRFocus,* May 1995, p. 7; and J. R. Goldon, *A Diagnostic Approach to Organizational Behavior,* 2nd ed. (Boston: Allyn and Bacon, 1987), p. 230.

50. C. Vinzant, "Messing with the Boss' Head," *Fortune,* May 1, 2000, pp. 329–331.

51. M. Price, "Effective Communication Begins with Listening," *Reno Gazette-Journal,* November 27, 2000, p. 1F.

52. D. Stiebel, *When Talking Makes Things Worse! Resolving Problems When Communication Fails,* reported in O. Pollar, "Talk Is Cheap If You Have Big Disagreements," *San Francisco Examiner & Chronicle,* February 21, 1999. p. J-3.

53. M. Just, P. A. Carpenter, and M. Masson, reported in J. Meer, "Reading More, Understanding Less," *Psychology Today,* March 1987, p. 12.

54. K. Alesandrini. *Survive Information Overload* (Homewood, IL: Irwin, 1992), pp. 191–202.

55. Alesandrini, 1992, p. 197.

56. K. Tyler, "Toning Up Communications," *HR Magazine,* March 2003, pp. 87–89.

57. T. Alessandra and P. Hunsaker, *Communicating at Work* (New York: Fireside, 1993), p. 231.

glossary

Terms and definitions printed in *italic* are considered business slang, or jargon.

A

absenteeism When an employee doesn't show up for work.

accommodative approach One of four managerial approaches to social responsibility; management does more than the law requires, if asked, and demonstrates moderate social responsibility.

acquired-needs theory Theory that states that there are three needs—achievement, affiliation, and power—that are the major motives determining people's behavior in the workplace.

action plan Course of action needed to achieve a stated goal.

adjourning One of five stages of forming a team; the stage in which members of an organization prepare for disbandment.

administrative management Management concerned with managing the total organization.

affective component of an attitude The feelings or emotions one has about a situation.

affirmative action The focus on achieving equality of opportunity within an organization.

American dream *Americans' hope for a better quality of life and a higher standard of living than their parents had.*

Americans with Disabilities Act Passed by the U.S. in 1992, act that prohibits discrimination against the disabled.

analyzers Organizations that allow other organizations to take the risks of product development and marketing and then imitate (or perhaps slightly improve on) what seems to work best.

anchoring and adjustment bias The tendency to make decisions based on an initial figure.

assessment center Company department where management candidates participate in activities for a few days while being assessed by evaluators.

Association of Southeast Asian Nations (ASEAN) Trading bloc consisting of ten countries in Asia.

attitude A learned predisposition toward a given object; a mental position with regard to a fact, state, or person.

authority The right to perform or command; also, the rights inherent in a managerial position to make decisions, give orders, and utilize resources.

availability bias Tendency of managers to use information readily available from memory to make judgments; they tend to give more weight to recent events.

B

B2B *Business to business.*

B2C *Business to consumer.*

balance sheet A summary of an organization's overall financial worth—assets and liabilities—at a specific point in time.

balanced scorecard Gives top managers a fast but comprehensive view of the organization via four indicators: (1) customer satisfaction, (2) internal processes, (3) the organization's innovation and improvement activities, and (4) financial measures.

base pay Consists of the basic wage or salary paid employees in exchange for doing their jobs.

been there, done that *Having prior experience with a situation or task.*

behavior Actions and judgments.

behavioral component of an attitude Also known as *intentional component,* this refers to how one intends or expects to behave toward a situation.

behavioral leadership approach Attempts to determine the distinctive styles used by effective leaders.

behavioral science Relies on scientific research for developing theories about human behavior that can be used to provide practical tools for managers.

behavioral viewpoint Emphasizes the importance of understanding human behavior and of motivating employees toward achievement.

behavioral-description interview Type of structured interview in which the interviewer explores what applicants have done in the past.

behaviorally anchored rating scale (BARS) Employee gradations in performance rated according to scales of specific behaviors.

benchmarking A process by which a company compares its performance with that of high-performing organizations.

benefits (fringe benefits) Additional nonmonetary forms of compensation.

Big Five personality dimensions They are (1) extroversion, (2) agreeableness, (3) conscientiousness, (4) emotional stability, and (5) openness to experience.

birth stage The nonbureaucratic stage, the stage in which the organization is created.

bit of kick *A rather strong or spicy taste added to a product or beverage.*

black mark *A negative evaluation.*

blended value The idea that all investments are understood to operate simultaneously in both economic and social realms.

blue flu *Calling in sick when you're really not. The blue refers to the color of the uniform some workers wear.*

bonuses Cash awards given to employees who achieve specific performance objectives.

bossy *Telling employees what to do and not listening to their suggestions.*

bottom line *The last line in a profit and loss statement; it refers to net profit.*

bought into *To have accepted completely.*

bounded rationality One type of nonrational decision making; the ability of decision makers to be rational is limited by numerous constraints.

bowing to competition *Following what competition does.*

break-even analysis A way of identifying how much revenue is needed to cover the total cost of developing and selling a product.

break-even point The amount of sales revenue at which there is no profit but also no loss to your company.

brick-and-mortar stores *Stores with traditional physical buildings as opposed to stores on the Internet.*

budget A formal financial projection.

buffers Administrative changes that managers can make to reduce the stressors that lead to employee burnout.

bureaucratic control The use of rules, regulations, and formal authority to guide performance.

burnout State of emotional, mental, and even physical exhaustion.

C

cannibalized business *One franchise pulls business away from another franchise.*

cascading Objectives are structured in a unified hierarchy, becoming more specific at lower levels of the organization.

causal attribution The activity of inferring causes for observed behavior.

celebrity stargazers *Customers that attend the opening of a new business hoping to see or meet a celebrity.*

centralized authority Organizational structure in which important decisions are made by upper managers—power is concentrated at the top.

change agent A person inside or outside the organization who can be a catalyst in helping deal with old problems in new ways.

charisma Form of personal attraction that inspires acceptance and support.

clan control Shared values, beliefs, rituals, and trusts emanating from a common culture.

classical viewpoint In the historical perspective, the viewpoint that emphasizes finding ways to manage work more efficiently; it has two branches—scientific and administrative.

climbed the ladder *Promoted to higher-level jobs.*

closed system A system that has little interaction with its environment.

code of ethics A formal, written set of ethical standards that guide an organization's actions.

coercive power One of five sources of power; the power held by all managers, which results from their authority to punish their subordinates.

cognitive component of an attitude The beliefs and knowledge one has about a situation.

cognitive dissonance Term coined by social psychologist Leon Festinger to describe the psychological discomfort a person experiences between what he or she already knows and new information or contradictory behavior, or by inconsistency among a person's beliefs, attitudes, and/or actions.

cohesiveness The tendency of a group or team to stick together.

collaborative computing Using state-of-the-art computer software and hardware to help people work better together.

collective bargaining Negotiations between management and employees regarding disputes over compensation, benefits, working conditions, and job security.

command economy In a planned economy or a central-planning economy, the government owns most businesses and regulates the amounts, types, and prices of goods and services.

common purpose A goal that unifies employees or members and gives everyone an understanding of the organization's reason for being.

communication The transfer of information and understanding from one person to another.

compensation Payment comprising three parts: wages or salaries, incentives, and benefits.

competitive intelligence Gaining information about competitors' activities so that one can anticipate their moves and react appropriately.

competitive advantage The ability of an organization to produce goods or services more effectively than its competitors do, thereby outperforming them.

competitors People or organizations that compete for customers or resources.

computer-assisted instruction (CAI) Training in which computers are used to provide additional help or to reduce instructional time.

conceptual skills Skills that consist of the ability to think analytically, to visualize an organization as a whole and understand how the parts work together.

concurrent control Control that takes place while operations are going on and is intended to minimize problems as they occur.

conflict Process in which one party perceives that its interests are being opposed or negatively affected by another party.

conglomerate structure The fourth type of organizational structure, whereby divisions are grouped around similar businesses or activities.

consensus General agreement; group solidarity.

constructive conflict Functional conflict that benefits the main purposes of the organization and serves its interest.

contemporary perspective In contrast to the historical perspective, the business approach that includes three viewpoints—systems, contingency, and quality-management.

contingency approach to leadership The belief that the effectiveness of leadership behavior depends on the situation at hand.

contingency design The process of fitting the organization to its environment.

contingency leadership model Fiedler's theory (1951) that leader effectiveness is determined by both the personal characteristics of leaders and by the situations in which leaders find themselves; the leader's style is either task-oriented or relationship-oriented, and it must be determined which style fits the situation at hand.

contingency planning Also known as *scenario planning* and *scenario analysis;* the creation of alternative hypothetical but equally likely future conditions.

contingency viewpoint In opposition to the classical viewpoint; a manager's approach should vary according to—that is, be contingent on—the individual and the environmental situation.

continuous improvement Ongoing, small, incremental improvements in all parts of an organization.

continuous-process technology A highly routinized technology in which machines do all of the work, to produce highly routinized products.

control process The four steps in the process of controlling: (1) establish standards; (2) measure performance; (3) compare performance to standards; and (4) take corrective action, if necessary.

control standard The first step in the control process; the performance standard (or just standard) is the desired performance level for a given goal.

controlling Monitoring performance, comparing goals, and taking corrective action as needed.

coordinated effort The coordination of individual efforts into a group or organization-wide effort.

core principles of TQM In total quality management, (1) everyone involved with the organization should focus on delivering value to customers (people orientation), and (2) everyone should work on continuously improving the work processes (improvement orientation).

cost-leadership strategy One of Porter's four competitive strategies; keeping the costs, and hence prices, of a product or service below those of competitors and targeting the wider market.

cost-focus strategy One of Porter's four competitive strategies; to keep the costs, and hence prices, of a product or service below those of competitors and to target a narrow market.

countertrading Bartering goods for goods.

counting on it *Expecting it.*

cross-functional team A team that is staffed with specialists pursuing a common objective.

culture A shared set of beliefs, values, knowledge, and patterns of behavior common to a group of people.

culture shock Feelings of discomfort and disorientation associated with being in an unfamiliar culture.

customer division A divisional structure in which activities are grouped around common customers or clients.

customers Those who pay to use an organization's goods or services.

D

360-degree assessment A performance appraisal in which employees are appraised not only by their managerial superiors but also by peers, subordinates, and sometimes clients.

database Computerized collection of interrelated files.

dead duck *Something doomed to failure.*

deal *A special price or some other benefit that not all people receive.*

decentralized authority Organizational structure in which important decisions are made by middle-level and supervisory-level managers—power is delegated throughout the organization.

deciding to decide A manager agrees that he or she must decide what to do about a problem or opportunity and take effective decision-making steps.

decision A choice made from among available alternatives.

decision making The process of identifying and choosing alternative courses of action.

decision-making style A style that reflects the combination of how an individual perceives and responds to information.

decision tree Graph of decisions and their possible consequences, used to create a plan to reach a goal.

decisional role One of three types of managerial roles: managers use information to make decisions to solve problems or take advantage of opportunities. The four decision-making roles are entrepreneur, disturbance handler, resource allocator, and negotiator.

decline stage The fourth stage in the product life cycle; period in which a product falls out of favor, and the organization withdraws from the marketplace.

decoding Interpreting and trying to make sense of a message.

defenders Experts at producing and selling narrowly defined products or services.

defensive approach One of four managerial approaches to social responsibility; managers make the minimum commitment to social responsibility—obeying the law but doing nothing more.

defensive avoidance When a manager cannot find a good solution and follows by (a) procrastinating, (b) passing the buck, or (c) denying the risk of any negative consequences.

defensive strategy Also called *retrenchment strategy;* one of three grand strategies, this strategy involves reduction in the organization's efforts.

delegation The process of assigning managerial authority and responsibility to managers and employees lower in the hierarchy.

Delphi group A problem-solving technique in which a group of physically dispersed experts fills out questionnaires to anonymously generate ideas; the judgments are combined and averaged to achieve a consensus of expert opinion.

democratic governments Governments that rely on free elections and representative assemblies.

demographic forces Influences on an organization arising from changes in the characteristics of a population, such as age, gender, ethnic origin, and so on.

developed countries Countries with a high level of economic development and generally high average level of income among their citizens.

development The education of professionals and managers in the skills they will need to do their jobs.

devil's advocacy Taking the side of an unpopular point of view for the sake of argument.

diagnosis Analysis of underlying causes.

dialectic method The process of having two people or groups play opposing roles in a debate in order to better understand a proposal.

differentiation The tendency of the parts of an organization to disperse and fragment.

differentiation strategy One of Porter's four competitive strategies; offer products or services that are of a unique and superior value compared to those of competitors and to target a wide market.

discrimination Prejudicial outlook; when people are hired or promoted—or denied hiring or promotion—for reasons not relevant to the job.

distributor A person or an organization that helps another organization sell its goods and services to customers.

diversification Strategy by which a company operates several businesses in order to spread the risk.

diversity All the ways people are unlike and alike—the differences and similarities in age, gender, race, religion, ethnicity, sexual orientation, capabilities, and socioeconomic background.

division of labor Also known as *work specialization;* arrangement of having discrete parts of a task done by different people. The work is divided into particular tasks assigned to particular workers.

divisional structure The third type of organizational structure, whereby people with diverse occupational specialties are put together in formal groups according to products and/or services, customers and/or clients, or geographic regions.

downsizing *The process of eliminating some managerial and nonmanagerial positions.*

downward communication Communication that flows from a higher level to a lower level.

duck the opportunity *Avoid the opportunity.*

ducks in a row *To have all one's tasks lined up (organized) and ready to be executed.*

dug down *Worked hard and diligently.*

dumping A foreign company's practice of exporting products abroad at a price lower than the home-market price, or even below the costs of production, in order to drive down the price of the domestic product.

E

e-business Using the Internet to facilitate every aspect of running a business.

e-commerce Electronic commerce; the buying and selling of goods and services over computer networks.

e-mail Electronic mail; text messages and documents transmitted over a computer network.

e-mail snooping *Reading other people's e-mail messages.*

e-leadership Leadership that involves one-to-one, one-to-many, and within- and between-group and collective interactions via information technology..

economic forces General economic conditions and trends—unemployment, inflation, interest rates, economic growth—that may affect an organization's performance.

economic pie *The money available in the economy.*

effect uncertainty One of three types of uncertainty; when the effects of environmental changes are unpredictable.

effective To achieve results, to make the right decisions and to successfully carry them out so that they achieve the organization's goals.

efficient Using resources—people, money, raw materials, and the like—wisely and cost-effectively.

embargo A complete ban on the import and/or export of certain products.

emotional intelligence The ability to cope, to empathize with others, and to be self-motivated.

employee assistance program Program designed to help employees overcome personal problems affecting their job performance.

employment tests Tests legally considered to consist of any procedure used in the employment selection process.

encoding Translating a message into understandable symbols or language.

entrepreneur Someone who sees a new opportunity for a product or service and launches a business to try to realize it.

entrepreneurship The process of taking risks to try to create a new enterprise.

Equal Employment Opportunity (EEO) Commission U.S. panel whose job it is to enforce anti-discrimination and other employment-related laws.

equity theory In the area of employee motivation, the focus on how employees perceive how fairly they think they are being treated compared to others.

escalation of commitment bias When decision makers increase their commitment to a project despite negative information about it.

ethical behavior Behavior accepted as "right" as opposed to "wrong" according to recognized ethical standards.

ethical dilemma A situation in which you have to decide whether to pursue a course of action that may benefit you or your organization but that is unethical or even illegal.

ethics Generally accepted standards of right and wrong that influence behavior; these standards may vary among countries and cultures.

ethics officer A person trained about matters of ethics in the workplace, particularly about resolving ethical dilemmas.

ethnocentric managers Managers who believe that their native country, culture, language, and /or behavior are superior to others.

ethnocentrism The belief that one's native country, culture, language, abilities, and/or behavior are superior to those of another culture.

European Union (EU) Union of 25 trading partners in Europe.

exchange rate The rate at which one country's currency is exchanged for another country's currency.

expatriate manager A manager living or working in a foreign country.

expectancy The belief that a particular level of effort will lead to a particular level of performance.

expectancy theory Theory that suggests that people are motivated by two things: (1) how much they want something and (2) how likely they think they are to get it.

expert power One of five sources of power; the power resulting from one's specialized information or expertise.

explicit knowledge Information that can be easily put into words, graphics, and numbers and shared with others.

exporting Producing goods domestically and selling them outside the country.

expropriation A government's seizure of a foreign company's assets.

external audit Formal verification by outside experts of an organization's financial accounts and statements.

external dimensions of diversity Human differences that have an element of choice; they consist of the personal characteristics that people acquire, discard, or modify throughout their lives.

external recruiting Attracting job applicants from outside the organization.

external stakeholders People or groups in the organization's external environment that are affected by it. This environment includes the task environment and the general environment.

extinction The withholding or withdrawal of positive rewards for desirable behavior, so that the behavior is less likely to occur in the future.

extranet An extended intranet that connects internal employees with selected customers, suppliers, and other strategic partners.

extrinsic reward The payoff, such as money, that a person receives from others for performing a particular task.

F

the Fed *Refers to the Federal Reserve Bank.*

feedback The receiver's expression of his or her reaction to the sender's message. Also, the information about the reaction of the environment to the outputs that affect the inputs; one of four parts of a system, along with inputs, outputs, and transformational processes.

feedback control Control that takes place after operations are finished; it is intended to correct problems that have already occurred.

feedforward control Control that takes place before operations begin; it is intended to prevent anticipated problems.

financial statement Summary of some aspect of an organization's financial status.

first-line managers One of three managerial levels; also called *supervisory managers;* they make the short-term operating decisions, directing the daily tasks of nonmanagerial personnel.

fixed budget Allocation of resources on the basis of a single estimate of costs.

focused-differentiation strategy One of Porter's four competitive strategies; to offer products or services that are of unique and superior value compared to those of competitors and to target a narrow market.

forced ranking performance review systems Performance review systems whereby all employees within a business unit are ranked against one another, and grades are distributed along some sort of bell curve, like students being graded in a college course.

forecast A projection of the future.

Foreign Corrupt Practices Act of 1977 An act that makes it illegal for employees of U.S. companies to bribe political decision makers in foreign nations.

formal appraisals Appraisals conducted at specific times throughout the year and based on performance measures that have been established in advance.

formal communication channels Communications that follow the chain of command and are recognized as official.

formal group A group, headed by a leader, that is established to do something productive for the organization.

forming One of five stages of forming a team; the first stage, in which people get oriented and get acquainted.

four management functions The management process that "gets things done": planning, organizing, leading, and controlling.

franchising A form of licensing in which a company allows a foreign company to pay it a fee and a share of the profit in return for using the first company's brand name and a package of materials and services.

free market economy Economic model in which production of goods and services is controlled by private enterprise and the interaction of the forces of supply and demand rather than by the government.

free trade The movement of goods and services among nations without political or economic obstruction.

freelancers *People who work independently of a firm and offer their work to anyone who is willing to pay.*

from scratch *Original; made from something completely new.*

full-range leadership Approach that suggests that leadership behavior varies along a full range of leadership styles, from take-no-responsibilty (*laissez-faire*) "leadership" at one extreme through transactional leadership, to transformational leadership at the other extreme.

functional managers Managers who are responsible for just one organizational activity.

functional structure The second type of organizational structure, whereby people with similar occupational specialties are put together in formal groups.

fundamental attribution bias Tendency whereby people attribute another person's behavior to his or her personal characteristics rather than to situational factors.

G

gainsharing The distribution of savings or "gains" to groups of employees who reduce costs and increase measurable productivity.

general environment Also called *macroenvironment*; in contrast to the task environment, it includes six forces: economic, technological, sociocultural, demographic, political-legal, and international.

general managers Managers who are responsible for several organizational activities.

geocentric managers Managers who accept that there are differences and similarities between home and foreign personnel and practices and that they should use whatever techniques are most effective.

geographic division A divisional structure in which activities are grouped around defined regional locations.

glass ceiling The metaphor for an invisible barrier preventing women and minorities from being promoted to top executive jobs.

global economy The increasing tendency of the economies of the world to interact with one another as one market instead of as many national markets.

global outsourcing Using suppliers outside the United States to provide labor, goods, and/or services.

global village The "shrinking" of time and space as air travel and electronic media make it easier for the people of the globe to communicate with one another.

globalization The trend of the world economy toward becoming a more interdependent system.

go for the gold *To work to be the very best (figuratively winning a gold medal).*

goal displacement The primary goal is subsumed to a secondary goal.

goal-setting theory Employee-motivation approach that employees can be motivated by goals that are specific and challenging but achievable.

goof off *(1) Taking unauthorized time off from work. (2) Doing things at work not associated with the job, such as talking with others at the drinking fountain.*

government regulators Regulatory agencies that establish ground rules under which organizations may operate.

grand strategy Second step of the strategic-management process; it explains how the organization's mission is to be accomplished. Three grand strategies are growth, stability, and defensive.

grapevine The unofficial communication system of the informal organization.

greenfield venture A wholly-owned foreign subsidiary that the owning organization has built from scratch.

group Two or more freely interacting individuals who share collective norms, share collective goals, and have a common identity.

group cohesiveness A "we feeling" that binds group members together.

groupthink A cohesive group's blind unwillingness to consider alternatives. This occurs when group members strive for agreement among themselves for the sake of unanimity and avoid accurately assessing the decision situation.

growth stage The second stage of the product life cycle. This, the most profitable stage, is the period in which customer demand increases, the product's sales grow, and (later) competitors may enter the market.

growth strategy One of three grand strategies, this strategy involves expansion—as in sales revenues, market share, number of employees, or number of customers or (for nonprofits) clients served.

H

halo effect An effect in which we form a positive impression of an individual based on a single trait.

heavy hitters *People with power and influence—and probably money.*

helped turn around *Helped reverse the downward trend.*

hero A person whose accomplishments embody the values of the organization.

heuristics Strategies that simplify the process of making decisions.

hierarchy of authority Also known as *chain of command*; a control mechanism for making sure the right people do the right things at the right time.

hierarchy of needs theory Psychological structure proposed by Maslow whereby people are motivated by five levels of needs: (1) physiological, (2) safety, (3) belongingness, (4) esteem, and (5) self-actualization.

high gear *Going at full strength.*

high tech *Anything having to do with advances in technology, such as computers, computer software, pagers, scanners, and the like.*

historical perspective In contrast to the contemporary perspective, the view of management that includes the classical, behavioral, and quantitative viewpoints.

horizontal communication Communication that flows within and between work units; its main purpose is coordination.

hot second *Immediately.*

human capital Economic or productive potential of employee knowledge, experience, and actions.

human relations movement The movement that proposed that better human relations could increase worker productivity.

human resource (HR) management The activities managers perform to plan for, attract, develop, and retain a workforce.

human skills The ability to work well in cooperation with other people in order to get things done.

hybrid structure Fifth type of organizational structure, whereby an organizational form uses functional and divisional structures in different parts of the same organization.

hygiene factors Factors associated with job dissatisfaction—such as salary, working conditions, interpersonal relationships, and company policy—all of which affect the job context or environment in which people work.

I

import quota A trade barrier in the form of a limit on the numbers of a product that can be imported.

importing Buying goods outside the country and reselling them domestically.

in the black *Profitable.*

in the red *Unprofitable.*

in the right hands *With the person who can give you the most help.*

incentives Benefits used to move people to action, such as commissions, bonuses, profit-sharing plans, and stock options.

income statement Summary of an organization's financial results—revenues and expenses—over a specified period of time.

incremental budgeting Allocating increased or decreased funds to a department by using the last budget period as a reference point; only incremental changes in the budget request are reviewed.

incremental innovations The creation of products, services, or technologies that modify existing ones.

incremental model One type of nonrational model of decision making; managers take small, short-term steps to alleviate a problem.

indigenization laws Laws that require that citizens within the host country own a majority of whatever company is operating within that country.

individual approach One of four approaches to solving ethical dilemmas; ethical behavior is guided by what will result in the individual's best long-term interests, which ultimately is in everyone's self-interest.

informal appraisals Appraisals conducted on an unscheduled basis and consisting of less rigorous indications of employee performance than those used in formal appraisals.

informal communication channels Communication that develops outside the formal structure and does not follow the chain of command.

informal group A group formed by people seeking friendship that has no officially appointed leader, although a leader may emerge from the membership.

information overload An overload that occurs when the amount of information received exceeds a person's ability to handle or process it.

informational role One of three types of managerial roles: managers receive and communicate information with other people inside and outside the organization as monitors, disseminators, and spokespersons.

infrastructure The physical facilities that form the basis of a country's level of economic development.

innovation Introduction of something new or better, as in goods or services.

inputs The people, money, information, equipment, and materials required to produce an organization's goods or services; one of four parts of a system, along with outputs, transformation processes, and feedback.

instrumentality The expectation that successful performance of the task will lead to the outcome desired.

integration The tendency of the parts of an organization to draw together to achieve a common purpose.

interacting group A problem-solving technique in which group members interact and deliberate with one another to reach a consensus.

internal audit A verification of an organization's financial accounts and statements by the organization's own professional staff.

internal dimensions of diversity The human differences that exert a powerful, sustained effect throughout every stage of people's lives (gender, age, ethnicity, race, sexual orientation, physical abilities).

internal locus of control The belief that one controls one's own destiny.

internal recruiting Hiring from the inside, or making people already employed by the organization aware of job openings.

internal stakeholders Employees, owners, and the board of directors, if any.

international forces Changes in the economic, political, legal, and technological global system that may affect an organization.

international management Management that oversees the conduct of operations in or with organizations in foreign countries.

International Monetary Fund (IMF) One of three principal organizations designed to facilitate international trade; its purpose is to assist in smoothing the flow of money between nations.

Internet Global network of independently operating but interconnected computers, linking hundreds of thousands of smaller networks around the world.

interpersonal role One of three types of managerial roles; managers interact with people inside and outside of their work units. The three interpersonal roles include figurehead, leader, and liaison activities.

intervention Interference in an attempt to correct a problem.

intranet An organization's private, internal Internet.

intrapreneur Someone who works inside an existing organization who sees an opportunity for a product or a service and mobilizes the organization's resources to try to realize it.

intrinsic reward The satisfaction, such as a feeling of accomplishment, a person receives from performing a task.

introduction stage The first stage in the product life cycle; a new product is introduced into the marketplace.

intuition model Form of nonrational decision making whereby a manager quickly sizes up a situation and makes a decision based on his or her experience or practice.

IOUs *Debt; abbreviation for "I owe you."*

is the heart *Is the most important part of something; the central force or idea.*

ISO 9000 series Set of company quality-control procedures, developed by the International Organization for Standardization in Geneva, Switzerland, that deals with all activities—from purchasing to manufacturing to inventory to shipping—that can be audited by independent quality-control experts, or "registrars."

J

jargon Terminology specific to a particular profession or group.

job analysis The determination of the basic elements of a job.

job characteristics model The job design model that consists of five core job characteristics that affect three critical psychological states of an employee that in turn affect work outcomes—the employee's motivation, performance, and satisfaction.

job description A summary of what the holder of the job does and how and why he or she does it.

job design The division of an organization's work among its employees and the application of motivational theories to jobs to increase satisfaction and performance.

job enlargement Increasing the number of tasks in a job to increase variety and motivation.

job enrichment Building into a job such motivating factors as responsibility, achievement, recognition, stimulating work, and advancement.

job involvement The extent to which one is personally involved with one's job.

job posting Placing information about job vacancies and qualifications on bulletin boards, in newsletters, and on the organization's intranet.

job satisfaction The extent to which one feels positively or negatively about various aspects of one's work.

job simplification The process of reducing the number of tasks a worker performs.

job specification Description of the minimum qualifications a person must have to perform a job successfully.

joint ventures Organizations that join forces to realize strategic advantages that neither could have achieved alone; a U.S. firm may form a joint venture, also known as a *strategic alliance,* with a foreign company to share the risks and rewards of starting a new enterprise together in a foreign country.

joke around *To tell jokes and generally act less than professional.*

jump at the idea *To respond positively to a new idea.*

jumped headfirst *Began quickly and eagerly, without hesitation.*

justice approach One of four approaches to solving ethical dilemmas; ethical behavior is guided by respect for impartial standards of fairness and equity.

K

key player *Important participant.*

kick back and relax *To take a rest.*

knowledge management Implementation of systems and practices to increase the sharing of knowledge and information throughout an organization; also, the development of an organizational structure—and the tools, processes, systems, and structures—that encourages continuous learning and sharing of knowledge and information among employees, for the purpose of making better decisions.

L

large-batch technology Routinized products made by highly mechanized organizations; mass-production assembly-line technology.

the last laugh *Comes from the expression, "He who laughs last, laughs loudest," because he or she has been proven right.*

leadership The ability to influence employees to voluntarily pursue organizational goals.

leadership grid model Blake and Mouton's leadership training model; the ideal leadership style has a high concern for (1) production, the job aspects of subordinates' behavior, and (2) people, the human aspects of their behavior.

leading Motivating, directing, and otherwise influencing people to work hard to achieve the organization's goals.

lean Six Sigma Quality-control approach that focuses on problem solving and performance improvement—speed with excellence—of a well-defined project; *see also* Six Sigma.

learned helplessness The debilitating lack of faith in one's ability to control one's environment.

learning organization An organization that actively creates, acquires, and transfers knowledge within itself and is able to modify its behavior to reflect new knowledge.

legitimate power One of five sources of power; all managers have this power, which results from their formal positions with the organization.

less-developed countries Also known as *developing countries;* nations with low economic development and low average incomes.

Level 5 leadership Leadership situation in which an organization is led by a Level 5 executive who possesses the paradoxical characteristics of humility and a fearless will to succeed, as well as the capabilities associated with levels 1–4: highly capable, contributing, competent, effective.

licensing Company X allows a foreign company to pay it a fee to make or distribute X's product or service.

line managers Managers who have the authority to make decisions and usually have people reporting to them.

locus of control Measure of how much people believe they control their fate through their own efforts.

loss Total costs exceed total sales revenue.

M

maintenance role Relationship-related role consisting of behavior that fosters constructive relationships among team members.

management The pursuit of organizational goals efficiently and effectively by integrating the work of people through planning, organizing, leading, and controlling the organization's resources.

management by exception Control principle that states that managers should be informed of a situation only if data shows a significant deviation from standards.

management by objectives (MBO) Four-step process in which (1) managers and employees jointly set objectives for the employee, (2) managers develop action plans, (3) managers and employees periodically review the employee's performance, and (4) the manager makes a performance appraisal and rewards the employee according to results.

management by wandering around (MBWA) Style of management whereby a manager literally wanders around the organization and talks with people across all lines of authority.

management process Performing the planning, organizing, leading, and controlling necessary to get things done.

management science Sometimes called *operations research;* branch of quantitative management; method of solving management problems by using mathematics to aid in problem solving and decision making.

maquiladoras U.S. manufacturing plants allowed to operate in Mexico with special privileges in return for employing Mexican citizens.

market control The use of market mechanisms—pricing, competition, market share—to guide performance.

marriage of software, hardware, etc. *Combination of various technologies.*

matrix structure Sixth type of organizational structure, which combines functional and divisional chains of command in a grid so that there are two command structures—vertical and horizontal.

maturity stage A stage when the organization becomes very bureaucratic, large, and mechanistic.

maturity stage The third stage in the product life cycle; period in which the product starts to fall out of favor, and sales and profits fall off.

means-end chain A hierarchy of goals; in the chain of management (operational, tactical, strategic), the accomplishment of low-level goals are the means leading to the accomplishment of high-level goals or ends.

measuring stick *Tool used to evaluate something.*

mechanistic organization Organization in which authority is centralized, tasks and rules are clearly specified, and employees are closely supervised.

media richness Indication of how well a particular medium conveys information and promotes learning.

medium The pathway by which a message travels.

Mercosur The largest trade bloc in Latin America, with four core members: Argentina, Brazil, Paraguay, Uruguay.

message The information to be shared.

meta-analysis Statistical pooling technique that permits behavioral scientists to draw general conclusions about certain variables from many different studies.

middle managers One of three managerial levels; they implement the policies and plans of the top managers above them and supervise and coordinate the activities of the first-line managers below them.

midlife stage A period of growth evolving into stability when the organization becomes bureaucratic.

mine the knowledge *Make maximum use of the knowledge employees have.*

mission An organization's purpose or reason for being.

mission statement Statement that expresses the purpose of the organization.

mixed economy An economy in which most of the important industries are owned by the government, but others are controlled by private enterprise.

money laundering *Making illegal money appear legal by passing it through a bank or a legal business.*

monochronic time The standard kind of time orientation in U.S business; preference for doing one thing at a time.

moral-rights approach One of four approaches to solving ethical dilemmas; ethical behavior is guided by respect for the fundamental rights of human beings.

more than meets the eye *There's more to something than can be seen.*

most favored nation This trading status describes a condition in which a country grants other countries favorable trading treatment such as the reduction of import duties.

motivating factors Factors associated with job satisfaction—such as achievement, recognition, responsibility, and advancement—all of which affect the job content or the rewards of work performance.

motivation Psychological processes that arouse and direct goal-directed behavior.

muddy the water *Make things unclear.*

multinational corporation Business firm with operations in several countries.

multinational organization Nonprofit organization with operations in several countries.

N

National Labor Relations Board Legislated in 1935, U.S. commission that enforces the procedures whereby employees may vote to have a union and for collective bargaining.

need-based perspectives Also known as *content perspectives;* theories that emphasize the needs that motivate people.

needs Physiological or psychological deficiencies that arouse behavior.

network structure Eighth type of organizational structure, whereby a central core is linked to outside independent firms by computer connections, which are used to operate as if all were a single organization.

no-haggle pricing *Situation in which prices are fixed and cannot be negotiated with the seller.*

noise Any disturbance that interferes with the transmission of a message.

nominal group A group whose purpose it is to generate ideas and evaluate solutions by writing down as many ideas as possible. The ideas are listed on a blackboard, then discussed, then voted on.

nonprogrammed decisions Decisions that occur under nonroutine, unfamiliar circumstances.

nonrational model of decision making A model of decision-making style that explains how managers make decisions; they assume that decision making is nearly always uncertain and risky, making it difficult for managers to make optimum decisions.

nonverbal communication Messages in a form other than the written or the spoken word.

norming One of five stages of forming a team; stage three, in which conflicts are resolved, close relationships develop, and unity and harmony emerge.

norms General guidelines or rules of behavior that most group or team members follow.

North American Free Trade Agreement (NAFTA) Formed in 1994, the trading bloc consisting of the United States, Canada, and Mexico.

not bat an eye *To not seem to see; to not react.*

O

objective appraisal Also called *results appraisal;* form of performance evaluation that is based on facts and that is often numerical.

obstructionist approach One of four managerial approaches to social responsiblity; managers put economic gain first and resist social responsibility as being outside the organization's self-interest.

open system System that continually interacts with its environment.

operational control Monitoring performance to ensure that operational plans—day-to-day goals—are being implemented and taking corrective action as needed.

operational goals Goals that are set by and for first-line managers and are concerned with short-term matters associated with realizing tactical goals.

operational planning Determining how to accomplish specific tasks with available resources within the next 1-week to 1-year period; done by first-line managers.

operations management A branch of quantitative management; effective management of the production and delivery of an organization's products or services.

opportunities Situations that present possibilities for exceeding existing goals.

organic organization Organization in which authority is decentralized, there are fewer rules and procedures, and networks of employees are encouraged to cooperate and respond quickly to unexpected tasks.

organization A group of people who work together to achieve some specific purpose. A system of consciously coordinated activities or forces of two or more people.

organization chart Box-and-lines illustration of the formal relationships of positions of authority and the organization's official divisions of labor.

organization development (OD) Set of techniques for implementing planned change to make people and organizations more effective.

organizational behavior (OB) Behavior that is dedicated to better understanding and managing people at work.

organizational culture Sometimes called *corporate culture;* system of shared beliefs and values that develops within an organization and guides the behavior of its members.

organizational life cycle Four-stage cycle with a natural sequence of stages: birth, youth, midlife, and maturity.

organizational opportunities The environmental factors that the organization may exploit for competitive advantage.

organizational size Measurement of a group's size according to the number of full-time employees.

organizational strengths The skills and capabilities that give the organization special competencies and competitive advantages in executing strategies in pursuit of its mission.

organizational threats The environmental factors that hinder an organization's achieving a competitive advantage.

organizational weaknesses The drawbacks that hinder an organization in executing strategies in pursuit of its mission.

organizing Arranging tasks, people, and other resources to accomplish the work.

orientation Process of helping a newcomer fit smoothly into the job and the organization.

out of the office loop *Not included in everyday workplace communication.*

outputs The products, services, profits, losses, employee satisfaction or discontent, and the like that are produced by the organization; one of four parts of a system, along with inputs, transformation processes, and feedback.

outsourcing Subcontracting of services and operations to an outside vendor. Using suppliers outside the company to provide goods and services.

owners Those who can claim the organization as their legal property.

P

panic Situation in which a manager reacts frantically to get rid of a problem that he or she cannot deal with realistically.

paradigm Generally accepted way of viewing the world.

participative management (PM) The process of involving employees in (1) setting goals, (2) making decisions, (3) solving problems, and (4) making changes in the organization.

path–goal leadership model Contingency approach that holds that the effective leader makes available to followers desirable rewards in the workplace and increases their motivation by clarifying the paths, or behavior, that will help them achieve those goals and providing them with support.

pay for knowledge Situation in which employees' pay is tied to the number of job-relevant skills they have or academic degrees they earn.

pay for performance Situation in which an employee's pay is based on the results he or she achieves.

perception Awareness; interpreting and understanding one's environment.

performance appraisal Assessment of an employee's performance and the provision of feedback.

performing One of five stages of forming a team; stage 4, in which members concentrate on solving problems and completing the assigned task.

perks *Short for perquisites; compensation in addition to salary, such as day care or a company car.*

personality The stable psychological traits and behavioral attributes that give a person his or her identity.

personalized power Power directed at helping oneself.

philanthropy Donation of money to worthwhile recipients, to promote human welfare.

pick up the tab *Pay for something.*

piece of the action *Part of the opportunities.*

piece rate Pay based on how much output an employee produces.

get a pink slip *To be fired from a job; derived from the days when employers gave workers written notices (on pink paper) that their jobs were terminated.*

pitch in *To help as needed.*

planning Setting goals and deciding how to achieve them. Also, coping with uncertainty by formulating future courses of action to achieve specified results.

planning/control cycle A cycle that has two planning steps (1 and 2) and two control steps (3 and 4), as follows: (1) Make the plan. (2) Carry out the plan. (3) Control the direction by comparing results with the plan. (4) Control the direction by taking corrective action in two ways—namely, (a) by correcting deviations in the plan being carried out, or (b) by improving future plans.

played his/her last card *Tried the last thing he/she could think of.*

political risk The risk that political changes will cause loss of a company's assets or impair its foreign operations.

political-legal forces Changes in the way politics shape laws and laws shape the opportunities for and threats to an organization.

polycentric managers Managers who take the view that native managers in foreign offices best understand native personnel and practices, and so the home office should leave them alone.

polychronic time Kind of time orientation common in Mediterranean, Latin American, and Arab cultures; preference for doing more than one thing at a time.

Porter's four competitive strategies (four generic strategies) (1) Cost-leadership, (2) differentiation, (3) cost-focus, (4) focused-differentiation. The first two strategies focus on wide markets, the last two on narrow markets.

positive reinforcement The use of positive consequences to encourage desirable behavior.

power The measure of the extent to which a person is able to influence others so that they respond to orders.

privatization The making private of business activities, as when state-owned activities are performed by private enterprise.

proactive approach One of four managerial approaches to social responsibility; managers actively lead the way in being socially responsible for all stakeholders, using the organization's resources to identify and respond to social problems.

proactive change Planned change; making carefully thought-out changes in anticipation of possible or expected problems or opportunities; opposite of *reactive change.*

proactive personality Someone who is apt to take initiative and persevere to influence the environment.

problems Difficulties that inhibit the achievement of goals.

process innovation A change in the way a product or service is conceived, manufactured, or disseminated.

process perspectives Theories of employee motivation concerned with the thought processes by which people decide how to act: expectancy theory, equity theory, and goal-setting theory.

product division A divisional structure in which activities are grouped around similar products or services.

product innovation A change in the appearance or the performance of a product or a service or the creation of a new one.

product life cycle A model that graphs the four stages of a product or service during the "life" of its marketability: (1) introduction, (2) growth, (3) maturity, and (4) decline.

profit The amount by which total revenue exceeds total costs; a valuable return.

profit sharing The distribution to employees of a percentage of the company's profits.

program A single-use plan encompassing a range of projects or activities.

programmed conflict Conflict designed to elicit different opinions without inciting people's personal feelings.

programmed decisions Decisions that are repetitive and routine. Contrast *nonprogrammed decisions.*

project A single-use plan of less scope and complexity than a program.

project life cycle Cycle of a project with four stages from start to finish: definition, planning, execution, and closing.

project management Achieving a set of goals by planning, scheduling, and maintaining progress of the activities that constitute a project.

project management software Programs for planning and scheduling the people, costs, and resources to complete a project on time.

project planning Preparation of single-use plans, or projects.

prospectors Managers who develop new products or services and seek out new markets, rather than waiting for things to happen.

provided the spark *Supplied the energy that motivated others.*

punishment The application of negative consequences to stop or change undesirable behavior.

Q

quality The total ability of a product or service to meet customer needs.

quality assurance A means of ensuring quality that focuses on the performance of workers, urging employees to strive for "zero defects."

quality circles Small groups of volunteer workers and supervisors who meet intermittently to discuss workplace and quality-related problems.

quality control A means of ensuring quality whereby errors are minimized by managing each state of production.

quality-management viewpoint Perspective that focuses on quality control, quality assurance, and total quality management.

quantitative management An evolutionary form of operations research, whereby quantitative techniques, such as statistics and computer simulations, are applied to management. Two branches of quantitative management are management science and operations management.

create quite a stir *Cause a situation in which people are all excited.*

R

radical innovations New products, services, or technologies that replace existing ones.

ratio analysis The evaluation of financial ratios (the relationship of two or more things); includes liquidity ratios, debt management ratios, asset management ratios, and return ratios.

rational model of decision making Also called the *classical model;* the style of decision making that explains how managers should make decisions; it assumes that managers will make logical decisions that will be the optimum in furthering the organization's best interests.

reactive change Change made in response to problems or opportunities as they arise. Compare *proactive change.*

reactors Managers who make adjustments only when finally forced to by environmental pressures.

readiness The extent to which a follower possesses the ability and willingness to complete a task.

realistic job preview A picture of both positive and negative features of the job and organization given to a job candidate before he or she is hired.

receiver The person for whom a message is intended.

recruiting The process of locating and attracting qualified applicants for jobs open in the organization.

reduced cycle time The reduction of steps in the work process.

referent power One of five sources of power; power deriving from one's personal attraction.

reinforcement Anything that causes a given behavior to be repeated or inhibited; the four types are positive, negative, extinction, and punishment.

reinforcement theory The belief that behavior reinforced by positive consequences tends to be repeated, whereas behavior reinforced by negative consequences tends not to be repeated.

related diversification Strategy by which an organization under one ownership operates separate businesses that are related to one another.

relaxed avoidance The situation in which a manager decides to take no action in the belief that there will be no great negative consequences.

relaxed change The situation in which a manager realizes that complete inaction will have negative consequences but opts for the first available alternative that involves low risk.

representativeness bias The tendency to generalize from a small sample or a single event.

response uncertainty One of three types of uncertainty; when the consequences of a decision are uncertain.

responsibility The obligation one has to perform the assigned tasks.

the rest is history *What happens next is well known.*

reward power One of five sources of power; all managers have this power, which results from their authority to reward their subordinates.

rites and rituals The activities and ceremonies, planned and unplanned, that celebrate important occasions and accomplishments in an organization's life.

role A socially determined expectation of how an individual should behave in a specific position; set of behaviors that people expect of occupants of a position.

roller coaster ride *Volatile; refers to the resemblance to the rapid change between extreme high and low points on an amusement park ride.*

rookie mistakes *A newcomer's errors; errors made by someone inexperienced.*

run on the banks *When people are uncertain whether or not their funds are safe in banks, they may rush to take their money out before other people do and there is none left.*

S

sales commissions The percentage of a company's earnings as the result of a salesperson's sales that is paid to that salesperson.

satisficing model One type of nonrational decision-making model; managers seek alternatives until they find one that is satisfactory, not optimal.

scab *A person who crosses a union picket line to assume the job of a striking worker.*

scientific management Management approach that emphasizes the scientific study of work methods to improve the productivity of individual workers.

seat-of-the-pants start-up *A new business that has very few resources.*

selection process The screening of job applicants to hire the best candidate.

selective perception The tendency to filter out information that is discomforting, that seems irrelevant, or that contradicts one's beliefs.

self-efficacy Personal ability to do a task.

self-esteem Self-respect; the extent to which people like or dislike themselves.

self-fulfilling prophecy Also known as the *Pygmalion effect;* the phenomenon in which people's expectations of themselves or others leads them to behave in ways that make those expectations come true.

self-managed teams Groups of workers who are given administrative oversight for their task domains.

self-monitoring Observing one's own behavior and adapting it to external situations.

self-serving bias The attributional tendency to take more personal responsibility for success than for failure.

semantics The study of the meaning of words.

sender The person wanting to share information.

servant leaders Leaders who focus on providing increased service to others—meeting the goals of both followers and the organization—rather than on themselves.

sexual harassment Unwanted sexual attention that creates an adverse work environment.

shared leadership Simultaneous, ongoing, mutual influence process in which people share responsibility for leading.

simple structure The first type of organizational structure, whereby an organization has authority centralized in a single person, as well as a flat hierarchy, few rules, and low work specialization.

single-product strategy Strategy by which a company makes and sells only one product within its market.

situational interview A structured interview in which the interviewer focuses on hypothetical situations.

situational leadership theory Leadership model that holds that leaders should adjust their leadership style according to the readiness of the followers.

skunkworks A project team whose members are separated from the normal operation of an organization and asked to produce a new, innovative product.

small-batch technology System in which goods are custom-made to customer specifications in small quantities.

SMART goal A goal that is Specific, Measurable, Attainable, Results oriented, and has Target dates.

social capital Economic or productive potential of strong, trusting, and cooperative relationships.

social loafing The tendency of people to exert less effort when working in groups than when working alone.

social responsibility Manager's duty to take action that will benefit society's interests as well as the organization's.

socialized power Power directed at helping others.

sociocultural forces Influences and trends originating in a country, society, or culture; human relationships and values that may affect an organization.

spam Unsolicited e-mail jokes and junk mail.

span of control The number of people reporting directly to a given manager.

special-interest groups Groups whose members try to influence specific issues.

special-purpose team A team that meets to solve a special or one-time problem.

stability strategy One of three grand strategies, this strategy involves little or no significant change.

staff personnel Staff with advisory functions; they provide advice, recommendations, and research to line managers.

stakeholders People whose interests are affected by an organization's activities.

start-up business *A new company.*

state uncertainty One of three types of uncertainty; when the environment is considered unpredictable.

statistical process control A statistical technique that uses periodic random samples from production runs to see if quality is being maintained within a standard range of acceptability.

stereotype A standardized mental picture resulting from oversimplified beliefs about a certain group of people.

stereotyping The tendency to attribute to an individual the characteristics one believes are typical of the group to which that individual belongs.

stock options The right to buy a company's stock at a future date for a discounted price; often a benefit given to key employees.

storming One of five stages of forming a team; stage two, the emergence of individual personalities, roles, and conflicts within the group.

story A narrative based on true events, which is repeated—and sometimes embellished upon—to emphasize a particular value.

strategic allies Describes the relationship of two organizations that join forces to achieve advantages that neither can perform as well alone.

strategic control Monitoring performance to ensure that strategic plans are being implemented and taking corrective action as needed.

strategic goals Goals that are set by and for top management and focus on objectives for the organization as a whole.

strategic human resource planning The development of a systematic, comprehensive strategy for (1) understanding current employee needs and (2) predicting future employee needs.

strategic management A five-step process that involves managers from all parts of the organization in the formulation and implementation of strategies and strategic goals: establish the mission and the vision; establish the grand strategy; formulate the strategic plans; carry out the strategic plans; maintain strategic control.

strategic planning Determining what an organization's long-term goals should be for the next 1–10 years with the resources it expects to have available; done by top management.

strategy A large-scale action plan that sets the direction for an organization.

strategy formulation The process of choosing among different strategies and altering them to best fit the organization's needs.

strategy implementation The execution of strategic plans.

stress The tension people feel when they are facing or enduring extraordinary demands, constraints, or opportunities and are uncertain about their ability to handle them effectively.

stressor The source of stress.

structured interview Interview in which the interviewer asks each applicant the same questions and then compares the responses to a standardized set of answers.

subjective appraisal Form of performance evaluation based on a manager's perceptions of an employee's traits or behaviors.

subsystems The collection of parts that make up the whole system.

supplier A person or organization that provides supplies—raw materials, services, equipment, labor, or energy—to other organizations.

SWOT analysis The search for the Strengths, Weaknesses, Opportunities, and Threats that affect an organization.

symbol An object, act, quality, or event that conveys meaning.

synergy Situation in which the economic value of separate, related businesses under one ownership and management is greater than the businesses are worth separately.

system A set of interrelated parts that operate together to achieve a common purpose.

systems viewpoint Perspective that regards the organization as a system of interrelated parts.

T

tactical control Monitoring performance to ensure that tactical plans—those at the divisional or departmental level—are being implemented and taking corrective action as needed.

tactical goals Goals that are set by and for middle managers and focus on the actions needed to achieve strategic goals.

tactical planning Determining what contributions departments or similar work units can make with their given resources during the next six months to two years; done by middle management.

tacit knowledge Knowledge that is individual-based, intuitive, acquired through considerable experience, and hard to express and to share.

take the plunge *To finally get started.*

talking the talk *Promising things to people but not following through with action.*

tariff A trade barrier in the form of a customs duty, or tax, levied mainly on imports.

task environment Eleven groups that present you with daily tasks to handle: customers, competitors, suppliers, distributors, strategic allies, employee groups, local communities, financial institutions, government regulators, special-interest groups, and mass media.

task role Behavior that concentrates on getting the team's task done.

team A small group of people with complementary skills who are committed to a common purpose, performance goals, and approach to which they hold themselves mutually accountable.

team-based structure Seventh type of organizational structure, whereby teams or workgroups, either temporary or permanent, are used to improve horizontal relations and solve problems throughout the organization.

technical skills Skills that consist of the job-specific knowledge needed to perform well in a specialized field.

technological forces New developments in methods for transforming resources into goods or services.

technology All the tools and ideas for transforming material, data, or labor (inputs) into goods or services (outputs). It applies not just to computers but any machine or process that enables an organization to gain a competitive advantage in changing materials used to produce a finished product.

telecom *Short for* telecommunications.

telecommute To work from home or remote locations using a variety of information technologies.

telephone tag *Playing back-and-forth with leaving telephone messages; leaving a telephone message when you attempt to respond to a message left for you.*

thorny issue *An issue that can cause pain (as a thorn on a rose bush may).*

time in the trenches *Working with the other employees and experiencing what they contend with as opposed to managing from an office and relying solely on reports about what is happening in the workplace.*

tip of the iceberg *Only a little bit of the issue or the problem; there is much more to the issue than what appears on the surface.*

top managers One of three managerial levels; they make the long-term decisions about the overall direction of the organization and establish the objectives, policies, and strategies for it.

total quality management (TQM) A comprehensive approach—led by top management and supported throughout the organization—dedicated to continuous quality improvement, training, and customer satisfaction. It has four components: (1) Make continuous improvement a priority. (2) Get every employee involved. (3) Listen to and learn from customers and employees. (4) Use accurate standards to identify and eliminate problems.

totalitarian governments Governments ruled by a dictator, a single political party, or a special-membership group.

trade protectionism The use of government regulations to limit the import of goods and services.

trading bloc Also known as an *economic community;* a group of nations within a geographical region that have agreed to remove trade barriers with one another.

training Educating technical and operational employees in how to better do their current jobs.

trait approaches to leadership Attempts to identify distinctive characteristics that account for the effectiveness of leaders.

transactional leader One who focuses on the interpersonal transactions between managers and employees.

transactional leadership Leadership style that focuses on clarifying employees' roles and task requirements and providing rewards and punishments contingent on performance.

transformation processes The organization's capabilities in management and technology that are applied to converting inputs into outputs; one of four parts of a system, along with inputs, outputs, and feedback.

transformational leadership Leadership style that transforms employees to pursue organizational goals over self-interests.

trend analysis A hypothetical extension of a past series of events into the future.

turnover The movement of employees in and out of an organization when they obtain and then leave their jobs.

two-factor theory Herzberg's theory that proposes that work satisfaction and dissatisfaction arise from two different work factors—work satisfaction from so-called motivating factors and work dissatisfaction from so-called hygiene factors.

U

underemployed Working at a job that requires less education than one has.

unrelated diversification Operating several businesses that are not related to one another under one ownership.

unstructured interview Interview in which the interviewer asks probing questions to find out what the applicant is like.

up front *To be forthcoming, to be honest from the start.*

upward communication Communication that flows from lower levels to higher levels.

utilitarian approach One of four approaches to solving ethical dilemmas; ethical behavior is guided by what will result in the greatest good for the greatest number of people.

V

valence The value or the importance a worker assigns to a possible outcome or reward.

value system The pattern of values within an organization.

values Abstract ideals that guide one's thinking and behavior across all situations; the relatively permanent and deeply held underlying beliefs and attitudes that help determine a person's behavior.

variable budget Allowing the allocation of resources to vary in proportion with various levels of activity.

variable costs Expenses that vary directly depending on the numbers of the product that one produces and sells.

videoconferencing Using video and audio links along with computers to enable people located at different locations to see, hear, and talk with one another.

virtual bank A bank with no building to go to; an Internet bank.

vision statement Statement that expresses what the organization should become and where it wants to go strategically.

W

walking the walk *Doing what you say you will do.*

wannabes *Individuals who want to be something but who aren't.*

watching over someone's shoulder *Looking at everything someone does.*

whistleblower An employee who reports organizational misconduct to the public.

wholly owned subsidiary A foreign subsidiary, or subordinate section of an organization, that is totally owned and controlled by the organization.

work teams Teams that engage in collective work requiring coordinated effort; they are of four types, which may be identified according to their basic purpose: advice teams, production teams, project teams, and action teams.

World Bank One of three principal organizations designed to facilitate international trade; its purpose is to provide low-interest loans to developing nations for improving transportation, education, health, and telecommunications.

World Trade Organization (WTO) One of three principal organizations designed to facilitate international trade; it is designed to monitor and enforce trade agreements.

Y

you get what you pay for *If you pay a low price, you'll probably get a low-quality product.*

youth stage The stage in which the organization is in a prebureaucratic phase, one of growth and expansion.

Z

zero-sum game *A game in which, if one side wins, the other side must lose—as opposed to a game where both sides can win, which is called a win-win game.*

zero-based budgeting (ZBB) Forcing each department to start from zero in projecting its funding needs for the coming budget period.

Credits

CHAPTER 1

Photos: Page 4t, © Image Source/ImageState; 4bCourtesy of Burrston House; 5, © Tim Boyle/Getty Images; 6, © Liu Jin/AFP/Getty Images; 7, © 1995–2000 FedEx. All Rights Reserved; 8, © PhotoDisc/Getty Images; 9, © Rudi Von Briel/PhotoEdit; 10, © Brian Williams & Stacey Sawyer; 11, AP/Wide World Photos; 12, © AbleStock/IndexStock Imagery; 13t, Courtesy of Microsoft; 13b, 14t, © PhotoDisc/Getty Images; 14b, Rosemary Hedger; 15, 16, AP/Wide World Photos; 17, Courtesy of Focus: Hope; 18t, © PhotoDisc/Getty Images; 18b, 19, 20, AP/Wide World; 22, © PhotoDisc/Getty Images; 23, © Joyce Tenneson.

Text/Illustrations/Logos: Management in Action, from "In the Lead: The Confident Boss Doesn't Micromanage or Delegate Too Much," *The Wall Street Journal* by Carol Hymowitz. Copyright 2003 by Dow Jones & Co. Inc. Reproduced with permission of Dow Jones & Co. Inc. via Copyright Clearance Center.

CHAPTER 2

Photos: Page 34, © PhotoDisc/Getty Images; 36t, © PhotoDisc/Getty Images; 36b, 68t, © Bettmann/CORBIS; 38b, © Underwood & Underwood/CORBIS; 39, © Sean Gallup/Getty Images; 40t, © PhotoDisc/Getty Images; 40b, © Bettmann/CORBIS; 41, Courtesy of AT&T Corporate Archives; 42t, © Bettmann/CORBIS; 42b, Courtesy of Debra's Natural Gourmet; 43, © Kent Dayton Photography; 44t, © PhotoDisc/Getty Images; 44b, © Najlah Feanny/CORBIS SABA; 46, © Don Carstens/Brand X Pictures/PictureQuest; 47, AP/Wide World Photos; 48, © Mark Richards/PhotoEdit; 49, Courtesy of Burrston House; 50, © Stockbye/PictureQuest; 51, Cyndy Freeman/© Starbuck Coffee Co. All Rights reserved.; 52t, © Masterfile Royalty Free/Masterfile; 52b, AP/Wide World Photos; 53, With permission of the W. Edwards Deming Institute; 54, © PhotoDisc/Getty Images.

Text/Illustrations/Logos: Costco logo, reprinted with permission; Management in Action, excerpt from Brian Bremner and Chester Dawson, "Can Anything Stop Toyota?," *BusinessWeek,* November 17, 2003, pp. 116, 177, 120, 122; Ethical Dilemma, excerpt from Joan O'C. Hamilton, "Journey to the Center of the Mind: Functional MRI Is Yielding a Clearer Picture of What Thoughts Look Like," *BusinessWeek,* April 19, 2004, pp. 78-80.

CHAPTER 3

Photos: Page 66t, © Randy Allbritton/Getty Images; 66b, © Mark Peterson/CORBIS; 68, Courtesy of United Airlines Archives; 70, © PhotoDisc/Getty Images; 71, © Tim Boyle/Getty Images; 72, Debra McClinton; 73, AP/Wide World Photos; 74, © Nick Gunderson/Getty Images; 75, © Ron Wurzer/Getty Images; 76t, © Royalty-Free/CORBIS; 76b, 79, AP/Wide World Photos; 80, © Arthur S. Aubry/Getty Images; 81, AP/Wide World Photos; 82, Brian Williams & Stacey Sawyer; 83, AP/Wide World Photos; 84, © PhotoDisc/Getty Images; 86, © Michael Newman/PhotoEdit; 87, AP/Wide World Photos; 88, © Bob Daemmrich/Stock Boston; 89, Courtesy of Johnson & Johnson; 90t, © Kent Knudson/PhotoLink/Getty Images; 90b, Courtesy of Skype; 91, Courtesy of 3M; 92, © 2002 Morton Buildings, Inc./Courtesy of Woodward Camp; 93, Courtesy of Ebay.

Text/Illustrations/Logos: Bagel Works logo, reprinted with permission; Figure 3.2, from L. Gardenswartz and A. Rowe, Diverse *Teams at Work: Capitalizing on the Power of Diversity*. Published by the Society for Human Resource Management, 2003. Reprinted with permission; Management in Action, from "Financial Surgery: How Cuts in Retiree Benefits Fatten Companies," *The Wall Street Journal* by Ellen E. Schultz and Theo Francis. Copyright 2004 by Dow Jones & Co. Inc. Reproduced with permission of Dow Jones & Co. Inc. via Copyright Clearance Center.

CHAPTER 4

Photos: Page 102t, © Duncan Smith/Getty Images; 102b, © Helen King/CORBIS; 104, Brian Williams & Stacey Sawyer; 105, © AFP/Getty Images; 106t © Chad Baker/Ryan McVay/Getty Images; 106b, © Jacobs Stock Photography/Getty Images; 108, © PhotoDisc/Getty Images; 109, Courtesy of Burrston House; 110t, © Janis Christie/Getty Images; 110b, Courtesy of Home Depot © Homer TLC, Inc.; 111, © MANDM, Inc./The Image works; 115, AP/Wide World Photos; 116t, © PhotoDisc/Getty Images; 116b, © P. Chickering/Photo Researchers; 117, © Deborah Harse/The Image works; 118, © Royalty-Free/CORBIS; 120t, © Comstock Images; 120b, AP/Wide World Photos; 121, © James Marshall/The Image works; 124t, © PhotoDisc/Getty Images; 124b, Aaron C. Anderer; 125, Rosemary Hedger; 127, © Tom Wagner/CORBIS SABA; 129, Courtesy of Mercedes Benz.

Text/Illustrations/Logos: Amazon.com logo, Amazon.com and the Amazon.com logo are registered trademarks of Amazon.com, Inc. or its affiliates; Management in Action, from "Lesson in India: Not Every Job Translates Overseas," *The Wall Street Journal* by Scott Thurm. Copyright 2004 by Dow Jones & Co. Inc. Reproduced with permission of Dow Jones & Co. Inc. via Copyright Clearance Center; Ethical Dilemma, from "Tough Tactics: European Regulators Spark Controversy with 'Dawn Raids'," *The Wall Street Journal* by Philip Shishkin. Copyright 2002 by Dow Jones & Co. Inc. Reproduced with permission of Dow Jones & Co. Inc. via Copyright Clearance Center.

CHAPTER 5

Photos: Page 140, © David Chasey/Getty Images; 141, 142, 143, AP/Wide World Photos; 144, © Stockbye/PictureQuest; 150, © PhotoDisc/Getty Images; 151, Rosemary Hedger; 152, © Royalty-Free/CORBIS; 154, © PhotoDisc/Getty Images; 155, © Catherine Karnow/CORBIS; 156, © Jim Arbogast/Getty Images; 157, © Bill Bachmann/The Image Works; 158, Courtesy of Wal-Mart.

Text/Illustrations/Logos: SouthWest Airlines logo, Courtesy Southwest Airlines, Co.; Management in Action, from "Get in Line," *Workforce Management* by Joe Mullich. Copyright 2003 by Crain Communications, Inc. Reproduced with permission of Crain Communications, Inc., via Copyright Clearance Center.

CHAPTER 6

Photos: Page 170t, Ryan McVay/Getty Images; 170b, © Kevin Lee/Getty Images; 172, Brian Williams & Stacey Sawyer; 174t, © Donovan Reese/Getty Images; 174b, © Michael Newman/PhotoEdit; 176, © Reuters/CORBIS; 178, AP/Wide World Photos; 179, © PhotoDisc/Getty Images; 180, © Ryan McVay/Getty Images; 181, Rosemary Hedger; 182, © Chapman/The Image Works; 183, Courtesy of Southwest Airlines; 184, © PhotoDisc/Getty Images; 185, © Stephen Chernin/Getty Images; 187, Brian Williams & Stacey Sawyer; 190t, © Royalty-Free/CORBIS; 190b, Courtesy of The Container Store; 193, © PhotoDisc/Getty Images.

Text/Illustrations/Logos: Excerpt–Motorola's CEO, excerpted from Adam Lashinsky, "Can Moto Find Its Mojo?" *Fortune,* March 21, 2004. Copyright © 2004 Time Inc. All rights reserved; Excerpt–Are American Companies Getting Away with Tax Murder?, excerpt from Mortimer B. Zuckerman, "An Intolerable Free Ride," U.S. News & World Report, May 17, 2004, p. 80. Copyright 2004 US News & World Report, L.P. Reprinted with permission; Ethical Dilemma, from "Space Case: U.S. Probes Whether Boeing Misused a Rival's Documents," *The Wall Street Journal* by Anne Marie Squeo and Andy Pasztor. Copyright 2003 by Dow Jones & Co. Inc. Reproduced with permission of Dow Jones & Co. Inc. via Copyright Clearance Center.

CHAPTER 7

Photos: Page204t, © PhotoDisc/Getty Images; 204b, AP/Wide World Photos; 205, Tina-Marie Lacava/Courtesy of Camden County College; 207, Courtesy of Southwest Airlines; 208, © PhotoDisc/Getty Images; 210, © Danny Lehman/CORBIS ; 211, © Reuters/CORBIS; 213, © Joseph Sohm/Photo Researchers; 214, © Nick Koudis/Getty Images; 219, © Gene Blevins/LA Daily News/CORBIS; 220, Rosemary Hedger; 222, © PhotoDisc/Getty Images; 223, ©Phillippe Gontier/The Image Works; 224, © PhotoDisc/Getty Images; 225, © Royalty-Free/CORBIS; 228, AP/Wide World Photos; 229, © Roger Ressmeyer/CORBIS.

Text/Illustrations/Logos: Figure 7.5, reprinted by permission of *Harvard Business Review*. Exhibit from "The Ethical Leader's Decision Tree," by C.E. Bagley, February 2003. Copyright © 2003 by the Harvard Business School Publishing Corporation; all rights reserved; Figure 7.6, from K. Hodgson, *A Rock and a Hard Place: How to Make Ethical Business Decisions When the Choices Are Tough,* 1992, pp. 69–73. Reprinted with permission of Kent Hodgson.

CHAPTER 8

Photos: p. 240t, © PhotoDisc/Getty Images; 240b, © Ryan McVay/Getty Images; 241, Courtesy of Hewlett-Packard Company; 243, © PhotoDisc/Getty Images; 244t, © Ryan McVay/Getty Images; 244b, Courtesy of Hewlett-Packard Company; 247, 248, 252t, 252b, © PhotoDisc/Getty Images; 253, AP/Wide World Photos; 255, Courtesy of Burrston House; 256, © Kim Kulish/CORBIS; 260t, © Ryan McVay/Getty Images; 260b, Courtesy of JetBlue Airlines; 261, Courtesy of McDonald's; 262, Melanie Dunea/CPI; 263, Courtesy of Mitsubishi; 265, © Auntie Anne's, Inc.; 266t, © PhotoDisc/Getty Images; 266b, Courtesy of Peter Guber.

Text/Illustrations/Logos: Grameenphone logo, reprinted with permission; Figure 8.1, adapted from "Concepts of Culture and Organizational Analysis," by L. Smircich published in *Administrative Science Quarterly,* Vol. 28, No. 1, March 1983, by permission of Administrative Science Quarterly; Excerpt–Southwest Airlines Organizational Culture, excerpted from Andy Serwer, "Southwest Airlines: The

Hottest Think in The Sky," *Fortune,* March 8, 2004. Copyright © 2004 Time Inc. All rights reserved; Excerpt–Should Drug Salespeople Be Allowed to Give Doctors Free Drug Samples as Gifts?, excerpt from D. Lavoie, "Drug Firm Sales Reps Go on Trial," *Associated Press,* April 13, 2004. Reprinted with permission of Associated Press and Valeo IP; Ethical Dilemma, excerpt from John A. Byrne, Mike France, and Wendy Zellner, "The Environment Was Ripe for Abuse," *BusinessWeek,* February 25, 2002, pp. 118–120.

CHAPTER 9

Photos: Page 278t, © PhotoDisc/Getty Images; 278b, Photo by Stef Barber–Mueller, SAS; 280, Courtesy of Burrston House; 281, Courtesy of Wachovia; 282, © PhotoDisc/Getty Images; 284, © Steve Cole/Getty Images; 289, Lafayette Instrument Company, Inc.; 290t, © PhotoDisc/Getty Images; 290b, © 1995-2000 FedEx. All Rights Reserved.; 293, 294t, 294b, 298t, 298b, © PhotoDisc/Getty Images; 299, © Royalty-Free/CORBIS; 300, © PhotoDisc/Getty Images.

Text/Illustrations/Logos: Management in Action, from "Almost Curtains," *Workforce Management* by M. Hammers. Copyright 2003 by Crain Communications, Inc. Reproduced with permission of Crain Communications, Inc., via Copyright Clearance Center; Ethical Dilemma, from "Companies Want the FBI to Screen Employees for Suspected Terrorists," *The Wall Street Journal* by Ana Davis. Copyright 2002 by Dow Jones & Co. Inc. Reproduced with permission of Dow Jones & Co. Inc. via Copyright Clearance Center.

CHAPTER 10

Photos: Page 316, © PhotoDisc/Getty Images; © Francis Dean/Dean Pictures/The Image Works; 321, © Edward Bock/CORBIS; 322, © PhotoDisc/Getty Images; 324, Courtesy of Southwest Airlines; 326t, © PhotoDisc/Getty Images; 326b, Courtesy of Burrston House; 329, © Esbin-Anderson/The Image Works; 330t, © Nick Koudis/Getty Images; 330b, AP/Wide World Photos; 333, © PhotoDisc/Getty Images.

Text/Illustrations/Logos: Wal-Mart logo, used with permission of Wal-Mart Stores, Inc.; Kodak logo, used with permission of Eastman Kodak Company; Tylenol logo, reprinted with permission; #M logo, reprinted with permission of 3M; Management in Action, excerpt from Diane Brady, "Pepsi's Thousand and One Noshes," *BusinessWeek,* June 14, 2004, p. 54, 56.

CHAPTER 11

Photos: Page 346, © PhotoDisc/Getty Images; 248, Courtesy of New School University, NY, NY; 350, © PhotoDisc/Getty Images; 351, Ben Van Hook; 352t, © PhotoDisc/Getty Images; 352b, © Peter L. Chapman/Stock Boston; 356, © PhotoDisc/Getty Images; 357, Courtesy of Nova Wines, Inc.; 358, © China Tourism Press/Getty Images; 359, © Jon Feingersh/Masterfile; 361, © Martin Rogers/Stock Boston; 362t, © PhotoDisc/Getty Images; 362b, © Andrew Levine/Photo Researchers; 364, © David Sacks/Getty Images.

Text/Illustrations/Logos: Management in Action, from "Reveille Has Its fans, But for Late Risers 9-to-5 Days Are A Pain," *The Wall Street Journal* by Jared Sandberg. Copyright 2004 by Dow Jones & Co. Inc. Reproduced with permission of Dow Jones & Co. Inc. via Copyright Clearance Center; Group Exercise, the ten values in this exercise were taken from the 36 values listed in the *Rokeach Value Survey,* 1967, 1982 by M. Rokeach. Reprinted by permission of Halgren Tests, N.W. 1145 Clifford, Pullman, WA 99163; (509) 334-5636; Ethical Dilemma, from "En-Ruse? Workers at Enron Say They Posed as Busy Traders to Impress Visiting Analysts," *The Wall Street Journal* by Jason Leopold. Copyright 2002 by Dow Jones & Co. Inc. Reproduced with permission of Dow Jones & Co. Inc. via Copyright Clearance Center.

CHAPTER 12

Photos: Page 376, © PhotoDisc/Getty Images; 378t, © Masterfile Royalty Free/Masterfile; 378b, © Tony Freeman/PhotoEdit; 384t, © PhotoDisc/Getty Images; 384b, © Chuck Savage/CORBIS; 386, AP/Wide World Photos; 389, © Jeff Zaruba/CORBIS; 390t, © Creatas/PictureQuest; 390b, © Nina Leen/TimePix/Getty Images; 392, © PhotoDisc/Getty Images; 393, © Chuck Kennedy/Knight Ridder Tribune; 394, © Royalty-Free/CORBIS; 396, 398t, © PhotoDisc/Getty Images; 398b, © Eric Millette Photography; 401, © PhotoDisc/Getty Images.

Text/Illustrations/Logos: Management in Action, from "Getting Engaged," *HR Magazine* by Steve Bates. Copyright 2004 by Society for Human Resource Management. Reproduced with permission of Society for Human Resource Management via Copyright Clearance Center; Ethical Dilemma, excerpt from Margaret Popper, "Lost Job, Lost Spouse: Being Fired Can Lead to Divorce," *BusinessWeek,* December 17, 2001, p. 26.

CHAPTER 13

Photos: Page 412, © Jim Arbogast/Getty Images; 413, AP/Wide World Photos; 416, Courtesy of Burrston House; 418t, © PhotoDisc/Getty Images; 418b, © Royalty-Free/CORBIS; 419, Courtesy of Boeing; 420, © PhotoDisc/Getty Images; 421, © Digital Vision/SuperStock; 423, © Kevin Horan/Stock Boston; 424, Courtesy of Volvo Car Corporation; 425, © Jon Feingersh/CORBIS; 426, 428t, © PhotoDisc/Getty Images; 428b, Courtesy of NASCAR Public Relations; 431, Courtesy of GM Saturn; 432, © Scott Olson/Getty Images; 435, AP/Wide World Photos.

Text/Illustrations/Logos: Great Little Box Co. logo, reprinted with permission; Management in Action, eExcerpt from Faith Keenan and Spencer E. Ante, "The New Teamwork," *BusinessWeek,* e.biz, February 18, 2002, pp. EB12-EB16.

CHAPTER 14

Photos: Page 444, © Comstock Images/Getty Images; 445, © Thomas Engstrom/Getty Images; 447, 448, AP/Wide World Photos; 450, © Alan and Sandy Carey/Getty Images; 454t, 454b, 456, © PhotoDisc/Getty Images; 457, © Royalty-Free/CORBIS; 458t, © C Squared Studios/Getty Images; 458b, © PhotoDisc/Getty Images; 462, AP/Wide World Photos; 464t, © Digital Vision; 464b, © PhotoDisc/Getty Images; 466, © Greg Wood/AFP/Getty Images; 468, © Image Source/Index-Stock Imagery.

Text/Illustrations/Logos: Figure 14.11, *from Good to Great: Why Some Companies Make the Leap and Others Don't* by Jim Collins. Copyright © 2001 by Jim Collins. Reprinted by permission of HarperCollins Publishers, Inc.; Figure 14.12, tips are offered by don MacRae, Business Week Online, September 6, 2001; Management in Action, excerpt from Diane Brady, "Act II," *BusinessWeek,* March 29, 2004, pp. 73–76.

CHAPTER 15

Photos: Page 484t, © PhotoDisc/Getty Images; 484b, © Ryan McVay/Getty Images; 485, 487, 488t, 488b, 490, 492, 493, 496t, 496b, 498, 499, 500, © PhotoDisc/Getty Images; 502, © Zigy Kaluzny/Getty Images; 504t, © Digital Vision/SuperStock; 504b, 506, © PhotoDisc/Getty Images; 508, AP/Wide World Photos.

Text/Illustrations/Logos: Management in Action, from "In the Lead: Missing From Work: The Chance to Think, Even to Dream a Little," *The Wall Street Journal* by Carol Hymowitz. Copyright 2004 by Dow Jones & Co. Inc. Reproduced with permission of Dow Jones & Co. Inc. via Copyright Clearance Center; Excerpt–Are Camera Cellphones Creating Ethical Problems?, excerpt from Yuri Kageyama, "Cellphones with Cameras Creating Trouble: Concerns Include Voyeurism," *Associated Press,* July 10, 2003. Reprinted with permission of Associated Press and Valeo IP.

CHAPTER 16

Photos: Page 520, © Nick Koudis/Getty Images; 521, © PhotoDisc/Getty Images; 522, © Martyn Vickery/Alamy; 526, © PhotoDisc/Getty Images; 527, Courtesy of Burrston House; 528, © Brand X Pictures/Getty Images; 529, AP/Wide World Photos; 530, © Mark Richards/PhotoEdit; 531, Courtesy of Hoodoo Ski Area/Leon Pearson; 532t, © PhotoDisc/Getty Images; 532b, © Oscar Sabetta/Getty Images; 533, Courtesy of Burrston House; 535, © Frank Micelotta/Getty Images; 536, © Lawrence Lawry/Getty Images; 537, 538, AP/Wide World Photos; 540, Rosemary Hedger; 542t, © Royalty-Free/CORBIS; 542b, Courtesy of Instituto Pro-Natura; 544, © Massimo Borchi/Photo Researchers; 545, © P. Chickering/Photo Researchers; A1, © Mitch Kezar/Getty Images; A6, © PhotoDisc/Getty Images.

Text/Illustrations/Logos: Management in Action, excerpt from John Carey and Michael Arndt, "Making Pills the Smart Way," *BusinessWeek,* May 3, 2004, pp. 102-103, Ethical Dilemma, excerpt from Paula Dwyer, "The SEC to Top Execs: Read the Fine Print," *BusinessWeek*, July 26, 2004, p. 33.

H

I

T

U

V

W

Y

Z